Second Edition

Law

Second Edition

M J GRIFFITHS and J S WILLIAMS

PUBLISHED BY LONGMAN GROUP UK LTD IN CO-OPERATION WITH THE CHARTERED ASSOCIATION OF CERTIFIED ACCOUNTANTS

© Longman Group UK Ltd 1990

ISBN 0 85121 562—9

Published by

Longman Professional and Business Communications Division
Longman Group UK Limited
21–27 Lamb's Conduit Street, London WC1N 3NJ

Associated Offices

Australia	Longman Professional Publishing (Pty) Limited 130 Phillip Street, Sydney, NSW 2000
Hong Kong	Longman Group (Far East) Limited Cornwall House, 18th Floor, Taikoo Trading Estate, Tong Chong Street, Quarry Bay
Malaysia	Longman Malaysia Sdn Bhd No 3 Jalan Kilang A, Off Jalan Penchala, Petaling Jaya, Selangor, Malaysia
Singapore	Longman Singapore Publishers (Pte) Ltd 25 First Lok Yang Road, Singapore 2262
USA	Longman Group (USA) Inc 500 North Dearborn Street, Chicago, Illinois 60610

All rights reserved. No part of this publication may be reproduced, stored in a retrieval system, or transmitted, in any form or by any means, electronic, mechanical, photocopying, recording or otherwise, without either the prior written permission of the copyright holder for which application should be addressed in the first instance to the publishers or a licence permitting restricted copying issued by the Copyright Licensing Agency Ltd, 33–34 Alfred Place, London WC1E 7DP.

A CIP catalogue record for this book is available from the British Library.

Printed in Great Britain
by Mackays of Chatham

For further information and enquiries please contact your local Longman office.

Europe, Latin America, Iran
Please contact our International
Sales Department
Longman House
Burnt Mill
Harlow
Essex CM20 2JE

Arab World
Longman Arab World Centre
Butros Bustani Street
Zokak el Blat
PO Box 11-945
Beirut
Lebanon

New Sphinx Publishing Co. Ltd.
3 Shawarby Street
Kasr el Nil
Cairo
Egypt

Librairie Sayegh
Salhie Street
PO Box 704
Damascus
Syria

Longman Arab World Centre
Al-Hajairi Building
Amir Mohammed Street
PO Box 6587
Amman
Jordan

Longman Arab World Centre
15th Street
PO Box 1391
Khartoum
Sudan

Cameroon
M A W Ngoumbah
BP 537
Limbe
Cameroon

Australia
Longman Cheshire Pty Ltd
Longman Cheshire House
Kings Gardens
91-97 Coventry Street
South Melbourne
Victoria 3205

Botswana
Longman Botswana (Pty) Ltd.
PO Box 1083
Gaborone

Canada
James D Lang
Marketing Manager
Carswell Legal Publications
2330 Midland Avenue
Agincourt
Ontario
M1S 1P7

Ghana
Sedco Publishing Co. Ltd.
Sedco House
PO Box 2051
Tabon Street
North Ridge
Accra

Hong Kong
Longman Group (Far East) Ltd.
18th Floor Cornwall House
Taikoo Trading Estate
Tong Chong Street
Quarry Bay

India
Orient Longman Limited
5-9-41/1 Bashir Bagh
Hyderabad 500 029

UBS Publishers Distributors
5, Ansari Road
PO Box 7051
New Delhi 110 002

Japan
Longman Penguin Japan Co. Ltd.
Yamaguchi Building
2-12-9 Kanda Jimbocho
Chiyoda-ku
Tokyo 101

Kenya
Longman Kenya Ltd.
PO Box 18033
Funzi Road, Industrial Area
Nairobi

Lesotho
Longman Lesotho (Pty) Ltd.
PO Box 1174
Maseru, 100

Malawi
Dzuka Publishing Co. Ltd.
Blantyre Printing & Publishing
Co. Ltd. PMB 39
Blantyre

Malaysia
Longman Malaysia Sdn, Berhad
No. 3 Jalan Kilang A
Off Jalan Penchala
Petaling Jaya
Selangor

New Zealand
Longman Paul Ltd.
Private Bag
Takapuna
Auckland 9

Nigeria
Longman Nigeria Ltd.
52 Oba Akran Avenue
Private Mail Bag 21036
Ikeja
Lagos

Pakistan
Tahir M Lodhi
Regional Manager
Butterworths
7 Jahangir Street
Islamia Park
Poonch Road
Lahore

Singapore
Longman Singapore
Publishers Pte Ltd.
25 First Lok Yang Road
Off International Road
Jurong Town
Singapore 22

South Africa
Maskew Miller Longman (Pty) Ltd.
PO Box 396
Howard Drive
Pinelands 7405
Cape Town 8000

Swaziland
Longman Swaziland Ltd.
PO Box 2207
Manzini

Tanzania
Ben & Co. Ltd.
PO Box 3164
Dar-es-Salaam

USA
Longman Trade USA.
Caroline House Inc.
520 North Dearborn Street
Chicago
Illinois 60610

Transnational Publishers, Inc.
PO Box 7282
Ardsley-on-Hudson
NY 10503

West Indies
Longman Caribbean (Trinidad) Ltd.
Boundary Road
San Juan
Trinidad

Longman Jamaica Ltd.
PO Box 489
95 Newport Boulevard
Newport West
Kingston 10
Jamaica

Mr Louis A Forde
'Suncrest'
Sunrise Drive
Pine Gardens
St Michael
Barbados

Zimbabwe
Longman Zimbabwe (PVT) Ltd.
PO Box ST 125
Southerton
Harare

The content of this title has been fully approved and endorsed by a specially constituted Advisory Board, whose members are:
Professor Susan Dev, MSc, FCCA, ATII, Professor Emeritus at the London School of Economics and Political Science
Professor Roger Groves, B Com, MSc, Phd, FCA, Professor of Accounting at the Cardiff Business School
Hymie Lipman, BA, MSc (Econ), FCCA, FCA, Head of Accounting and Finance at the Kingston Business School
Anthea Rose, MA, Deputy Secretary of the Chartered Association of Certified Accountants

Preface

This book has been written specifically for students preparing for the 1.4 Law paper of the Chartered Association of Certified Accountants. It should also be useful for students on other foundation accounting or similar professional courses. In writing it, we have sought to provide a book which will enable the reader to meet the objectives of the revised syllabus as specified by ACCA. These are:

- how civil justice is administered through the courts, tribunals and arbitration;
- the main sources of law;
- basic principles of legal reasoning;
- the major principles governing the creation, content and termination of simple contracts, and their application;
- the rules relating to contracts for the sale of goods, contracts for the supply of services, hire purchase and consumer credit agreements and of employment, and their application;
- the nature and purpose of negotiable instruments, the form of cheque and banker/customer relationships;
- basic concepts of legal personality including partnerships and limited liability companies; the major rules of agency and the application of them;
- the potential liability of an accountant for professional negligence and methods of protection against risk;
- when to seek the advice of a solicitor.

    We have also sought to equip the reader to cope successfully with an examination based on a syllabus which aims, according to the Study Guide issued by ACCA to 'understand...basic legal principles and...apply them in various situations'.

    We have tried to assume no prior knowledge of the law and so have sought to build gradually, particularly in the earlier chapters. We have been particularly careful to try to explain clearly those areas which in our experience students find difficult.

    Knowing that many readers will have limited access to personal tutorial assistance we have provided a glossary of technical expressions and a large number of worked examination type problems and self-assessment questions in the text. The book also contains the most recent (June 1988) examination paper with worked solutions.

    In writing this preface we acknowledge with gratitude the encouragement to write this book given by the Chartered Association of Certified Accountants and hope that the finished text does not fall short of their initial hopes. Various parts of the book were looked at by colleagues within the School of Legal Studies at The Polytechnic, Wolverhampton, Frank Sharman, Nicola Dickens and Andrew Ganley who made a number of useful suggestions and generally showed a kindness and sympathy not always bestowed upon the ignorant by the learned. Any errors which remain are, of course, exclusively our own. The typing was done by Mrs Gwen Morris, who, having technically retired from full-time work, managed to keep the typescript flowing through with remarkable speed and accuracy; once again it is our pleasure to acknowledge with thanks all her help. Finally, we remember with gratitude (since not many others do) the Parliamentary draftsmen without whose miscellaneous efforts, such as the Misrepresentation Act 1967 and the Unfair Contract Terms Act 1977, the book would have been considerably shorter.

Michael Griffiths
Stuart Williams

October 1989

Contents

	Page
Preface	vii

1	**Introduction to the study of law**	1
	1.1 Introduction	1
	1.2 The study of law	1
	1.2.1 How to study a topic	2
	1.2.2 How to make notes	2
	1.2.3 Problem answering	2

2	**The nature and classification of English law**	3
	2.1 What is law?	3
	2.2 The characteristics of English law	3
	2.3 The growth of one system from Saxon times	3
	2.4 Absence of a code of laws	4
	2.5 Judicial character of English law	4
	2.6 The accusatorial procedure	4
	2.7 Limited influence of Roman law	5
	2.8 The doctrine of precedent	5
	2.9 The classification of English law	5
	Summary	5
	Self-test questions	6
	Exercises	6

3	**Historical development of English law**	7
	3.1 Origin and development of the Common Law	7
	3.2 The early courts	7
	3.3 The early development of Equity	8
	3.3.1 Remedy at common law	8
	3.4 The Judicature Acts 1873–1875	9
	3.5 The relationship today between Common Law and Equity	10
	Summary	11
	Self-test questions	11

4	**The system of courts and personnel of the law**	13
	4.1 The work of the courts	13
	4.1.1 Courts of record and not of record	13
	4.1.2 Superior and inferior courts	13
	4.1.3 Courts of first instance and of appeal	13
	4.1.4 Civil and criminal courts	13
	4.2 Civil court structure	13
	4.3 Civil courts (first instance)	14
	4.3.1 Magistrates' courts	14
	4.3.2 County courts	14
	4.3.3 High Court	15
	4.3.4 The Restrictive Practices Court	17
	4.4 Civil courts of appeal	18
	4.4.1 High Court	18
	4.4.2 Court of Appeal (Civil Division)	18

4.4.3	House of Lords	18
4.4.4	European Court of Justice	19
4.4.5	Judicial Committee of the Privy Council (JCPC)	20
4.5	Criminal court structure	20
4.6	Criminal courts (first instance)	21
4.6.1	Magistrates' courts	21
4.6.2	Crown courts	22
4.7	Criminal courts of appeal	23
4.7.1	Crown Court	23
4.7.2	Divisional Court of the Queen's Bench Division	24
4.7.3	Court of Appeal (Criminal Division)	24
4.7.4	House of Lords	25
4.8	Alternatives to the courts	25
4.8.1	Introduction	25
4.8.2	Administrative tribunals	25
4.8.3	Domestic tribunals	27
4.8.4	Arbitration	27
4.9	Personnel of the law	28
4.9.1	The Bar	28
4.9.2	Solicitors	29
4.9.3	Legal executives	29
	Summary	29
	Self-test questions	30
	Exercises	31

5 Sources of law 33

5.1	The sources of law	33
5.2	Custom	33
5.3	The nature of judicial precedent	34
5.3.1	Law reports	34
5.3.2	The citation of cases	35
5.3.3	The Authority of the Courts	35
5.3.4	The House of Lords	36
5.3.5	Court of Appeal	36
5.3.6	Divisional courts	36
5.3.7	High Court	37
5.3.8	Other courts	37
5.4	Statute law	37
5.4.1	Acts of Parliament	37
5.4.2	The process of legislation	38
5.4.3	Delegated legislation	39
5.4.4	The advantages and disadvantages of delegated legislation	40
5.5	Subsidiary sources	40
5.5.1	The law merchant	40
5.5.2	Canon law or Ecclesiastical law	41
5.5.3	Roman law	41
5.5.4	Text books	41
5.5.5	The European Communities	41
5.5.6	Evidence	42
5.5.7	Law reform	42
	Summary	43
	Self-test questions	43
	Exercises	43

6 Judicial precedent and statutory interpretation 45

6.1	Ratio decidendi and obiter dicta	45
6.2	Treatment of a judicial decision	46
6.3	Do judges make law?	46

6.4	Advantages and disadvantages of judicial precedent	47
6.5	Persuasive and binding precedent	47
6.6	The interpretation of statutes	47
6.6.1	The Literal Rule	47
6.6.2	The Golden Rule	48
6.6.3	The Mischief Rule	48
6.6.4	The Eiusdem Generis Rule	49
6.6.5	Expressio unius est exclusio alterius	49
6.6.6	Noscitur a sociis	49
6.7	Statutory presumptions	49
6.8	Intrinsic aids to interpretation	51
6.9	A comparison between statute law and judicial precedent	51
	Summary	51
	Self-test questions	51
	Exercises	52

7 Contract—formation of a contract 53

7.1	Introduction	53
7.2	Offer	54
7.2.1	The nature of an offer	54
7.2.2	Communication of offer	56
7.2.3	Termination of offer	56
7.3	Acceptance	58
7.3.1	The nature of acceptance	58
7.3.2	Silence cannot constitute acceptance	60
7.4	Certainty of terms	60
7.5	Consideration	61
7.5.1	The meaning of consideration	61
7.5.2	Past consideration	61
7.5.3	Consideration must move from the promisee	62
7.5.4	Consideration need not be adequate	63
7.5.5	Consideration must, however, be sufficient	63
7.6	Equitable estoppel	65
7.7	Privity of contract	65
7.8	Collateral contracts	66
7.9	Intention to create legal relations	66
7.9.1	Domestic and social arrangements	67
7.9.2	Commercial arrangements	67
7.9.3	Collective bargaining agreements	68
7.10	Capacity	68
7.10.1	Introduction	68
7.10.2	Minors	68
7.11	Mentally disordered and drunken persons	70
7.12	Assignment	71
7.12.1	Introduction	71
7.12.2	Assignment by act of parties	71
7.12.3	Assignment by operation of law	72
	Summary	73
	Self-test questions	73
	Exercises	74

8 Form and contents of a contract 75

8.1	Form of a contract	75
8.1.1	Introduction	75
8.1.2	Simple contracts which have to be in writing	76
8.1.3	Simple contracts which have to be evidenced in writing	76
8.1.4	Contracts which must be under seal	77
8.2	Contents of a contract	77

8.2.1	Introduction	77
8.2.2	Terms and representations	78
8.2.3	Express terms	80
8.2.4	Implied terms	80
8.2.5	Classification of terms	82
8.2.6	Exclusion clauses	84
	Summary	92
	Self-test questions	92
	Exercises	93

9 Matters affecting the validity of a contract — 95

9.1	Definitions	95
9.1.1	Valid contracts	95
9.1.2	Voidable contracts	95
9.1.3	Void contracts	95
9.2	Misrepresentation	96
9.2.1	Introduction	96
9.2.2	What constitutes a misrepresentation?	96
9.2.3	Types of misrepresentation	100
9.2.4	Remedies for misrepresentation	101
9.2.5	Exclusion of liability for misrepresentation	105
9.3	Mistake	105
9.3.1	Introduction	105
9.3.2	Mistakes which do not affect a contract	105
9.3.3	Common mistake	106
9.3.4	Mutual mistake	108
9.3.5	Unilateral mistake	108
9.3.6	Mistake as to the nature of the document signed	110
9.3.7	Relief granted by Equity	111
9.4	Duress and undue influence	112
9.4.1	Introduction	112
9.4.2	Duress	112
9.4.3	Undue influence	113
9.5	Illegality	114
9.5.1	Introduction	114
9.5.2	Contracts illegal by statute	115
9.5.3	Contracts which are illegal at common law	115
9.5.4	The effects of illegality	116
9.5.5	Contracts void by statute	119
9.5.6	Contracts void at common law	120
9.5.7	The effect of contracts which are void at common law	123
	Summary	123
	Self-test questions	124
	Exercises	124

10 Discharge of the contract and remedies for breach — 125

10.1	Discharge	125
10.1.1	By performance	125
10.1.2	By agreement	127
10.1.3	By frustration	128
10.1.4	By breach	132
10.2	Remedies for breach of contract	133
10.2.1	Introduction	133
10.2.2	Damages	133
10.2.3	Specific performance	138
10.2.4	Injunction	139
10.2.5	Rescission	140
10.2.6	Rectification	140

	10.2.7 Quantum meruit	140
	10.2.8 Limitation of actions	141
	Summary	141
	Self-test questions	142
	Exercises	142

11 Sale and supply of goods and services — 143

11.1	Sale of goods	143
11.1.1	Introduction	143
11.1.2	Contracts covered by the Sale of Goods Act 1979	143
11.1.3	Implied terms	146
11.1.4	Transfer of property and possession	156
11.1.5	Transfer of title	161
11.1.6	Performance	162
11.1.7	Personal remedies	165
11.1.8	Real remedies	166
11.2	Supply of goods	168
11.2.1	Introduction	168
11.2.2	Supply of goods under the SGSA	169
11.2.3	Terms implied by the SGSA	170
11.3	Supply of services	170
11.3.1	Introduction	170
11.3.2	Contracts covered by the Act	170
11.3.3	Terms implied by the Act	170
	Summary	172
	Self-test questions	172
	Exercises	173

12 Consumer credit — 175

12.1	Types of consumer credit	175
12.2	Credit activities covered by the Act	176
12.2.1	Credit brokers	176
12.2.2	Debt counsellors and debt adjusters	176
12.2.3	Debt collecting agencies	176
12.2.4	Credit reference agencies	176
12.3	Terminology	176
12.3.1	Restricted and unrestricted use credit	177
12.3.2	Debtor-creditor-supplier and debtor-creditor agreements	177
12.4	Agreements covered by the Act	179
12.4.1	Introduction	179
12.4.2	Regulated consumer credit agreements	179
12.4.3	Linked transaction (s19)	180
12.4.4	Agreements excluded in whole or in part from the Act	181
12.5	Protection of debtor before he enters the agreement	181
12.5.1	Introduction	181
12.5.2	Debtor cannot bind himself to enter the agreement (s59 CCA)	182
12.5.3	Creditor's liability for pre-contractual statements	182
12.5.4	Debtor may withdraw from the contract (s57 CCA)	183
12.6	Protection of the debtor in relation to the contract itself	183
12.6.1	Formalities	183
12.6.2	Copies	183
12.6.3	Implied terms	184
12.6.4	Liability of the creditor	184
12.6.5	Debtor's right to have information	186
12.6.6	Extortionate credit bargains	186
12.6.7	Loss of credit token	186
12.7	Rights to end the contract	187
12.7.1	Cancellation	187

	12.7.2	Rescission for misrepresentation	189
	12.7.3	Debtor's right to repudiate for breach of condition	189
	12.7.4	Debtor's right to pay off early	190
	12.7.5	Debtor's right to terminate an H-P or conditional sale agreement	190
	12.7.6	Creditor's right to terminate for debtor's breach	190
	12.7.7	Creditor's right to terminate on the debtor's default	191
	12.8	Protection of the debtor by the court	191
	12.8.1	Time orders	191
	12.8.2	Other orders	191
	12.8.3	Recovery of goods	192
		Summary	192
		Self-test questions	193
		Exercises	193

13 The contract of employment — 195

	13.1	Employees and independent contractors	195
	13.2	Formation of the contract of employment	197
	13.3	The Section 1 statement of employment	197
	13.4	The employer's duties	197
	13.5	The employee's duties	200
	13.5.1	Act reasonably and co-operate	200
	13.5.2	Personal service	200
	13.5.3	Obedience	200
	13.5.4	Good faith	201
	13.5.5	Reasonable care	202
	13.6	Termination of employment—an outline	202
	13.7	Common law termination	203
	13.7.1	Passage of time	203
	13.7.2	Impossibility of performance	203
	13.7.3	Insolvency etc of the employer	204
	13.7.4	Notice	205
	13.7.5	Dismissal without notice	205
	13.7.6	Remedies at common law	207
	13.8	Redundancy payments	208
	13.8.1	Qualifying employees	209
	13.8.2	Redundancy	209
	13.8.3	Offer of alternative employment	210
	13.8.4	Calculation of redundancy payment	210
	13.8.5	Redundancy procedure	211
	13.9	Unfair dismissal	211
	13.9.1	Qualifying employees	211
	13.9.2	Valid reasons for dismissal	212
	13.9.3	Was the employer's action reasonable?	214
	13.9.4	Inadmissable reasons for dismissal	215
	13.9.5	Dismissal of strikers	215
	13.9.6	Written reasons for dismissal	215
	13.9.7	Remedies for unfair dismissal	215
	13.10	Summary of remedies for dismissal	216
		Summary	216
		Self-test questions	217
		Exercises	217

14 Negotiable instruments—introduction — 219

	14.1	Development of the bill of exchange	219
	14.1.1	Assignment of a debt	220
	14.1.2	Development of negotiable instruments	220
	14.1.3	The negotiable instrument	221
	14.2	The characteristics of negotiability	221

14.3	Definition of a bill of exchange	222
14.4	Holder, holder for value and holder in due course	223
14.5	Holder for value	224
14.6	Holder in due course	225
14.7	Liability on a bill of exchange	226
14.8	Indorsement of a bill of exchange	226
14.8.1	Indorsement in blank	226
14.8.2	Special indorsement	226
14.8.3	Conditional indorsement	226
14.8.4	Restrictive indorsement	227
14.8.5	Indorsement sans recours	227
14.8.6	Forged indorsements	227
14.9	Dishonour of the bill of exchange	227
	Summary	227
	Self-test questions	228
	Exercises	228

15 Cheques 229
15.1	The cheque form	229
15.2	Crossings	229
15.2.1	General crossings	230
15.2.2	Special crossing	230
15.2.3	Not negotiable crossing	231
15.2.4	Account payee crossing	231
15.3	Modern clearing	232
15.4	Duties of a customer	232
15.5	Duties of the banker	232
15.6	Protection of the paying banker	234
15.7	Protection of the collecting banker	235
	Summary	236
	Self-test questions	236
	Exercises	237

16 The concept of legal personality 239
16.1	Creation of corporations	239
16.2	Consequences of incorporation	239
16.3	Companies	240
	Summary	241
	Self-test questions	241
	Exercises	241

17 Agency 243
17.1	Creation of agency	243
17.1.1	Introduction	243
17.1.2	Agency created by agreement	244
17.1.3	Agency created by ratification	245
17.1.4	Agency created by estoppel	248
17.1.5	Agency created by operation of law	249
17.2	Duties of an agent	250
17.2.1	Introduction	250
17.2.2	To perform what he has contracted to perform	250
17.2.3	To act with care and skill	250
17.2.4	To perform his duties in person	250
17.2.5	Not to deny principal's title to money or property	251
17.2.6	To act in good faith	251
17.2.7	To account to the principal for all sums received	252
17.3	Rights of an agent	252
17.3.1	A right to indemnity	252

17.3.2	A right to remuneration	252
17.3.3	A right of lien	253
17.4	Effects of agency	254
17.4.1	Where the agent acts for a disclosed principal	254
17.4.2	Where the agent acts for an undisclosed principal	255
17.4.3	Agent's liability to a third party	256
17.5	Termination of agency	257
17.5.1	An agency may be terminated in the following ways	257
17.5.2	Limits on the right to terminate	258
17.5.3	Effects of termination	258
	Summary	259
	Self-test questions	259
	Exercises	260

18 The law of partnership — 261

18.1	Introduction	261
18.2	Definition of a partnership	261
18.3	Creation of a partnership	264
18.3.1	Illegal partnerships	264
18.3.2	Capacity	264
18.3.3	The name of the firm	264
18.3.4	The partnership agreement	265
18.3.5	The continuance of the partnership after the expiry date	266
18.4	Agency of the partners	267
18.5	Liability of the partners	268
18.5.1	Liability in contract	268
18.5.2	Liability in tort	268
18.5.3	The duration of a partner's liabilities	269
18.6	Termination of the partnership	270
18.6.1	Dissolution without a court order	270
18.6.2	Dissolution by order of the court	271
18.6.3	The consequences of dissolution	272
18.7	Differences between companies and partnerships	272
	Self-test questions	274
	Exercises	274

19 Professional negligence and the accountant — 275

19.1	Vicarious liability	275
19.2	Introduction to negligence	276
19.3	Economic loss	279
19.4	Exclusion of liability	280
19.5	The position of auditors	281
19.6	Insurance against risk	284
	Summary	284
	Self-test questions	285
	Exercises	285

Solutions to questions — 287

Additional questions — 347

December 1989 ACCA Accounting Examination Questions — 363

Author's model answers to December 1989 examination — 365

Glossary — 379

Table of cases — 385

Index — 391

CHAPTER ONE

Introduction to the study of law

Why law is important to accountants

There are many courses: accountancy, estate agency, business studies, etc, on which some introductory law has to be studied. You may well ask yourself the question, why study law? Had you wanted to become lawyers you would not have chosen to study accountancy. The answer to this is that law regulates business, and accountancy is concerned with business. You need to understand something about law because business has to operate within the constraints imposed by the law.

Much of this book is concerned with the law of contract and its application to business; sale of goods, consumer credit, agency, partnership, employment and negotiable instruments are all practical applications of the law of contract. You will need in practice to have some understanding of the law on all these topics.

Having said this, and returning to our opening comments, we appreciate that you have no desire to become lawyers and we equally have no desire to turn you into lawyers; in this regard we have too much respect for the thought and care which you have put into your choice of career.

1.1 INTRODUCTION

Many of the rules of law which you will be learning may well be forgotten by you shortly after your examination. What we want you to take forward after Level 1 is two things. Firstly, we want you to have a sound understanding of the general principles of the law of contract. This is because if you have this sound grounding you will probably not find Company Law as daunting as the less well-equipped students. The significance of a good comprehension of Company Law, the rules which apply to corporate businesses, is obvious to you if you wish to become an accountant in business. Secondly, we want you to have a sound grasp of how to deal with legal materials, statutes and decisions of the courts. If you know how to interpret an Act of Parliament you will be in an excellent position to understand Revenue Law. In this regard, every year Parliament passes the Finance Act which implements the Government's budget for the year, with the accompanying changes to tax legislation. Whatever sort of accountancy work you eventually do, you will almost certainly have to deal with the interpretation of tax statutes.

So law is something which must be studied. It has a relevance both to business life and to your immediate future career. What we shall try to do is to make it as interesting and as relevant to accountancy as we can, we promise you, we are not in the business of missionary work trying to convert you to become lawyers!

1.2 THE STUDY OF LAW

When we first started to study law we were both told that there was no substitute for hard work. You must have experienced the sort of talks that are so frequently given by encouraging headmasters and benevolent celebrities at school prize days: 'keep working hard and you will succeed'. Unfortunately this is said so often that it almost becomes meaningless. And this is equally unfortunate and sad in this context because it is very much the case with law that hard work is necessary for success. You cannot guess what the law is. You either know a rule of law or you do not know it. Law is often not a matter of common sense. So the sensible guess of the intelligent layman as to what the law is on a particular matter is as likely to be wrong as it is to be right. In a way this is one of the good points about law as an examination subject. No great imagination or flair is needed, simply hard work. If you have done the ground work and understood it, examination success is virtually certain.

1.2.1 How to study a topic

Because law is a complex body of rules, it is very easy for a beginner to lose his way at the beginning of a new topic. The key to success is to get to understand at an early stage exactly what the topic is about. You all know the expression about 'not being able to see the wood for the trees', law is rather like that. You have first to see the wood; after this you can fill in the detail about the various trees. One of the best ways of approaching a new chapter is firstly to read through only the paragraph headings. This will show you the structure of the chapter. After this, read through the text. At this stage it is perhaps as well not to make notes. Simply read the chapter through, making no attempt to memorise any individual rules. After this, and bearing in mind the paragraph headings, decide how you are going to break down your learning into manageable segments. Having done this, you might start to make a few notes.

1.2.2 How to make notes

Because law consists of rule after rule, it is seductively easy to make lots of notes. This is usually a mistake, because when you do this you frequently find yourself writing out the textbook. It is better simply to make a few notes, leaving a lot of space for further notes to be added at a later stage. Leave wide margins on either side of the page, and leave plenty of lines between paragraphs.

Having developed your basic notes in this way, start to work through examination questions. There are typical questions at the end of each chapter, and also a past examination paper with this book. When you answer a question, mark in your notes (a) that you have answered a question on this point, and (b) any particular points of law raised by the question which you have not included in your first attempt at making the notes.

Work through as many questions as you can. This will highlight the important points on any particular topic, and, if you annotate your notes as we have suggested, you will ultimately have a useful set of notes from which to revise.

Having produced these notes, you should try to read them through regularly. Revision should not be left to the last minute. It is good practice to set aside a set period of time, say an hour once a fortnight, when you can quickly read through your law notes. Even without consciously trying to remember individual rules, you will be surprised at how much knowledge you begin to acquire.

On the subject of note-taking, we finish with what should be your key principle: take note rather than notes.

1.2.3 Problem answering

Something which newcomers to the study of law find difficult is problem solving. This is where a question is asked by means of a short case-study. The candidate is presented with a short set of facts and asked how he would deal with them.

Although at first sight problems might appear more difficult than essays, they are in fact much easier to score marks on. This is because each point raised by the problem should remind you of a rule of law which you are required to mention. In other words, problems should prompt you as to what you should be writing. As a result of this, you will probably find it easier to avoid omitting crucial points in your answers with problems than with straightforward essay questions.

When answering problems you should ensure that your attempt at an answer goes through four stages. Firstly, you should identify the point in issue. This need only be a couple of sentences. Simply state what you see as the object of the question. Secondly, outline the relevant law. This part of your answer should go into some depth into the law on the topic identified in your opening sentences. Thirdly, apply the law to the problem in hand. All too frequently students feel that it is sufficient merely to state the law. This is not the case. You must ensure that you show how the law applied to the problem set. Finally, answer the question in the terms set. If you are asked to advise someone, then you should conclude your answer in those terms.

It would be meaningless at this stage to try to give an example of how this applied to a specific problem. This must wait until you have studied some law. However, throughout this book there are numerous problems and suggested solutions. As and when you come to these, please note how the four stages just referred to are dealt with.

CHAPTER TWO

The nature and classification of English law

This chapter is an introduction to the subject of law. Many of you are probably studying law for the first time and so your first question may well be 'What is law?' When we have answered this question, we shall then look at the characteristics of English law as it is this law which you are studying for the examination. Finally we shall consider some of the possible classifications of English law.

2.1 WHAT IS LAW?

The word '**law**' is used in many different senses. For example, there are laws of science, moral laws, and the laws of sport. In this book we are going to be considering the general principles of English law as it is applied in the courts. There is no generally accepted definition of what law is in this sense, but a useful working definition is 'the body of principles recognised and applied by the State in the administration of justice'. This may also be expressed slightly differently as the set of rules recognised and acted on by the Courts of Justice.

The type of law with which we are concerned is that which regulates the conduct of men and women in a particular community. It may affect them as private individuals or on a business basis. It may regulate their conduct as citizens, for example, in the maintenance of official secrets. The law is accepted and obeyed by most of the people whose conduct it regulates and is enforceable by the sovereign authority within the community.

2.2 THE CHARACTERISTICS OF ENGLISH LAW

'English law' means the law of England. England (which in this context includes Wales but not Scotland, Northern Ireland, the Isle of Man or the Channel Islands) is a smaller geographical unit than the United Kingdom. The United Kingdom is a parliamentary union and for international purposes is the State. England and Wales is a smaller unit and has to be clearly identified as different from Great Britain, which is a union of the kingdoms of England and Scotland. This is because Scotland has her own legal system. Scots law is quite different from English law. This book and your syllabus confines itself to English law.

English law has a number of distinct characteristics. In the following paragraphs they will be considered in detail. They include:

1   A single system of law from Saxon times
2   The absence of a code of law
3   The judicial character of English law
4   Accusatorial procedure
5   Limited influence of Roman law
6   The doctrine of precedent

2.3 THE GROWTH OF ONE SYSTEM FROM SAXON TIMES

To a foreign observer, probably the most striking characteristic of English law is its antiquity and continuity. Most of the countries on the continent of Europe have modern legal systems which have emerged over the past 200 years or so. Many came about following a revolution within the country concerned. English law, on the other hand, has an unbroken history which can be followed right back to Ethelbert who was King of Kent from 560 to 616. The law has been evolved and recorded since this time without any fundamental change in the system. This, of course, is not to say that the law has not changed. It has altered and developed to meet changing needs of society. However the change and development has been a continuous process. One early English writer, John Selden, said that English law was like 'the ship by often mending had no piece of the first material'. In other words, the law itself had changed in detail, but the body of law had continued to exist throughout the entire period. Another aspect of this characteristic is that a rule of law does not cease to exist merely because it is not used for a long time. Thus, however old a case is when it is considered by the court, it is still evidence of what the law is, so long as it has not been overruled by either another case or a statute.

2.4 ABSENCE OF A CODE OF LAWS

Codification may be said to have two different meanings, firstly the enshrining in a single document all the basic law and secondly the enshrining in a single statute all the law on one particular topic. English law has never been codified in the first of these senses. In English law, a unified system was reached at an early stage in its development. To produce a complete code of English law would be a very difficult and probably unnecessary task today, though there has been some movement towards codification in specific areas, such as sale of goods, partnership and bankruptcy.

Other areas of law, such as land law and company law, have been consolidated by Act of Parliament. Consolidation means the bringing together of all statutory provisions into a single statute. This is different from codification which involves the bringing together into a single statute not only statutory provisions but also all other relevant law from whatever source, such as cases and custom.

2.5 JUDICIAL CHARACTER OF ENGLISH LAW

As has been said, English law is uncodified. Closely tied in with this is its judicial character. English case law is made by the judges and this body of case law forms the basis of the English legal system. Acts of Parliament assume the existence of case law, and unless a clear intention is shown to the contrary, it is assumed that statute does not alter the established case law. When a case comes to court, both existing case law and statutes on the particular subject in question have to be interpreted by the judges. In a later chapter we shall consider how the judges interpret cases and statutes. At this stage it is sufficient to note that, because the judges do have this duty to interpret existing law, they have always played a most significant role in the development of the law.

2.6 THE ACCUSATORIAL PROCEDURE

In English law, the judge remains neutral throughout the procedure and hears the argument put forward by both sides in civil and criminal cases. This is called the accusatorial or adversarial method of procedure. In some foreign legal systems, it is for the court itself to adduce evidence which will be heard and considered. This is known as the inquisitorial procedure.

It follows from this that there are always two sides in every case. What the sides are called depends upon the type of case. For example, in a criminal case the one party will be the prosecutor and the other the accused. In a civil action, for example, in negligence or breach of contract, the party bringing the action will be the plaintiff, and the one being sued, the defendant. In some company cases the one side will be the petitioner and the other the respondent. Whatever the sides are known as, they can always be divided between the one bringing the case and the one opposing it. This is reflected in the way in which the case is cited (ie the title given to it in the Law Report and textbooks). For example, when you come to look at the law of negligence, you will consider the case of *Donoghue* v *Stevenson* (1932). This indicates that one party to the action was called Donoghue and the other Stevenson. Having said this, sometimes cases will be cited by a single name, for example, *The Wagon Mound* (1961). This case, you will discover, again when you consider the law of negligence, concerned a ship. Most Admiralty cases are cited in this way. However, even in a case cited like this there are two sides.

THE NATURE AND CLASSIFICATION OF ENGLISH LAW: CHAPTER TWO

2.7 LIMITED INFLUENCE OF ROMAN LAW

Roman law was one of the first complete systems of law to be fully recorded in textbooks. It was a highly developed and highly sophisticated system of law, and it formed the basis of the legal systems of many countries on the continent of Europe. Scots law also reflects the influence of Roman law. However, the impact of Roman law on the English legal system has been minimal.

2.8 THE DOCTRINE OF PRECEDENT

Since the 13th century, the English courts have adopted a system of interpreting past cases. This system is known as the doctrine of binding judicial precedent. Under this, the decisions of certain courts must in principle be followed by other courts. The doctrine is central to English law and will be considered in detail in a later chapter.

2.9 THE CLASSIFICATION OF ENGLISH LAW

There are many different ways in which the law can be classified. First it may be classified by reference to the subject matter of a dispute. For example, a major distinction can be drawn between criminal and civil law. When most people who have not studied law think of the work of lawyers they think of the criminal law, the prosecution of murderers and thieves, the punishment of car drivers who break the law etc. Curiously, however, civil law is by far the larger body of law, applying in almost every area of human activity, for example, when we buy a newspaper, when we are injured in a road accident, when we vote in an election, when we rent accommodation or when we die.

The aims of the criminal law may be said to be the suppression of crime, the protection of society, and the punishment of criminals. On the other hand, the aims of the civil law are the enforcement of obligations, the compensation of injured parties, and the recovery of property not in the hands of the true owner. The distinction between civil and criminal law is to be found in the purpose of the action rather than the action which gives rise to the case. In civil actions compensation by way of damages is usually sought. In criminal actions it is the punishment of the offender which is desired. There are some situations in which conduct will give rise to both criminal and civil liability. For example, if a person drives his car recklessly and causes injury to some other road user, he may be prosecuted for reckless driving and sued by the injured person for compensation in negligence. Similarly, if one person steals property belonging to another, he may be prosecuted in a criminal court and also sued in a civil court by the true owner of the property either for the recovery of the property itself or, if this is not possible, for its value.

Another way of categorising the law is between public law and private law. Private law in this regard is the law which applies to private individuals such as the law of contract, the law of tort, (ie, civil wrongs such as negligence or defamation) and family law. Public law on the other hand is law directly relevant to the State such as constitutional and administrative law, planning law and highway law, and criminal law.

Yet another division is between substantive law and procedural law. Substantive law is the body of those rules of law, whether civil or criminal, which define civil wrongs and criminal offences. Procedural law, on the other hand, lays down the rules governing how rights are enforced under civil law or crimes prosecuted under the criminal law.

SUMMARY

This chapter has been simply an introduction to the nature and classification of English law. You may find some of the ideas which have been expressed rather difficult to understand. This is often the nature of a preliminary chapter. As you progress through this book, what is said here will make more sense to you and so you are advised to read this again when you have dealt with more of the subject. The characteristics of English law are particularly important and you should make every effort to understand these characteristics, though some, such as the doctrine of precedent, will be fully understood only when the doctrine has been examined in more detail.

LAW

SELF-TEST QUESTIONS

2.1 List six of the characteristics of English law

2.2 Why has English law not been fully codified?

2.3 Jones has stolen some goods from Green. The police prosecute Jones for theft and Green sues him for the return of the goods

(a) Will the action by the police be in
   (i) criminal law? or
   (ii) civil law?

(b) In this action, will Jones be called
   (i) the defendant?
   (ii) the respondent?
   (iii) the accused?

(c) Will the action brought by Green be in
   (i) criminal law? or
   (ii) civil law?

(d) In this action will Jones be called
   (i) the defendant?
   (ii) the respondent?
   (iii) the accused?

2.4 **Complete the following sentence:**
'English law may be classified into

(a) Criminal and ____;
(b) Public and ____;
(c) ____ and procedural'.

Answers on page 289

EXERCISES

Exercise 2.1

Explain the difference between codification and consolidation of the law and give examples of each.

Exercise 2.2

What are the main characteristics of English law?

Answers on page 289

CHAPTER THREE

Historical development of English law

In this chapter we are going to consider the historical development of English law. It is dealt with very much in outline and is intended as no more than background reading. However, some knowledge of the development of law is essential especially in order to understand the complicated concept of the equitable jurisdiction of the courts today.

3.1 ORIGIN AND DEVELOPMENT OF THE COMMON LAW

The term '**common law**' in its strictest sense means those laws which have been developed by the common law courts as distinct from the rules developed by the courts of equity. The expression has other meanings, depending upon how it is being used. For example, it can mean English law as opposed to the law of another State. It can mean law created by the custom of the people as opposed to statute law.

Prior to the Norman Conquest in 1066 the population of what is now the United Kingdom was essentially tribal. No central government was in existence and there was no uniform legal system such as exists today. Most areas of population which were usually to be found in townships throughout the country such as Chester, Lancaster and Durham had their own customs and rules. They also had their own methods of applying these. Justice would be administered within the community by the local chief (by whatever name he was called) either arbitrarily by himself or through a court over which he presided. It was only after the Conquest that attempts were made to develop a system of centralisation.

The process was begun by William the Conqueror. He developed the existing feudal system. This system was based on land ownership throughout the country. Each person held his land as a tenant of another person, with the King himself as the ultimate owner. Some time after the Conquest as part of the centralisation of Government, the system developed whereby disputes were settled by itinerant justices who were sent out by the King to tour the country to try cases for the crown. The justices took their authority from a commission given them by the King, and from the reign of Henry II (1154–1189) they went out at regular intervals.

At first they would go into a tribal community and administer both royal justice and those customs peculiar to that community. First, of course, they would have to learn what the local customs for the particular tribal community were. These frequently they would learn with the help of a jury. Having learned them they would then apply them to the case. Over the years the justices refused to apply bad customs, and, no doubt following discussions between themselves, would apply the best customs throughout the country. Thus over a period of time some local customs gained the force of general law as the justices applied the best customs in this way. This was the origin of the common law: the law common to the entire country.

3.2 THE EARLY COURTS

The courts in which the justices exercised their judicial functions throughout the land were known as assize courts, the judges being known as commissioners of assize. In addition to these courts, there were three other courts established in London. The Court of King's Bench dealt mainly with criminal matters and also certain civil matters in which the king had an interest. The Court of Common Pleas (or Common Bench) dealt with civil actions brought by one subject against another. The Court of Exchequer dealt with revenue matters and with a few civil matters. These courts, which were established in about the 12th century, lasted until they were abolished by the Judicature Act in 1875.

No action at common law could commence without the service of a writ on the defendant. This was a formal document obtained, on payment, from the administrative offices of the Chancery, the secretarial department of state. As the writ set out the allegation in the case, it was essential that the correct writ should be chosen otherwise no action could be pursued. In the early days there was no limit to the types of writ which could be issued. However, the Provisions of Oxford (1258) and the Statute of Westminster (1285) had the effect of preventing the issue of new writs unless they could be shown to be similar to existing ones. Thus there crept into the law a rigidity and inflexibility which prevented many injured parties from obtaining a remedy.

3.3 THE EARLY DEVELOPMENT OF EQUITY

In ordinary language the word 'equity' means 'fairness' or 'justice'. However in law the word has a specialised meaning. It refers to the rules, developed by the Court of Chancery, which themselves were originally based upon the ideas of fairness.

The early common law system had a number of significant defects which were all too apparent by the 15th century. As was said in the previous section, an action could not be commenced unless there was an appropriate writ. In the early development of the common law it used to be said that where there was a right there was a remedy. This meant that where someone had a grievance then there was an appropriate writ. By the 15th century the situation had changed so that where there was a remedy there was a right. In other words an aggrieved citizen could commence proceedings only if there were a writ which fitted his particular case. In other words, however much a litigant had been wronged, if there was no writ to cover the situation, then he had no remedy. Besides this, there were other defects. There was no proper system of appeals. The litigant, dissatisfied with the decision reached by the court in which he originated his case had no possibility of appealing to a higher court. Trial was always by jury. As has been said, in the early days of the legal system the jury used to assist the commissioners of assize to discover what the customary law was in a particular locality. It seems curious today, when the jury must be seen to be impartial and have no connection with or knowledge of the litigant, that in the early times the role of the jury was the exact opposite. They would know the litigants and this was thought to assist them in deciding which side to believe. There was the very real risk in this situation that a juror might be influenced by a powerful litigant.

3.3.1 Remedy at common law

Finally, the only common law remedy was damages. The award of damages is a monetary compensation paid to a person for some loss which he has suffered. This obviously is a useful remedy where, for example, a neighbour's cattle have trespassed on the plaintiff's land and caused damage. However, there are times when an injunction (an order prohibiting a course of conduct) or specific performance (an order enforcing a particular action) would be more desirable. For example, suppose a neighbour's cattle regularly trespassed over land, then while damages would help compensate for the damage caused, an injunction, ordering the neighbour to restrain his cattle on pain of punishment would obviously be more useful.

THE CONCEPT OF EQUITY

Thus, over the years, the practice developed for a litigant who had failed to obtain a satisfactory result at common law to petition the King for a remedy. The King would pass such petitions on to his chief minister, the Chancellor, for his attention. This became so popular a way of seeking redress that in the 15th century a permanent Court of Chancery was established to hear them. In the early days, the Chancellor would decide each case on the basis of what he felt was fair in the circumstances of the case. There was a saying that equity varied with the length of the Chancellor's foot. However, by the 17th century, the doctrine of precedent was firmly established even in the Court of Chancery, and this had a limiting effect on the discretionary powers of the Chancellor. As the doctrine of precedent had its impact, the Court of Chancery became preoccupied with procedural formalities. The Court of Chancery had one further unique feature. Until the 19th century there was only one judge who sat in the Court of Chancery, the Chancellor himself. This obviously resulted in delay before cases were heard.

In spite of this, equity made important contributions to English law. It recognised rights and concepts which were unknown to the common law. For example, it recognised the concept of a trust whereby legal and equitable ownership could be divided. If A holds property on trust for B the legal ownership of the property is A's but the beneficial ownership is B's. This means that if the property consists of money in a deposit account, then although the investment is in A's name, the right to the dividend is B's. Another concept which it recognised was the mortgage. Prior to this the only means of security was the pledge. This involved the deposit of property with the lender as security. The borrower was therefore deprived of the use of the property. Equity recognised a mortgage, whereby the borrower remained in possession of the property though (at least before 1925 when property law was radically reformed) the ownership lay in the lender, so that in the event of the borrower defaulting on his obligations under the mortgage to repay principal and to pay interest, the lender could realise his security (ie sell the property in order to recover what he was owed). At common law the only possible remedy was damages. As has been seen, damages is a satisfactory remedy where the plaintiff is suing to recover for a loss which he has sustained. Equity recognised the remedies of injunction and specific performance used respectively to restrain a person from doing something or requiring him to act according to his undertaking. It also modified or extended many common law rules, such as allowing a contract to be set aside on the grounds of fraud or mistake.

3.4 THE JUDICATURE ACTS 1873–1875

The 18th century was a sad period in the history of English law; it was a time of stagnation and complacency. It gave birth, however, to the great jurist Jeremy Bentham, who was born in 1748 and who lived to be nearly 90. Throughout his life he devoted himself to the criticism of legal institutions and the suggestion of how reform could take place. His followers continued his work after his death and eventually his labours bore fruit. There were a number of defects in the English legal system in the first half of the 19th century. Law and equity were dealt with in different courts. This resulted in a litigant who wanted both an equitable and a common law remedy having to take two separate sets of proceedings in two different courts. His common law claim for damages might, for example, be pursued in the Court of King's Bench, while his claim for an injunction, an equitable remedy, would be pursued in the Court of Chancery. Matters such as matrimonial causes and probate were dealt with in a separate ecclesiastical court, having its own unique procedure. No adequate system of appeals existed. Procedure both in the Court of Chancery and the Common Law Court was antiquated. Finally, although equity had developed as a system of law to mitigate the harshness of the common law, some of its rules had by this time developed in such a way as to conflict directly with the rules of common law.

The second half of the 19th century saw a number of important reforms. The Court of Probate Act 1857 abolished the probate jurisdiction of the ecclesiastical courts and established a new Court of Probate. In the same year the Matrimonial Causes Act transferred the matrimonial jurisdiction of the ecclesiastical courts to a specially created divorce court. The Chancery Procedure Act 1852 and the Common Law Procedure Act 1854 allowed the respective courts of common law and equitable jurisdiction to apply the remedies of the other jurisdiction in certain cases, and today, as a result of these and later changes, equity and Common law are now applied in the same courts. However by far the most radical change was seen in the Supreme Court of Judicature Act 1873–1875. These Acts abolished both the old common law courts and the Court of Chancery and replaced them with a single new court, the Supreme Court of Judicature, which incorporated the jurisdiction of the former courts. In fact the use of the word 'supreme' is somewhat misleading. It was adopted because at the time it was intended to abolish the right of appeal to the House of Lords. The Supreme Court consisted of two branches, the higher branch, the Court of Appeal, and the lower branch, the High Court of Justice. The new system came into being on 1 November 1875. The High Court consisted of five divisions, the Queen's Bench Division, (for by now Queen Victoria was on the throne), the Chancery Division, the Common Pleas Division, the Exchequer Division and the Probate, Divorce and Admiralty Division.

The Queen's Bench Division replaced the old common law courts. The Chancery Division replaced the Court of Chancery. The Probate, Divorce and Admiralty Division (now itself replaced by the Family Division) replaced the separate specialist courts which earlier in the century had dealt with these matters. Each division had jurisdiction over any matter coming before it, though for administrative reasons the business of a particular division fell mainly within its particular area of expertise.

The Judicature Acts were themselves amended by and consolidated in the Judicature Act 1925 though the broad structure of the courts remained intact until the major reforms brought about by the Administration of Justice Act 1970 and the Courts Act 1971. The structure of the Supreme Court is now to be found in the Supreme Court Act 1981.

Incidentally the county courts, which were established in 1846 to deal with small civil matters, are not part of the Supreme Court and have not been significantly affected by these Acts.

3.5 THE RELATIONSHIP TODAY BETWEEN COMMON LAW AND EQUITY

As has been seen, the common law developed as a complete system of law. By its nature, equity assumes the existence of the common law. It is sometimes described as a gloss on the common law. It was developed to deal with some of the defects of the common law and as such it cannot exist in isolation. Equity presupposes the existence of the common law and this is very much reflected in the relationship between the two systems today.

Both common law and equity have developed in the broad context of the English legal system, and so both rely heavily upon the doctrine of judicial precedent and both have been partly embodied in statutes such as the Sale of Goods Act 1979 and the Trustee Act 1925. There are, however, still a number of significant differences between common law and equity.

1. Equity is not in itself a complete system of law. The common law is a complete system, though equitable rules have developed from time to time to supplement the common law when necessary.

2. Equity is said to act *in personam* (on the person) whereas common law is said to act *in rem* (on the thing ie legal rights are enforceable against everyone). This has two different meanings.

    Firstly equitable remedies are given against the person and are enforceable ultimately by imprisonment of that person. An injunction, for example, is essentially an order to a specified person or persons not to do something. It is not made against the world at large. Common law remedies, on the other hand, are in the form of damages and as such are against property.

    Secondly, common law rights are enforceable against anyone and everyone. On the other hand, equitable rights are enforceable only against those persons who are bound in conscience and in law to recognise them, such as persons having knowledge that the right exists. So the equitable remedy of rescission (the right to set aside a contract) cannot be used if a third party has paid for and acquired an interest in the property which is the subject matter of the dispute and has obtained this interest without notice of the defect in title.

    This sounds complex but it is easily illustrated. We shall see when we come to look at the law of contract that a party who enters into a contract as a result of a misrepresentation (ie a false statement of fact designed to induce him to enter into the contract) may set the contract aside or claim damages. So if A buys a car from a garage as a result of the salesman saying that it had covered only 20,000 miles when in fact it had covered 60,000, A could ask to rescind that contract. However, if A had acquired the car as a result of a part exchange deal and had traded in his old car and the garage had then sold that car to a third party who knew nothing of the earlier misrepresentation, A would not be able to claim rescission. All he could claim would be damages.

3. The common law remedy of damages is available as of right given that the plaintiff proves his case. No matter how unmeritorious his claim, if it is justified in law then he is entitled to damages. Equitable remedies are only available at the discretion of the courts. So, for example, if a person claiming an injunction has not himself acted with complete integrity in the transaction then the court will not order the injunction for him against the defendant.

4. At common law an action must be commenced within the limitation period. The law will not allow a plaintiff to commence proceedings too long after the occurrence of the incident giving rise to the claim. Thus, for example, an action for personal injuries suffered as a result of the alleged negligence of the defendant must be commenced within three years of the injuries being caused. An action for breach of contract must generally be commenced within six years of the breach. Equitable remedies are not subject to such a mathematical restriction. They must be sought without undue delay. In equity there is a doctrine known as *laches*. This means that if the plaintiff delays for too long then his claim will be thrown out. What is 'too long' is essentially a matter for the court to determine. However, it is certainly a shorter period of time than the common law limitation period.

5 If there is a conflict or variance between the rules of equity and the rules of common law then the rules of equity must prevail. An example of this is the case of:

Walsh v Lonsdale (1882)

Here there was a written agreement for a lease between A and B. One of the terms of the lease was that a deed should be executed containing a covenant to pay one year's rent in advance. B went into possession under the agreement and paid rent for some time though never in advance. Subsequently A claimed rent from B in advance. At common law, because the deed had never been executed, A was not entitled to enforce the provision requiring rent in advance. However, it was held by the court that since an agreement to execute a deed such as existed here would be specifically enforceable in equity (in other words A could take B to court and obtain an order of specific performance against him to make him enter into the agreement) and since the Judicature Act provided that where there was a conflict between law and equity, equity should prevail, A was entitled to claim the rent in advance.

There are no examination questions on this chapter since it is essentially background reading and does not form part of the examination syllabus.

SUMMARY

In this chapter we have been looking at the historical development of English law which, although very much background reading, is nevertheless very necessary for an understanding of much of present day law. A prime characteristic of English law is its continuous development over a long period of time, indeed since long before the Norman Conquest. First there existed customs unique to a particular locality. Then there came the development of the common law. Finally, superimposed upon this to meet some of the defects of the common law, was the system of equity. Probably the most important thing to draw from this chapter is an understanding of the inter relationship of common law and equity today.

SELF-TEST QUESTIONS

3.1 Which of the following sentences is true?

(a) The common law cannot exist without equity
(b) Equity cannot exist without the common law

3.2 What were the major defects in early common law which lead to the creation of equity?

3.3 What are the main contributions of equity to British law?

3.4 What are the key distinctions between the common law and equity?

3.5 How does the case of *Walsh v Lonsdale* (1882) deal with the relationship between the common law and equity?

Answers on page 290

The system of courts and personnel of the law

There are a number of different ways of classifying English courts. They may, for example, be divided into courts of record and courts which are not of record; or into superior and inferior courts; or courts of first instance and courts of appeal; or civil and criminal courts.

4.1 THE WORK OF THE COURTS

4.1.1 Courts of record and not of record

Historically, a court of record was a court which maintained a record of its proceedings. The phrase now means a court which has a power to punish for contempt. This power is available to courts such as the county court, the High Court, the Court of Appeal and the House of Lords.

4.1.2 Superior and inferior courts

The superior courts are the House of Lords, Court of Appeal, High Court, Crown Court, Restrictive Practices Court, Employment Appeal Tribunal and the Judicial Committee of the Privy Council. All courts not within the above category are inferior courts, and include the county courts and magistrates' courts.

The jurisdiction of superior courts is not limited either in geographical terms or in terms of the value of the subject matter in dispute. A distinctive feature of inferior courts is that they are subject to the supervisory jurisdiction of the High Court exercised by prerogative order. The High Court also has power to supervise the Crown Court in the exercise of its appellate jurisdiction, even though the Crown Court is a superior court.

4.1.3 Courts of first instance and of appeal

This is not a satisfactory distinction as, although some courts, such as the House of Lords and Court of Appeal, exercise a purely appellate jurisdiction, and others, such as the magistrates' courts have no appellate jurisdiction, many courts, especially the High Court and the Crown Court, exercise both original and appellate jurisdiction.

4.1.4 Civil and criminal courts

For the sake of convenience, this is the categorisation we will use in this chapter.

You will remember that civil law deals with actions by one person against another, criminal law with actions by the State against a person who acts contrary to the rules imposed by the State, for example, a person who commits a crime. As we will see, some courts, such as the House of Lords, Court of Appeal, High Court, Crown Court and the magistrates' courts exercise jurisdiction in both civil and criminal matters.

4.2 CIVIL COURT STRUCTURE

The hierarchy of the civil courts is shown below. The arrows show the courts to and from which appeals may be made. It is important to know the court structure as it is on this that an effective doctrine of precedent depends.

The functions and grounds for appeal from each court will be explained in relation to this diagram.

DIAGRAM 4.2

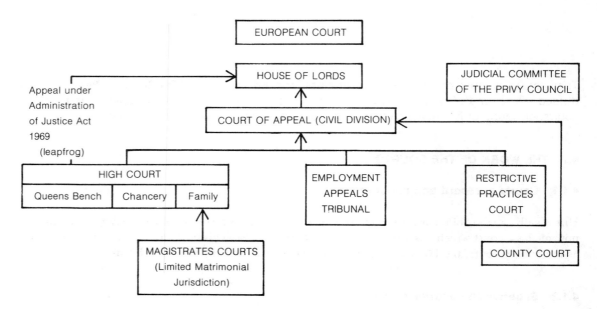

4.3 CIVIL COURTS (FIRST INSTANCE)

4.3.1 Magistrates' courts

Magistrates' courts have a limited civil jurisdiction. This is mainly concerned with matrimonial matters such as:

1. Matrimonial disputes (other than divorce petitions)
2. Guardianship and adoption
3. Affiliation
4. Actions for unpaid rates
5. Licensing of, for example, premises for the sale of alcohol

Appeal from the magistrates' courts on matrimonial proceedings lies to the Family Division of the High Court; on matters relating to licensing to the Crown Court.

4.3.2 County courts

County courts are governed by the County Courts Act 1959 (as amended) and the County Court Rules which are a form of delegated legislation and which give the procedure to be followed in these courts.

There are over 400 county courts in England and Wales.

1 PERSONNEL OF THE COUNTY COURTS

Each county court has a judge assisted by a Registrar. A county court judge is either a circuit judge or a Recorder both of whom are ex officio county court judges or exceptionally a judge of the High Court or the Court of Appeal. Normally, circuit judges will hear the cases and will sit alone. He may however sit with a jury of 8 people if the action relates to a charge of fraud or if it is a defamation action remitted from the High Court. The Registrar acts as clerk of the court but he will also hear the smaller cases, especially under the small claims procedure. He must be a solicitor of at least 7 years' standing.

2 FUNCTION OF THE COUNTY COURTS

The county courts were established to deal with small civil claims within their area. These courts deal with the majority of civil law cases heard in the United Kingdom.

Each court's jurisdiction is limited to the locality in which it is situated. Thus, actions in a county court may be brought only if the defendant lives or carries on business within that court's district or if it was in that district that the cause of action arose.

3 JURISDICTION OF THE COUNTY COURTS

As we said earlier, county courts are designed to hear small local actions so, as well as being restricted geographically in their jurisdiction, they are also limited in relation to the value of the claims they may hear.

The county courts' jurisdiction includes:

1. Actions in contract where the sum claimed is less than £5,000. If, however, both parties to an action agree to waive this limit the court may hear claims for higher amounts.
2. Actions in tort where the amount claimed does not exceed £5,000. This limit does not apply in the case of defamation actions.
3. Equitable matters such as trusts, dissolution of partnerships and actions relating to mortgages where the sum involved is less than £30,000.
4. Unlimited jurisdiction to deal with insolvencies is granted to some county courts outside London. These courts will also have jurisdiction to wind-up companies with a paid-up share capital of less than £120,000.
5. Actions relating to the title to, and recovery of possession of, land the net annual rateable value of which does not exceed £5,000.
6. Undefended divorces.
7. Matters required by statute to be dealt with by the county court. For example, the Consumer Credit Act 1974 states that actions under the Act will be brought in the county court.

4 THE SMALL CLAIMS PROCEDURE

In order to make the courts more accessible and to establish a quicker, cheaper and more efficient means of dealing with small claims, an arbitration procedure was established. This arbitration is carried out under guidelines set out by the Lord Chancellor and is usually heard by the Registrar although it may be conducted by a judge or an outside arbitrator if application for this to happen is made.

The small claims procedure applies to claims of £500 or less and, in fact, any action within this limit is automatically referred to arbitration. Such a referral will be rescinded by the Registrar following application by one of the parties only if:

1. The action involves complicated issues of law or fact, or,
2. Fraud is alleged in the case, or,
3. Both parties agree to the case going to trial, or,
4. In the light of the subject matter of the claim or of the interests of the parties or of the circumstances of the case, arbitration would be unreasonable.

The procedure in small claims is kept simple. It starts with an attempt to reach agreement between the parties and only if this fails will the action proceed to a hearing. The arbitrator may adopt any procedure he thinks would be both effective and fair to the parties. Solicitor's charges are not normally allowed in this type of arbitration. The only costs that are allowed are those relating to the cost of the summons, the costs of enforcing any award made, and any legal expenses which have been incurred because the party ordered to pay the costs has behaved unreasonably.

4.3.3 High Court

The High Court has jurisdiction to try any case other than those allocated by statute to the county or another court. For administrative reasons, the High Court is split into three divisions, each of which deals with different types of case.

The three divisions are:

QUEEN'S BENCH DIVISION (QBD)

This division deals with common law cases and matters not dealt with in the other divisions. In particular, it deals with claims in contract and tort for sums exceeding £5,000, and, as part of its function, has jurisdiction over Admiralty and Commercial matters.

CHANCERY DIVISION (Ch D)

This division deals with trusts, mortgages, bankruptcy, company and partnership matters, specific performance of contracts and disputes relating to wills, for example, cases relating to the validity or otherwise of a will, to the meaning of a will and, if there is no will, cases relating to the estate of the deceased.

FAMILY DIVISION (Fam D)

This division deals with family matters such as contested divorce cases, annulment of marriages, judicial separations and wardship cases.

Each of the three divisions has its own head. There are something just below 100 puisne (ie lesser) judges in the High Court each of whom is assigned to a division by the Lord Chancellor. The QBD is headed by the Lord Chief Justice and has approximately 40 puisne judges; the Chancery Division is headed by the Vice-Chancellor and has 10 puisne judges; and the head of the Family Division is called the President. Family Division has 16 puisne judges.

Procedure in both the High Court and the Court of Appeal is governed by the Rules of the Supreme Court. These are a form of delegated legislation having been drawn up by the Rules Committee. This Committee is made up of judges, barristers and solicitors. A case is usually heard by a judge sitting alone, although either party to an action relating to defamation, malicious prosecution or false imprisonment may require the case to be heard by a jury. If the action involves fraud, the defendant may demand trial by jury.

The High Court is situated in London but High Court judges may hear cases anywhere in England or Wales at centres determined by the Lord Chancellor.

PREROGATIVE ORDERS

One of the Queen's Bench Division's important functions is to prevent an abuse of power by inferior courts and tribunals or by national or local government departments or even by individuals. In other words, the QBD has a duty to protect individuals against injustice. It does this by means of the prerogative orders. These orders derive their name from the fact that, originally, they were issued under the royal prerogative. Now they are dealt with by the QBD under the procedure known as 'judicial review'.

Application for review is made under the procedure set out in Order 53 of the Rules of the Supreme Court. The prerogative orders are as follows:

MANDAMUS

This literally means 'we summon' and is an order of the QBD to require an individual, body or organisation to carry out its duty under the law. For example, an order of mandamus may be made against:

1. a local authority, to make it produce its accounts for inspection.
2. a lower court, requiring it to hear a case which it has wrongly refused to hear.
3. a government department, to make it carry out its legal obligations to an individual.

An order of mandamus, however, will be issued only if the individual, body etc has a legal duty to carry out the act in question. It will not be issued when the body merely has a discretion as to whether it will act. Furthermore, mandamus will be issued only where there is no other satisfactory remedy.

PROHIBITION

This is an order issued to prevent a court, tribunal or other judicial or quasi-judicial body from exceeding its jurisdiction. It will be issued, for example, if a tribunal tries to hear a case which it has no power to hear; if, in other words, it acts beyond its powers or *ultra vires*.

The QBD may issue a prohibition to prevent it acting in this way. Such an order, however, will not lie against a non-statutory body, such as a social club, nor where a final decision has been reached. In this last case, the aggrieved party will have to apply for an order of *Certiorari* (see later).

An example of prohibition, as well as mandamus, is shown in the case of:

Re Godden (1971)

G was a Chief Inspector in the Kent police force. He made certain allegations against a superior but, on investigation, these were not upheld. Pornographic material had been found in G's desk and this, together with the report on G's allegations, led the Chief Medical Officer of the Kent force, Dr Crosbie Brown, to certify G as being unfit for duty because of mental disorder.

G's own consultant psychiatrist was not permitted to see the report and certified G as being 'completely normal'. The Kent police, wishing to retire G compulsorily, appointed Dr Brown to decide whether G was 'permanently disabled' under the Police Pensions Regulations 1971. G's representatives applied to the court and an order of prohibition was issued disqualifying Dr Brown from determining the matter. The ground for the order was that, as Dr Brown had already committed himself to a view he could not be impartial in performing the quasi-judicial function of making a decision under the Pensions Regulations.

There was also an order of mandamus issued compelling the police authority to disclose their report to G's medical advisers.

CERTIORARI

By this order, the QBD requires inferior courts and certain tribunals to bring a case which it has decided to send to the High Court for the High Court to decide whether the lower court or tribunal has acted in excess of its jurisdiction, or mistakenly in law, or in breach of the principles of natural justice. If the QBD finds that this has happened, the matter may be returned to the inferior court or tribunal with a direction to reconsider it and to reach a decision in accordance with the QBD's findings.

The rules of natural justice are the rules which the common law imposes on all courts and on any person who in any way claims to act judicially. They are designed to ensure a fair hearing. For example, it is a rule of natural justice that both parties to a case are entitled to be heard and put their arguments. Another rule is that no man may be a judge in his own cause. That is, no-one can act in a judicial capacity if he has a monetary interest in the case or if there is a bias or a reasonable suspicion of bias in the judge (eg if he has a personal friendship with or a personal dislike of one of the parties). It is also a principle of natural justice that, wherever practicable, justice must be seen to be done.

An example of a breach of natural justice occurred in the case of:

Dimes v Grand Junction Canal Proprietors (1852)

An action relating to the canal company was heard by the Lord Chancellor. After the Lord Chancellor had reached a decision, it was discovered that he had shares in the canal company and his decision was set aside on the grounds that it violated natural justice. The Chancellor had a pecuniary interest in the case.

HABEAS CORPUS

This means 'you have the body' and it is a prerogative *writ* used to obtain the release of a wrongfully detained person. It may be used, for example, to secure the release of a person held in police custody for longer than the permitted period without being charged, or the release of a person detained under the Mental Health Act without justification. If the need is urgent and a case is made out, the QBD may make an order absolute, which secures the individual's immediate release. Otherwise, the court will make an order nisi which enables the opposing party to give his arguments. If these are not accepted the order will then be made absolute.

4.3.4 The Restrictive Practices Court

This court was established under the Restrictive Practices Act 1956 and deals with cases under the Restrictive Trade Practices Act 1976. It decides whether an agreement comes within this Act and, if so, whether it can be justified on one of the grounds given in the Act. It also deals with cases under the Resale Prices Act 1976. The court is staffed by High Court judges and a number of laymen selected because of their experience in industry, commerce or public affairs. Quorum is a judge and two other members. The judge decides questions of law; questions of fact are decided on a majority decision. Appeals on points of law go to the Court of Appeal (Civil Division). This court ranks with the High Court as a part of the Supreme Court structure, though it is not actually part of the High Court.

4.4 CIVIL COURTS OF APPEAL

4.4.1 High Court

Each division of the High Court hears appeals. They are heard by a divisional court (consisting of two or three High Court judges) of the relevant division. In other words, appeals are heard by a divisional court of the relevant High Court division.

1. **QBD** hears appeals from Rent Tribunals though its main function is to hear appeals relating to criminal matters.
2. **Chancery Division** hears appeals from bankruptcy courts outside London. Insolvency proceedings within the London area heard by Chancery itself with appeal to the Court of Appeal (Civil Division). Chancery also hears appeals from the decisions of the Special Commissioners of Income Tax.
3. **Family Division** hears appeals from decisions on matrimonial matters made by the magistrates' courts.
4. **The Employment Appeal Tribunal**
   This tribunal hears appeals almost exclusively on points of law from Industrial Tribunals on applications under various pieces of employment legislation. Therefore, it will hear matters relating, for example, to redundancy payments, equal pay, trade unions and labour relations and sex discrimination. The tribunal is staffed by judges nominated by the Lord Chancellor and by lay members selected from both sides of industry. A quorum is a judge and two lay members. It is on a level with the High Court.

4.4.2 Court of Appeal (Civil Division)

The Court of Appeal hears appeals from the High Court, other superior courts, and county courts. The appeal may be on questions of law and fact. The court will consider the whole case that was argued before the lower court, using the notes made by the shorthand writer and the judge, and in its decision the Court of Appeal may uphold, reverse or amend the lower court's decision, or order a new trial for the case.

The Court of Appeal comprises the Master of the Rolls and 16 Lord Justices of Appeal. In practice, three judges will hear a case.

4.4.3 House of Lords

The House of Lords has two functions—legislative (to make laws) and judicial (to act as the highest court of appeal in the country). In its judicial capacity the House of Lords is in fact a Standing Committee which comprises the Lord Chancellor, nine Lords of Appeal in Ordinary and any other members of the House who have held high judicial office. Collectively these are known as the Law Lords.

APPEALS FROM THE COURT OF APPEAL

The House of Lords is the highest civil court of appeal for the United Kingdom. It hears appeals from the Court of Appeal only if the person bringing the appeal (the appellant) can obtain leave to appeal from either the Court of Appeal or from the House of Lords itself. Leave to appeal will be granted only if the point of law involved in the case is one of general public importance. In this way only the most legally significant points of law are dealt with by the Lords.

APPEALS FROM THE HIGH COURT

Since the Administration of Justice Act 1969, it is possible, in limited cases, to appeal directly from the High Court to the House of Lords. This is known as the 'leap-frog' procedure.

Such an appeal will be allowed when a High Court judge certifies that a sufficient case for direct appeal has been established. He will do this by showing that:

1   The point of law involved either relates to the interpretation of a statute or a statutory instrument or is based on a decision of the Court of Appeal or the House of Lords. Thus, under the doctrine of precedent, it binds both the High Court judge and the Court of Appeal.
2   The point of law involved is one of general public importance.

Such a leap-frog appeal will arise therefore if, in trying a case, a High Court judge finds himself bound by a previous decision of the Court of Appeal. If he believes that the point of law is one of general public importance and if, for example, he believes that in the light of changed circumstances that decision is now wrong, he will certify that the case should be allowed to 'leap-frog' the Court of Appeal and go straight to the House of Lords. There would be no point in him requiring the appellant to follow the normal procedure and appeal to the Court of Appeal as, in general, the Court of Appeal is bound by its own previous decisions. Before the procedure may be used, both the House of Lords and the parties must also agree to it. The procedure is in fact very seldom used, normally in no more than half a dozen or so cases per year.

4.4.4 European Court of Justice

The Court of Justice of the European Communities, known as the European Court, is the only court of law of the EEC.

Although the European Commission has certain powers to resolve disputes it is not acting as a court when it does so. It is exercising quasi-judicial powers. An appeal from the Commission's decision is to the European Court but, in hearing the appeal, the court is acting as a court of first instance. This will be the first time the dispute has been heard by a court. There is no appeal from the European Court. Thus the court is, at one and the same time, both a court of first instance and the ultimate court of appeal.

As well as hearing appeals from decisions of the European Commission, the European Court has a vital role to play in interpreting the provisions of the Treaty of Rome 1957 and the secondary legislation arising from it. This interpretation will be undertaken for the benefit of the national courts of the member states.

THE PURPOSE OF THE EUROPEAN COURT'S INTERPRETATIVE ROLE

Each member state has different methods of and rules for interpreting statutes. Thus, in the United Kingdom, the system is based on the Common Law, in France on the Napoleonic Code which is itself Roman Law based. If the courts in each member state could interpret the Treaty of Rome according to their own rules, it would be impossible to have a uniform application of the Treaty throughout the Common Market. By giving this interpretative role to the European Court, this problem is overcome. Whatever a member state's rules of interpretation might be, the meaning of the Treaty of Rome will be governed by the principles followed by the European Court and will therefore be constant.

PROCEDURE FOR INTERPRETATION

By Article 177, Treaty of Rome, if a point of EEC law arises in a case being heard by the highest court in a member state that court **must** refer the issue to the European Court for a ruling on the interpretation of the relevant point of law.

For example, if in the United Kingdom the House of Lords is hearing a case which involves a provision of the Treaty of Rome it must refer to the European Court for a ruling on how the provision should be interpreted. The European Court will make its interpretation and then refer the matter back to the House of Lords to apply the provision. The ruling will be enforced by means of national enforcement machinery.

Article 177 is part of English law by virtue of s2 European Communities Act 1972.

Courts other than the highest appeal court in a member state *may*, but do not have to, refer questions of interpretation of EEC law to the European Court. Thus the rather odd position is that, although the Lords have to make a reference for interpretation, an Industrial Tribunal, for example, does not have to and can validly apply its own interpretation to the law involved.

COMPOSITION OF THE EUROPEAN COURT

Judges of the court are drawn from member states. They are assisted by Advocates-General whose function is to summarise the facts of and the law relating to a particular case and to present this to the judges. Because the Court is a court of first instance, it does not have the advantage of having before it the reasoned decision of a lower court. The Advocates-General provide this information and guidance.

4.4.5 Judicial Committee of the Privy Council (JCPC)

FUNCTION OF THE JCPC

The JCPC gives 'advice' to the Queen and this is the form its judgments take. Other than hearing appeals from the findings of professional disciplinary bodies such as the General Medical Council, the JCPC plays no role in the English judicial system.

Its main function is to deal with appeals from the courts of countries which are in some way connected with the United Kingdom, such as certain Commonwealth countries. It also hears appeals from the courts of the Isle of Man, the Channel Islands and the Cayman Islands. The JCPC has both civil and criminal jurisdiction. Its decisions have persuasive effect on English courts. That is, English courts are not bound to follow a precedent set by the JCPC.

COMPOSITION

The JCPC comprises the Lord Chancellor, the Law Lords and any Privy Councillor who has held high judicial office in the United Kingdom. It also comprises certain Commonwealth judges who have been appointed to the Privy Council.

4.5 CRIMINAL COURT STRUCTURE

As can be seen from the diagram below, the criminal trial and appeal procedure is slightly more complicated than that applying in the civil courts. The reason for this is that some courts, ie the magistrates' and the Crown courts have a dual function. The magistrates' courts act as both trial and examining courts. The Crown Court acts both as an appeal court and a court of first instance.

4.6 CRIMINAL COURTS (FIRST INSTANCE)

4.6.1 Magistrates' courts

INTRODUCTION

Magistrates' courts are concerned mainly with criminal matters although, as we saw earlier, they do have a limited civil jurisdiction. In London and certain other places, some magistrates' courts are presided over by stipendiary magistrates, who are barristers or solicitors of at least seven years' standing and who usually sit alone. Other magistrates' courts, however, are presided over by justices

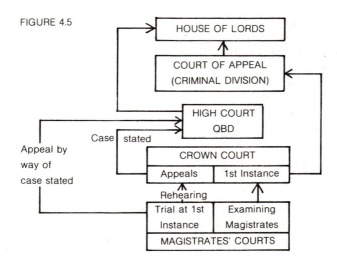

FIGURE 4.5

of the peace (JPs) sitting in panels. JPs do not have to have any legal qualifications. They are advised on points of law and procedure by the Clerk of the Court who is a barrister or solicitor of at least five years' standing. Stipendiary magistrates are paid a salary, JPs are unpaid.

A case in the magistrates' court will usually be heard by either three to seven lay justices (JPs) or one stipendiary.

CRIMINAL JURISDICTION

Criminal offences are divided into three categories:

1   Offences triable only summarily
2   Offences triable only on indictment
3   Offences triable either way

We will deal with each of these in turn

1 Offences triable only summarily
These are the least serious criminal offences such as speeding violations, or obstructing free passage along the highway. These must be tried in the magistrates' court. If the accused is found guilty, the magistrates may fine him up to £2,000 and/or sentence him to six months' imprisonment. If, however, they feel that the accused deserves greater punishment than this, the magistrates may refer the case to the Crown Court for sentencing. The Crown Court's sentencing powers are limited only by the maximum punishment allowed for the offence by statute.

2 Offences triable only on indictment
These are the more serious offences such as murder, rape, and blackmail. These crimes have to be tried by a jury in the Crown Court. An indictment is a formal document, prepared by Crown Court officials in the Queen's name, specifying the offence which the accused is alleged to have committed. If there is more than one offence, each is set out in a separate paragraph known as a 'count'.

Before such a case is heard by the Crown Court, there has to be a committal hearing before a magistrates' court. Traditionally this involved a preliminary hearing of the evidence and a decision whether a *prima facie* case has been made against the accused. We will look at the rules relating to committal proceedings later.

3 Offences triable either way
These are all other indictable or summary offences which may be tried either by the magistrates or in the Crown Court. These offences are listed in the Magistrates' Courts Act 1980 and the method of trial adopted will depend on a number of factors.

If the offence is serious, prosecution will usually be taken by the Director of Public Prosecutions (DPP). If he requires trial in the Crown Court then the accused will be indicted.

If, however, the DPP is not involved, or if he does not specify trial on indictment then the matter will go first to the magistrates' court to decide which would be the most suitable method of trial. It will hear representations as to the proper method of trial from both the prosecution and the defence and, in the light of these representations and of the gravity of the alleged offence and the limits on the court's sentencing powers, will decide where the case should be heard.

If it is decided that a summary trial is suitable, the decision must be explained to the accused. He will then have a right to demand a jury trial and, if he does, he will be indicted.

Offences which may be tried either way include, for example, theft. If the theft is relatively trivial, or a first offence, it may be decided to try it summarily. If it is serious, it may be decided that trial on indictment is the most suitable method.

EXAMINING MAGISTRATES

Before he can be tried on indictment, a person must appear before one or more magistrates traditionally to decide whether a *prima facie* case to which the accused must answer. In other words, the magistrates are not trying the case, they are merely undertaking a preliminary examination of the evidence to decide whether it is sufficient to justify a trial; whether, on first appearance, there is evidence to support the charge. These are known as committal proceedings. The prosecution must call its witnesses and show the magistrates the evidence it wishes to put before a jury. The accused may, if he wishes, tell the magistrates what defence he is submitting. The witnesses' evidence will be written down and signed by both the witness and one of the magistrates. This record of the evidence is known as a deposition. Having heard the evidence, the examining magistrates must decide:

either that a sufficient case has been made against the accused. They will then commit him for trial to the Crown Court;
or that no *prima facie* case has been established. In this event, they will release the accused.

To avoid any prejudice to a subsequent trial, s8 Magistrates' Courts Act 1980 makes it an offence to publish details of the committal proceedings other than the basic facts such as the name of the accused, his alleged offence, decision, legal aid and so on. The accused may however request that reporting restrictions be lifted. He may do this, for example, to try to publicise the matter to bring more witnesses forward.

However by s6 of the 1980 Act, if an accused is legally represented and does not plead that there is no case to answer, the examining magistrates may commit him for trial on the evidence of written statements. When this happens they do not even have to consider the evidence. This procedure is used in the vast majority of cases today as it saves substantial amounts of time.

JUVENILE COURTS

These are courts made up of a maximum of three JPs, at least one of whom must be a woman, selected from a special panel of magistrates. The juvenile courts hear cases involving children (from 10 to 14 years) and young persons (up to 17 years old). The court will try the juvenile for any offence except either homicide or any offence for which the juvenile is likely to be imprisoned for a long period. In this case the juvenile will have to be committed for trial. The juvenile court will also deal with cases where the juvenile's health, development or education are being neglected or if he or she is exposed to moral danger or is beyond parental control.

The emphasis in juvenile courts is on informality. The public are excluded from the hearings and the juvenile must not be named in the press unless the court or the Home Secretary order otherwise.

4.6.2 Crown courts

Crown Courts were established by the Courts Act 1971. Crown Courts are part of the Supreme Court and have buildings all over the country. A Crown Court may sit anywhere in England and Wales. The court's service is divided into 6 circuits: Northern; North-eastern; Wales and Chester; Midland and Oxford; South-eastern; and Western. Each circuit has towns designated as first-, second-, and third-tier centres.

THE SYSTEM OF COURTS AND PERSONNEL OF THE LAW: CHAPTER FOUR

1. First-tier centres deal with civil and criminal cases. They are served by both High Court and circuit judges.
2. Second-tier centres deal with criminal matters only. They are served by High Court and circuit judges.
3. Third-tier centres also deal exclusively with criminal matters and are served by circuit judges and recorders.

CLASSIFICATION OF OFFENCES FOR THE CROWN COURT

For the purposes of trial in the Crown Court, criminal cases may be classified into

1. **Class 1 Offences**
   These include the most serious offences such as murder and those offences which carry the death penalty such as treason and piracy with violence. They also include incitement, attempt or conspiracy to commit any of these offences.
   Class 1 offences must be tried by a High Court judge.
2. **Class 2 Offences**
   These include manslaughter, infanticide, child destruction, rape, mutiny and piracy and incitement, attempt or conspiracy to commit any of these. These offences must be tried by a High Court judge unless the judge presiding over the particular circuit provides otherwise.
3. **Class 3 Offences**
   These include all indictable offences other than those in classes 1, 2 or 4. So, for example, they include robbery or assault with intent to rob, wounding, or causing grievous bodily harm with intent. They may be tried by a High Court judge, a circuit judge, or a recorder.
4. **Class 4 Offences**
   These comprise mainly the offences which may be triable either on indictment or summarily (see earlier), for example, causing death by reckless driving, burglary etc and any incitement, attempt or conspiracy to commit these offences.
   They may be fixed by a High Court or circuit judge or a recorder. They are normally tried by one of the last two.

COMPOSITION OF THE CROWN COURT

The jurisdiction of the Crown Courts may be exercised by a High Court judge, a circuit judge or a recorder.

A circuit judge is an existing county court judge. New circuit judges may be appointed from barristers of ten years' standing or recorders with three years' experience.

A recorder is a part-time judge appointed from the ranks of either barristers or solicitors of ten years' standing.

When sitting in the City of London, the Crown Court is called the Central Criminal Court and the Lord Mayor and Aldermen of the City of London are entitled to sit with the professional judge.

All indictable offences are triable by a judge and a jury of normally 12 persons.

4.7 CRIMINAL COURTS OF APPEAL

4.7.1 Crown Court

The Crown Court hears appeals from the magistrates' courts' decisions. The appeal may be made against conviction or on the grounds of excess of jurisdiction. There is also an appeal against the sentence imposed by the magistrates (if the accused pleaded guilty in the magistrates' court this is the only appeal allowed). The appeal may be on a point of law or fact and may be made by the defence although not the prosecution.

COMPOSITION OF THE CROWN COURT WHEN HEARING APPEALS

When hearing appeals from the magistrates' courts, the Crown Court will comprise one professional judge sitting with two to four lay justices.

POWERS OF THE CROWN COURT

The appeal from the magistrates' court will involve a complete retrial of the case. All witnesses will be required to give evidence again and questions of fact and law will be re-decided.

The court may confirm the conviction or allow the appeal. On an appeal against sentence it has the power to confirm, reduce, vary or increase the sentence within the limits allowed to the magistrates' court. It may also remit the case (ie send it back) to the original court with its opinion on the law and facts involved, or make such other order as it thinks fit.

4.7.2 Divisional Court of the Queen's Bench Division

The divisional court of the QBD will hear appeals from both the magistrates' and the Crown Courts.

APPEALS FROM MAGISTRATES' COURTS

An appeal from the magistrates' court must be made by way of 'case stated' and may be lodged by either the prosecution or the defence. The appeal will be on a point of law only. There can be no direct appeal to the QBD on points of fact.

A 'case stated' means that, on the request of either party, the magistrates must 'state a case'. That is, they must write down their findings of fact and identify the point of law about which there is dispute. The findings of fact will form the basis of the appeal on the point of law. The divisional court will not enquire into the facts of the case. It may affirm, reverse or amend the magistrates' decision or remit the case to the magistrates' court with its opinion in which case the magistrates must deal with the accused on the basis of the divisional court's ruling on the law.

APPEALS FROM CROWN COURT

This again must be by way of 'case stated' and again may involve only questions of law. This right will lie only when the accused has appealed to the Crown Court from a decision of the magistrates.

4.7.3 Court of Appeal (Criminal Division)

The Court of Appeal hears appeals from the Crown Court when it is acting as a court of first instance.

If the appeal is against conviction and is based exclusively on a question of law it is granted as of right. In other words, the accused has an absolute right to appeal to the Court of Appeal.

If, however, the appeal against conviction is based on a question of fact, or on mixed fact and law, it will be permitted only if the Court of Appeal grants leave to appeal or if the trial judge certifies that an appeal should be allowed.

An appeal against sentence lies only by leave of the Court of Appeal. The court may refuse an appeal if it believes that there has been no miscarriage of justice.

WHO MAY APPEAL?

Appeal may be made by the accused. The Court of Appeal can confirm or reverse the decision or, if fresh evidence has come to light and the Court of Appeal is unsure how a jury would react to it, the court can require that the accused be tried again.

Where the jury has acquitted an accused, the Attorney General may refer the case to the Court of Appeal for its opinion on the point of law involved by means of case stated. This, however, is not an appeal as such. The jury's 'Not Guilty' verdict stands whatever the Court of Appeal's decision. The ruling is simply declaratory of the law for future cases.

COMPOSITION OF THE COURT OF APPEAL (CRIMINAL DIVISION)

Most appeals will be heard by three judges. These will be drawn from amongst the Lord Justices of Appeal and may also include judges of the QBD, who may sit at the request of the head of the Court of Appeal (Criminal Division), the Lord Chief Justice, acting after consultation with the Master of the Rolls (head of the Court of Appeal (Civil Division)). Appeals against sentence may be heard by two judges, but, if they disagree, the case must be re-argued before at least three.

There is no jury trial in the Court of Appeal.

4.7.4 House of Lords

The House of Lords may hear appeals from the Court of Appeal or the Divisional Court of the Queen's Bench Division. It will hear appeals on points of law only and such an appeal may be instituted by the prosecution or the defence.

For an appeal to the House of Lords to be permitted:

1. The court whose decision is being appealed must certify that a point of law of general public importance is involved, and
2. Either this court or the House of Lords gives leave to appeal. Such leave will be granted only where it is felt that it is desirable that the House of Lords should hear the appeal.

The House of Lords has the same membership as for civil appeals and its decisions may be by majority verdict. Appeals will always be heard by an odd number of Law Lords.

For the requirements of direct appeal from the High Court to the Lords, see the discussion on the Civil Courts' appeal procedure.

4.8 ALTERNATIVES TO THE COURTS

4.8.1 Introduction

In the event of a dispute, the courts are not the only means whereby the parties may sort out their differences. In some cases, such as matters relating to social legislation, administrative rather than legal action is what is required. Thus there is a system of administrative tribunals established to deal with these matters and with other disputes involving government departments or public authorities.

There are also domestic tribunals which are, in effect, disciplinary committees exercising jurisdiction over groups of people such as members of a particular profession or club or other association.

Finally, it is possible in certain circumstances to resolve a dispute by taking it to arbitration. This has certain advantages over legal action and is often required in commercial contracts and in the standard form contracts of many industries, such as construction and civil engineering.

4.8.2 Administrative tribunals

These are tribunals established to deal with the administration of Acts of Parliament and delegated legislation. They are quite separate from the courts of law and deal with disputes arising from the application of statutory provisions. There are many different types of such tribunals such as the Social Security Appeal Tribunals, the Rent Tribunals, the General and Special Commissioners of Income Tax, and Industrial Tribunals.

The majority deal with disputes involving government departments and other public bodies, but some, such as the rent and the industrial tribunals deal with problems between individuals, and a few do not deal with disputes at all but have a licensing role, such as the Traffic Commissioners.

COMPOSITION

The composition of tribunals varies greatly but, as a general rule, it will comprise a chairman, a clerk, who is usually a civil servant from the relevant government department, and a number of lay members, some of whom will be expert in the subject with which the tribunal is concerned. The lay members are often unpaid.

Sittings may be in public or in private and legal representation may be allowed. Evidence is rarely taken on oath.

For example, the Social Security Appeal Tribunals hear appeals from decisions of adjudicating officers of the Department of Health and Social Services. The tribunal comprises a legally qualified chairman and two lay members. Decisions are taken on a majority vote. The tribunal will hear appeals relating to claims for unemployment benefit, sickness benefit and supplementary benefit.

Claimants are rarely represented by a lawyer. An appeal from the tribunal lies to the Social Security Commissioners.

Industrial tribunals also comprise a legally qualified chairman and two lay members. These tribunals hear most disputes relating to employment matters such as redundancy, unfair dismissal, equal pay and discrimination. In most cases, appeal lies to the Employment Appeal Tribunal only on points of law. Unlike most other tribunals, the industrial tribunals appear to have many characteristics of a court.

CONTROL OF TRIBUNALS

Certain controls over tribunals are provided by the Tribunals and Inquiries Act 1971. Under this legislation there is operated a Council on Tribunals. The Council's function is to review and report on the constitution and working of certain tribunals specified in the Schedule to the Act and to be consulted before procedural rules are made for these tribunals. It also has to consider and report on any matters referred to it concerning any tribunal.

The Council, however, may not involve itself in the issues to be decided nor does it have the power to overrule any decisions made by tribunals.

The Act also provides that, if it is requested to do so, a tribunal must give reasons for its decision and, if a party to proceedings has a ground of appeal on a point of law he may appeal to the High Court or require the tribunal to state a case for the High Court to give an opinion. The High Court also has control of tribunals by the use of the prerogative orders of mandamus and certiorari.

Many tribunals are governed by statutes which lay down a procedure for appeal.

Another way in which tribunals are to some extent controlled lies in the fact that, for certain tribunals, the chairman has to be selected from a panel appointed by the Lord Chancellor. Only the Lord Chancellor may remove a member of a specified tribunal from office. If a Minister of State wishes to remove such a member, he may do so with the Lord Chancellor's consent.

Finally, tribunals are controlled by the common law rules of natural justice. They are acting in a quasi-judicial manner and so must comply with the basic judicial standards. These rules, which have been dealt with earlier, require that, for example, each side to the action is heard and that no man may be a judge in his own cause.

ADVANTAGES OF TRIBUNALS

The advantages of tribunals over courts of law are that:

1. tribunals provide a quick, cheap, flexible and informal method of settling disputes. As tribunals are not governed by the doctrine of judicial precedent they have a wide discretion to judge each case on its merits. In dealing with problems arising from social legislation it is essential that the relevant body has a wider discretionary power than the courts can exercise.
2. as many of the statutes which have created tribunals do not give much guidance as to the way the tribunals are to deal with the cases, tribunals have developed their own policies based on justice, expediency and social policy. Such freedom is not available to the law courts.
3. tribunals are often comprised of people with relevant qualifications such as doctors, who can determine disabilities, and others who have expert knowledge in the particular field under review. This expertise helps hearings decide matters accurately and efficiently.
4. tribunals relieve the courts of a large work-load which would certainly swamp them. The tribunals remove from the courts the need to hear constantly recurring and relatively minor problems. They can hear and deal with these problems much more quickly than the courts.

DISADVANTAGES OF TRIBUNALS

1. Too much discretionary power can result in tribunal decisions being unpredictable and inconsistent.

2 Although technical experts save much time and make for a more efficient resolution of disputes, they can not always be relied upon to be as impartial as they should be.
3 Most tribunals receive little publicity so their operation is not widely known or understood.
4 The reasons for a tribunal's decisions are not always made known.
5 There are wide variations in the rights to appeal against a tribunal's decision.

4.8.3 Domestic tribunals

This phrase covers disciplinary committees of professions and other groups of people. Thus professional bodies such as those relating to accountants, doctors and lawyers have disciplinary committees to deal with infringements of rules of professional conduct. Trade organisations and many social clubs and associations also have their own tribunals. These are controlled by the High Court by the use of the prerogative orders.

4.8.4 Arbitration

Many commercial agreements require disputes to be referred to arbitration. That is, the disputes have to be determined by one or more arbitrators either named in the contract or appointed in a way specified by it.

If there is an arbitration agreement in the contract and one of the parties ignores it and commences proceedings in the courts, the other party may apply for and be granted an order stopping the action and requiring the matter to be referred to arbitration. Statutes sometimes require disputes to go to arbitration.

CONDUCT OF AN ARBITRATION

By the Arbitration Act 1950, arbitrations must be conducted in a judicial manner. Arbitrators may, for example, take evidence under oath. The arbitrator's decision is called an award and it is enforceable by the successful party. He can treat the award as if it were an order of the county court (if the sum involved is within the limits for the county court's jurisdiction) or he can seek leave for the award to become an order of the High Court. An application to one of the courts precludes application to the other.

SUPERVISION OF ARBITRATION

By the Arbitration Act 1979, the High Court has the power to determine points of law involved in the arbitration. Application for such determination may be made by one of the parties with the consent of the arbitrator or of all the other parties. It will be allowed only if it might produce substantial savings in costs to the parties and provided the point of law is one on which leave to appeal would be likely to be granted (see below).

As a general rule, the arbitrator's decision is final. Leave to appeal against the award will be granted only in certain circumstances:

1 There must be consent to the appeal by all the other parties or leave to appeal must be granted by the court.
2 Leave of the court will be granted only if the decision on the question could substantially affect the rights of one or more of the parties.
3 Leave will also only be granted if, except in certain circumstances, the parties have not agreed to exclude the right of appeal to the court.

The High Court may confirm, vary, set aside or remit the award. There is an appeal from the High Court's decision to the Court of Appeal provided:

1 leave to appeal is granted by either court; and
2 the High Court certifies that the point of law is one of general public importance or is one which, for some special reason, should be considered by the Court of Appeal.

ADVANTAGES OF ARBITRATION

1. It is generally relatively cheap. Arbitrators' fees may be high but there is no court cost and no expense need be incurred in preparing pleadings.
2. It is quick. There is no delay waiting for the arbitration. If the case is going to court, it has to wait its turn in the lists (the order of business for the court). Thus it could take many months before an action is heard.
3. The arbitrator can be appointed because of his expertise in the subject matter of the case. This saves the time and expense of having to call expert witnesses.
4. The time and place of the arbitration can be arranged so as to suit the convenience of all the parties.
5. Arbitrations are held in private and thus, especially in commercial cases, will avoid potentially harmful publicity.
6. Proceedings, although keeping within the general rules of evidence, are informal and thus less daunting.

DISADVANTAGES OF ARBITRATION

1. It is unsuitable for legally complicated matters of dispute. For this type of case, action in the court is more useful.
2. If an appeal against the award is allowed, litigation could ensue and the savings made by the use of arbitration will be lost.

4.9 PERSONNEL OF THE LAW

4.9.1 The Bar

In England law is practised by a split profession: lawyers are divided into barristers and solicitors. Probably the best way to explain the role of the barrister is to regard him as a trial lawyer ie the lawyer who appears in court. Sometimes his position in relation to a solicitor is compared with that of a medical consultant as opposed to a general practitioner. The main part of the barrister's work lies in the presentation of issues in court and the giving of opinions on points law submitted to him by solicitors on behalf of their clients for clarification. Although solicitors may appear in the lower courts, barristers have an almost exclusive right of audience in the higher courts. The barrister is not employed directly by his client. The client first approaches a solicitor who refers him on to the barrister. The split profession is almost unique to England, and is said to have two distinct advantages. Firstly it enables the client to be referred to a specialist in a particular area of law. Secondly it ensures that the barrister does not become personally involved with the party whom he represents and so is able to act completely impartially. Besides appearing in court, a barrister does some 'office work'. He drafts the paperwork for cases, and writes opinions on specific questions of law which are referred to him. A person cannot practise as a barrister unless he has been 'called to the Bar' and become a member of an Inn of Court.

There are four Inns of Court, the Inner Temple, the Middle Temple, Lincoln's Inn and Gray's Inn. Each Inn has its own hall, where its members dine, and its own library for the use of its members. The administration of the Inn is under the control of its Bench, comprising senior members and judges who are Benchers or Masters of the Inn. The Inns of Court no longer have any direct responsibility for the education of barristers, as they did in earlier times. This is dealt with by the Council of Legal Education and the Inns of Court School of Law. Moreover the control of the profession has become centralised in the Senate of the Inns of Court and Bar.

Barristers work from offices known as 'chambers'. These are sets of rooms shared by barristers, headed by a senior barrister (the Head of Chambers) and managed by a clerk. They may not enter into partnership and practise simply on their own account. It is a convention that a barrister may not sue for fees owing to him. Even today in the gown which the barrister wears there is a small pocket into which traditionally the client would slip an honorarium (a gift) as a reward for representing him in a case. The most senior barristers are known as Queen's Counsel (QC). To become a Queen's Counsel a barrister will 'take silk'. This means that he will be entitled to wear the silken, as opposed to stuff, gown. To become a QC a barrister must apply to the Lord Chancellor and, if the application is granted, the barrister gains the considerable advantage of not having to prepare pleadings. QC's account for about 10% of the profession. All barristers who are not QC's are known as 'juniors'. By no means all barristers apply or even desire to become QC's and it would be wrong to suppose that a junior is an inferior grade of barrister. He is simply a barrister who has not taken silk.

When a solicitor instructs a barrister he does so by way of what is known as a brief. This is a statement by the solicitor by way of either an outline of the case which the barrister is requested to present or a specific reference to the point of law on which the barrister is requested to give an opinion. The brief can in complex cases run to many pages in length and should be accompanied by copies of all relevant documents.

4.9.2 Solicitors

To return to the medical analogy, solicitors are the general practitioners of the profession, and it is to the solicitor that the client initially goes. If necessary the solicitor refers the client on to the barrister for specialist advice and attention. However, the analogy should not be carried too far. While it is certainly accurate to refer to the traditional family solicitor as a general practitioner, solicitors are increasingly working together in very large partnerships in just the same way as are accountants. Within such partnerships, and indeed within almost all medium sized firms of solicitors as well, individual solicitors specialise in specific areas of law. The work of solicitors is extremely varied. They deal with a wide variety of domestic matters such as the purchase and sale of land and anything built thereon; the preparation of wills and the winding up of the estates of deceased persons; and divorce and related matters such as the sorting out of property disputes following divorce. It is to them that litigants in civil cases and defendants in criminal cases go. In this regard, many solicitors spend much time in the lower courts, such as the magistrates' courts and the county courts, acting as advocates. When, however, a case goes to the High Court the solicitor must normally instruct a barrister to act as the advocate. This does not, however, mean that the solicitor has no further interest in the case. He still has to supervise his client's case, and in particular get the case ready for trial.

The profession of solicitor is overseen by the Law Society, centred at the Law Society's Hall in Chancery Lane, London. The control of the profession is with the Council of the Law Society which supervises the work of a Secretary General and a permanent staff. A person may not act as a solicitor unless he has been admitted by the Law Society. This means that his name must be entered on the Roll of Solicitors kept by the Law Society. He must also have a practising certificate issued by the Law Society. Training of solicitors takes place at the College of Law or at one of the Polytechnics authorised to provide education for the profession. Rather perversely, Law Society exams are regarded as being harder than Bar examinations.

4.9.3 Legal executives

In the old days solicitors used to have working for them, clerks who were not solicitors themselves. Senior clerks were known as managing clerks and had their own Solicitors' Managing Clerks' Association. From this there developed, in 1963, the Institute of Legal executives. Qualified members of the Institute are called fellows, and must have served 8 years in employment with a solicitor and also have passed the examinations of the Institute. Legal Executives tend to restrict themselves (as indeed now do most solicitors) to a single area of the law such as conveyancing, personal injury claims, probate etc.

SUMMARY

In this chapter, we have looked at the various systems which may be used in the settlement of disputes and in the prosecution of crimes. As we will see later, the structure or hierarchy of the courts plays a vital part in the application of the doctrine of judicial precedent and, in reading about this, you must refer back to the diagrams in this chapter.

You will realise that the English court structure provides a sort of filtering process for cases. Of the thousands of cases that come before the courts each year, the vast majority are heard in the lower courts—the magistrates' courts in the case of crimes and the county courts and small claims courts in the case of civil matters. By the time these cases have been filtered through the various levels of court by means of appeals, only a very small number will be heard by the House of Lords.

Outside the court system, tribunals also play a large part in the filtering process, hearing the vast majority of claims made under the various pieces of social legislation. Arbitration, too, deals with many actions which would otherwise have to be tried in court. Bear in mind that it is by far the minority of cases which are taken from the lowest to the highest courts in the hierarchy. The higher they reach, the more important the point of law involved in the case becomes as a precedent for later cases. The filtering process, therefore, is vital to ensure that only the most important points of law are considered by the higher courts and, because the number of cases they deal with is relatively small, these courts can spend more time considering, expounding and developing the principles involved in the cases with which they actually deal.

Finally we considered briefly the various persons who work within what can loosely be described as the legal professions. For the client, a solicitor is usually his first contact with the law. If more specialist advice is required, the client is referred to a barrister. It should not be forgotten, however, that there are other personnel working with the law including legal executives and licensed conveyancers, and also barristers and solicitors in commerce and industry and central and local goverment.

SELF-TEST QUESTIONS

4.1 In which courts will the following cases be heard?

(a) A claim of £4,500 for breach of contract
(b) A request for an order of mandamus against a local authority
(c) A charge of murder
(d) An appeal from an Industrial Tribunal's decision on a claim for redundancy payment?

4.2 The prerogative orders are:

(a)
(b)
(c)

4.3 When will these orders be granted?

4.4 When will the House of Lords hear civil appeals?

4.5 What is the function of the European Court of Justice in the British legal system?

4.6 List the functions of the magistrates' courts

4.7 Distinguish between barristers and solicitors

4.8 Which of the following statements is correct?

(a) A person must qualify and practice as a solicitor before he can become a barrister
(b) A person may be both a barrister and a solicitor at the same time
(c) Barristers and solicitors are separate branches of the legal profession

Answers on page 291

EXERCISES

Exercise 4.1

Describe the work of the county court and explain its importance within the English legal system.

Exercise 4.2

Describe the jurisdiction of the civil courts of first instance and explain the system of appeals in civil cases.

Answers on page 291

32 LAW

CHAPTER FIVE

Sources of law

As was said in Chapter 2 (see especially sections 2.4 and 2.5) English law is not a codified system of law. During its development it was substantially judicial in character. Because of this there is no single source of law. Instead we have to look at a variety of sources, including judicial precedent and statute law and also a number of other sources such as custom and the European Communities.

5.1 THE SOURCES OF LAW

The sources which we are going to be considering are set out below:

THE SOURCES OF LAW

1	Custom		
2	Judicial Precedent		
3	Statute Law	(a)	Acts of Parliament
		(b)	Delegated legislation
4	Subsidiary Sources	(a)	Law Merchant
		(b)	Canon law
		(c)	Roman law
		(d)	Text books
5	European Communities	(a)	Regulations
		(b)	Directives
		(c)	Decisions

5.2 CUSTOM

Custom is the oldest source of law in England. It has its origin in the usage or practice of people in doing a certain thing in a certain way. At one time, and particularly in the early stages of the development of the common law, it was the major source of law in England. It has now, however, largely been absorbed into the common law and is no longer a creative source of law. There used to be two main types of custom: general customs which applied throughout the entire country and local customs which were limited in their application to a particular part of the country. Today almost all general customs have been absorbed into judicial precedent or legislation. Although local custom is of no major significance, the courts will recognise the existence of a local custom and apply it to a case being considered so long as the following criteria are satisfied:

1. It must have existed continuously from time immemorial. For this purpose 'time immemorial' means 1189, which is regarded by the law as the maximum period in which legal memory can go back. Of course, it is almost impossible to prove something has existed continuously since 1189.

    Accordingly the courts are willing to accept as proof that a custom has existed continuously since 1189 the fact that no evidence is produced to show that it was not in existence during that period.

2. It must be limited to a particular locality.
3. It must be reasonable.
4. It must be certain and clearly defined.
5. It must be consistent with the existing law.

These concepts are difficult to grasp in the abstract. They may be better understood by considering the criteria in the following cases which have from time to time come before the courts:

Mercer v Denne (1905)

Denne owned part of a beach. He intended building houses on this land. Some local fishermen tried to prevent this, claiming that they had a local customary right to dry their fishing nets on the land. Witnesses were called to prove that the custom of the fishermen drying their nets on this spot was known to date back some seventy years. In the absence of any evidence to the contrary the court was willing to assume that it had existed since 1189. It was held that the local customary right existed at the time of the action, had existed since time immemorial, and therefore the court was prepared to refuse to allow Denne to build the houses.

Contrast:

Simpson v Welles (1872)

Welles was accused of obstructing a public footpath by setting up a refreshment stall upon it. His defence was that he did so by virtue of a custom which originated in the Statute of Labourers 1361. It was held that Welles should be convicted since he had been unable to establish that the customary right which he put forward as his defence had existed since 1189.

Note also:

Wolstanton's case (1940)

A landowner permitted mining under the house of a tenant. The mining resulted in the house being severely damaged. When the tenant sought compensation from the landlord, the landlord put forward the defence that there existed a customary right for the lord of the manor to take minerals from under a tenant's land without making compensation for subsidence and damage to buildings. It was held that the tenant could succeed in his claim. The landlord's defence failed since clearly such a custom would be unreasonable.

As well as local customs, there are also trade customs. Sometimes these are referred to as 'convential usage'. They are almost never encountered today, but an example is to be found in the case of:

Smith v Wilson (1832)

This case concerned the lease of a rabbit warren. The lessee (the tenant) agreed under the lease to leave 10,000 rabbits in the warren at the end of the period of the lease. It was held that by local trade custom 1,000 meant 1,200 in such a situation.

5.3 THE NATURE OF JUDICIAL PRECEDENT

The English judge is bound by the doctrine of precedent. This is the principle whereby a decision made by one court must be followed in subsequent cases by lower courts. As will be seen there are a number of exceptions to this, but the doctrine of precedent is recognition that decided cases are authoritative of the existence of a legal rule. Precedent may be of two types, binding and persuasive. A binding precedent is one which a lower court must follow. A persuasive precedent is authoritative but the court is not bound to follow it. The doctrine of precedent has been applied in the English courts since the 13th century, though it is only since the 19th century that the doctrine of binding precedent has been firmly established in English law. The doctrine of precedent will be dealt with in Chapter 6. There are however a number of important elements on which the doctrine depends and these elements are examined in the following paragraphs.

5.3.1 Law reports

It is self-evident that the existence of a doctrine of precedent is dependent upon the accurate reporting of judicial decisions. Ever since the doctrine of precedent came into being, law reports have been produced. It is, however, only since 1855 that 'official' reports have been published. The history of law reporting divides into three periods. From 1283 to 1535 there were what is known as the Year Books. These were notes of cases compiled largely by students of law who were present in court when the cases were decided. Not least because of their age, they are not of great use today. The next period, from 1535 to 1865, was the period of private reporting. These were reports produced and published by individuals such as judges or barristers and published under the name of the particular reporter. They are of variable quality and, therefore, use. Some, by great lawyers such as Sir Edward Coke, are highly regarded. Others are of less value. For example, it was said of one reporter, Espinass, that he heard only half of what went on in a case and reported the other half.

Modern law reports have existed from 1865 with the establishment of the General Council of Law Reporting. Before publication of these reports, the judges whose decisions are reported, read and revise the reports of their judgment. Thus the report may be safely relied upon. The General Council of Law Reporting has existed continuously since 1865, changing only in name to the Incorporated Council of Law Reporting for England and Wales. The reports are produced in five series as shown below:

The Law Reports

(produced by the Incorporated Council of Law Reporting for England and Wales)

AC	Appeal Cases, decided by the House of Lords and the Judicial Committee of the Privy Council.
QB	Cases decided by the Queen's Bench Division of the High Court, and on appeal from here to the Court of Appeal.
Ch	Cases decided by the Chancery Division and on appeal from here to the Court of Appeal.
Fam	Cases decided by the Family Division and on appeal from here to the Court of Appeal.
ICR	Industrial Cases decided by the Employment Appeal Tribunal and other courts.

There are a number of private reports also published which are popular with lawyers including the All England Law Reports, the Common Market Law Reports and Lloyds Law Reports. These private reports are not necessarily checked by the judges concerned and so have the advantage of speedy publication. They also include many cases which do not appear in the official law reports.

5.3.2 The citation of cases

As was said in Chapter 2 (see 2.6) English law is accusatorial in its nature. This means that in any case there are two sides. In a civil case, at first instance, there will be a plaintiff and a defendant. For example, in the first case considered in this chapter, *Mercer v Denne*, Mercer was the plaintiff and Denne the defendant. Suppose that Denne had decided to appeal the decision against him, then the case would have been cited as *Denne v Mercer*, with Denne being the appellant and Mercer the respondent.

In a criminal case there are also two sides, the first is the prosecutor and the other the defendant. A criminal case is often cited as *R v Jones*. R is the abbreviation for Regina or Rex which is Latin for the Queen, or King, as the case may be. As has been seen in Chapter 2 (2.9), crime is a wrong against society and so punishment is usually sought in the name of the Queen as the representative of society.

5.3.3 The authority of the courts

The importance of a judicial decision depends upon the status of the court in which the case was decided. As a general rule, the higher the court where the decision was made, the more likely the decision is to be binding in a lower court. Table 5.3.3 sets out the authority of the courts:

TABLE 5.3.3 **The Authority of the Courts**

Court where decision made:	Courts bound by decision:
House of Lords	Itself (subject to 1966 Practice Direction) and all lower courts.
Court of Appeal (both Civil and Criminal Divisions).	Itself (subject to certain exceptions) and all lower courts.
Divisional Court of the High Court.	Itself generally and all lower courts.
High Court (Queen's Bench Division, Chancery Division and Family Division) and Crown Courts.	All lower courts but not itself
County Courts and Magistrates Courts.	No courts bound.

5.3.4 The House of Lords

In the case of *London Street Tramways Company Limited* v *London County Council* (1898), the facts of which are unimportant here, it was stated that the House of Lords was bound by its own previous decision. The reason for this was that it was felt that the decisions of the highest court should be final and definite. However, there was criticism of this rule and in 1966 a Practice Statement was issued by the House of Lords. This provided that although normally previous decisions of the House were to be binding, the House could now depart from a previous decision where it appeared right to do so.

In a Press Notice released by the House of Lords at the time of the issuing of the Practice Statement, it was stressed that while the statement was of great significance, it should not be many cases where the House would regard it as proper that it should not follow its own precedent. It would, however, be proper to depart from precedent if it were considered that the earlier decision had been influenced by conditions which no longer prevailed and that in the current climate of opinion the law should be different. Thus the relaxation of the rule would, for example, allow the House of Lords to pay greater attention to the decisions of superior courts throughout the Commonwealth.

The statement was widely welcomed by a majority of lawyers, though, as anticipated, the power to depart from its own previous decisions, has only been exercised by the House of Lords on very rare instances.

The first time that the power was exercised was in *Conway* v *Rimmer* (1968) when the House overruled its previous decision in *Duncan* v *Cammell Laird & Co* (1942). In the earlier case the House had ruled that an English court would not itself inspect the documents which were the property of a Crown department and in respect of which the appropriate department claimed privilege (ie the right not to produce them to the court). In *Conway* v *Rimmer* the House held that when privilege was claimed, the court itself could inspect the documents to decide whether the documents should be produced or not.

More recently in *Miliangos* v *George Frank (Textiles) Ltd* (1976) the House was influenced by changes in regard to foreign exchange and the instability of sterling and ruled that a money judgment could be expressed in a foreign currency. This decision expressly overruled the earlier decision in *Re United Railways of Havana and Regla Warehouses Ltd* (1961).

Decisions of the House of Lords are binding on all lower courts.

5.3.5 Court of Appeal

As we saw in Chapter 4, (4.4 and 4.5) the Court of Appeal has both a Civil Division and a Criminal Division. The general rule is that the decisions of both Divisions are binding upon the court itself and upon all lower courts. This general rule is, however, subject to exceptions in the two courts. In the Civil Division an earlier Court of Appeal decision is not binding in the following circumstances:

1. Where there are two conflicting previous decisions. In this situation, the decision which is not followed is deemed to be overruled.
2. Where there is a previous decision of the Court of Appeal (Civil Division), which, although not expressly overruled, is inconsistent with a later House of Lords decision.
3. Where an earlier decision was given *per incuriam* (ie through lack of care). This only happens where some relevant binding precedent or statute which would have affected the earlier decision was overlooked by the court in the case. It is very rare that this will happen. *Per incuriam* involves the overlooking of some authority which would affect a decision. Mere errors in reasoning are insufficient.

In the Criminal Division the three exceptions (above) apply together with one further exception. When the court sits as a 'full court' (ie a court with more judges than usual), the Criminal Division may overrule a previous decision of itself on the ground that the law has been misunderstood or misapplied.

5.3.6 Divisional courts

Divisional Courts are bound by previous decisions of the House of Lords and of the Court of Appeal. There is an exception to this where a Court of Appeal decision was *per incuriam* in circumstances where a relevant decision of the House of Lords was not considered. A Divisional Court is bound by its own previous decisions unless one of the three exceptions referred to above in connection with the Court of Appeal (Civil Division) applies.

5.3.7 High Court

A judge sitting in the High Court is bound by the decisions of all the above courts. He is not bound by decisions of other High Court judges, though such previous decisions are of persuasive authority and will only not be followed where the judge is satisfied that the earler decision is wrong.

5.3.8 Other courts

Other courts such as County Courts, Magistrates Courts and Administrative Tribunals are bound by the decisions of all the courts mentioned above. The decisions of these courts are not binding in subsequent cases decided in courts of this level.

5.4 STATUTE LAW

5.4.1 Acts of Parliament

Statute Law is that part of English law which is made either by Parliament itself or under its authority. Law made under Parliament's authority is known as 'delegated legislation'. As has been seen, the earliest source of English law was the common law as applied by the judges. It follows from this that Statute Law is not in itself a complete system of law. It is merely superimposed on the common law to modify and improve it. It is said by many lawyers today that legislation is the only source of law. This is subject, however, to the need to consider whether judges make law (see Chapter 6 section 6.3).

In the British Constitution the supreme power of the country is vested in Parliament and in theory the power of Parliament to make law is almost unlimited. Indeed not many years ago one famous writer on Constitutional Law wrote that the British Parliament could pass a law making it unlawful for a Frenchman to smoke in the streets of Paris. Although this would be unthinkable in practice, it does illustrate the power which Parliament was thought to have. There are, however, two restrictions on this power which should be borne in mind. Firstly, because of our membership of the European Communities, some of our legislative authority has passed to those Communities. Secondly, no Parliament will pass a law which is going to be disobeyed by all of the people and which cannot be enforced.

During the course of the last century, Statute Law has been used increasingly. In particular it has been used for the following purposes:

1. The amendment and updating of existing law where this has become out-of-date or inapplicable to modern needs.
2. The creation of new law to deal with situations not dealt with by the common law. In particular it has intervened in areas of social legislation such as the Inheritance (Provision for Family and Dependents) Act 1975 which allowed persons who were dependent for their living and income upon a person who had died but failed to provide for them by his will to claim against his estate (ie the property which he had left). Another example is the Housing (Homeless Persons) Act 1977 which imposes an obligation upon local authorities to provide accommodation for people who are homeless in certain circumstances.
3. Consolidation which is the process whereby the provisions contained in a number of statutes are brought together and re-enacted in a single statute. Examples of this are the Income and Corporation Taxes Act 1970 and the Companies Act 1985.
4. Codification which is the process whereby all the law, whether derived from statute or precedent, on a single area is brought together into a single comprehensive code. Examples of this are the Sale of Goods Act 1979 and the Partnership Act 1890.
5. The raising of revenue, principally the Finance Act which is passed each year to implement the Government's Budget proposals.

5.4.2 The process of legislation

Parliament consists of two Houses, the House of Lords and the House of Commons. The members of the House of Lords are the Lords Spiritual and the Lords Temporal. The Lords Spiritual are the Archbishops of Canterbury and York, the Bishops of London, Durham and Winchester and 21 other senior bishops of the Church of England. The Lords Temporal are the Peers of the Realm whose entitlement to sit is either hereditary (ie passed from one generation to another) or for life. Life peerages first came into being under the Life Peerages Act 1958. This entitled the Queen to confer a life peerage upon an individual and such an appointment to a life peerage allows that individual to sit and vote in the House of Lords. The sort of individuals upon whom life peerages are bestowed are former Government ministers, leading trade union figures and other people who have had distinguished careers in public life.

The House of Commons consists of Members of Parliament who are elected locally as representatives of a constituency. Since the Representation of the People Act 1969 everyone over the age of 18 has been allowed to vote so long as they are not disqualified from so doing. Amongst the people who may not vote are peers, clergy of the Church of England and Roman Catholic churches, full-time judges, members of the regular armed forces, and offenders who have been sent to prison for more than one year and who are still detained in prison. Voting is by means of a secret ballot, and has been so since the Ballot Act 1872.

The passage of a Bill through Parliament is illustrated by the following diagram.

The passage of a Bill through Parliament (commencing in the House of Lords)

BILL → HL → First Reading → Second Reading → Committee → Report → Third Reading → HC → First Reading → Second Reading → Committee → Report → Third Reading → Royal Assent → ACT

NB When a Bill commences in the House of Commons, it passes first through this and then through the House of Lords.

From the diagram you see that a Bill may be introduced in the House of Lords (HL). It will then progress through a first reading, second reading, committee, report and third reading. It will next go to the House of Commons (HC) and pass through the same processes, and afterwards go to the Queen for the Royal Assent and thereupon become an Act. In the alternative a Bill may be produced in the House of Commons and then, having gone through the same processes, will pass to the House of Lords and go from there for the Royal Assent. Until the Royal Assent has been received, legislation being considered by Parliament is known as a Bill. Once the Royal Assent has been granted, it is known as an Act.

Generally Bills may be introduced into either House depending on how busy a particular House is at the time of introduction. However, Money Bills, meaning Bills which seek to impose a charge on the public revenue, must be introduced in the House of Commons.

The first reading of a Bill is in fact not a reading at all. It is merely a formality with the title of the Bill being read to the House. Once this has been done the Bill is printed. The second reading is again not a full reading of the Bill but a debate on the broad merits of the intended legislation. At this stage there may be no amendments to the legislation. Committee stage is where the detail of the proposed legislation is considered. The Committee of Members which considers the Bill usually consists of between 16 and 50 members of the particular House. After the Committee has subjected the Bill to a detailed review, it then reports upon it to the House. At this point the House reconsiders the main issues of the Bill and may debate amendments which have been made or new clauses inserted in Committee. Following this there is the third reading during which only verbal alterations may be proposed. After this the Bill goes to the other House (ie whichever House it has not passed through) and it passes through similar stages there.

The direct power of the House of Lords is extremely limited in relation to legislation. If a Bill has passed through the House of Commons and the House of Lords then makes amendments, those amendments must be returned to the House of Commons for its approval. The Parliament Act 1911 provides that any bill which has been designated a Money Bill must be introduced in the House of Commons and, having been passed by this House, must be passed by the House of Lords without amendment within one month of the time it is received by the Lords. Should the House of Lords fail to pass the Bill, then it will nevertheless receive the Royal Assent and so become law without their consent.

The Parliament Act 1949 further diminished the direct power of the House of Lords. Bills may be divided into two main categories, public bills and private bills. Public bills are concerned with matters of public importance. Once a public bill has passed through the House of Commons in two successive sessions (ie years of sitting) and has been rejected by the House of Lords in each session, it may nevertheless be presented for the Royal Assent without the agreement of the House of Lords.

Private bills deal with local matters or matters affecting individuals. There is also a third category, the Private Members Bill, which may be introduced by an individual Member of Parliament on a matter in which he has a particular interest.

The granting of the Royal Assent is now a formality. It is unlikely that there would be circumstances when the Queen would withhold her consent to a Bill which has passed through the Parliamentary process.

Perhaps at this point we should consider the relationship between Parliament and Government. Parliament, consisting as it does of the House of Lords and the House of Commons, is made up of individuals of almost all political persuasions. It is Parliament not Government which passes legislation. The Government consists of senior members of whichever political party enjoys a majority in the House of Commons. The Government is primarily responsible for deciding what business is conducted in Parliament. Accordingly it is the Government which decides what new legislation is to be considered by Parliament. So although the Government does not pass legislation, it is responsible for the bulk of the legislation which is enacted by Parliament.

5.4.3 Delegated legislation

Delegated legislation is law made under authority of Parliament. Various bodies or institutions such as Government ministers, public corporations and local authorities have limited power to make subordinate legislation. The legislation is known by a variety of different names including rules, regulations, byelaws and orders in council. Within Britain, the supreme law-making power lies with Parliament. A subordinate body may only legislate under specific powers conferred by Parliament. There are a number of reasons why delegated legislation is necessary:

(a) Parliament does not have sufficient time to discuss in full all matters on which it wishes to legislate.
(b) Many areas of legislation deal with technically detailed areas.
(c) In a time of emergency the law may usually be introduced more quickly by, for example, an order of a Minister than by an Act of Parliament.
(d) Parliament, which is concerned with matters on a national scale, should perhaps not have its time taken up with dealing with matters confined to a specific locality, eg byelaws concerning the opening of public paths in a particular town or city.

A major difference between legislation enacted by Parliament and delegated legislation is that while a court cannot consider the validity of an Act of Parliament, it can question the validity of a piece of delegated legislation. In particular delegated legislation is subject to the doctrine of *ultra vires*. This means that all delegated legislation must fall clearly within the powers to make such legislation enjoyed by the body purporting to make it. For example:

A G v Fulham Corporation (1929)

The Fulham local council established a municipal laundry. Various Acts of Parliament empowered it to establish baths, bathing-places and wash-houses. It was not, however, empowered to establish a laundry. A ratepayer challenged the running of the laundry. It was held that the local council were clearly acting ultra vires and accordingly an injunction should be granted restraining the council from this conduct.

It would be wrong to think that there is no control of delegated legislation within Parliament itself. The Statutory Orders (Special Procedure) Acts 1945 and 1965 establish a special procedure whereby instruments may be made subject to 'special parliamentary procedure by the Act under which they are made'. This involves opportunity being given for objections to the raised to the order at a local enquiry and also by petition to Parliament. More frequently, Parliamentary scrutiny is secured by the statutory instrument being made subject to some requirement of 'laying' before Parliament. Sometimes the Act requires that the statutory instrument should be laid before Parliament before it comes into force. Sometimes in addition to the requirement that the instrument be laid before Parliament an affirmation resolution is needed to be passed by the House before the instrument comes into force. On other occasions the instrument is made so that it comes automatically into force having been laid before Parliament so long as a negative resolution is not passed by Parliament during a period of forty 'sitting' days.

In addition to this procedure there is also a Joint Select Committee on Statutory Instruments to which members of both Houses of Parliament belong. It is charged with considering every statutory instrument which is laid or laid in draft before Parliament with a view to seeing whether the notice of Parliament should be drawn to the instrument on one of a variety of grounds including (a) that all wording used in the instrument is obscure, (b) that the instrument appears to impose charges on the subject or on the public revenue or (c) that the instrument has retrospective effect in circumstances where this was not envisaged by the statute under which it was made.

5.4.4 The advantages and disadvantages of delegated legislation

There are both advantages and disadvantages in delegated legislation. These are illustrated by the following table:

TABLE 5.4.4 **Advantages and Disadvantages of Delegated Legislation**

	Advantages		Disadvantages
1	Saving of Parliamentary time.	1	Loss of Parliamentary control.
2	May be enacted quickly.	2	May be insufficiently considered.
3	Matters of detail better dealt with.	3	Tendency towards excessive legislation.
4	Withdrawal or amendment easier.	4	Inadequate publicity.

Considering first the advantages, there is obviously a major saving of Parliamentary time if another person or body is authorised to make some of the legislation which otherwise would be Parliament's responsibility. Delegated legislation may be enacted quickly as it does not have to go through the rather laborious procedure of readings which are required for an Act of Parliament. Delegated legislation is a much better medium with which to deal with matters of detail and its withdrawal or amendment is very much easier than effecting similar changes in an Act of Parliament. There are, however, disadvantages. Obviously there is a loss of Parliamentary control. The fact that delegated legislation does not go through the full Parliamentary procedure means that, on occasions, it is perhaps insufficiently considered. It certainly leads towards excessive legislation. During the course of a year the number of Acts of Parliament passed tends to be in the region of 150, whereas there are thousands of pieces of delegated legislation. This obviously makes law more complex and bulky. Finally, there is often inadequate publicity given to delegated legislation, thereby making it difficult for even lawyers to keep up-to-date with new legislation.

5.5 SUBSIDIARY SOURCES

5.5.1 The law merchant

The law merchant, or mercantile law, was described in the case of *Goodwin* v *Robarts* (1875) as 'neither more nor less than the usages of merchants and traders ... ratified by the decisions of the courts of law which, upon such usages being proved before them, have adopted them as settled law'. It was originally a separate branch of law based upon the custom of merchants, which in turn was based upon Roman law. Over the centuries it has been absorbed into the common law, for example in the Sale of Goods Act 1893 (now 1979) and the Bills of Exchange Act 1882 and it is today dealt with by the Queen's Bench Division of the High Court.

5.5.2 Canon law or Ecclesiastical law

Immediately following the Norman Conquest in 1066 the Ecclesiastical Courts were of great importance dealing, amongst other things, not only with matters involving clergy discipline and offences by clergy against church doctrine, faith and morality but also with things which concerned ordinary individuals such as marriage, legitimacy of children and wills of property other than land. These matters now form part of the jurisdiction of the High Court and are almost entirely regulated by statute.

5.5.3 Roman law

Unlike the law of almost all other European countries, English law was little influenced in its development by Roman law, although a number of principles in our law are expressed in Latin terminology. Roman law was for many centuries taught in England, but formed no part of the training given to common lawyers. As has been seen, the English common law developed in a far more haphazard way as and when the need for its application to the practicalities of business and affairs arose.

5.5.4 Text books

In the English courts it used to be the case that text books were not treated as authorities, no matter how eminent their authors. In *Bastin* v *Davies* (1950), Lord Goddard C J said that the court would 'never hesitate to disagree with a statement in a text book, however authoritative or however long it had stood, if it thought right to do so'. This is, of course, not to say that text books are not used by lawyers in preparing their arguments, nor that they are not quoted by counsel in their arguments in court. Even this is subject to a rather odd rule. It used to be the case that living authors could not be cited by name. However, the modern approach of the courts is that death in itself does not affect the authority of a particular writer.

5.5.5 The European Communities

By the European Communities Act 1972, the United Kingdom became a full member of the European Communities. These are the European Coal and Steel Community, the European Economic Community, and the European Atomic Energy Community. Much of English domestic law, such as contract, tort, family law and land law is not affected by membership of the European Community. However, in the field of economics, restrictive trade practices, the free movement of labour, capital and services, agriculture and business developments, we are considerably affected. The United Kingdom is now subject to obligations which are imposed upon it by Community legislation, and enjoys rights given by such legislation. If there is a conflict between Community law and English law, the former prevails, and it is applied in the British court in just the same way as British law.

The power of the Community to make law is vested in the Council of Ministers. It is exercised by means of regulations, directives and decisions. These will be considered in the following paragraphs.

REGULATIONS

Once a regulation passed by the Council of Ministers has come into effect it is immediately law within all the member states of the European Communities. There is no need for individual member states to enact it, and indeed they must not do so. In the same way as an Act of Parliament, a regulation may impose obligations and confer rights upon individuals.

DIRECTIVES

A directive passed by the Council of Ministers orders that the domestic legislation of member states of the Communities should achieve certain results. It can only be implemented by domestic legislation, and so, while it is binding upon member states, it is not binding upon their subjects until such time as it is enacted by their national legislatures.

DECISIONS

Decisions are not of general application but merely settle actual situations brought before the Council for consideration. They are mainly used where a State seeks permission from the Council to depart from certain pieces of Community legislation and when the Commission has investigated infringements of the Treaty by individuals or companies.

5.5.6 Evidence

Evidence is the manner in which facts are proved in a case. What we are concerned with in this syllabus is firstly what is called the burden of proof and secondly presumptions.

In English law the prime rule of evidence is that 'he who asserts must prove'. In other words, whoever makes an allegation in a case must prove it. Put another way, in a civil case it is for the plaintiff to prove his case; in a criminal case it is for the prosecution to prove his. The next logical step from this is to consider to what degree of certainty a case must be proved. Clearly very rarely can something be proved with absolute certainty. For example, often a crime can only be proved to have been committed by a person by means of circumstantial evidence; only the very careless criminal allows himself to be caught in the act. In a criminal case, the facts alleged must be proved beyond reasonable doubt. In a civil case proof is on the balance of probabilities. 'Beyond reasonable doubt' means just what it says. The prosecution must prove its case in order to establish the defendant's guilt. There is no need for the prosecution to anticipate and deal with every argument which the defence might raise. The jury may entertain some very slight doubts but certainly no significant doubts. It must be satisfied 'beyond reasonable doubt' that the prosecution has proved its case. 'On the balance of probabilities' in a civil case is a rather lower standard. The plaintiff must prove that it is more likely than not that his allegations are true.

Once certain facts have been established in court they may give rise to what is known as a presumption, of which there are three kinds: presumptions of fact, irrebuttable presumptions of law, and rebuttable presumptions of law. Circumstantial evidence affords an example of a presumption of fact. If a person is known to have been alone in a room at the time when a theft took place from a safe in that room there is a presumption of fact that he committed the theft. Presumptions of fact can always be rebutted, and so, for example, if it can be shown that there was a hole in the back of the safe and also in the wall behind the safe, the presumption that it was the person in the room who committed the theft may be rebutted.

An example of an irrebuttable presumption of law is that a child below the age of 10 cannot commit a crime. The court cannot deny this. A child of this age is incapable of committing a crime. An example of a rebuttable presumption of law is that a child aged between 10 and 14 cannot commit a crime. In other words, while a child of this age is presumed to be incapable of committing a crime, evidence can be adduced to prove that the child knew what he was doing and had a criminal intent when he acted so as to rebut (or displace) the presumption of innocence.

5.5.7 Law reform

While the Law Commission the main body making recommendations as to how this law should be reformed today is not itself a source of law, it is a significant influence on the development of the law today. The Law Commission is an official body whose task it is to consider the existing law and to make proposals for its reform. It was established under the Law Commissions Act 1965, and consists of five members appointed by the Lord Chancellor. Its function is to keep the whole of the law under review with a view to its systematic development and reform and in particular its simplification and modernisation. To this end, the Law Commission may consider proposals for law reform referred to them, prepare programmes for the examination of different branches of the law, undertake the examination of the particular branches and formulate proposals for reform by means of draft bills.

SUMMARY

In this chapter we have considered the main sources of English law. By far the most important are the common law and statute. It should, however, never be forgotten that there are other sources of importance. The sources of law were illustrated at the beginning of this chapter in tabular form. They should now be memorised.

SELF-TEST QUESTIONS

5.1 List the main sources of law

5.2 What are the main factors on which the doctrine of binding precedent depends?

5.3 List the courts bound by decision in:

(a) The House of Lords
(b) The High Court

5.4 When may the Court of Appeal decide not to follow its own previous decisions?

5.5 What is statute law?

5.6 Why is delegated legislation necessary?

5.7 How do the courts control delegated legislation?

5.8 How do the following EEC laws take effect in the legal systems of member states:

(a) Regulations
(b) Directives?

5.9 Distinguish between:

(a) Consolidation and codification of law
(b) Public and private bills

5.10 What is the most important modern source of law?

Answers on page 295

EXERCISES

Exercise 5.1

What are the main sources of English law today?

Exercise 5.2

What is the difference between (a) the civil burden of proof and (b) the criminal burden of proof?

Answers on page 295

CHAPTER SIX

Judicial precedent and statutory interpretation

Whenever evidence is brought to court it has to be interpreted by the court. This applies even with a simple piece of factual evidence. For example, in a case where someone is accused of having stolen goods from a shop, there may be evidence that the accused was actually seen taking the goods. Even this evidence has to be interpreted by the court. The court must consider whether the person giving the evidence is reliable; was he at the time of the alleged offence in a position to see the accused taking the goods; is he a person who is known habitually to tell untruths? The judge must also interpret sources of law which are cited before him by counsel. In particular he has to interpret past judicial precedents, especially those binding upon him, and statutory provisions. This chapter will consider these two areas, judicial precedent and statutory interpretation.

6.1 RATIO DECIDENDI AND OBITER DICTA

Not everything in the decision reached by a judge in a case carries the same weight. The only part of the decision which may be binding (depending upon the authority of the court involved), is the actual decision of the court based upon the material facts of the case. This is referred to by the Latin expression *ratio decidendi* which means the reason for deciding. The remainder of the judgment is described as *obiter dicta* which means things said by the way. (The singular of *obiter dicta* is *obiter dictum*, literally a thing said by the way). Nothing other than the *ratio decidendi* may be regarded as binding. The most that an *obiter dictum* can be is persuasive.

In order to understand the difference between *ratio decidendi* and *obiter dicta*, it is necessary to consider the form taken by a judgment in court. This is illustrated by the following table.

TABLE 6.1 **Contents of a Judgment**

1. A summary of all relevant facts.
2. A review of the relevant law.
3. (Sometimes) a review of counsel's arguments in relevant precedents.
4. (Sometimes) a review of the judge's reasoning in relevant precedents.
5. Application of the relevant law to the relevant facts.
6. Decision: which may be broken down into:
   (a) Obiter dicta—things said by the way;
   (b) Ratio decidendi—the reason for the decision.

In giving judgment, a judge does not stick rigidly to this pattern but he will usually cover all of these areas. He will summarise the facts which are before him. He will also review the relevant law. In doing this he will often consider the argument put to him by counsel and also the reasoning of the judges in precedents cited to him. He will then apply the relevant law as he understands it to the relevant facts as he sees them. This will enable him to come to a decision which may be broken down into the *ratio decidendi* and *obiter dicta*.

The difference between *ratio decidendi* and *obiter dicta* can perhaps be illustrated by the following simple example. In English law it is an offence to drive a motor vehicle while under the influence of alcohol. This is, on the face of it, a simple concept. But what is meant by driving a motor vehicle? Let us suppose that Smith, having drunk far more than he should, attempts to drive his car. The car will not start and so Smith gets some friends to push the car along the road while he sits in the driving seat and steers. While this is happening he is arrested by a policeman. Subsequently he appears in court charged with driving a motor vehicle while under the influence of alcohol. In giving his judgment the judge says that Smith was driving the car, not withstanding that the engine was not running and that he was merely steering. However, the judge goes on to say that if Smith had been outside the car, merely helping his friends to push it, he would not have been driving. The *ratio decidendi* in this judgment is that a person is driving a motor vehicle if he is sitting inside the car steering while others are pushing. The *obiter dictum* is that he would not be regarded as driving if he were outside the vehicle helping to push it. This is a very simplistic example and it must be said that it is frequently very difficult to distinguish between *ratio decidendi* and *obiter dicta*, and frequently judges themselves cannot agree exactly as to what constitutes the *ratio decidendi* in a particular case. Often the statements made by the judge in regard to the principles in the case before him may be far wider than in fact warranted by the precise facts of the case. When we come to examine consideration in the law of contract, we shall come to the case of *Central London Property Trust Ltd* v *High Trees House Ltd* (popularly known as the 'High Trees Case') (1947) (Chap 6 para 11). It is interesting to note that the statement made by Denning J about promissory estoppel was obiter since it was made in respect of facts found not to exist in the particular case before the court. Likewise, when we come to the liability for negligent mistatements, we shall look at *Hedley Byrne & Co Ltd* v *Heller & Partners Ltd* (1964) (Chap 19 para 4). Here the House of Lords stated that the person who makes a statement of fact owes a duty of care to the person to whom he makes the statement if he expects that person to reply upon the statement and fails to put a disclaimer of liability with the statement. This expression of the law was infact obiter since it was found in the case itself that there had been no breach of duty because the statement under consideration had been made with a disclaimer. This may not be a very meaningful statement at this point, but a reminder to turn back to this is included in the text later when these cases are dealt with.

6.2 TREATMENT OF A JUDICIAL DECISION

When a judicial decision comes to be considered by the court, it may be treated in a variety of ways:

1. The losing party in the case may choose to appeal. When the case goes to appeal, the higher court may either affirm or reverse the decision of the lower court. When this happens, the decision of the lower court ceases to have any authority as a precedent.
2. The decision may be considered in a subsequent and different case. Sometimes it will be followed in the subsequent case. Each time it is followed its importance as a precedent is increased.
3. It may, on the other hand, be overruled by a higher court in a subsequent case. When this happens it will usually no longer be regarded as a precedent. (Incidentally the overruling of a decision should not be confused with the reversing of a decision. A case is only reversed on appeal. When a case is overruled, it is really the principle of law in that case which is overruled. The overruling has no effect on the outcome of the earlier case). A precedent may also be overruled by a subsequent statutory provision which reverses the effect of it.
4. When a judge finds that a precedent which has been referred to him is not absolutely relevant to the facts of the case which he is presently considering, he may distinguish the earlier decision.
5. If the decision of an earlier case is directly relevant to the facts of the case before the judge, but is not binding upon him, he can simply choose not to follow it. In this case there will be a conflict of precedent which will ultimately have to be resolved by some higher court.

6.3 DO JUDGES MAKE LAW?

In strict legal theory, judges do not make law. In reaching a decision in a case, they merely state how the existing law applies to the case before them. However, it can be argued that they make law in the following limited ways:

1. Where there is no existing precedent which is directly relevant to the case before them, then they must extend the existing law to cover the new situation by analogy.
2. Where they overrule an existing precedent, frequently because there are other conflicting precedents.
3. Where they distinguish precedents cited before them, and so limit the scope of the previous rule.

6.4 ADVANTAGES AND DISADVANTAGES OF JUDICIAL PRECEDENT

Professor Geldart has listed the advantages and disadvantages of the system of judicial precedent. These advantages and disadvantages are illustrated by the following diagram:

TABLE 6.4 **Advantages and Disadvantages of Judicial Precedent**

Advantages	Disadvantages
Certainty	Rigidity
Flexibility	Inconsistency
Attention to detail	Vast bulk
Practical nature	

The advantages are perhaps fairly obvious. Particularly where a precedent comes from the House of Lords, there is a considerable degree of certainty in the law. There is also flexibility in the system, in that the judges are free to adapt existing law to new situations. The system pays great attention to detail, with an enormous wealth of rules covering most circumstances. Because of the way in which the common law system has evolved, the law is of an extremely practical nature.

There are, however, corresponding disadvantages. The fact that certain precedents, particularly from the higher courts, are binding may in some instances limit the discretion enjoyed by a judge. There is a danger of inconsistency since a judge will sometimes seek to avoid a rule contained in an established precedent which would otherwise result in hardship in the case before him. The very nature of the doctrine of precedent leads to a vast bulk of law. In English law there are well over a thousand volumes of law reports and over half a million cases.

6.5 PERSUASIVE AND BINDING PRECEDENT

Those precedents which a judge must follow are called binding precedents. All others are merely persuasive. Probably the most numerous persuasive precedents are all *obita dicta* and also the decisions of judges of the High Court. Such decisions, it will be recalled, are not binding in subsequent High Court cases. Other persuasive precedents are decisions of the Judicial Committee of the Privy Council and decisions of the courts of Commonwealth countries.

6.6 THE INTERPRETATION OF STATUTES

The function of judges in relation to legislation is to apply it in the case before them. Language is, however, in some respects an imperfect means of communication and sometimes the intention of Parliament is not completely clear in the legislation which it passes. In interpreting a statute, a judge is assisted by certain rules of interpretation and by some presumptions. There are also some intrinsic and extrinsic aids to construction. These rules, presumptions and aids are referred to collectively as the principles of statutory interpretation and they will be examined in the following paragraphs.

6.6.1 The Literal Rule

The literal rule very simply states that the wording of the statute must be interpreted in accordance with its literal meaning. Sentences must be given their grammatical meaning. This is so even though the result of this literal interpretation may be a decision of the court which was not intended by Parliament. This is illustrated in the following cases:

Inland Revenue Commissioner v Hinchy (1960)

Section 25(3) of the Income Tax Act 1952 stated that 'a person who neglects or refuses to deliver ... a true and correct list, declaration or return ... shall (a) if proceeded against by action in any court forfeit the sum of £20 and treble the tax which he ought to be charged under this Act'. In his return, Hinchy stated that he had received savings bank interest of £18 instead of the amount actually received, £51. The tax due on the amount omitted was £14. Hinchy's income tax for the whole year was £139 (including the £14). The Inland Revenue Commissioners claimed £438, this being 3 times the £139 + £20. The House of Lords upheld the Commissioner's claim. The wording of the statute was perfectly clear. A tax payer who had declared only part of the interest received by him is liable to pay treble the whole tax charges for the year and not merely treble the tax on the income which he had failed to declare.

In applying the literal rule it is important that the court bears in mind that technical words must be given their normal technical meaning. For example:

Unwin v Hanson (1891)

The Highways Act 1835 allowed a Borough Surveyor to prune and lop any trees excluding light from the highway. The plaintiff brought proceedings against the Borough Surveyor who had cut the top from the plaintiff's trees. Evidence was admitted to show that pruning meant the removal of surplus branches to improve growth, and lopping meant to cut branches from the side of the tree. The Court of Appeal held therefore that the Borough Surveyor had acted unlawfully, since topping the trees was different from pruning or lopping.

In determining the meaning of words, the court is free to consult a dictionary.

6.6.2 The Golden Rule

The Golden Rule is generally regarded as simply a modification of the literal rule. It states that if applying the literal rule results in an interpretation which has either no meaning or an absurd meaning then the literal rule is disregarded and some other rule applied. An excellent, if amusing, example of this is the case of:

Adler v George (1964)

The Official Secrets Act 1920 provided that a person would be guilty of an offence if he obstructed HM Forces 'in the vicinity of' a prohibited place. A prosecution was brought under the Act against a person found actually in an RAF base, a prohibited place. To have applied the words 'in the vicinity of' literally would have meant that the defendant would have been acquitted. This would have been an absurdity. The Act was clearly passed to prevent persons getting into such places as RAF bases. Accordingly the Divisional Court determined that the defendant was guilty of an offence.

6.6.3 The Mischief Rule

This rule, sometimes referred to as the rule in Heydon's case (1584) is that if there is any doubt as to the meaning of a statutory provision, the court can look behind the statute at the mischief or defect in the law which the statute sought to remedy and interpret the statute to suppress that mischief. The application of the rule is seen in the following cases:

Corkery v Carpenter (1951)

The Licensing Act 1872 provided that a person found drunk in charge of a 'carriage' on the highway could be arrested without a warrant. The defendant in this case was arrested without a warrant having been found drunk in charge of a bicycle. It was held by the Divisional Court that a bicycle was a 'carriage' for the purposes of the Act. Accordingly the defendant was properly arrested. The mischief which the Act sought to make unlawful was the presence on the highway of drunken persons in charge of some form of transport. Had the court applied the literal rule, the result might have been different since it could almost certainly be argued that a bicycle is not a carriage within the normal meaning of the word.

Maidstone Borough Council v Mortimer (1980)

The Town and Country Planning Act 1971 made it an offence to cut down any tree protected by a preservation order. Mortimer cut down an oak tree which he did not realise was protected by such an order. It was held by the Divisional Court that the offence had been committed regardless of whether the accused had knowledge of the order. The mischief which the statute had been passed to prevent was just such cutting down of protected trees without the consent of the local planning authority.

6.6.4 The Eiusdem Generis Rule

This rule provides that when general words are used by way of summary after a number of specific words forming a category, the general words are taken to refer only to things of the kind which fall within the category. This is illustrated by the following cases:

***Powell v Kempton Park Racecourse Company* (1899)**

The Betting Act 1853 prohibited the keeping of any 'house, office, room or other place' for the purpose of betting with persons resulting thereto. The court had to consider whether Tattersall's Ring, an outdoor place at a racecourse, fell within the meaning of 'some other place'. It was held by the House of Lords that since the specific places mentioned were all indoor places, the words 'other place' must be similarly interpreted. Therefore an uncovered enclosure was not an 'other place'.

6.6.5 Expressio unius est exclusio alterius

This rule means that where certain things are expressly mentioned and they are not followed by any general word, then there is no extension by implication of the specific things to other similar things. This is illustrated by:

***Tempest v Kilner* (1846)**

Section 17 (which has now been repealed) of the Statute Frauds 1677 required that a contract for the sale of 'goods, wares and merchandise' for £10 or more should be evidenced in writing. It was held that this did not apply to a contract for the sale of stocks and shares. These were not 'goods, wares and merchandise' and were clearly excluded since they received no express mention.

6.6.6 Noscitur a sociis

This rule means that an Act must be read as a whole. The meaning of words and phrases is determined by their context. A good example is:

***Pengelly v Bell Punch Company Limited* (1964)**

The case concerned the interpretation of the word 'floors' in s28(1), Factories Act 1961. The word was held not to cover those parts of the factory floor which were properly being used for the purpose of storage. The Act was concerned with 'floors, steps, stairs, passages and gangways'. They were required to be kept free from obstruction. Diplock L J explained 'it will be observed that the last four are places used for the purpose of passage. The expression "floors" in this context and in the light of the word "obstruction" which means "blocking or being blocked; making or becoming more or less impassable" is, in my view, limited to those parts of the factory floor from which workmen are intended or likely to pass and re-pass'.

6.7 STATUTORY PRESUMPTIONS

Although the power of Parliament to legislate is almost without limit (see Chapter 5 section 5.4), Parliament is presumed not to intend to pass certain laws without express words. The most important presumptions include the following:

AN ACT OF PARLIAMENT APPLIES TO THE UNITED KINGDOM

This is because Parliament is the Parliament of the United Kingdom. If Parliament intends to exclude some part of the United Kingdom it must say so expressly. Thus sections 440 and 441 of the Insolvency Act 1986 expressly provide that only specific parts of the Act apply to Scotland and Northern Ireland. Conversely, if it is Parliament's intention that an Act should apply to territories or acts done outside the United Kingdom, this also must be expressly stated.

AN ACT OF PARLIAMENT DOES NOT BIND THE CROWN

An Act of Parliament has no application to the Crown, nor to Crown servants while performing their official duties, nor to property occupied by the Crown for public purposes unless it expressly says so.

Thus for example the Health and Safety at Work etc Act 1974 expressly states that the Crown is bound by certain provisions therein.

PRESUMPTION AGAINST AN ALTERATION OF THE COMMON LAW

An Act of Parliament is presumed only to alter the Common Law if it expressly states that it does so. The basis of English law is still the Common Law. Statutes are essentially additions and corrections to it, though of increasing importance as each year goes by.

PRESUMPTION AGAINST REPEAL OF EARLIER ACTS

There is a presumption against an implied repeal of an earlier act by a later one, though if a later act is clearly inconsistent with an earlier act then there is a repeal of the earlier legislative provisions.

PRESUMPTION AGAINST DEPRIVATION OF LIBERTY

If Parliament wishes to deprive a person of his liberty then clearly expressed words to this end must be used. For example:

Morris v Beardmore (1981)

The accused in this case had been involved in a motor accident. Uniformed police officers went to his house to interview him and were admitted to the house by his son. The accused at the time was upstairs in his bedroom, and refused to come downstairs though he sent a message through his son asking the police officers to leave the premises as they were trespassers. The officers, however, went to the accused's bedroom and asked him to take a breath test because they suspected him of having been drinking. When he refused he was arrested and taken to a police station. The House of Lords held that he was not guilty of refusing to provide samples of breath contrary to the Road Traffic Act 1972 because the police officers were in fact trespassing in his house, since the Act did not permit them to go into the house in the way in which they had.
  Therefore the accused did not have to comply with their request.

PRESUMPTION AGAINST DEPRIVATION OF PROPERTY OR INTERFERENCE WITH PRIVATE RIGHTS

When a statute encroaches upon the rights of an individual subject, that statute must be interpreted so as to respect the rights involved. Lord Warrington of Clyffe explained in *Colonial Sugar Refining Co Limited* v *Melbourne Harbour Trust Commissioners* (1897) that 'a statute should not be held to take away private rights of property without compensation unless the intention to do so is expressed in clear and unambiguous terms'.

INTENTION IS REQUIRED FOR CRIMINAL LIABILITY

Unless the statute expressly provides to the contrary, criminal offences require an intention on the part of the accused. (There are some offences, such as exceeding the speed limit in a motor vehicle or parking in a restricted area which do not require any mental element to be shown; it is sufficient for the prosecutor simply to show that the alleged incident took place). The need for a mental intention is obviously of great importance for the protection of the liberty of the subject. A good example of this presumption arose in the case of:

Sweet v Parsley (1970)

Section 5, Dangerous Drugs Act 1955 (now repealed) provided that it was an offence to be concerned in the management of premises used for the smoking of cannabis. The defendant in this case was the owner of a house which she had let to tenants. The tenants used it for smoking cannabis, though the defendant knew absolutely nothing about this. It was held by the House of Lords that she was not guilty of the offence. She did not know the premises were being used for an unlawful purpose and she did not intend them to be used in this way.

PRESUMPTION AGAINST RETROSPECTIVE EFFECT

As a general rule legislation regulating conduct ought to be introduced to deal with future conduct. It should not have an effect on acts done or rights acquired prior to that date. Clear words must be used in a statute if it is to be retrospective. For example:

R v Miah (1974)

Sections 24 and 26, Immigration Act 1971 created the offences of being an illegal immigrant in the United Kingdom and being in possession of a false passport. It was held by the House of Lords that the offences did not apply to acts done some 14 months before the Act was passed.

Retrospective legislation is possible, however, and it is only commonly found in the realm of tax legislation. Here retrospective legislation will frequently be passed to block a tax loophole which has been exploited to the benefit of taxpayers.

6.8 INTRINSIC AIDS TO INTERPRETATION

All but the most simple of statutes contain definition sections which state the meaning to be given to certain words and phrases which are used in the Act. An Act of Parliament has two titles, the short title and the long title. The short title is merely the name such as the Companies Act 1985 or the Misrepresentation Act 1967. The long title is part of the Act itself and is a concise indication of the general aims of the Act. Lord Simon of Glaisdale said in *Royal College of Nursing of United Kingdom* v *DHSS* (1981) that it provided the 'plainest of all guides to the general objective of a statute.'

There is also some guide to interpretation provided by the Interpretation Act 1978. This contains definitions of a number of standard words and phrases and lays down certain general rules of interpretation. It provides, for example, that 'the male includes the female gender', so any reference to a man is taken to mean also a reference to a woman unless the statute expressly says otherwise.

6.9 A COMPARISON BETWEEN STATUTE LAW AND JUDICIAL PRECEDENT

By way of a summary of what we have considered in this chapter, we will compare statute law and judicial precedent. It is done in the following diagram:

TABLE 6.9 **Comparison between Statute Law and Judicial Precedent**

Statute	Precedent
Creates new law. Makes rules to govern future conduct. Is formal and imperative.	Generally thought not to create new law. Applies existing rules to past conduct. Based upon reasoning.

SUMMARY

While statute creates new law, precedent is generally thought not to do so. Statute generally makes rules applicable to future conduct, whereas precedent applies existing rules to past conduct. Statute is formal and imperative, whereas precedent is based upon a reasoned application of the law to a given situation.

SELF-TEST QUESTIONS

6.1 Distinguish between:
(a) (i) a ratio decidendi and (ii) an obiter dictum
(b) (i) overruling a decision and (ii) reversing a decision

6.2 Why does the doctrine of judicial

precedent have the advantage of certainty?

6.3 List the rules of statutory interpretation

6.4 How is the literal rule applied?

6.5 Why was it necessary to use the Golden Rule of interpretation in the case of *Adler* v *George* (1964)?

6.6 How was the mischief rule applied in *Corkery* v *Carpenter* (1951)?

6.7 The provisions of a certain act apply to 'cats, dogs and other animals' Would the act apply to

(a) horses?
(b) hamsters?

6.8 Section 1 of an (imaginary) Act provides that cars and lorries must have an off-side wing mirror and that lorries must also have a near-side mirror. On principles of statutory interpretation, why does the position as the near-side mirrors not apply to cars?

6.9 Which presumption was used in the case of *Sweet* v *Parsley* (1970)?

6.10 What are the intrinsic aids to interpretation of statutes?

Answers on page 298

EXERCISES

Exercise 6.1

Explain the English doctrine of judical precedent. What, in your view, are the main advantages of the doctrine?

Answers not supplied.

Exercise 6.2

Describe the main principles of interpretation of statutes.

Answers on page 299

Contract—formation of a contract

A contract may be defined as a legally binding agreement between two or more persons. This area of law forms a major part of this syllabus and will be considered in the next few chapters.

7.1 INTRODUCTION

Under the contractual agreement rights are acquired by one party in return for something received by the other party. Usually this consists of a positive act by the other party, though it may be a forbearance. A typical contract arises when a person goes into a shop and buys a commodity which the shop is selling. An example of a forbearance situation would be where a teacher promises a pupil that if the pupil will not go out with his girlfriend during the three weeks prior to an important examination he, the teacher, will give the pupil £10.

There are a number of elements necessary for a binding contract to come into existence. For convenience they are listed below, though you will not fully understand them until you have finished studying the chapters on contract. At this stage they will serve merely as an extended index to illustrate what we are going to cover. While you are working through contract, they may serve as a useful indicator as to how the subject comes together. When you have finished contract, you may find them useful as a summary of what you have been doing.

1. A contract is made between two or more persons. One party must have made an offer to the other in which he indicated his willingness to be bound by a contractual agreement on certain items whether express or implied.
2. The other party must have accepted that offer in its precise terms, without himself adding any further terms or conditions.
3. The parties must have had an intention to create legal relations. In other words, the parties must have intended, whether consciously or subconsciously, that the agreement would be enforceable in a court of law if things went badly wrong.
4. Each party must have given consideration. This means that each party to the contract must have suffered a detriment in return for the benefit received. For example if Adam buys some sweets from a shop, the consideration moving from Adam to the shop is the price for the sweets and from the shop to Adam, the sweets themselves. There is an exception to this rule where the contract takes the form of a deed.
5. If there is a requirement that the contract be in a particular form, then this requirement must be complied with. For example, it will be seen that contracts of guarantee must be evidenced in writing, otherwise they are not enforceable in the courts of law.
6. Both parties to the contract must have contractual capacity. Corporations must act within the powers conferred upon them by their constitution (see further Chapter 16). There are limitations on the contractual capacity of minors (persons under the age of 18), persons of unsound mind and persons under the influence of drink.
7. Both parties must have freely consented to enter the contract.
8. The contract must not have been induced by means of a mistake recognised in law, nor by a misrepresentation.
9. The contract must not be one which is treated by the law as illegal. This is rather wider than a contract the carrying out of which would constitute a criminal offence. It also includes contracts which are contrary to public policy, which means contracts which the court feels, as a matter of policy, should not be enforceable.
10. The contracts must be capable of being performed at the time it is entered into.

A contract which does not satisfy these requirements may be treated by the courts as being void, voidable or unenforceable. Again, at this stage, these terms will not mean much to you. However, it is as well to introduce you to the terms at this stage and, for the time being, the definitions given should simply be learnt.

1. A void contract is a contract which does not exist and which has never existed. It is of no legal effect. Neither party can enforce it against the other. An example of this is a contract which is affected by a mistake recognised by law as being sufficient to vitiate the contract.
2. A voidable contract is a contract which, when entered into, was valid, but which is capable of being treated as void by one of the parties thereto if he so elects. An example of a voidable contract is one which is entered into as a result of undue influence exerted by one party on the person seeking to avoid the contract.
3. A contract which is unenforceable is one which is valid at the time of its formation and which remains valid if the parties perform it. It is, however, incapable of being enforced by legal action if either party fails to perform it.

7.2 OFFER

7.2.1 The nature of an offer

An offer is a definite indication of the willingness of the person making the offer (the offeror) to be bound by an agreement with the person to whom the offer is made (the offeree) if he agrees to the terms of the offer. An offer may be oral or written. In appropriate circumstances, it may also be implied from the conduct of the offeror. For example, if a person goes into a hotel and books accommodation for the night, he impliedly agrees to pay for that accommodation even though he may be unaware of the exact price.

As has just been said, an offer is a definite indication of a willingness to be bound. As such it is the penultimate step before acceptance by the offeree. It must be distinguished from an invitation to treat, which is a preliminary step in negotiations which may or may not lead to a definite offer being made. The essential difference between an offer and an invitation to treat is that whereas an offer result in a binding contract coming into existence upon its being accepted, an invitation to treat cannot do so. In the following paragraphs are examples of invitations to treat.

DISPLAY OF GOODS

Where goods are displayed in a self-service store or a shop window, the display constitutes an invitation to treat rather than an offer. The same is true of goods advertised in catalogues. This is illustrated by:

Pharmaceutical Society of Great Britain v Boots Cash Chemists (Southern) Ltd (1952)

By Pharmacy and Poisons Act 1933, s18, it was unlawful to sell specified drugs 'unless the sale is effected under the supervision of a registered pharmacist'. The defendant chemists were the proprietors of a self-service store. Drugs which could only be sold under the supervision of a registered pharmacist were displayed on the shelves. There was no pharmacist at the display shelves, though there was one present at the cash desk. The Pharmaceutical Society brought proceedings against Boots claiming that they were in breach of the Pharmacy and Poisons Act in that the display of goods on the shelves was an offer which was accepted by the customer when he put an article into his basket. It was held by the Court of Appeal, however, that the display of drugs on the shelves was merely an invitation to treat. The offer was made by the customer when he presented the goods at the cash desk. The acceptance took place when the transaction was completed at the cash desk.

This, of course, has important implications for shoppers. If you go into a supermarket and place items in the basket provided and then find that you have forgotten your money, you can simply replace the goods on the shelves and walk out. Were the placing of the goods in the basket in itself an acceptance, as the Pharmaceutial Society contended, you would in these circumstances be obliged to pay for the goods. It also has important implications for the shopkeeper. For example, it is an offence in England for a shopkeeper to sell cigarettes to a person under the age of 16. The request by an under-age customer for cigarettes on display is therefore an offer which the shopkeeper is free to decline. Similarly an advertisement in a newspaper for goods for sale is an invitation to treat.

Partridge v Crittenden (1968)

The appellants advertised in a magazine for cage bird enthusiasts 'Bramblefinch Cocks and Hens, 25s'. They were charged, and convicted by the court at first instance, with offering for sale a wild live bird which is a criminal offence. The Divisional Court quashed the conviction holding that the advertisement in the magazine was no more than an invitation to treat. Thus the offence of offering the bird for sale was not committed.

INVITATIONS TO SUPPLIERS FOR TENDERS

Sometimes an invitation is made to a tradesman or supplier to make tenders for the supply of goods or services. An example of this might arise where a school requires a further 100 desks. It writes to a number of suppliers asking them to tender to supply the desks. In this situation it is the tender itself which is the offer. The acceptance of the offer comes when the order for the desks is placed.

STATEMENT OF SELLING PRICE

A statement of selling price may be an invitation to treat. It is not necessarily an offer. The leading case on this is:

Harvey v Facey (1893)

Harvey telegraphed to Facey in regard to a particular piece of land 'Will you sell us Bumper Hall Pen? Telegraph lowest cash price.' To this Facey replied 'Lowest price for Bumper Hall Pen, £900'. Harvey responded by telegraph 'We agree to buy Bumper Hall Pen for £900 asked by you'. The question was whether this was sufficient to bring a contract into existence. It was held by the Judicial Committee of the Privy Council that Harvey's first question had been merely a request for information. Facey's reply had been merely a statement as to the lowest price which he would accept in the event of his deciding to sell. It was not an offer to sell. Thus no legally binding agreement had been entered into.

In a situation such as this, it is essentially a matter of construction for the court to determine whether or not a contract has come into existence. *Harvey* v *Facey* was distinguished in the case of:

Bigg v Boyd Gibbins Ltd (1971)

Boyd Gibbins offered to buy a property from Bigg. Bigg replied 'As you are aware that I paid £25,000 for this property, your offer of £20,000 would appear to be at least a little optimistic. For a quick sale I would accept £26,000'. Boyd Gibbins replied 'I accept your offer'. It was held that this exchange of letters was intended to achieve the formation of a contract. In this case the statement of selling price, £26,000, was an offer.

A particular problem concerning the interpretation of pre-contractual statements arose in:

Gibson v Manchester City Council (1979)

In 1970, Manchester City Council which was under Conservative control, was selling council houses to the tenants living in them. Gibson was a council tenant who wrote to the Council asking whether he could purchase his house. In response the Council wrote to him that it 'may be prepared to sell the house to you at a purchase price of £2,725 less 20% equals £2,180 freehold'. The letter continued 'If you would like to make formal application to buy your council house please complete the enclosed application form and return it ... as soon as possible'. The application form itself was headed 'Application to buy a council house'. Gibson duly completed the form and returned it to the Council. Before a formal contract had been prepared, the Council changed from Conservative to Labour control and the new leaders adopted the policy that they would only sell houses where legally binding agreements were already in existence. Gibson sought an order for specific performance of the contract (ie an order from the court that the Council should complete the sale to him). It was held by the House of Lords that no contract had come into existence. The letter from the Council had been merely setting out the financial terms on which the Council would be prepared to consider the sale and purchase in due course. The offer had come from Gibson himself and, since it had not yet been accepted by the Council, there was no binding contract.

DECLARATION OF INTENTION

A declaration of intention, such as a newspaper advertisement specifying that an auction will be held, does not constitute an offer:

Harris v Nickerson (1873)

Nickerson, an auctioneer, advertised that he would be selling certain goods, including some office furniture, at an auction sale to be held in Bury St. Edmunds. Harris made the journey from London to attend the sale with the intention of bidding for the office furniture. In the event, although the auction was held, the office furniture was withdrawn from sale. It was held that Harris could not recover from the auctioneer the money which he had expended on travelling to attend the auction. The advertisement was merely a statement of intention to hold the auction, not an offer which was capable of acceptance by a person attending it.

At an auction sale the call by an auctioneer for bids is an invitation to treat. The bids are made by those who attend the auction wishing to purchase the goods. Acceptance is effective by the fall of the auctioneer's hammer. This principle is now contained in statute. Section 58, Sale of Goods Act 1979 states that a sale of goods by auction is completed by the fall of the hammer and until that time a lot may be withdrawn.

7.2.2 Communication of offer

It is, perhaps, a statement of the obvious that an offer cannot be accepted unless it is known to the offeree. Thus an offer must be communicated by the offeror to the offeree. When an offer is sent by post, it is made when the letter is received by the offeree. Usually an offer is addressed to a specific person, in which case only that person may accept so as to create a legally binding contract. When it is addressed in this way, a purported acceptance by someone else does not give rise to a legally enforceable contract. Although this is the usual method of making an offer, it is possible for an offer to be made to a limited group of persons or even to the world at large. When it is made to a group of persons it may be accepted by any one within the group who knows of the offer. When it is made to the world at large it may be accepted by any one who, knowing of the offer, accepts it. For example in:

Carlill v Carbolic Smoke Ball Co (1893)

An advertisement was issued by the Carbolic Smoke Ball Co extolling the virtues of a carbolic smoke ball (a medicament) made by them. The advertisement stated that if the ball was used in accordance with their instructions the user was almost guaranteed not to catch influenza. To 'show their sincerity in this matter' they stated that they had deposited £1,000 with their bankers and that they would pay £100 from this to any person who used the smoke ball as instructed and still caught influenza. Mrs Carlill, having read the advertisement, bought and used the carbolic smoke ball as instructed. In spite of this she caught influenza. It was held by the Court of Appeal that the advertisement constituted an offer to the world at large and as such was capable of acceptance by any one using the ball in accordance with the instructions. Since Mrs Carlill had acted in this way, there was an acceptance by her.

A question sometimes considered is the problem of identical cross-offers. This is where two offers couched in identical terms are made simultaneously by two persons to each other. It was said, in *Tinn* v *Hoffman & Co* (1893) that identical cross-offers would not constitute a contract. The reason for this was stated to be that neither party would know if he were bound by the contract. Although there has never been a legal decision exactly on this point, it is suggested that identical cross-offers would in practice bind the parties since it is hardly likely that the parties would have any objection to being so bound.

7.2.3 Termination of offer

Once an offer has been made, it remains capable of being accepted until such time as it terminates. An offer may be terminated in the following ways:

REVOCATION

An offer may be revoked by the offeror at any time prior to acceptance by the offeree. Although as will be seen below (see 7.3.1) acceptance of an offer by post is deemed to be made when the letter of acceptance is posted, a letter revoking an offer must actually be received by the offeree. Unless and until the revocation is communicated, it is of no effect:

Byrne v Van Tienhoven (1880)

Byrne, the plaintiff, was based in Cardiff and Van Tienhoven, the defendant, was based in New York. On 1 October the defendants wrote to the plaintiffs offering to sell them 1,000 boxes of tinplates. The plaintiffs received this letter on 15 October and accepted it by letter on the same day. Meanwhile on 8 October the defendants had written again to the plaintiffs revoking the offer of 1 October. This letter did not actually reach the plaintiffs until 20 October. It was held that the contract had been made at the date of posting the acceptance, 15 October. Thus the contract had already been formed by the time that the revocation was received.

There is in fact no requirement that the revocation should be made by the offeror so long as it is communicated to the offeree by a reliable source:

Dickinson v Dodds (1876)

Dodds offered to sell a house to Dickinson for £800. The written offer stated that the offer would remain open until 9.00 am on Friday 12 June. In fact on Thursday 11 June Dodds sold the house to a third party. Dickinson was informed of the sale later in the day by a source which he knew to be reliable. Notwithstanding this, at 7.00 am on Friday 12 June, Dickinson handed Dodds a letter purporting to accept the offer and then sought to enforce the sale, arguing that the original offer had not been revoked and that therefore Dickinson's acceptance brought a valid contract of sale into existence. It was held that the offer had been revoked and that accordingly Dickinson could not enforce the contract. There was no need for the revocation actually to be communicated by Dodds himself to Dickinson.

These cases concern what are sometimes referred to as bilateral offers. This is a situation where an offeror expresses a willingness to be bound by a promise in return for a promise by the offeree. The same principles apply in the case of a unilateral offer which arises where an offeror promises to be bound if the offeree acts in a certain way. In this case the question which has to be addressed is whether the offer may be withdrawn at any time prior to complete acceptance or whether it becomes incapable of withdrawal once the offeree has commenced performance of the act which is capable of becoming acceptance. This was considered in the case of:

Errington v Errington & Woods (1952)

A father bought a house for his daughter and son-in-law to live in. He provided one-third of the purchase price by cash, the remainder to be paid by mortgage. He then offered that so long as the daughter and son-in-law paid the mortgage instalments, he would give them the house once it was paid for. They duly paid the instalments and the father then sought to revoke his offer to convey the house to them. It was held by the Court of Appeal that the father's offer could not be revoked once the daughter and son-in-law had commenced performance in the specified manner. There must be a term implied into the contract that the offer would be irrevocable once performance had commenced.

REJECTION OF THE OFFER

Once an offer is rejected by the offeree then it comes to an end. To be effective, the rejection must reach the offeror. There is also an implied rejection if the offeree makes a counter-offer on terms which are at variance with those proposed by the offeror. Once he has made a counter-offer, an offeree cannot revive the rejected offer:

Hyde v Wrench (1840)

Wrench offered to sell to Hyde a farm for £1,000. Hyde rejected this offer, stating instead that he was prepared to pay £950. Wrench would not accept the reduced price contained in the counter-offer and Hyde thereupon purported to accept the original offer of £1,000. It was held that no contract to sell the farm had come into existence. The counter-offer of £950 had rejected the original offer and such rejection having been made there was no way in which the original offer could be revived by the offeree's action.

It is important in this context to differentiate between a counter-offer and a mere request for more details of the offer. A request for details does not constitute a rejection:

Stevenson v McLean (1880)

McLean offered to sell some iron to Stevenson at £2 per ton. Stevenson sent a telegram asking whether he would be permitted to pay for the iron over a period of time. Receiving no reply, he thereupon accepted the original offer. McLean failed to deliver, having sold the iron to a third party. It was held that since the original offer had not been withdrawn, its acceptance by Stevenson brought into being a binding contract. There had been a breach of this contract and Stevenson was entitled to succeed in his action for damages. The request as to whether Stevenson could pay for the iron over a period of time was merely a request for information and not a new offer.

LAPSE OF TIME

If an offer is stated to remain open for a specified period of time, then termination occurs automatically upon the expiration of that time. If there is no stipulated time limit, an offer remains open only for a reasonable time:

Ramsgate Victoria Hotel Co v Montefiore (1866)

Montefiore offered to purchase some shares in the Ramsgate Victoria Hotel Company. He sent his letter of application to the company on 8 June. He received no response until 23 November when the company sent him a letter purporting to accept his offer. Montefiore refused after so long a time to pay for the shares and the hotel company brought proceedings against him for the price of the shares. It was held that the lapse of time had been so long as to bring the offer to an end, and therefore no acceptance was possible. Therefore there was no contract and no liability upon Montefiore to pay for the shares.

NON-OCCURRENCE OF AN EXPRESS OR IMPLIED CONDITION

Sometimes an offer is made subject to a condition. In the event of that condition not being satisfied, the offer cannot be accepted. For example, a customer may agree to buy a second-hand car from a garage so long as certain repairs are carried out to the car. If those repairs are not effected, then no contract will come into existence and the offer to buy will terminate. An example of this is:

Financings Ltd v Stimson (1962)

Stimson offered to buy a car on hire-purchase. After he had made the offer but prior to its acceptance, the car was severely damaged when a third party crashed into it outside the garage. It was held by the Court of Appeal that no contract had come into existence since there must be an implied term that until acceptance took place the car would remain in substantially the same condition as at the date of the offer.

DEATH OF OFFEROR OR OFFEREE

If an offeror dies after making an offer, whether that death terminates the offer depends upon the nature of the intended contract. If the contract envisages something which is essentially personal, such as the writing of a book or the painting of a picture then the death will obviously terminate the offer. On the other hand, if the offer was not referable specifically to the offeror personally, then his death would probably not affect the continuance of the offer and its capability of acceptance.

7.3 ACCEPTANCE

7.3.1 The nature of acceptance

Acceptance is an agreement by the offeree to all the terms of the offer. Until there has been an acceptance, no contract exists and in consequence any action by either of the parties to enforce the contract will fail. Acceptance may be by oral or written statement. It may also be by conduct, though the mere mental decision of the offeree to accept is not enough. A useful discussion of acceptance by conduct took place in:

Brogden v Metropolitan Railway Co (1877)

Brogden supplied the Metropolitan Railway Company with coal. This had been going on for several years and the two parties decided to draw up a formal agreement. The Metropolitan Railway Company drew up the agreement in draft and sent it to Brogden for his approval. Brogden made some slight alterations and returned the draft marked 'approved'. No further action was taken upon the contract but for the next two years coal was supplied and paid for in accordance with the terms of the amended draft agreement. Brogden then refused to supply any more coal to the railway company, claiming that there was no binding contract. The House of Lords held that while mere mental assent by the railway company to the terms of the amended draft was not a valid acceptance, a binding contract had been created in this particular case by the railway company and Brogden acting upon the terms of the draft contract.

On the other hand, conduct is not acceptance of an offer, if the offer itself states specifically the form that acceptance should take:

Western Electric Ltd v Welsh Development Agency (1983)

The Development Agency offered Western Electric a licence to occupy factory premises. The letter of offer stated 'if you accept this licence on the above terms, will you please complete the acknowledgement and acceptance at the foot of the enclosed copy and return it to us at your earliest convenience'. Western Electric never completed the acknowledgement though they did take up occupation of the premises. It was held that the mere occupation of the premises was not an acceptance since the offer made by the Welsh Development Agency had expressly stated how acceptance should take place.

In *Carlill* v *Carbolic Smoke Ball Co* (above) the question was also considered whether an offer could be accepted by simply being acted upon. It was held by the Court of Appeal that Mrs Carlill, in using the smoke ball in accordance with the instructions, was exempted from the need of communicating the fact of acceptance to the company.

When acceptance is by post and telemessage, it is generally deemed to occur as soon as the letter or telemessage of acceptance is posted or handed in as the case may be. This was decided in:

Adams v Lindsell (1818)

Lindsell wrote to Adams offering to sell him some wool. Adams immediately posted his acceptance of the offer, but the acceptance did not reach Lindsell until two days later than it might have been expected to. In the period of time between posting and receipt of the acceptance, Lindsell had sold the wool to a third party. It was held that the contract had come into existence as soon as the letter of acceptance had been posted.

It should be noted, however, that the offeror can exclude this unique postal acceptance rule by specifying in the offer that the acceptance must be actually communicated to him:

Holwell Securities Ltd v Hughes (1974)

Hughes granted to Holwell Securities a six month option to purchase property, the option being exercisable by notice in writing to Hughes. Solicitors acting for Holwell Securities sent a letter purporting to accept the option though the letter was never delivered. Holwell Securities sought an order of specific performance of the contract. It was held by the Court of Appeal that the provision in the option that it was exercisable by notice in writing to Hughes indicated that the parties never intended that the posting of the letter should constitute the exercise of the option. Thus the postal rule of acceptance had been varied by the express terms of the contract and so no order for specific performance of the contract would be made.

As a general rule, acceptance may be by any method which is at least as effective and expeditious as the offer. Thus an offer by letter could be accepted by letter, face-to-face oral communication or by telephone message. However, it is possible for an offeror to insist upon a particular method of acceptance and in this case acceptance by any other means is of no effect. It should be noted that the postal rule of acceptance is applicable only to letters and telegrams. It does not apply, for example, where communication is by telex:

Entores v Miles Far East Corporation (1955)

Entores was a London company and Miles Far East Corporation was an American firm with agents in Amsterdam. Both Entores and the Amsterdam agent used telex machines. Entores offered to purchase certain goods from the Amsterdam agent by telex. This offer was accepted by the Amsterdam agent also by telex. The question was whether the contract was made in England or Holland. It was held by the Court of Appeal that the acceptance took place when it was received (ie in London) rather than when the telex was sent (in Holland). Accordingly the contract was made in England and so subject to English law.

This was confirmed in:

Brinkibon Ltd v Stahag Stahl (1982)

Brinkibon was an English company, Stahag an Austrian company based in Vienna. The Austrian company offered to sell some steel to Brinkibon. Acceptance of this offer was sent by telex to Stahag in Vienna. The contract was never performed and the question arose as to whether the contract was made in England or Austria. It was held by the House of Lords that since the acceptance emanated from England it was received in Austria. Therefore the contract was made in Austria and so was subject to Austrian law.

7.3.2 Silence cannot constitute acceptance

An offeror cannot impose liability on an offeree by stating that an offer will be regarded as having been accepted unless it is rejected within a certain time nor can he impose silence as being acceptance. For example in:

Felthouse v Bindley (1862)

Felthouse and his nephew, were negotiating for the sale of the nephew's horse. They had not reached an agreement as to the price when Felthouse wrote to the nephew saying 'if I hear no more about him I consider the horse is mine for £3.15.0d'. Although the nephew decided to accept this offer, he never replied. He was in the course of selling certain farm stock through an auctioneer, Bindley, whom he instructed not to sell the horse since a private sale had already been arranged. By mistake, Bindley sold the horse and was subsequently sued by Felthouse for conversion, a tort which comprises wrongfully dealing with someone else's goods. It was held that the auctioneer was not liable. At the time the auction had taken place no contract had been concluded between Felthouse and his nephew since silence cannot constitute acceptance. Therefore Bindley, the auctioneer, had done no wrong to Felthouse.

It should be noted that not only can an offeror not impose liability on an offeree by stating that silence is deemed to be acceptance, the Unsolicited Goods and Services Act 1971 provides also that a person receiving unsolicited goods may in some circumstances treat them as though they were an unconditional gift to him.

A contract cannot come into existence if the terms of an offer are fulfilled by a person who is in fact ignorant of the offer. If a person finds and returns a lost dog to its owner not knowing that the owner had offered any reward for its return, then the finder cannot claim the reward. The returning of the dog was an act of kindness rather than an acceptance of the offer. (This point was made in para 7.2.2 to which you might find it useful to refer).

7.4 CERTAINTY OF TERMS

Even though an offeror and an offeree may intend making a contract, the contract may fail because of uncertainty. There must be agreement between the parties on the material terms of the contract. It is not the job of the court to spell out the terms of a contact if the parties were too idle to do so:

Bushwall Properties Ltd v Vortex Properties Ltd (1976)

Vortex Properties agreed to sell 51½ acres of land to Bushwall Properties for £500,000. This price was due to be paid in three instalments, a first instalment of £250,000 followed by two further instalments at twelve-monthly intervals of £125,000. The agreement stated that 'on the occasion of each completion a proportionate part of the land shall be released forthwith' to Bushwall Properties. There was no machinery provided in the contract for the allocation of the proportionate part. It was held by the Court of Appeal that the agreement was void because of uncertainty.

On the other hand, the court only destroys a contract as a very last resort. It will, for example, ignore terms in a contract which are meaningless. In:

Nicolene Ltd v Simmonds (1953)

Nicolene Ltd offered to buy some steel bars from Simmonds. Simmonds replied accepting the offer but adding 'I assume that we are in agreement that the usual conditions of acceptance apply'. There were in fact no usual conditions which could be implied either from the nature of the business concerned or from any previous dealings between the parties. It was held by the Court of Appeal that the term in question was meaningless and so it could be severed from the contract as a whole. There was a considerable element of public policy behind this. The courts would not allow a party to avoid his obligations under a contract simply by having a term which has no meaning whatever and arguing that this rendered the whole agreement void for uncertainty.

Accordingly, Simmonds in this case, was liable for his failure to deliver the steel bars.

In the same way the court is happy to look at trade customs or previous dealings between the parties in order to clarify vague terms. For example in:

Hillas & Co v Arcos Ltd (1932)

Hillas agreed to buy '22,000 standards of softwood goods of fair specification over the season 1930' from Arcos. The agreement contained an option under which Hillas could buy a further 100,000 standards in 1931, though without any mention of the kind of timber or manner of shipment. There were no problems with respect to the original purchase in 1930. However, when, in 1931, the buyers sought to exercise the option for that year, the sellers asserted that the lack of detail rendered the contract so vague as not to be binding. It was held by the House of Lords that, having regard to the previous course of dealing between the parties, there was a clear intention to be bound. Any ambiguities could be resolved by reference to previous dealings between these parties.

7.5 CONSIDERATION

7.5.1 The meaning of consideration

Consideration is essential for the validity of a simple contract (ie a contract which is not contained in a deed). The classic definition of consideration is to be found in the case of *Currie v Misa* (1875) as any 'right, interest, profit or benefit accruing to one party, or some forbearance, detriment, loss or responsibility given, suffered or undertaken by the other'. This is the generally quoted definition but it is not one which is particularly easy to understand. What it means is that each party to the contract must suffer some loss or detriment in return for some benefit or advantage conferred upon him. For example, if we go into a shop and buy a packet of sweets the price for the sweets which we pay to the shop is consideration moving one way and the sweets coming from the shop to us is consideration moving the other way. Perhaps a better definition of consideration is 'the price for the promise'. Contracts which are contained in deeds (also known as specialty or formal contracts) do not require consideration for their validity. So long as the contract makes it clear by its wording that is intended to be a deed, and is signed by the party or parties making it and these signatures are witnessed, and is delivered as a deed, a valid contract is made. (It used to be the case that a deed had to be sealed by the parties to it. This requirement by 5.1 of the Law of Property (Miscellaneous Provisions) Act 1989.) Certain contracts, such as a conveyance of land, a legal mortgage of land or a transfer of a British ship need to be contained in a deed otherwise they are invalid. These are discussed in Chapter 8. The majority of contracts are simple contracts.

Consideration may be divided into three types, executory, executed and past. Executory consideration occurs where, if you wish to receive the benefit of a contract you must do something in order to gain that benefit. For example, I offer to pay you £5 if you will clean my car. Thus the undertaking to pay you £5 and the undertaking to clean the car is in the future and is executory. Once you have cleaned the car then that part of the consideration becomes executed. Likewise once I have paid you the £5 my part of the bargain is executed. In many contractual situations, such as where you go into a shop to buy a newspaper, the distinction between the consideration being executed and executory is a very fine one and somewhat artificial, whereas, with more important and continuing agreements, such as a contract by a painter and decorator to paint a house, analysis of the consideration into executory and executed is simple to make.

7.5.2 Past consideration

As a general rule, consideration must not be past. Past consideration is consideration which is already performed before the agreement is made. For example, I get home from work one day and find that my neighbour has dug my garden for me. There was no agreement between us that he would do this but I say to him I will pay him £10 when I receive my next pay packet. When I do in fact get paid I refuse to pay my neighbour. He has no right to sue me for the money because, at the time I promised him the £10, the consideration which he had given was past. This is illustrated by:

Re McArdle (1951)

Mr McArdle, by his Will, left a bungalow to his wife for her life and provided that, after her death, it should be sold and the proceeds divided equally between his children. After Mr McArdle's death, while the widow was still living, one of Mr McArdle's sons, together with his wife, went to live at the bungalow with the widow. The daughter-in-law spent money on improving the house and subsequently the other children promised her £188 to reimburse her the cost of the work. The promise was never kept. Proceedings were brought by the son and daughter-in-law in an attempt to enforce payment. It was held by the Court of Appeal that there was no obligation on the other children to keep their promise. All the improvements had been completed before the promise of payment was made. The work was accordingly past consideration. Thus an obligation to pay never arose.

There are a number of exceptions to this rule. Firstly, maybe there is an implied promise imputed to one party that he will pay for some action of the other party. In other words it was assumed all along that one party would be paid. For example in:

Re Casey's Patents (1892)

Stewart was the owner of certain patent rights. Casey worked for him as a manager and, when Casey had spent two years working promoting the invention which was protected by the patent, Stewart wrote to him saying that 'in consideration of your services as manager' Casey would be given a one-third share in the patent rights. The promise was never fulfilled so subsequently Casey sued to enforce it. The Court of Appeal held that the promise of a share in the patent rights was enforceable. There was a clear implication that Casey would be rewarded for the work which he was doing in respect of the patent.

Secondly, s27, Bills of Exchange Act 1882 provides that consideration, whenever given on a bill or cheque, is deemed to be good consideration.

This is an example of what might be referred to as genuinely past consideration being good consideration at law. Another such example arises under the Limitation Act 1980. As a general rule debts become statute-barred six years after they have been made (in other words no action can be brought to enforce a contract once the contract is six years old). However, if one party to a contract acknowledges in writing his liability upon the contract after it is six years old, this has the effect of reviving the claim of the other party.

7.5.3 Consideration must move from the promisee

It is not enough that consideration is present for a simple contract to be enforceable. It is also necessary for the person who seeks to enforce the contract to show that he himself provided consideration. This is closely connected, but different from, the principle of privity of contract which is that only a person who is a party to a contract may enforce it by means of legal action. Although the rule that consideration must move from the promisee and the rule that only a person who is a party to a contract may enforce it are very similar, they are different. For example, Arnold and Bertram, Colin's two grandfathers each agreed to pay Colin £1,000 a year while Colin studied to become an accountant. The terms of the agreement were that Arnold and Bertram would each pay the money over so long as the other also did so. If Bertram failed to make the payment as promised but Arnold did in fact pay, Colin could not sue Bertram since Colin provided no consideration in return for Bertram's promise.

Moreover he is not a party to the contract. Even if Colin were expressly joined as a party to the contract, he would still fail in his action since he had given no consideration personally. It would, of course, be different had the agreement been made by deed and Colin joined as a party to it, since it is not necessary to show that consideration has been provided to enforce contracts under seal.

Although consideration must move from the promisee, there is no need for consideration to move from the promisee to the promisor. While the person seeking to enforce a contract must show that he has provided consideration there is no need for the consideration to have gone to the person against whom the contract is sought to be enforced. For example, Stephen, a butcher, undertook to John to deliver a turkey to Martin. So long as Stephen has delivered the turkey to Martin, Stephen can sue John for the price of the turkey even though it was not John himself who received the goods.

7.5.4 Consideration need not be adequate

So long as there is consideration in a contract, the courts will not question whether the agreement is fair. In other words, so long as the consideration has some sort of economic value, the courts will not question its adequacy. For example:

Mountford v Scott (1975)

Mountford paid Scott £1 for an option to purchase Scott's house for £10,000. Subsequently Mountford sought to exercise the option but Scott refused to go through with the sale, claiming that the £1 consideration was a mere token and insufficient to support a legally enforceable contract. It was held by the Court of Appeal that the £1 which Mountford had paid for the option to purchase, although small in comparison with the value of the house was adequate to support the contract.

Similarly in:

Chappell & Co Ltd v Nestlé Co Ltd (1960)

Nestlé sold gramophone records to purchasers of their chocolate bars in return for 1/6d plus three chocolate bar wrappers. The question arose as to whether Chappell, the copyright owner of the music on record, was entitled to a royalty based on 1/6d or on 1/6d plus three chocolate bar wrappers. It was found as a question of fact that, while Nestlé would not have supplied a record for a customer who simply sent in the 1/6d, they destroyed the chocolate bar wrappings as soon as they received them. It was held by the House of Lords that the chocolate bar wrappings were obviously accorded some value by Nestlé and thus they formed part of the consideration.

7.5.5 Consideration must, however, be sufficient

The law will not recognise certain types of action or promise as good consideration. For example, if a person is already under a duty imposed upon him by law to do something then he cannot claim additional consideration for performing that duty:

Stilk v Myrick (1809)

Two seamen deserted their ship during the course of a voyage. The captain agreed to divide the wages of these deserters amongst the remaining crew so long as they would finish the voyage shorthanded. On completion of the voyage the captain failed to honour his promise and the crew sued. It was held that the promise of extra remuneration was not binding. The members of the crew were bound by the terms of their contract to do the work which they had done and so they had provided no additional consideration for the captain's promise of extra remuneration.

It would have been different if the desertions had resulted in the remainder of the voyage becoming dangerous. For example in:

Hartley v Ponsonby (1857)

This case again concerned the desertion of members of the crew of a ship. However the desertions were such as to render the ship unseaworthy because of undermanning. The captain again promised to divide the wages of the deserters amongst the remaining crew members. It was held that the remaining crew members here had an enforceable contract since they had provided good consideration for the employer's promise. They were working over and above what had been contemplated in their contract of employment.

The court will permit a party seeking to enforce a contract to do so provided he can establish that the consideration which he has given in excess of what he was legally obliged to do. For example in:

Glasbrook Bros Ltd v Glamorgan County Council (1925)

At the time of a miners' strike, Glasbrook Bros asked for permanent police protection for their colliery. The protection sought by the company was greater than the police felt necessary. Because of this the police agreed to provide a permanent guard only so long as Glasbrook Bros would make some additional payment. Subsequently the company refused to pay and Glamorgan County Council, the employers of the police, sought to enforce the contract. It was held by the House of Lords that the company had to pay. The police had exceeded their legal duty in that they had provided a degree of protection which was greater than they considered necessary.

This case was considered in:

Harris v Sheffield United Football Club (1987)

As a result of the violent behaviour of spectators at the defendant football club's ground, it became necessary to have a substantial police presence at the ground to maintain law and order. Under the Police Act 1964, the police authority could charge a fee for providing 'special police services'. The club denied liability claiming that in attending such matches, the police were merely carrying out their duties. The Court of Appeal held that since the club staged matches for its own purposes and police were required to attend in substantial numbers to deal with potential violence, the police were providing special police services for which the club had to pay. The police therefore were acting in excess of their existing legal duty.

Payment of a smaller sum does not discharge a debt for a greater amount. For example, if James owes Harry £10,000 and Harry agrees to accept £5,000 from James in full satisfaction of the £10,000 debt, then so long as James does not give Harry any further consideration, Harry can break his promise at common law and claim the balance outstanding:

Foakes v Beer (1884)

Foakes had obtained a judgment against Beer, and agreed to accept payment by instalments. Foakes was to pay her £500 at once and the balance in instalments. In return for this Foakes would not 'take any proceedings whatever on the judgment'. As a matter of law, every judgment debt carries interest. In other words the longer it is outstanding the more the judgment debtor has to pay. Beer paid the sum due and in the agreed manner. Foakes then sued him for the interest. It was held by the House of Lords that the interest had to be paid.

In practice, it is a very difficult area for persons seeking to enforce debts. On the one hand a credit controller needs to collect money and to do so, he sometimes has to offer incentives such as a discount for prompt payment. On the other hand this should not mean that debtors are allowed to get away with their obligations. A good example of this dilemma is to be found in:

D & C Builders Ltd v Rees (1965)

D & C Builders had done some work for Mr and Mrs Rees in respect of which they were owed £482. Mrs Rees knew that D & C Builders were in some financial difficulty themselves and offered a cheque for £300 in full and final settlement. She made it quite clear to the builders that if they did not accept that £300 then they would certainly not be paid the £482. D & C Builders agreed and then sued for the balance of £182. It was held by the Court of Appeal that they were entitled to recover the balance. Because of the pressure which Mrs Rees had put upon them to accept the cheque for £300 there was no real agreement on the part of the builders that they would accept the smaller sum, nor had Mrs Rees provided any extra consideration.

In some circumstances payment of a smaller sum will amount to a sufficient consideration to discharge the whole debt. This usually occurs where at the request of the creditor some fresh element is introduced into the bargain, as where a smaller sum is accepted as payment at an earlier date than that on which the account is due to be settled. Similarly, the payment of a smaller sum but at a different place from that at which it was due will discharge a debt as will the giving of a chattel in addition to the smaller sum. An altered method of payment may discharge a debt, again so long as the creditor agrees. For example if Paul is owed £25 by Simon he might accept a book from Simon having a market value only of £10. So long as there is agreement between the parties this would discharge the obligation. In *D & C Builders* v *Rees* one of the arguments put up by Mrs Rees was that there had been an altered mode of payment in that £482 was due in cash whereas she had paid by cheque. The Court of Appeal would not accept this argument. There is no discharge when the smaller sum is paid by cheque. A cheque is regarded in this context as the equivalent of cash.

There are two further cases where the payment of a smaller sum will discharge a debt. The first is where a creditor accepts a smaller sum from a third party in full settlement of a debt. This occurred in:

Welby v Drake (1825)

Drake owed Welby £18. Drake's father paid Welby £9 which Welby accepted in full and final settlement of the debt. Welby subsequently sued Drake for the balance. It was held that he had no right to recover. His consideration for the money paid him by Drake's father was the release of Drake from his liability.

The second is where a composition is reached with creditors. In this situation a debtor who is unable to meet all his debts gets his creditors to agree to accept part payment in full and final satisfaction of their respective claims. In both these situations the rationale is that it would be a fraud on the third party or, in the second case, on the other creditors, were the one creditor subsequently able to sue for the full debt due to him after having agreed to a composition.

7.6 EQUITABLE ESTOPPEL

Equitable estoppel is a doctrine whereby a person may be estopped (or prevented) from denying a statement of fact which he has made and which has subsequently been relied upon by someone else to that person's detriment. Estoppel is simply a rule of evidence which prevents a statement which has been made in these circumstances from subsequently being denied. The leading case is:

Central London Property Trust Ltd v High Trees House Ltd (1947)

In 1937 Central London Property Trust let a block of flats to High Trees House on a long lease at a rent of £2,500 per annum. In 1940, because of the impact of the war, many of the flats were empty and the landlords agreed to reduce the annual rental to £1,250. The rent was paid at this level until 1945 when the flats were again fully occupied. Thereupon Central London Property Trust stated that they wished to revert to the full rent being paid in the future and sued for the full rent for the last two quarters of 1945. It was held that they were entitled to receive the full rent as from the time when the flats were once again fully occupied, though it was stated (obiter) that if the Central London Property Trust had sued for the full rent for the time when the flats were only partially occupied they would have been estopped since High Trees acted upon the promise to receive the reduced rent. A promise had been made to reduce the rent. When the promise was made it was clearly known to Central London Property Trust that High Trees House would act upon the promise. Therefore it would be inequitable to allow Central London Property Trust to go back on their word. It was, however, found as a matter of fact that the promise was understood by both parties only to apply so long as the flats were empty or merely partially let. Thus when the flats became fully occupied in early 1945, the promise to accept a reduced rent ceased to be binding upon Central London Property Trust.

In *D & C Builders Ltd* v *Rees* (1966) one of the arguments put forward by Mr and Mrs Rees was that D & C Builders were estopped from suing for the full amount due. However, the pressure exerted upon the builders by Mrs Rees was such that it would be inequitable to permit the estoppel to operate here.

Equitable estoppel may be pleaded only as a defence. It can never give rise to a cause of action. Thus in:

Combe v Combe (1951)

During the course of divorce proceedings a husband promised his wife that he would pay her an allowance of £100 per annum. Relying upon this promise the wife did not apply to the courts for a maintenance order against her husband. When subsequently the husband failed to honour his promise the wife sued. Amongst other grounds she sought to rely on the principle of estoppel, claiming that the husband was estopped from denying that he had made her a promise to pay her an allowance. It was held that the action should fail. The wife had given no consideration for the promise from her husband. Estoppel could not be used as a course of action. In the words of Birkett L J estoppel is 'a shield and not a sword'; in other words it may only be a defence.

7.7 PRIVITY OF CONTRACT

A person can neither sue nor be sued on a contract to which he is not a party. Put another way this means that a contract cannot impose obligations or confer benefits upon a person who is a stranger to the contract. This is illustrated by:

***Dunlop Pneumatic Tyre Co Ltd* v *Selfridge & Co Ltd* (1915)**

Dunlop sold tyres to a wholesaler, Dew & Co, on the condition that they would not be resold at below a set price. As part of the bargain which Dew & Co. made with Dunlop, Dew & Co promised to obtain a similar undertaking on maintaining the agreed price from any retailer to whom they sold the tyres. They sold some tyres to Selfridge who agreed to observe the price fixing agreement. Subsequently Selfridge sold tyres in breach of the agreement and Dunlop sued them for breach. It was held by the House of Lords that the action must fail since Dunlop had not been a party to the agreement between Dew & Co and Selfridge.

7.8 COLLATERAL CONTRACTS

One way of getting around the principle of privity of contract which has been developed by the courts is the concept of the collateral contract. For example, when a car is acquired from a garage on hire-purchase, the customer does not in fact make a contract with the garage. What happens is that the garage sells the car to a finance company and the finance company then lets the car on hire-purchase to the customer. In this situation the court may be prepared to find that because benefit does pass to the garage from the customer, albeit indirectly, that there exists a collateral contract between these two parties. For example in:

***Andrews* v *Hopkinson* (1957)**

Andrews acquired a car on hire-purchase from a finance company, having been told at the garage where it was displayed for sale that it was 'a good little bus'. Subsequently because of defects in the car it crashed and Andrews was injured. It was held that a collateral contract existed between Andrews and the garage. Andrews' consideration was that he had agreed to obtain the car from the finance company and this in turn had meant that the garage had a sale of the vehicle to the finance company. The garage's consideration was its promise as to the reliability of the car.

Similarly in:

***Shanklin Pier Ltd* v *Dettel Products Ltd* (1951)**

Shanklin Pier employed contractors to paint their pier. They had enquired of Dettel, a firm of paint manufacturers, which paint would be best and had been advised by Dettel that a specified paint would last for 7 to 10 years. On the strength of this Shanklin Pier instructed the contractors to buy and use this paint. In fact it began to deteriorate almost immediately and the pier needed repainting after only three months. It was held by the House of Lords that although Shanklin Pier could not sue on the contract of sale of the paint, since the paint had been acquired by the contractors, as the plaintiff had specified exactly what type of paint should be used, they could sue on a collateral contract between themselves and Dettel. Having given orders for this specific paint to be used by the contractors, Shanklin Pier were indirectly causing a benefit to go to Dettel, the manufacturers of the paint. This was Shanklin Pier's consideration for the manufacturer's promise as to the paint's quality.

7.9 INTENTION TO CREATE LEGAL RELATIONS

Even where there is offer, acceptance and consideration present, the intention of the parties may be such as to indicate that there is no wish for them to enter into a legally binding obligation. For example if Gordon asks Veronica to meet him for dinner one night, while there may be an offer by Gordon, and acceptance by Veronica and consideration in that both are suffering some detriment while gaining some advantage, there would not be an intention between them to enter into a legally binding agreement. Thus if Veronica fails to turn up at the appointed place and time, Gordon would have no right to sue her for breach of contract. In this context there are three distinct types of arrangement which have to be looked at:

1. Domestic and social arrangements.
2. Commercial arrangements.
3. Collective bargaining agreements.

These will now be considered.

7.9.1 Domestic and social arrangements

There is a general presumption in English law that a husband and wife do not intend to make a legally binding contract with each other. For example in:

Balfour v Balfour (1919)

The husband was a civil servant based in Ceylon. He came to England on leave with his wife and subsequently returned to Ceylon, his wife remaining in England because she had health problems. The husband promised to pay the wife £30 per month as maintenance, but failed to honour this promise.

Subsequently the wife sued. It was held that the wife must fail in her action because she had provided no consideration for the promise and, even if she had, there was no intention to create legal relations. Where the contracting parties are husband and wife the onus is upon the plaintiff in an action such as this to rebut the presumption that in domestic arrangements there is no intention to enter into a legally binding agreement.

Similarly in relation to parents and their children:

Jones v Padavatton (1969)

Mrs Padavatton was living and working in America. Her mother, Mrs Jones, offered her a monthly allowance if she would give up her job, go to England and read for the Bar. This Mrs Padavatton did though without success in the examinations. Mrs Jones subsequently bought a house in London and allowed the daughter to live there and, instead of actually paying the monthly allowance, allowed the daughter to receive rent from other tenants living in the house. Three years later Mrs Jones sought possession of the house and the daughter counter-claimed for breach of the agreement to pay the monthly allowance. It was held that even though the agreement initially may have been made with both parties intending to enter into a legally binding relationship, it had only been for a reasonable time so as to enable the daughter to pass the Bar examinations. Thus it had lapsed by expiration of time. The subsequent agreement, allowing the daughter to live in the house, had been simply a domestic arrangement and there was no intention whatever to create legal relations. Thus the mother's action to recover the house succeeded.

On the other hand, if the husband and wife are not living together, there may well be an intention to enter into legal relations. For example, in:

Merritt v Merritt (1970)

A husband who was separated from his wife agreed that he would transfer the matrimonial home out of their joint names into her name alone so long as she paid off the outstanding mortgage. When the husband failed to transfer the home the wife sued. The husband's defence was that there was no legally binding agreement. It was held, however, that the husband's promise was legally binding. This was an 'arms' length transaction' entered into with a clear intention to be bound.

Similarly in:

Simpkins v Pays (1955)

Mrs Pays was a grandmother who, together with her granddaughter and Simpkins, a lodger in Mrs Pays house, entered a weekly newspaper competition. All three contributed to the stakes but the entry was in Mrs Pays' name. Eventually a prize of £750 was won with one of the entries. Mrs Pays refused to share the prize with the other two collaborators and Simpkins sued for one third of the prize money. It was held that he was entitled to succeed. This had been a joint enterprise between the three and there was a clear intention that any prize should be shared between them.

7.9.2 Commercial arrangements

There is a presumption in the case of commercial arrangements that there is an intention that they should be legally binding. However, this presumption can be rebutted if a contrary intention is clearly expressed. An example of this arose in:

Rose and Frank Co v Crompton & Bros Ltd (1925)

A commercial agreement provided 'this agreement is not entered into ... as a formal or legal agreement, and shall not be subject to legal jurisdiction in the law courts'. It was held by the House of Lords that this agreement was not a legally enforceable contract. Thus when Crompton refused to honour its obligations under the agreement, Rose & Frank had no remedy.

Another decision where the intention was not found was:

Kleinwort Benson Ltd v Malaysic Mining Corporation Bhd (1989)

The plaintiff Bank granted a loan facility to a subsidiary company of the defendant. As part of the arrangement the defendants gave the plaintiffs two 'letters of comfort' stating 'it is our policy to ensure that the business (of the subsidiary) is at all times in a position to meet its liabilities to you.' The subsidiary went into liquidation and the plaintiffs tried to enforce the letters of comfort. It was held by the Court of Appeal that the plaintiffs were not entitled to recover because there was no intention on the part of the defendant to create legal relations.

However, whether a party to a contract has discharged the presumption that it is legally binding is essentially a question of fact in every case. For example in:

Esso Petroleum v Commissioners of Customs & Excise (1976)

Esso Petroleum, in a sales promotion, supplied garages with coins commemorating the World Cup Football Series with the intention that one coin should be given away to motorists when they bought petrol. This case concerned whether the handing of the coins to the motorists constituted a sale. It was held by the House of Lords that in fact there was no sale, though a majority of the Lords thought that there was a contract for the supply of the coins. They reached this decision because Esso Petroleum had failed to prove that there was no contractual intent.

7.9.3 Collective bargaining agreements

These are agreements made between a trade union and an employer. They are concerned with negotiating conditions of service including wages. By s18 Trade Union and Labour Relations Act 1974, there is a presumption that a collective agreement between an employer and a trade union is not legally binding unless there is an express statement to the contrary in the agreement in which case it is legally enforceable to the extent stated.

7.10 CAPACITY

7.10.1 Introduction

For a contract to be valid the parties to it must have capacity. Capacity means the legal ability in law to enter a contract. The common law is based on the assumption that the average person is an adult who is of sound mind. In looking at the law of capacity we will examine those parties who do not comply with this norm, that is, those who in some way lack contractual capacity or whose capacity is limited. The two main types of person we will look at are minors and mentally disordered persons.

7.10.2 Minors

INTRODUCTION

A minor is a person who is under 18 years of age. The law relating to minors' capacity to enter a contract is contained in the common law and in the Minors Contracts Act 1987. A minor's contract may be either valid or voidable. Those contracts of minors which are voidable are subdivided into those contracts which are enforceable by and against the minor unless and until he avoids them, and those which are enforceable by the minor to a limited extent but which are unenforceable against him. We will deal with each of these in turn.

VALID CONTRACTS

A valid contract is one which may be enforced by and against the minor. There are two types of minors' contract which are valid: contracts of necessaries and beneficial contracts of service.

Contracts for necessaries are contracts whereby the minor acquires 'goods suitable to the condition in life of the minor and to his actual requirements at the time of sale and delivery' (s3 Sale of Goods Act 1979). So, for goods to be necessary, they must be suitable both to the minor's condition in life and to his actual requirements. If, therefore, the minor already has an adequate supply of the goods at the time of sale these goods will not be necessaries even though they are of a type essential to support life (eg food) and even though the supplier is unaware of the fact that the minor already has a sufficient supply. This is shown in the case of:

Nash v Inman (1908)

Inman was a minor studying at university. He ordered and received 11 fancy waistcoats from a tailor and then refused to pay for them. The tailor sued for the agreed purchase price. The court held that this type of garment was necessary to maintain the minor in the standard of living to which he was accustomed. However, on proof that the minor was already adequately supplied with similar items of clothing, it was held that these waistcoats were surplus to his actual needs at the time of sale and delivery and therefore the contract was not binding on the minor.

If the goods are necessaries the minor need only pay what the court considers a reasonable price. This need not be the contract price. Furthermore the minor will only be liable for goods which are necessaries if they have actually been delivered to him. While the contract is still executory he is not bound by the agreement. Examples of necessaries would include food, clothing and medical supplies. A married minor is also liable to pay for necessaries supplied for his wife and children.

Beneficial contracts of service are also valid and binding on a minor if, taken as a whole, the contract is beneficial to him. In the case of:

Roberts v Gray (1913)

The minor wished to become a professional billiards player and he made an agreement with the plaintiff, a leading professional, to go on a tour. The plaintiff organised the tour but then, following a dispute, the minor refused to proceed with it. The court held that the contract was for the minor's benefit as it was designed to train him for a career as a billiards player. He was therefore liable in breach of this contract.

If, however, the contract, although one of apprenticeship, has terms which are unduly onerous on the minor it will not be enforceable.

This was shown in the case of:

De Francesco v Barnum (1890)

Two minors made a contract with the plaintiff for him to teach them stage dancing. The contract was to last for 7 years. By the agreement, the minors undertook that they would not accept any engagements without the plaintiff's consent; that they would not marry during the apprenticeship; and that they could be sent abroad to perform if the plaintiff so chose. They were to be paid a nominal amount per performance and were not to be paid whilst they were unemployed. The plaintiff did not undertake to find them any engagements. Furthermore, the plaintiff had the right to terminate the contract if he felt that the minors were unsuitable for a dancing career.

The minors accepted an engagement with the defendant and the plaintiff brought this action against the defendant for inducing the minors to break the contract they had made with him. The court held that this agreement, taken as a whole, was unreasonable and was therefore unenforceable against the minors. The defendant, therefore, was not liable as there was no contractual relationship between the minors and the plaintiff with which he could have interfered.

VOIDABLE CONTRACTS WHICH ARE VALID AND ENFORCEABLE AGAINST THE MINOR UNLESS AND UNTIL HE REPUDIATES THEM

These are contracts which bind the minor unless and until he avoids them. He may do this either during his minority or within a reasonable time of attaining his majority. Contracts within this category are those in which the minor acquires an interest in subject matter of a permanent nature. They include leases, sales and purchases of land, purchases of partly paid-up shares in companies and contracts whereby a minor becomes a partner in a firm.

In all these cases the minor is bound unless and until he repudiates. If he does not repudiate he is bound by the contract. If, however, he does effectively repudiate he ceases to be bound in the future. He will be unable to recover any money already paid unless he can show that he has received nothing whatsoever for this money. For example, in the case of:

Corpe v Overton (1833)

A minor agreed to enter into a partnership and deposited £100 with the defendant as security for his performance of the contract. Before the partnership came into being however the minor repudiated the contract. The court held that the minor could recover the £100 as he had not received any benefit, never having been a partner.

If, however, the minor has had some benefit he cannot recover his money. This is shown in the case of:

Steinberg v Scala (Leeds) Ltd (1923)

In this case, a minor applied for shares in a company and paid the amounts due on allotment. When the company called for the balance of the purchase price of the shares, the minor was unable to pay this. She repudiated the contract for the purchase of the shares and claimed back the money she had already paid. The court held that her claim should fail, as there had not been a total failure of consideration. The minor had not received dividends on her shares but she had received some benefits in that the shares had been allotted to her. By obtaining the shares she had also obtained the right to attend and vote at the company meetings if she so wished.

VOIDABLE CONTRACTS WHICH ARE ENFORCEABLE BY THE MINOR TO A LIMITED EXTENT BUT WHICH ARE UNENFORCEABLE AGAINST HIM

By the Minors Contract Act 1987, contracts which do not fall within either of the above categories are voidable by the minor but are unenforceable against him. This category therefore covers, for example, contracts for the purchase of non-necessaries, trading contracts entered into by the minor, and loans which the minor has received. The minor can enforce these contracts but he cannot be sued on them. On attaining full age, however, a minor can either ratify such contracts or make fresh agreements to be bound by them. The contract would then be fully enforceable by and against the minor.

By the s3 Minors Contracts Act 1987, the supplier of goods under this type of contract may apply to the court for an order to recover his property from the minor. The order will be granted if the court is satisfied that it will be 'just and equitable' to require the minor to return the goods or 'any property representing it'. So, for example, if the minor has sold the goods acquired under this type of contract and is still in possession of the actual purchase price he received for them, the supplier of the goods may recover this money if the court believes that this would be just and equitable. Equally if the minor has exchanged the goods he acquired under the contract for other goods the court may order these other goods be handed over to the original supplier.

LIABILITY IN TORT

A minor cannot be sued in tort if this action is being used as a way of enforcing a contract which would otherwise be unenforceable against the minor. This is shown in the case of:

Leslie Ltd v Sheill (1914)

A minor borrowed £400 by falsely claiming he was of full age. Under the pre-1987 law this contract was void. The moneylender sued the minor for the recovery of the loan, claiming the amount as damages for the tort of deceit. The court held that the claim should fail as the moneylender was merely attempting to recover by action in tort what he could not recover by an action in contract.

If, therefore, the minor entered a contract that was unenforceable against him the other party to the agreement could not sue the minor in tort to enforce rights which he could not have enforced by an action in contract.

7.11 MENTALLY DISORDERED AND DRUNKEN PERSONS

If a person was so mentally disordered or was so drunk that he did not know that he was contracting, and the other party was aware of his disability, the contract is voidable at the suit of the mentally disordered or drunken person. If, however, the contract was for necessaries the mentally disordered or drunken person will be bound to pay a reasonable price even though it can be shown that he was unaware of the nature of the transaction and the other party knew this. If the otherwise voidable contract is ratified during a lucid period then it will be valid and binding. The contract will also be binding if the other party was unaware of the disability at the time he entered the agreement.

7.12 ASSIGNMENT

7.12.1 Introduction

In the section of this Chapter which dealt with consideration we said that only a person who has given consideration for a promise can sue on that promise. There are, however, a number of exceptions to this general rule. As we shall see later on in this book a person can enter into a contract through an agent and the agreement thus made is binding on the person who so acted even though he was not a party to the negotiations. In the chapter on Negotiable Instruments you will see that a holder in due course can sue any prior party to a bill even though that party was not in a direct contractual relationship with him. Another case where a person who is not a party to the original contract can nevertheless sue on that contract occurs when the rights under the agreement are assigned to him. In this section we will look at the law relating to assignment.

Assignment is the way in which a person transfers his rights under a contract to a third party. Assignments may take place through the acts of the parties or by the operation of law. They may be legal or equitable in form.

7.12.2 Assignment by act of parties

There are two ways in which rights can be assigned by act of the parties: by legal assignment or by equitable assignment. The effect of both these methods is that the rights under the contract are transferred from one person to another. The difference between the two is in the method in which these rights are enforced. As we will see, the assignee (the one to whom the right is transferred) under a legal assignment can sue to enforce the contract in his own name whereas an equitable assignee has to sue in the name of the assignor (the person whose rights are being transferred).

LEGAL ASSIGNMENTS

For legal assignments the three requirements of s136(1) Law Property Act 1925 must be satisfied. These requirements are that:

1 **The assignment must be absolute.** In other words the assignor must transfer his entire interest unconditionally to the assignee. The assignee must have complete ownership of this right. For example, if a right is assigned as security for repayment of a debt and is to be re-assigned if the debt is repaid this will not be an absolute unconditional assignment. In the case of:

Durham Bros v Robertson (1898)

A builder, who was owed £1,080 pounds under a contract, borrowed some money. He assigned the right to the £1,080 to the lender as security for the loan 'until the money (lent) ... be repaid'. The court held that this was not an absolute assignment. It was conditional upon the money lent to the builder not being repaid by him and so it could not take effect as a legal assignment.

In other words, the assignor must assign the whole of his interest and not retain any rights whatsoever for there to be a legal assignment.

2 **The assignment must be in writing** and signed by the assignor.
3 **Express notice of the assignment in writing must be given to the debtor.** This notice must clearly instruct the debtor to pay the assignee. Notice may be given by the assignor or the assignee at any time before action is brought. If the notice is posted however it will take effect only when it is received by the debtor.

If all three of these requirements are satisfied there will be a valid legal assignment of the right. The assignee of the right can exercise all the legal and other remedies in respect of that right which could be exercised by the assignor. So, for example, the assignee can enforce the right by suing in his own name. In other words there is privity of contract between the assignee and the original debtor.

An example of how this would work would be if Alan owes Ben £100 and Ben owes Clive £100. Ben can assign his right to receive £100 from himself to Clive and, as long as the assignment is absolute, and is in writing, and express notice of the assignment is given to Alan, then Alan must pay Clive. The contract in the eyes of the law is now between Alan and Clive. Clive can sue Alan in his own name to obtain the money.

EQUITABLE ASSIGNMENTS

If an assignment does not satisfy one or more of the three requirements of s136 Law of Property Act then it cannot take effect as a legal assignment. It may however take effect as an equitable assignment. So, for example, an assignment may not take effect in law because it is not in writing or because notice in writing is not given to the debtor. This assignment, however, may still take effect in equity. All that equity requires for a valid assignment is that there is a clear **intention** to assign.

So long as this intention is clear, a right can be effectively assigned in equity by any words whether oral or written. There is no particular form of words required nor does the debtor have to be given notice, although it is advisable to do so in that it would prevent the debtor paying the assignor. If the debtor did pay the assignor without having been told of the assignment the assignee will have no right of action against the debtor.

Notice will also give the assignee priority over any later assignee of the same right. For example, if Alan owes Ben £100 and Ben assigns the right to receive this money to Clive but does not tell Alan about this assignment this can take effect only as an equitable assignment. If Ben later, wrongly, assigns the same rights to Dan the person entitled to claim the money from Alan will be the first to give him notice of the assignment. So if Dan is the first to give Alan notice, Dan will be entitled to receive the money as priority depends, not on the order of the assignment, but rather on the order in which notice of assignment is received by the debtor.

The effect of an equitable assignment is the same as a legal assignment except that the assignee can enforce his right only by using the name of the assignor. In other words, in order to sue on the debt the assignee must join the assignor to his action as co-plaintiff. If the assignor will not join as co-plaintiff (if for example he disputes the assignment) he can be joined as co-defendant.

ASSIGNMENTS ARE SUBJECT TO EQUITIES

Whether the assignment is legal or equitable, the assignee takes subject to any defects in the assignor's title and subject to any claim the original debtor may have against the assignor. In other words, an assignee receives no better but no worse title than the assignor had.

So, for example, if in the above example Alan owes Ben £100 for goods that he has received from Ben and Ben assigns the rights to the £100 to Clive, Clive will take no better but no worse title than Ben had to this money. So if Alan disputes the £100 debt on the grounds that the goods were faulty he can use this as a defence in any action Clive may bring against him.

RIGHTS WHICH CANNOT BE ASSIGNED

There are certain rights which are not capable of assignment. For example, some contracts state that rights under them cannot be assigned. If, despite this, an assignment of rights under the contract is made, the assignee would be unable to enforce the contract against the debtor. Personal contracts are also not capable of being assigned. A personal contract is one which has been made because of one of the party's skill, special knowledge, experience or reputation. In these circumstances the rights under this contract cannot be assigned. For example:

Cooper v Micklefield Coal and Lime Co Ltd (1912)

The benefit of a contract to supply coal on credit to a retail coal merchant (who had considerable business experience in a particular neighbourhood) was held by the court not to be assignable to another coal merchant who lacked this type of experience. In making the contract the suppliers had relied on the original dealer's skill and experience. If the suppliers were forced to deliver to a new purchaser they would be subjected to an entirely different risk from that for which they had contracted.

7.12.3 Assignment by operation of law

A number of assignments may occur by operation of law and the most important of these are:

1. **Assignment upon death.** The benefit and burden of a contract, except one of a personal nature, passes to the deceased's personal representative. The personal representative can sue and be sued in respect of debts due and breaches of contract committed during the lifetime of the deceased. He is, however, only liable for debts and damages up to the total value of the estate he is administering.
2. **Assignment upon bankruptcy.** Property belonging to a bankrupt passes to his trustee in bankruptcy. This property includes rights under a contract and the right to bring an action for breach of contract.

    The trustee thus becomes the assignee of the benefit of the bankrupt's contracts. He may also execute work which the bankrupt has agreed to execute. If, however, the trustee believes that the contract is burdensome, that is, it will involve the estate in expense, or will not benefit the estate, he may disclaim such agreements. If he does this, then the rights and liabilities of the bankrupt in the contract cease and any person injured by the disclaimer must prove in the bankruptcy for whatever loss he has sustained.

SUMMARY

In this Chapter, we have discussed the way in which a simple contract is created. This type of contract takes effect from its substance rather than from the form in which it is made. In other words, if any of the requirements given in this chapter are missing, there will not be a valid contract. You must know these requirements, which are listed in the introduction, as they form the basis of most of the contracts we will be discussing later in this book. For a valid contract to come into existence there has to be offer, acceptance, consideration and an intention to create legal relations. The offer comes from one party and the acceptance from the other. It is essential that they relate to the same subject matter. An offer must be communicated before it can be accepted. Obviously a person cannot purport to accept an offer of which he is not aware. Acceptance must generally also be communicated, though there are exceptions in the case of acceptance by conduct and of acceptance by post. Consideration is the price for the promise. It must always be present in contracts other than those taking the form of deeds. So long as consideration is there, the court will not question the value which the parties themselves put upon it. In some respects consideration itself signifies an intention by the parties to enter into a legally binding agreement. There is always a presumption that a commercial agreement is legally binding, though there is a presumption in the case of domestic agreements that they are not legally binding. In either case, the presumption can be rebutted by evidence to the contrary.

It is essential that this is thoroughly understood before you move on to consider the remainder of the law of contract because not only are questions asked solely on the areas covered in this chapter, they are sometimes asked in respect of matters covered in later chapters in such a way as to draw in some of this preliminary work on the formation of contract.

SELF-TEST QUESTIONS

7.1 List the requirements of valid, simple contract

7.2 Distinguish between void, voidable and unenforceable contracts

7.3 Distinguish between an offer and an invitation to treat

7.4 How may an offer be terminated?

7.5 What is the ratio in:

(a) *Brogden* v *Metropolitan Railway Co* (1877)

(b) *Western Electric Ltd* v *Welsh Development Agency* (1983)

(c) *Adams* v *Lindsell* (1818)

(d) *Brinkibon Ltd* v *Stahat Stahl* (1982)

(e) *Felthruse* v *Bindley* (1862)

7.6 How will the courts resolve uncertainties in contracts?

7.7 Distinguish between:

(a) Executory consideration
(b) Executed consideration
(c) Past consideration

7.8 Why was there not a binding contract in *Stilk* v *Myrick*?

7.9 When can payment of a smaller sum be satisfaction for a larger debt?

7.10 'Equitable promissory estoppel' is 'a shield not a sword'—what is meant by this?

7.11 What is meant by privity of contract?

7.12 Was an intention to create legal relations found in

(a) *Balfour* v *Balfour* (1919)
(b) *Merrit* v *Merrit* (1970)
(c) *Rose and Frank Co* v *Crompton Bros Ltd* (1925)?

7.13 Complete the following passage:

'A minor's contract may be either valid or voidable. Valid Contracts are (a) _____ and (b) _____. Minors' voidable contracts may be divided into two types: those which are (c) _____ and those which are (d) _____. Voidable contracts in the first category are those whereby the minor acquires (e) _____. Those within the second category of voidable contracts are (f) _____.

7.14 For a legal assignment of a legal right the following requirements must be satisfied:

(a)
(b)
(c)

7.15 Why is legal assignment described as an exception to the doctrine of privity?

Answers on page 301

EXERCISES

Exercise 7.1

Explain the rules governing consideration. In particular distinguish between executory, executed and past consideration.

Exercise 7.2

Explain what you understood by an intention to create legal relations. Illustrate your answer with examples.

Exercise 7.3

J invited tenders for the supply of fuel oil. K submitted a tender in which he offered to supply fuel oil 'in such quantities and at such times as required.' J accepted K's tender.
   Consider the legal situation if:

1   J never placed an order for fuel oil
2   J ordered a quantity of fuel oil but K was not able to supply it.
3   K informed J that he no longer intended to supply him with fuel oil.

Answers on page 302

Form and contents of a contract

In this Chapter we will look at two aspects of the contract: the form the contract must take and the ways in which the courts deal with the various terms of the contract.

In the previous Chapter, we discussed the requirements for a valid, simple contract. There must be intention, offer, acceptance, consideration and capacity for such a contract to be enforceable. For the majority of agreements, this is sufficient. The fact that there is no written evidence of the contract is irrelevant to its validity. For some contracts, however, statute requires that they are either entirely written down or are evidenced in writing in order to be enforceable. Other contracts are required to be in the form of a deed. In this Chapter we will look at those contracts which have to be put into some special form.

We will then examine the law dealing with the contents of the contract; in other words at the ways in which the courts decide what terms the parties have actually agreed in their contract and how a breach of these terms is treated.

8.1 FORM OF A CONTRACT

8.1.1 Introduction

So far we have dealt with the formation of a simple contract. Such a contract takes effect from its substance rather than its form. In other words, in deciding whether such a contract is or is not valid, the court will look, not at the form the agreement takes, but at whether it has all the necessary ingredients; whether there is offer, acceptance, intention, consideration and capacity and whether the parties have reached a true agreement. The form of the contract is irrelevant. It may be in writing or completely oral. This will make no difference to its validity.

Some simple contracts, however, are required by Act of Parliament to be completely reduced to writing in order to be valid, whereas others have to be evidenced in writing to prove their existence. Without such written evidence these contracts are unenforceable by action in court.

As well as simple contracts, the law also recognises another form of contracting: specialty contracts or deeds. These contracts take their effect from their form rather than their substance. In other words, the courts will look, not at the contents of the contract, but at the form in which the contract is made.

A deed must be signed, witnessed and delivered. So, for such a contract, the agreement must be in writing; it must be signed; it must be witnessed and it must clearly show by its wording that it is intended to be a deed; finally, the document must be delivered ie handed over with the intention of creating rights for the other party.

The court will look at the form and not the content of deeds in deciding whether or not it is valid. So, for example, if an agreement lacks consideration it can not be a simple contract. If, however, the agreement is contained in a deed, the court will regard it as valid and binding as long as the form of the contract is correct. If the promise lacks consideration, however, specific performance of the obligation will not be ordered.

As we said earlier, simple contracts generally can take any form as long as their substance is valid.

As we also said, however, there are exceptions to this general rule, that is, contracts which, by statute, require some special form. We will now deal with these.

8.1.2 Simple contracts which have to be in writing

Where a statute requires a contract to be in writing, the writing is an essential part of the contract. Without it, the contract is of no effect, just as it is if there is no consideration. The simple contracts which have to be in writing in order to be valid, and the statutes which impose this requirement, are:

1. The transfer of shares in registered companies (Companies Act 1985).
2. Negotiable instruments (Bills of Exchange Act 1882).
3. Contracts of marine insurance (Marine Insurance Act 1906).
4. Legal assignments of contractual rights (Law of Property Act 1925).
5. Assignments of copyrights (Copyright Act 1956).
6. Contracts for the sale or other disposition of an interest land (Law of Property (Miscellaneous Provisions) Act 1989).

Under the Consumer Credit Act 1974, certain regulated agreements have to be in writing in order to be enforceable. If these agreements do not comply with the formalities laid down by the 1974 Act, although they satisfy all the requirements of a valid simple contract, they can be enforced only by court order.

8.1.3 Simple contracts which have to be evidenced in writing

Certain simple contracts are required by statute to be evidenced by some note or memorandum in writing in order to be enforceable by action in court. Even without this written evidence they are still valid contracts, so if both parties perform their sides of the bargain the lack of evidence will be irrelevant. If, however, one of the parties breaks the contract, and the other wishes to sue him, the injured party will have to show written evidence, signed by the party in breach, admitting the existence of the alleged contract. Without such evidence, the contract is unenforceable.

The rule as to evidence in writing applies only to guarantees.

GUARANTEES

The requirement that guarantees should be evidenced by some written note or memorandum is contained in s4 of the Statute of Frauds 1677. Under a contract of guarantee, one party (the guarantor or surety) promises to be answerable to the other for the debt, default or miscarriage of a third party.

Example 8.1

Ben wants to obtain a loan from the Northern Bank plc, but the Bank is unwilling to lend him money unless he obtains a financially sound person to guarantee his repayments. Ben persuades George to enter a contract with the Bank to act as guarantor. Ben, however, remains primarily liable to repay the money and the Bank must first try to obtain it from him. It is only if Ben defaults that George will be liable to pay. In other words, George, the guarantor is secondarily liable in the event of the person he is guaranteeing failing to honour his obligations. In these circumstances, George must pay the Bank. He will then be able to try to recover the money from Ben.

To be enforceable, George's contract with the Bank would have to be evidenced in writing. There have to be three parties to a guarantee. These parties are:

1. The debtor (principal debtor).
2. The creditor (the person to whom the money is owed).
3. The guarantor (secondary debtor).

There will **not** be a guarantee (and therefore evidence in writing will not be required to make the contract enforceable) where one person takes over primary liability for the debt of another.

Example 8.2

If, in Example 8.1 above, George says to the bank 'let Ben have the money and I will repay you' this will not be a guarantee. George is assuming primary liability. The Bank's consideration is to provide the money to Ben; George's is his promise to repay the money directly to the Bank.

This is known as a contract of indemnity. Although three parties are involved, only two, George and the Bank, are contracting parties. Ben would have no rights under this contract. Unlike a guarantee, a contract of indemnity does not have to be evidenced in writing to be enforceable.

An illustration of the distinction between a guarantee and indemnity is shown in the case of:

Mountstephen v Lakeman (1874)

A local board of health intended to connect the drains of some houses to the main sewerage system. L, who was chairman of the board, told M, a builder, to do the work. M asked how he was going to be paid and L said, 'Do the work and I'll see you paid'. There was no written note of this arrangement.

M did the work, but the board refused to pay him as it had not authorised him to do the job. M sued L in contract, but L argued that his promise was a guarantee and, as it had not been evidenced in writing, it was unenforceable.

The House of Lords, however, held that, as the board had never authorised M to do the work it had no primary liability which could be guaranteed by L. Therefore, L's words formed the basis of a contract of indemnity and written evidence was unnecessary. M had sufficient oral evidence to prove his case and so could enforce L's promise.

A feature of guarantees which distinguishes them from other contracts whereby a person assumes responsibility for another's liability is that, in a guarantee, the guarantor must be totally unconnected with the contract except by virtue of his promise to pay the debt. If the promise is part of a wider transaction between the 'guarantor' and the 'creditor' it will not be a guarantee within the meaning of the Statute of Frauds 1677 and will therefore not have to be evidenced in writing.

For example, a *del credere* agent is not treated as a guarantor. A *del credere* agent is one who, in return for extra commission, agrees that, if the person he introduces to his principal wrongfully refuses to pay then he, the agent, will accept liability for this debt. This promise to reimburse the principal is part of a larger transaction ie agency, and so it will not be regarded as a guarantee. It will, in fact, be a contract of indemnity and will not have to be evidenced in writing to be enforceable.

Another example of a case where the promise to pay is part of a larger transaction and is therefore not a guarantee is:

Fitzgerald v Dressler (1859)

A sold goods to B who failed to pay the agreed price.

A refused to transfer the goods to B until payment had been made. In other words, A exercised a lien over the goods. In the meantime, however, B sold the goods to C. In order to obtain the goods from A, C made A an oral promise that, if B did not pay the amount owing, he (C) would settle the outstanding debt. A agreed to this and handed over the goods to C. B did not pay, but when A asked C to settle the account C refused, arguing that he had given a guarantee which, lacking evidence in writing, was unenforceable.

The court held that C's promise was incidental to a larger transaction and was given to protect his own property rather than to guarantee payment of B's debt. He was making the promise to buy-off A's lien and the contract with A was therefore outside the Statute of Frauds. There was no need for written evidence of the contract. A could demand payment of B's debt from C.

8.1.4 Contracts which must be under seal

1 Contracts made without valuable consideration.
2 Conveyance of land, legal mortgages of land and leases for more than three years.
3 Transfers of British ships or of shares therein.
4 Conditional bills of sale.

8.2 CONTENTS OF A CONTRACT

8.2.1 Introduction

Having established that the parties have made a valid contract, it is then necessary to decide what are the parties' rights and obligations under this contract. To do this, the courts will have to look at the terms of the contract.

Terms may be either express (that is, actually stated in the contract, whether orally or in writing) or implied (that is, terms not actually agreed by the parties but brought into the contract by

Act of Parliament or by the court itself). All terms, whether express or implied, will be regarded as conditions or warranties or intermediate terms. We will look at how the categorisation is made later in this Chapter.

A type of term which requires special attention is one which attempts to exclude liability for breach of contract. These are known as exclusion clauses. The use and application of exclusion clauses is controlled very carefully by both the courts and Parliament by means of the Unfair Contract Terms Act 1977.

In dealing with the contents of the contract, however, the first matter that has to be decided is: which of the statements made before the contract is concluded are part of that contract and which are merely representations?

8.2.2 Terms and representations

INTRODUCTION

The distinction between terms and representations is important in that, if a statement proves to be incorrect, the innocent party's remedy will depend on whether the statement is incorporated in the contract (in which case, the remedy will lie in breach of contract) or whether it is a mere representation (in which case the remedy will lie in misrepresentation). If the statement is classified as a mere representation, the innocent party will only have a right to damages if the statement was made fraudulently or negligently, but not if it was made innocently. The right to treat the contract as ended is available for all types of misrepresentation but it may be lost if, for example, the innocent party has, in the court's opinion, left it too late to bring his action. The remedy for misrepresentation is an equitable remedy and is therefore granted at the court's discretion. The remedy for breach of a term of contract is a common law remedy and is therefore available 'as of right'.

From the point of view of the remedies available to the innocent party, therefore, it is necessary to draw a distinction between those statements which are mere representations and those which are incorporated into the contract as terms.

To make the distinction, the courts use the following guidelines:

DID THE MAKER OF THE STATEMENT HAVE SPECIAL KNOWLEDGE COMPARED WITH THE OTHER PARTY?

If he did, then the court is likely to treat the statement as a term of the contract; if he did not, it will probably be treated as a mere representation.

Compare the following two cases:

Dick Bentley (Productions) Ltd v Harold Smith (Motors) Ltd (1965)

In recommending a car to a prospective purchaser, a dealer described the particular vehicle as 'one of the nicest cars we have had in for quite a long time' and said that it had had a replacement engine and gear box and had been driven only 20,000 miles since the new parts had been fitted. On the strength of these statements, the purchaser bought the car, but found it to be generally unsatisfactory. It was discovered that the statements about the car's mileage were untrue, although the dealer had not made the claim fraudulently. He had believed that the mileage shown on the mileometer was accurate. Had the statement been a mere representation, the purchaser's remedy would have been to ask the court to rescind the contract. This being an equitable remedy, it would be granted only at the court's discretion. The purchaser, however, argued that the statement was a term of the contract and claimed damages.

The Court of Appeal held that, as the statement was made by someone with a technical knowledge not possessed by the other party, it was a term of the contract. The purchaser was therefore entitled to claim damages as of right for breach of contract.

Oscar Chess Ltd v Williams (1957)

A private person selling his car to a garage in part exchange for another car innocently misrepresented the age of his car. He was relying on the car's registration book which was forged, although the seller was unaware of this. The Court of Appeal held that, as the maker of the statement had less knowledge than the person to whom it was made the statement was a mere innocent misrepresentation. The garage therefore was not entitled to damages.

IF THE MAKER OF THE STATEMENT SUGGESTS THAT THE OTHER PARTY CHECKS ON ITS ACCURACY HIMSELF, THE STATEMENT WILL BE A MERE REPRESENTATION

The courts will regard this as not being part of the contract, as the maker of the statement is obviously not trying to persuade the other person to enter the contract on the strength of it.

So, for example, if in selling a car the vendor describes it as having a 'good, sound engine' but suggests that the prospective purchaser employs an independent engineer to look at the vehicle, the statement will be treated as a representation rather than as a term of the contract.

If a pre-purchase check by an independent person is normal practice in a particular case then again statements made by the vendor will be treated as representations rather than terms. For example, in the case of house purchases, it is usual for the prospective purchaser to have the property examined by an independent surveyor before he buys. In these cases, pre-contractual statements will not be treated as terms of the contract.

IF THE STATEMENT IS MADE WITH THE INTENTION OF DISSUADING THE OTHER PARTY FROM CHECKING ON ITS ACCURACY AND IS SUCCESSFUL IN THIS AIM, IT WILL BE TREATED AS A TERM OF THE CONTRACT

This is illustrated in the case of:

Schawel v Reade (1913)

S was looking at a horse which he was thinking of buying for stud purposes. R, the seller, said 'You need not look for anything, the horse is sound. If there was anything the matter with the horse, I should tell you.' S therefore stopped his examination and, relying on the seller's statement, bought the horse. The animal was not sound.

The House of Lords held that the seller's statement was a term of the contract, for breach of which S could recover damages. The words and actions of the parties showed that it was understood that responsibility for the horse's condition rested on the seller.

IF THE ACCURACY OF THE STATEMENT IS VITAL TO THE MAKING OF THE CONTRACT IT WILL BE TREATED AS A TERM

In other words, a statement will be a term if the other party would not have entered the contract unless the statement had been made and was accurate. In the case of:

Bannerman v White (1861)

W was thinking of buying some hops from B but said that, if sulphur had been used in the cultivation of the crop, he would not even bother to ask the price. B assured him that no sulphur had been used although in fact it had. W bought the crop. The court held that B's assurance that sulphur had not been used was a term of the contract, as W had made it clear that he would contract only on those terms. The fact that the assurance was false, therefore, was a good defence to W when B sued him for failure to pay the price of the hops.

IF THE STATEMENT IS MADE SOME TIME BEFORE THE CONTRACT IS CONCLUDED, IT MAY BE REGARDED AS A REPRESENTATION

The longer the lapse of time between the making of the statement and the making of the contract, the more likely the court is to regard it as a representation rather than a term. The reason for this, is that if there is a lapse of time, it will show that the statement was merely part of the preliminary negotiations. It is a question of fact in each case. For example:

Routledge v McKay (1954)

During the course of negotiations for the sale of a motor cycle, the seller, in answer to a question of the buyer, wrongly stated that the motor cycle was a 1941 or 1942 model. The registration book gave the original date of registration as 1941 but, in fact, the true date was 1930. The seller was not responsible for this mistake. Seven days later, the parties made a contract for the sale of the motor cycle although the written terms of the sale did not mention the vehicle's date of registration.

The court held that the statement concerning the original date of registration was a representation. The buyer therefore could not claim damages for breach of contract.

IF AN ORAL STATEMENT IS NOT INCLUDED IN THE LATER WRITTEN CONTRACT, THE COURTS TEND TO REGARD IT AS A MERE REPRESENTATION

This is based on the assumption that, if the parties put their contract in writing, they will include in that writing all those parts of the negotiations they intend to be part of the contract. This is not an invariable rule. As with all guidelines the basic question is one of fact.

THE EFFECT OF THE MISREPRESENTATION ACT 1967

Before 1967, if a statement was a mere representation, the innocent party would have a right of action in damages only if the representor had acted fraudulently. The only other remedy was the discretionary one of rescission of the contract. The right to rescind could be lost through no fault of the innocent party.

Before 1967, therefore, it was important for the innocent party to show that a statement made before contract was a term and not merely a representation. The 1967 Act, however, introduced a right of damages for negligent misrepresentation, so the representee's position is not as weak as it was. The need to prove that a statement is a term rather than a representation is now less important, although the limits on the representee's right to rescind remain.

The law of misrepresentation will be discussed in greater detail in Chapter 9.

8.2.3 Express terms

DEFINITION

Express terms are those parts of the contract which contain the parties agreed obligations. It is from the express terms that the basis of the agreement can be discovered.

Example 8.3

Simon agrees to sell a car to Brian for £1,000, delivery to take place on 1 June. It is agreed that the car will be fitted with four new tyres and will have a current Ministry of Transport certificate.

The express terms of this contract are:

1. Simon will deliver the car to Brian.
2. Delivery will take place on 1 June.
3. The car will have four new tyres.
4. The car will have a current Ministry of Transport certificate.
5. Brian will pay Simon £1,000.

WHAT ARE THE TERMS OF THE CONTRACT?

The question is, how does the court discover what are the express terms of the contract?

If the contract is contained in a deed or, if it is a simple contract, it is wholly in writing, there is generally no difficulty. The terms of the contract are all written in the document. The general rule is that the court will not allow the parties to give oral evidence 'to add to, vary or contradict' the written agreement. The parties' rights will be restricted to those obligations which are actually set out in the writing unless oral evidence is necessary to prove a custom or trade usage; or to show that the contract was not intended to come into effect until the occurrence of an event which has not yet occurred; or if, as the court often finds is the case, the parties have not reduced all the agreement into writing and must therefore bring oral evidence to prove the unwritten parts.

If the contract is unwritten, of course, then the express terms can be discovered only by oral (or parol) evidence.

In interpreting and construing a contract the courts apply the same principles as they use in relation to statutory interpretation (see Chapter 6).

8.2.4 Implied terms

As well as terms agreed by the parties, the law also implies terms into certain contracts. In other words, the parties are bound both by the actual undertakings they have given each other and by undertakings annexed to the contract by statute, or by Common Law, or by custom. Even though the parties may be unaware of these implied terms, they are nevertheless as bound by them as if they had actually agreed to them.

For example, in the lease of a house, there is an implied term that the house will be habitable. In a contract for the sale of a house which is being built, there are implied terms that the house will be completed with sound materials and in a workmanlike manner and that, when finished, it will be fit for habitation.

TERMS IMPLIED BY STATUTE

Certain Acts of Parliament imply terms into some contracts. For example, the Sale of Goods Act 1979 implies terms into contracts for the sale of goods and the Supply of Goods and Services Act 1982, implies terms into those contracts within its scope (see Chapter 11). The Supply of Goods (Implied Terms) Act 1973 implies terms into contracts of hire-purchase (see Chapter 12).

TERMS IMPLIED BY COMMON LAW

The courts have a common law power to imply terms into a contract to give that contract business efficacy. Such a term will be implied only where the court feels it is necessary to give effect to the parties' presumed intention. They must have intended the provision to apply but had not troubled to state it. The term implied must, in the court's opinion, be an obvious oversight. The way in which this doctrine operates is shown in the case of:

The Moorcock (1889)

The appellant owned a jetty. The respondent owned a ship, The Moorcock. The parties made a contract whereby The Moorcock was to be discharged and loaded at the appellant's jetty. There was nothing in the contract stating that the jetty would be a safe place at which to moor the ship although both parties realised that, when the tide was out, the ship would rest on the river bed. The ship was damaged when the tide went out and the vessel settled on a ridge of hard ground beneath the mud on the river bed.

The Court of Appeal implied a term into the contract that the jetty would be a safe place at which the ship could moor. The appellants were liable to pay damages for breach of this implied term. Such an undertaking, said the court, must obviously have been intended by the parties and had to be implied in order to give the contract business efficacy.

The courts will not imply a term merely to make better sense of the agreement or to make it more workable. For example, in the case of:

Trollope and Colls Ltd v NW Metropolitan Regional Hospital Board (1973)

The parties had contracted that certain work was to be completed in phases. The completion dates of each phase were given, but no provision was made for what would happen in the event of the first phase overrunning its completion date. The first phase was late in being completed, but the court refused to imply a term into the contract to cover this eventuality. The court's function was not to imply terms to make a contract more workable. It would not re-write the contract for the parties even though this would have been an improvement.

The express terms were clear and unambiguous, and so the court would apply these even though it believed that some other terms would have been more suitable.

TERMS IMPLIED BY CUSTOM

If there is a particular custom or trade usage, this will be implied into the contract even though the parties have not expressly mentioned it. For example, in the case of:

Hutton v Warren (1836)

H was the tenant of a farm owned by W. H was given 3 months' notice to quit but was told that he had to cultivate the land for the period of notice. This he did and claimed a fair allowance for the seeds and labour he had used and for which he had received no benefit as he had to leave the farm before harvest. Evidence was brought to show that, by custom, a tenant was bound to farm for the whole of his tenancy but, when he quit, he was entitled to a fair allowance for the seeds and labour. The court therefore implied this term into the contract and awarded H compensation.

8.2.5 Classification of terms

INTRODUCTION

Whether a term is express or implied, the court has to consider its importance in relation to the contract as a whole. Not all terms are of equal importance. Breach of some will have a more serious effect on the contract than breach of others.

Some terms are so basic to the contract that, if they are broken, the main purpose of the contract is defeated. Such terms are called conditions. Other terms are subsidiary to the main purpose of the contract and, although they may be broken, the main purpose of the contract will be left intact. These terms are called warranties. The deciding factor is the intention of the parties as gathered from the wording of the contract and the circumstances surrounding its making.

If the parties have indicated that a particular undertaking is to be a condition, the courts will, in general, abide by this indication. This is not, however, an invariable rule. Even though the parties have described a term as a condition, if the court believes that the matter is trivial it will treat the term as a warranty. For example, in the case of:

L Schuler AG v Wickham Machine Tool Sales (1973)

S made a contract with W, giving W the exclusive right to sell S's panel presses in England. The agreement stated that it was a condition of the contract that W's representatives should visit and solicit orders from six named firms each week. W's representatives occasionally failed to keep to this schedule and S, arguing that any failure to comply with this term gave them the right to treat the contract as repudiated, purported to end the agreement.

The House of Lords, however, said that although the term was described in the contract as a condition, the minor breaches by W did not give S the right to treat the contract as repudiated. To treat this term as a condition, said the Lords, would be so unreasonable that the parties could be said not to have intended it to be so.

In reality, of course, S did so intend, but the court used its common law power to construe the contract in such a way as to give what it considered to be a reasonable construction of the agreement.

CLASSIFICATION DEPENDS ON THE PARTIES' INTENTIONS

The parties to the contract may themselves classify the term into a condition or warranty but, as we have seen, this classification is not final. The court may disregard what the parties have said and treat the term in a way that it believes the parties must have intended. The consequences of the way the term is classified lie in the remedies available to the innocent party.

Example 8.4

Rob undertakes to supply goods to Tom, delivery on 1 July. Rob does not deliver until 10 July. Obviously he is in breach of contract but the question that arises is: Can Tom refuse to accept and pay for the goods or does he have to accept delivery and merely claim compensation from Rob? The answer will depend on whether the stipulation as to time is a condition or a warranty.

If, in ordering the goods, Tom had said to Rob: 'if you cannot deliver these goods by 1 July I will not order them from you', then it may be inferred by this emphatic statement that the time of delivery is a condition. Late delivery would then give Tom the right to treat the contract as repudiated. He will not be obliged to accept or pay for the goods. If he has already paid, he may recover the sum from Rob and also sue him in breach of contract.

If, however, the stipulation as to time was an incidental term of the contract, Tom must treat its breach as a breach of warranty. He must accept and pay for the goods when they are delivered. Any damage he has suffered by reason of the delay will be set-off in a reduction of the price.

If it is not possible to classify the term as a condition or a warranty whether from the contract itself, or from surrounding circumstances or from statute or custom, the court will treat the term as innominate (or intermediate). In this case the court will 'wait and see' the effect of the breach and award a remedy accordingly. In other words, if a term cannot be categorised as a condition or a warranty there is no automatic remedy available if that term is broken. The court will see how badly affected the innocent party is by the breach and, if the consequences are severe, allow him to repudiate it, if trivial merely allow him damages.

We will now look at conditions, warranties and innominate terms in more detail.

CONDITIONS

A condition is a term which goes to the root of the contract and which is so fundamental that, if it is broken, will enable the innocent party to treat the contract as ended and recover any money he has paid. He will incur no further liability under the agreement. If he has suffered any loss because of the breach he may also be able to recover compensation for this.

For example:

Poussard v Spiers and Pond (1876)

An actress was taken ill and so was not able to fulfil her contract to play the leading part in an operetta from the beginning of its run. By the second week of the operetta she had recovered, but by this time a substitute had been employed to take her part. The court held that the actress was in breach of condition and that therefore the producers were entitled to treat the contract as discharged.

If, however, despite the breach of condition, the innocent party continues with the contract he will be said to have affirmed it and will have lost the right to repudiate. The breach of condition will have to be treated as a breach of warranty. The contract will continue and the buyer's remedy will be in damages.

So, if in the *Poussard* case (above), the theatre management had allowed the actress to return to the operetta, they could not later have treated the contract as repudiated by her initial breach. All they could have done would have been to obtain damages from her for any extra expense they had incurred by reason of her breach. They would have treated the breach of condition as a breach of warranty. If the subject matter of the contract is goods and the transaction is covered by the Sale of Goods Act 1979 affirmation is known as 'acceptance' (See Chapter 11). The effect, however, is the same. There will also be affirmation if there is too long a delay in claiming the remedy for breach of condition.

In summary, therefore, if there is a breach of condition the innocent party may:

1. treat the contract as discharged, return any goods received, recover any money paid and claim damages for any extra loss; or
2. treat the contract as continuing, keep any benefit received, pay the amounts owing under the contract, and merely sue in damages for breach; or
3. if there has been delay in claiming the right to repudiate or, if the subject matter of the contract is goods and these cannot be returned to the other party (because, for example, the innocent party has already sold them or has destroyed or consumed them) there will be no choice in the matter. The innocent party must treat the breach of condition as a breach of warranty and merely claim damages.

WARRANTIES

A warranty is a term of the contract which is subsidiary to the main point of the contract and which, if broken, will leave the contract intact. The innocent party must fulfil his side of the bargain and claim compensation for the breach by an action in damages.

In the case of:

Bettini v Gye (1876)

An opera singer who had been engaged for the whole season turned up for rehearsals only 3 days before the opening night instead of, as the contract required, 6 days before. The court held that, as the rehearsal requirement was subsidiary to the main point of the contract (which was for him to appear for the whole season), the singer's employers, although entitled to damages for breach of warranty, were not entitled to treat the contract as repudiated.

INNOMINATE TERMS

As we said earlier, a term may be categorised as a condition or a warranty by the parties or by the court or even by mercantile custom. If, however, the terms are not so categorised they will be innominate (or intermediate) terms. That is, they are not conditions or warranties and a breach will not automatically give the innocent party the right to treat the contract as repudiated or to sue in damages.

If an innominate term is broken, the innocent party's remedy will depend on the seriousness of the breach. The court adopts a 'wait and see' approach. If, in fact, the breach has a serious effect on the contract the innocent party will be entitled to treat the contract as repudiated. If, however, the effect of the breach is not serious, the innocent party's remedy will be in damages. The contract will remain valid.

The way in which the court deals with innominate terms is shown in the case of

Cehave NV v Bremer Handelsgesellschaft mbH (1975)

There was a contract for the sale of citrus pulp pellets to be shipped from America to Rotterdam, Holland. One of the terms of the contract was that the pellets were to be 'shipped in good condition'. When the goods arrived at Rotterdam it was discovered that part of the consignment had been damaged. The buyers, who had paid in advance of delivery, rejected the pellets for breach of the term that they should be shipped in good condition, and claimed recovery of the money they had paid. The sellers refused. Whilst the parties were arguing, the court appointed an official to sell the cargo. The money was to be paid into court pending the outcome of the case between the sellers and the buyers. The goods were sold to a Mr. Baas who immediately resold them to the original buyers at the price he (Baas) had paid and which was substantially less than the original contract price, the market price for citrus pulp pellets having fallen considerably. The buyers used the pellets for the purpose for which they had originally bought them and brought this action claiming the return of the money they had paid the sellers under the original contract.

The Court of Appeal held that the buyers should fail in their action. The term 'shipped in good condition' could not be categorised as a condition either from the terms of the contract or by custom. It was an innominate term and the remedy to be given depended on the effect of its breach on the contract. As the buyers had acquired the pellets and used them for their original purpose they showed that the effects of the damage were not serious. They were entitled to claim damages for the deterioration in quality, but the contract stood. They therefore could not recover the purchase price they had paid.

A term will be innominate, therefore, when it has not been classified as a condition or a warranty by the parties, the court or custom. When, and only when, it is categorised as innominate will the courts adopt a 'wait and see' approach and award a remedy accordingly. If the parties have described a term as a condition, and the courts accept this classification, then any breach of that term, however trivial the consequences, will entitle the innocent party to treat the contract as repudiated.

If, however, the term has not been so classified the courts will 'wait and see' the effects of breach. So if, for example, in the *Cehave* case, the goods had been so damaged that they could not have been used for their originally intended purpose, the buyers would have been entitled to recover the purchase price they had paid the sellers.

In later chapters of this book we will look at terms implied into contracts by statutes such as the Sale of Goods Act 1979 and the Supply of Goods (Implied Terms) Act 1973. These Acts categorise the terms into conditions and warranties and the courts must follow this categorisation. There is no question of a term described as a condition by a statute being treated as an innominate term. So, however minor the effects of breach, if a term classed as a condition by an act is broken the innocent party will have the right to treat the contract as repudiated.

8.2.6 Exclusion clauses

INTRODUCTION

An exclusion clause is one which attempts either to exclude entirely or in some way limit one party's liability to the other for breach of contract. For example, in a contract for the sale of goods, the seller may insert a clause stating that he will not be liable in breach of contract if the goods he delivers are in any way defective. This will be an exclusion clause. A clause will also be treated as an exclusion clause if it attempts in some way to limit the innocent party's right to make a claim or discourages him from doing so.

For example, if a term restricts the seller's liability to a refund of the purchase price paid by the buyer should the goods bought prove defective, this will be an exclusion clause, as will a requirement that any claims be made within 14 days of the contract.

The courts have always been reluctant to enforce exclusion or limiting clauses and have based their attacks on them by looking carefully at whether the clause has been properly incorporated into

FORM AND CONTENTS OF A CONTRACT: CHAPTER EIGHT 85

the contract and, if it has, whether it covers the event which has occurred. Since 1977, the Unfair Contract Terms Act has added further limitations on the effectiveness of exclusion clauses. We will deal with each of these points in turn.

INCORPORATION OF EXCLUSION CLAUSES INTO CONTRACTS

Whether or not an exclusion or limiting clause has been incorporated into a contract depends on several common law rules. The position differs depending on whether or not the contract was signed.

If the contract is signed, the person signing is bound by its terms even if he has not read the contract. For example, in the case of:

L'Estrange v Graucob (1934)

L bought a cigarette vending machine for her café. She signed, without reading, the sales agreement, one of the terms of which was that 'any express or implied condition, statement or warranty ... is hereby excluded'. The machine did not work properly, but when L sued the suppliers in breach of contract the court held that she should fail. By signing the agreement, she had agreed to all the terms included in it even though she had not read them.

A signatory may avoid liability only if it can be shown that the signature was induced by misrepresentation or that the document was signed under a non-negligent mistake as to its nature (see Chapter 9—mistake as to the nature of the document signed).

For example, in the case of:

Curtis v Chemical Cleaning and Dyeing Co (1951)

C took a white satin wedding-dress to the cleaners. She was given a slip of paper to sign but, before she did so, she asked the assistant to explain one of the clauses on the paper. The assistant said that it meant that the firm was not liable for damage to beads and sequins on clothes given in to be cleaned. This statement was literally true but what was not mentioned was that the document excluded liability for 'any damage howsoever arising'. The dress was returned stained, due to the cleaners' negligence, but when C sued for damages the company relied on the exclusion clause and claimed that it was not liable. The court held that the company could not rely on the clause to avoid liability. The assistant's innocent misrepresentation as to the extent of the exclusion limited its effect to cover damage only to beads and sequins.

If the contract is unsigned, that is if it is contained for example in a ticket or notice, reasonable steps must have been taken to bring any exclusion clause it contains to the notice of the party entering the contract.

The person trying to rely on the exclusion must show:

1   that the document was an integral part of a contract which could be expected to contain terms. In the case of:

Chapleton v Barry UDC (1940)

C hired a deck-chair and, having paid the fee, was given a ticket which referred him to the conditions of hire, one of which was an exclusion clause. C did not read the ticket. The deck-chair collapsed and C was injured but when he sued Barry UDC., the council claimed that the exclusion clause exempted it from liability. The court held, however, that the ticket was a mere receipt, given after the contract had been made. The exclusion clause, therefore, had not been incorporated into the contract and so did not bind C. He was entitled to damages for his injuries.

If, however, the unsigned document is contractual, any exclusion clause which it contains or to which it refers will apply to the transaction even if the plaintiff is unaware of the existence of the clause because, for example, he had not read the document. In the case of:

Thompson v LMS Railway (1930)

T bought a railway ticket which referred to the conditions under which passengers were carried by the railway company. One of these conditions was an exclusion of liability for the death of or personal injury to passengers. T could not read the ticket because she was illiterate. She was injured and claimed damages. The court held that she should fail in her claim. The fact that she could not read the ticket was irrelevant: 'illiteracy is a misfortune not a privilege'. The railway company had taken reasonable steps to bring the exclusion clause to the notice of its passengers by incorporating it into a contractual document (the ticket). So all passengers were bound by the exclusion whether or not they were aware of its existence.

Note that, since the Unfair Contract Terms Act 1977, any attempt to exclude liability for death or personal injury caused by negligence is absolutely void. *Thompson's* case however remains good authority for the meaning of reasonable notice of terms of a contract.

2   that, if no notice of the exclusion is given, the clause has been incorporated into the contract by a previous course of dealings.

A person who wishes to escape liability by pleading an exclusion clause must show either that the exclusion was drawn to the other party's attention before the contract was made, or that there has been a previous course of dealings between him and this other party and that an exclusion clause had been incorporated in these dealings. In other words, he must show that, although the exclusion clause was not part of the present dealings, previous transactions had incorporated such a term in such a way that the other party must have known that it would apply in the present circumstances. The argument is that the previous dealings will give constructive notice of the exclusion.

In transactions where the plaintiff is an individual, rather than a commercial undertaking, the doctrine of constructive notice is unlikely to be applied by the courts. The fact that previous dealings between the parties incorporated an exclusion clause will not help the defendant avoid liability if such a clause was not brought to the plaintiff's attention as part of the transaction in dispute. For example:

Hollier v Rambler Motors (1972)

Each time H had had his car repaired by R he had signed a form which excluded R's liability for damage caused to customers' cars whilst they were in R's possession. On one occasion, however, H left his car for repair but was not asked to sign the form. His car was damaged by fire caused by R's negligence. When H sued for damages, R argued that, because of the previous course of dealings, H must be taken to know of the exclusion and thus be bound by it. H, it was claimed had constructive notice.

The court held that H was not bound by the exclusion. The fact that there had been a previous course of dealings was not enough to incorporate the exclusion into the present contract. Furthermore, said the court, the wording used was not sufficiently precise or clear to exclude liability for negligence. H was entitled to damages for the damage to his car.

Constructive notice, therefore, will generally not be enough to incorporate an exclusion clause into a consumer transaction. In a commercial transaction, however, the court may allow a plea of constructive notice to succeed. In such a dealing, where both parties are acting in the course of business, terms used in previous dealings between the parties or which are commonly used in the relevant industry, may be incorporated into a contract by constructive notice. In the case of:

British Crane Hire Corp Ltd v Ipswich Plant Hire (1974)

The defendants hired a crane from the plaintiffs under an oral contract. Following the contract, the defendants were sent a form by the plaintiffs. The defendants were to sign and return the form which, amongst other things, contained a clause requiring the hirers of the crane (the defendants) to indemnify the owners (the plaintiffs) for all expenses incurred in connection with the use of the crane. A clause similar to this was in common use in the industry. Before the defendants signed the form the crane was damaged through no fault of the defendants. The plaintiffs had to carry out expensive repairs to the equipment and they brought this action claiming the right to be indemnified by the defendants. The defendants argued that, when the oral contract was made, the clause imposing this liability had not been incorporated and that they were therefore not bound by it. The court held, however, that as:

1   The parties were in an equal bargaining position; and
2   The defendants knew that similar clauses were commonly used in the industry.

There was a common understanding that the contract was made on these terms. It had been incorporated into the contract by constructive notice and the defendants were therefore obliged to indemnify the plaintiffs.

FORM AND CONTENTS OF A CONTRACT: CHAPTER EIGHT

THAT NOTICE OF THE EXCLUSION WAS GIVEN BEFORE OR AT THE TIME OF THE CONTRACT

If notice of the exclusion clause is given after the contract is made, the clause will be ineffective to protect the party relying on it. This is because he will have given no consideration for its incorporation into the transaction. His consideration will be past (ie the making of the contract).

In the case of:

Olley v Marlborough Court Ltd (1949)

O booked in at the hotel and paid for a room in advance. When he and his wife went to the room they saw a notice excluding the hotel's liability for any articles left in the room. Such articles had to be handed to the management for safe custody. O's wife left a fur coat in the room and the coat was stolen. The hotel denied liability relying on the notice in the room.

The court held that the hotel was liable. The contract with O had been made at the reception desk and no subsequent notice could alter O's rights under that contract.

Although not strictly a case on exclusion clauses, a recent decision of the Court of Appeal is important on the incorporation of terms into a contract:

Interfoto Picture Library Ltd v Stiletto Visual Programmes Ltd (1988)

The defendants were an advertising agency. They needed some photographs of the 1950's for some work they were doing. They telephoned the plaintiff photo library and were sent 47 transparencies. Accompanying the transparencies was a delivery note saying that £5.00 per day would be charged for each transparency retained beyond fourteen days. There was a delay in the defendants returning the transparencies and the plaintiff submitted an invoice for over £3,500 for the retention of them.

The Court of Appeal held that while in principle the contract between the parties was on the terms of the delivery note, where a condition in a contract was particularly onerous or unusual then the party seeking to rely on it had to show that it had been fairly and reasonably brought to the other party's attention. In the circumstances it was not sufficient simply to incorporate the term in a delivery note. Accordingly the defendants were not liable.

CONSTRUCTION OF EXCLUSION CLAUSES

The courts are very strict in their interpretation of exclusion clauses. For example, the party relying on the exclusion must show that it covers the loss which has occurred. If it does not, or if it is ambiguous or uncertain, the courts will construe it against the interests of the party seeking its protection.

This is known as the:

1 Contra proferentem rule

We have already seen an application of this rule in the case of *Hollier* v *Rambler Motors* (above), where the court held that the exclusion clause was not sufficiently specific to avoid liability for negligence and so could not be used by the garage to enable it to escape the customer's claim. The general wording of the exclusion was construed against the interests of the party seeking to rely on it.

Another illustration of the rule is contained in the case of:

Houghton v Trafalgar Insurance (1954)

A five-seater car crashed whilst it was carrying 6 passengers. The owner's contract of insurance excluded the insurers' liability for any damage caused whilst the car was 'carrying any load in excess of that for which it was constructed'. Relying on this exclusion, the insurers refused to pay for the damage caused in the crash.

The court held, however, that the word 'load' in the clause was ambiguous. It could not be taken to refer to passengers but rather to cases where a specified weight must not be exceeded, as in relation to vans and lorries. The insurance company therefore could not avoid liability and had to pay compensation in respect of the accident.

Again in the case of:

Andrews v Singer (1934)

A contracted to buy some 'new Singer cars' from S. The contract contained a clause which excluded 'all conditions, warranties and liabilities, implied by statute, common law, or otherwise'. When the cars were delivered, one of them turned out to be a used car. When A sued in breach of contract, S tried to rely on the exclusion clause but the Court of Appeal held that A should succeed in his claim. The term 'new Singer car' was an *express* condition of the contract and breach of this term was not covered by the exclusion clause, which protected S only from liability for breach of *implied* conditions.

If, however, the exclusion clause is clear, comprehensive and unambiguous the *contra proferentem rule* cannot help the injured party. See, for example, the clause in *L'Estrange* v *Graucob* (above).

2 The main purpose rule

In construing an exemption clause, the courts act on the presumption that it was not intended to defeat the main purpose of the contract. For example, in the case of:

Glynn v Margetson & Co (1893)

Oranges were to be shipped from Spain to the United Kingdom. A clause in the contract of carriage permitted the ship to call at virtually any port in Europe and Africa. The ship loaded the oranges and then went east from Spain on some other business, returned to Spain and only then travelled to the United Kingdom. By the time it arrived, the cargo of oranges had deteriorated because of the delay. The House of Lords held that, despite the clause giving them the right to deviate from the route, the carriers were liable. The wide wording used had to be cut down so that it did not defeat the main object of the contract—the carriage of oranges from Spain to the United Kingdom. The clause would only justify the carrier calling at ports en route between the two countries.

This, however, is only a presumption and may, therefore, be rebutted. That is, the party relying on the exclusion may show that the words used are sufficiently precise and strong to cover this eventuality. The main purpose rule of construction is given statutory support by s3 Unfair Contract Terms Act 1977 (see later).

3 Oral representations

If a contracting party or his agent makes oral representations these may override an exemption clause on which the representor is seeking to rely. For example, in the case of:

Mendelssohn v Normand Ltd (1969)

M left his car in N's garage and was given a ticket, which he did not read. The ticket contained a clause excluding N's responsibility for the loss of the contents of the car. One of N's attendants told M to leave the car doors unlocked and, on being given the keys to the car by M, promised to lock the car after he had moved it. M's suitcase was stolen from the car but when M sued, N relied on the exclusion clause. The court held that the oral statement of N's employee, made with the apparent authority of N, took priority over the printed conditions, which therefore could not be relied upon by N. Furthermore, the garage had carried out the contract in a way not envisaged by the parties.

Also, in the case of:

J Evans & Son (Portsmouth) v Andrea Metzario (1976)

The defendants imported machinery from Italy for the plaintiffs. The machinery was shipped below decks in crates. In 1967, the defendants started to use containerised transport. Their contract with the plaintiffs gave them complete freedom in relation to the method of transportation used, but they gave the plaintiffs oral assurances that the plaintiffs' containers would continue to be shipped below decks. On one occasion, a container holding machinery for the plaintiffs was carried on the deck of the ship and was washed overboard. The court held that the plaintiffs were entitled to damages. The defendants' oral promise overrode the printed conditions.

4 Fundamental breach

A fundamental breach of contract occurs where the effect of the breach is such that performance of the contract is totally different from that contemplated by the parties. Until 1966 it was thought that, if there was a fundamental breach, the whole basis of the contract had been destroyed and all the clauses in the contract, including any exclusion clauses, were of no effect. Such an argument was used by a party to a contract whose claim came within a valid exclusion clause and whose only hope to recover compensation, therefore, was to show that the whole contract, including the exclusion, had ceased to exist because of a fundamental breach.

In 1966, however, in the case of:

Suisse Atlantique Société D'Armement Maritime SA v NV Rotterdamsche Kolen Centrale (1967)

(The facts of which do not concern us), the House of Lords held that there is no rule of law that an exemption clause can never apply to cover a fundamental breach. It is a question of construction in each case whether the wording of the exemption clause covers what has happened.

Following *Suisse Atlantique*, however, the Court of Appeal tried to modify this ruling, but the principle in the case was affirmed, again by the House of Lords, which overruled the intervening Court of Appeal decisions. They did this in the case of:

Photo Production Ltd v Securicor Transport Ltd (1980)

P owned a factory which was guarded at night and over weekends by S, under a contract which contained a clause excluding S's liability for 'any injurious act or default by any employee' of S. One of S's employees lit a small fire inside P's factory. The fire got out of control and P's factory and all its stock, worth in total over £600,000, was destroyed. When P sued S, S relied on the exclusion clause to avoid liability.

The House of Lords held that, although S was clearly in breach of its obligation to operate its service with due care and skill and with proper regard for the safety and security of P's premises, the court's function was to construe and apply the exclusion clause. The clause in this contract was clearly and unambiguously covering the circumstances that had arisen. S, therefore, was protected from liability. There was no question of S's breach preventing it relying on the exclusion.

The position with regard to fundamental breach, therefore, is that it is a question of construction of an exclusion clause whether it operates to cover the case that has arisen. If the wording of the clause clearly and unambiguously deals with what has occurred, the fact that the underlying purpose of the contract has been destroyed will not prevent the party in breach from relying on the exclusion to avoid liability.

UNFAIR CONTRACT TERMS ACT 1977

The Unfair Contract Terms Act 1977 (UCTA) severely restricts the way in which parties to certain contracts may exclude or limit their liability for breach by the use of exclusion clauses. The Act, however, does not apply to those contracts listed in Schedule I. These are:

1   Contracts of insurance.
2   Contracts for the creation or transfer of an interest in land.
3   Creation or transfer of patents.
4   Company formations, transactions in securities and other rights and obligations of the corporators.

In these cases the pre-1976 law will apply.

UCTA does apply, however, to all other exemption clauses which purport to exclude or limit liability in contract or tort. In general, it applies only to business liability, that is, when the person seeking the protection of an exemption clause is acting in a business capacity. The main provisions of the Act are as follows:

1   Avoidance of liability for negligence (s2 UCTA)

A person acting in the course of business cannot exclude his liability for negligence resulting in death or personal injury. Any attempt to do so will be void.

Such a person can exclude liability for *other damage*, that is damage to goods or economic loss, caused by negligence, only if the term or notice containing the exclusion is fair and reasonable in the light of the circumstances which were, or ought reasonably to have been, known to or in the contemplation of the parties when the contract was made. So, for example, if the exemption clause limits liability to a specified sum, in deciding whether this provision is reasonable, the courts will take account of the resources of the party relying on the limitation and on whether he could have covered himself by taking out insurance.

The fact that the person who is harmed by the negligence agrees to, or is aware of, a term restricting the other party's liability does not of itself show that he voluntarily accepted the risk. In the County Court decision of:

Woodman v Proto Trade Processing (1987)

Woodman had taken photographs of a friend's wedding intending to give these pictures as a wedding present. He took the film to Dixons to be developed, but Dixons lost the film. When sued, Dixons sought to rely on an exclusion clause which was part of the contract made with W. This limited Dixons' liability to the cost of replacing the film.

It was held that this exclusion was unreasonable and so void. All developers of films had similar exclusions and therefore W had no real choice but to enter a contract on these terms and also it is unreasonable that everyone, whatever the value of the films given in for developing, should have to take the risk of the film being lost. W was awarded £75 compensation.

2 Avoidance of liability arising from the sale or other supply of goods (ss5–7 UCTA)

These sections deal with attempts by sellers to avoid liability which arises from their breach of the implied terms in the Sale of Goods Act 1979 (SGA) and the Supply of Goods and Services Act 1982. These terms are discussed fully in Chapter 11 but for the moment it is sufficient to say that in all contracts covered by the 1979 Act, there are certain terms automatically implied. There are implied conditions that:

(a) The seller owns the goods he is selling (s12 SGA).
(b) If the goods are sold by description, they will correspond with that description (s13 SGA).
(c) If the seller sells goods in the course of a business, that the goods will be of merchantable quality and fit for the buyer's specific purpose (s14 SGA).
(d) If the goods are sold by sample they will correspond with the sample (s15 SGA).

The effect of UCTA on attempts to exclude liability for these sections depends on whether or not the dealing is a consumer dealing. A sale will be a consumer dealing if all three of the following requirements are satisfied:

(a) The buyer does not buy or hold himself out as buying in the course of business.
(b) The seller sells in the course of business.
(c) The goods are of a type ordinarily supplied for private use or consumption.

If all three of these requirements is satisfied, the sale will be a consumer dealing and any attempt to exclude liability for breach of the implied terms relating to goods in either the 1979 or the 1982 Act will be absolutely void.

If, however, one or more of the three is not satisfied, the sale will be a non-consumer dealing, in which case there can be no exclusion of the condition as to ownership. The other implied terms may be excluded or limited however, but only if the court is satisfied that reliance on the exclusion clause is fair and reasonable.

So, for example, if the buyer buys as part of his business, such as an accountant buying furniture or equipment for the office, or holds himself as buying in this way, as when a private person obtains a trade discount for the goods he is buying, the sale will be a non-consumer sale and the seller may exclude his liability for ss13–15 SGA provided he can show that reliance on the clause is fair and reasonable. Likewise, if the seller sells privately, or if the goods are not of a type ordinarily sold for private use or consumption (eg a van, an office computer), exclusion of liability may be possible.

As we said, however, in a non-consumer dealing the person relying on an exclusion must show that reliance on the exclusion is fair and reasonable. Schedule 2 UCTA gives guidelines as to what is fair and reasonable. The court will look at:

(a) The relative bargaining strength of the parties (the stronger the position of the seller, the less likely the court will be to allow an exclusion).
(b) Whether the buyer received an inducement to agree to the clause (if, for example, he received a price reduction) the courts are likely to regard the clause as fair and reasonable.
(c) Whether the buyer could have made a contract with other suppliers without such a term, but chose instead to make it with this particular seller despite the exclusion.
(d) Whether the buyer knew or ought reasonably to have known of the term.
(e) If liability is made conditional on compliance with some requirement (eg seller accepts liability only if the faulty goods are returned within 14 days of the fault occurring) whether such compliance is reasonable.
(f) Whether the goods were made or adapted to the special order of the buyer (in which case, the court will be more willing to allow the exclusion).

Schedule 2 requires the court to take account of these guidelines but gives it the general duty to examine the reasonableness of the exclusion in the light of all other factors. For example, in the case of:

George Mitchell (Chesterhall) Ltd v *Finney Lock Seeds Ltd* **(1983)**

The buyers, farmers, bought cabbage seed from the defendants, seed merchants, under a contract which contained a clause limiting the defendants' liability for defective seed to the amount of the purchase price. The seeds were completely defective and the buyers lost over £60,000 profit on the crop. The sellers tried, as was their custom, to negotiate a settlement but, when they were unsuccessful in this, they relied on the exclusion clause and claimed that their liability was limited to the purchase price of the seed which was about £200.

The court held that, in trying to negotiate a settlement, the seed merchants had shown that even they did not believe that their limitation clause was fair and reasonable. The clause therefore could not be justified and the buyers were entitled to recover their lost profit as damages.

3 Guarantees (s5 UCTA)

If goods are of a type ordinarily supplied for private use or consumption the manufacturer cannot, by the use of a guarantee, exclude his liability for loss or damage arising from the goods proving defective while in consumer use, if this loss or damage results from the negligence of a person concerned in the manufacture or distribution of the goods.

So, it is no longer possible for a manufacturer to use a guarantee to extract a binding undertaking from the purchaser of the manufacturer's goods not to sue the manufacturer in negligence in return, for example, for the manufacturer's promise to replace any faulty parts.

4 Contracts made on one party's standard terms (s3 UCTA)

Where a person deals on the suppliers' standard terms of business, whether this person is a private consumer or not, the supplier's liability can be excluded only if he can show that the exclusion is reasonable. The burden of proving reasonableness again lies on the party seeking to rely on the clause.

The requirement that the clause must be shown to be reasonable will also apply to any provision by which the supplier claims the right to perform the contract in a manner which is substantially different from that which could reasonably be expected of him. This covers situations within the 'main purpose rule' (see above). Furthermore, the Act provides that, where the requirement of reasonableness applies, a term which can be shown to satisfy that requirement will remain effective even if the contract in which it is contained has been terminated by breach (s9(1) UCTA). This covers cases of fundamental breach (see above) and will apply to such cases as *Photo Production* (above). As the contract on which the action in *Photo Production* was brought was made before 1977, UCTA did not apply to the case.

5 Avoidance of liability for misrepresentation (s8 UCTA)

Any attempt to exclude liability for misrepresentation must be justified as being reasonable.

6 The scope of UCTA

The requirements of the Act apply, not just to the terms of the actual contract of sale, but also to the terms of any other contract which attempts to exclude the seller's liability in relation to the sale. For example, if A agrees to sell goods to B only if B enters a subsidiary or collateral contract to exclude A's liability in the event of the goods proving defective, this collateral contract will be subject to UCTA's control, even though the main contract for the sale of goods has no exclusion clause in it.

The Act will also apply to non-contractual notices containing exclusion clauses eg notices displayed at the point of contract which exclude liability.

Furthermore, the phrase 'exemption clause' includes attempts to make liability or the enforcement of a right of action subject to restrictive or onerous conditions (such as the obligation to return the defective goods within a certain time in order to claim a right). It also covers cases where the buyer's claim would result in him losing a benefit he would otherwise enjoy, such as a loss of favourable credit terms. This will be treated as an attempt by the supplier to limit or avoid his liability and will come within the scope of UCTA.

SUMMARY

In this Chapter we have looked at the form of contracts and their contents. In relation to form, remember that the majority of simple contracts do not have to be in any particular form. They can be made orally or in writing. The court will be concerned only with the substance of the contract; the way in which the contract was made and what it contains. Those simple contracts which do require a special form, whether they have to be completely written or merely evidenced in writing, are the exceptions to the general rule. All these exceptions are created by statute.

In relation to the contents of the contract make sure that you understand the following distinctions:

1. Conditions, warranties, innominate terms.
2. Express and implied terms.

These are very important when we discuss specific contracts such as those covered by the Sale of Goods Act 1979. Note, too, the meaning and effect of exclusion clauses and see how their application is controlled by the courts and by statute. If there is an exclusion clause, you must look, firstly, at whether it has been properly incorporated into the contract under the rules of common law. If it has been, you must then see whether it is covered by UCTA and, if so, if it is void or not under the provisions of the Act. If it is valid, you must decide whether it could be justified as being reasonable. In deciding whether it is reasonable, or even whether it applies at all to the event that has happened, you will use the common law rules of construction. Reasonableness will also be judged in relation to the guidelines in Schedule 2 UCTA.

The law contained in the 1977 Act will be relevant when we come to discuss the Sale of Goods Act 1979, the Supply of Goods and Services Act 1982, and the Supply of Goods (Implied Terms) Act 1973.

SELF-TEST QUESTIONS

8.1 In the case of
(a) *Mountstephen* v *Lakeman* (1874) and
(b) *Fitzgerald* v *Dressler* (1859),
Why was the arrangement entered into by the parties not a guarantee?

8.2 Lack of evidence in writing of a guarantee makes that contract
(a) void?
(b) voidable?
(c) unenforceable?
(d) valid?

8.3 Complete this sentence:

'A contract under seal takes effect from its (a) ____ rather than its (b) ____.

8.4 'If the maker of a statement has special knowledge compared with the other party, that statement may be regarded as a term of the contract, rather than a mere representation.'

Is this ratio of:

(a) *Oscar Chess Ltd* v *Williams* (1957), or
(b) *Dick Bentley (Productions) Ltd* v *Harold Smith (Motors) Ltd* (1965)?

8.5 What is the ratio of *Bannerman* v *White* (1861)?

8.6 Compare:

(a) *The Moorcock* (1889), and
(b) *Trollope and Colls Ltd* v *N W Metropolitan Regional Hospital Board* (1973)

8.7 Distinguish

(a) conditions
(b) warranties
(c) innominate terms

8.8 Why could the party in breach not rely on his exclusion clause in the following cases:

(a) *Curtis* v *Chemical Cleaning and Dyeing Co* (1951)
(b) *Hollier* v *Rambler Motors* (1972)
(c) *Olley* v *Marlborough Court Ltd* (1949)
(d) *Andrews* v *Singer* (1934)
(e) *Glynn* v *Margetson & Co* (1893)

8.9 By the Unfair Contract Terms Act 1977, the following exclusions are void:

(a)
(b)
(c)
(d)

8.10 Define a consumer dealing in the Unfair Contract Terms Act 1977

Answers on page 306

EXERCISES

Exercise 8.1

Explain how the terms of a contract may be categorised into conditions, warranties and innominate terms.

Exercise 8.2

Distinguish between:

1. Contracts under seal
2. Simple contracts which must be in writing
3. Simple contracts which must be evidenced in writing.

Answers on page 307

Matters affecting the validity of a contract

As we saw in Chapter 7, a contract is based on agreement. It therefore follows that, if there is no true agreement, the contract will be defective and can be set aside. So, for example, if one of the parties made a false statement to the other, to induce this other to enter the contract, the one so induced may have the right to set the contract aside and thus escape any liability under it. Likewise, if the parties contracted under a mistake, and the mistake is such that it means that no real agreement has been reached, the contract will be invalid.

The right to set the contract aside also arises when one of the parties was forced into the contract by, for example, the use of physical, moral or economic pressure by the other.

Finally, whether true agreement exists or not, if the contract made by the parties is illegal in the eyes of the law it will be void and no rights whatsoever can be obtained under it.

In this chapter, we will examine the meaning and effect of misrepresentation, mistake, duress, and illegality. Before we do, however, we must review the meanings of valid, voidable and void contracts.

9.1 DEFINITIONS

9.1.1 Valid contracts

These are contracts which are complete and regular in all respects and which are enforceable by action in the courts.

9.1.2 Voidable contracts

A voidable contract is one which is in some way defective but not so defective as to be treated as void. If a contract is voidable, the party who is innocent of the defect has a choice of actions. He may avoid the contract (in which case neither party has any liability under it for the future) or he may affirm it (in which case the contract continues to bind both parties). The contract, however, is valid and enforceable unless and until it is avoided.

Contracts entered into following a misrepresentation are voidable as are contracts entered into under duress. If a person has been induced by a misrepresentation to make a contract, therefore, he has the option of either avoiding the contract, in which case he is released from any future liabilities under it, or of affirming it, in which case the contract continues to operate despite the misrepresentation. There are, however, limits on the rights to avoid. For example, if, before steps are taken to set the contract aside, an innocent third party acquires an interest in the subject matter of the contract, the right to avoid will have been lost.

9.1.3 Void contracts

A void contract is really no contract at all. Because of some basic flaw in the agreement, neither party has any rights or liabilities under it. Such an agreement cannot be enforced by action. Contracts made under an operative mistake will be void as will those which are illegal, that is which involve the performance of something forbidden by common law or statute or which are contrary to public policy.

Contracts entered into by a corporate body and which are outside that body's powers will also be void. The corporate body will have acted *ultra vires*.

9.2 MISREPRESENTATION

9.2.1 Introduction

In the course of negotiations leading to the making of a contract, one of the parties may make a statement which is designed to and does induce the other to enter the agreement. Some of these statements may be incorporated into the contract and thus become contractual terms (see Chapter 8). In this case, if the statement turns out to be false, the innocent party will have a right to sue the maker of the statement (the representor) in breach of contract.

Other pre-contractual statements may be held to form the basis of a collateral contract (see Chapter 8). In return for the representor promising that what he says is true, the person to whom the statement is made (the representee) enters the main contract. If the statement turns out to be untrue, the representee will have a right of action in breach of the collateral contract.

If, however, the pre-contractual statement is not incorporated into either the main contract or a collateral contract, it will be treated as a mere representation and, if it is untrue, (ie a misrepresentation), the representee's remedy will lie, not in breach of contract, but rather in misrepresentation.

A misrepresentation, therefore, is a false statement of fact which, although it induces a person to enter the contract, is not part of the contract itself. A misrepresentation may be either fraudulent, negligent or purely innocent.

9.2.2 What constitutes a misrepresentation?

As we said in the last section, a misrepresentation is a false statement of fact which induces the representee to enter a contract. For a representation to be actionable, therefore, the following points must be satisfied.

THE STATEMENT MUST BE MORE THAN MERE SALES TALK

Words which no reasonable person would take as being factual will not be misrepresentations eg 'This car is the finest in the world'. These are words which could not be taken as having a factual basis. They are mere sales talk and no reasonable person would rely on them in entering the contract. They would not be actionable by the representee.

THE STATEMENT MUST BE ONE OF FACT NOT LAW

To be actionable as a misrepresentation, a statement must be of fact, not law. So, for example, if S persuades B to buy goods for cash by telling him that the law does not permit the sale of such items on credit, this will be a statement of law and, even if it is incorrect, it will not be an actionable misrepresentation.

THE STATEMENT MUST BE ONE OF FACT NOT OPINION

The statement must be capable of being true or false when it is made. A mere opinion by the representor cannot therefore be a representation. This was shown in the case of:

Bisset v Wilkinson (1927)

The seller of a farm in New Zealand told the prospective purchaser that, in his opinion, the land would support 2,000 sheep. Both the vendor and the purchaser of the farm knew that it had never been used to rear sheep. The land was not capable of supporting this number of sheep. The court held that the statement was one of opinion and therefore did not amount to a representation.

If however, the statement of opinion contains an element of fact and the person making the statement, who knows the facts best, does not hold the opinion or has no reasonable grounds for claiming to hold it, there will be a misrepresentation if the opinion is unfounded. For example, in the case of:

***Smith v Land and House Property Corporation* (1884)**

The seller of a hotel described it as let to 'Mr Flack, a most desirable tenant'. In fact, Mr Flack paid his rent only occasionally and under pressure. The court held that the seller's statement was not just a mere statement of opinion. It was an actionable misrepresentation. The seller was impliedly stating that he knew facts which justified his opinion.

An apparent statement of opinion will also be treated as a statement of fact where the representor is in a position to have expert knowledge about the circumstances of the claim. This was shown in:

***Esso Petroleum Co Ltd v Mardon* (1976)**

In this case, Esso was opening a new garage. M was considering taking the tenancy on the garage, and was told by Esso that he would sell 200,000 gallons of petrol from the site over a three year period. M doubted this, but when he questioned Esso's estimate, he was assured that it was accurate. M took the tenancy but when he found that he did not sell the quantity of petrol estimated by Esso he sued the company in misrepresentation. Esso claimed that the estimate was a mere opinion, but the Court of Appeal held that, as Esso were experts in this field, they could be taken to have based their estimate on accurate facts. The company was therefore liable in misrepresentation.

THE STATEMENT MUST NOT MERELY BE ONE OF INTENTION

If the statement is merely a declaration of future intention by the person making it, it is not capable of being true or false at the time it is made and will not therefore be an actionable misrepresentation if, later, the intention is not put into effect. If, however, at the time he makes the statement, the representor has no such intention at all, it will be an actionable misrepresentation. This is illustrated in the case of:

***Edgington v Fitzmaurice* (1885)**

The directors of a company invited the public to lend money to the firm stating that the sums raised would be used to improve the company's premises and to extend its operations. In fact, the directors' real intention in raising the loan was to pay off the company's existing debts. The court held that the directors had made a misrepresentation. They had claimed to have an intention which was, at the time of the statement totally untrue. The statement of their present intention was a statement of fact. As the judge hearing the case, Bowen L J said:

'... the state of a man's mind is as much a fact as the state of his digestion.'

THE STATEMENT MUST BE UNTRUE

The statement can take any form; it may be oral, or in writing or even by conduct, as where the representor dresses up, for example, as a policeman and thus obtains credit. It must however be untrue to constitute a misrepresentation.

SILENCE CANNOT, IN GENERAL, CONSTITUTE MISREPRESENTATION

As a general rule, there must be some active misleading by the representor. Merely keeping quiet will not constitute misrepresentation. For example, in the case of:

***Fletcher v Krell* (1873)**

A woman who applied for and obtained the post of governess was held not liable in misrepresentation merely because she did not reveal that she had been divorced (in the 19th century, such a fact would have disqualified her from this appointment).

In certain circumstances, however, silence will constitute misrepresentation. This will occur in the following cases:

1. Where there is a change of circumstances
   If a statement, although true when made, later becomes untrue before the contract is entered into, the representor must tell the representee of the change in circumstances. If he does not do so, he will be liable in misrepresentation. This is shown in the case of:

***With v O'Flanagan* (1936)**

The defendant was selling his medical practice. The plaintiff entered into negotiations in the January. At the time, the practice was worth £2,000 and the plaintiff was told this. Before the actual sale occurred, however, the doctor fell ill and the practice became virtually worthless. He did not tell the plaintiff of this change. The court held that the defendant's silence in these circumstances amounted to misrepresentation.

2 Where the statement is a half-truth
Although what the representor says is true, what he leaves unsaid may be a misrepresentation if it would alter the effect and meaning of the statement made. For example, in the case of:

***Nottingham Patent Brick and Tile Co* v *Butler* (1886)**

The prospective purchasers of a piece of land asked the vendor's solicitor whether the property was subject to a restrictive covenant. The solicitor said that he was not aware of any. He was telling the truth because he had not read the relevant documents. He did not disclose this fact to the prospective purchasers, who decided to buy the land. When the purchasers discovered that, in fact, there were restrictive covenants over the land they brought an action to rescind the contract. The court held that, although what the solicitor had said was true, what he had left unsaid altered the effect of his statement. The purchasers, therefore, were entitled to rescind the contract for misrepresentation.

3 Where there is a fiduciary relationship between the parties
In certain relationships, there is a duty to make full disclosure. Some relationships, such as parent and child, require more than full disclosure (see section 4 of this Chapter) but in others, the fiduciary duty is limited to a duty to make full disclosure.
   Such relationships include contracts between principals and agents; between partners; and between the promoters of a company and the company itself.

4 Where the contract is of the utmost good faith
Contracts *uberrimae fidei* (of the utmost good faith) require a full disclosure of all material facts. Failure to disclose such a fact would make the contract voidable. These are contracts in which one of the parties is in a much better position than the other to know the relevant facts and so must disclose these facts before the contract is made. The main examples of contracts of the utmost good faith are:

(a) Contracts of insurance.
   The insured, being in possession of all facts relevant to the proposed insurance, must disclose these facts to the insurer before the contract of insurance is made. Material facts in this context are those which would influence the mind of the prudent insurer in deciding whether to give insurance and if so, at what premium. Thus, any facts relevant to the insurance must be disclosed even if the insurer does not specifically ask for the information. For example, if A wanted to insure his house against fire, he would have to disclose that he had been convicted of arson in the past, even if this question was not on the proposal form. This fact would influence the insurer in deciding whether or not to insure and, if so, at what premium.
      If the insured does not disclose a material fact, the insurance company may avoid the contract, even though the undisclosed information is not the cause of any loss which occurs.

(b) Contracts of family arrangement.
   In contracts between members of the same family, for example, to settle property on the children, all facts must be disclosed. Failure to be completely frank will result in the agreement being voidable at the instance of the party harmed. For example:

***Gordon* v *Gordon* (1821)**

Two brothers agreed to divide the family estate. The division was made on the basis of the elder brother's mistaken belief that he was illegitimate. The younger brother knew that his brother was legitimate but said nothing.
   Nineteen years after the division of the estate the elder brother discovered the truth and, in a subsequent action, the court held that the agreement should be set aside.

(c) Contracts of guarantee and partnership.
   Although neither of these contracts is of the utmost good faith while they are being formed, once they have been made they become *uberrima fides*. Thus, for example, once a

partnership has been formed, each partner owes a duty to his fellow partners to make full disclosure of all material facts in his dealings with them.
- **(d)** Contracts for the sale of land.
  There is a duty on the seller of land to disclose all defects in his title to the property.
- **(e)** Contracts to subscribe for shares in a company.
  Promoters of a company have a duty to make full disclosure of all material facts in any prospectuses which invite the public to subscribe for shares. If full disclosure is not made, the resulting contracts are voidable.

5   In cases of concealed fraud. In:

Gordon v Selico Co Limited (1986)

The case concerned a sale of a flat within a block of flats which had been conveyed by a developer to G on a 99-year lease. Shortly after moving in he discovered dry rot.

It was held by the Court of Appeal that the deliberate concealment by the developer of the existence of dry rot constituted a fraudulent misrepresentation for which G could recover damages.

THERE MUST BE RELIANCE ON THE MISREPRESENTATION

However false a pre-contractual statement may be, the representee will have no right of action unless he relied on the statement in entering the contract, that is, unless it induced him to make the contract. In other words, the representee cannot avoid the contract if it can be shown that he knew that the representation was untrue, or that he was unaware of the representation in the first place, or if he or his agent made their own investigations to test the statement's truth. For example:

Horsfall v Thomas (1862)

The buyer of a gun did not examine it before he bought. A defect in the gun had been concealed but, as he had not examined the weapon, this concealment had not affected his decision to purchase. The court held that there was no misrepresentation.

Note the case of:

Attwood v Small (1838)

The sellers of some mines and iron works made certain claims about the undertaking's earning capacity. The prospective purchasers employed their own experienced agents to check the truth of these claims. The agents confirmed the sellers' claims and the sale was completed. Six months later, however, the purchasers discovered that the claims had been exaggerated and tried to have the contract rescinded for misrepresentation.

The court held that, as the purchasers had not relied on the sellers' answers they could not claim to have been induced by them. The action for rescission, therefore, failed.

If, however, the representee is given the chance of checking the truth of the statement but does not do so, he does not lose his right to claim rescission. This was shown in the case of:

Redgrave v Hurd (1881)

The plaintiff, a solicitor, advertised for a partner who would also buy his house. When the defendant answered his advertisement the plaintiff claimed that the practice earned about £300 a year and offered the defendant various accounts to examine. The defendant did not examine them. Had he done so he would have discovered that the practice was worthless. The defendant agreed to enter the partnership and to buy the house but, when he discovered the true position he refused to complete the purchase. The plaintiff sued him but the Court of Appeal held that the action should fail. The misstatement was a misrepresentation as the defendant had entered the contract in reliance on it. The fact that he had rejected the opportunity to discover its truth was irrelevant.

So, as long as the representee relies on the statement in entering the contract, he will have an action in misrepresentation if it later turns out that the statement was untrue. This is the position even if the misstatement is only one of the factors persuading the representee to enter the contract. In other words, to give him a right in misrepresentation, the misstatement does not have to be the only reason why the representee made the transaction. This is illustrated in the case of:

Edgington v Fitzmaurice (1885) (see above)

The plaintiff took debentures in the company, partly because of the misstatement in the prospectus as to how the money was to be used but also because he wrongly believed that debenture holders would obtain a charge on the company's property. This belief was due to his own mistake and, he admitted, he would not have sent the money but for this belief.

Despite this, the court held that he could claim the misstatement in the prospectus as a misrepresentation entitling him to set the contract aside. It was one of the factors which induced him to lend the money to the company.

9.2.3 Types of misrepresentation

INTRODUCTION

There are three types of misrepresentation—fraudulent, negligent and wholly innocent. A fraudulent misrepresentation is one made either in the knowledge that it is false or reckless. If the misrepresentation is not fraudulent it is presumed to be negligent unless the representor can show that he did believe and had reasonable grounds for believing in the truth of his statement. If he can do this, the representation will be wholly innocent.

As we shall see, the importance of the distinction lies in the remedies available for each type. Although the innocent party can avoid the contract whatever type of misrepresentation is involved, he has a right to damages only if the misstatement was made fraudulently or negligently. Furthermore, the basis of this claim differs depending on the nature of the misrepresentation.

In this section we will look at the different types of misrepresentation and, in the next section, at the remedies available for each.

FRAUDULENT MISREPRESENTATION

A fraudulent misrepresentation is a false statement of fact made by a representor who either knows it is false, or makes it without believing it to be true, or makes it recklessly, careless whether it is true or false. All other misrepresentations are innocent.

This definition of fraudulent misrepresentation was given in the case of:

Derry v Peek (1889)

A company was permitted by Act of Parliament to operate horse-drawn tramcars in Plymouth. The Act also provided that, subject to Board of Trade approval, the company could also operate steam-powered tramcars in Plymouth. The directors of the company, believing that the Board of Trade's approval was a mere formality, issued a prospectus stating that the company had a right to use steam-powered tramcars. Shares in the company were bought in reliance on the prospectus. The Board of Trade later refused permission to the company to use steam-powered tramcars and the company was wound up. Many investors lost money and sued the directors in the tort of deceit.

The House of Lords held that, as the directors genuinely believed that the Board's consent was a mere formality, they were inaccurate but not dishonest. Inaccuracy cannot amount to fraud.

So, fraudulent misrepresentation will occur when the representor lies, or where he is grossly careless or deliberately does not make an investigation because he, in effect, knows what he would discover and chooses not to do so.

If there is a fraudulent misrepresentation, the representee may avoid the contract and/or claim damages in the tort of deceit. We will deal with these remedies in the next section.

NEGLIGENT MISREPRESENTATION

If the representor is not fraudulent, he is presumed to be negligent. In other words, if there is no fraud involved in the misstatement there is an automatic assumption that it was made in the belief that it was true but without reasonable care being taken to discover whether it was in fact true.

The burden of proof then shifts to the representor to show that he did believe and had reasonable grounds for believing in the truth of his statement. If he can do this, the representation will be wholly innocent.

An expert must verify statements which he makes in a proper professional manner. On the other hand, a person without expert knowledge may rely on the apparent expertise of a person who may be expected to have this information. For example in:

***Humming Bird Motors v Hobbs* (1986)**

Hobbs was a young man who occasionally bought and sold motor cars not so much as a business but as more of a sideline. He bought a car from a dealer who told him that its recorded mileage was 34,900 miles. Hobbs then sold it to the plaintiffs and in all innocence assured them that the mileage was accurate. It turned out that the car had done over 80,000 miles. The plaintiffs tried to recover damages for negligent misrepresentation. The Court of Appeal, however, held that Hobbs had not been negligent. He was no more than an amateur repeating what he had been told by an expert. Thus he had reasonable grounds for making the statement which he had.

This type of misrepresentation was introduced by s2(1) Misrepresentation Act 1967. The remedies available to the representee are to avoid the contract and/or claim damages under the 1967 Act. Damages may also be available under the tort of negligence. We will deal with these remedies in the next part of this Chapter.

WHOLLY INNOCENT MISREPRESENTATION

If the representor can show that he did believe and that he had reasonable grounds for believing in the truth of what he was saying, the misrepresentation will be wholly innocent. In this case, the representee may avoid the contract but he has no right to damages. By s2(2) Misrepresentation Act 1967, however, in cases of wholly innocent misrepresentation, the *court* has the discretion to award damages instead of rescission. That is, the court may consider that, in the circumstances, the contract should be allowed to continue and the representee compensated by an award of damages. It must be stressed, however, that this is entirely at the court's discretion. There is no right in the representee to claim damages for wholly innocent misrepresentation.

9.2.4 Remedies for misrepresentation

INTRODUCTION

The remedy available for all types of misrepresentation is, as we have seen, for the representee to avoid the contract. He may also apply to the court for the formal order of rescission. In the case of fraudulent and negligent misrepresentation he will also be entitled to damages. In the case of innocent misrepresentation damages may be awarded instead of rescission.

We will deal with each of these remedies in turn.

TO AVOID THE CONTRACT

In all cases of misrepresentation, the innocent party may avoid the contract. In other words, misrepresentation makes the ensuing contract voidable.

The representee will have several courses of action which he may take:

1. If he decides that, despite the misrepresentation, the contract operates to his advantage, the innocent party may decide to enforce it. Being voidable, the contract is valid and enforceable unless and until it is avoided. The representee therefore may choose the course of action which best suits him.
2. If he decides that he does not wish to be bound by the contract because of misrepresentation, the representee may simply refuse to perform his side of the bargain and, if the other party sues him in breach, he will plead the misrepresentation as a defence.
3. Alternatively, if he wishes to avoid the contract, the representee may give notice by words or conduct to the representor, telling him that the contract is being set aside.

    The effect of the notice, assuming that there is good cause to repudiate, is that the contract is thereupon cancelled. You will recall that, unless and until it is avoided, a voidable contract is valid and enforceable. So, for example, if a buyer misrepresents his identity in order to induce a seller to allow him to pay for goods by means of a cheque and to take the goods away before the cheque is cleared, the buyer will have a voidable title. In other words, he will have a valid title which the seller may avoid by informing the buyer that the contract is being set aside. If the cheque is dishonoured, the seller may avoid the contract and recover the goods. If, however, before the transaction is set aside the buyer sells the goods to an innocent purchaser, that purchaser will obtain good title. He had bought from a person who himself had a good title which had not yet been avoided.

4   If the representor is a rogue, of course, the representee may find it difficult to inform him that the contract is being avoided. In these circumstances, the contract may be avoided by the representee doing everything necessary in the circumstances to show that he is setting the contract aside.

For example:

Car and Universal Finance Co v Caldwell (1965)

A seller was induced by the fraud of the buyer to sell him a car, to accept payment by cheque, and to allow the buyer to take the car away before the cheque was cleared. The cheque was dishonoured and, because he could not find the rogue, the seller told the police and the Automobile Association, asking them to find the car. Later, the rogue sold the car. It was held by the court that the seller had done all he could in the circumstances to avoid the contract and that it had therefore been avoided before the rogue sold it to the third party. So the seller was able to recover his vehicle.

RESCISSION

Instead of, or as well as, giving notice of the fact that he is avoiding the contract, the representee may apply to the court for an order of rescission. Such an order means that the court formally cancels the contract. The parties are put in the position they were in before the contract was made—it is as if they had never entered the contract in the first place. There must be a 'giving back and taking back' on both sides.

Rescission is an equitable remedy and is therefore granted at the court's discretion. There is no right to an order of rescission and the right to rescind will be lost in certain circumstances.

THE RIGHT TO RESCIND IS LOST:

1   When the innocent party affirms the contract. If the representee carries on with the contract, or takes no steps to rescind it, after he discovers the misrepresentation, he will be denied an order of rescission. By not taking action he has impliedly affirmed the contract. He may also expressly affirm it by telling the representor that he is continuing with the transaction.

2   When there is an unreasonable lapse of time. The representee must act swiftly to rescind the contract. In the case of fraudulent misrepresentation time starts running from the discovery of the fraud, but in the case of any non-fraudulent misrepresentation the time will run from the date of the contract. In other words, if the misrepresentation is innocent and the representee does not discover it until some time after the contract, he may find that he has lost his right to rescind. This was illustrated in the case of:

Leaf v International Galleries (1950)

The seller innocently misrepresented a picture as having been painted by John Constable. The buyer discovered the truth five years after the sale and immediately brought an action to have the contract rescinded. The court held that it was too late to rescind. Although there was no evidence of affirmation, as the buyer had only just discovered the misrepresentation, he had lost his right to rescind because of lapse of time.

3   When restitution is impossible. Rescission requires a giving back and taking back on both sides. This is known as *restitutio in integrum*. If, therefore, it is not possible to restore the parties substantially to their original positions rescission will not be permitted. There does not have to be precise restoration. For example, the fact that goods bought following a misrepresentation have been used or have deteriorated will not stop the court granting rescission. If, however, the goods have been used to the point of being totally useless this will stop the order being made.

For example:

Vigers v Pike (1842)

A company bought and partly paid for the lease of a mine. The contract had been made following a misrepresentation by the owners of the property, but by the time the company brought an action for rescission for misrepresentation the mine had been substantially worked. The court held that, as the parties could not be substantially restored to their original positions (the mine by now being virtually valueless) an order of rescission would not be granted.

In the case of fraudulent misrepresentation, however, the representee need only hand back what he has received under the contract if he himself sues for rescission. If he does nothing, but waits for the representor to sue him in breach of contract, he can claim the fraud as a defence *and* keep what he obtained under the contract. There does not have to be restitution on his side. So, for example, if a contract of insurance was obtained following a fraudulent misrepresentation by the insured, the insurance company could refuse to pay out on a claim under the policy, and wait for the insured to sue the company in breach of contract. The insurers would have a good defence because of the insured's fraud *and* would be able to keep all the premiums he had already paid. If, unusually, the insurance company sued the insured to have the contract rescinded, it would then risk being required to return all the instalments paid.

4   When a third party has acquired an interest in the property. As long as this third party has acted in good faith and for value, he will obtain good title to the property and the representee will have lost the right to rescind. This is because, as we said earlier, until a voidable contract is avoided it is valid and enforceable and therefore the person with such good title can pass good title to an innocent purchaser.

5   When the court considers that damages would be more appropriate. Under s2(2) Misrepresentation Act 1967, the court has the power to decide that it would be more equitable to award damages instead of rescission in cases of non-fraudulent misrepresentation. If the court makes this decision, an order of rescission will be refused and the contract will continue to operate. This discretion of the court may be exercised only in cases of negligent or wholly innocent misrepresentation. In relation to negligent misrepresentation these damages may be claimed in addition to the statutory or common law damages (see the next section of this Chapter) but in assessing the amount of these damages the amount granted under s2(2) will be taken into account.

In relation to wholly innocent misrepresentation the damages awarded instead of rescission are the only compensation the representee will receive. If the right to rescind has been lost, the court's power to award damages instead is also lost.

An illustration of the court's decision to award damages in the place of rescission occurred in the case of:

Gosling v Anderson (1972)

The plaintiff bought a flat from the defendant. Before the sale, the plaintiff had said that she would buy only if she could have a garage built and the defendant's agent had told her that planning permission for garages had been granted. The agent honestly believed that this was true although in fact he was wrong. The court held that the plaintiff was entitled to damages instead of rescission. This, said the court, was the equitable solution to the case.

The representee may request an order of rescission either as well as, or instead of, taking his own steps to avoid the contract. If he is granted the order, this will, of course, mean that the contract is avoided. If, however, the representee has already avoided the agreement he may still ask the court to order rescission if he is finding it difficult to recover his property or money from the representor. In making the order to rescind, the court will also order the representee to give back the benefits he has received.

An order of rescission has two further advantages:

1   It will formally release the representee from any further liability, for example, from liability for future calls on shares, if the contract which has been induced following the misrepresentation was one for the purchase of shares in a company.

2   It will enable the representee to recover compensation for any money he has *necessarily* spent under obligations imposed on him by the contract. This is not a claim for damages, but rather an indemnity for all the expenses necessarily incurred in the performance of the contract; expenses which had to be met under the agreement.

This point is illustrated in the case of:

Whittington v Seale-Hayne (1900)

The plaintiff took a lease of property after the defendant's agent had assured him that the premises were in a sanitary condition and in a good state of repair. The plaintiff established a poultry farm on the property. It was later discovered that the premises were very insanitary and the water supply was poisoned. As a result, most of the poultry died and the plaintiff's manager became seriously ill and had to receive hospital treatment. Furthermore, the local authority declared the premises unfit for human habitation and ordered the plaintiff to repair the drains. As he was required under the lease to do any repairs or work required by the local authority, the plaintiff carried out the necessary work.

The plaintiff then sought an order for rescission of the contract on the grounds of the agent's misrepresentation. The plaintiff claimed compensation for:

(a) the value of the stock he had lost.
(b) the cost of his manager's medical treatment.
(c) loss of profits.
(d) rent.
(e) rates.
(f) cost of the repairs ordered by the local authority.

The court held that he was entitled to be indemnified only for those expenses necessarily incurred in his performance of the contract ie the rent, rates and cost of necessary repairs. Although the rest of his losses resulted from the contract, they were not necessarily incurred under it. The plaintiff did not have to bring poultry or a manager onto the premises, but he did have to pay the rent etc.

DAMAGES

The representee will have a right to an action in damages for both fraudulent and negligent misrepresentation. As we have already mentioned, there is no right to damages for wholly innocent misrepresentation but the court may award damages instead of rescission under the Misrepresentation Act 1967, s2(2).

1 Damages for fraudulent misrepresentation
When the representee has entered a contract following a fraudulent misrepresentation, he will have a right to avoid the contract and to claim damages in the tort of deceit. ('Deceit' is another word for 'fraud' in tort). This right to damages is generally available whether the injured party has repudiated or affirmed the contract, but he must prove that he has suffered actual loss as a result of the misrepresentation. If, however, the contract was for the subscription of shares in a company, the innocent party may claim damages only if he rescinds the contract.

As the action is in tort, the amount of damages will be all the loss flowing from the breach. This may be much wider in scope than the measure of damages in contract. For example:

Doyle v Olby (Ironmongers) Ltd (1969)

Following fraudulent misrepresentations made by the vendor, the plaintiff purchased an ironmonger's business. When he discovered the fraud he sued in damages. His damages were assessed as covering all the loss flowing from the breach, including the reasonable expenses he incurred in running the business. The court calculated the sum according to tortious rather than contractual rules.

2 Damages for negligent misrepresentation
A representee who has entered a contract following a negligent misrepresentation may sue for damages either at common law or under s2(1) Misrepresentation Act 1967.
(a) Damages at common law.
The right to claim damages at common law for a negligent misrepresentation is based on an obiter of the House of Lords in the case of *Hedley Byrne & Co Ltd v Heller & Partners Ltd* (1964) (the facts of which are not relevant here). The Lords said that, if, in the course of business and in response to a request, a person gives advice or information in circumstances where a reasonable man would know that such advice or information could be relied upon, a duty of care is imposed on this person to take reasonable care to ensure the advice etc is accurate. If he fails to do so and damage is thereby suffered by the representee, the representee will have a right of action for damages.

The Hedley Byrne principle was applied to pre-contractual misstatements in the case of *Esso Petroleum Co Ltd v Mardon* (1975) (see above 9.2.2) in which it was held that a duty of care will arise when, in pre-contractual negotiations, one party with relevant special knowledge or expertise makes a statement to the other party who lacks this special knowledge or expertise. If this statement is wrong and is made negligently and induces the representee to enter the contract with the 'expert', the expert will be liable to an action in the tort of negligence.

The advantages of an action in negligence as opposed to one brought under the 1967 Act are that in the common law action the plaintiff does not have to show that a contract was entered into with the misrepresentor (which he has to prove in an action under the 1967 Act). The burden of proof is on the plaintiff to show that, because of the special relationship between him and the defendant, there is a duty of care and that this duty has been broken and has resulted in financial loss to the plaintiff.

(b) Damages by statute.

A person who has entered a contract following a negligent misrepresentation may have an action under the Misrepresentation Act 1967, s2(1). The burden of proof is on the defendant to show that he did believe and had reasonable grounds for believing in the truth of what he was saying. Only if this can be shown will the claim for damages fail. Compare this with the action at common law where the duty is on the plaintiff to show a duty of care and breach of that duty with damage resulting.

See the case of *Gosling* v *Anderson* (1972) (above). The right of action under s2(1), however, is available only to a person who has entered into a contract with the misrepresentor.

9.2.5 Exclusion of liability for misrepresentation

By the Misrepresentation Act 1967, s3, as amended by the Unfair Contract Terms Act 1977, any attempt to exclude liability for misrepresentation must be justified as being reasonable by the person relying on the exclusion.

Such an exclusion could not be justified as being reasonable in relation to fraudulent misrepresentation. In the case of innocent (ie non-fraudulent) misrepresentations the question of reasonableness depends on the facts of each particular case.

9.3 MISTAKE

9.3.1 Introduction

If either or both of the parties have made a mistake when they enter the contract and the mistake is such that there is no real agreement, the contract will be void. Not every mistake will have this effect. As we shall see, a mistake as to the quality of the subject matter will have no effect on the contract nor, in general, will a mistake as to the value of the goods, services etc being bought. To make a contract void, the mistake must be an operative mistake. That is, a mistake recognised by the law as, in effect, preventing the parties reaching true agreement.

What is referred to as an operative mistake is one which goes to the root of the contract and which means that, although the parties are apparently in agreement, they are in reality at cross-purposes. There is no real consent. At common law, the genereal rule is that mistake does not affect the contract. The situations where it does have this effect are exceptions to this rule. Equity, however, will give some relief in cases where the parties have contracted under a mistake but can obtain no remedy at common law. Mistake, in fact, provides a good example of the way in which Equity provides a gloss on the common law by giving a remedy where none exists at law.

In this section we will look firstly at the general rule that mistake does not affect a contract. We will then look at the exceptions to this rule ie at those mistakes which will render a contract void. These may be categorised as common, mutual and unilateral mistakes and mistake as to the nature of the document signed. Finally we will examine the relief granted by Equity to parties who have contracted under a mistake.

9.3.2 Mistakes which do not affect a contract

As we said in the introduction to this section, the majority of mistakes will not affect a contract. Even though either or both of the parties have entered the agreement under a mistake as to some matter, the general rule of common law is that the contract will be enforced on the terms upon which apparent agreement has been reached.

For example, the general rule of common law is *caveat emptor*. This means 'let the buyer beware'. It is up to the buyer to ensure that he is obtaining the bargain he wants. He must protect himself. So, if a person agrees to buy a painting, thinking it is by a famous artist, but later discovers that he has made a mistake and has in fact paid ten-times what the painting is worth he will have no remedy at all! (unless of course the seller has in some way misled him). The principle of *caveat emptor* will apply. The mistake the buyer has made is not an operative mistake. In the eyes of the law it would not go to the root of the agreement in such a way as to render that agreement void.

An illustration of this reluctance of the courts to find an operative mistake occurs in the case of:

Bell v Lever Bros Ltd (1932)

B was the chairman of the board of a company controlled by L. B was made redundant when the company was amalgamated with another firm and he was paid £30,000 compensation. Later, however, L discovered that B had committed breaches of duty (by making secret profits out of the company's transactions) and could have been dismissed without receiving any compensation at all. L therefore brought an action against B to recover the £30,000 claiming that it had been paid under a mistake.

The court held that the contract was not void for mistake. L had obtained what they had bargained for—the release from B's contract of employment. They had wanted to end B's contract and had ended it. The fact that they were in error as to whether or not they had to pay to obtain this release was a question of quality not substance. It did not affect the basic agreement reached.

So, errors of judgment will not constitute operative mistake. Further, mistakes of law (as opposed to fact) will not affect the contract.

This is shown in the case of:

Sharp Bros and Knight v Chant (1917)

It was agreed by the landlord and tenant that the rent of the property let should be increased by 6d per week. The tenant paid this increased rent for a time and then discovered that under rent restriction regulations the landlord had had no right to make the increase. The court held that the payment had been made under a mistake of law. This was therefore not an operative mistake and the rent could not be recovered by the tenant. The payments already made could be kept by the landlord.

Having established that, in general, mistake does not affect a contract, we will now examine the cases which provide an exception to this rule ie those instances where the law will regard a mistake as operative. In these cases, the contract will be treated as absolutely void and no rights of ownership will pass. The transferor of any property under such a contract will be able to recover it. As we said, there are four kinds of operative mistake—common, mutual, unilateral and as to the nature of the document signed.

9.3.3 Common mistake

This arises where an agreement has been reached but both parties have made the same mistake as to the subject matter of the contract. This mistake must go to the root of the contract to be operative. As a general rule, such a mistake will have no effect on the contract. Both parties will be bound. For example, in the case of:

Leaf v International Galleries (1950) (see 9.2.4)

Although both the seller and the buyer of the painting wrongly believed that it had been painted by Constable this was not sufficient to constitute an operative common mistake. The buyer's only remedy would be for misrepresentation but, as you will remember, the fact that he discovered the error five years after the sale meant that he had lost his right to repudiate.

The Common Law, however, does recognise certain categories of common mistake as affecting a contract. These are:

COMMON MISTAKE AS TO THE EXISTENCE OF THE SUBJECT MATTER

If, at the time of the contract, the subject matter does not exist, because, for example, it has perished, the contract will be void for common mistake. The contract is said to be for *res extincta*. For example, A agrees to sell B a car. Unknown to both parties, the car had been destroyed by fire before the contract was made. This is an example of *res extincta* and the contract will be void, provided neither party is to blame for the destruction. This is illustrated in the case of:

Couturier v Hastie (1856)

A cargo of corn was being shipped to the United Kingdom. The bill of lading (the document issued when the goods are loaded on board ship and which is taken to represent the goods and to enable the person holding it to deal with the goods) was sent overland and, using it, the seller's agent sold the goods to the buyer. Unknown to both parties, the corn had become overheated and the captain had put into an intermediate port and had sold the cargo. In other words, at the time the contract for the sale of the corn had been made, it had in fact already been sold and had therefore ceased to exist for the purposes of the contract of sale made in the United Kingdom. The House of Lords held that there was no contract.

This situation is now covered by s6 Sale of Goods Act 1979 which provides that, where there is a contract for the sale of specific goods but, at the time of the contract and unknown to either the buyer or the seller the goods have perished, the contract is void.

A recent decision on common mistake was:

Associated Japanese Bank (International) Limited v Credit du Nord FA (1988)

Jack Bennett entered into a contract to sell four machines to the plaintiff's bank and then lease them back from it. For this he was to be paid £1m. The defendant bank guaranteed the transaction. Obviously both banks believed that the machines actually existed. Bennett did not own the machines. He failed to keep up the payments under the lease and the plaintiff bank claimed the outstanding balance from the defendant. The defendant refused to pay claiming that the guarantee was subject to either an express or implied condition precedent that the machines were in existence and that accordingly the guarantee was void for common mistake.

It was held that the guarantee was indeed subject to an express condition precedent as to the existence of the machines. Thus since the machines did not exist, the plaintiff bank's claim had to fail and must therefore be dismissed. A contract is void *ab initio* for common mistake if a mistake by both parties to the contract renders the subject matter of the contract significantly different from that which both parties believed at the time the contract was executed.

COMMON MISTAKE AS TO THE EXISTENCE OF A STATE OF AFFAIRS

If a contract is entered into on the basis of a state of affairs which has either never existed or has ceased to exist, the contract will be void for common mistake. For example:

Strickland v Turner (1852)

There was a contract for the sale of an annuity on the life of a person who was, in fact, dead at the time the contract was made. The court held that the contract was void for mistake.

Again, in the case of:

Galloway v Galloway (1914)

A man and woman entered into a deed of separation. It was later discovered that, in fact, the couple had never been validly married. The court held that the separation agreement was void as it had been made on the basis of a state of affairs which had never existed.

COMMON MISTAKE AS TO THE OWNERSHIP OF PROPERTY

This will arise when a person contracts to buy property which, unknown to both him and the seller, already belongs to the buyer. This is known as a case of *res sua* (literally: 'his own thing'). Such a situation arose in:

***Cooper v Phibbs* (1867)**

C agreed to take the lease of a fishery from P. Unknown to both parties, however, C already owned the fishery. When he discovered the true state of affairs, C brought an action to have the lease set aside.

The court held that the contract was void for common mistake. It is not possible in law for a person to contract to acquire property which already belongs to him.

9.3.4 Mutual mistake

This arises where both parties are mistaken but each has made a different mistake.

For example, A offers to sell his car to B. A has two cars. He is offering to sell car 1, B accepts thinking A means car 2. Outwardly there is agreement but genuine consent is lacking.

In these circumstances, the court will ask itself what a reasonable third party would make of these negotiations. If, objectively, it would appear that a reasonable person would take the contract as meaning what A intended it to mean, it will be enforced on those terms. If B's understanding of the agreement is, objectively, more reasonable, the contract will be taken to mean what B thought it meant.

In the above example, if car 1 was a brand new Rolls Royce and car 2 a ten year old Ford Escort and A said to B 'I will sell you my car for £100' (meaning car 2), and if B accepted, thinking A meant the Rolls Royce, the court would decide what a reasonable man would make of these facts. It would decide that, objectively, the contract could be taken to be for the purchase of car 2 and enforce it on those terms. This is shown in the case of:

***Wood v Scarth* (1858)**

The case concerned the granting of a lease of a public house. The defendant, who owned the property, had intended to offer the lease at a rent and to charge the plaintiff a premium of £500 when the lease was taken up. During the negotiations, however, the premium was not mentioned and the plaintiff, unaware of the premium, agreed to take the lease 'on the terms already agreed'. When the defendant discovered the mistake he refused to convey the property. The plaintiff sued.

The court held that, in applying the objective test, it was reasonable for the plaintiff to assume that there was no premium to be payed. A contract had therefore come into existence on the terms understood by the plaintiff. He was entitled to damages for breach.

The court, however, refused to grant specific performance of the contract as this would have been unduly harsh on the defendant.

If, objectively, the court cannot find the sense of the parties' promise, the contract will be void. In effect, no contract will have come into existence as the parties could not be said to have reached agreement. This was held in the case of:

***Raffles v Wichelhaus* (1864)**

The seller agreed to sell the buyer a consignment of cotton to arrive on board the 'SS Peerless from Bombay'. There were two ships called the SS Peerless sailing from Bombay. The one was to sail in the October the other in the December. The buyer thought that the cotton was to be delivered on the October ship, the seller meant the cotton on the December ship. The court held that in these circumstances it was impossible to find the sense of the promise. There were no indications as to whose understanding was correct. The contract, therefore, was void for mutual mistake. Neither party was liable. The whole issue was too uncertain to constitute a contract.

9.3.5 Unilateral mistake

This arises where one of the parties is mistaken as to some fundamental fact concerning the contract and the other party knows, or ought to know, of this mistake. This is illustrated in the case of:

***Legal and General Assurance Society v General Metal Agencies* (1969)**

The plaintiffs, who were the defendants' landlords, served notice of termination of the lease on the defendants. The county court refused to grant the defendants a new lease at it was proved that they had been persistently late in paying the rent.

Some time later, however, the plaintiffs mistakenly sent the defendants a demand for one quarter's rent in advance.

MATTERS AFFECTING THE VALIDITY OF A CONTRACT: CHAPTER NINE

The plaintiff's general manager signed the demand which had been printed in error by the company's computer. The defendants sent a cheque for this rent and, when the cheque was paid into the plaintiff's account, the defendants claimed that a new tenancy had been created by implication. The plaintiffs brought this action to recover possession of the premises.

The court held that the plaintiffs should succeed. The rent demand had been sent and the payment had been accepted by mistake. This mistake was known to the defendants. There had been no intention to create a new tenancy.

If, however, the fact that one of the parties is mistaken is not known to the other, there will be no operative mistake and the contract will be enforced. This was held in the case of:

Higgins (W) Ltd v Northampton Corporation (1927)

The plaintiff agreed to build houses for the defendant at an agreed price. In calculating the price, however, the plaintiff had made a mistake, deducting a certain sum twice. The defendant, believing that the price quoted was correct, entered the contract.

The court held that the contract was valid and binding. Furthermore the court refused to rectify the contract (see later) as rectification is possible only where there is a common, rather than unilateral, mistake. In this case, as there had been no fraud or other misrepresentation, the written agreement had to stand.

There are two main areas in which unilateral most often occurs. These are:

MISTAKE AS TO THE IDENTITY OF THE OTHER PARTY

For such a mistake to be operative and to make the contract void, it has to be shown that:

1. At the time of making the contract, the mistaken party regarded the identity of the other as being of vital importance
2. That he intended to deal with some person other than the one he actually dealt with and took reasonable steps to check on the alleged identity
3. That the other party was aware of all these facts (this point is usually not difficult to prove as the other party is often a rogue).

An illustration of how this operates in practice is shown in the case of:

Cundy v Lindsay (1878)

A person named Blenkarn ordered goods from Lindsay and signed the order in such a way as to make it appear that it came from Blenkiron, a reputable firm which was known to Lindsay. Lindsay sent the goods to Blenkarn. He did not pay for them but sold them to Cundy. Blenkarn was later convicted of fraud. Lindsay sued Cundy for conversion of the goods, claiming that, as Lindsay's contract with the rogue was void for mistake, the rogue had no title, and so no title could have been passed by him to Cundy.

The court held that Lindsay should succeed. Lindsay's contract with the rogue was void for unilateral mistake.

The identity of the rogue must be of vital importance to the mistaken person. The mere fact that a contract is made with someone who claims to be a different person than he actually is, will *not* make the contract void if the mistaken party has not heard of either the rogue or the person the rogue claims to be.

This is the difficulty experienced when a contract is made following face-to-face negotiations. The assumption is that the mistaken party intended to deal with the person in front of him, regardless of that person's actual or alleged identity. The fact that a person may claim to be someone else may make the contract voidable for fraudulent misrepresentation, but it will not be void for unilateral mistake.

The distinction is important, in that if the rogue has a voidable title to goods etc he may pass good title to an innocent purchaser as long as he acts before the original contract is avoided. If, however, the original contract is void for unilateral mistake, the rogue cannot pass any title to another, however innocent that other may be.

In the case of face-to-face negotiations, the courts tend to treat the contract as voidable for fraud but not void for unilateral mistake.

This was shown in the case of:

Lewis v Averay (1971)

L advertised his car for sale. The advertisement was answered by a rogue who claimed to be a television actor, Richard Green. L agreed to sell the car to the rogue who paid by cheque, signed 'R A Green', and who, after producing a pass to Pinewood Studios in the name of Green was allowed to take the car away. The cheque was dishonoured. The rogue sold the car to A, from whom L tried to recover it in this action. The Court of Appeal held that L should fail. The identity of the rogue was not important to L from the point of view of the contract—L would have sold it to anyone prepared to buy, regardless of who they were. The identity was important to him only in relation to the purchaser's ability to perform the contract ie to pay for the car. The contract, therefore, was not void for unilateral mistake. It was merely voidable for fraudulent misrepresentation. As the rogue had sold the car to A before L had avoided the contract, A obtained good title. L's only action now lay against the rogue.

The one case in which, in face-to-face negotiations, the mistaken party showed to the court's satisfaction that the identity of the rogue was of vital importance was that of:

Ingram v Little (1961)

The plaintiffs advertised their car for sale and the advertisement was answered by a rogue. In the course of negotiations the rogue said he wished to pay by cheque at which point the plaintiffs called the whole deal off. The rogue then claimed to be P G M Hutchinson and gave an address which the plaintiffs checked in the telephone directory. Finding a P G M Hutchinson at the address given, the plaintiffs then re-opened negotiations and sold the car to the rogue, accepting payment by cheque and allowing the rogue to take the car away. The cheque was dishonoured. The rogue, however, had already sold the car to the defendant and had disappeared. The plaintiffs sued the defendant for the return of the car, claiming that their original contract with the rogue was void for unilateral mistake. The court held that the plaintiffs should succeed. The identity of the rogue was a matter of importance for the plaintiffs, not just for the question of his credit-worthiness but, on the facts, in the entering of the contract itself.

Ingram v *Little*, however, should be regarded as an exceptional case. The general rule is that, in face-to-face negotiations, the mistaken party is regarded as having intended to deal with whoever is in front of him. At most, his contract with the rogue will be voidable for fraud.

MISTAKE AS TO THE INTENTION OF THE PARTIES

If one of the parties makes a fundamental mistake in stating his intention and the other party either knows, or is taken to know, that this has happened the contract will be void. This was shown in the case of:

Hartog v Colin and Shields (1939)

An offer was made for the sale of hare-skins at a price 'per pound' instead of 'per piece'. This meant that the skins were being sold at a price which was substantially lower than the price such goods would normally fetch. The offer was accepted, despite the fact that the acceptor could not reasonably have supposed that it expressed the offeror's true intention. The court held that the contract was void for mistake. The offeree/acceptor must have known that the offeror had made a mistake.

9.3.6 Mistake as to the nature of the document signed

You will remember from the last chapter that, when a person signs a contract, he is taken to have agreed to all the terms of that contract whether he knows of them or not.

One of the ways in which he can escape from liability is by showing that he made an operative mistake as to the nature of the document signed. This defence is known as a plea of '*non est factum*'—'it is not my deed'. The requirements for a successful plea of *non est factum* were laid down in the case of:

Saunders v Anglia Building Society (1970)

Mrs G signed a document which she was told was a deed of gift of her house to her nephew. She did not read the document before signing but believed what she had been told by the person asking her to sign (a business colleague of her nephew's). In fact, the document was an assignment of Mrs G's leasehold interest in the house to the nephew's business colleague. This colleague later mortgaged the interest to the Anglia Building Society. Mrs G asked for the assignment to be set aside on the grounds that she was mistaken as to the nature of the document signed.

The House of Lords held that the action should fail. Mrs G's case did not satisfy the requirements for a successful plea of *non est factum*. To be successful, the Lords held, it has to be shown that:

1 The signature was induced by a trick or fraud.
2 The document signed is substantially different in nature or character from that which the signer thought he was signing. In *Saunder's* case the document Mrs G thought she was signing would have transferred the house from herself to another (her nephew) and the document she actually signed transferred the house (to the nephew's colleague). There was therefore not a sufficiently substantial difference in nature or character between the two documents to found a plea of *non est factum*.
3 The person signing the document must show that he had not been negligent in doing so.

In effect, the plea of *non est factum* will be available only to a person who, through no fault of his own, is either temporarily or permanently unable to understand the nature of the document he is signing. This inability may be the result of illness, defective education or some disability such as blindness. Even in these cases, it must be shown that the person signing was not negligent in doing so, but had, for example, asked to have the document read to him.

9.3.7 Relief granted by Equity

The rules of common law provide that if a contract is entered into under a mistake it is void; if there is no operative mistake, the contract is valid. There is no middle ground at common law even though, in some cases, the remedy available will be unjust. Equity, as a gloss on the common law, provides remedies to cover this 'middle-ground'.

Having said that, however, it must be noted that, in cases of mistake, Equity generally follows the common law. Thus if a contract is void at common law for common mistake, Equity will not grant an order of specific performance. In cases of mutual mistake, Equity will look for the 'sense of the promise' and enforce the contract accordingly.

The way in which Equity assists parties who have entered a contract under a mistake is in relation to the remedies it provides. These remedies are as follows:

RESCISSION ON TERMS

As we saw in relation to misrepresentation, rescission is an equitable order setting the contract aside. Equity may grant this order, but impose terms on the parties to ensure that each is treated fairly. For example:

Cooper v Phibbs (1867) (see 9.3.3)

The contract to take a lease of the fishery was held void for common mistake. In granting the order of rescission, however, Equity gave the person who wrongly believed that he was the owner a lien over the property for the improvements he had made during the time he believed that he owned it. The actual owner could discharge the lien by compensating this person for the improvements.

Even though an agreement is not regarded as void at common law, however, Equity may still treat it as voidable if this would be a just solution. This occurred in the case of:

Solle v Butcher (1950)

A landlord leased a flat to a tenant at a yearly rent of £250. Both the landlord and tenant believed that the property was not controlled by the Rent Restriction Acts, under which the rent would have been £140. The flat was, in fact, under the control of the Acts but, under this legislation, provided he gave notice before the tenancy commenced, the landlord could have increased the rent by 8% of the cost of any repairs and improvements he had undertaken on the property. He had in fact carried out extensive renovations before he let the premises and 8% of the cost of these would have brought the rent up to the £250 he actually charged. Not believing that the Act applied to the lease, however, no notice had been given by the landlord, and the tenant, discovering that he had been overpaying, sued for the return of the balance of the rent. The landlord counterclaimed for rescission of the lease on the grounds that it was void for mistake.

The court held that, although the parties had been operating under a common mistake of fact it was not an operative mistake at common law. Applying the rules of Equity, however, the court held that the lease would be rescinded. To avoid causing harm to the tenant, however, the court gave him a choice of actions. He could either surrender the lease entirely or remain in the flat as a mere licensee until a new lease had been drawn up. In the meantime, the landlord could serve the necessary statutory notice which would enable him to charge the protected rent plus a sum for repairs which would bring the lawful rent up to £250 a year.

REFUSAL OF SPECIFIC PERFORMANCE

Even though the contract is valid at common law, Equity may nevertheless refuse to grant specific performance if this would result in an injustice. This has already been mentioned in relation to the case of *Wood* v *Scarth* (1858) (see 9.3.4).

Equity may also grant specific performance subject to terms. For example, if a contract is not void at common law, Equity may grant specific performance subject to the mistake under which the contract was made being rectified.

RECTIFICATION

This will be granted where the parties have reached a clear, oral agreement, but when this agreement is put in writing the written contract does not accurately express what the parties had agreed verbally. The court may order the written contract to be altered to bring it into line with the oral agreement. Thus in the case of:

Craddock Bros Ltd v Hunt (1923)

An oral agreement was made for the sale of a house, excluding an adjoining yard. The written agreement and the conveyance included the yard. The court rectified both the written agreement and the conveyance to bring them into line with the oral agreement.

For rectification, however, the writing must fail to reflect the previous oral agreement. The fact that it fails to reflect the *intentions* of the parties will not be a ground for rectification. For example, in the case of:

Frederick Rose (London) Ltd v William Pim & Co Ltd (1953)

The plaintiffs received an order for 'feveroles'. Not knowing what 'feveroles' were, the plaintiffs asked the defendants who said that they were horse beans and that they could supply them. The plaintiffs therefore gave the defendants an oral order for 'horse beans' and the contract was later put into writing. The plaintiffs received the horse beans from the defendants and sent them to the customer who had ordered the 'feveroles'. It was found that the horse beans supplied were not 'feveroles'.

The court refused to rectify the written contract. The oral agreement had been for horse beans and this was accurately reflected in the written contract. The fact that the parties' intention was not correctly expressed was not a ground for rectification.

9.4 DURESS AND UNDUE INFLUENCE

9.4.1 Introduction

Duress means actual violence or the threat of violence to the person of the contracting party or to the person of someone else who is a member of his immediate family. Undue influence arises where a person uses his influence in such a way as to exclude the exercise of the free reasoned judgment of the person subjected to it.

Contracts made under duress or following the application of undue influence are voidable at the instance of the party affected.

9.4.2 Duress

As we said in the introduction, duress arises where there is actual or threatened violence to a person unless that person enters a contract. The party thus forced into the agreement may avoid the contract when the threat is removed. As this is a common law remedy, it is available as of right. For example, in the case of:

***Friedeberg-Seeley* v *Klass* (1957)**

The defendants refused to leave the defendant's flat until she signed a receipt for a jewel-case and its contents. She eventually did as she was required and the defendants left with the jewel-case. The plaintiff later found that they had left her a cheque for £90.

The court held that the transaction for the sale of the goods was voidable for duress and that therefore the plaintiff could avoid it.

9.4.3 Undue influence

Because the application of duress was limited, Equity developed the principle of undue influence. This will arise where the party coerced has pressure put on him, which pressure, although not amounting to duress, nevertheless prevents him exercising free choice as to whether or not he enters the contract.

Equity recognises two types of undue influence: cases where the party alleging undue influence has to prove it, and cases where, because of the relationship between the parties and the influence the one has over the other, influence is presumed.

WHERE UNDUE INFLUENCE HAS TO BE PROVED

This proof must be given where there is no special relationship between the parties. Whether such influence has been exerted is a question of fact. For example, in the case of:

***Williams* v *Bayley* (1866)**

A son forged his father's signature on several negotiable instruments which came into the possession of the son's bank. The banker called a meeting with the father and implied that, if the matter was not satisfactorily resolved, there was the possibility of the son being convicted and transported. The father therefore agreed to give the bank security in return for the bank handing over the negotiable instruments. It was held that the father's promise to give security was voidable as it had been made following the exploitation by the bank of the father's natural concern and anxiety for his son.

WHERE UNDUE INFLUENCE IS PRESUMED

The presumption will be made where the parties to the contract are in some special relationship whereby one has influence over the decisions and actions of the other. Examples of such special relationships are doctors and patients, religious advisers and those they advise, trustees and beneficiaries, solicitors and clients, guardians and wards, and parent and child. There is no such special relationship to give rise to the presumption of undue influence in the relationship between husband and wife.

When people in these relationships make contracts with each other, there is presumed to have been undue influence unless the person who is alleged to have exercised such influence can show that the other party was in a position to form a free, unfettered judgment, possibly by obtaining independent advice.

In recent years the courts have extended the principle of undue influence to cover cases where there is a substantial inequality of bargaining power and the duress is economic. This is shown in the case of:

***Lloyd's Bank Ltd* v *Bundy* (1975)**

A father and son both banked at the same branch of Lloyd's. The son's business was in severe debt and the bank informed the father that his existing guarantee of his son's company's overdraft would have to be extended if the bank was to continue allowing the company overdraft facilities. This advice was given by the bank's assistant manager. The father had already secured the overdraft but, following the advice he had received from the assistant manager, he increased the guarantee to £11,000 charging his home to the bank as security. This amount represented the sum total of all the father's assets.

By agreeing to this course of action, the father was benefiting not only his son, but also the bank, as it had security for the son's debts. The son's company later went into receivership and the bank proceeded against the father on his guarantee and the charge on his home.

The Court of Appeal held that a special relationship existed between the bank's assistant manager and the father. The bank had a duty to the father to ensure that he was aware of the need to obtain independent advice before he entered the transaction, especially as this transaction also benefited the bank. The charge was set aside on the grounds that it had been procured by undue influence exerted by the bank on a person who was in a much weaker economic position and who was likely to be strongly influenced by his son's problems when he executed the charge on his property.

This decision has to some extent been limited by the case of:

National Westminster Bank v Morgan (1983)

A wife executed a charge over her share in the matrimonial home in order to secure a loan which would be used to clear a building society mortgage on the house. In so doing she obtained no legal advice and was assured by the bank manager that the charge would not be used to secure any advances to her husband's business. In fact it did secure such advances. Notwithstanding this the bank had no intention of using the charge in any other way other than in clearing the building society mortgage and in fact no advances were made to the husband's business.

It was held by the House of Lords that the bank manager was in these circumstances not obliged to advise independent legal advice. Even though his explanation as to the legal effect of the charge had been wrong, he had correctly stated the intention of the bank. The security thus constituted no disadvantage to Mrs Morgan since it had been used only for what she had wanted, namely the clearing of the building society mortgage. The courts will not protect persons simply against mistakes arising as a result of inequality of bargaining power. There must be actual disadvantage for undue influence to be pleaded.

A similar situation arose in:

Midland Bank v Shepherd (1988)

The husband's account with the plaintiff bank became overdrawn. He arranged with the bank to transfer the overdraft to a new joint account held by both himself and his wife. The mandate was signed by both husband and wife and referred to 'any loan or overdraft . . . being our joint and several responsibility . . . ' Subsequently the husband borrowed £10,000 from the bank on overdraft from this joint account for business purposes, though the wife had no part in this arrangement. The husband became bankrupt and the bank sued the wife. It was held by the Court of Appeal that there was no evidence of the husband having exercised any dominant influence over the wife and thus the wife could not escape liability to the bank.

THE EFFECTS OF UNDUE INFLUENCE ON A CONTRACT

If there has been undue influence exerted in obtaining a contract, the transaction is voidable. If, however, the innocent party has affirmed the contract after the influence ceased or after the relationship giving rise to the presumption has ended, he will have lost his right to avoid. He will also have lost his right to end the contract if he delays in bringing an action for rescission or if, before steps to rescind are taken, a third party acquires an interest in the subject matter of the contract in good faith and for value.

9.5 ILLEGALITY

9.5.1 Introduction

Although the parties may have reached agreement on all aspects of the contract, it may nevertheless be unenforceable in whole or in part because either statute or common law provides that such undertakings are illegal. The word 'illegal' in this context has several meanings. It includes contracts which are unlawful in the general sense of the word eg a contract to commit a crime. It also includes those agreements which statute or common law render unenforceable by action by either one or both of the parties. These could be described as technically illegal rather than illegal in the ordinary meaning of the expression.

In this section we will look at contracts which are illegal by statute, those which are illegal at common law and those which are made void by statute or common law. We will also examine the effects of illegality.

9.5.2 Contracts illegal by statute

Some contracts are expressly prohibited by statute. Thus, for example, it is illegal to insure the life of a person in whom the person taking out the policy has no insurable interest (Life Assurance Act 1774). An insurable interest in this context means a pecuniary interest. In other words, unless the person effecting the policy stands to lose financially by the death of the person whose life is insured the policy will be illegal and void. No rights can be claimed on this contract.

If a contract is affected by statute, the court will look at the reason why the law makes this provision. If it is intended to prevent this type of contract altogether (as in the case of the Life Assurance Act 1774, which was designed to prevent people using life assurance as a form of gambling) the whole contract will be illegal and void. If, however, the object of the Act is to raise revenue then non-compliance may not affect the contract itself. For example:

Smith v Mawhood (1845)

Statute required that sellers of tobacco should be licensed. A tobacconist sold tobacco without a licence. The purchaser broke the contract and the court held that the tobacconist could sue him despite his lack of a licence. The object of the act was not to make contracts for the unlicensed sale of tobacco void, but rather to raise revenue for the State.

See also the case of:

Archbolds (Freightage) Ltd v Spanglett Ltd (1961)

Contrary to legislation, a carrier contracted to transport goods without obtaining the necessary licence to permit him to do so. The court held that this contract was valid, as the purpose of requiring a carrier to be licensed was to help in the administration of road transport. It was not designed to prevent such contracts being made.

In other words, whether or not a statute affects the validity of contract is a question of construction to be decided by the court.

9.5.3 Contracts which are illegal at common law

The common law regards certain contracts as being against public policy and therefore void. The judges decide whether an agreement comes within this category. Their decisions are based on what they consider to be in the best interests of the public at the time, taking account of current morality and social and economic conditions. Public policy, therefore, is a flexible idea, changing with changes in society. As Parliament is increasingly taking over the role of protector of the public, however, so the judges are becoming more reluctant to create new categories of contract affected by public policy considerations. In general, the courts apply the existing law in this area. They do not create new rules.

Amongst those contracts which are illegal at common law are the following:

CONTRACTS TO COMMIT A CRIME OR A TORT

A contract to commit a crime or a tort are illegal and completely unenforceable. For example, if A promises B £100 to assault C, B will be unable to enforce this contract if he does the act and A refuses to pay. A and B will also be liable to prosecution at criminal law. Contracts to defraud the Revenue fall within this category. For example:

Miller v Karlinsky (1945)

The defendant employed the plaintiff at a weekly wage of £10 plus expenses. The 'expenses' were to include the income tax the plaintiff had to pay on his £10. The plaintiff sued the defendant to recover 10 weeks' arrears of salary, plus his expenses for this period. The sum claimed for expenses included the amount of tax the plaintiff would have to pay on his salary for the 10 weeks. The court held that the contract was illegal as it defrauded the Revenue. The plaintiff was not entitled to recover either his expenses or his salary. All these payments were tainted with the illegality of the original contract.

CONTRACTS THAT ARE SEXUALLY IMMORAL

This category includes contracts which are in themselves sexually immoral and those which, although innocent in themselves, have an immoral purpose. For example, in:

Pearce v Brooks (1866)

A coach builder who hired a carriage to a prostitute, knowing that she intended to use the vehicle in the course of her business, was held by the court to be unable to recover the hire charges. The contract was illegal.

CONTRACTS WHICH HARM NATIONAL SECURITY OR RELATIONS WITH FRIENDLY STATES

Contracts which are harmful to national security, such as trading with the enemy in time of war, are illegal and void as are contracts which prejudice the relations between the United Kingdom and a friendly country. This includes contracts which have as their object the commission of an offence in such countries. The case of:

Foster v Driscoll (1929)

A contract was made to export whisky to the USA at a time when the prohibition laws prevented any dealing in alcohol in that country. The court held that this contract was illegal and void and could not be enforced in the British courts.

CONTRACTS PREJUDICIAL TO THE ADMINISTRATION OF JUSTICE

A contract not to prosecute is illegal if the prosecution is for an offence that concerns the public (ie a crime). If it concerns the infringement of a private right, however, a contract not to prosecute will be enforceable. In the case of:

Fisher & Co v Apollinaris Co (1875)

The court held that a contract not to prosecute for an infringement of trademark was valid and enforceable. The prosecution did not relate to a matter which harmed the public generally. The offence committed was of a private nature.

If, however, the contract is designed to defeat law which is designed to protect society generally, it will be unenforceable.

John v Mendoza (1939)

The defendant was made bankrupt owing the plaintiff money. The defendant asked the plaintiff to say that the money owing him had been given as a gift. If the plaintiff did this, the defendant promised, the plaintiff would be paid in full regardless of the amounts received by the other creditors.

Acting on his promise, the plaintiff did not prove in the defendant's bankruptcy.

It later turned out that the defendant could pay all his creditors in full. He did so and the bankruptcy was annulled. He did not, however, pay the plaintiff who brought this action for the money he was owed. The court held that the action should fail. By not proving in the bankruptcy, the plaintiff had lost all right to recover his debt and the defendant's promise to pay him in full was unenforceable as it was designed to defeat the bankruptcy laws.

CONTRACTS PROMOTING CORRUPTION IN PUBLIC LIFE

A contract to procure a public office by improper means or to bribe an official will be illegal and void.

Parkinson v College of Ambulance Ltd (1925)

The plaintiff was told that, if he made a contribution to the charity he would receive an official honour, probably a knighthood. The plaintiff made a substantial donation but did not receive his honour. He sued the charity to recover his donation but the court held that he should lose. The agreement to buy an honour was illegal and void. No action could be brought under it.

9.5.4 The effects of illegality

CONTRACTS WHICH ARE ILLEGAL AS FORMED

Where the actual creation of the contract is prohibited, it will be illegal from the outset and, as a general rule neither party can sue or be sued upon it.

Re Mahmoud and Ispahani (1921)

A statutory order provided that no-one could buy or sell linseed oil unless he had first obtained a licence to do so. The seller, who was licensed, sold some oil to the buyer, who fraudulently told the seller that he too had a licence. The court held that the contract was illegal from its inception. The statutory order prohibited the making of unlicensed contracts for the oil. The fact that the seller was innocent was irrelevant and his action for non-acceptance failed.

If the contract is made illegal by statute, of course, the statute itself may make provision as to what the effects of breach are to be. For example, under the *Resale Prices Act 1976* it is unlawful:

1. For two or more suppliers to agree to withold supplies from dealers who do not comply with resale price conditions;
2. Or to agree to supply such dealers on terms which are less favourable than those given to other dealers who do agree to observe the price restrictions.

It is also unlawful for dealers to agree to refuse to place orders with or to discriminate against those suppliers who will not enforce resale price maintenance. The 1976 Act provides sanctions to be enforced against people who enter this type of transaction. The sanctions are that the Crown may apply to the court for an injunction or 'other appropriate relief'. The statute, in other words, contains remedies for breach of its provisions and the court will enforce these remedies.

CONTRACTS WHICH ARE ILLEGAL AS PERFORMED

These are contracts which, although not illegal in the way in which they are formed, are performed by one of the parties in a way in which is prohibited by statute.

In these circumstances, the party who performed the contract illegally has no rights or remedies under the contract.

Anderson Ltd v Daniel (1924)

There was a contract for the sale of artificial fertiliser. By statute, the seller had to give the buyer an invoice which contained information as to the percentage of certain chemicals contained in the fertilizer. The seller in this case failed to comply with this statutory duty and the court held that he was not allowed to sue for the price of the goods.

If, however, the other party is innocent of the illegality, his rights will remain unaffected. For example:

Marles v Philip Trant and Sons Ltd (No 2) (1953)

A contracted to sell spring wheat to B, but in fact delivered winter wheat. B innocently resold the wheat as spring wheat to C, but this contract was illegal as performed in that B did not supply an invoice with the goods to C as required by statute. The court held that C could sue B and B could sue A for the breach of the contracts of sale.

RECOVERY OF MONEY OR PROPERTY PASSED UNDER AN ILLEGAL CONTRACT

As a general rule, title to money or goods transferred under an illegal contract will pass to the transferee despite the illegality. Such property, therefore, cannot be recovered (*Parkinson* v *College of Ambulance Ltd* (1925)—see 9.5.3 above).

There are, however, exceptions to this general rule. These are as follows.

1. If the transferor can make his claim without relying on the illegality.
   If the plaintiff brings an action relying on rights other than those contained in the illegal contract, he will succeed.

Bowmakers Ltd v Barnet Instruments Ltd (1944)

The plaintiffs hired certain machine tools to the defendants under hire-purchase agreements. These agreements were illegal, as war-time regulations required all sellers of machine tools to be licensed and the plaintiffs had not obtained such a licence. The defendants failed to keep up the hire-purchase instalments on the tools, some of which they sold. They refused to hand back the rest to the plaintiffs. The plaintiffs sued, not on the illegal hire-purchase agreements, but in conversion in that the defendants had wrongly dealt with the plaintiff's property.

The Court of Appeal held that, although the hire-purchase contract was illegal, the plaintiffs' action should succeed. They were suing, not in breach of contract, but as owners. In other words, their action did not depend on the illegality.

2 If the parties are not in *pari delicto* (equally at fault).

If the plaintiff can show that, although the contract was unlawful on the face of it, he had entered it because of the defendant's fraud, duress or undue influence he may be able to recover his property from the defendant.

Atkinson v Denby (1862)

The plaintiff, who was in financial difficulties, offered to pay his creditors 5 shillings in the £. This was agreed to by every creditor except the defendant, who said that he would accept this arrangement only if the plaintiff paid him £50. The plaintiff agreed to this, fearing that, unless the defendant was a party to the scheme it would fail totally. The court held that the plaintiff could recover his £50 as he had been coerced into defrauding his creditors.

3 If the transferor genuinely repents the illegality.

If the transferor can show that he repents the illegality he will be able to recover the property he has transferred under the agreement. Such repentance, however, must be genuine and not just undertaken for the sake of convenience.

Bigos v Bousted (1951)

In contravention of the Exchange Control Act 1947, the plaintiff agreed to supply the defendant with £150 worth of Italian currency to be handed over in Italy in return for payment of £150 in England. The defendant handed over a share certificate as security. The plaintiff did not supply the Italian money and the defendant demanded the return of the share certificate. The plaintiff refused to hand it over and brought this action to obtain the £150 which she claimed she had lent to the defendant. The defendant counter-claimed for the return of his certificate saying that, although the contract was illegal, he had repented the illegality. The plaintiff abandoned her claim and the court held that the defendant should fail in his counter-claim. The repentance was not genuine. It was 'but want of power to sin'. In other words the repentance was the result of his inability 'to sin' as, had the lire been made available in Italy, he would certainly have accepted them.

For a plea of repentance to succeed the claimant must have only partly, rather than substantially, performed the contract. Compare the following two cases:

Kearley v Thomson (1890)

The plaintiff, who was friendly with a bankrupt, paid the defendant £40 to stay away from the friend's public examination and not to oppose the discharge. The defendant, who was likely to oppose the discharge, did stay away from the public examination but, before an application for discharge had been made, the plaintiff brought this action claiming the recovery of his £40, alleging that he had changed his mind and had repented the illegality.

The court held that the plaintiff should fail. The illegal scheme had already been substantially effected and therefore repentance was too late.

Taylor v Bowers (1876)

The plaintiff, who was being pressurised by his creditors, assigned to A some machinery he owned in order to put it out of his creditors' reach. He then called a creditors' meeting and, not disclosing the machinery as part of his assets, tried to persuade them to settle for less than the amount of their debts. The creditors refused to do so and the plaintiff brought this action to recover the machinery from the defendant who had obtained it from A.

The court held that the plaintiff should succeeed. The illegal fraud on the creditors had not been executed.

4 If the transferor belongs to a class which the statute was designed to protect.

If the statute makes certain contracts illegal in order to protect a class of people, a member of that class may be able to sue on the contract. He will not be regarded as equally blameworthy as the other party. The parties, in other words, will not be in *pari delicto*.

In the case of:

Barclay v Pearson (1893)

A newspaper's competition was held to be an illegal lottery under the Gaming Act 1802. This Act had been passed to protect people who entered lotteries against those who organised such schemes. The court held that, as the competitors were the class of persons the law was designed to protect, they could recover their entry fee although they could not obtain the prize money.

9.5.5 Contracts void by statute

Contracts which are made void by either statute or common law do not involve any moral wrongdoing. They are made void (and therefore, in general, unenforceable by either party) on the grounds of public policy, that is, that Parliament or the courts believe that they would have undesirable social or economic consequences. There is less sense of blame attaching to these contracts than to those which are treated as illegal.

For our purposes, the main contracts declared void by statute are wagering contracts and contracts within the scope of the Restrictive Trade Practices Act 1976.

WAGERING CONTRACTS

By the Gaming Act 1845, a wagering contract is void. No action may be brought for either the bet or the winnings. A wager may be defined as an agreement between two persons or two groups of persons whereby one will win and the other lose a stake on the outcome of a future uncertain event in which neither has any other interest. It follows from this definition that if three or more persons are involved in the agreement it will not be a wager (if, for example, A, B and C each put £5 into a fund to be given to the one who has chosen the winning horse in a race, this will not be a wager).

Furthermore, as both parties must stand to win or lose, a football pools competition will not be a wager. If a person wins with his football coupon, the promoters will return the stake money they have received, less their commission. In other words, the pools companies do not stand to lose. The agreement is not a wager and is therefore valid. That is why pools companies insert the phrase 'binding in honour only' to prevent the transaction being enforceable against them. Without this phrase, there would be a valid binding contract. The future uncertain event refers either to an occurrence which has not yet happened or to an uncertainty in the parties' minds. For example, it will be a wager if the parties placed a stake on the resolution of a dispute as to how many countries there are in the world. Although this is a certain fact, there is uncertainty in the parties' minds. The number to be finally discovered by them is the future uncertain event.

Finally, to be a wager, neither party must have any interest in the outcome of the event other than the stake money they might win. This distinguishes a wager from a contract of insurance which is valid only if the insured has an interest in the event not occurring. So, for example, if a person insures his house against fire he has an interest in the house not burning down. His insurance is designed to compensate him if this unlooked for event occurs. Thus it is not a wagering contract.

The effect of a wagering contract is that it is void. No action may be brought for the winnings or for the bet itself. Once the bet has been paid or the winnings collected, however, they are irrecoverable because, by making payment, the payer has waived the protection of the Gaming Act 1845.

CONTRACTS WITHIN THE RESTRICTIVE TRADE PRACTICES ACT 1976

Under this Act, agreements between two or more persons to fix prices and/or regulate the supplies of goods or services are void unless the parties to the agreement can justify it in one of the ways specified in the Act. Such agreements must be registered with the Director General of Fair Trading and, if the parties wish to justify their restrictive undertakings, they will have to do so before the Restrictive Practices Court.

The grounds on which justification can be argued are, in effect, what the 1976 Act prescribes as the public interest in this area. For example, the parties may argue that the agreement is necessary to prevent unemployment in an area where unemployment is already high, or that it is necessary to protect export markets.

All restrictive agreements within the definition in the Act are *prima facie* void. If the parties do not try to justify their agreement, or if their attempted justification fails, they are required to end the agreement. If they do not do so voluntarily, they can be required to do so by an injunction obtained by the Director General of Fair Trading.

Restrictive agreements which affect trade between Member-states within the European Economic Community are also made void by virtue of Article 85 Treaty of Rome 1957. Unlike the position in the United Kingdom's domestic law, however, firms in the EEC which act in this way may also be subjected to fines.

9.5.6 Contracts void at common law

The two main types of contract made void at common law are contracts to oust the jurisdiction of courts and contracts in restraint of trade.

CONTRACTS TO OUST THE JURISDICTION OF COURTS

A contractual provision designed to remove the right of one or both of the parties to bring an action in a court of law is void. For example:

Baker v Jones (1954)

The rules of the British Amateur Weightlifters' Association provided that the only body empowered to interpret the Association's rules was its central council. It was also provided that the council's decisions were final. The court held that this provision was against public policy and was therefore void.

In an arbitration agreement, however, it is perfectly valid for the parties to be required to submit their case to arbitration rather than go to court. If there is such an arbitration agreement made and, in breach of its provisions, one of the parties takes his case straight to court, the court may refuse to hear the action, referring it to the arbitrator for decision. In arbitration proceedings, however, each party may refer points of law to the courts for them to rule on the legal principles involved.

CONTRACTS IN RESTRAINT OF TRADE

Contracts in restraint of trade are those which in some way restrict a person's freedom to exercise his trade, business or profession as he chooses. In other words, they are restrictions on a person's freedom to act as he chooses in the exercise of his calling. Such restraints of trade are *prima facie* void (that is, initially presumed to be void) unless the party relying on them can show that they are reasonable both in the interests of the parties (ie that they do not give a wider protection than can be justified) and in the interests of the public (ie that they do not harm the public good).

There are three categories of contract in restraint of trade:

1 Restraints imposed upon employees.
2 Restraints imposed when a business is sold.
3 Restraints accepted by retailers in relation to the goods they sell.

We look at each of these in detail. At this stage, we should mention that, although this area is referred to as 'contracts in restraint of trade' the restriction is usually contained within a covenant (or promise) *within* a contract.

1 Restraints imposed upon employees.
   As with all contracts in restraint of trade, it must be shown that there is an interest worthy of protection and that the restraint is reasonable in the interests of both the parties and the public. The restriction usually occurs as a clause in the contract of employment. For example, Green & Co employ Henry as a sales representative. In the contract of employment, along with the terms as to his rate of pay, his holiday entitlement and so on there is a clause preventing Henry working as a sales representative in any similar business for 5 years after leaving Green's employment. This is a covenant in restraint of trade. The covenant will become relevant only if Henry leaves his job and then takes up employment with a competing business within 5 years. The court will have to decide whether the covenant, which is *prima facie* void, can be justified and therefore be allowed to stand.

The burden of proving that it is reasonable as between the parties lies on the employer (in the example, Green & Co.). That it is unreasonable in the interests of the public must be shown by the employee (in the example, Henry).

For the agreement to be allowed, it must be shown that:

(a) There is an interest worthy of protection. Merely trying to stop a former employee from using his skill will not be allowed, even if that skill had been acquired in the employer's service.

The interests worthy of protection in contracts of employment are trade secrets and influence over clients. Thus, if an employee had been given access to his former employer's business secrets, or had been put into a position where he could influence this employer's customers he may validly be prevented from doing so, even if this meant that the former employee's competitiveness was thereby reduced.

(b) The restraint must be reasonable in the interests of the parties. This means that the geographical area covered and the length of time for which the restriction is to operate must be no more than is necessary to protect the employer's interests. For example:

Littlewoods Organisation Ltd v Harris (1978)

By his contract of employment, a divisional director of the plaintiffs, a mail-order business, was, for 12 months after leaving his employment, prevented from working for Great Universal Stores (GUS), Littlewoods' main competitors. In the course of his employment for Littlewoods the director had gained detailed knowledge of the firm's bi-annual catalogue. Such catalogues are crucial to the success of mail-order businesses. The director left Littlewoods and, within 12 months, obtained employment with GUS. In this action, Littlewoods sought an injunction to prevent him taking up this job.

The Court of Appeal held that Littlewoods had an interest worthy of protection. The details of the catalogue constituted a trade secret which the company was entitled to protect. The 12 month period for which the restriction was to operate was also reasonable but there was some dispute as to the reasonableness of the geographical area covered. Littlewoods' business was restricted to the United Kingdom, whereas GUS's business was worldwide. The restriction on the ex-director of Littlewoods referred to working for GUS generally. The Court of Appeal held that the restriction could be construed to cover only GUS's mail-order business in the United Kingdom. The restraint was therefore held reasonable and an injunction against the former director was granted.

Compare this case with:

Empire Meat Co Ltd v Patrick (1939)

The contract of employment of an employee of a retail butchers provided that, on leaving his employment, he should not be employed in, or carry on the business of, retail butchery within 5 miles of his employer's place of business. This was held to be too wide a restriction. The employer's trade was drawn from a much smaller area.

(c) The restraint must be reasonable in the interests of the public.

What is in the public's interest is a question for the judge to decide. It will depend, for example, on the job in which the employee was engaged and the judge's perception of its value to society. In the case of:

Hensman v Traill (1980)

A restriction on a doctor, who was a partner in a general practice, that for 5 years after leaving the firm he should not practice within 7 miles of the practice was held to be void. Not only was the restraint too wide, it also operated against the public interest as it meant that that particular community was deprived of the services of this doctor.

2   Restraints imposed on the sale of a business

Again, such a restriction will be void unless it can be shown that there is an interest worthy of protection and that the restraint is reasonable in the interests of the parties and the public.

The main interest worthy of protection in these cases is the sale of the goodwill of the business. For example, if A sells both his business and the goodwill of that business to B, B would be able to enforce a promise by A not to operate a similar business within a reasonable radius. To refuse to allow such a restriction would make the sales of businesses very difficult. The purchaser could not otherwise be guaranteed that he would receive what he had paid for.

There must, however, be a genuine sale of the business. The restraint must have a stronger basis than merely a bare attempt to prevent competition.

In the case of:

Vancouver Malt and Sake Brewing Co Ltd v Vancouver Breweries Ltd (1934)

A company which was licensed to brew beer but which in fact did not do so agreed to sell the goodwill of this business and to refrain from brewing beer for 15 years. The court held that, as the vendors did not in fact brew beer, they had no goodwill to sell. The restriction therefore amounted merely to an agreement not to compete and was illegal.

Even where there is a genuine sale, the restriction must be no wider than is reasonably necessary to protect the purchaser of the business. For example, in:

British Reinforced Concrete Engineering Co Ltd v Schelff (1921)

The plaintiffs manufactured and sold 'BRC Road Reinforcements', the defendants sold 'Loop Road Reinforcements'. The defendants sold their business to the plaintiffs and, in the contract of sale, agreed not to compete with them in the manufacture or sale of road reinforcements. The court held that all the defendants had sold was the business relating to 'Loop' reinforcements and it was only in relation to this type that a restriction was justifiable. The covenant, therefore, was void.

In other words, the reasonableness of the restriction depends on the business being sold. For example, in:

Nordenfelt v Maxim Nordenfelt Guns and Ammunition Co (1894)

N had a world-wide business for the manufacture and sale of guns and ammunition. When he sold this business he agreed that, for 25 years, he would not manufacture guns or ammunition anywhere in the world or carry on any other business competing with the purchaser in any way. The court held that the world-wide restriction was valid—the business sold had a world-wide market. The non-competition clause, however, was too wide and would be severed (see later).

3   Restraints accepted by retailers in relation to the goods they sell.
These arise when a retailer agrees to sell only one brand of goods. Such agreements are known as *solus agreements* and are particularly common in the petrol industry. They may be part of a mortgage or a lease or entered into quite separately from any other arrangement. So, for example, if an oil company gives a loan to a garage to enable the garage to improve its facilities, the oil company may take a mortgage over the garage premises and make it a condition of the mortgage that, until the loan has been repaid, the garage will sell only the oil company's petrol. It is, however, not necessary that the *solus agreement* be held to a mortgage or loan—it can be a straightforward contract whereby the retailer agrees to stock and sell only one manufacturer's goods in return for that manufacturer giving the retailer an increased discount on the wholesale price of the goods.

Whatever form it takes, however, a *solus agreement* falls within the doctrine of restraint of trade and is therefore *prima facie* void. The party relying on the agreement will have to justify it by showing that he has an interest worthy of protection and that the restriction is reasonable in the interests of the parties and of the public.

For example, in the case of:

Petrofina (GB) Ltd v Martin (1966)

The defendant agreed that, for a period of 12 years, he would sell only Petrofina petrol. In return, Petrofina gave him a rebate on the petrol sold. Martin agreed that, if he sold the business, he would require the purchaser to enter a similar agreement with Petrofina. Martin broke the agreement and started selling other firms' petrol. Petrofina brought this action asking the court to grant an injunction against Martin to stop any further breaches. The Court of Appeal, however, refused the application. The agreement could not be justified. The obligation to sell the business only to a person who would enter a similar solus agreement with Petrofina was unreasonable as it could make the garage unsaleable. Furthermore, the period of 12 years for which the tie was to operate was unreasonably long.

The whole question of the application of the doctrine of restraint to *solus agreements* was reviewed in the case of:

***Esso Petroleum Co Ltd v Harper's Garage (Stourport) Ltd* (1967)**

This case concerned a garage company which owned and operated two garages. It entered two *solus agreements* with Esso. The agreement relating to the first garage was for 4 years 5 months and the one relating to the second was for 21 years. The House of Lords held that the 4 year 5 month restraint was valid, but the 21 year restraint was unreasonable and therefore void. The Lords said that, in relation to solus agreements, the oil companies' competitive position in the market was an interest worthy of protection. Solus ties helped the companies secure this position by giving them guaranteed outlets for their petrol and by enabling them to plan their production effectively.

Furthermore, in deciding whether such agreements were reasonable, the public, rather than the parties', interest was the soundest basis for decision. Both parties to the agreement negotiated it from a position of relatively equal bargaining strength. The agreement must have suited both the oil company and the garage when it was negotiated. It was only when, later, the garage discovered it could obtain better discounts elsewhere that it attempted to break the agreement.

So, said the House of Lords, the public interest was the surer way of deciding the validity of *solus agreements*. In the Esso case, the Lords referred to the recommendations of the Monopolies and Mergers Commission which had published a report on the solus system in the petrol industry in 1965. The report of the Commission had recommended that solus ties for a maximum of 5 years benefited the public in that, amongst other things they kept the price of petrol down. Any longer than 5 years, however, took the agreement beyond the period of what was reasonably foreseeable in the industry. The House of Lords applied these recommendations in their judgment in the Esso case.

9.5.7 The effect of contracts which are void at common law

Insofar as the contract contravenes public policy it will be void. If, however, only part of the contract operates against public policy that part may be severed (ie cut out) from the contract and the remaining, valid, parts of the agreement allowed to stand.

For example, if a contract of employment contains a restrictive clause which cannot be justified as being reasonable, that clause may be severed from the contract. The rest of the contract, however, will continue to be valid and enforceable. Thus, even though his contract of employment contained an invalid restraint, an employee could still enforce the valid sections relating, for example, to the payment of his salary.

If the restriction is essentially the whole point of the contract, however, unless this term can be justified the whole contract will fail.

In applying the doctrine of severance to a contract, the courts will not re-write the contract. The offending part must be capable of being removed from the contract leaving the remaining, valid sections as a sensible, cohesive agreement. In other words, the contract must be so drafted that the judges can, in effect, put a line through the void parts and yet leave the nature of the contract as a whole unaltered.

SUMMARY

In this Chapter, we have looked at the various ways in which a contract may be invalidated. Such invalidity may arise in the course of the formation of the contract, that is, if there is misrepresentation or mistake, or if duress or undue influence is used, or it may arise from within the contract itself as when the agreement is illegal or void because of public policy.

Note the differing effects these invalidating factors have on the contract and consider how the various defects in its formation or content are interrelated. Thus, for example, if a contract is induced by a misrepresentation, this misrepresentation may, but does not necessarily have to, lead to an operative mistake. As a misrepresentation merely makes the contract voidable, the party who was misled will be unable to recover the property if, before he rescinds the contract, the rogue has sold the goods to an innocent purchaser who takes without notice of the initial misrepresentation. The victim's only hope in these circumstances is to show that the contract is void for operative mistake. If he is able to do this, then the rogue received no title and therefore no title can be obtained by a third party, however innocent that person may be.

SELF-TEST QUESTIONS

9.1 When may an apparent statement of opinion be treated as a misrepresentation?

9.2 When will silence constitute misrepresentation?

9.3 Distinguish between
(a) fraudulent,
(b) negligent, and
(c) wholly innocent misrepresentation

9.4 A misrepresentation makes the resulting contracts voidable. The representee may also have the contract rescinded by order of the court. What is the relationship between avoiding and rescinding the contract?

9.5 Why was the right to rescind lost in
(a) *Leaf* v *International Galleries* (1950)
(b) *Vigers* v *Pike* (1842)

9.6 Distinguish between:
(a) Common mistake
(b) Mutual mistake

9.7 Distinguish between the ratio of:
(a) *Lewis* v *Averay* (1971), and
(b) *Ingram* v *Little* (1961)

9.8 What are the requirements for a plea of non est factum?

9.9 How does Equity grant relief in cases of mistake?

9.10 Distinguish between the effects of contracts which are
(a) illegal as formed, and those which are
(b) illegal as performed

9.11 Compare
(a) *Kearley* v *Thomson* (1890), and
(b) *Taylor* v *Bowers* (1876)

9.12 What must be shown in order to justify a covenant in restraint of trade?

Answers on page 310

EXERCISES

Exercise 9.1

What do you understand by an 'operative mistake' in the law of contract? What is the effect of such a mistake on a contract?

Exercise 9.2

James is an antique dealer who is an authority on eighteenth century English furniture. Paul has recently bought an old country house and wishes to acquire some antique furniture for it. He sees and admires a set of dining chairs which are in James' antique shop. James tells him that the chairs are 'beyond doubt eighteenth century.' Moreover they 'might well have come from Chippendale's own workshop.' Paul pays £5,000 for the chairs and they are delivered shortly afterwards to his home. Some days later Paul is dusting one of the chairs when he sees a label on the underside of the seat which reads 'Made by CAR Penter, Watford 1937.' Paul investigates this further and confirms that the chairs were indeed made by a tradesman, CAR Penter in Watford in 1937, and are in fact worth only about £500. The error made by James was an honest mistake which had occurred because he bought the chairs in a sale at an old country house and had not had time to examine them properly.
    Explain what remedies Paul may have against James.

Answers on page 311

Discharge of the contract and remedies for breach

A contract will be discharged when the parties are released from their obligations under it. Once a contract is discharged, neither party can rely on its terms. They can enforce only those rights which may arise from the discharge.

The most usual way in which a contract is discharged is when the parties have performed their obligations under it. For example, A offers to sell his car to B for £100. When A has delivered the car and B has handed over the £100 both parties have performed their obligations and both are discharged. A contract may also be discharged, even before complete performance, if the parties make a new agreement to release each other or to vary each other's obligations. If some outside cause makes it impossible to perform the contract further the contract may then be discharged by frustration. Finally, if one of the parties breaks the contract the other party may treat the contract as discharged by breach. In this case the innocent party will be given certain remedies. He may, for example, sue for damages to compensate him for the loss he has suffered because of the breach or he may claim an order of specific performance, requiring the party in breach to perform his obligations.

10.1 DISCHARGE

10.1.1 By performance

THE GENERAL RULE

The general rule is that for contracts to be discharged by performance that performance must be precise and exact. In other words both parties must have performed precisely and exactly what they contracted to perform under the agreement. So, for example, a contract for the sale of a car will be discharged by performance when the car has been handed over and the buyer has paid the money. If, however, there are some hidden defects in this vehicle the seller will not have fully performed his obligations and is therefore not discharged. The buyer's right to sue under the contract remains.

This general rule, that performance must be precise and exact, applies to entire contracts. These are contracts under which one party must perform all that he has contracted to perform before he can claim the other party's performance. So, for example, when a person has undertaken to do some work for a sum of money his right to payment will be conditional on his having completed the work. So, if Brickit Ltd agree to build a house for Adam for £10,000, Brickit will not be entitled to receive the £10,000 or any part of it until they have completed the construction. If Brickit start the work and then voluntarily abandon it, again the firm will not be entitled to payment for the portion they have executed. Another example would be if an employee is engaged at a wage of £100 per week. His right to be paid is conditional on his having served the complete period of a week and if therefore he leaves in the middle of the week without justification he cannot claim payment for the days he has worked. This point is illustrated in the case of:

Sumpter v Hedges (1898)

The plaintiff had agreed to erect two buildings for the defendant for a total price of £565. The plaintiff did part of the work (valued at £333) but then abandoned the construction. The defendant completed the buildings. The plaintiff claimed that he was entitled to be paid for the work he had actually done. The Court of Appeal held, however, that the defendant had occupied his own land with the partly completed buildings on it but he had no real option whether to take the benefit of the work done or not. He could not leave the buildings in the state in which the plaintiff had abandoned them and therefore he had a right to go in and complete the work. The plaintiff had not performed precisely and exactly what he contracted to perform and therefore was not entitled to payment.

If, however, the innocent party has a free choice whether or not to accept the partial performance and he chooses to accept it then he must pay for the work he accepts. In *Sumpter* v *Hedges* as we said earlier, the landowner had no choice but to accept the partial work so he was not liable to pay for it. In completing the work, however, he used certain materials which had been left by the plaintiff on the site. The court held that he was liable to pay the plaintiff a reasonable price for these materials as he had had a free choice whether or not to use them.

The general rule therefore is that for discharge, performance must be precise and exact. There are, however, a number of exceptions to this general rule, that is, cases where although one of the parties has not completely performed what he contracted to perform he can nevertheless claim payment from the other.

EXCEPTIONS TO THE GENERAL RULE

1   Divisible contracts

A divisible contract is one which can be divided into promises which are independent of each other. For example, a tenant's covenant to pay rent is independent of the landlord's covenant to repair the premises. So unlike the position in relation to entire contracts, one of the parties to a divisible contract can demand the other's performance without himself having to perform his own side of the bargain. Thus even though the landlord does not repair the property the tenant is not discharged from his obligation to pay rent. The tenant must pay and bring an action to enforce the landlord's covenant. The two promises are divisible.

Another example of a divisible contract will occur when there is an agreement to deliver goods by instalments, each instalment to be separately paid for. For example, A agrees to buy 100 tonnes of coal from B, delivery to be made in 10 instalments of 10 tonnes per instalment, payment to be made on delivery of each instalment. This will be a divisible contract; one that can be divided into a series of 10 separate obligations. In this case payment will keep pace with performance. So if three instalments have been delivered and then the seller does not deliver any further consignments the purchaser may be required to pay for the instalments already delivered. If, however, the contract provided that although delivery was to be by instalments payment was to be made upon delivery of the final instalment, this would be an entire contract and the seller would have to deliver the full 100 tonne consignment before he could demand payment from the buyer.

2   Acceptance of partial performance

If there is partial performance and the promisee has a choice either to accept or reject this performance and he chooses to accept it, he must pay for that part of the work he has thus adopted. This was shown in *Sumpter* v *Hedges* (above) in relation to the builders' materials that the defendant used in completing the work.

3   Prevention of complete performance by other party
In the case of:

***Planché v Colburn* (1831)**

P agreed to write a book on costume and ancient armour for 'The Juvenile Library'. This was a series of books to be published by C. P was to be paid £100 on completion of the work. He collected materials and wrote part of the book but before publication the series was discontinued. The court held that P was entitled to a reasonable remuneration for the amount of work he had undertaken. The money was awarded on a *quantum meruit* basis. This is a quasi-contractual claim operating independently of the original contract (see later).

4   Substantial performance

If the contractor has substantially completed the contract, even though there are some deficiences or imperfections in his work he may be entitled to receive payment. In other words if the contract has been completed in the ordinary sense of the term, payment cannot be refused because there are slight defects or omissions. This is shown in:

***Hoenig v Isaacs* (1952)**

The plaintiff had agreed to decorate the defendant's flat for £750. As the work progressed the defendant made part payments to the plaintiff but when the plaintiff claimed to have finished the work and demanded the balance, the defendant, claiming that the work had some defects in it, refused to pay. The plaintiff sued for the balance of the money owing him. The court held that as the defective work would cost £55 to put right, the defects were not serious and could be easily remedied. The plaintiff therefore had substantially complied with the terms of the contract and was entitled to receive the contract sum less the cost of remedying the defects.

What is substantial performance is a question of fact in each case. For example in:

Bolton v Mahadeva (1972)

B agreed to install a central heating system in M's house for £560. The fitting of the system was faulty and the amount of heat given out was 10% less than had been expected. Furthermore a defective flue caused fumes to permeate the living rooms of the house. The cost of remedying the defects would be £174. The defendant refused to pay the price of the work and was sued by the plaintiff who claimed substantial performance. The court held that the plaintiff was *not* entitled to recover the contract price of £560 with a deduction of £174 as damages for bad workmanship. The defects could not be cured by slight adjustments to the central heating system. Taking into account the cost of repairs in relation to the total price for completion of the work, it was impossible to maintain that the contract had been substantially performed. Not only was the work shoddy, it was also generally ineffective for its primary purpose.

TIME OF PERFORMANCE

Time of performance of a contract is generally not a condition. If, therefore, one of the parties is late in performing his obligations, the other party cannot treat the contract as ended. All he can do is sue for damages. Time of performance, however, may be made a condition if, following a delay, the promisee informs the promisor that the contract must be performed by a certain date otherwise it will be treated as repudiated. The promisee is providing consideration by impliedly waiving his right to sue for damages for the delay in return for the term as to time being made a condition. Time of performance can also be made a condition:

1   By an express stipulation to this effect in the contract.
2   Where the surrounding circumstances or the subject matter of the contract show that the parties obviously intended this to be a condition. For example, in a contract for the sale of highly speculative shares it is necessary that the agreement be performed on the date stated in the contract.

10.1.2 By agreement

BILATERAL DISCHARGE

As a contract is made by agreement it can be ended or varied by an agreement which in itself will be a binding contract. Bilateral discharge will occur where the contract is wholly or partly executory on both sides. Discharge by agreement in these circumstances may take one of three forms:

1   By termination of the original contract.
2   By termination of the original contract and substitution of a new agreement.
3   By variation of the original contract.

A mere oral agreement is sufficient to effect all of these unless the original contract was one that required written evidence (see Chapter 8). In this case any new agreement or variation in an agreement must be evidenced in writing to be enforceable. This is shown in:

Goss v Nugent (1833)

In this case there was a written contract for the sale of land. One of the terms of the contract required the vendor to make good title. The purchaser, however, agreed orally not to insist on title being made to part of the land. Later, however, he changed his mind and declined to go through with the purchase of the property. The vendor sued him in breach. The court held that the vendor should fail as he was unable to deliver the title that had been agreed in the original contract. The original contract stood, as the oral variation was of no effect.

When a contract is discharged by a bilateral agreement there is consideration present to make a new contract, as each party has given up what he was entitled to receive from the other under the original agreement. If, however, one party alone agrees not to insist upon precise performance by that other party, (for example, he says that he will not object if the goods are delivered one week late) then there is no consideration. This unilateral undertaking will not operate to discharge or vary the contract. However, if the other party relies on this voluntary forbearance and alters his position by doing so then the doctrine of equitable promissory estoppel (see Chapter 7) may allow that party a good defence to an action under the original contract. You will remember however that this forbearance to sue may be withdrawn as long as reasonable notice of its withdrawal is given.

UNILATERAL DISCHARGE

Where the contract has been wholly performed by one of the parties, any release of the other party has to be either under seal or supported by consideration. In other words, release in these circumstances has to be in the form of either a deed or a simple contract. If it takes the form of a simple contract there will be accord (that is the agreement to release the party who has not fully performed) and satisfaction (the consideration given in return for the release). So, for example, if A owes B £500 and B agrees to take £400 in full satisfaction of the debt, A will not be released from liability. If, however, B agrees to take £400 at a date earlier than the contract date then A will be released from making further payment. The agreement to pay the smaller sum at an earlier date is the accord and the payment at a time earlier than the contract requires is the satisfaction.

Payment in the form of a cheque for a smaller sum than that due under the original contract will not be a good discharge of the debt. This was shown in the case of *D & C Builders* v *Rees* (1965). The law relating to accord and satisfaction has been dealt with in detail in Chapter 7.

BY CONDITION SUBSEQUENT

A contract may provide for its own discharge on the happening of a particular event. For example, a contract of employment provides that it may be ended by the giving of notice by either the employer or the employee. Leases of land may also make provision for their termination by the giving of notice on either side. In these cases, however, statutes provide some control over the freedom of the parties to end their contracts as they choose by, for example, providing minimum periods of notice which must be given to employees who are being dismissed. An example of a contract which provides for its own discharge occurred in:

Head v Tattersall (1871)

H bought from T a horse 'guaranteed to have been hunted with the Bicester hounds'. The understanding was that H could return the horse up to the following Wednesday if it did not conform to the description. Within the time limit allowed by the contract the horse was injured and it was then discovered that it had never hunted with the Bicester hounds and the plaintiff returned it and claimed to recover the purchase price. The court held that the plaintiff could succeed. The option to return the horse was a condition subsequent and it made no difference that the horse had been injured through no fault of the plaintiff whilst in the plaintiff's possession. The plaintiff could therefore cancel the contract and recover the purchase price.

NOVATION

Novation occurs when obligations under the contract are transferred from one person to another. For there to be a valid novation there must be a three-sided contract. For example, if A has undertaken to do some work for B and A is selling his business to C and wishes to transfer the duty to do the work to C the parties will, if they choose, enter a novation. B agrees to release A from his obligation to perform the contract in return for A persuading C to enter a contract with B to perform the work. B's consideration for C's promise is his release of A from the terms of the original contract.

10.1.3 By frustration

1   A party will not be excused from his obligations under a contract merely because circumstances have arisen which have made his promise more difficult or less profitable to fulfill or have made it incapable of fulfilment. So, for example, if a contractor undertakes to complete work by a

given date he will not be excused if by reason of strikes or bad weather or lack of materials or labour he finds it impossible to finish the work at the agreed time. For example in the case of:

Tsakiroglou & Co Ltd v Noblee and Thorl GmbH (1961)

T agreed to sell Sudanese groundnuts to N. The nuts were to be shipped from Port Sudan to Hamburg between November and December 1956. As a result of the Suez crisis, however, the Suez Canal was closed from 2 November 1956 until April 1957. T failed to deliver the groundnuts, arguing that shipment around the Cape of Good Hope (which was the only route available following the closure of the Canal) was commercially and fundamentally different from what the parties had contracted for. The House of Lords held, however, that the contract was not frustrated and that T were liable for breaking the contract. The changing circumstances had not made a sufficiently fundamental or radical difference to the terms of the original contract. 'An increase of expense is not a ground of frustration' (per Viscount Simonds).

2   Definition of frustration
    A contract will be frustrated therefore when, without the fault of either party, the obligation becomes incapable of performance because circumstances have arisen which would make that performance something radically different from the contractual undertaking. You will see that for frustration neither party must be to blame and that the situation that has arisen must have made further performance of the contract impossible. The frustrating event must be the result of some inevitable outside cause.

3   Frustrating events
    It is not possible to classify all the circumstances which will frustrate a contract but the following are the most common examples:

    (a) Personal services
         A contract for personal services will be frustrated by the death or incapacity of the promisor. So, for example, a contract of employment for a skilled worker will be frustrated if he is deprived permanently or for a long time of the use of his hands. This is shown in:

Condor v The Barron Knights Ltd (1966)

C was a drummer engaged to play in a pop group. He was contractually bound to work seven nights a week when work was available. After he had suffered an illness, however, C was advised by his doctor that it was only safe for him to work on four nights a week. The group had to engage another drummer who could safely work seven nights a week. The court held that C's contract had been frustrated in the commercial sense. It was impractical to engage a substitute for the three nights a week when C could not work, as this would involve double rehearsals of the group's music and comedy routines.

    (b) The non-occurrence of an event
         If a contract has been made on the basis of some future event then the contract will be frustrated if in fact that event does not take place. For example, in:

Krell v Henry (1903)

H agreed to rent K's premises to view the Coronation procession of Edward VII. The procession was not mentioned in the agreement. Because the King took ill, the Coronation had to be postponed. The procession did not take place and H did not occupy the premises. K sued H for the rent. The Court of Appeal held that though the procession had not been mentioned in the agreement it was the basis of the contract and the contract was therefore frustrated when the event did not take place.

The contract will not be frustrated, however, if the event is not the sole basis of the contract. This occurred in:

Herne Bay Steam Boat Co v Hutton (1903)

H Co agreed to hire a steamboat to the defendant for a period of two days in order to take passengers to Spithead to cruise around the Fleet and to see the Naval Review which was to take place on the occasion of Edward VII's Coronation. Because the Coronation was cancelled so was the Review, although the Fleet had already assembled. The steamboat therefore could have been used to cruise around the Fleet. The Court of Appeal held that the contract was not frustrated. The holding of the Naval Review was not the only event upon which the intended use of the boat depended. Another object of the contract was to cruise around the Fleet and this object remained capable of being fulfilled.

(c) By changes in the law
A common cause of frustration, especially in time of war, is interference by the Government or legislature. Acts contemplated by the contract may be prohibited or restricted or become impossible to perform. For example, in:

Re Shipton Anderson & Co v Harrison Bros Arbitration (1915)

The contract was made for the sale of a quantity of wheat lying in a warehouse. Before the wheat had been delivered, however, and before ownership had passed to the buyer under the contract, the Government requisitioned the wheat using wartime emergency regulations which empowered it to control food supplies. The House of Lords held that the seller was excused further performance of the contract as it was now impossible to deliver the goods because of the Government's lawful requisition. The contract in other words had been frustrated.

In:

Metropolitan Water Board v Dick Kerr & Co (1918)

A contract to construct a reservoir was frustrated by a wartime order which forbade constructional work and required contractors to place labour and plant at the disposal of the Ministry.

Compare this case with:

Tamplin (FA) Steamship Co Ltd v Anglo-Mexican Petroleum Products Co Ltd (1918)

In this case a vessel was chartered for five years from December 1912. In February 1915 the Government requisitioned the ship for use in the transport of troops. The owners claimed that the contract was frustrated. The charterers were willing to continue to pay the agreed freight (the rental for the ship) as they wished to receive the larger sum paid by the Government by way of compensation. The owners, however, claimed that the contract was frustrated in which case the ship would return to their control and they would receive the Government compensation. The House of Lords held that the requisitioning of the ship did not have the effect of frustrating the charter party. In view of the time still to run on the charter the interruption could not be described as sufficient to discharge the contract. There might be many months during which the ship would be available for commercial purposes before the remainder of the charter expired.

(d) Destruction of the subject matter
If the specific thing essential to the performance of the contract is destroyed, the contract will be frustrated.
For example, in the case of:

Appleby v Myers (1867)

Contractors had undertaken to erect certain machinery on the defendant's premises. Whilst the work was in progress the premises were destroyed by fire. The fire was not due to the fault of either party. The contract was held to be frustrated.

4   Events which will not frustrate a contract
A contract will not be frustrated where

(a) Performance is merely made more difficult or expensive.
This was shown in the case of
Tsakiroglou & Co Ltd v *Noblee and Thorl* (see above).
(b) The frustration is self-induced.
This is shown in the case of:

Maritime National Fish Ltd v Ocean Trawlers Ltd (1935)

M chartered a vessel from O. The ship could operate only with an otter trawl. Both parties realised that it was an offence to use such a trawl without first obtaining a Government licence. M was granted three such licences but chose to use them in respect of three other vessels. The result of this was that O's vessel could not be used. The court held that the charter party had not been frustrated and M was liable to pay the charter fee. M had freely chosen not to license O's vessel and therefore its inability to use it was a direct result of its own deliberate act.

(c) The parties provide for the frustrating event in the contract.
If the contract states what will happen in the event of the occurrence arising the contract will not be regarded as frustrated. If, however, this event is more extreme than

was envisaged by the contract, the court will decide on construction of the terms of the agreement, whether or not the event has been provided for. In the case of:

Jackson v Union Marine Insurance Co Ltd (1874)

A ship was chartered in November 1871 to proceed with all possible despatch, dangers and accidents of navigation excepted, from Liverpool to Newport. It was to load a cargo of iron rails at Newport for transport to San Francisco. The ship sailed on the 2 January 1872 but the next day it ran aground in Caernarvon Bay. It was refloated by the 18 February and taken to Liverpool where it underwent extensive repairs which lasted until August. On the 15 February the charterers repudiated the contract. The court held that the time it took to have the ship repaired was so long as to frustrate the original adventure. In a commercial sense the speculation entered upon by the shipowner and the charterers had been frustrated. The express exceptions in the contract were not intended to cover an accident which caused such extensive damage.

(d) Possibly the doctrine of frustration does not apply to a lease. A lease is regarded as more than a contract. The lease gives the lessee an estate in land which continues to exist whatever happens.
In:

Cricklewood Property & Investment Trust Ltd v Leighton's Investment Trust Ltd (1945)

A building lease was entered into in 1936 for a term of 99 years. Under the lease the tenants were to build a number of shops to form a shopping centre. Before the work was completed, war broke out and the Government imposed restrictions on building and the supply of materials. The tenants refused to pay the rent reserved by the lease on the basis that the lease had been frustrated by these restrictions. The House of Lords held that the tenants were obliged to pay the rent. The interruption of building work did not destroy the identity of the arrangement or make it unreasonable to carry out the building work as soon as the restrictions were lifted. The House of Lords based their decision on the fact that a six year interruption from 1939 to 1945 was not long enough to frustrate the lease but they did not deal with the general position regarding frustration of leases. There were, however, several points made obiter in the case and the general view of the House of Lords was that a lease could never be frustrated unless, for example, the lease was for land on which building was to take place but later the land was declared a permanent open space before building took place.

5   The effects of frustration
When frustration has been established, the contract is at an end and neither party is liable to perform obligations which arise after the date of frustration. The question of compensation for the parties in the event of frustration is governed by the Law Reform (Frustrated Contracts) Act 1943. This Act provides that:

(a) All sums paid before the frustrating event can be recovered (whether consideration has either totally or partially failed).
(b) Money which was due to be paid but which had not yet been paid ceases to be payable.
(c) If the party who has received the money or to whom the money is due under the above two points has incurred expenses in carrying out his part of the contract, the court may allow him to retain or recover the whole or part of the money expended. In estimating these expenses the court may include a reasonable sum for overheads or personal services.
(d) A party who has received a valuable benefit must pay for it such amounts as the court considers just having regard to all the attendant circumstances. Amongst these circumstances will be the expenses incurred by the beneficiary in the performance of his part of the contract.

The 1943 Act has certain limitations. The right to recover expenses is limited to those cases where money has been spent or is payable under the contract *before* frustration has occurred. The court has a discretion concerning the sum to be allowed and will disallow expenditure prematurely or unreasonably incurred. A number of contracts are specifically excluded from the provisions of the Act. It has, for example, no application to contracts for the carriage of goods by sea, to voyage charter parties, to contracts of insurance, or to contracts for the sale of goods which perish before the risk passes to the buyer.

The parties themselves may agree to exclude the provisions of the Act by the terms of their agreement. If the parties provide as to rights and liabilities in the event of frustration the courts will enforce this term. For example, the standard form of building contract makes provision for contingencies created by the outbreak of war. If such a frustrating event occurs, the 1943 Act will not apply—the terms of the contract will govern the situation.

10.1.4 By breach

Breach of contract will occur when one of the parties fails or refuses to perform his obligations under the agreement. In these cases the other party will always be entitled to damages and, if the failure or refusal is serious, he may also be entitled to treat the breach as a repudiation of the contract by the defaulting party. In other words, if the breach is serious he may regard the contract as discharged. Alternatively, the innocent party may choose to treat the contract as continuing and rely on his remedy in damages and insist on the other party performing the contract. This can be seen in:

White & Carter (Councils) Ltd v McGregor (1961)

M, a garage proprietor, agreed with W, advertising contractors, for the display of advertisements for the garage for three years. The day the contract was made, M decided not to go through with it and asked W to cancel the contract. W refused to do this and displayed the advertisements as agreed. W later sued for the full amount due under the contract. The court held that W was entitled to claim the full amount. M had committed an anticipatory breach of contract and W was entitled to accept this breach as repudiation or to treat the contract as continuing. There was no obligation on them to accept the breach. The contract therefore survived.

The innocent party may treat the breach as discharging a contract where there is:

ANTICIPATORY BREACH

Anticipatory breach will occur when one of the parties renounces his obligations either before the time for performance has arrived or before the contract has been completely performed. For example, in:

Hochster v De La Tour (1853)

H was engaged to act as a courier for T. The contract was made in April, the work was to commence in June. In May however T told H that his services would not be required. H brought this action in breach. The court held that H was entitled to damages even though the time for performance had not yet arrived.

In:

Cort v Ambergate Railway Co (1851)

The contract was for the supply of 3,900 tons of railway chairs which C was to deliver to A Co in certain quantities on certain dates. C delivered 1,787 tons which A accepted but then A refused to take any further deliveries. C brought this action but A Co argued that the mere fact that C was ready to deliver the balance was not sufficient. For an action in breach, argued A Co, actual delivery was necessary. The court held, however, that A Co was wrong. C had a right to sue immediately without showing actual delivery.

If there is an anticipatory breach of contract, the innocent party has a choice of actions. He may either accept the breach and treat the contract as repudiated and claim damages there and then or as in *White & Carter (Councils) Ltd v McGregor*, treat the contract as still continuing and thus allow the party in breach to have second thoughts. The danger of this, however, is that if in the meantime the contract becomes frustrated the party in breach will be relieved from liability. This occurred in the case of:

Avery v Bowden (1855)

The contract concerned a charter party of a ship. Under the terms of the contract a cargo of wheat was to be loaded at Odessa within 45 days. When the ship arrived at Odessa the charterer informed the owner's captain that there was no cargo and advised him to sail home. The captain refused to accept the refusal, hoping that the charterer would find a cargo. Before the 45-day period expired, however, the Crimean War broke out thus making any trade with Russia illegal. The owner sued the charterer for breach of the charter party. The court held that the owner's action should fail. The captain had refused to accept the charterer's anticipatory breach as a discharge and, before the time for performance had arrived the contract had been discharged by frustration. The defendant therefore had a good defence.

If there is acceptance of an anticipatory breach but between this time and the date fixed for performance of the contract something occurs which would have frustrated the contract were it still in existence and would therefore have relieved the party in breach of his obligations, the innocent party will be entitled only to nominal damages. This occurred in:

The Mihalis Angelos (1970)

A ship, The Mihalis Angelos, was chartered to load mineral ore at Haiphong on 1 July and to carry this ore to Hamburg. The contract provided that if the vessel was not available for loading on 20 July the charter party could be cancelled. On 17 July, however, Haiphong was bombed and the charterers repudiated the contract. This anticipatory breach was immediately accepted by the vessel owners. In fact, the vessel was still in Hongkong harbour on 23 July and thus the charter party could have been cancelled in any event by the charterers. The court held that the owner could recover only nominal damages for the breach. The fact that they could not have performed the contract on 20 July was a contingency that had to be looked at in deciding the amount of damages to be awarded.

IMPLIED REPUDIATION BY THE OTHER PARTY

If one of the parties acts in such a way as to prevent himself performing the contract, he will be regarded as having impliedly repudiated the contract. For example, if a person has agreed to sell goods to the buyer but then sells them to a third party he will have impliedly repudiated. As above this may occur either before performance or during the time the contract is being performed.

FAILURE OF PERFORMANCE

If one of the parties fails to carry out a vital part of the contract, in other words commits a breach of condition, the innocent party may regard himself as discharged from his own obligations and may also claim damages if he has suffered loss. If, however, the failure to perform is only with regard to a minor part of the contract, ie is a breach of warranty, the innocent party will not be discharged but can merely claim damages for the breach.

If there has been a breach of condition but the innocent party chooses to treat the contract as continuing he will be said to have affirmed the agreement. This means that he has elected to treat the breach of condition as a breach of warranty. His only remedy then is to sue in damages. He cannot treat the contract as repudiated by the breach. On the distinction between conditions and warranties see Chapter 8.

10.2 REMEDIES FOR BREACH OF CONTRACT

10.2.1 Introduction

When a contract is broken the innocent party has a number of remedies. He will, for example, have a right of action for damages. He may also be able to claim specific performance of the contract to require the other party to perform what he has undertaken to perform. To prevent a breach of contract an injunction may be granted. If the contract has been entered into following misrepresentation or under duress or undue influence, the innocent party may ask for an order of rescission and, if there is an error in the written contract, for rectification. If one of the parties has obtained a benefit under the contract, the other may ask the court to order the beneficiary to pay for this advantage he has obtained. This will be granted on a *'quantum meruit'* basis.

Finally, all actions in breach must be brought within the period specified by the Limitation Act 1980. Any action not brought within this time will be unenforceable.

We will examine each of these remedies in detail.

10.2.2 Damages

If there has been a breach of contract, the innocent party may claim damages as of right. In other words, the remedy is at common law and therefore does not depend on the court exercising its discretion. In deciding the amount of damages to be awarded, the court follows certain principles. These are as follows:

DAMAGES MUST NOT BE TOO REMOTE

It is not all the loss which can be traced to the breach which is taken into account in the assessment of damages. When a contract is broken, it may create a chain of events which has far-reaching and unanticipated effects. The loss for which damages will be awarded is that which is immediate rather than too remote.

For example, an employee who is unfairly dismissed suffers the immediate consequence of a loss of wages. As a result, he may fail to pay his mortgage and be ejected from his house. These are remote consequences. The immediate consequences are those which can be readily foreseen as likely to follow from the breach. The remote consequences do not arise naturally from the breach but are the result of special attendant circumstances.

The test for remoteness of damage, that is, for deciding which consequences of a breach the innocent party may recover damages, was given in:

Hadley v Baxendale (1854)

The drive shaft of the plaintiff's mill in Gloucester was broken. He employed the defendant, a carrier, to take the shaft to the makers in Greenwich for it to be used as the model for the manufacture of a new one. The defendant delayed delivery of the shaft and was therefore in breach of contract and the mill remained idle for much longer than was necessary. The plaintiff brought this action in breach of contract claiming as damages the loss of profits during the period of additional delay. The court held that the plaintiff could not recover damages for this extra loss of profits. It was too remote.

The test for remoteness formulated in the case was that:

1. Damages will be awarded only for losses arising naturally from the breach or otherwise within the reasonable contemplation of the parties when they made the contract as the probable result of the breach.
2. Damages will be awarded for losses outside the natural course of events only when the special circumstances which caused the loss are within the defendant's actual or constructive knowledge at the time he makes the contract.

In the *Hadley* case, the extra loss of profits did not arise in the usual course of things. It was reasonable for the defendant to suppose that the miller had a spare drive shaft. The special loss that would result from the delay (ie that the mill would be completely idle and all profit would be lost) had not been disclosed to the defendant at the time the contract had been made.

WHAT WILL BE REASONABLY WITHIN THE CONTEMPLATION OF THE PARTIES?

This is a question of fact in each case. For example, a loss of profit arising from breach of a trading contract will be recoverable, if the contract is made between experienced parties who can be taken to understand the ordinary practices and circumstances of each other's business. For example, in:

Czarnikow Ltd v Koufos ('The Heron II') (1967)

K, shipowners, contracted to carry a cargo of sugar for C to Basrah. K knew that there was a sugar market at Basrah and also that C were sugar merchants. K did not actually know, however, that C intended to sell the sugar at Basrah market as soon as it was landed. The ship deviated from its normal course in order to carry out some other work for the shipowners and, as a result, was 9 days late in arriving at Basrah. The sugar was sold immediately, but fetched £4,000 less than it would have fetched had it been delivered on the date required in the contract. The court held that C could recover this £4,000 as damages for breach of the contract of carriage. K must have realised that the sugar would be sold immediately on arrival and that the price of the goods would probably fluctuate. The loss therefore was in the ordinary course of events and was within the reasonable contemplation of the parties.

Under the first head of the rule in *Hadley* v *Baxendale*, therefore, loss will be too remote if it is not of the type or kind that could be within the reasonable contemplation of the parties. The party in breach does not have to know of the actual loss that will be suffered as long as he is aware, or should be aware, that this type of loss may ensue. In:

Wroth v Tyler (1974)

The defendant contracted to sell his house to the plaintiffs for £6,000, the sale to be completed in October 1971. In July 1971, the defendant wrongfully repudiated the contract. By the October of that year, the house was worth £7,500. The plaintiffs sued for specific performance of the contract (ie for an order to make the defendant proceed with the sale) and for damages. Judgment was given in January 1973, by which time the value of the house had increased to £11,500.

The court held that, although the plaintiffs were not entitled to an order of specific performance, they were entitled to damages. The defendant argued that, as he could not have foreseen the very large rise in house prices 1971 to 1973 this loss was too remote. The court disagreed. It held that the defendant knew the plaintiffs had no resources other than the £6,000 they had raised to buy the house and that therefore they could not act on their knowledge of the breach to make a substitute purchase on a rising market. The defendant knew that there would be some loss of the type or kind suffered even if he could not know the full extent of this loss. He was therefore liable to pay damages assessed on the basis of the value of the house at the date of judgment, not at the date of breach. In other words, the plaintiffs were awarded £5,500 rather than £1,500 damages.

WHEN WILL 'SPECIAL' DAMAGES BE AWARDED?

By the second branch of the rule in *Hadley* v *Baxendale*, a defendant will be liable for losses which arise outside the normal course of events (ie special damages) only when the special circumstances which caused the loss were within his actual or constructive knowledge at the time the contract was made.

The way in which this rule operates is seen in the following two cases:

Simpson v London & North Western Railway Co (1876)

The defendant railway company collected S's samples of cattle food from a showground in Bedford in order to transport them to another showground in Newcastle. S, who were manufacturers of cattle food, told the railway company that the goods 'must be at Newcastle on Monday certain'. The samples were not delivered until after the show in Newcastle had ended and S, who had travelled to Newcastle to display the goods, claimed damages for his loss of profit and loss of time.

The court held that S should succeed in his claims. The railway company knew of the special circumstances and had entered the contract on that basis.

Victoria Laundry Ltd v Newman Industries Ltd (1949)

The plaintiffs ordered a new boiler from N. N was five months late in delivering the boiler and, as a result, the plaintiffs lost their normal business profits during the period of delay and the profits from a lucrative dyeing contract they were offered during the period. N knew that the plaintiffs needed the boiler for immediate use.

The court held that the loss of normal profits arose naturally from the breach and could therefore be recovered. The loss of profits on the dyeing contract, however, could not be recovered as N knew nothing about this offer and so could not be said to have foreseen the loss.

THE PURPOSE OF DAMAGES IS TO COMPENSATE THE INNOCENT PARTY

Damages are designed to put the injured party in the same financial position as if the contract had been properly performed. In other words, the purpose of damages is to compensate the innocent party, not to enable him to make a profit.

So, if the breach of contract causes the innocent party no loss, he will obtain only nominal damages—usually £1. For example, if A agrees to buy a car from B but B then sells the car to C in breach of his contract with A, the amount of damages A will recover will depend on whether he can buy a similar vehicle elsewhere. If he can do so and pays no more for it than he was going to pay B, he will have a right of action against B but, because he has suffered no loss, he will receive only nominal damages.

If, on the other hand, he has to pay much more for a similar car when he buys it elsewhere, he will be awarded the difference between the price he was going to pay B and the price he has to pay to acquire a similar vehicle from another source.

Another illustration of the point that the purpose of damages is to compensate is that, in an action for loss of earnings arising from a breach of contract, the court will reduce the amount awarded by the amount of tax the plaintiff would have had to pay had he earned the money. In:

Beach v Reed Corrugated Cases Ltd (1956)

The plaintiff had a 15-year contract with the defendants. He was to be paid a salary of £5,000 per year. After four years, he was wrongfully dismissed. He could have expected to earn a further £55,000 had he been kept on in employment. The court held, however, that in awarding him damages, account had to be taken of the income tax he would have paid on this money and the tax he would have had to pay on his private investments. The plaintiff therefore was awarded £18,000 damages. This represented the amount he would actually have received from his earnings. The amount deducted to take account of taxation does not go to the Inland Revenue. It reduces the damages the employer has to pay. The reduction is made to ensure that the innocent party is merely compensated for his loss.

THE INJURED PARTY MUST MITIGATE HIS LOSS

This means that the innocent party cannot merely sit back and do nothing following the breach. He must try to make good his loss by, for example, trying to obtain the goods from elsewhere, or by trying to find a new job, or by, in some other way, attempting to rectify the position in which he has found himself. The court may even hold that he should accept a new contract with the party in breach. In:

Brace v Calder (1895)

The defendants, a partnership, agreed to employ B as manager of a branch of their business for two years. Five months after the contract, however, the partnership was dissolved by the retirement of two of the partners and the business was transferred to the remaining partners, who offered to employ B on the same terms as before. B refused. The dissolution of the partnership constituted wrongful dismissal of B, and he sued the firm claiming, as damages, the amount he would have earned had he served the full contractual period.

The court held that B had behaved unreasonably in rejecting the offer of continued employment. He had not taken the opportunity of mitigating his loss. He was therefore entitled only to nominal damages.

DIFFICULTIES IN ASSESSING THE AMOUNT OF LOSS WILL NOT PREVENT AN ACTION

The courts are not deterred from awarding damages merely because the loss suffered is difficult to quantify. The courts are prepared to award damages based on an estimate of loss. This was shown in:

Chaplin v Hicks (1911)

C agreed with H, a theatrical manager, to attend an interview at which 12 girls would be chosen from 50 applicants to be employed by H for a term of three years. H did not give C sufficient notice of the interview to enable her to attend and she therefore lost her opportunity to be selected. She claimed damages for this lost opportunity.

The court held that, although the assessment of loss was very difficult (eg there was no telling whether, had she attended the interview, the plaintiff would have been selected), nevertheless she was entitled to damages for the breach. She was awarded £100.

In certain circumstances, the court will include in the damages a sum to compensate the injured party for mental distress and inconvenience. For example, in the case of:

Jarvis v Swan's Tours Ltd (1973)

J booked a winter-sports holiday with the defendants on the strength of representations in the defendants' brochure. The advertised facilities were not available. The brochure claimed amongst other things that there would be an English-speaking hotelier, a representative throughout the holiday and that a house-party would be held. None of these materialised and J was very disappointed. He sued for damages for breach of the contract to provide the promised holiday. The court held that J could recover damages for mental distress—in this type of case, both parties contemplated that, on breach, there might be mental inconvenience such as frustration, annoyance, and disappointment. Difficulties in putting a price on such matters would not prevent the court making an award.

The court in the *Jarvis* case, however, said that such an award would be made only in suitable cases. Examples of other suitable cases are seen in:

Jackson v Horizon Holidays Limited (1975)

J booked a holiday for himself, his wife and two of their children. The brochure described the hotel as having first class facilities and J made it clear that he wanted the holiday to be of the highest standard. In the event the facilities were sadly lacking, the bathroom in the children's room was unusable. There was dirty linen on the bed. The food was distasteful. Jackson sought damages in respect of the loss of his holiday for himself, his wife and the two small children. The Court of Appeal held that he was entitled to recover damages for all members of the party. This decision has been criticised since the wife and children were clearly not parties to the contract. However, it has to be said that in the event it seems a fair result.

Heywood v Wellers (1976)

H went to the defendant solicitors to ask them to institute proceedings to recover a £40 debt that she was owed and to obtain an order to stop the debtor molesting her. The solicitors gave her the wrong advice as to the court in which her action should be taken and when, despite the non-molestation order, the debtor again molested H, her solicitors failed to take him to court. H sued her solicitors. The court held that the solicitors could not recover their costs from H as they had failed completely to fulfil their side of the contract. Their advice had been useless. Furthermore, H was entitled to damages for the disappointment, upset and mental distress she had suffered as a result of the solicitors' breach of contract. They had broken their duty of care to her by not preventing her being molested.

LIQUIDATED DAMAGES AND PENALTIES

The contract may provide for the payment of an agreed sum in the event of breach. Such a fixed sum is known as 'liquidated damages'. The amount agreed, however, must be a genuine attempt to pre-estimate the loss that will be suffered in the event of breach. If it is an amount fixed to deter a person from breaking a contract it will be a penalty and will not be enforced.

If the sum is a genuine pre-estimate of the loss, it will be enforced even though the actual loss is greater or smaller than the actual loss.

Cellulose Acetate Silk Co Ltd v Widnes Foundry Ltd (1933)

The defendant, W, agreed to build a plant for C by a certain date. The contract provided that W would pay C £20 a week for every extra week taken to finish the work beyond the contract date. C was 30 weeks late in completing the plant. S claimed for their actual loss, which was £5,850. The court held that the amount agreed in the contract was a genuine attempt to pre-estimate the loss. The plaintiffs therefore were entitled to recover only these liquidated damages of £20 per week. They could claim only £600.

The distinction between liquidated damages and penalties was discussed in the case of:

Dunlop Pneumatic Tyre Co Ltd v New Garage & Motor Co Ltd (1915)

N, who were wholesalers, agreed not to sell D's tyres at below the list price. The contract provided that liquidated damages of £5 would be paid for every tyre sold below this price. The House of Lords held that the requirement to pay £5 per tyre was a genuine pre-estimate of loss and therefore represented liquidated damages. Precise estimation of loss was difficult in the circumstances, but the agreed figure was not extravagant and represented an honest attempt by the parties to provide for the breach.

Although the question as to whether a fixed payment is a penalty or a genuine attempt to pre-estimate loss depends on the parties' intentions, Viscount Dunedin in the *Dunlop Case* laid down a number of guidelines:

1. The sum will be a penalty if it is extravagant in relation to the greatest loss that could conceivably be proved to have followed from the breach.
2. It will be a penalty if the breach consists only in not paying a sum of money, and the sum to be paid is greater than the sum which ought to have been paid.
3. There is a presumption that the agreed payment is a penalty when a single lump sum is payable by way of compensation on the occurrence of one or more of several events, some of which may cause serious damages others of which may cause only slight loss. In:

***Ford Motor Co (England) Ltd v Armstrong* (1915)**

A was a retailer who sold F's cars. In his agreement with F, A undertook:

(a) not to sell any of F's cars or spares at below list price;
(b) not to sell F's cars to other dealers in the motor trade;
(c) not to exhibit any car supplied by F without F's permission.

For any breach of the agreement, A agreed to pay F £250, being the damage which the plaintiff would 'sustain' by the breach.

The defendant broke the agreement.

The Court of Appeal held that the £250 was in the nature of a penalty and not liquidated damages. It was payable for different types of breach which were not likely to produce the same loss. The size of the payment also suggested that it was not a genuine pre-estimate of loss.

4   the fact that the consequences of the breach are difficult to quantify in advance does not stop the sum agreed being an attempt at a genuine pre-estimate of loss and therefore enforceable
5   the fact that the parties call an agreed sum a penalty or liquidated damages is not conclusive. The court may reach its own conclusion on the matter.

10.2.3 Specific performance

A decree of specific performance is an order of the court compelling a party to a contract, on pain of imprisonment for contempt, to perform his side of the bargain. Specific performance will not be granted where damages would be an adequate remedy. So, for example, most contracts for the sale of goods will not be specifically enforceable. The buyer could generally obtain similar goods elsewhere and sue the seller for the difference between the price he was going to pay and the price he actually had to pay for these goods.

Specific performance is an equitable remedy and is therefore granted at the court's discretion.

CONTRACTS WHICH ARE SPECIFICALLY ENFORCEABLE

Specific performance will be granted for those agreements which are of a positive character and for breach of which the remedy of damages would be inadequate as no-one but the defendant can perform what he has contracted to perform.

A contract will be specifically enforceable if it is:

1   For the sale of land or of an interest in land
2   For the sale of goods which are unique, or rare, or in short supply.

In the case of:

***Sky Petroleum Ltd v VIP Petroleum Ltd* (1974)**

In March 1970 a contract was made between S and VIP whereby S agreed to buy all the petrol it required from VIP for a period of at least 10 years. In 1973 VIP purported to terminate the contract for an alleged breach of its terms by S. This was a time of acute national shortage of petrol following an embargo on oil exports by Arab countries supplying the UK. S would be unable to find alternative sources of supply at that time. The court granted S an injunction to stop VIP withholding petrol. The injunction was granted because the court could order specific performance of a contract to sell and purchase chattels which were not specific or ascertained in cases where damages would not provide a sufficient remedy, as was the case here.

CONTRACTS WHICH CANNOT BE SPECIFICALLY ENFORCED

An order of specific performance will not be granted if the performance cannot be effectively supervised by the court. So, a decree of specific performance will not be granted:

1   For contracts which require day-to-day performance by one party of continuous, successive acts. The court cannot supervise the party's actions to make sure that the decree is obeyed. So,

contracts of employment and contracts of service cannot be specifically enforced. For example, in:

Lumley v Wagner (1852)

W agreed to sing for L at Her Majesty's Theatre during a given period, and not to sing elsewhere without L's permission. W refused to sing for L, but agreed to sing for another promoter at Covent Garden.

The court refused to grant L a decree of specific performance to compel W to sing at his theatre as this was a contract for personal services and could not be specifically enforced. The court did, however, grant L an injunction to stop W singing at Covent Garden otherwise people who liked her singing might go there to the disadvantage of L and to the advantage of his competitor.

2   Contracts to build or repair property. Again, execution of the work cannot be controlled. The exception to this occurs when

  (a) The building work is clearly defined.
  (b) The plaintiff has a substantial interest in the performance of the work and the interest is such that damages would not provide adequate compensation.
  (c) The defendant is in possession of the land on which the work is to be done and this prevents the employment of a substitute builder.

In:

Wolverhampton Corporation v Emmons (1901)

The Corporation had acquired land for redevelopment. It had sold part of the land to the defendant who had covenanted to demolish houses on the land and build new property in their place. The defendant demolished the houses and submitted plans for the new work. These plans were approved, but the defendant failed to start building. The Corporation applied for a decree of specific performance which the court granted. The defendant's obligations were precisely defined by the plans; damages would be an inadequate remedy, as the Corporation was losing rates on the houses which should have been built on the town centre site; and, as the defendant had possession of the site, the Corporation could not get the work done by employing another builder.

3   Contracts for the loan of money. The loan can be raised elsewhere and damages obtained for any losses incurred.
4   Contracts for the sale of goods which are not unique, rare or in short supply.

10.2.4 Injunction

An injunction will be granted to enforce a negative undertaking. It will be used to prevent a party from doing what he has agreed not to do, as in the *Lumley* v *Wagner Case* (above). It will also be granted to prevent a person breaking a contract. In a contract of employment, the employee can be prevented from engaging in work similar to that involved in the contract which has been broken, but it will not be ordered to prevent the employee doing other kinds of work. In:

Warner Brothers Pictures Inc v Nelson (1936)

N (whose stage name was Bette Davis) agreed that for a specified period she would act for W; that, during this period, she would not act for anyone else; and that she would not engage in any other occupation without W's consent. During the period, N contracted to act for another person in breach of the agreement. The court granted W an injunction against N stopping her acting for this other person. The court, however, would not grant an injunction to prevent her from engaging in any other occupation as this would force her to perform her contract or remain idle.

In other words, as in the case of a decree of specific performance, an injunction will not be granted to stop a person leaving their employment. Nor will it order an employer not to dismiss an employee unless damages would be an inadequate compensation for losses suffered as a result of the dismissal.

An injunction is an equitable remedy and is subject to the same criteria as a decree of specific performance.

10.2.5 Rescission

This again is an equitable remedy, available at the court's discretion to a person who wishes to avoid a contract affected by misrepresentation, mistake, duress or undue influence. The effect of an order of rescission is to put the parties back to the position they were in before the contract was made.

For a more detailed discussion of rescission, see Chapter 9.

10.2.6 Rectification

This order will be granted when an oral contract has been put into writing but the writing does not reflect what had been verbally agreed. Again, see Chapter 9 for a more detailed discussion of this remedy.

10.2.7 Quantum meruit

Quantum meruit means 'how much is deserved'. In other words, an award made on a *quantum meruit* basis will be of such amount as the court believes the plaintiff has earned or deserves in respect of work completed or services undertaken for the benefit of another party. A claim on the basis of *quantum meruit* may be made in the following circumstances:

WHERE THE CONTRACT DOES NOT PROVIDE HOW MUCH THE PLAINTIFF IS TO BE PAID

If a person has delivered goods or performed a service under a contract which makes no provision as to how much he is to be paid, the court will award what it believes to be a reasonable sum in the light of all the circumstances.

WHERE THE CONTRACT DOES NOT MAKE FULL PROVISION FOR PAYMENT

An award on a *quantum meruit* basis will be made where one of the parties has performed more onerous duties at the request of the other party than were covered in the contract. For example, in:

Parkinson & Co Ltd v Commissioners of Works and Public Buildings (1950)

Contractors agreed to erect work for payment of the cost of the work (estimated at £5 million) plus £300,000. During the course of the work, the Commissioners exercised their contractual right to ask for additional works costing £1.5 million over the original £5 million estimate. The court held that the express provision providing payment of £300,000 was referable only to the cost of the original £5 million project. The contractors therefore could claim extra payment on a *quantum meruit* for the additional £1.5 million works.

MINORS' CONTRACTS FOR NECESSARIES

Although such a contract is valid and binding on a minor, he need only pay what the court considers to be a reasonable sum for the goods even though the contract provides for the payment of a greater sum.

WHERE PLAINTIFF IS PREVENTED FROM COMPLETING HIS WORK BY THE OTHER PARTY'S BREACH

In other words, if one party starts to perform the contract but is stopped from fully performing his obligations because the other party breaks the contract, the innocent party can claim payment on a *quantum meruit* basis as an alternative to suing for damages. The amount awarded may be based, where possible, on the contract rate. See the case of *Planché* v *Colburn* (page 126).

WHERE THERE IS PARTIAL PERFORMANCE OF A CONTRACT

If the contract is partly performed and this partial performance is voluntarily accepted by the other party he must pay for the benefit he has thus obtained. The amount he can claim will be based on a *quantum meruit* basis. See, for example, *Sumpter* v *Hedges* (page 125).

WHERE ONE PARTY HAS PERFORMED WORK UNDER A CONTRACT SUBSEQUENTLY FOUND TO BE VOID FROM THE OUTSET

For example, in the case of:

Craven-Ellis v Canons Ltd (1936)

The plaintiff was employed as managing director by the defendant company. The Articles of the company required directors to have qualification shares which they had to obtain within 2 months of their appointment. The plaintiff never acquired the shares so his contract of employment was void. The court held that, despite this, the director was entitled to a reasonable sum by way of remuneration on the basis of a *quantum meruit*.

10.2.8 Limitation of actions

By the Limitation Act 1980, an action for breach of simple contract must be brought within 6 years of the cause of action accruing, ie within 6 years of the breach occurring. Actions for breach of a contract under seal must be brought within 12 years of the breach. At the end of these periods, the contract is not discharged, it merely becomes unenforceable by action in court.

These statutory periods will not start running against a plaintiff who is under some disability in the eyes of the law (eg who is a minor, or a mentally disordered person) until the disability ceases eg until the minor reaches the age of 18, or the mentally disordered person recovers.

REVIVAL OF CAUSE OF ACTION

A claim which is outside the limitation period may be revived if the debtor or someone representing him acknowledges the liability in writing and such acknowledgement is communicated to the other party, or if the debtor makes any part payment of the debt.

THE EFFECTS OF FRAUD

If the plaintiff's right of action is concealed by fraud, the period of limitation does not begin to run until the plaintiff has discovered the fraud or, by reasonable diligence, could have found it. In this context, 'fraud' will cover any deliberate concealment of a breach of contract which is not likely to be discovered for a long time.

EQUITABLE CLAIMS

Claims in equity eg for injunction or specific performance, are not normally governed by the Limitation Act. They are covered instead by the equitable doctrine of 'laches'. This means that delay may defeat equity. In other words equitable remedies must be sought by the plaintiff as quickly as possible. The courts considering an equitable remedy, however, may apply the 1980 Act by analogy where there is both a common law and an equitable remedy.

SUMMARY

In this chapter we have looked at the various ways in which a contract may be ended. The principles we have studied apply in general to all contracts, whatever their subject matter. So, for example, a contract of agency will be ended when the agent has performed what he agreed to perform. If the subject matter of the agency is destroyed through no fault of either party the agency is frustrated.

The remedies for breach also are of general application. For example, the rules as to remoteness of damage as stated in the case of *Hadley* v *Baxendale* are included in the provisions of the Sale of Goods Act 1979.

In other words, the law in this chapter and, indeed, in this whole section on contract, applies to all the specific contracts we will be studying later. You must make sure that you understand the basic principles before you move on to look at the way these principles are applied to particular types of undertaking.

SELF-TEST QUESTIONS

10.1 How may a contract be discharged?

10.2 Distinguish between the decisions in
(a) *Sumpter* v *Hedges* (1898), and
(b) *Hoenig* v *Isaacs* (1952)

10.3 Define frustration

10.4 Why was the contract frustrated in the following cases?
(a) *Condor* v *The Barron Knights* (1966)
(b) *Krell* v *Henry* (1903)
(c) *Metropolitan Water Board* v *Dick Kerr & Co* (1918)

10.5 Which Act determines the rights and duties of parties to a frustrated contract?

10.6 Define anticipatory breach and describe the remedies available to the innocent party in the event of such a breach occurring

10.7 What is the test for remoteness of damages in contract?

10.8 Compare the decisions in
(a) *Simpson* v *London & North Western Railway Co* (1876), and
(b) *Victoria Laundry Ltd* v *Newman Industries Ltd* (1949)

10.9 What is the purpose of damages?

10.10 What do the cases of *Jarvis* v *Swan's Tours Ltd* (1973), *Cox* v *Philips Industries Ltd* (1975), and *Heywood* v *Wellers* (1976) show?

10.11 Distinguish between liquidated damages and a penalty

10.12 Which contracts cannot be specifically enforced and why?

10.13 When will a claim on a *quantum meruit* basis be made?

10.14 Under the Limitation Act 1980, what are the limitation periods for actions for
(a) breach of simple contract
(b) breach of contracts made under seal?

Answers on page 315

EXERCISES

Exercise 10.1

How may a valid contract be discharged by frustration? What is the effect of such a discharge?

Exercise 10.2

1 Describe the rules governing remoteness of damage and the measure of damages in the law of contract.

2 H promised to deliver goods to J on a specified date. There was a term in the contract which provided for the payment of liquidated damages of £500 in the event of a breach of contract by H.

    H delivered goods of the correct quality and quantity but two weeks late. J accepted the goods. Later J decided to sue H for breach of contract and to claim £500 damages.

Advise J.

Answers on page 316

Sale and supply of goods and services

This chapter will deal with the rights and duties attaching to the transfer of ownership of goods from one person to another. A sale of goods covered by the Sale of Goods Act 1979 will occur when the seller sells goods to the buyer in return for the buyer paying a money consideration called the price. In other words, the 1979 Act applies only when the buyer pays for the goods by cash (or by cheque or credit card). If there is no cash involved, as where the buyer exchanges his goods for the seller's, the Sale of Goods Act will not apply to the transaction. Nor will it apply where, for example, the buyer must perform some act in order to obtain the goods (eg 'buy 20 litres of petrol and obtain a 'free' wine glass.' Again, the buyer's consideration for the glass is not the payment of cash; it is the act of buying the petrol). These contracts are covered by the Supply of Goods and Services Act 1982. It does, however, apply to part-exchange contracts, for example, when a person exchanges his old car for a new one and pays cash for the balance.

Both the 1979 and 1982 Acts imply certain terms into the contracts of sale (SGA) and supply (SGSA), but the Sale of Goods Act also gives rules relating to the passing of property, performance of the contract and remedies available for breach. These rules apply only to sale of goods contracts and will be dealt with in this chapter. If the contract is one for the supply rather than sale of goods, the rules relating to the passing of property etc will be dealt with by the common law.

Finally, this chapter will deal with the terms implied into a contract for the supply of services by the Supply of Goods and Services Act 1982.

11.1 SALE OF GOODS

11.1.1 Introduction

Sales of goods are covered by the Sale of Goods Act 1979. The Act applies to all contracts whereby the seller transfers or agrees to transfer property in goods to the buyer for a money consideration called the price (SGA 1979 s2(1)). To decide when the Act applies it is necessary to analyse the definition.

11.1.2 Contracts covered by the Sale of Goods Act 1979

CONTRACT

For the Act to apply, there must be a contract between the buyer and the seller. The Act does not lay down the requirements for this contract. It assumes that a contract has been formed according to the general common law rules set out in this book. Unless the Act specifically contradicts these rules they will apply to all contracts for the sale of goods.

The reason why the Act gives no definition of a contract is that it is intended to be a general code covering every type of transaction which involves the sale of goods, from the sale of a box of matches to the sale of a multi-million pound computer, from sales between private individuals, to sales between multi-national companies.

PROPERTY

Property in this context means ownership of the goods. The purpose of a contract for the sale of goods therefore is to pass ownership in these goods from the seller to the buyer.

Property or ownership may pass as soon as the contract is made.

EXAMPLE 1

Sam offers to sell his car to Ben at a certain price. Ben accepts the offer and a contract therefore comes into existence. Property passes at this time.

Or, property may pass at some later stage as when, for example, the contract is made subject to a condition:

EXAMPLE 2

Ben agrees to buy Sam's car subject to Sam fitting four new tyres. This is an agreement to sell and will become a sale when the condition is satisfied and the buyer is notified. Thus property remains with Sam until he has fitted the four new tyres and Ben has been notified. At this stage, property passes to Ben.

It is only if property has passed that the seller will be able to sue the buyer for the price of the goods if the buyer refuses to pay. If the contract is an agreement to sell, the seller will be able to sue the buyer for damages for breach but not for the purchase price of the goods (see later).

EXAMPLE 3

In Example 2 (above) if, before Sam fits the new tyres, Ben says that he no longer wants the car, Sam's only action will be to sue Ben for damages for breach of contract. The purpose of damages is to compensate the innocent party (Sam) so Sam will receive the difference in value (if any) between the price Ben had agreed to pay and the market value of the car. If, however, Ben says that he does not want the car *after* Sam has fitted the tyres and told Ben that the car is ready for collection, property will have passed and Ben can be made to pay the price he has agreed.

Also, whoever has property in the goods will bear the risk of any accidental loss of or damage to these goods. Thus, if property has not passed, the seller will bear this risk; when property has passed, however, the risk will be with the buyer (see later).

EXAMPLE 4

If, in Example 2, before Sam has fitted the tyres the car is destroyed in a crash, Sam the seller will have to bear the loss and Ben will not be liable. If, however, the car is destroyed after the tyres have been fitted and Ben has been notified, Ben will have to pay for the vehicle even though he had not yet been to collect it. Property, and therefore risk, had passed to him when the condition had been fulfilled and he had been notified.

GOODS

Goods includes anything that can be touched or moved and which is visible and of which physical possession can be taken. The word therefore covers everything that would generally be understood to be goods. It does not include land or rights such as debts, or shares in a company (which cannot be physically transferred), nor does it include money which is exchanged as currency. If, however, money is being bought and sold for its curio value, for example by a person who collects coins, then it will be classed as goods and the Sale of Goods Act will apply to the transaction. In deciding whether a coin has been transferred as currency or for its curio value, the court will see what the parties to the contract intended. So, for example, if you go to a bank and buy some American dollars to take on holiday to the USA with you, the dollars will have been transferred as part of a currency transaction and the Sale of Goods Act will not apply. If, however, one of the notes you acquire has a flaw in it and you sell this note to a collector, the intention of the parties will be to transfer it as goods, not currency, and the Sale of Goods Act will apply to this contract.

Goods may be categorised as either specific or unascertained.

SPECIFIC GOODS

Specific goods are 'goods identified and agreed upon at the time a contract of sale is made' (SGA 1979 s61(1)). In other words, if the contract states the actual goods which are to be sold, so that these goods and no others are the subject matter of the contract, the goods will be specific.

UNASCERTAINED GOODS

Unascertained goods are any goods which are not specific. The term includes future goods (that is, goods which are not yet in existence such as a crop which is to be grown or a car which is to be made); goods which are sold by description (as when you go into a shop and ask for 'a box of matches', leaving it to the assistant to choose the box which is to be sold rather than choosing it yourself); and goods which form part of a larger consignment (as, for example, when the buyer buys two tonnes of wheat out of a consignment of 100 tonnes). When the goods are identified in accordance with the contract they become ascertained, and it is only then that property will pass. Thus, in the example of the purchase of the wheat (above) property stays in the seller until the two tonnes of wheat have been ascertained. When they have been ascertained, that is, when the tonnes have been set aside to be delivered to the buyer and to no-one else, property passes to the buyer.

This point was discussed in:

Re Wait (1927)

The buyers agreed to buy 500 tons of wheat out of a consignment of 1,000 tons on board a particular ship. The buyer paid in advance but before he could take delivery, the seller went bankrupt. The question before the court was whether the buyer could claim his 500 tons. He could do so only if property in the 500 tons, which at the time of the seller's bankruptcy had not been removed from the total consignment, had passed to him.

It was held that the 500 tons were unascertained goods, property in which could pass only when they became ascertained, that is when a particular 500 tons and no other were to pass to the buyer under the contract. Therefore, no property had passed to the buyer despite his payment in advance and he had no right to claim 500 tons of wheat. All he could do was to prove as an unsecured creditor in the seller's bankruptcy.

The distinction between specific and unascertained goods is of particular importance in relation to the transfer of property (ie ownership of the goods) which will be discussed in more detail later.

'A MONEY CONSIDERATION CALLED THE PRICE'

For a contract to come within the Sale of Goods Act, a buyer must pay money for the goods. Contracts of part-exchange (where the buyer pays the contract price partly in goods and partly in money) will also be covered.

EXAMPLE 5

A buyer agrees to buy a new car for £5,000. He pays the purchase price by transferring his old car (worth £2,000) to the seller and paying the £3,000 balance in cash. This transaction will be covered by the Sale of Goods Act.

SGA 1979 s8 states that the price may be fixed by the contract or it may be left to be decided in a way agreed upon in the contract or it may be based on prices charged by the parties in previous dealings. If the contract says nothing about the price, the courts have the power by s8(2) to require the buyer to pay a reasonable price. If, however, the agreement states that the parties are to agree a price at a later date, this will mean that they are still in the process of negotiation and the court will hold that no contract has yet been made.

May and Butcher v R (1934)

It was held that an agreement for the sale of goods at a price to be fixed by the parties at a later date was not a concluded contract at all.

CONTRACTS TO WHICH THE SALE OF GOODS ACT WILL NOT APPLY

There are several types of contract by which property in goods passes but which do not come within the definition in SGA 1979 s2(1) and which therefore do not fall within the scope of the Act. The most important of these are:

HIRE-PURCHASE CONTRACTS

The ultimate aim of both hire-purchase and sale contracts is the same—the transfer of ownership in goods from one person to another. The ways in which these aims are achieved, however, are different.

In a contract of hire-purchase, the hirer bails the goods and, at the end of the hire period, he has the option to purchase. It is not until the option to purchase has been exercised that a contract of sale occurs. Until this time, the hirer may end the contract without incurring any liability in breach.

In a contract of sale, on the other hand, the buyer is bound to buy the goods even though there may be a delay in the passing of property. In other words, in a sale, the ultimate destination of the goods is known.

Hire-purchase contracts are governed by the Consumer Credit Act 1974. This will be discussed in the next chapter.

CONTRACTS FOR WORK AND MATERIALS

A distinction has to be made between those contracts which have as their main object the sale of goods, and those whose main object is to provide skill as well as goods for the purchaser. The Sale of Goods Act 1979 will apply to the former but not to the latter.

A broad distinction may be drawn by asking: What was the parties' main intention? If the main intention was to buy and sell goods and the skill involved in the contract was incidental to this, then the transaction will be covered by the Sale of Goods Act. If, however, the main purpose of the contract was that the 'buyer' should receive the benefit of the 'seller's' skill and the transfer of goods was only incidental to this, then the transaction will be a contract for work and materials.

EXAMPLE 6

Ben buys a radio for his car from Sam's shop. For an extra payment, Sam agrees to fit the radio in the car. In answer to the question: What was the parties' main intention?, the answer would be: to buy and sell a radio. The fitting of the radio was only incidental to this, so the transaction would be covered by the Sale of Goods Act 1979 as it is a contract for the sale of goods.

Contrast that situation with:

EXAMPLE 7

Ben takes his car to Sam's garage for a service. As part of the service, Sam puts fresh oil and new filters into the car and charges Ben for these, as part of the service price. Is the transaction for the oil and the filters covered by the Sale of Goods Act? The question is: What was the parties' main intention? Here, the main intention was to improve Ben's car by servicing it.

The sale of the oil and the filters was only incidental to this, not the main purpose of the contract. The contract is therefore one of work and materials.

Other examples of work and materials contracts would be a contract to paint a portrait (the buyer is buying the skill of the painter, not just the materials he uses); a contract for a plumber to come to fix a burst pipe (even though the plumber uses, and charges for, new piping, the main purpose of the contract is to provide a service).

The importance of the distinction lies in the fact that contracts for the supply of work and materials are covered by the Supply of Goods and Services Act 1982. This Act implies terms which are identical to those implied by the Sale of Goods Act 1979 (see the next part of this chapter) but does not deal with other matters such as the transfer of property and possession or remedies. In contracts for work and materials, these issues are dealt with by the common law rather than by Act of Parliament.

The Supply of Goods and Services Act 1982 also covers contracts for the supply of goods which do not come within the Sale of Goods Act definition. For example it will cover contracts for the supply of goods where there is no money consideration as where the transaction is based on an exchange of one article for another. The 1982 Act will be dealt with later in this chapter.

11.1.3 Implied terms

INTRODUCTION

Certain terms are automatically implied into all contracts covered by the Sale of Goods Act 1979. There are implied conditions that the seller has the right to sell the goods (s12); that goods sold by description will correspond with the description (s13); that the goods will be of merchantable quality and fit for the purpose (s14); and that, if goods are sold by sample, the bulk will correspond with the sample (s15). These terms apply to all Sale of Goods Act contracts, whether the parties are aware of them or not.

TYPES OF TERMS

The Sale of Goods Act divides the implied terms into conditions and warranties.

1. A **condition** is a term which, if broken, gives the buyer a choice of actions. He can *either* treat the contract as ended, return the goods and recover the purchase price plus damages if he has suffered any extra loss, *or* decide to keep the goods and sue the buyer for damages.
2. A **warranty** is a less important term. If the seller is in breach of warranty the buyer's only remedy is to sue the seller for damages. The buyer must keep the goods. The amount of damages which may be claimed will be the difference in value between the goods as they are delivered and the value they would have had if there had been no breach of warranty.

ACCEPTANCE

If the buyer has accepted the goods, he has to treat any breach of condition as a breach of warranty. In other words, if the buyer has accepted goods which it is later discovered are not of merchantable quality, the buyer will not be able to treat the contract as repudiated. His only remedy will be to keep the goods and sue the seller for damages (s11(4)).

A buyer will be said to have accepted the goods in the following three cases (s34 and s35):

1. When the buyer clearly and unequivocally tells the seller that he accepts the goods by, for example, signing a note to this effect; or
2. When, after a reasonable opportunity for examining the goods, the buyer acts in a way which prevents him returning any faulty goods to the seller in substantially the same condition they were in when they were delivered to him. Thus, the buyer will be said to have accepted the goods when, after a reasonable opportunity for examining them, he sells them to another person or when he uses the goods, together with other materials, to make a new object; or
3. When the buyer keeps the goods for a reasonable time without telling the seller that he intends to reject them.

What are a reasonable time and a reasonable examination were discussed in the case of:

Bernstein v Pamsons Motors (Golders Green) Ltd (1987)

B bought a new Nissan car from the defendants. For three weeks after the purchase, B took the car on a series of short journeys in order to test it. He drove a total of 142 miles. The car's engine then failed completely and had to have lengthy and expensive repairs done to it. The buyer wanted to reject the car, but the High Court held that he had accepted the car and therefore his only action was for damages. The court said that a buyer will have accepted goods when he has had a reasonable time to inspect the goods and to try them out generally. The fact that a defect was serious and could only be discovered after the goods had been used for some time was irrelevant. In this case, B had had time to try out the car generally and had therefore accepted it.

The time for examination starts running from the first reasonable opportunity for examination (*Long* v *Lloyd* (1958)).

IMPLIED TERMS AS TO TITLE (SGA 1979 S12)

s12 contains a number of implied terms relating to title; an implied condition that the seller has the right to sell; implied warranties that the buyer will have quiet possession of the goods and that the goods will be free from any charge or encumbrance; and warranties given when the seller sells a limited title.

1. Implied condition that the seller has the right to sell (s12(1)):
   In all contracts for the sale of goods, there is an implied condition that the seller has the right to

sell. This means that, when a person sells goods, he impliedly promises that he is the owner of these goods and that he has the power to transfer rights to them to the buyer.

In:

Rowland v Divall (1923)

The plaintiff bought a car from the defendant. Several months after the sale, it was discovered that the defendant had not owned the car but had, in fact, bought it from a thief. The defendant was completely innocent in the matter. The car was returned to the true owner and the plaintiff claimed the return of the full purchase price from the defendant. The defendant argued that, as the plaintiff had had the use of the car for several months, he should be said to have accepted it and his remedy therefore should lie only in damages. In calculating the damages, the defendant argued, the court should take account of the use the plaintiff had had of the car and should accordingly reduce the amount awarded.

The court rejected the defendant's argument. When a person buys goods, he is paying for ownership. If the seller does not own the goods then he cannot pass any ownership to the buyer and the buyer has therefore received nothing for the purchase price he has paid. There is, in fact, a total failure of consideration. The buyer could not be said to have accepted the goods, as there was nothing to accept. The buyer was therefore entitled to recover the full purchase price from the seller.

So, if the seller is in breach of s12(1) because he does not own the goods he is selling, there will be a total failure of consideration and the buyer may recover the full purchase price. In these circumstances, the buyer cannot choose to accept the goods and merely sue for damages; his only remedy is to treat the contract as repudiated.

There is, however, another interpretation of 'the right to sell'. This is that the seller will be in breach of s12(1) if, even though he actually owns the goods he is selling, he does not have the ability in law to transfer possession of these goods to the buyer.

This point was made in:

Niblett Ltd v Confectioners' Materials Co Ltd (1921)

The seller sold the buyer 3,000 tins of condensed milk which were being shipped to the United Kingdom from the USA. The cans were labelled 'Nissly' which was an infringement of the Nestlé trademark. Customs refused to release the cans to the buyer until the offending labels had been removed and destroyed. This the buyer did and then sold the unlabelled tins for the best price he could obtain. The court held that the sellers were liable in breach of s12(1) as, although they owned the cans of milk, they did not have the right to sell them at the time property was to pass. Because of the infringement of another's trademark, the seller did not have the power to transfer the milk to the buyer.

Whether the seller commits a breach of s12(1) because he does not own the goods he is selling, or because he does not have the power or ability to sell, his liability is strict. The fact that he is completely innocent is no defence to an action by the buyer, as was shown in *Rowland* v *Divall* (above).

2 Implied warranties (s12(2)):

Section 12(2) implies two warranties into all contracts covered by the Sale of Goods Act. There is an implied warranty that the seller will transfer the goods free from any charge or encumbrance not disclosed or known to the buyer at the time of sale. In other words, there is an implied warranty that the goods supplied will be free of any third-party rights such as lien. There is also an implied warranty that the buyer will receive quiet possession of the goods; ie that there will be no physical interference with the buyer's possession of the goods. In *Niblett's* case, it was suggested that the buyer having to remove the labels from the tins was a breach of the warranty of quiet possession. In the case of:

Microbeads v Vinhurst Road Markings Ltd (1975)

In January 1970, the sellers sold a number of road marking machines to the buyer, both parties being unaware that another firm had applied for letters patent for similar machines. As part of the patenting process, the complete specification for the machine was published in November 1970 and the letters patent were granted in 1972. Under patent law, a person applying for a patent is granted rights and privileges in respect of the patent only after publication of the complete specification and it is only after letters patent have been granted that the owner can bring action against anyone using the patented invention without permission.

In 1972, therefore, the patentee of the machine sued the buyer of the road markers for using the machines in breach of patent. The court held that this interference with the buyer's use of the goods constituted a disturbance of his quiet possession and therefore constituted a breach of the warranty in s12(2). The seller was therefore liable to the buyer. This warranty, said Lord Denning, was a continuing warranty. It applies not just at the time of sale but also in the future. Thus whereas s12(1) can be broken only at the time of sale, s12(2) will be broken whenever a third person lawfully interferes with the buyer's quiet possession.

3   Sale of a limited title (s12(3)–(5)):
    Section 12(3)–(5) applies whenever it is clear from the terms of the contract or the circumstances of the sale, that the seller is lawfully selling goods which do not belong to him. In these cases, the seller will not be liable provided he has disclosed all charges and encumbrances over the goods which he knows about and the seller does not, and provided that he has the right to sell such title that he is transferring.

EXAMPLE 8

Under the Torts (Interference with Goods) Act 1977 (T(IG)A 1977), a person in possession of goods which he has been given to repair or service or clean etc (the bailee) may sell these goods if the person who gave the goods to him (the bailor) does not collect them.

Thus, if a person takes his watch into a jeweller's shop to be repaired and then does not return to collect it at the given time, the jeweller (the bailee) may give notice to the customer (bailor) of his intention to sell the watch. If the bailee has not given notice, he must show that he has taken reasonable steps to find the bailor to give such notice or, alternatively, that he has obtained a court order for sale. If the bailor satisfies one of these conditions he may then sell the uncollected watch and pass to the purchaser such title as the bailor possessed.

Thus, if the bailor owned the watch, the purchaser from the jeweller will obtain good title and the jeweller will have to account to the bailor for the money he received, less the cost of repair and sale. If, on the other hand, the bailor did not own the watch but was, in fact, buying it on hire-purchase, the finance company will be able to recover the watch from the purchaser. If it is clear that the sale by the jeweller is a sale of a limited title, the purchaser is acquiring just such title as the bailor possessed. If he possessed none, then the purchaser acquires none and must return the watch to the finance company. If the jeweller had a legal right to sell (which he does under the 1977 Act) and as long as he declares all charges and encumbrances over the goods of which he is aware (if he knows of none he cannot declare any) then the purchaser of the watch is left without any right of action at all against the jeweller. The weakness in the title which he is acquiring will be reflected in the price he pays for the watch.

This is explained in the following:

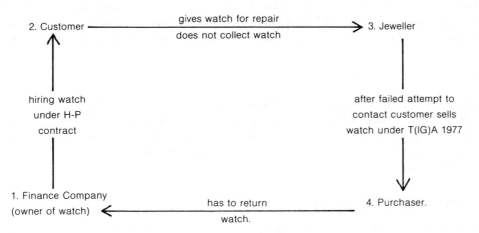

The purchaser is left without any action against the jeweller as long as the jeweller was unaware of the fact that the customer was hiring the goods on H-P and complied with the pre-sale requirements of the T(IG)A 1977. If, however, the jeweller did not comply with the Act's requirements, or if he knew of the H-P contract and did not disclose it he would be liable to the purchaser in breach of s12(4) and (5) SGA.

IMPLIED CONDITION IN A SALE BY DESCRIPTION (SGA S13)

In every sale of goods by description, there is an implied condition that the goods will correspond with the description.

1 A sale will be by description when:
 (a) The goods are unascertained.
 (b) Or although specific, the goods are bought as 'a thing corresponding with a description'.

For example in:

***Grant v Australian Knitting Mills* (1936)**

The buyer went into a shop and asked for a pair of long woollen underpants. The goods were displayed on the counter in front of him and the sales assistant selected a pair which the buyer bought. The underpants contained a chemical, used in the clothes' manufacture, which caused the buyer to develop a severe skin disorder. The chemical should have been removed before the goods were sold but had not been in this particular pair of underpants. It was held that this was a sale by description. Although the underpants had been displayed in front of the buyer, he had bought the particular pair as goods complying with the description 'long woollen underpants'. (Note that the buyer's action was based on a claim that the underpants were not of merchantable quality (s14(2)). Until 1973, a purchaser could succeed in an action for breach of s14(2) only if the sale was by description. Hence the need for the plaintiff to show that he bought these goods by reference to their description.)

Similarly in:

***Beale v Taylor* (1967)**

The defendant advertised his car for sale in a newspaper, describing it as a 'Herald (1200) Convertible, White, 1961'. The plaintiff answered the advertisement and went to inspect the car. He noticed that there was a 1200 disc on the back of the vehicle. The plaintiff bought the car but later discovered that, although the back half was indeed a 1961 Herald, the front half was part of a much earlier model which had been cleverly welded on. He sued the seller for breach of s13.

The defendant claimed that, as the plaintiff had examined the car, he could not claim that the sale was by description. The court held, however, that the buyer had bought the goods relying on the description in the advertisement and on the 1200 disc on the back of the car. There was therefore a breach of s13. The car, by the disc, described itself as being the model claimed.

By s13(3) a sale will not be prevented from being a sale by description merely because the goods, being exposed for sale, are selected by the buyer. This brings within the scope of s13 sales of goods in supermarkets when the buyer chooses the actual goods himself. These goods may be described, for example, by their wrapping, or by the marking on the shelf on which they are stacked.

2 The meaning of description

Even though a sale may be by description, however, not all the words which relate to the goods are necessarily part of the description for the purposes of s13. The early cases on the original Sale of Goods Act, which was passed in 1893, seemed to suggest that the courts would adopt a broad approach to the question of what constituted words of description.

For example in:

***Re Moore & Co and Landauer & Co* (1921)**

The buyer ordered a number of cans of fruit to be packed in crates containing 30 cans per crate. When the goods arrived, although the correct number of cans was delivered some of the crates contained only 24 cans. The court held that the way in which the goods were to be packed was part of the description and therefore the buyer was entitled to reject the goods for breach of s13 even though, in fact, he was not in any way affected by the wrong packing. He merely wanted an excuse to avoid the contract.

In later cases, however, the courts have adopted a much narrower approach. They now suggest that words of description are only those words necessary to identify the nature of the goods. Other words, such as words of purpose and words of quality are not part of the description but fall to be decided under other sections of the Sale of Goods Act.

This was stated in the case of:

***Ashington Piggeries Ltd v Christopher Hill Ltd* (1972)**

The sellers manufactured animal food-stuff. The buyers were breeders of mink and they ordered a food-stuff called 'King Size' from the sellers. The buyers provided a formula for this 'King Size', one of the ingredients of which was herring meal. The sellers were told that the 'King Size' was to be fed to mink.

The herring meal used for the King Size had been stored in a chemical which, unknown to the sellers, had reacted with the herring to create a poisonous substance which was particularly harmful to mink. The buyers fed the King Size to their mink which died. The buyers sued the sellers claiming, amongst other things, breach of s13 in that as they had asked for King Size for mink and as the King Size had poisoned the mink there was a misdescription. The House of Lords held that there was no breach of S13. Words of description are those words necessary to identify the nature of the goods, and the purpose of the goods (ie 'for mink') was not relevant to the identification of the King Size. Whatever use the King Size was to be put to its identity remained the same. The purpose of the goods fell to be considered under s14.

The words 'for mink' would be part of the description only if there were different types of King Size, some suitable for mink, others suitable for, eg, cattle. Then and only then would the words 'for mink' be necessary to distinguish this type of King Size from King Size for cattle. Only in these circumstances would words of purpose be necessary to describe the identity of the goods.

3   Remedies for breach of s13

As s13 is a condition, breach of the term entitles the buyer to treat the contract as repudiated and return the goods and recover the purchase price. Alternatively the buyer may choose to keep the goods and sue for damages (as he did in *Beale* v *Taylor*). Section 13, however, is subject to the common law rule *de minimis non curat lex* (the law does not take account of small discrepancies). Thus, if there is only a slight deviation from the contract description the court may decide that this is too small to constitute a misdescription and refuse to find a breach of s13.

EXAMPLE 9

Ben orders 10 tonnes of steel from Sam. When the steel is delivered Sam discovers that it is 5 kilograms short of 10 tonnes. The court could apply the *de minimis rule* and decide that the shortage is too small to matter and refuse to allow Ben to treat the contract as repudiated.

The application of the *de minimis rule* is at the court's discretion. If, for example, the court decides that the discrepancy could have been further reduced it will not allow the *de minimis rule* to apply. In other words, the rule is designed to enable business contracts to proceed smoothly rather than to protect the lazy seller.

IMPLIED CONDITION THAT THE GOODS WILL BE OF MERCHANTABLE QUALITY (SGA S14(2))

Section 14(2) provides that where goods are sold in the course of a business there is an implied condition that the goods will be of merchantable quality. This condition will not apply, however, in relation to defects which are specifically drawn to the buyer's attention before sale or, if the buyer has examined the goods before sale, as regards defects which that examination ought to have revealed.

It is necessary to analyse the various parts of this definition.

1   The goods must be sold in the course of a business

For the condition to apply to the sale, the seller must sell in the course of a business. In other words, it will not apply to private sales. For the purpose of s14(2), the buyer's capacity does not matter. Whether he buys in the course of business or for his private use is irrelevant.

Compare this section with sections 12 and 13 which apply to *all* sales, regardless of the capacity of the seller.

2   The condition applies to 'the goods supplied under the contract'

In the case of:

***Wilson v Rickett, Cockerell & Co* (1954)**

A coal merchant supplied the plaintiff with a ton of Coalite. The Coalite contained a detonator which, when put on the fire, exploded. When the plaintiff sued, the defendant argued that the Coalite itself was of merchantable quality and that the detonator should be disregarded. The Court of Appeal held, however, that the condition in s14(2) applied to the total consignment. A ton of Coalite which included a detonator could not be said to be a consignment of merchantable quality. The plaintiff therefore was awarded damages.

3   The goods must be of merchantable quality

Merchantable quality is defined in s14(6) as meaning goods which are as fit for the purpose or purposes for which such goods are commonly bought as it is reasonable to expect having regard to the description applied to them, the price (if relevant) and all other relevant circumstances.

Thus, to be of merchantable quality, the goods must be fit for their ordinary purpose or purposes even if this is not the purpose for which the buyer bought them. The goods need only be fit for one of their normal purposes. They do not have to be fit for all the purposes for which goods of this type could be used. This was held in:

M/S Aswan Engineering Establishment Co v Lupdine (1987)

The buyer bought some heavy duty plastic pails in which to transport a liquid waterproofing compound to the Middle East. The pails, filled with the compound, were stacked up to six high in the shipping containers and, on arrival at their destination, Kuwait, were left, still stacked up to six high, in full sunshine on the quayside. Eventually, the extreme heat caused the pails to collapse and all the compound was lost. The buyer sued the seller claiming that the pails were not of merchantable quality as, it was argued, they should be fit for all the purposes for which goods of this type would commonly be used.

The Court of Appeal rejected this argument. The court held that for goods to be unmerchantable they had to be unfit for *any* purpose for which goods sold under the contract description would normally be used. These pails could be used for export shipment to many parts of the world, albeit not to the Middle East if they were left in exceptional heat stacked up to six high. The buyer lost his action.

Thus, to be merchantable, the goods need only be fit for one of their normal purposes.

The definition also covers the sale of second-hand goods. The price will be relevant here. As a general rule, the less you pay for second-hand goods the more defects you must expect before you can claim that the goods are not of merchantable quality. Thus a person who buys a second-hand car for £50 must expect more defects than one who pays £5,000 for a car. In other words, merchantable quality is a relative idea. It depends on how the goods were described, how much was paid for them and all other relevant circumstances. If the goods were new, the buyer may expect far fewer defects than if they were second-hand. In:

Rogers v Parish (Scarborough) Ltd (1987)

The Court of Appeal held that a new car is bought, not just to be driven from one place to another, but to enable the owner to do so with the appropriate degree of comfort, ease of handling, reliability and pride in the vehicle's outward and inward appearance.

The question to be asked is: 'What, in view of the description, price, etc was the plaintiff entitled to think he was buying?' If the goods do not comply with what he was entitled to think he was buying, they will be unmerchantable.

The goods have to be merchantable at the time of sale and delivery if they are intended for immediate use but, if the reasonable person would apply some process to them before use, they need be merchantable only when this process has been applied. Compare the following cases:

Grant v Australian Knitting Mills (1936)

It was held that the long woollen underpants were intended for immediate use and therefore had to be merchantable at the time of sale. Because the underpants bought contained a chemical, they were not of merchantable quality.

Heil v Hedges (1951)

The buyer bought pork chops which she ate after only part-cooking them. The chops contained a parasitical worm which would have been killed and thus made harmless had the chops been fully cooked. As it was, the worm was alive and made the buyer ill. The court held that the chops need only be merchantable after they had been fully cooked. The seller, therefore, was not liable for breach of s14(2). The chops could not be said to be unmerchantable.

Once it is shown that s14(2) applies to a particular case, the seller has strict liability. It is no defence to an action for him to show that he took all reasonable care to avoid committing an offence.

4 When s14(2) will not apply

As said earlier s14(2) will not apply when the seller sells the goods privately, that is, not in the course of a business. It will also not be implied in relation to defects which are specifically drawn to the buyer's attention before he buys the goods. Thus, for example, a buyer goes into a garage to buy a car and sees a particular model that he likes but, before he buys, the seller points out some patches of rust on the vehicle. If the buyer, knowing of these defects, goes ahead and buys the car, he cannot later reject the car because of these patches of rust. He has made his purchase in the full knowledge of the defects which have been pointed out to him. Of course, if there are other serious faults in the vehicle which have not been drawn to his attention he can reject the car because of these other defects, and if the defects which have been drawn to his attention are, in fact, substantially more serious than he had been led to believe he would be able to reject because of these.

In:

Bartlett v Sydney Marcus Ltd (1965)

A buyer was offered a car but, before the sale, he was told that the vehicle had a faulty clutch. The seller offered the buyer the car with the faulty clutch for £550 or said that he could have the clutch repaired before purchase, in which case the car would cost £575. The buyer chose to buy the car as it stood for £550, but when he later had the clutch repaired discovered that the repairs cost £45. He brought this action claiming that the seller was in breach of s14(2) as the defect was more serious than he had been led to believe. The court held that the car was of merchantable quality. The defect had been pointed out to the seller before sale and was not substantially worse than the buyer had been told. The buyer therefore lost his action.

The court in *Bartlett's* case in fact said that second-hand cars will be merchantable as long as they are usable, regardless of any other defects. This statement was made before there was a statutory definition of merchantable quality, however, and would not be followed today as it takes no account of, amongst other things, the price paid for the car.

The other exception to s14(2) states that, if the buyer examines the goods before the contract is made, the implied condition will not apply to any defects which the actual examination undertaken should have revealed. In other words, the question has to be asked whether the buyer had examined the goods before he bought them? If he did, it then has to be asked: what was the extent of the examination? Finally it must be discovered what that actual examination ought to have revealed to a reasonable person. The buyer will not be able to reject for any defects which ought to have been revealed by his examination (whether he in fact noticed them or not).

EXAMPLE 10

Ben went to a garage to buy a car. He examined the car by looking in the engine (although he knew nothing about engines) and by taking the car for a test drive. He bought the car. Later Ben discovered that the car had a defective engine and faulty steering. The defect in the engine could have been seen by a reasonable person by merely looking under the bonnet of the car and the defective steering noticed on a test drive by a reasonably competent driver. Ben was neither of these and had noticed nothing. Ben would be unable to reject the car for breach of s14(2).

In his situation, Ben would have been better not examining the car at all. If he had not done so, he would have retained full rights to reject the vehicle for breach of s14(2).

In other words, it is better not to examine goods at all than to examine them without knowing what you are doing or negligently. The law, in this instance, protects the lazy buyer. There is no requirement that the buyer should examine the goods and, in many cases, he retains more rights if he does not do so.

IMPLIED CONDITION THAT THE GOODS WILL BE FIT FOR THE BUYER'S PURPOSES (S14(3))

Section 14(3) provides that if goods are sold in the course of business and the buyer expressly or impliedly makes known the purpose for which he requires the goods there is an implied condition that the goods supplied will be reasonably fit for that purpose. The condition does not apply where the buyer does not rely, or it is unreasonable for him to rely, on the seller's skill and judgment.

In analysing s14(3), therefore, it will be seen that the following points arise:

1 The sale must be in the course of business

This requirement is the same as for s14(2).

2 The condition applies to 'the goods supplied'

Again as in s14(2) the condition applies to the whole consignment.

3 The buyer must make known the purpose for which he is buying the goods. He can do this either expressly or impliedly.

Implied notification will occur if the goods have only one purpose in the normal course of events and the buyer is buying them for this purpose. By asking for the goods, the buyer is impliedly notifying the seller of the purpose for which the goods are required (ie their normal purpose) and, if they are not fit for this purpose, the buyer can reject them for breach of s14(3).

In:

Preist v Last (1903)

The buyer bought a hot-water bottle. He intended to use it for its normal purpose but did not tell the seller this. The bottle burst in bed, scalding the buyer's wife. The court held that there was a breach of s14(3) because hot-water bottles had only one purpose in the ordinary course of events and the buyer wanted it for this purpose. Therefore, by asking for a hot-water bottle the buyer was impliedly telling the seller of the purpose for which he required the goods.

In some cases, however, in order to rely on s14(3) the buyer must expressly notify the seller of the purpose for which the goods are required. This express notification is necessary when the goods have more than one purpose as when, for example, the buyer orders 'animal food' he should specify the type of animal for which he requires the food in order to be able to rely on s14(3). If he does not give such express notification and is sold food which is not suitable for his particular animal but is suitable for other animals he will have no right to sue the seller under s14(3).

The buyer must also give express notification of the purpose for which he requires the goods if he wants goods, which normally have only one purpose, for some special, unusual purpose. This occurred in:

Griffiths v Peter Conway Ltd (1939)

A woman bought a Harris tweed coat without disclosing that she had very sensitive skin. The coat caused her to develop a skin disorder and she sued the sellers claiming breach of s14(3). The court held that she should fail in her action as she had not told the sellers that she wanted the coat for an unusual purpose (ie to be worn by someone with abnormally sensitive skin). The coat was perfectly all right to be worn by someone with normal skin and, as she had not made her particular purpose known, she could not claim to have been relying on the sellers' skill and judgment.

4 The goods must be reasonably fit for the specific purpose

The goods do not have to be absolutely fit for the buyer's purpose. Thus, second-hand goods do not have to be as fit for the buyer's purpose as new goods would have to be. They need only be reasonably fit second-hand goods. For example, in:

Crowther v Shannon Motor Co (1975)

The buyer bought a second-hand Jaguar motor car from the defendant car dealers. The car was eight years old and showed over 80,000 miles on the odometer. Before the sale, the buyer had been assured by the seller that, for this type of car, 80,000 miles was of little consequence and the car's engine could be expected to last for a long time yet. Three weeks later the engine seized up completely and had to be replaced. The buyer sued for breach s14(3), and the court held that the seller was liable. The car was not reasonably fit for its purpose. Although the purchaser of a second-hand car must expect defects, he was entitled to require that the goods be reasonably fit for the purpose. This car was not.

So, second-hand goods will be reasonably fit for the purpose even though there are some defects but not if the defect is too serious. In that event, they will not be reasonably fit second-hand goods.

5   The time for judging whether the goods are fit for the purpose is the time of sale and delivery. In *Crowther's* case, the fact that the car broke down only three weeks after sale showed that it must have been unfit at the time it was bought.

6   The condition will not apply when there is no reliance on the seller's skill and judgment or when such reliance would be unreasonable. The buyer cannot claim breach of s14(3) if the seller disclaims all knowledge of the goods. In the *Ashington Piggeries* v *Christopher Hill* case (above) the sellers told the buyers that they had never provided mink food before. If the food supplied had only affected mink, therefore, the sellers would not have been liable for breach of s14(3). As it was, however, the poison in the herring meal harmed all animals (although it was particularly harmful to mink) and therefore the sellers were liable. There will also be no breach of s14(3) if the buyer has greater knowledge of the goods than the seller. In the case of:

Teheran-Europe Co Ltd v ST Belton (Tractors) Ltd (1968)

The sellers sold the buyers air-compressors for resale in Iran. Because of certain design details, the compressors could not be resold on the Iranian market but, when the buyers sued the sellers for breach of s14(3), the court held that they should fail. The sellers had sold their standard compressors and, as the buyers regularly dealt in Iran, they knew the state of the market much better than the sellers did. It was therefore unreasonable for them to rely on the seller's skill and judgment.

There will also be no reliance implied where the buyer fails to give the sellers sufficient detail as to what the buyer's purpose is, as where the buyer merely asks the seller for 'animal food'.

The fact that the buyer only partly relies on the seller's skill and judgment, however, will not prevent an action under s14(3). In:

Cammel Laird & Co v Manganese Bronze and Brass (1934)

The buyer ordered ships propellers, giving the sellers full details about these goods. The only detail left to the seller's discretion was how thick the blade should be. The propellers supplied were of the wrong thickness and were therefore noisy in operation. The court held that there was a breach of s14(3) in that there had been at least partial reliance on the seller's skill and judgment to provide a propeller suitable for the vessel for which it was intended.

7   Section 14(3) imposes strict liability

Once breach of s14(3) is shown, it is no defence for the seller to show that he had done everything possible to avoid committing the breach. For example, in:

Frost v Aylesbury Dairies (1905)

The buyer bought some milk from the defendant milk suppliers. The sellers took all precautions known at the time to keep the milk free from germs but this particular milk contained typhoid germs. The buyer's wife drank the milk and died of typhoid. The court held that the defendants were liable for breach of s14(3) as the milk was not fit for human consumption. The fact that all possible reasonable care had been taken to ensure the milk's purity was no defence to the action.

THE RELATIONSHIP BETWEEN S14(2) AND S14(3)

Both the conditions refer to fitness for purpose. The difference between the two is that, for s14(2) the goods must be fit for their general purpose whereas for s14(3) they must be fit for the buyer's specific purpose. In many cases, of course, the buyer will want the goods for their general purpose. For example, when you buy a car you want it for driving around towns, through the country etc. Thus, if the car is not fit for these purposes the seller will be liable in breach of both s14(2) and (3).

If, however, the buyer has examined the goods before he bought them and has overlooked a defect which his examination ought to have revealed he will have lost his right of action under s14(2) but may still have an action under s14(3) if the goods prove unsuitable because of this defect.

On the other hand, if, for example, the buyer buys a car having told the seller that he wants it for rallying, but the seller says he knows nothing about any special requirements for this sport and the car turns out to be useless for the buyer's purpose, the buyer will have no action under s14(3) (the seller has disclaimed knowledge) but may have rights under s14(2) as the car is not fit for its ordinary purpose, having regard to its description (for rallying).

IMPLIED CONDITION THAT THE BULK OF THE GOODS SOLD BY SAMPLE WILL CORRESPOND WITH THAT SAMPLE (S15)

A sale by sample will occur where the contract says that it is such a sale (eg 'as per sample') or where the buyer buys goods intending to rely on the sample he has been shown.

If the sale is by sample, there is an implied condition that the bulk of the goods will correspond with the sample both in description and in quality. The buyer must be given a reasonable opportunity of comparing the bulk with the sample and the section implies a condition that the goods will be free of any defect which would make them unmerchantable and which would not be apparent on a reasonable examination of the sample.

In:

Godley v Perry (1960)

A child bought a catapult which, because of its faulty construction, broke in use and caused the child to lose his eye. He successfully sued the shopkeeper for breach of sections 14(2) and 14(3). The shopkeeper, who had bought the catapults by relying on a sample which he had tested by pulling back the elastic, sued the wholesaler who had supplied him, claiming breach of s15. The court held that the shopkeeper had made a reasonable examination and the defect had not been revealed by this examination. The wholesaler was therefore liable for breach of s15 in that he had supplied goods in a contract of sale by sample and these goods were not free of a defect which was not apparent on a reasonable examination of the sample.

11.1.4 Transfer of property and possession

INTRODUCTION

'Property' in goods means ownership of the goods. The general rule governing the transfer of property is that it will pass from the seller to the buyer when the parties intend it to pass (s17). If no such intention can be discovered in the contract or from the surrounding circumstances, the SGA provides certain rules to be applied to decide whether property is still with the seller, or whether it has been transferred to the buyer. As we will see later, the fact that the seller has retained, or the buyer has obtained, physical possession of the goods does not of itself mean that he also has property in the goods. Property can pass without possession and possession without property. Furthermore, property can pass without the buyer having paid the purchase price.

Only if property has passed, however, can the seller claim the purchase price for the goods from the buyer, and even though property may have passed to him the buyer is not entitled to possession of the goods until he has paid or tendered the purchase price. The most important effect of the transfer of property is that the risk of accidental loss or damage to the goods passes with the property.

RISK

By s20, unless it is otherwise agreed, the risk of accidental loss or damage lies with the seller until property passes. The risk will then pass to the buyer. This rule, however, will bind the parties only if they have not agreed otherwise in the contract. In other words, the parties themselves may say where risk lies regardless of who has property in the goods. There may also be an allocation of risk from the surrounding circumstances of the sale.

Further, s20(2) provides that, if delivery has been delayed because of the fault of either party, and the goods are lost or damaged because of the delay, the party at fault must bear this loss or damage regardless of whether or not property has passed. This point is shown in the case of:

Demby Hamilton & Co Ltd v Barden (1949)

The contract was for the sale of 30 tons of apple juice which the seller was to keep on his premises until the buyer came to collect it. This was a sale of unascertained goods, so by the s18 Rules (see later) the property in the juice remained in the seller. The buyer collected about two-thirds of the juice but then delayed in giving instructions for the remainder. The juice remained in the seller's possession and eventually went bad. The court held that, although property in the juice was in the seller, the loss was the result of the buyer's delay in collecting it. The buyer therefore had to bear the risk and had to pay the agreed price.

Finally, regardless where property lies, if the possessor of the goods fails to take reasonable care of them, then he will have to bear the risk of their accidental loss or damage.

We must now discuss the rules relating to the passing of property. These are contained in sections 16 to 19 of the Sale of Goods Act. The rules distinguish between the passing of property in specific goods and the passing of property in goods which are unascertained. We have already discussed specific and unascertained goods (see 11.1.2). SGA s18 Rules 1–4 deals with the passing of property in specific goods, s18 Rule 5 with the passing of property in unascertained goods.

The governing principle in relation to the passing of property, however, is contained in SGA s17.

PROPERTY PASSES WHEN THE PARTIES INTEND IT TO PASS (SGA S17)

Section 17 provides that in a contract for the sale of specific or ascertained goods property passes when the parties intend it to pass. Such intention may be discovered from the terms of the contract, the conduct of the parties and the circumstances of the case. This section applies to specific and ascertained goods. Ascertained goods are goods which were unascertained at the time of the contract but which have been identified in accordance with the contract. In fact, by s16 there can be no passing of property in unascertained goods unless and until these goods have been ascertained.

Because s17 is worded in such general terms, the parties and the court have wide powers to decide just when property is to pass. So, for example, where the buyer is a consumer not acting in the course of business, the courts generally hold that the parties did not intend property to pass until the buyer obtained physical possession of the goods. The reason why the courts imply such a contrary intention is that they accept that the majority of people would not realise that ownership, and therefore risk, may pass before possession and would therefore not realise that they bore the risk of the goods being accidentally destroyed or damaged. Thus, they would not think it necessary to insure the goods as soon as the contract was made. The courts, accepting this, use s17 and imply a term that the parties do not intend property to pass until the buyer is actually in possession of the goods.

An important example of the use the parties make of s17 is in relation to the so-called Romalpa clause. This clause was first considered by the court in:

Aluminium Industrie Vaassen BV v Romalpa Aluminium Ltd (1976)

The sellers sold some aluminium foil to the defendant buyers under a contract which provided that ownership of the foil would not pass to the buyers until they had paid all the money they owed the sellers both for this and for any other transactions. The buyers were given the power to sell any objects they made with the foil, but, if they did so, they had to assign to the plaintiff sellers the benefit of any claim against the sub-buyers. The contract also provided that the buyers could be required to store the foil in such a way as to make it clear that it was the property of the sellers by, for example, keeping it separate from other foil. The purpose of these provisions was to protect the sellers in the event of the buyers going bankrupt before they had paid all that they owed the sellers. The sellers were attempting to retain ownership of the foil until they had been paid in full and if in the meantime it had been mixed with other material and sold by the buyers, to have these rights transferred to the purchase price paid for the goods.

The buyers went bankrupt still owing the sellers some money. Of the funds remaining to the buyers, over £35,000 represented the proceeds of sale of unmixed foil supplied by the plaintiffs to the defendants and sold by them to third parties.

The court held that the plaintiff sellers could recover this money in priority to any creditors of the defendant buyers. To give the contract business efficacy, the court implied a power in the buyer to sell mixed as well as unmixed aluminium foil and gave the sellers the right to recover the proceeds of such a sale. The third parties who had bought the foil from the defendant buyers obtained absolute title to it.

Thus the sellers achieved all that they had hoped to achieve and, following this case, many other firms, seeing the advantages they could obtain by retaining ownership in goods even though they had transferred possession of them to a buyer, adopted similar provisions in their contracts. As long as the clause is carefully worded, following the Romalpa pattern, sellers obtain priority in recovery of their debts from an insolvent buyer. In other words, a seller who has put a successful

Romalpa clause in his contract of sale obtains more security for his rights than the buyers' other creditors in the event of the buyers' insolvency. It is this securing of an advantage by private agreement that causes the courts to interpret Romalpa clauses very narrowly. The only other way in which a creditor can obtain such an advantage is by having the debtor grant a charge over his (the debtor's) property. The effect of this charge is that, in the event of the debtor becoming insolvent, the creditor obtains payment before other creditors. The creditor is made a secured creditor. Such charges, however, have to be registered otherwise they are void against the debtor's liquidator. Once registered, they can be inspected by anyone who goes to Companies House in London. A Romalpa clause gives the creditor the same advantages without the attendant publicity.

Another case in which a Romalpa clause was successfully used was:

Clough Mill v Martin (1984)

The buyer bought yarn to use in the manufacture of fabrics. The buyer was given credit. Clause 12 of the contract of sale provided that until full payment for the yarn was received, ownership of the yarn remained with the seller and, if the buyer was late in making payment, the seller could recover the yarn and was given the right to enter the buyer's premises for that purpose. It was further provided that, if the buyer became insolvent, payment would become due immediately and that, if any of the yarn was incorporated into other goods before payment had been made the seller would obtain property in these new goods.

Before he had made full payment for the yarn, the buyer became insolvent and a receiver was appointed. The receiver seized a quantity of unused yarn and refused to allow the seller to obtain possession of it, claiming that, in fact, Clause 12 was a charge which was void for non-registration. The seller sued the receiver for damages for wrongfully depriving the seller of possession of the yarn.

At first instance, the judge decided for the receiver on the grounds that the sole purpose of Clause 12 had been to provide security for payment. Property in the yarn had passed to the buyer on delivery and the buyer had granted a charge over what were now his goods to the seller. This charge was void for non-registration. The seller appealed and the Court of Appeal reversed the decision of the lower court. The court held that the seller had retained title to the yarn after delivery to the buyer and was therefore entitled to recover all the identifiable and unused yarn still in the buyer's possession. The buyer had never acquired ownership of the yarn and therefore the question of whether he had granted a charge did not arise. The seller was entitled to damages.

In an obiter, however, the Court of Appeal stated that, if the yarn had been incorporated into other goods, these new goods would then belong to the buyer and any rights of the seller would arise by virtue of a charge granted in his favour. This charge would have to be registered to be valid.

In many cases, the parties do not make any provision as to when property will pass, nor do the courts imply any intention into the contract. In these circumstances, the Sale of Goods Act s18 Rules 1–5 provides the means for ascertaining when property will pass. Section 18 Rules 1–4 deal with the passing of property in specific goods, s18 Rule 5 with the passing of property in unascertained goods.

SECTION 18 RULE 1

This rule states that where there is an unconditional contract for the sale of specific goods in a deliverable state, property passes to the buyer when the contract is made whether or not payment and/or delivery are postponed.

For Rule 1 to apply, therefore, a number of requirements must be satisfied. Firstly, the contract must be unconditional. This means that the contract must not be subject to any condition which suspends the passing of property. So, for example, it would not apply to a contract to buy a car 'subject to the seller fitting four new tyres'. This would be a condition which must be satisfied before the contract can become binding.

Secondly, the goods must be specific. This has been discussed in 11.1.2.

Thirdly, the goods must be in a deliverable state, which is defined in SGA s61 as being 'in such a state that the buyer would under the contract be bound to take delivery of them.' In other words, the goods must be in such a state that they can be handed over to the buyer without anything having to be done to them.

EXAMPLE 11

Jones contracts to buy a van for his business from Smith's garage. The contract is made on the Wednesday and Jones says that he will send someone to collect the vehicle on the Friday. In the meantime the van is to remain on Smith's premises. On the Thursday, the garage is damaged by fire. The van is destroyed. Who has to bear the loss?

The contract is unconditional (Smith does not have to do anything to the van); the van is specific goods; it is in a deliverable state (it is ready to be collected); and therefore property and risk passed to Jones as soon as the contract was made on the Wednesday. Jones has to bear the loss and pay for the van.

SECTION 18 RULE 2

This rule provides that where there is a contract for the sale of specific goods but the seller has to do something to the goods to put them in a deliverable state, property passes when this has been done and the buyer is notified.

'Deliverable state' has the same meaning as in Rule 1. Thus, Rule 2 will apply if, for example, the seller has to pack the goods ready for delivery to the buyer, or if the goods have to be assembled before the buyer takes possession. Another example of goods having to be put in a deliverable state occurred in:

Underwood Ltd v Burgh Castle Brick and Cement Syndicate (1922)

The contract was for the sale of an engine, which weighed 30 tons and was set in a concrete emplacement. It took two days to disconnect the machine and two weeks for it to be dismantled and made ready for delivery to the buyer. The engine was damaged as it was being loaded by the sellers onto a railway wagon for shipment to the buyer.

The court held that the engine was not in a deliverable state when the contract was made and so Rule 1 did not apply. Property in the goods was still with the seller at the time of the accident and therefore he had to bear the loss. Section 18 Rule 2 applied.

It is not enough for property to pass that the goods are put in a deliverable state. The buyer must also receive notice that this has been done. The notice must be actual notice, but it will be enough that the buyer knows that the goods have been put in a deliverable state. The Rule does not require that the seller is the one who gives the notice.

SECTION 18 RULE 3

This rules applies to contracts for the sale of specific goods in a deliverable state where the seller has to weigh, measure, test or do something else in relation to the goods in order to ascertain the price. Property passes when this has been done and the buyer is notified. This Rule applies only where the *seller* is required to do the weighing etc. If the buyer is required to do this, property will probably pass on the making of the contract. This was shown in:

Nanka Bruce v Commonwealth Trust Ltd (1926)

The seller sold the buyer cocoa at an agreed price per unit of weight. It was agreed that the buyer would re-sell the cocoa, the sub-buyer would weigh it, and the original buyer would pay the seller according to the results of the weighing. The court held that the weighing by the sub-buyer did not make the sale conditional, it was merely to check whether the goods fitted the weights as reported. Property had passed to the buyer as soon as the contract had been made. In other words, s18 Rule 1 applied to the contract.

SECTION 18 RULE 4

This rule deals with the passing of property in cases where the goods are delivered to the buyer on approval or on a 'sale or return' basis. The rule provides that, in these situations, property passes

1. When the buyer says he accepts the goods.
2. When he does some act to adopt the transaction (by, for example, selling the goods and thus behaving as if he were the owner).
3. When he keeps the goods beyond the time fixed for their return, or if no time is fixed, beyond a reasonable time.

Until the buyer does one of these three things, the goods remain at the risk of the seller.

EXAMPLE 12

Bill sees an advertisement in a newspaper which offers electric razors on 14 days free trial. He sends off for a razor which is delivered. During the 14 day period, the razor is accidentally damaged. Bill cannot be made to pay for it. The risk is still with the seller. If, however, during the period, Bill sold the razor to a friend, this would be an act adopting the transaction and property would pass to Bill. He would thereupon become liable to pay for the goods. Risk would also pass to him if he kept the razor for longer than the 14 day period without telling the seller that he was rejecting the goods.

SECTION 18 RULE 5

This rule relates to the passing of property in unascertained goods. You will remember that, under s16, no property in unascertained goods can pass unless and until the goods are ascertained. The mere fact that the goods are ascertained, however, does not mean that property in them has passed. There have to be further steps taken for this to occur. These further steps are stated by Rule 5.

Rule 5 says that property in unascertained goods passes when goods which are of the contract description and which are in a deliverable state are unconditionally appropriated to the contract. The appropriation may be done by either the seller or the buyer acting with the other's assent. This assent may be express or implied and may be given either before or after the appropriation is made.

So, for property in unascertained goods to pass they must first be ascertained and then unconditionally appropriated to the contract with the mutual assent of both parties. Unconditional appropriation occurs when the goods which have been set aside and no others are to be transferred to the buyer under the terms of the contract. The mere fact that the seller sets aside goods which he expects to use under the contract is not enough. He must act in such a way as to show that these are the goods which are going to go to the buyer. In:

Aldridge v Johnson (1857)

The contract was for the sale of a certain quantity of barley out of a larger consignment in the seller's granary. Under the contract the buyer was to send his own sacks which the seller was to fill. The sacks were sent to the seller who filled most of them. The seller then realised that he was on the point of insolvency, so he emptied the barley in the sacks back onto his pile of grain. The court held that the buyer was entitled to that much of the barley as had been sacked in the buyer's sacks. The unascertained goods had been ascertained and unconditionally appropriated to the contract when the barley had been put in the buyer's sacks.

Compare this with:

Carlos Federspiel & Co SA v Charles Twigg & Co Ltd (1957)

A British bicycle manufacturer contracted to sell a number of bicycles to a foreign buyer. Under the contract, the seller was to load the goods onto a ship for transportation to the buyer. The seller packed the bicycles into crates marked with the buyer's name and address but before they could be despatched the seller went into liquidation. The court held that property had not passed to the buyer and that therefore he was not entitled to claim the bicycles. Until the seller had done all that he had to do under the contract (ie put the bicycles on board the named ship) it could not be said that these bicycles and no others were the subject matter of the contract. Only when the goods had been loaded on the ship would they have been unconditionally appropriated.

The unconditional appropriation may be carried out by either party with the assent of the other. This assent may be express or implied as in:

Pignataro v Gilroy and Son (1919)

The seller sold 140 bags of rice to be delivered in two consignments of 125 bags (situated at a certain wharf) and 15 bags at the seller's premises. Complying with the buyer's request, the seller sent the buyer a delivery order for the 125 bags and told the buyer that the remaining 15 bags were also ready for collection. The buyer collected the 125 but did not go to collect the 15 for some weeks after the delivery date. When he did eventually arrive to collect them he found that they had been stolen.

The court held that property and therefore risk had passed to the buyer as, in asking for the delivery order, the buyer had assented in advance to the seller's appropriation. There was also subsequent assent shown by the fact that the buyer had done nothing for several weeks in response to an appropriation made at his request.

11.1.5 Transfer of title

INTRODUCTION

SGA s16–20 deal, as we have seen, with the passing of property. This is important mainly because it shows where the risk of accidental loss or damage lies. The sections assume that the seller has title to (or owns) the goods he is selling. If there is some dispute about title, then the courts will have to refer to sections 21–26 to resolve the dispute.

The general rule of common law, stated again in the SGA, is *nemo dat quod non habet* (no-one can give what he does not have). In other words, a person without title cannot pass title to another. If a thief steals your books and sells them to another person that person cannot obtain title to the books, even though he is innocent of the original theft. The thief had no title so he cannot create title in anyone else. Sections 21–26 give a number of exceptions to this general rule ie cases where, although the seller had no title, the buyer can obtain good title to the goods. It must be emphasised however that these are no more than exceptions. The general *nemo dat* rule remains the guiding principle of law.

The exceptions to the *nemo dat* rule are:

AGENCY (SGA S21(1))

If the seller is an agent of the owner and sells within the authority granted him by the owner, the buyer will obtain good title. Agency will be dealt with in Chapter 17.

MERCANTILE AGENTS (SGA S21(2)(A))

A mercantile agent is one who, in the ordinary course of his business, buys or sells goods or raises money on the security of goods. If such an agent is in possession of goods with the consent of the owner for some purpose connected with sale, then any sale by the agent in the ordinary course of business operates to transfer a good title in the goods to the buyer as long as the buyer acts in good faith and without notice of any limits on the mercantile agent's powers.

EXAMPLE 13

Ann takes her car to Brian's garage for him to sell on her behalf at not less than £2,000. Brian often buys and sells cars on behalf of customers. Brian sells Ann's car to Cliff for £1,500. Cliff acts in good faith, not knowing that Brian is disobeying Ann's instructions. Ann is bound by the sale to Cliff. All she can do is to sue Brian for the £500 balance.

Brian is a mercantile agent in possession of the goods with the owner's consent for some purpose connected with sale. He sells to a purchaser who takes in good faith and without notice of the limit of Brian's authority. The owner Ann cannot recover the car from Cliff.

ESTOPPEL (S21(1))

Where the true owner of the goods acts in such a way as to make it appear to the buyer that the person selling the goods has the right to sell and the buyer acts on this appearance, the true owner will be estopped from denying the seller's right to sell. The buyer again must act in good faith and without notice of the seller's lack of title.

SALE IN MARKET OVERT (S22(1))

A market overt is any open, public and legally constituted market established by Act of Parliament, Royal Charter or prescription. If goods are sold in market overt according to the usages of the market, the buyer acquires good title even though the seller had none. Again, to claim title, the buyer must act in good faith and without notice of the seller's lack of a right to sell. Thus, any purchase in a market overt (including in shops in the City of London) will give an innocent buyer titled good against the whole world, even though the seller had no title to transfer (eg because he had stolen the goods).

VOIDABLE TITLE (S23)

If an innocent buyer, acting in good faith, buys goods from a seller who has a voidable title which has not been avoided, the buyer obtains good title. So, for example, if Ben buys a car from Sam and pays for it by means of a cheque which is dishonoured Ben will have a voidable title. If he sells the car to Clive before Sam avoids the contract (which Sam can do, for example, by telling the police of Ben's fraud) then Clive will obtain good title. Clive must have bought the car in good faith and without notice of Ben's fraud. Sam is left with an action in damages against Ben. Misrepresentation gives the representee a voidable title. See Chapter 9.

SALE BY A SELLER IN POSSESSION (S24)

If a person sells goods to a buyer but remains in possession of them with the buyer's consent and sells them again to another person who takes in good faith and without notice of the original sale, the second buyer obtains title, provided he obtains physical possession of the goods. The original buyer is left with an action for damages against the seller. He cannot, however, claim the goods.

SALE BY A BUYER IN POSSESSION (S25)

If a person who has bought or agreed to buy goods obtains possession of them with the consent of the seller, then any sale by this person to another buyer who takes without notice and is given actual possession of the goods operates to give the second buyer good title. The original seller loses his goods and is left with an action for damages against the original buyer.

It must be emphasised that all these are merely exceptions to the general rule relating to title: *nemo dat quod non habet*.

11.1.6 Performance

INTRODUCTION

The seller's duty in performing the contract is to deliver the goods, the buyer's to accept and pay for them according to the contract. The duty to deliver and the duty to accept and pay are concurrent conditions. In other words, neither party has the power to require the other's performance until he is willing and able to perform his own part of the contract. This is, however, subject to contrary intention in the contract.

SELLER'S DUTY TO DELIVER

Delivery is defined as the 'voluntary transfer of possession from one person to another' (s61(1)). Delivery may take one of several forms:

1. The transfer of actual physical possession of the goods.
2. Symbolic delivery. When, for example, goods are stored in a warehouse, delivery of the key to the warehouse with the intention that the buyer will have the right to enter and remove the goods, will operate as symbolic delivery of the goods.
3. When the seller retains physical possession, delivery occurs when the seller agrees to hold the goods on behalf of the buyer ie when he changes his role from that of seller to that of warehouseman.
4. Where goods are in the possession of a third person at the time of sale, delivery to the buyer occurs when the third person acknowledges that he is holding the goods for the buyer.
5. When documents of title to the goods are transferred to the buyer. Documents of title are documents which represent the goods eg bill of lading.
6. If, under the contract of sale, the seller delivers goods to an independent carrier in order to have them transported to the buyer, this is *prima facie* deemed to be delivery of the goods to the buyer. This will not apply if the carrier is employed by the seller—delivery in this case will occur when the goods are handed over to the buyer. The seller is required to make a reasonable contract of carriage.

In the absence of any agreement to the contrary, the place of delivery is the seller's place of business or, if there is no place of business, the seller's residence. If the seller is required by the contract to deliver the goods to the buyer's premises, he will have discharged his duty by delivering them there without negligence to a person who appears to be authorised to receive them.

THE TIME OF DELIVERY

The time of delivery is covered by s10(1), which provides that, whether a term as to time of delivery is a condition or a warranty depends on the terms of the contract.

If the seller is late in delivering the goods, the buyer may specify a new time limit. In return for his agreeing by implication not to sue the seller in breach, the buyer may treat this time as a condition. This was shown in:

Rickards (Charles) Ltd v Oppenheim (1950)

Seller agreed to sell a car chassis to the buyer. The chassis was to be ready at the latest by 20 March. It was not ready on this date and the buyer, having pressed the seller for delivery on several subsequent occasions, eventually said on 29 June that he would not accept delivery after 25 July. The chassis was not ready until 18 October. The buyer refused to accept it. The court held that the buyer was entitled to reject. He had given the seller reasonable notice that delivery had to be made by a certain date thus making time of delivery a condition. While he continued to press for delivery, the buyer could not reject the goods. He had waived his right to do so. Once he gave a firm date, however, he ended the period of waiver.

DELIVERY OF WRONG QUANTITIES

Subject to the *de minimis rule* (see the section on sale by description) the Sale of Goods Act requires the seller to deliver the correct quantity of goods ordered. If the seller delivers less than the contract amount the buyer may, by s30(1):

1   Reject the goods, or
2   Accept the short delivery and pay a proportion of the contract price.

For example, in:

Behrend v Produce Brokers (1920)

The contract was for the sale of 700 tons of cotton seed to be delivered on board the ship the 'Port Inglis' at London. The ship arrived in London, discharged 37 tons of seed and then left for Hull in order to discharge other goods which had been loaded on top of the remainder of the seed. Without any delay the ship returned to London to discharge the rest of the cotton seed. The buyer refused to accept the balance of the goods and the court held that he was entitled to do so. He could accept the part actually delivered and reject the rest, paying for the part accepted at the contract rate.

If the seller delivers more than he contracted to deliver, the buyer may, by s30(2) and (3)

1   Reject the whole consignment, or
2   Accept the whole consignment and pay for it at the contract rate, or
3   Accept the contractual amount and reject the rest.

If the seller delivers goods of the contract description mixed with goods of a different description, the buyer may, by s30(4)

1   Reject the entire consignment, or
2   Accept the goods complying with the contractual description and reject the rest. The meaning of 'contractual description' is the same as for s13 (see earlier).

INSTALMENT DELIVERY

As the seller is bound to deliver the correct quantity of goods, it follows that the buyer does not have to accept delivery by instalments unless he agrees to do so. For an instalment delivery to be binding on the buyer, therefore, there must be an agreement to that effect either expressed in the contract or implied from construction of the contractual terms.

A contract to deliver goods by instalments may be either entire or divisible (or severable). The importance of the distinction between the two lies in the remedies available for breach. If a contract is entire, a serious breach with regard to one instalment could give the buyer the right to treat the whole contract as repudiated. Breach of one instalment in a divisible (or severable) contract, however, does not necessarily give this right. The courts will look at such factors as whether the breach is liable to be repeated and, in deciding the remedy to be awarded act on the presumption that the parties intended the payment of damages rather than rescission. It is therefore necessary to distinguish between entire and divisible contracts for the sale of goods by instalments.

1 Entire contracts

A contract for delivery of goods by instalments will be entire if the seller is required to deliver all the goods before he can demand payment from the buyer. In other words, if full and complete delivery is a condition precedent to liability to pay, the contract will be entire.

If the contract is entire, then breach of condition with regard to any instalment will entitle the buyer to reject all the goods. By the same token, if the buyer has accepted one or more instalments he will not be able to reject the goods even if a later instalment is faulty. Because he has accepted part of an entire contract he must treat any later breach of condition as a breach of warranty and merely sue for damages.

EXAMPLE 14

Ben orders 100 tonnes of Grade A coal from Sam, the coal to be delivered in 10 instalments of 10 tonnes per instalment, payment to be made on delivery of the final instalment. This is an entire contract; the seller must deliver all the goods before he can claim payment. If the first four instalments are satisfactory but the fifth is of Grade B coal, Ben can treat the whole contract as repudiated. If, however, Ben has already used the first four instalments which have been delivered he will be said to have accepted the contract. He will be unable to reject and will only have a right of action in damages.

2 Divisible contracts

A divisible or severable contract for the sale of goods by instalments is a contract whereby payment keeps pace with performance. In other words, an instalment contract will be divisible when each delivery is to be separately paid for. Because the remedies for breach of divisible contracts are more flexible, the courts wherever possible will construe an instalment contract as divisible rather than entire.

If a divisible contract is broken, the court will decide the remedy which should be granted by looking at the seriousness of the breach in relation to the contract as a whole and at the likelihood of the breach being repeated. If the breach is not very serious in relation to the contract and is not likely to be repeated, the remedy for the injured party will be damages. Otherwise, the remedy will be to permit him to treat the contract as repudiated. The distinction between these two points is illustrated by the following cases:

Maple Flock Co Ltd v Universal Furniture Products (Wembley) Ltd (1934)

The contract was for the sale of 100 tons of rag flock to be delivered in three loads per week, each delivery to be separately paid for. The first 15 loads were satisfactory, the 16th did not comply with the contractual requirements, but the buyers took four more loads (all of which were satisfactory) before they tried to treat the contract as repudiated. The court held that the buyers were not entitled to refuse further deliveries. The breach had affected only a small portion of the flock delivered and there was no probability that the breach would be repeated.

Compare that case with:

Munro & Co Ltd v Meyer (1930)

The contract was for the sale of 1,500 tons of meat and bone meal, delivery to be made at the rate of 120 tons a month. After over half the total quantity had been delivered and had been found to be seriously defective, the buyer claimed to treat the contract as repudiated. The court held that he could do so. The breach was substantial and serious and had been so persistent that the buyer could treat the whole contract as being at an end.

BREACH OF DUTY TO DELIVER

If the seller fails to deliver, or delivers at the wrong date or in some other way wrongly, the buyer has a right of action for damages (s51(1)).

BUYER'S DUTY TO ACCEPT

We have discussed acceptance in 11.1.3. If the buyer wrongfully refuses to accept the goods he is liable to the seller in an action for damages (s50(1)).

BUYER'S DUTY TO PAY

Payment has to be made in accordance with the terms of the contract.

11.1.7 Personal remedies

A personal remedy is a remedy in damages (as opposed to a real remedy, which is a right of action based on the goods themselves). The seller will have a right to sue the buyer for the price of the goods where the buyer wrongfully neglects or refuses to pay and either property has passed to the buyer, or the price is payable on a day certain regardless of the passing of property. If property has not passed to the buyer, or the price is not payable on a day certain, the seller's remedy for the buyer's wrongful non-payment will be an action in damages.

The buyer will have a right of action for damages against the seller if the seller wrongfully refuses or neglects to deliver the goods (s51(1)).

THE MEASURE OF DAMAGES

The general rule for assessing how much damages should be awarded for breach by either the seller or the buyer is that the innocent party may claim the estimated loss directly and naturally resulting in the ordinary course of events from the breach. This is a statement of the common law rules as given in the case of *Hadley* v *Baxendale* (1854). See Chapter 10.

AVAILABLE MARKET

The Act, however, gives a *prima facie* rule for assessing damages. The rule states that, if there is an available market for the goods in question, the measure of damages is the difference between that available market price and the contract price at the date of the breach of contract.

By available market, the Act means that the goods can be readily bought and sold and the price they fetch is fixed by the law of supply and demand. So, for example, there will not be an available market where the goods can be sold only at a price fixed by the manufacturer. The court will ask whether the goods, or similar goods, could easily be bought or sold within a reasonable time and within a reasonable distance. If this is the case, the court will hold that there is an available market for the goods, will discover how much they would be worth on this market, and will award damages based on the difference between this price and the price agreed in the contract.

The available market rule, however, is only a *prima facie* way of assessing damages. The court will dispense with it if it is felt that it is inappropriate to apply the test or if the law of supply and demand does not affect the price obtainable for the goods. In these circumstances, the court will apply the general rule of assessment and award the innocent party damages based on the loss directly and naturally resulting from the breach.

Compare the following cases:

Thompson (WL) Ltd v *Robinson (Gunmakers) Ltd* (1955)

The plaintiff car dealers agreed to sell a new Vanguard car to the defendant at a price fixed by the car's manufacturers. The buyer refused to take delivery of the car when it arrived. At the time of breach, the supply of Vanguards exceeded the demand in the locality, although not in other localities.

When he was sued, the buyer argued that only nominal damages should be awarded as there was no difference between the contract price and the price at which the goods were normally sold (as the cars were always sold at the price fixed by the manufacturer). In other words, he argued, the available market price was the same as the contract price. The court, however, held that the plaintiffs were entitled to obtain as damages their loss of profit on the sale of the car, as they had sold one car less than they would otherwise have done. Even if the 'available market' rule took in the whole of the country (in which case there may be an available market) it would be unjust to apply it in this case and the court refused to do so. It also refused to do so because the retail price was fixed. The damages awarded therefore were based on the loss arising directly and naturally from the breach ie the loss of profit.

Charter v Sullivan (1957)

The plaintiff car dealer agreed to sell a Hillman Minx car to the defendant at the fixed retail price. At the time of the sale the demand for such cars exceeded the supply. The only limits on the numbers the plaintiff could sell were those imposed by the fact that he could obtain only a limited number of the cars from the manufacturer.

The defendant refused to accept delivery of the car but, within ten days of this refusal, the plaintiff had sold it to another buyer at the same retail price. The court again held that, as there was a fixed retail price for the goods the available market test would not apply and therefore the measure of damages would have to be based on the loss arising directly and naturally from the breach. As they had suffered no loss, the plaintiffs were awarded nominal damages—they could sell every Hillman Minx they could obtain from the manufacturers and so they had sold the same number of cars and made the same amount of profits as they would have sold and made had the defendant not broken his contract.

DAMAGES IF THE BUYER HAS LOST A SUB-SALE

If the buyer has resold the goods before he receives them from the seller and the seller fails to deliver, the question arises whether the buyer is able to claim damages for the loss of this sub-sale. If there is no available market for the goods in question, he will be able to recover his lost profit provided the seller was aware of the sub-sale. This loss of a sub-sale will be a direct and natural consequence of the seller's breach.

If, however, there is an available market for the goods in question, the buyer should not lose the sub-sale. By definition he could easily obtain the goods from elsewhere to honour his bargain. The only time he can claim his loss of profit on a sub-sale when there is an available market for the goods is when he can show that the possibility of a re-sale was known to the seller at the time of the original contract and that he had made the sub-sale on the basis that the actual goods he was buying from the seller would be the goods delivered to the sub-buyer. This would occur, for example, when the goods were being shipped by the seller to the buyer and the buyer had received the bill of lading for the goods and had used this bill to make his sub-sale. This would mean that unless the buyer delivered the actual goods represented by the bill to the sub-contractor there would necessarily be a breach of contract.

11.1.8 Real remedies

These are remedies available to an unpaid seller and are exercised against the goods themselves. Real remedies are lien, stoppage in transit and re-sale of the goods.

UNPAID SELLER (S38(1))

A seller will be regarded as unpaid when either:

1 The whole of the purchase price has not been paid or tendered to him, or
2 When he was given conditional payment, eg a cheque, and the condition has not been satisfied, eg the cheque has been dishonoured.

Thus a seller who has been paid part of the price has the right to exercise his real remedies unless he has agreed to allow the buyer credit or unless the contract provides for delivery by instalments and is treated as divisible. In this last case, the unpaid seller's rights are treated separately in relation to each instalment. Each instalment, in other words, gives the buyer a separate obligation to pay.

LIEN (SS41–43)

A lien is the right to retain physical possession of the goods. Thus it cannot be exercised if the seller has lost physical control of the goods. By exercising a lien, the unpaid seller is refusing to hand over the goods to the buyer until the buyer pays him for them. A lien does not end the contract. The goods remain the buyer's during the exercise of the lien.

A lien will be lost:

1. When the buyer or his agent lawfully obtains possession of the goods. If the buyer unlawfully obtains possession, by, for example, breaking into the seller's premises and taking the goods, the seller can recover the goods and continue the exercise of the lien.
2. When the seller delivers the goods to a carrier to have them sent to the buyer.
3. When the seller waives his right of lien by, for example, accepting security for payment from the buyer.
4. When the buyer pays what he owes.

STOPPAGE IN TRANSIT (SS44–46)

This is a right given to an unpaid seller who has handed the goods to an independent carrier for the purpose of having them transported to the buyer to recover the goods from the carrier and to hold them until the buyer pays the price. As with lien, this right does not end the contract of sale but, unlike lien, it may only be exercised if the buyer is insolvent.

For the purpose of stoppage, a buyer will be insolvent if he either cannot or has ceased to pay his debts as they fall due. It is not necessary for the seller to wait until insolvency proceedings have been started against the buyer before he exercises his right of stoppage.

The right to stop exists for as long as the goods are in the hands of the independent carrier. The seller may exercise the right at any time before the goods are handed over to the buyer or before the carrier acknowledges to the buyer that the goods are being held for him.

Stoppage will be carried out by the unpaid seller giving notice to the carrier, altering the original instructions. The carrier must obey this notice and the seller must pay the expenses of re-delivery.

RETENTION OF THE GOODS

Both lien and stoppage give the unpaid seller the right to retain the goods until the buyer pays. They are also the first stage in the process that must be undertaken before the seller can sell the goods to another purchaser.

The fact that the buyer has re-sold the goods to another person does not affect the seller's rights, so long as the seller did not actually assent to the sub-sale. The unpaid seller's right to retain the goods continues despite any such sub-sale (s47).

EXAMPLE 15

Smith sold goods to Jones. Jones paid a deposit but has not yet paid the balance. As required by the contract, Smith handed over the goods to an independent carrier for them to be sent to Jones's factory but Smith later discovered that Jones had stopped paying his debts. Smith immediately served notice on the carrier and had the goods re-delivered to his (Smith's) premises. Smith has now been told by Green that Jones had in fact sold the goods to him. Green is claiming the goods from Smith.

Smith does not have to hand them over to Green. Smith had not assented to the sub-sale by Jones and therefore may continue to exercise his unpaid seller's rights.

If, however, the unpaid seller actually assents to the sub-sale by the buyer he will be bound by it and will have to hand over the goods to the sub-buyer. There must be actual assent to the sub-sale. Merely knowing that the buyer has sold the goods to another person is not sufficient to defeat the unpaid seller's rights (*Mordaunt Brothers* v *British Oil and Cake Mills Ltd* (1910)).

EXAMPLE 16

If, in example 15, Smith had agreed to Jones's sale to Green (because, for example, he thought that this was the only way in which the buyer could obtain enough money to pay) then Smith would be obliged to hand over the goods to Green.

If, however, Smith knew of, but did not assent to, the sale he may retain the goods until he has been paid for them.

In:

Mount (D.F.) Ltd v Jay and Jay (Provisions) Co Ltd (1960)

The sellers sold goods in the possession of a wharfowner to the buyer and agreed that the buyer would pay the price of the goods out of money to be received by the buyer from sub-sales of these goods. The buyer sold some of the goods to a sub-buyer who paid the buyer. The buyer, however, failed to pay over this money to the sellers and the sellers instructed the wharfowner to refuse to allow the sub-buyer to collect the goods.

The court held that as the sellers had actually assented to the sale to the sub-buyer they were bound by it and could not exercise their rights against the goods. They had to allow the sub-buyer to collect the goods from the wharf.

If, however, the seller has transferred the document of title to the goods to the buyer and the buyer has re-sold the goods by transferring this document of title, the unpaid seller will have lost his real remedies against the goods and must hand them over to the sub-buyer.

RIGHT OF RESALE (S48)

As we said earlier, lien and stoppage in transit are the first stage in the unpaid seller's right of resale. In certain circumstances the unpaid seller may re-sell the goods. If he does so, the second buyer obtains good title and the original buyer's right to the goods is defeated.

The circumstances in which the unpaid seller may re-sell the goods are:

1. Where the goods are perishable, or
2. Where the unpaid seller gives notice of his intention to re-sell if the buyer does not, within a reasonable time, pay or tender the price and the buyer does not do so, or
3. Where, in the contract, the seller reserves the right to dispose of the goods if the buyer does not pay and the buyer does not do so.

Under s48(3) and (4), and following the decision in the case of *RV Ward Ltd* v *Bignall* (1967) resale by the seller operates to rescind the original contract. Thus, if the seller makes extra profit on the second sale the original buyer has no right to claim it. If, on the other hand, the seller makes a loss he may sue the original buyer to recover this loss.

11.2 SUPPLY OF GOODS

11.2.1 Introduction

The Sale of Goods Act 1979 applies only to those contracts where the seller transfers or agrees to transfer property in goods to the buyer for a money consideration called the price (SGA s2(1)). As we pointed out earlier, however, there are other ways in which ownership of goods can be transferred: for example, there can be a contract of exchange where no money changes hands, or the transfer of ownership in goods in return for the performance of another contract, for example a customer is given a wine glass with every 20 litres of petrol he buys. There are also contracts which involve not just the transfer of goods but the provision of a service as well as when, for example, a person takes his car into a garage to have the engine overhauled. Although this will involve the sale of engine oil, this sale is only incidental to the main purpose of the contract—that of providing skill in improving the 'buyer's' engine. For example, in:

Young and Marten Ltd v McManus Childs Ltd (1968)

Building contractors sub-contracted some roofing work to the appellants and instructed them to use 'Somerset 13' tiles. These tiles were made by only one manufacturer. The appellants bought and used the tiles as instructed. After they had been exposed to the weather, however, the tiles were shown to be defective and the building contractors sued the appellants in damages. The House of Lords held that this was a contract for work and materials not a sale of goods. The main purpose of the contract was the provision of the appellants' skill not the sale of the tiles. The Lords, however, implied terms into the contract which were identical to those implied by the Sale of Goods Act and held the appellants liable for breach of the implied undertaking that the goods supplied should be of merchantable quality.

In all these cases, because the transaction in question does not come within the Sale of Goods Act definition of a sale the contract is not covered by the 1979 Act. For the sake of convenience we shall call these transactions contracts for the supply of goods. As we saw in the case of *Young and Marten* (above), however, even though the Sale of Goods Act did not apply to these cases the courts implied terms identical to those in the SGA into these transactions. In other words, even if the transaction was one for the supply of goods and not sale, the court dealt with the seller's obligations in the same way.

This approach of the common law to contracts for the supply of goods was put into statutory form in the Supply of Goods and Services Act 1982 (SGSA). The SGSA covers three types of transaction: contracts for the supply of goods; contracts for the hire of goods; and contracts for the supply of services.

11.2.2 Supply of goods under the SGSA

The Act applies to all contracts for the transfer of property in goods, whether or not services are also provided, and regardless of the nature of the consideration, *except*:

1. Contracts covered by the Sale of Goods Act 1979. If a transaction comes within the definition of sale in the 1979 Act, this Act will apply to the contract.
2. Contracts of hire-purchase. These are covered by the Consumer Credit Act 1974 (see next chapter).
3. Contracts of exchange for trading stamps. These transactions are covered by their own legislation, the Trading Stamps Act 1964.
4. Contracts for the transfer of property in goods by deed, there being no other consideration for the transaction. Thus if the transfer of the goods is, in effect, a gift but is given formal effect by the execution of a contract under seal, the SGSA will not apply to the transaction.
5. Contracts intended to operate by way of mortgage, charge, pledge or other security. In other words, the Act will not apply to cases where, although ownership is transferred from one person to another, it is intended that there will be a transfer back to the transferor when he has, for example, paid what he owes.

The SGSA, therefore, will cover all other contracts for the supply of goods. It will govern contracts where the goods are exchanged for other goods; or where the contract is one for work and materials as in the *Young and Marten* case; or where goods are given in return for the performance of an act as, for example, when a wine glass is given for every 20 litres of petrol bought.

In all cases, however, the Act will apply only if there is a contract in existence. The transfer of goods other than by contract will not be covered. For example, in:

Esso Petroleum Co Ltd v *Commissioners of Customs and Excise* (1975)

Esso dealers gave customers a 'free' world cup coin with every four gallons of petrol they bought. The Commissioners of Customs and Excise, claiming that the coins had been 'purchased' by the public, demanded £200,000 arrears of purchase tax on them. Purchase tax was payable 'on articles of a kind produced in quantity for general sale'.

The House of Lords held that the coins had not been sold as such and were therefore not liable to purchase tax. The Commissioners lost their action. Lord Denning in the Court of Appeal described the transaction relating to the coins as 'a pure gift unattended by any taint of sale'. If this were the case, the 1982 SGSA would not apply to the transaction as there was no contract. In the House of Lords it was argued that the supply of coins was not a sale (no money consideration) but it was a contract, the customer's consideration being his entry into the collateral contract to buy the necessary quantity of petrol. In this case, the transaction would be a contract for the supply of goods now covered by the SGSA.

In:

Pfizer Corp. v *Minister of Health* (1965)

The House of Lords held that the supply of drugs to a member of the public under the National Health Service, whether by a hospital or a pharmacist, was not a sale, even though the person obtaining the drugs had to pay a prescription charge. There was no contract here as there was no element of bargain or agreement. The patient had a right by statute to demand the drug on payment of the prescription charge and the hospital had a statutory duty to supply it on receipt of such payment. Thus there was no contract at all in the true sense.

Therefore neither the 1979 nor the 1982 Act would apply to this transaction.

11.2.3 Terms implied by the SGSA

In relation to contracts for the supply of goods covered by the SGSA, the Act implies terms which are identical to those implied by the Sale of Goods Act 1979.

- s2 Implied condition as to title; implied warranties as to quiet possession and freedom from encumbrances; and implied warranties in the sale of a limited title.
- s3 Implied condition that, in a sale by description, the goods will correspond with the description.
- s4 Implied conditions that the goods supplied will be of merchantable quality and reasonably fit for the buyer's purpose.
- s5 Implied conditions imposed on a sale by sample.

As the Act implies terms identical to those in the 1979 Act the remedies will be the same too.

11.3 SUPPLY OF SERVICES

11.3.1 Introduction

Before 1982 the duties of a person carrying out a service were laid down by the common law. A person who held himself out as being prepared to carry out a service had to exercise the skill of a reasonably competent member of the trade or profession which usually carried out such services. The pre-1982 Act decisions were all based on the idea of reasonableness and all related to obligations which arose in the course of business. The common law courts derived their authority to imply terms into these contracts from the case of *The Moorcock* (1889). This case established the principle that, in business contracts, the law will give effect to the parties' presumed intentions, and thus give the contract business efficacy, by implying terms into the transaction.

The SGSA, in fact, is a restatement of the law as contained in the pre-1982 cases. Thus the Act does not affect private obligations as when a service is provided as an act of friendship and not in the course of business. The Act also uses the concept of reasonableness to decide how much care and skill must be shown in the carrying out of the service.

11.3.2 Contracts covered by the Act

Section 12 SGSA defines a contract of service as one under which the 'supplier' agrees to carry out a service other than a contract of service or apprenticeship. A contract will be for the supply of a service under the Act whether or not goods are also transferred or to be transferred or bailed or to be bailed by way of hire under the contract. The Act will apply whatever the nature of the consideration for the service. There must, however, be a contract undertaken in the course of business.

The Act therefore does not apply to contracts of employment or apprenticeship, but it does apply to any other type of contract under which a service is provided to the customer. Thus, for example, it will apply to a contract for a garage to service or repair a car or to a contract between a householder and a plumber called in to mend broken water pipes or an electrician employed to replace faulty wiring. In order to cover as many services as possible, there is no definition of contract and no definition of service.

11.3.3 Terms implied by the Act

REASONABLE CARE AND SKILL (SGSA S13)

Where the supplier of a service is acting in the course of a business there is an implied term that he will carry out the service with reasonable care and skill.

This section will cover such pre-1982 cases as:

Kimber v William Willett Ltd (1947)

The defendants, a firm of expert carpet layers, agreed to take up and clean the plaintiff's carpet. The carpet to be cleaned was attached to the hall carpet by being sewn to a 'tongue' of the hall carpet which stretched under the door into the room.

The defendants took up the carpet, but left the 'tongue' of hall carpet protruding under the door. They did not nail this piece of carpet down and the plaintiff tripped over it, fell and was injured. The court held that in a contract such as this between an ordinary householder and a firm of expert carpet layers there was an implied term that the work would be done in a workmanlike and safe way. The defendants were therefore liable to pay damages for breach of this implied term.

Levison v Patent Steam Carpet Cleaning Co (1977)

The plaintiff handed over his valuable Chinese carpet to the defendants for them to clean. The carpet was stolen whilst it was in the defendants' possession. The court held that the defendants were liable for breach of the implied term that they would take reasonable care of the goods in their control.

Curtis v Chemical Cleaning and Dyeing Company (1951)

The defendants were held liable for breach of the implied term that they would exercise reasonable care and skill in the performance of their duties when they spilled chemicals on, and stained, a white satin wedding dress given in for cleaning.

The standard of care required under s13 is that of the reasonably competent person who undertakes the type of work in question in the course of his business.

You will notice that the Act refers to an implied *term* and does not categorise the terms into conditions or warranties. This gives the court scope as to the remedy it will award in a particular case. If the effect of the breach is serious, and it is appropriate to do so, the court will allow the customer to treat the contract as repudiated. If, however, damages would be an appropriate remedy this is what the court will award.

If the contract involves both goods and services, the customer's remedy will depend on where the fault lies. If it is the goods supplied which are faulty, the remedy will lie under sections 2–5 of the SGSA. If it is the way in which they were fitted, the remedy will be under s13 of the same Act. If both the goods and the services are to blame for the loss, the action will lie under both parts of the 1982 Act although it must be remembered that, as the purpose of damages is to compensate, the customer can never make more than his actual loss.

TIME (SGSA S14)

When a supplier is acting in the course of business and no time for performance is agreed in the contract, nor is it left to be agreed in a manner specified in the contract, nor can it be determined by a course of dealings between the parties, then there is an implied term that the supplier will carry out the service within a reasonable time. What is a reasonable time is a question of fact. An illustration of how the court fixes a 'reasonable' time is shown in:

Charnock v Liverpool Corporation (1968)

A garage took 8 weeks to repair a car when a 'normally competent' repairer would have taken 5. The court held that this was an unreasonable delay and awarded damages to the plaintiff. The amount of damages was based on the cost of hiring another car for the 3 weeks between the time the car should have been repaired and the time it was actually ready.

If a reasonable time has elapsed, the customer may serve a notice fixing the time for performance of the contract. The time limit must be reasonable but, subject to this, the customer may treat the contract as repudiated if the supplier fails to meet the deadline. See the case of *Rickards (Charles) Ltd v Oppenheim* dealt with earlier in 11.1.6.

CONSIDERATION (SGSA S15)

If no price is fixed in the contract, nor is it left to be agreed in a manner specified in the contract nor can it be determined by a course of dealings between the parties, there is an implied term that the party contracting with the supplier will pay a reasonable price.

This section applies only where no consideration has been or can be fixed by the contract. If a price has been agreed, the customer has no power to re-open the negotiation even if this agreed price turns out to be excessive.

SUMMARY

In this chapter we have discussed specific contracts relating to the sale and supply of goods and services. Each of these contracts has to be formed according to the common law rules relating to contract except where the governing Act specifies otherwise (eg the Sale of Goods Act 1979 requiring the consideration to be in the form of money). In other words, these contracts have to be understood against the background of the common law of contract.

What the various Acts governing these contracts do, is to add to the law as it applies to the transactions in question. In all the Acts we have covered it does this by implying certain terms into the contracts and, in the case of the Sale of Goods Act 1979, by making further provision as to the passing of property, the duties of performance and the remedies of the sellers.

In the main, the Acts put into statutory form the existing rules of common law and mercantile custom. The original Sale of Goods Act 1893 (which was repealed and to a large extent re-enacted by the 1979 Act) codified existing law including mercantile custom and the Supply of Goods and Services Act 1982 codified the common law relating to the supply and hire of goods and services. The reason for such codification is that it makes for certainty and clarity in the law. It also gives greater ease of reference, cutting out the need to refer to a series of cases in order to make a point. Finally, and especially in the case of the 1982 Act, the restatement of existing obligations had the advantage of drawing the public's attention to them. It helped the public realise that there was a certain amount of protection available to it by virtue of the terms implied into contracts for the supply of goods and, especially, services.

SELF-TEST QUESTIONS

11.1 Define a contract for the sale of goods

11.2 Distinguish between
(a) express and
(b) implied terms

11.3 When will a buyer be said to have accepted goods under the SGA 1979?

11.4 What is the effect of acceptance?

11.5 What are the terms implied into contracts for sale of goods by the 1979 Act?

11.6 What, according to *Rowland* v *Divall* (1923) is the basic aim of a contract for the sale of goods?

11.7 When will a sale be by description for the purpose of s13 SGA?

11.8 What is meant by 'words of description'?

11.9 Complete the following definition of merchantable quality.

'Goods will be of merchantable quality if they are as (a) _____ for which such goods are commonly bought as it is
(b) _____ to expect having regard to (c) _____, the (d) _____ (if relevant), and all other relevant circumstances' Section (e) _____ Sale of Goods Act 1979

11.10 How does the case of *M/S Aswan Engineering Establishment Co* v *Lupdine* (1987) assist in the interpretation of the definition of merchantable quality?

11.11 Compare *Grant* v *Australian Knitting Mills* (1936) and *Heil* v *Hedges* (1951)

11.12 Charles bought a car from Ace Garage, telling the garage that he wanted to go on a driving holiday to the Swiss mountains in the vehicle. The car he bought overheated so badly, however, that it could not be used for its ordinary purpose of driving around Britain, let alone in the Swiss mountains. Which of the following points related to Charles's case?:
(a) His action would be for breach of
 (i) s 13
 (ii) s 14 (2)
 (iii) s 14 (3)
 (iv) s 14 (6)?
(b) The garage is in breach of
 (i) condition
 (ii) warranty?

(c) Would you answer to (a) differ and why, if, before he bought the car, Charles had taken it for a test drive and the engine had overheated, but Charles had not noticed this?
 (i) Yes
 (ii) No

11.13

(a) **When does property pass under the Sale of Goods Act?**
(b) **What is the effect of property passing?**

11.14 What is the significance of the distinction between entire and divisible contracts?

11.15 What are the remedies available to an unpaid seller?

11.16 John's water-pipes in his bathroom burst. He called in Fred, a plumber, who replaced the faulty pipe. A day later the new pipe started leaking. Advise John

(a) If the new pipe was faulty, would his action lie
 (i) In the Sale of Goods Act 1979, or
 (ii) In the Supply of Goods and Services Act 1982?
(b) If the fitting of the new pipe was faulty, would John's action lie in breach of
 (i) s 13
 (ii) s 14
 (iii) s 15
of the Supply of Goods and Services Act 1982?

Answers on page 320

EXERCISES

Exercise 11.1

1 What are the rules governing the passing of property and risk in a contract for the sale of goods?
2 L, a printer, asked M, a paper merchant to supply him with paper. M agreed and L selected a quantity of paper. L also asked M to put on one side and store for him a similar quantity of paper. M telephoned L to say that this second order of paper had been stored and would be delivered at L's request. Before either of the orders of paper could be delivered they were severely damaged by flood water.

Advise M.

Exercise 11.2

1 Explain the meaning of the rule *nemo dat quod non habet* contained in the Sale of Goods Act 1979. What are the major exceptions to the rule?
2 L went to M's shop to buy a second-hand typewriter. He explained to M that he wanted a machine that was suitable for beginners. M recommended a machine and told him that it had a minor fault that needed repair. L purchased the machine for £100. He later discovered that the machine was too complicated for him to operate and that the cost of repairing the fault was £50. Moreover, certain of the letters did not print properly.

Advise L.

Answers on page 321

174 LAW

Consumer credit

In this chapter we will look at the law relating to consumer credit, whether such credit is given in the form of a loan or overdraft or whether it involves credit cards or hire purchase, credit or conditional sale agreements.

The law is contained in the Consumer Credit Act 1974 (CCA), a statute passed to cover all forms of consumer credit transactions and to give protection to individuals who enter credit agreements. This protection comes in two forms:

1   A requirement that people or firms giving credit be licensed and
2   A requirement that consumer credit agreements follow the form set out in the Act; a form designed to give the debtors maximum information.

The Act also protects the debtor both before he enters the agreement and during the life of the agreement itself. It also deals with the various ways in which such an agreement may be ended.

Because the Consumer Credit Act was designed to cover all credit transactions, it was necessary to introduce new terminology into the law so as to give concepts which are general enough to cover a large range of transactions and yet which are sufficiently precise to prevent unscrupulous creditors from abusing the system. We will look at the terminology of the Act in the next section of this chapter.

12.1   TYPES OF CONSUMER CREDIT

There are a large number of different types of consumer credit. They range from contracts of hire purchase, whereby a person hires goods from the owner with the option to purchase at the end of the hire period, to credit sales, which are sales of goods, ownership in which passes immediately to the buyer but the price for which is payable at a later stage (eg purchases from mail order catalogues where the price of goods is paid after delivery). The expression consumer credit also covers conditional sales, under which the purchase price of the goods is payable in instalments but ownership is not to pass to the buyer until certain conditions (such as full payment) are satisfied. These, you will see, are virtually indistinguishable from hire purchase contracts and, in fact, the 1974 Act treats them in much the same way as it does H-P agreements. The key difference is that a conditional sale agreement is a *sale* of goods and therefore the buyer may pass title in the goods in certain circumstances to an innocent third party (see Chapter 11, 11.1.5 'Transfer of Title'). In a contract of hire-purchase, the hirer in most cases has no power to transfer ownership in the goods to another. If he attempts to do so, the finance company may recover the goods.

EXAMPLE 1

H is hiring a television set under a contract of hire purchase with the Quick Finance Company. H sells the set to G, his neighbour, who does not know of the hire-purchase transaction. The Quick Finance Company may recover the set from G. It remains the property of the finance company until H has paid all the instalments due and exercises his option to purchase the set. If, however, H is buying the set under a conditional sale agreement and the sale by him to G comes within one of the exceptions to the *nemo dat quod non habet* rule in the Sale of Goods Act 1979 (eg H sold as a buyer in possession), G obtains good title. (See the chapter on Sale of Goods for further illustration of this point.)

Other types of consumer credit covered by the Act include personal loans, overdrafts given by banks, budget accounts in shops, and credit card transactions under which a buyer buys goods or services from a supplier and the supplier is paid for them by the credit card company to whom the buyer subsequently pays the price.

12.2 CREDIT ACTIVITIES COVERED BY THE ACT

Those who give credit are covered by the Act and are required to comply with certain formalities and to obtain licences to operate. The Act also covers people and undertakings who carry on business which is in some way connected with credit. These also have to be licensed under the Act and are subject to various requirements and regulations relating, for example, to the seeking and carrying out of their business. If any person trades without a licence when the Act requires he be licensed, the contracts he enters into will be unenforceable unless a court order is obtained.

Examples of activities which are related to the giving of credit are:

12.2.1 Credit brokers

A credit broker is one who introduces individuals seeking credit to those whose business involves giving credit. This 'introduction' does not have to be a person's main business. So, for example, a motor dealer who arranges finance for a customer with a finance company will be a credit broker, as will an estate agent who, as part of his business, introduces a prospective house purchaser to a building society to help him obtain a mortgage.

The motor dealer and the estate agent are credit brokers and thus will be subject to the 1974 Act's provisions relating to licensing and the restrictions it places on the way in which they seek business etc.

One exception to this occurs in relation to individuals who, not operating from trade premises, and not acting as an employee of a finance company, effect introductions of individuals seeking credit to those willing to provide it. As long as this person does not by any other method effect introductions so as to bring him within the definition of credit brokers, he will not be covered by the restrictions in the Act. This exemption, in other words, applies to individuals who act as part-time agents for mail-order companies. These individuals will not be treated as credit brokers even though they introduce people wanting credit (customers ordering from the catalogue) to a firm willing to give it (the mail-order company).

12.2.2 Debt counsellors and debt adjusters

Debt counsellors are those who give advice on how to deal with consumer credit debts, such as bankers, solicitors, and advice agencies. These must all be licensed although for voluntary organisations such as Citizens' Advice Bureaux it is possible to obtain a group licence.

Debt adjusters are those who negotiate with the provider of the finance (the creditor) on behalf of a debtor in order to agree ways in which the debtor can pay off what he owes. For example, if a debtor has entered an H-P agreement and then loses his job and cannot pay the full H-P instalment each month, he may ask his adviser to negotiate with the finance company to allow him to pay smaller instalments over a longer period. The adviser will be a debt adjuster. Another example of debt adjustment occurs when a firm takes over all the debtor's liabilities in return for payments to the firm by the debtor.

12.2.3 Debt collecting agencies

These are firms which collect debts for creditors, usually in return for commission.

12.2.4 Credit reference agencies

These are firms which collect and sell information about the financial standing of individuals.

12.3 TERMINOLOGY

As we saw in the last section, the 1974 Act has introduced new terminology and new concepts into the law. We will now look at this new terminology so that when we deal with the various ways in which the Act controls consumer credit, you will understand how the protection varies according to the type of transaction involved. In going through the terminology note how certain types of credit (eg credit cards) may come within more than one of the definitions used.

12.3.1 Restricted and unrestricted use credit

Some of the provisions of the Act distinguish between restricted use credit (abbreviated to R-U-C) and unrestricted use credit (abbreviated to U-U-C).

RESTRICTED USE CREDIT

R-U-C is credit which is given to finance a particular purchase or transaction and which is given in such a way that the creditor can make sure that it will be used only for the purchase or transaction in question.

1   Thus, for example, the agreement will be for R-U-C where the person supplying the credit also supplies the goods.

EXAMPLE 2

Mary goes to Rose's Garage and sees a car she wishes to buy. Rose introduces her to the Fast Finance Company and Mary enters a contract to buy the car on H-P from Fast Finance. The effect of this contract is that Rose's Garage sells the car to Fast Finance which in turn hires it to Mary on H-P. Fast Finance is therefore supplying both the goods and the credit. Obviously it can control how Mary spends the credit (she does not, of course, receive any actual money at all). This is therefore an R-U-C agreement.

2   An agreement will also be for R-U-C where the creditor, in advancing money to the debtor for the purchase, actually pays the price directly to the supplier and not to the debtor. For example, if in Example 2, instead of obtaining the car on H-P from Fast Finance, Mary had gone to her bank for a loan for the purchase price and the bank had paid the amount of the loan directly to Rose's Garage, this transaction with the bank would be for R-U-C; though not if the bank had credited Rose's current account with the amount of the loan, in which case it would be unrestricted use credit.
3   An agreement where the creditor, instead of advancing money to the debtor, gives him a token, such as a credit card, which is restricted in its use to a specified supplier or suppliers (ie those who accept the credit card).

UNRESTRICTED USE CREDIT

If there is no control over the way the debtor uses the finance the agreement will be for U-U-C. In other words, if the debtor can use the finance in any way he chooses, such as will be the case if he obtains an overdraft from a bank or a loan from a finance company, it will be U-U-C.

Loans will be unrestricted use, even though the debtor may have contracted to use the loan only for a specific purpose.

In Example 2 above, if Mary had obtained an overdraft from her bank to pay for the car this will be a U-U-C agreement even though, when she obtained the overdraft Mary promised that she would use it only to buy the car. Because the bank cannot ensure that she actually uses it in this way, the credit will be treated as unrestricted use. Similarly cash drawn by means of a credit card is U-U-C.

RELEVANCE OF THE DISTINCTION

The distinction between R-U-C and U-U-C is relevant in several ways. For our purposes, the most important relate to the debtor's right to cancel the agreement (see 12.7) and to the meaning of linked transactions (see 12.4.3).

12.3.2 Debtor-creditor-supplier and debtor-creditor agreements

This distinction is fundamental to the workings of the 1974 Act. It is, in effect, the distinction between loans which are connected to the supply of the goods or services in question (a debtor-creditor-supplier, or D-C-S, agreement) and those which are not (a debtor-creditor, or D-C agreement).

The key factor is the relationship between the *supplier* of the goods or services and the *creditor*. If these two parties are the same person, or, if different, have a pre-existing business link, the agreement will be a D-C-S agreement. If there is no link, it will be a D-C agreement.

D-C-S agreements are usually for R-U-C, and D-C agreements are usually for U-U-C, although this is not necessarily the case as we shall see.

We will now look at D-C-S and D-C agreements in more detail.

DEBTOR-CREDITOR-SUPPLIER AGREEMENTS

A D-C-S agreement is a connected loan agreement; an agreement where there is some connection between the creditor and the supplier. It is, perhaps, more clearly expressed as a debtor and creditor-supplier agreement. Such an agreement will arise:

1. Where the person who supplies the goods and the person who provides the credit are one and the same person. If you look back to Example 2 in this chapter (section 12.3.1) you will see that Fast Finance provides both the goods and the credit to Mary. The creditor and supplier are one and the same person and therefore this is a D-C-S agreement for R-U-C.

2. Where the creditor and supplier work together under business arrangements. For example, in the case of credit card transactions, restricted use credit is given to the debtor by the card company under a pre-existing arrangement between the card company and the supplier (the shop). The arrangement is that, in return for the supplier accepting payment by credit card, the credit card company will settle the customer's bill for the goods in question. Another illustration would occur where, again in Example 2, Mary, instead of acquiring the goods on H-P, obtains a loan from Fast Finance having been introduced to Fast Finance by the garage. There is therefore a link between the creditor (Fast Finance) and the supplier (Rose's Garage) and so this is a D-C-S agreement.

DEBTOR-CREDITOR AGREEMENTS

These are any agreements which are not D-C-S agreements. In a D-C agreement, the supplier of the goods or services has no connection with the person who provides the finance. For example, if a person obtained a bank overdraft and then bought a car with the money, there is no connection between the bank and the supplier of the car. Again in Example 2, if Mary obtains a loan from a finance company which she herself arranges and which has not been suggested to her by the garage, there would be no link between Rose's Garage and the finance company. This would be a D-C agreement. If the money was paid to Mary, it would be a D-C agreement for U-U-C. If the money was paid directly to Rose's Garage it would be a D-C agreement for R-U-C. In each of these instances, there is no existing connection between the finance company and the supplier.

THE IMPORTANCE OF THE DISTINCTION BETWEEN D-C-S AND D-C AGREEMENTS

As we said earlier, the distinction is vital to the operation of the 1974 Act. For our purposes, the importance lies in relation to the following points:

1. The debtor's exercise of a right to cancel a regulated agreement (see 12.7) also automatically cancels a linked transaction. If the main agreement is a D-C-S agreement, any transaction financed by the creditor is a linked transaction.

EXAMPLE 3

Safe Finance, under an arrangement with Green Motor Dealers, advances to one of Green's customers the purchase price of a car being bought by the customer from Green. If the customer can and does cancel the loan from Safe Finance under the provisions of the 1974 Act, the contract for the sale of the car between Green and the customer will also automatically be rescinded. Furthermore, Safe Finance will be jointly and severally liable with Green to repay to the debtor any money he has already handed over.

If, however, the car is bought with an unconnected loan (eg the customer arranges the loan himself from a company entirely unconnected with Green Motor Dealers) even if the customer cancels the loan agreement, the contract for the sale of the car still remains in force. The loan is a D-C agreement.

2   If the debtor under a D-C-S agreement has a right to sue the supplier for misrepresentation or in breach of contract, the creditor will be jointly and severally liable with the supplier (see 12.6). This joint and several liability does not arise in D-C agreements.

12.4 AGREEMENTS COVERED BY THE ACT

12.4.1 Introduction

If an agreement is regulated, it will be governed by the requirements and restrictions of the Act as will any transaction linked to the agreement. Furthermore, anyone wishing to carry on the business of granting credit under regulated agreements must be licensed by the Director-General of Fair Trading as must anyone wishing to carry on an ancillary credit business.

In this section, we will examine the definition of a regulated consumer credit agreement and the meaning and effect of linked transactions. We will also look at agreements which are exempt from the workings of the Act.

12.4.2 Regulated consumer credit agreements

Section 8 CCA defines a regulated consumer credit agreement as an agreement whereby a person (the creditor) provides credit not exceeding £15,000 to an individual or partnership (the debtor). There are therefore three parts to the definition each of which must be examined.

A PERSON (THE CREDITOR)

The word 'person' in this context covers every entity known to the law. The creditor therefore may be an individual, a partnership, or an incorporated or unincorporated association. The creditor is the person who provides the finance under the consumer credit agreement.

PROVIDES CREDIT NOT EXCEEDING £15,000

The word 'credit' includes a cash loan and any other form of financial assistance on terms of repayment either in cash or in any other form.

It is the credit that must not exceed £15,000 for the Act to apply. For this purpose the Act distinguishes between the credit and the total charge for credit. The credit means the amount of the loan or other financial accommodation given to the debtor. It does not include the total amount the debtor has to repay. In other words, the credit means the amount of the actual loan but not the interest or credit charges.

EXAMPLE 4

The Easy Finance Company (the creditor) makes a contract for the hire-purchase of goods with Green (the debtor). Under the agreement, Green is to make periodic payments to Easy Finance and, when he has paid a total of £17,500 and has exercised his option to purchase, ownership of the goods will pass to him.

The total H-P price of £17,500 includes £1,000 deposit paid by Green and £1,500 credit charges, including interest. The agreement therefore provides credit of £17,500 − (£1,500 + £1,000) = £15,000.

This is therefore a regulated consumer credit agreement, as the total amount actually advanced to Green is within the statutory limits.

The credit therefore is the amount granted to the debtor. This may be either:

1   **fixed sum credit**, where the amount is fixed at the beginning of the agreement, as in a hire-purchase contract or a fixed sum bank loan. In these cases, the amount of the credit is the capital sum. Any deposit or interest payable will not be included in assessing the credit amount (as in the previous example); or
2   **running account credit** (also known as revolving credit) by which the debtor is entitled to draw money up to an agreed credit limit. Each time the debtor withdraws money, the credit

available to him is accordingly reduced and any payment the debtor makes into the account in reduction of his debt restores the credit up to the amount of this payment.

Bank overdrafts, credit card arrangements and store budget accounts are all examples of running account credit. Such agreements will be regulated by the Act if the maximum debt allowed on the account during any agreed period does not exceed £15,000. Once again, in deciding whether the credit amount comes within the £15,000, no account will be taken of any deposit or finance charges.

TO AN INDIVIDUAL OR PARTNERSHIP (DEBTOR)

The word 'individual' includes a partnership or other unincorporated body of persons not made up entirely of bodies corporate. It also includes individuals in the ordinary sense of the word, and unincorporated clubs and unincorporated charities. In other words, the only type of debtor excluded from the protection of the Act is a body corporate; a company or other association which has an existence separate from its members. In determining whether the Act applies to a credit agreement, it is only the status of the debtor that is relevant; and even if the debtor is a body corporate it will fall within the protection of the Act if the body corporate has joined with an individual in making the agreement.

Thus, if the debtor is a company the Act will not apply to the credit transaction. If, however, the credit is obtained jointly by a company and an individual (eg a director of the company acting in his own right) the Act will apply to this agreement.

12.4.3 Linked transaction (s19)

A linked transaction is a transaction which is subsidiary to but in some way linked with the main credit transaction. A linked transaction is automatically cancelled or terminated if the main (or principal) credit agreement is cancelled or terminated. Section 19 gives three types of linked transaction:

1. Where a transaction is entered into in compliance with a term of the principal agreement.

   Thus, for example, if the principal agreement for the financing of a purchase of goods requires the debtor to insure the goods, or to have the goods serviced at his (the debtor's) own expense by the supplier, this will be a linked transaction. It is a transaction made in compliance with a term in the main contract and, if the main contract is cancelled (see later) or is terminated (see later) the linked transaction also falls.

2. Where the principal agreement is a three-party D-C-S agreement and the subsidiary transaction is financed by the principal agreement. This will be an agreement for R-U-C.

EXAMPLE 5

Jones enters into an agreement with Smith's Garage to buy a car. The purchase is funded by a regulated loan given to Jones by Easy Finance. Jones was introduced to Easy Finance by Smith's Garage (in other words, there was a pre-existing arrangement between the creditor and the supplier). The purchase of the car by Jones from Smith's is linked to the loan to Jones from Easy Finance. So, if the loan is cancelled by the debtor or is terminated, the contract for the sale of the car will also fail automatically.

3. Where the creditor tells the debtor that, if the debtor enters a particular contract, the creditor will then enter the principal credit agreement with the debtor.

EXAMPLE 6

Jones goes to Easy Finance for a loan. Easy Finance tells Jones that if he first takes out a life assurance policy which he can assign to the credit company, it will then grant him the loan (ie enter the principal agreement). Jones takes out the policy and Easy Finance then makes the contract to give him a loan. The life assurance contract is a linked transaction and, if the principal loan agreement fails, so, automatically, does the life assurance.

Section 19 CCA expressly excludes the provision of security, such as a guarantee, from its operation. A guarantee as to the debtor's performance therefore does not automatically fail with the principal contract which it is designed to secure.

12.4.4 Agreements excluded in whole or in part from the Act

The Act provides that certain agreements, which would otherwise be regulated, are excluded from the workings of the Act either in whole or in part. These agreements are (1) exempt agreements; (2) small agreements; and (3) non-commercial agreements. We shall deal with each of these in turn.

1. Exempt agreements

   Certain agreements are exempt from the workings of the Act by virtue of s16 and the Consumer Credit (Exempt Agreements) Order 1980. In other words, the following agreements do not have to comply with the requirements of the Act, nor does the debtor obtain the protection afforded by the Act when he enters such an agreement. The only ways in which the Act applies to these contracts, in fact, is if they are extortionate credit bargains (see later) and in relation to the controls on the lender seeking business.

   The categories of exempt agreements include:
   (a) Mortgages for house or land purchase where the lender is a building society, or a local authority or is one of the bodies listed in regulations made under s16 CCA eg insurance companies, charities, or organisations of employers or workers.
   (b) D-C-S agreements (other than H-P or conditional sale) for fixed-sum credit where the credit is repayable by four or fewer instalments. Thus the Act does not apply to many ordinary sales where the buyer is given time to pay eg where a shop allows the price of an item sold to be paid in say three instalments.
   (c) D-C-S agreements for running account credit where the debt has to be paid in a single payment eg Diners' Club Card and American Express, which have to be paid in full at the end of each month.
   (d) D-C agreements where the annual percentage charge for credit does not exceed the higher of either 13% or 1% above the highest base rate of the London and Scottish Clearing Banks. The purpose of this exemption is to encourage the provision of cheap credit as can occur when, for example, employers give loans to employees at low rates of interest. Without such exemption from the requirements of the Act, some lenders may be discouraged from making such arrangements.

2. Small agreements (s17(1))

   A small agreement is a regulated consumer credit agreement, which is either unsecured or secured only by a guarantee or indemnity, and which provides credit of £50 or less. Hire-purchase and conditional sale agreements are specifically excluded from this exemption which will apply, for example, to credit sale agreements where credit not exceeding £50 is repayable by instalments and property in the goods passes to the buyer immediately, eg purchases from a mail order catalogue where the purchase price is less than £50.

   Small D-C-S agreements for R-U-C within the scope of s17 are generally exempted from the Act's provisions relating to formalities and cancellation but are still subject to the Act as regards default, termination and control by the courts.

3. Non-commercial agreements (s189(1))

   These are consumer credit agreements not made by the creditor in the course of a business carried on by him. This will cover, for example, loans by one friend to another where the lender is not acting in any way as part of his business. These agreements are not affected by the formalities and cancellation provisions of the Act nor will the lender be liable under S75(1) (see later). The rest of the Act, however, will still apply to the transaction.

12.5 PROTECTION OF DEBTOR BEFORE HE ENTERS THE AGREEMENT

12.5.1 Introduction

Once we have established that a credit agreement is regulated, we must then decide whether it complies with the provisions laid down in the Act. The purpose of these provisions is to ensure that full information is given to all parties both before and at the time the agreement is made and that the contract itself follows the form required by the Act. If such further information is not given, or if the agreement is incorrectly executed, then the creditor will be able to enforce the agreement only by obtaining a court order. Even before he enters the contract, however, the debtor is given certain rights.

12.5.2 Debtor cannot bind himself to enter the agreement (s59 CCA)

Any agreement which attempts to bind a person to enter into a prospective regulated agreement is void. The mere option given to the debtor to take credit is valid, even though it binds the creditor.

In other words, the Act protects prospective debtors although not prospective creditors.

12.5.3 Creditor's liability for pre-contractual statements

In a D-C-S case, any antecedent negotiations conducted by the supplier or credit broker are conducted by him as agent for the creditor (s56 CCA). There can be no contracting out of this provision.

ANTECEDENT NEGOTIATIONS (s56(4))

Antecedent (or pre-contractual) negotiations begin when the negotiator and debtor first enter into communication. This includes communication by advertisement. The negotiations include any representations made by the negotiator to the debtor and any other dealings between them. With the phrase 'antecedent negotiations' being given such a wide meaning, you will see that all regulated agreements must have some prior communication and so all will be covered by s56.

THE NEGOTIATOR

For the purposes of s56, the negotiator includes:

1. The creditor or the owner or his agent or employee.
2. A dealer who introduces a customer to a finance company in order to enable the customer to acquire the goods he wants from the dealer by means of a hire-purchase contract with the finance company. The dealer will then sell the goods to the finance company which will hire them back to the customer.
3. A supplier selling goods against a credit card.
4. A dealer selling goods for cash advanced to the buyer by a finance company to whom the buyer has been introduced by the dealer.

Any person within these categories and who conducts negotiations is a negotiator within s56 and the negotiations he conducts are antecedent negotiations for the purpose of any representations and cancellation provisions (see later).

In other words, if a negotiator makes an actionable representation in relation to the goods, the creditor will be liable for this misrepresentation.

EXAMPLE 7

Dean goes to Fast Garages and sees a car which he wishes to buy. Fast Garages tells Dean that the car has had only one careful owner and that the mileage shown is accurate. Dean therefore decides to buy the car, but, because he cannot afford to pay cash for it he follows Fast Garages' suggestion and enters a hire-purchase contract with Easy Finance Co. Fast Garages provides him with Easy's forms and, when the H-P contract is concluded, Fast sells the car to Easy which lets it back to Dean on H-P.

Later Dean discovers that, in fact, the car has had several owners, two of whom have crashed it badly, and that the car has done at least double the mileage shown.

Because Fast Garages is a negotiator for the purposes of s56 (see point 2 above) and the misrepresentations are made during antecedent negotiations, Easy Finance is liable for Fast Garages' misrepresentations and Dean will have an action against the finance company even though it was not a party to, or aware of, the original wrongful statement.

12.5.4 Debtor may withdraw from the contract (s57 CCA)

This right exists until the finance contract has been executed (ie signed in compliance with all the formalities). Thus no binding contract can come into existence until all formalities have been completed.

Notice of withdrawal, whether oral or written, is effective if it is given

either to the creditor

or to the credit broker or supplier who is the negotiator in antecedent negotiations

or to any person who, in the course of a business, acts on behalf of the debtor in any negotiations for the agreement eg a dealer arranging finance for the customer with a finance company. The dealer is, in fact, the customer's agent, but by s57 notice of withdrawal to him operates as notice to the finance company.

12.6 PROTECTION OF THE DEBTOR IN RELATION TO THE CONTRACT ITSELF

12.6.1 Formalities

The Act provides that contracts whereby a debtor is provided with credit must comply with certain formalities. These are set out in sections 61–64 CCA and in Regulations made under the Act. If these formalities are not complied with, the agreement is 'improperly executed' and cannot be enforced by the creditor without a court order.

The formalities for proper execution are that:

1. The document must comply with the format prescribed by regulations. That is, it must be printed on paper of a certain colour, the lettering must be of the size and in the style prescribed; there must be no handwriting on the contract except to give details of the parties, the goods, the finance and the signature and date.
2. The contract must give the debtor notice of his rights, for example, to cancel or to terminate the agreement. This notice must be in the form laid down by regulations.
3. There must be a detailed disclosure of all relevant information. What is 'relevant' is again covered by the legislation and includes information relating to the cash price of the goods or services, the amount of deposit paid, any advance payments made, the total charge for credit expressed as an annual percentage rate (APR) and the amounts and timing of repayments.
4. The document has to be signed by the debtor in a 'signature box' which informs him of the nature of the transaction into which he is entering ('this document contains a consumer credit agreement; only sign it if you wish to be bound'). It must also be signed by or on behalf of the creditor. The debtor must sign *only* after all the relevant information has been entered onto the agreement (see point 3 above). If the debtor signs 'in blank', that is before the information has been inserted, this will be improper execution, even though the information is filled in later.
5. The agreement must contain all the terms of the agreement, other than the implied terms.
6. The agreement must be easily legible when it is presented or sent to the debtor for his signature.

12.6.2 Copies

As part of the aim of the Act to give the debtor full information and to ensure that he is aware of all that is happening there is a duty to provide him with copies of this agreement. Failure to comply with the requirements will mean that the agreement is not properly executed.

1. As soon as he signs the agreement, the debtor must be given a copy there and then.
2. If the agreement is not executed when the debtor signs it, he must be given or sent a copy of the executed agreement within 7 days of execution. An agreement is executed when both parties (ie debtor and creditor) have signed it. In most cases, the debtor will sign the agreement and then it will be sent to the finance company for it to sign. Only when the creditor (finance company) has signed will the agreement be executed. The debtor must be given or sent a copy of this agreement within 7 days of the creditor signing his part of the contract.
3. If the agreement is executed at the time the debtor signs (that is, if, unusually, the creditor signs

at the same time) a copy of the agreement must be given there and then to the debtor. This is the only copy he will be given unless the agreement is cancellable.

4   If the agreement is cancellable (see 12.7) the above rules (2)–(3) will be varied in certain ways.
  (a) All copies have to contain notices in the form prescribed by regulations informing the debtor of his right to cancel;
  (b) Any second copy has to be sent by post;
  (c) If the agreement is executed when or immediately after the debtor signs and the debtor is given only one copy, he has to be sent a separate notice setting out his right of cancellation. This second notice has to be sent *by post* within 7 days of making the agreement.

12.6.3 Implied terms

All contracts of hire purchase under the Consumer Credit Act 1974 have certain terms implied into them. These terms, which are contained in the Supply of Goods (Implied Terms) Act 1973 are, with necessary amendments to take account of the transaction being basically one of hire and not sale, the same as those implied by sections 12–15 Sale of Goods Act 1979. Thus:

1   There is an implied condition that the person transferring the goods under the H-P agreement will have the right to transfer ownership at the time when the hirer exercises his option to purchase.
2   There is an implied condition that where goods are hired by description they will correspond with the description.
3   There are implied conditions that the goods hired on H-P will be of merchantable quality and that, where the hirer's purpose has been made known either expressly or impliedly to the creditor or to the credit broker, the goods will be fit for that purpose.
4   Where goods are hired by sample there is an implied condition that the bulk will correspond with the sample.

These implied terms have the same effect as those in the Sale of Goods Act 1979. Thus if a person was acquiring a new car on H-P and the engine proved to be badly defective, he could treat the H-P contract as repudiated for breach of the implied conditions of merchantable quality and fitness for purpose. He could therefore reject the car and recover any money he had paid, provided he did not affirm the contract (that is, provided he did not keep using the goods after he became aware of his right to reject).

This is further illustrated in the case of:

Warman v Southern Counties Car Finance Corporation Ltd (1949)

The plaintiff was hiring a car on H-P. After he had paid some of the instalments he discovered that the finance company did not have the right to transfer ownership in the car. He had paid eight months' instalments when the true owner claimed return of the car. The plaintiff returned it and sued the finance company for breach of the implied conditions that they had or would have the right to transfer ownership in the car. The court held that the plaintiff should succeed in his claim. He was entitled to recover all the instalments he had paid, the legal costs involved in hiring the car and all other incidental expenses. The fact that he had used the car for eight months was held to be irrelevant. There was a total failure of consideration.

12.6.4 Liability of the creditor

Two of the main ways in which the creditor is made liable to the debtor for misrepresentation and breach of contract can be found in sections 56 and 75 CCA.

SECTION 56 CCA

Section 56 provides that any antecedent negotiations for a D-C-S agreement conducted by the supplier, are conducted by him as agent for the creditor.

So, for example, a dealer who negotiates with a 'customer' for the purchase by the 'customer' of goods on H-P, does so as agent of the finance company. You will recall that when a person acquires goods on H-P, the dealer will sell the goods to the finance company and this company will hire the goods to the debtor. The contract in these cases is between the debtor and the finance company. It is a two party D-C-S agreement, with the creditor and the supplier being the same person.

The creditor, of course, will have made no representations to the customer about the goods—this will have been done by the dealer who persuaded the customer to contract to obtain the goods in the first place. By s56, however, the dealer conducts these negotiations as agent of the finance company, so if he makes any misrepresentations about the goods the hirer can sue the finance company, as well as the dealer, for these.

'Antecedent negotiations' begin when the negotiator (in our example, the dealer) and the debtor first enter into communication. This includes communication by advertisement.

EXAMPLE 8

Mary goes to Rose's Garage and sees a car she likes. Rose makes some false statements about the car and, relying on these, Mary agrees to buy it on hire-purchase from Fast Finance Co, a company to whom she is introduced by Rose. Rose's Garage therefore sells the car to Fast Finance which hires it to Mary under the H-P contract. This, therefore, is a two-party D-C-S agreement. Fast Finance, of course, has made no mis-statements to Mary but, by virtue of s56, Rose is taken to have made the misrepresentations as agent of Fast Finance. Mary therefore has a right of action in misrepresentation against the finance company for Rose's mis-statements.

If, under the ordinary rules of contract, the mis-statement has been incorporated into the contract, Mary will have a right of action in breach of contract against the finance company.

There can be no contracting out of this provision.

SECTION 75 CCA

This section imposes liability on the creditor in a three-party D-C-S agreement. It provides that, in such an agreement, where the debtor has a claim against the supplier for misrepresentation or breach of contract, he has a like claim against the creditor who is made jointly and severally liable.

The creditor has a right to be indemnified by the supplier.

This section will apply only where:

1. The agreement is a three-party D-C-S agreement. In other words, it will apply only where the creditor and the supplier are different persons but there is some business connection between them.

    In Example 8, if, rather than entering into an H-P contract, Mary had borrowed money from Fast Finance and had bought the car from Rose's Garage with Fast Finance already having a pre-existing arrangement with Rose's Garage to fund sales, this would be a three-party D-C-S agreement. The creditor and supplier are different persons. Section 75 would apply to make Fast Finance liable in the same way as Rose's Garage. So, for example, if the car broke down after she had bought it, Mary could sue Rose's Garage in breach of s14(2) Sale of Goods Act 1979.

    She would also have a like claim against Fast Finance by virtue of s75.

2. The agreement is a commercial agreement (ie the creditor lends the money in the course of business).

3. The claim against the supplier relates to goods which the supplier has attached a cash price of between £100 and £30,000. As s75 applies only to three-party D-C-S agreements, it will not apply to impose liability on a creditor in a hire-purchase agreement (where the creditor will also be the supplier). In other words, s75 relates to cases where the debtor uses the credit supplied to finance a separate contract of supply. It will apply, for example, to purchases made by use of a credit card.

EXAMPLE 9

George books a holiday with Sunny Tours Ltd. He pays by credit card. There are lots of things wrong with the holiday. The hotel is not as advertised, and there are many other breaches of contract. Provided the holiday costs between £100 and £30,000, George will have a right of action against Sunny Tours and a like action against the credit card company, which is jointly and severally liable with the supplier of the service (that is, the holiday).

Thus, if Sunny Tours has gone into liquidation, George will still have a right of action against the creditor.

The fact that the debtor sues the supplier but does not obtain judgment, does not prevent him bringing an action against the creditor. If the debtor chooses to sue the creditor and succeeds, the creditor may claim indemnity against the supplier. The creditor is also entitled to any defences which would have been available to the supplier had he been sued by the debtor.

12.6.5 Debtor's right to have information

During the currency of the agreement, the debtor has the right to receive certain information from the creditor (sections 77–79) as to matters such as how much he has already paid and how much he still owes. He is also entitled to a further copy of the agreement if he needs one. The information has to be given within 12 working days. This period begins on the day after the request has been received.

A corresponding obligation on the debtor is to tell the creditor where the goods are if the agreement requires the debtor to keep the goods in his possession or control (s80).

12.6.6 Extortionate credit bargains

These are covered by sections 137–140 of the Act. Under these sections, the court has the power to re-open credit agreements which it regards as extortionate. This power applies to any credit agreement, not just those which are regulated under the Act. Thus it applies even where the credit exceeds £15,000 or where the agreement is exempt from the other provisions of the Act. It covers not just terms as to repayment but also minimum payment and forfeiture clauses.

THE COURT'S POWER TO RE-OPEN THE AGREEMENT

The power is available if the credit bargain is extortionate, that is, if the payments are grossly exorbitant, or if the agreement otherwise grossly contravenes the ordinary principles of fair dealing.
Factors the court must take into account include:

1. The prevailing interest rates.
2. The debtor's age, experience and business capacity.
3. The state of the debtor's health and the financial pressure on him.
4. The degree of risk accepted by the creditor.
5. The creditor's relationship to the debtor.
6. Whether an inflated cash price was quoted for the goods or services.

THE COURT'S POWER IF THE AGREEMENT IS EXTORTIONATE

If the court finds that the agreement is extortionate, it may re-open the transaction and adjust the rights and duties of the parties. The court may:

1. Set aside or reduce any obligation imposed on the debtor.
2. Require the creditor to repay all or any part of any sum paid under the credit bargain or any related agreement by the debtor or a surety.
3. Alter the terms of the credit agreement.

12.6.7 Loss of credit token

If the debtor loses his credit token (ie his credit card) he will not be liable for any misuse of the card:

1. After he has informed the creditor of his loss.
2. If the creditor has not given him notice of the name, address and telephone number of a person to be contacted in the event of such loss.

The debtor is liable for a maximum of £50 for misuse of the card before he reports its loss to the creditor, but if the card is misused by someone who obtained it with the debtor's consent, the debtor's liability extends to the full amount spent by this person.

12.7 RIGHTS TO END THE CONTRACT

Under the CCA, there are several ways in which the credit agreement may be ended. In certain circumstances it may be cancelled by the debtor; it may be rescinded by him if he entered the agreement following a misrepresentation; the hirer may treat it as repudiated for breach of condition; and the creditor may terminate it if the debtor defaults in his performance of his obligations. The creditor also has a right to pay off his debt early or to terminate the agreement at any time before he pays the final instalment and exercises his option to purchase.

We will deal with each of these in turn:

12.7.1 Cancellation

WHICH AGREEMENTS ARE CANCELLABLE?

An agreement will be cancellable if two requirements are satisfied:

1. oral representations are made in antecedent negotiations in the debtor's presence; *and*
2. the debtor signs other than at the place of business of the creditor, a negotiator or a party to a linked transaction.

So, to enable a debtor to cancel, there must have been oral representations made in his presence in the course of antecedent negotiations. These representations must have been made by an individual acting as, or on behalf of, the negotiator. 'Antecedent negotiations' has the same meaning as it has in relation to s56 (see 12.6.4).

Once it has been established that there have been antecedent negotiations it must then be shown that these negotiations included oral representations. If there are no face-to-face oral representations (if, for example, the negotiator merely has telephone discussions with the debtor) the cancellation provisions will not apply. As long as the debtor is present, however, it is sufficient if the representations are made to a third party who is also present.

The object of these provisions is to protect a prospective debtor who is subjected in person to sales-talk and sales-pressure, to give him a chance to 'cool-off'. The other requirement for cancellation is that the debtor signs at some place other than the creditor's place of business or the place of business of a negotiator or a party to a linked transaction. If he signs at any of these places, he will not have a right of cancellation.

Thus the debtor will have a right to cancel if he signs:

1. At the premises of some other dealer. Even if this dealer deals in goods of a similar description, this will not be sufficient to prevent the debtor being able to cancel.
2. At his own home.
3. At his own business premises.
4. At the offices of his solicitor.

The burden of proof is on the creditor to show that, because of the place at which the agreement was signed, the cancellation provisions do not apply.

METHOD OF CANCELLATION

Written notice of cancellation must be served

1. On the creditor, or
2. On a negotiator of the agreement, or
3. On the debtor's own agent in antecedent negotiations. This provision takes account of the fact that there are various types of broker, such as insurance brokers, who although not the debtor's agent in the eyes of the law are often taken to be such by the consumer. The debtor/consumer, therefore, might assume that communication to this broker is, in effect, equivalent to communication to the creditor. The 1974 Act gives effect to that assumption for the purpose of service of notice of cancellation.

CANCELLATION PERIOD

The notice must be served during the cancellation period. This period lasts until the end of the fifth day following the day upon which the debtor receives his second notice of cancellation, whether this is his second notice of a right of cancellation of an executed agreement, or whether it is the executed agreement itself, if the agreement was not executed when the debtor signed.

If the notice of cancellation or the second copy of the agreement is lost in the post and does not reach the debtor, his time for cancellation continues to run. If the notice etc never arrives, therefore, the debtor's cancellation period continues indefinitely.

If the debtor serves notice of cancellation by post, however, it takes effect from the time of posting, irrespective of whether or when the notice actually arrives at the creditor's.

EFFECTS OF CANCELLATION ON A D-C-S AGREEMENT FOR R-U-C

Cancellation ends both the finance agreement and any linked transaction. It also automatically withdraws any offer by the debtor or his relative to enter into a linked transaction. In other words, a cancelled agreement is treated as if it had never been entered into.

The debtor is released from liability for any payment, whether it has accrued due or whether it is payable in the future.

1 Debtor's rights
The debtor is entitled to:
(a) Repayment of any money paid under or in contemplation of the consumer credit agreement or any linked transaction.
(b) Recovery of any goods he has given in part-exchange. If these goods are not recovered within 10 days in substantially the same condition as when they were delivered by the debtor, he will be entitled to a sum equal to the part-exchange allowance.
(c) A lien on the goods he has received under the agreement until the above rights are satisfied.

Any security which has been given is treated as if it had never taken effect.

2 Debtor's duties
The debtor must return the goods *unless* they are perishable or consumable and either:
(a) have been consumed before cancellation, or
(b) before cancellation have been incorporated in land or in some other object not comprised in the cancelled agreement or linked transaction.

In 2(a), although the debtor can cancel, he does not have to restore the goods. In other words, he has the goods without paying for them. For example, if a debtor is hiring a freezer and food on H-P terms which cover both. If the debtor has the right to, and does, cancel the agreement, he must return the freezer but does not have to return the value of the food. In practice, the creditor may avoid this difficulty by postponing delivery until after the end of the cancellation period.
(c) Until the goods are re-delivered, however, the debtor must retain and take reasonable care of them. This duty comes to an end after 21 days unless the debtor is at fault for not making the foods reasonably available for collection by the creditor.

EFFECTS OF CANCELLATION ON A D-C AGREEMENT FOR U-U-C

If the agreement being cancelled is for a loan paid directly to the debtor which he can use as he wishes (even though such use may be in breach of the contract with the creditor) the cancelled agreement continues in force insofar as it relates to the repayment of credit already received and interest.

In other words, if the cancelled agreement is for U-U-C, the debtor must repay any parts of the loan which he has already received although he is not liable to take any future parts of the loan.

If the debtor either:

1 Repays within one month of cancellation; or
2 If the credit repayable by instalments, before the date the first instalment is due, he will not

have to pay any interest on the amount he has borrowed. If he does not repay within these time limits, the debtor may repay the amounts he has received over the contract period with re-calculated interest.

EXAMPLE 10

The debtor takes out a £3,000 loan with a finance company, the money to be paid to him in three £1,000 instalments, the total to be repaid over five years. The agreement was signed at the debtor's home and so it is cancellable. The debtor receives the first £1,000 when he signs but he later cancels the agreement. The effect of the cancellation is that:

1   The debtor does not have to take the final two instalments of the loan.
2   He must repay the £1,000 already borrowed. If he does so within one month of cancellation or before the date of his first repayment, he does not have to pay any interest.
3   If he does not or cannot repay the £1,000 within the time limits, he will be required to repay the sum over the agreed time period (ie in this example, 5 years). The interest he pays will be re-calculated to take account of the fact that the amount borrowed is only one-third of the amount originally agreed.

As the loan is for U-U-C, any transaction entered into by the debtor using the borrowed money remains unaffected by his cancellation of the loan agreement, unless there is a business connection between the creditors and the supplier (ie unless it is a D-C-S agreement).

The following example will illustrate how the rules relating to cancellation work:

EXAMPLE 11

George sees a car in Rose's Garage. The salesman takes George out in the car for a test-drive, during which the salesman explains that, if George cannot pay cash for the car the garage could arrange for him to hire the vehicle on H-P with Speedy Finance Company. George decides to acquire the car on H-P and, as the salesman happens to have the various forms with him, they pull into the side of the road and, still sitting in the car, George signs the H-P agreement for the car. The garage takes George's old car, worth £200, in part-exchange, allowing him £1,000 for it to induce him to enter the contract.

As George has signed at other than trade premises (he signed in the car at the side of the road) and as there were oral representations made to him in the antecedent negotiations (the salesman talking about the car during the test-drive) the agreement is cancellable. The agreement George signed must contain a notice of his rights of cancellation.

George must receive a copy of the executed agreement (ie the agreement as signed by the finance company) within seven days of its execution. He then has a further five days in which to cancel. He may cancel by giving written notice to Rose's Garage. The finance agreement will thereupon be treated as if it had never been made and the agreement to take the car will also fail.

George is also entitled to recover his own car that he gave in part-exchange. If Rose's Garage have, in fact, already disposed of this car they must give George the part-exchange allowance they made for it—ie £1,000.

12.7.2 Rescission for misrepresentation

If the supplier and the creditor are one and the same person and this person conducted the preliminary pre-contractual negotiations, any misrepresentation made will entitle the debtor to rescind the ensuing agreement under the ordinary rules of contract.

Also, by s56, which we have already discussed, any antecedent negotiations conducted by the supplier to a D-C-S agreement will be conducted by him as agent for the creditor (eg if a dealer conducts negotiations which lead to an H-P agreement between the debtor and the creditor, under which the creditor obtains the goods from the dealer and lets them on H-P to the debtor, then the dealer is regarded as the agent for the creditor. If the dealer has made an actionable misrepresenta-tion, the debtor will be able to rescind the contract with the creditor).

Also, by virtue of s75 (see earlier), in a three-party D-C-S agreement, if the debtor has a claim against the supplier for misrepresentation he will have a similar claim against the creditor.

12.7.3 Debtor's right to repudiate for breach of condition

Again, by virtue of s75, in a three-party D-C-S agreement, if the debtor has a claim against the supplier for breach of any condition, whether express or implied, he will have a similar claim against the creditor. So, for example, if the goods supplied under the D-C-S agreement are in breach of one or more of the terms implied by the Sale of Goods Act 1979 the debtor will be able to sue the supplier and/or the creditor.

If, of course, the creditor himself breaks a condition of the contract the debtor will be able to treat the contract as repudiated under ordinary principles of contract.

12.7.4 Debtor's right to pay off early

The debtor has the right at any time to settle early. In other words, he can pay off all he owes under the finance contract at any time he wishes. His right to do this cannot be excluded by any provision in the agreement.

The debtor may exercise his right to pay off early by giving written notice. This notice does not have to be signed and it may embody the exercise by the debtor of any option to purchase the goods which is given to him by the agreement.

If the notice is accompanied by payment of the outstanding balance, less the statutory rebate, it can take effect immediately. Alternatively, the debtor is entitled to specify any future settlement date he chooses, as long as it is not later than the contract date for completion of payment.

If the debtor settles early, he will obtain a rebate on the interest he is required to pay under the agreement. The method of calculating this rebate is given in Regulations made under the 1974 Act.

12.7.5 Debtor's right to terminate an H-P or conditional sale agreement

The debtor may, by sections 99–100 CCA, terminate his hire-purchase or conditional sale agreement at any time before he pays the final instalment and exercises the option to purchase.

If, however, the debtor exercises this right to terminate he must:

1. Pay all the instalments outstanding, and
2. He may have to bring the total amount he has paid to one-half of the total hire-purchase price (or less, if this is stated by the agreement or if the court so orders), and
3. He must allow the creditor to repossess the goods, and
4. He must pay damages if he has failed to take reasonable care.

EXAMPLE 12

George is buying a television set under an H-P agreement. The total cost of the set is £700. George loses his job and finds that he cannot keep paying the H-P instalments. He therefore decides to terminate the contract.

If he has already paid over half the total H-P price he will not have to pay any more money, although, of course, he will lose the money he has already paid. He will also have to allow the creditor to recover the set and pay damages if he has failed to take reasonable care of it.

If George has only paid £200, however, he may be required to pay the finance company a further £150 to bring the amount paid up to half the total hire-purchase price. He must also, once again, allow the creditor to repossess the goods and he will have to pay damages if he has failed to take care of the set. If, however, the agreement specifies that, in the event of termination, a hirer need pay less than half the total price, or if the court decides that a smaller amount would be fair, George will only have to pay that lesser sum.

12.7.6 Creditor's right to terminate for debtor's breach

The creditor has the right to terminate the contract if the hirer is in breach of any of its terms. This right, which is given by s98 CCA, relates to breaches other than the debtor's default in making repayments.

For example, a finance contract often provides that the creditor will have the right to terminate the agreement if:

1. The goods are destroyed or the insurers of the goods treat a claim relating to them on a total loss basis.

2   The debtor gave false information in connection with his entry into the contract.
3   The debtor has a receiving order made against him or becomes insolvent, or makes a composition with or calls a meeting of his creditors.
4   If execution is levied or attempted against any of his assets or income.

These grounds are usually stated expressly in the contract, which will also provide that, in the event of one of these events occurring, the creditor will have a right to repossess the goods (subject to the debtor's statutory protection—see later) and the debtor will have to pay all amounts he owes together with such further sums as are necessary to bring the total amount paid up to one-half of the total H-P price. In other words, the contract will be treated as if the debtor had terminated it.

For the creditor to be able to terminate in this way, he must give the debtor a minimum of seven days' notice in the prescribed form before any action is taken.

12.7.7 Creditor's right to terminate on the debtor's default

If the debtor defaults in his obligation (eg to pay his instalments etc,) the creditor is entitled to end the agreement.

Before he does so, however, the creditor must serve a notice of default on the debtor. The notice of default must specify:

1   The nature of the alleged breach.
2   If the breach is capable of remedy, what action is required to remedy it and the date before which that action is to be taken (eg how many instalments the debtor is owing and the date by which he must pay these arrears).
3   If the breach is not capable of remedy, the sum (if any) required to be paid as compensation for the breach.
4   The time within which the debtor has to rectify the breach or pay the compensation. This must be a minimum of 7 days.
5   The consequences of non-compliance with the notice.

If default notice is not served, the creditor cannot terminate the agreement nor can he recover the goods or any payments, nor can he enforce any guarantees he has been given under the agreement.

Once a default notice has been served, the debtor may apply to the court for a time order (s129). This order will fix a time for the debtor to pay the sums owing or to remedy the breaches he has committed.

In fixing the time, the court will have regard to the debtor's finances and to what it considers reasonable in the circumstances.

12.8 PROTECTION OF THE DEBTOR BY THE COURT

Actions on consumer credit must always be brought in the county court. The court may make the following orders:

12.8.1 Time orders

These are granted on the application of the debtor after he has received a default notice (see last section).

12.8.2 Other orders

In hire-purchase and conditional sales the court has the power, if it thinks it is just to do so, to:

1   Order the debtor to return all the goods to the creditor.

2   Order the creditor to transfer title in part of the goods to the debtor, and the debtor to return the rest to the creditor.

The court has the power, on re-application, to suspend any of the provisions it has made in an order.

12.8.3 Recovery of goods

CREDITOR'S POWER TO ENTER DEBTOR'S PREMISES

A creditor cannot enter any land to take possession of goods held under a regulated hire purchase or conditional sale agreement unless the creditor obtains an order of the court (s92).

If the creditor enters without such authority he will incur liability under s92(3).

PROTECTED GOODS

Goods will be 'protected goods' if, under a regulated hire-purchase or conditional sale agreement, the debtor:

1   Has paid one-third or more of the total H-P price; and
2   He is in breach of his contract; and
3   He has not terminated the agreement; and
4   Ownership of the goods is still in the creditor.

In these cases, the creditor cannot recover possession of the goods from the debtor without an order of the court. If the creditor does recover them without first obtaining the necessary court order, the agreement automatically terminates and the debtor can recover all the payments he has made.

In granting an order, the court may make any provisions it thinks fit as for example, in 12.8.2 above.

In all cases, however, if the Act requires that no action may be taken without an order of the court, the consent of the debtor given at the time will be equally effective.

Thus, for example, if the goods are protected, the creditor cannot recover them without a court order. If, however, the debtor voluntarily hands them over to the creditor he will be taken to have waived the protection of the court and his recovery of possession by the creditor will be valid.

SUMMARY

In this chapter, we have examined the ways in which the Consumer Credit Act 1974 protects people who enter credit transactions. We have seen that the ways in which such protection is granted is by licensing people who give credit, by making unlicensed dealers' contracts unenforceable without the court's permission, and by regulating the individual agreements made by debtors.

We have also seen that the Act is drafted in such a way as to cover as many different types of credit transaction as possible; hence the need for the new terminology and concepts. It is essential that you understand these in order to appreciate the control and protection afforded by the legislation. Note, too, that some of the provisions relate only to hire-purchase and conditional sale agreements. These parts of the Act will not apply to other credit transactions such as loans.

Finally, bear in mind that the purpose of the Act is to protect the consumer. Note how such protection is provided before, during and at the end of the contract but, in looking at how the agreement may be ended, consider the consequences to the debtor. If, for example, he cannot pay any more instalments he would be better advised to do nothing and wait for a notice of default (at which time he can apply to the court for a time order) rather than actually terminate the agreement (when he could be made to pay up to half the total hire-purchase price). Such is the protection afforded by the Act that the debtor would be best served by doing nothing and waiting for the creditor to take the initiative.

SELF-TEST QUESTIONS

12.1 Distinguish between:

(a) Restricted–Use–Credit and
(b) Unrestricted–Use–Credit

12.2 Complete the definition of a regulated consumer credit agreement

'A regulated consumer credit agreement is an agreement whereby a person (the (a) ____), provides credit not exceeding (b) ____, to an (c) ____ or (d) ____ (the debtor). Credit may be either (e) ____ or (f) ____ credit'

12.3 How is the debtor protected before he enters the contract?

12.4 Describe the rules as to copies of the agreement

12.5 The implied terms in hire-purchase contracts are contained in

(a) Sale of Goods Act 1979
(b) Supply of Goods and Services Act 1982
(c) Consumer Credit Act 1974
(d) Supply of Goods (Implied Terms) Act 1973

12.6 Complete the following sentence:

'By s 75 CCA, in a (a) ____ party D-C-S agreement, if the debtor has a claim against the supplier for (b) ____ or (c) ____, he has a like claim against the (d) ____ who is made (e) ____ and (f) ____ liable'

12.7 When will a credit bargain be treated as extortionate?

12.8 When will an agreement be cancellable?

12.9 Define the cancellation period

12.10 On what conditions may a debtor terminate an HP or conditional sale agreement?

12.11 Define 'protected goods'

Answers on page 324

EXERCISES

Exercise 12.1

James, one of your clients, is the proprietor of an electrical dealer's shop. He wishes to introduce hire purchase facilities into the shop. Explain to him what is meant by a hire purchase contract and what formalities are necessary for its valid creation under the Consumer Credit Act 1974. What are effects of a failure to comply with these formalities?

Exercise 12.2

1   How does the Consumer Credit Act 1974 protect an individual who acquires goods subject to a hire purchase agreement that is covered by the provisions of the Act from the risk of having those goods confiscated from him if his payment falls into arrears?
2   John was acquiring a television on hire purchase (total hire purchase price £180). Having paid £65 on this, he made a further agreement with the same creditor relating to the television set and a new cooker (total hire purchase price £330). John has paid a further £10 under this new agreement but has now fallen into arrears with his instalments. The creditor has written to John threatening to repossess if the arrears are not paid by return of post.

Advise John.

Answers on page 325

194 LAW

The contract of employment

In this chapter we are concerned with the Contract of Employment. Until relatively recently the relationship used to be referred to as one of master and servant. However, to reflect changing social attitudes, it is now customary to refer to it as employer and employee. In approaching the topic, the first thing which we must do is to distinguish between a contract of service and a contract for services. The relationship of employer and employee is known as a Contract of Service. That of employer and independent contractor is known as a Contract for Services. The importance of the distinction is that at common law an employer is vicariously liable (ie personally responsible) for whatever his employee does. Thus if the employee, in the course of his employment, causes injury to a third party, that third party may take action directly against the employer. It is seldom that an employer is vicariously liable for what is done by an independent contractor. Having looked at this we will consider the formation of the contract and its terms. We will conclude by examining the termination of the contract and the remedies available to the employee who feels himself to have been wrongly removed from his job for whatever reason.

13.1 EMPLOYEES AND INDEPENDENT CONTRACTORS

There are two main types of working relationship, the contract of service and the contract for services. Under the first, the person doing the work is known as the employee; under the second, as the independent contractor. At its most simple form the difference is easy to illustrate. If I am rich enough to employ someone to drive me about in my car, my chauffeur is an employee. If I hire a taxi to take me to the station, the taxi-driver is an independent contractor. Some of the differences between the two relationships are obvious. If I have a chauffeur, it is my responsibility to pay him wages, to pay his national insurance contributions and to find him work to do. In the case of the taxi-driver, once I have disembarked at the station and paid my fare, my obligations to the driver are at an end.

There are various reasons why the distinction is important including the fact that statutory provisions which protect employees do just that rather than assisting independent contractors. There are also taxation and insurance differences.

In law, however, probably the most important difference between the two relationships is that of vicarious liability. This, as has been said, is the liability of an employer for the wrongs of his employee. There are a number of reasons why an employer should be held vicariously liable for the wrongs of an employee. These are listed below:

1. The employer is the person with the ultimate control over the employee. If he asks him to do something which is dangerous and likely to cause injury to other people there is every reason why he should be personally liable.
2. The employer is in a far better position to insure against liability to third parties than an employee. The cost of the insurance can be disseminated amongst the employee's customers by means of a fractional increase in the price of goods or services supplied.
3. The employer is the person who ultimately makes any profits on the work done by the employee. It would be inequitable were the employer not to be made liable for any defaults of the employee.
4. There is a Latin maxim *qui fecit per alium, fecit per se* which means he who acts through someone else, acts directly himself. In other words the employee is merely an extension of the employer.

The significance of the difference between employer and employee is very much easier to illustrate than to explain. This is largely because over the years the courts have adopted a number of different tests in different cases for determining whether a worker is an employee or an independent contractor. The first test which they traditionally applied is the control test ie that the employer not only told the employee when and where to do his work, but also how to do it. This is an extremely simple and simplistic test. Its origins lay in the 19th century and was completely apt in the case of domestic, agricultural or manual workers. However, it is clearly insufficient in the case of highly skilled employees such as doctors, accountants, computer programmers and the like. Because of this the court had to determine another test, or more accurately, tests, to be applied in appropriate cases. One of these is the organisation or integration test. The question to be asked here was whether the worker was fully integrated into the employer's business. In the case of an independent contractor there is clearly no integration with the employer's business, since the worker is essentially doing his business on his own account. On the other hand, a doctor employed by a health authority or a computer programmer employed by an international company clearly satisfies the organisation test since they are essential cogs in the workings of the machinery of the employer. A recent example of the test arose in:

Hitchcock v Post Office (1980)

Hitchcock was a sub-postmaster whom the Post Office dismissed. He claimed compensation for unfair dismissal (see 12.9). It was held that he was not an employee of the Post Office and thus was not entitled to compensation for unfair dismissal. While the Post Office clearly exercised control over the manner of doing his work, the economic reality of the situation was that he was in business on his own account. The premises and much of the equipment belonged to him. He could delegate tasks to his own employees. Were his management successful, he would enjoy the profits.

The more modern approach of the courts has been towards adopting what is known as the multiple test. Here they do not rely on a single factor, such as control or integration, but look at the whole arrangement between the worker and the employer and infer from this what was their intention. Amongst the factors considered are the method of payment of wages, whether income tax or social security contibutions are deducted by the employer prior to the payment over of remuneration, which party provides the tools and equipment for the job, whether the worker may profit himself from his own management of the task, and whether the worker is regarded as an integral part of the employer's business. An excellent example of this arose in:

Ready Mixed Concrete (South East) Limited v Minister of Pensions and National Insurance (1968)

The Government introduced a payroll tax under which employers had to pay a set amount each week for every employee who worked for them. Ready Mixed Concrete sought to avoid this tax in the case of their lorry drivers. To achieve this they dismissed them as employees and then re-engaged them as independent contractors. Hire-purchase agreements were arranged under which drivers would purchase their own vehicles. The drivers were to be responsible for the maintenance and insurance of the vehicles. On the other hand, the vehicles were to remain in the company's house colours and could only be used for the purposes of the company's business. The drivers were to be paid by reference to the deliveries which they performed, though they could delegate this task if they so desired.

It was held that the drivers were independent contractors rather than employees, and accordingly the company need not pay national insurance contributions in respect of them. In reaching its decision the court had regard to all the factors. Some, such as the requirement that the lorries remain in the house colours of the company and could only deliver the company's products, pointed towards a contract of employment situation. Others, such as the acquisition by the drivers of their own lorries, their responsibility for the maintenance and insurance of the lorries, and the ability to delegate to others pointed towards an independent contractor situation. On balance, applying the multiple test, the court adopted the view that the drivers were independent contractors.

It is difficult to say which of these three tests the court will apply in a given situation. Although the control test is the oldest of the three, it is still sometimes used. This difficulty is the more pointed because in certain situations the application of different tests will lead to different results. A simple example is provided by a test pilot employed by an aircraft manufacturer. Suppose that the board of directors of the company are businessmen rather than pilots themselves, the control test would result in the pilot being an independent contractor. Clearly the board could not tell him how to do his job. On the other hand both the integration test and the multiple test would point towards his being an employee. The test pilot is clearly an integral part of the organisation. Taking all the factors of his employment into account, his payment of wages, his testing only of the company's products etc. he is clearly also an employee. There is little doubt that in this situation the court would find him to be an employee.

13.2 FORMATION OF THE CONTRACT OF EMPLOYMENT

By s1, Employment Protection (Consolidation) Act 1978, an employer must give to those of his employees covered by the Act a written statement of their contract of employment within thirteen weeks of the beginning of their period of employment. This is a formality subsequent to entry into the contract. As a general rule, the contract of employment itself comes into existence without any legal formalities. It may be created by oral arrangement, by written agreement or even by entry into the relationship. There are a few exceptions. For example, the Companies Act 1985 provides that a director's service agreement must be in writing. The Merchant Shipping Act 1970 requires that the crew of British merchant vessels have a written agreement with their employers.

13.3 THE SECTION 1 STATEMENT OF EMPLOYMENT

By s1, Employment Protection (Consolidation) Act 1978, an employer must provide employees within thirteen weeks of their commencement in employment a written statement containing the following provisions:

1. Identification of the parties.
2. The date on which the period of continuous employment commences, including a statement as to whether any employment with a previous employer counts as part of the period of continuous employment with the present employer, and if so, the date when such continuous period began.
3. The scale or rate of remuneration or the method of calculating such remuneration.
4. The intervals at which the remuneration is to be paid.
5. Details of hours of work.
6. Details of holiday entitlement and holiday pay.
7. Details of entitlement to sickness pay.
8. Details of pensions and pension schemes.
9. The length of notice which the employee is obliged to give and entitled to receive on termination of the contract of employment.
10. The title of the job which the employee has been employed to do.

This statement must generally be accompanied by particulars of any disciplinary rules which may be applied to the employee and grievance procedures which he may follow in the event of his being dissatisfied with the way in which he is treated by the employer. Any changes in these terms have also to be notified to the employee in writing within one month of the change.

This statutory statement is not a contract. It is merely evidence of the contract and gives details of certain terms of the contract. If, however, the employee has already been given a written contract which refers to all the matters required to be detailed in the statutory statement, he need not be given the statement, though he must be supplied with details of disciplinary and grievance procedures.

If an employee feels that the statement with which he has been supplied is incomplete or inaccurate, or indeed if no statement has been given to him at all, he may complain to an industrial tribunal for the tribunal to determine the missing details.

13.4 THE EMPLOYER'S DUTIES

THE PAYMENT OF WAGES

The employer is only required to pay wages if there is an express or implied provision in the contract to this effect. In practice, even if there is no express provision for the payment of wages, a right to remuneration will be implied from the employee performing his duties in the expectation of remuneration. It used to be the case that manual workers were entitled always to receive their wages in cash. However, this requirement was repealed by the Wages Act 1986. This Act also contains provisions which affect employees in regard to what deductions an employer may make from their wages. Generally an employer may not make a deduction unless it is either required or authorised by statute, or provided for by the contract of employment or by some prior written authorisation given by the employee. An example of a permitted statutory deduction is the withholding of income tax and national insurance contributions from the employee's gross wages by the employer. There are exceptions for the recovery of overpayments of wages or expenses from employees and in respect of certain disciplinary matters. If an employee is unhappy about the legality of a deduction made by an employer, he must complain to an industrial tribunal within 3 months of the deduction or payment. A complaint may also be made on the ground that the deduction was excessive.

Whether wages are payable to an employee during a period of absence from work because of illness traditionally depends on the terms of the contract. Should the contract be silent on the point, it would appear that wages are payable unless there is a contrary intention proved by the employer. This was the result of the case of:

Orman v Saville Sportswear Ltd (1960)

The case concerned a production manager who was employed at a factory manufacturing skirts. He was paid a wage of £30 per week + 2d for each skirt manufactured. This usually resulted in his weekly wage being approximately £50. His written contract was silent as to the payment of wages during illness. He was absent from work for several weeks through illness and on his return he claimed wages for the period of his absence. It was held that since his written contract was silent on the point, wages were payable during illness unless the employer was able to prove otherwise. The employer had failed to prove that wages were not payable and therefore Orman was entitled to his lost wages at a rate of £50 per week.

However, more recently in *Mears v Safecar Security Ltd* (1981) it was said that a term permitting the payment of wages during absence through illness will only be implied if the circumstances, including trade practices and custom, and the way in which the parties act warrant such implication.

In regard to the payment of employees during a period of absence from work through illness, it should be mentioned that sickness benefit is payable under the National Insurance Scheme for any day an employee is unavailable for work through illness. This is not a payment of wages but rather compensation under the National Insurance Scheme to which all employees contribute. Since April 1983, sickness benefit has only been payable after an initial period of 8 weeks. During the first 8 weeks of absence from work through illness, under the Social Security and Housing Benefit Act 1982, the employer of an employee who pays national insurance class 1 contributions must pay sickness benefit for the first 8 weeks of absence in any one period of sickness or in total in any tax year. Although this benefit is paid by the employer, it is totally different from the payment of wages during sickness and should not be confused with it.

THE PROVISION OF WORK

It is curious that the general view of English law has been that there is no duty upon an employer to provide work for his employee. The result of this is that an employer will not be in breach of contract if he fails to provide work. Thus, provided he pays wages in lieu of notice, he may dismiss an employee without requiring him to work throughout the period of notice. However, there are certain contracts where the opportunity to work is of the essence and so exceptions to the general negative duty to provide work have developed. For example, there may be an obligation to provide work for an actor for whom the publicity involved in performing in public is as important as the remuneration. Similarly if the employee is paid wholly or partly by commission the employer should provide work to enable him to earn it.

The traditional view that the employer is not under an obligation to provide work has never been expressly overruled. However, in conclusion on this point, it should be noted that in the case of *Langston v AUEW* (1974), the facts of which are not important for our purposes, all three members of the Court of Appeal were in agreement that it could at least be argued that a right to work should now be implied in contracts of service.

PROVISION OF A SAFE SYSTEM OF WORK

As part of the general law of negligence (see Chapter 19) every employer is under a duty at common law to take reasonable care for the safety of his employees. Failure to take this care may result in a claim in negligence against the employer. In addition to this there are other duties of care imposed upon employers (and indeed upon employees and other persons) by legislation such as the Factories Act 1961, the Offices, Shops and Railway Premises Act 1963, and the Health and Safety at Work etc Act 1974.

The common law duty to provide a safe system of work, breach of which may give rise to a claim in negligence, involves matters such as the selection of competent staff and the provision of proper supervision, the ensuring that premises, plant and materials are safe, and the overall requirement that all factors affecting employment fuse together to ensure a system whereby work may, with reasonable care, be carried out in safety. The crucial word in determining the duty owed by the employer is **reasonable**. In assessing reasonableness a variety of factors have to be borne in mind. These include the likelihood of risk of injury, the nature of the risk, the characteristics of the employee and the cost of prevention. The essence of negligence is fault. If the employer is not at fault he cannot be found liable in negligence. Thus in:

Davie v New Merton Board Mills (1959)

Davie was injured when a steel drift broke while he was using it. The drift had been negligently manufactured by its maker. The maker sold it to a supplier from whom the New Merton Board Mills, Davie's employer, bought it. The employer paid the normal price for the drift and had no means of knowing of the manufacturer's negligence. It was held that since the employer had bought the tool from a reputable supplier at a proper price he had performed his duty to his employee and thus was not liable.

It should be noted that although the principle in this case remains good law, the particular point at issue was altered by the Employers' Liability (Defective Equipment) Act 1969 which provides that if an employee is injured through a defect in equipment caused by the fault of a third party, that fault is deemed to be the negligence of the employer. Thus if the actual case were to arise today, the employee would be successful.

The employer's duty is not absolute. He has to take only reasonable care. This is illustrated by:

Latimer v AEC Ltd (1953)

A factory was flooded following a storm. When the flooding subsided, the employers took great care to ensure that the factory was safe for the next shift. 40 men were employed in spreading several tons of sawdust over the factory floor which had been left slippery as a result of the floodwater spreading grease and oil around. A small part of the factory floor was not treated with sawdust because the supply ran out. Latimer, a worker on the next shift, slipped on an untreated pool of oil. It was held by the House of Lords that AEC had not failed in their duty to provide safe premises. They had acted with reasonable care to make the factory safe, and could not be expected to completely close down the factory until the floor was fully cleaned.

The duty of care is owed to each employee individually. Thus the employer has to take greater care of young and inexperienced workmen than of the more skilled operatives. He has also to have regard to the physical attributes of individual employees. This is illustrated by:

Paris v Stepney Borough Council (1951)

Paris, an employee of Stepney Borough Council, was almost completely blind in one eye. This was known to the Council who employed him as a mechanic. One day while working on a vehicle, a piece of metal flew into his good eye making him blind. Paris claimed damages on the basis that goggles should have been provided. It was held by the House of Lords that Paris should succeed. The employers had failed to take reasonable care for his safety, even though goggles were not usually provided for the type of work which he was doing. The employers should have realised that the result of an eye injury to a man with sight in only one eye was far more serious than a similar injury to men with sight in both eyes.

As has been said, there are a large number of statutory provisions which regulate safety in industry. For example, s14, Factories Act 1961 requires that dangerous parts of machinery should be securely fenced. Breach of this duty is a criminal offence, for which the employer, supervisors employed by him and indeed the workman who may himself have been injured may be prosecuted. If a person is injured in circumstances where there has been a breach of statutory duty, he may sue the employer for the tort of breach of statutory duty. So for example if an employee is injured while working on a steel cutting machine which has inadequate fencing, he may sue the employer for damages for breach of statutory duty. In this regard the employer's liability is strict. In other words it does not matter that he has taken reasonable care to see that the machine was properly fenced. It is enough to prove that in fact it was not so fenced.

INDEMNITY

An employer must indemnify his employees against all liabilities and expenses which are incurred by the employee in the proper performance of his duties. Because the employee is working for someone else, it is perfectly reasonable that the person receiving the benefit should indeed indemnify him. This is so even where the acts of the employee are illegal provided that the employee was not aware of the illegality. For example in:

Gregory v Ford (1951)

An employee was required by his employer to drive a motor vehicle. Unknown to the employee it was not insured against third party risk. Subsequently the injured person successfully sued both the employer and the employee. The employee then sought an indemnity from the employer. It was held that the employer should indemnify the employee.

REFERENCES

An employer is under no duty to provide a reference for an employee. If he does give one and it proves to be false, he may incur liability in a variety of ways. If the reference is defamatory of the employee, the employee may sue the employer for damages in defamation. In such circumstances the employer may avoid liability by pleading a defence unique in defamation of qualified privilege, that is that he gave the reference without malice and believing in its truth. The opposite of defamation would arise where an employer gives a better reference than the employee is entitled to, knowing it to be untrue and intending that the person to whom it was given should act upon it and suffer damage. Here the employer may be liable for the tort of deceit. If a good reference is given negligently in circumstances where the employee is in fact not worthy of a good reference, liability may arise in negligence (see Chapter 19). An employer who wilfully makes false statements in a reference may also be prosecuted for a criminal offence under the Servants Characters Act 1792.

13.5 THE EMPLOYEE'S DUTIES

13.5.1 Act reasonably and co-operate

An employee must perform his duties in a manner which is in all the circumstances reasonable. Even where the employer has produced a rule book giving details of how work should be done, an employee must not interpret those rules in such a way as to defeat the smooth running of the employer's business. This is illustrated by:

Secretary of State for Employment v ASLEF (No.2) (1972)

Railway employees worked in strict observance of a rule book provided by British Rail. By so doing they caused serious delays in the running of trains. It was held that the employees were in breach of contract. While they were free to withdraw their goodwill they could not deliberately obstruct the employer's business.

13.5.2 Personal service

The relationship of employer and employee is essentially a personal one. Thus an employee may not, without the express or implied permission of his employer, delegate the performance of his duties to someone else.

13.5.3 Obedience

An employee must obey lawful orders given to him by his employer so long as what he is required to do falls within the scope of his contract of employment. He cannot, however, be required to perform an unlawful act, nor an act which would place him in personal danger, unless the risk of danger was envisaged in the contract, such as would be the case with a fireman or other rescue worker. The point about an employee not being required to do an act which would put him at risk is illustrated by the case of:

***Ottoman Bank* v *Chakarian* (1930)**

The Ottoman Bank requested Chakarian, who was an Armenian who had escaped while under sentence of death imposed on him by the Turks, to work at their branch in Constantinople. It was held by the House of Lords that he was justified in disobeying the order to work there since to have remained in the town would have put him under grave risk of recapture and execution.

13.5.4 Good faith

An employee is obliged to act in good faith in just the same way as an agent. An example of breach of good faith is the taking of bribes. This is illustrated in:

***Boston Deep Sea Fishing & Ice Co* v *Ansell* (1889)**

Ansell, the managing director of Boston Deep Sea Fishing, which was a fishing company, took secret bribes from a supplier. He also held shares in certain ice-making and fish-carrying companies who paid him secret commissions for causing Boston Deep Sea Fishing to enter into contracts with them. The company dismissed Ansell as managing director for reasons unconnected with these matters but later discovered the true facts. The managing director claimed that he had been wrongfully dismissed. It was held, however, that he had broken his duty of good faith by accepting the bribes and commissions and so the dismissal was valid.

Another example of breach of good faith occurs if an employee diverts customers of his employer from the employer's business. An example of this is:

***Sanders* v *Parry* (1967)**

Parry was an assistant solicitor in Sanders' employment. Amongst other things Parry looked after the affairs of a particular builder client. The builder told Parry that he was unhappy with dealing with Sanders and that if Parry could set up his own practice then he, the builder, would divert all his work to him. Accordingly Parry left Sanders' practice and started up by himself. It was held that Parry had gone in breach of his duty of good faith and damages of £500 were awarded against him in favour of his former employer.

Another aspect of the duty of good faith and one which has increasing importance is the development of industrial processes and inventions by an employee. As a general rule any invention or discovery made in the course of employment in circumstances where the employee is simply doing what he has been employed to do and is doing it in working hours and using the resources of his employer, belongs to the employer. Thus the employer may claim the benefit of an employee's invention if, to allow the employee to retain it, it would be a breach of his duty of good faith. This is illustrated by:

***British Syphon Co* v *Homewood* (1956)**

Homewood, a technician employed by British Syphon Co, invented a particular syphon system. He subsequently left the employment of the company and sought to patent the invention. The British Syphon Co sought an order that Homewood should assign his interest in the invention to them. It was held that the order should be made. To allow the employee to retain the invention would be a breach of the inventor's duty of good faith.

It should be added that s39, Patents Act 1977 specifies exactly what is the position of the employee in respect of inventions. An invention belongs to the employee except in two specific circumstances; these are:

1. Where the invention was made in the normal course of the employee's duties or in the course of duties which, although outside his normal duties, were specifically assigned to him, and in either case the circumstances were such that an invention might reasonably be expected to result from the carrying out of his duties; or
2. Where the invention was made in the course of the duties of the employee and at the time of making the invention, because of the nature of his duties, the employee had a special obligation to further the interests of the employer's undertaking.

By s42, any agreement which purports to diminish the employee's rights in an invention to which s39 relates is unenforceable insofar as it does diminish those rights. There is a statutory scheme for the payment of compensation by employers to employee inventors under ss41 and 42. Under these provisions an employee may make an application to the Patents Court or the Patents Office for an award of compensation (which may be by way of either a lump sum or periodic payments or both) if he makes an invention the benefit of which belongs to the employer under s39 and which confers 'outstanding benefit' to the employer or if he makes an invention which belongs to him but which he leases or assigns to his employer.

13.5.5 Reasonable care

Implied in every contract of employment is a term that the employee will perform his contract with reasonable care. If the employee fails to exercise this care then he must indemnify his employer for any loss which results. It should be added that it is very seldom that this duty is ever enforced since it is rare that an employee will be sufficiently wealthy to justify the employer taking action against him. An illustration of this is found in:

Lister v Romford Ice & Cold Storage Co Ltd (1957)

Lister was a driver employed by Romford Ice. While in the course of employment he negligently injured his father who was a fellow employee. The father obtained damages in an action against the company which was insured under an employers' liability policy. When an insurance company makes a payment under a policy it is subrogated to the position of the insured. This means that it enjoys exactly the same rights in respect of the incident giving rise to the claim as does the insured himself. Pursuant to this right the insurance company brought proceedings in the name of the company against Lister claiming that he owed a duty to them to exercise reasonable care in the performance of his duties. It was held by the House of Lords that the insurance company being subrogated to the position of Romford Ice could obtain compensation from Lister for the amount that the insurance company had had to pay out in respect of the father's claim.

13.6 TERMINATION OF EMPLOYMENT—AN OUTLINE

When an employee loses his job other than because of retirement or resignation, he will usually want compensation of some kind from his employer. Most of the remainder of this chapter will be concerned with looking at how that compensation may be obtained. The dismissed employee has three possible remedies:

1. Wrongful dismissal.
2. Redundancy payment.
3. Unfair dismissal.

It must be clearly understood at this point that there are several ways in which a job may be brought to an end other than by dismissal, including frustration, performance and mutual agreement. What we are mainly concerned with here is dismissal.

The above possible remedies will be looked at in some detail later. First, however, it is important to consider what sort of contract the contract of employment is. Before 1965 it was treated simply as a contract just like any other. As such it was enforced in accordance with its terms. So if the contract provided that the employee could be dismissed upon being given three months' notice, the employer could on 1st January give notice to his employee and expect him to cease work on 31st March. In the alternative he could dismiss him on 1st January and make him a payment of three months' wages in lieu of notice. Dismissal at common law was and still is as simple as this. Motive is irrelevant. An employer could dismiss because he did not like the employee, because of the employee's religion or race, because the employee supported the wrong football club, because the employee belonged to the wrong political party, because the employee was too good at his job, because the employee belonged to a particular trade union, because the employee was a pregnant woman, or for any other reason whether connected or not with the employment. This obviously was a very unsatisfactory state of affairs. Most people see employment as something rather different from a run of the mill contract. Employees are entitled to regard themselves as having some interest akin almost to a property right in their job. If they lose their job they are entitled to be compensated in some way. This interest which an employee has in his job was recognised first in the Redundancy Act 1965 (the provisions of which are now contained in an amended form in the Employment Protection (Consolidation) Act 1978). The concept of an interest in the employee's job was extended by the Unfair Dismissal Provisions of the Industrial Relations Act 1971 (which are also now contained in an amended form in the Employment Protection (Consolidation) Act 1978).

Whenever considering a problem involving the dismissal of an employee it is important always to think of these three remedies: wrongful dismissal, redundancy and unfair dismissal.

13.7 COMMON LAW TERMINATION

Termination of the contract of employment at common law will be examined under the following headings:

1. Passage of time.
2. Impossibility of performance.
3. Insolvency of the employer.
4. Notice.
5. Dismissal without notice.
6. Remedies at common law.

13.7.1 Passage of time

Just as with any other contract, a contract of performance can be brought to an end by performance. If an employee is taken on to work for one year his contract of employment comes to an end on the expiration of the year. Similarly if he is employed to do a specific act, such as to build a wall around his employer's premises, the contract comes to an end when he has satisfactorily built the wall. At common law an employee has no claim for damages when his job comes to an end in this way though as will be seen he may have some entitlement to a redundancy payment or to compensation for unfair dismissal.

13.7.2 Impossibility of performance

Again, just as with any other contract, a contract of employment may become frustrated by some external event which renders the performance of the contract impossible. A typical example of this is to be found in:

Morgan v Manser (1947)

Manser was a stage performer (he was in fact Charlie Chester). In 1938 he entered into a contract with Morgan who was to be his manager for the following 10 years. Shortly after this, war broke out and Manser was called up to serve in the Forces. This resulted in his being on active service for six years. It was held that such a prolonged period of absence from the stage was sufficient to frustrate the contract of employment.

The important point in this context about frustration is that when a contract of employment is frustrated no damages are payable to the injured party because the contract has simply come to an end as a result of the frustrating event. If on the other hand the contract is terminated by one party in the erroneous belief that it has been frustrated, then the injured party will be able to claim damages for wrongful termination. In this context, the effect of illness of an employee is important. Whether illness does frustrate the contract of employment depends upon the construction placed upon the illness by the court, which will look at factors such as how long the employee had been working prior to his illness, how long he has been away through illness and how long he is likely to be away in the future and the nature of the employment itself. In most employment situations where there is a long serving employee, his illness will not frustrate the contract. For example, in:

***Marrison v Bell* (1939)**

A vegetable salesman was absent from work for four months because of illness. It was held by the Court of Appeal that this was not sufficient to discharge his contract of service. Therefore the employee in this case was entitled to receive wages during his period of illness.

This should be contrasted with the case of:

***Poussard v Spiers & Pond* (1876)**

A singer who was due to take the lead in an opera was taken ill during the rehearsal period prior to the commencement of performances.

Because of her illness she missed the opening night and several subsequent performances. It was held that this was sufficient to frustrate the contract. Accordingly the employer could treat the contract as being at an end and was under no obligation to pay damages.

This was also the situation in:

***Condor v Barron Knights Ltd* (1966)**

C was the drummer in a pop group and was under contract with the group to work as and when required. Because of illness he was unable to play with the group more than four nights a week. At the time they had a full diary of engagements and were frequently playing seven nights a week. It was held that this illness was sufficient to frustrate the contract. The pop group could not be expected to operate other than on a fulltime basis and it was recognised that it was unrealistic to expect the group to obtain a part-time substitute for C when he was not available.

(*see page 129*)

13.7.3 Insolvency etc of the employer

When an individual or a partnership is unable to pay its debts, it becomes bankrupt. When this happens to a limited company it goes into liquidation. Rather curiously when an individual or partnership employer becomes bankrupt this does not automatically bring to an end any contract of employment which the individual or partnership may have with employees. Of course, because of the employer's insolvency the employee may choose to leave his job because of the likelihood of him not being paid for what he does. Usually in these circumstances however the employer will tell the employee that by virtue of his bankruptcy he will be unable to pay his wages and therefore the employee is dismissed. In this situation the employee will have a claim for wrongful dismissal because notice has not been given to him. Under s348, Insolvency Act 1986 when a bankruptcy order is made in respect of an individual who is the employer of an apprentice or articled clerk, then either the bankrupt or the apprentice or articled clerk may give notice to the trustee that he wishes to terminate the apprenticeship or articles.

The liquidation of a corporate employer may arise either because of a court order or following a resolution of the shareholders of the company. When the liquidation commences following a court order, the employees are automatically discharged. Thereupon they may claim damages for wrongful dismissal because they have not been given notice. If the company is put into liquidation following a shareholders' resolution then, if the reason for the liquidation is that the company is insolvent, there is again an automatic dismissal of employees who may claim damages for wrongful dismissal. It should be noted that sometimes limited companies operate through groups. A holding company at the head of the group carries out its various activities through subsidiary companies in which it controls all the shares. Often within a group situation some subsidiary companies are put into liquidation and their businesses transferred to other subsidiary companies. Here the liquidation of the subsidiary company arises not because of insolvency but just as a matter of convenience. In this circumstance the employees of the subsidiary company are not dismissed.

When a company's assets are used as security for a floating charge and the company fails to make repayments of principal and interest as and when they arise under that charge, the bank or other creditor having the benefit of the charge may appoint an administrative receiver. Usually the appointment is under the terms of the charge document itself. When this is the case and there is no court involvement, the employees of the company subject to the charge are not dismissed. Sometimes, however, an administrative receiver is appointed by the court, and whenever there is a court appointment there is usually an automatic discharge of employees. When there is this discharge, the employees may claim damages for wrongful dismissal.

If the employer is a partnership, then whether a change in the constitution of the partnership affects the continued employment of employees depends on two factors; firstly the nature of the contract of employment and secondly the nature of the change in the constitution of the partnership. If the contract is essentially of a personal nature, then a change in the constitution of the partnership will automatically bring to an end the contract of service of the employee. On the other hand, if the contract is not essentially personal then the change in constitution will not have this result. For example in:

Phillips v Alhambra Palace Co (1901)

Phillips was a music-hall performer under contract with the Alhambra Palace Co, a firm of three partners. When Phillips had entered into his contract with the partnership he did not know the identity of the partners. A partner died and Phillips tried to claim that the contract had been discharged by the change in constitution of the partnership resulting from the partner's death. It was held that since the contract was not a personal one (the identity of the partners was not of major importance) it survived the change in the constitution.

13.7.4 Notice

As a general rule a contract of employment may only be brought to an end if proper notice is given. Of course, this is not the case where either the employer or the employee has broken a major term of the contract so as to entitle the other simply to treat the contract as terminated (this will be considered below).

The common law rule is that in the absence of an express term which states what the required notice is, a contract of employment is terminable by either party giving reasonable notice. What reasonable means depends upon the circumstances of the case and includes factors such as the nature of the employment, the seniority of the employee and his length of service. The entitlement to reasonable notice has to be read in conjunction with s49 Employment Protection (Consolidation) Act 1978. This lays down minimum periods of notice and a contract term providing for a shorter notice period is void.

If the employee has been employed for more than 4 weeks and less than 2 years, he is entitled to receive one week's notice. If his continuous employment has been for 2 years or more, he is entitled to receive one week's notice for each year of service up to a maximum of 12 weeks. Thus an employee with 18 months continuous service is entitled to one week's notice. An employee with 8 years continuous service is entitled to 8 weeks notice. An employee with 20 years continuous service is entitled to 12 weeks notice. When an employee wishes to terminate his contract the minimum period of notice which he must give is one week, given that he has been employed for at least four weeks. Apart from this the employee's obligation to give notice is not related to length of service. Either party may forego his right to notice, or, in the alternative, accept a payment in lieu of notice.

In the event of the contract stating upon what grounds a contract may be brought to an end, those grounds are construed as exhaustive. For example, in:

McClelland v Northern Ireland General Health Services Board (1957)

McClelland was a clerk in the service of the board. Her service contract provided that she could be dismissed for 'gross misconduct' or if she proved 'inefficient and unfit to merit continued employment'. The contract went on to permit dismissal for failure to take or honour the oath of allegiance or for permanent ill-health or infirmity. If she wished to terminate her employment she could do so by giving one month's notice. The board dismissed her on the ground of redundancy having given her six months' notice. It was held by the House of Lords that the express powers to dismiss an employee were comprehensive and that no further power, even to dismiss on the ground of redundancy, could be implied. Accordingly, her contract had not been validly terminated.

13.7.5 Dismissal without notice

If an employer or an employee is in breach of his fundamental obligations under the contract of employment then the other party may treat the contract as terminated. When it is the employer who is in breach of his duty then the dismissal is known as constructive dismissal. For this to occur the conduct of the employer must constitute a breach which goes to the root of the contract. Examples of constructive dismissal which have arisen in the cases are:

1. Unilateral reduction in pay of the employee.
2. Change in the nature of the job, such as demotion.
3. Failure to maintain adequate working temperatures.
4. Change in the employee's place of work.

It used to be the case that whether there was a constructive dismissal depended upon whether the employer had in all the circumstances acted reasonably. However, this was generally thought to be too vague, and in *Western Excavating (ECC) Ltd v Sharp* (1978) the Court of Appeal held that the employee must show that the employer was guilty of repudiatory conduct. In other words the conduct must be such as to go to the root of the contract. We will now consider this case:

Western Excavating (EEC) Ltd v Sharp (1978)

An employee took time off work without permission. This eventually led to his being suspended from work without pay for five days. This caused him severe financial difficulties, and so he asked his employer for an advance against the holiday pay to which he was entitled. He also asked for a loan. Both requests were refused, whereupon he resigned, claiming that he had been constructively dismissed. It was held by the Court of Appeal that there had been no breach or repudiation of the contract by the employer and so there had been no dismissal.

Thus for there to be a constructive dismissal there must have been conduct going to the root of the contract. Examples of this would be the denial to an employee of a right to promotion or seniority or place of work such as to amount to a repudiation of the contract.

There has over recent years been a marked reduction in the number of cases of constructive dismissal coming before the courts. Doubtless this is directly connected with the high level of unemployment today and the difficulty which people who are out of work find in obtaining employment. The result has been that employees are generally prepared to endure a worsening of their conditions of service rather than claim that their employer has by his conduct dismissed them and then proceed to claim damages for wrongful dismissal and/or unfair dismissal.

If an employee by his conduct puts himself in breach of his duty of good faith (see 12.5.4) then, given that his conduct amounts to a repudiation of his obligations under the contract, his employer may dismiss him without notice. So, for example, in *Boston Deep Sea Fishing v Ansell* (1889), had the employer known of the managing director's breach of his duty of good faith prior to the termination of the contract of employment, he would have been entitled to dismiss him without notice. This is sometimes referred to as summary dismissal, and upon being dismissed in this way, the employee is entitled to no compensation in lieu of notice. Even misconduct outside the contract of service may justify dismissal if it is sufficient directly to affect the employer's business or the ability of the employee to perform his duties faithfully. For example, in:

Pearce v Foster (1886)

A clerk with a firm of merchants speculated heavily on the Stock Exchange. The amount involved was a figure of several hundred thousand pounds. His employer dismissed him and the clerk claimed damages for wrongful dismissal. It was held that the dismissal was lawful. In reaching this decision the court gave three reasons:

1. The clerk's duties included the giving of advice on investments. Because of his private dealings, there was a risk that the advice which he gave would not be completely disinterested.
2. Since the clerk was responsible for large amounts of money his Stock Exchange speculations may tempt him to steal.
3. If clients of the employers became aware of the clerk's private speculation they might have less confidence in dealing with them.

Disobedience of a lawful order will justify dismissal without notice if the disobedience is such as to amount to a repudiation of contractual obligations. However, the disobedience must be sufficiently serious to amount to a repudiation, and lesser conduct will not justify such dismissal. For example, in:

Laws v London Chronicle (1959)

Laws was an employee of the London Chronicle. She and her immediate superior to whom she was directly answerable were in a meeting with the managing director. Her superior walked out of the meeting telling Laws to follow him. The managing director told her to stay where she was. Laws followed her superior out and was subsequently dismissed by the managing director for disobedience. It was held by the Court of Appeal that the dismissal was wrongful. Laws had acted simply out of loyalty for her superior and her disobedience of the managing director's instruction did not constitute a repudiation of the contract.

Incompetence or neglect by an employee may justify dismissal if it causes serious loss to the employer or it occurs with unhappy regularity. For example, in:

Baster v London & County Printing Works (1899)

A printing machine was damaged because of gross negligence by an employee. This resulted in considerable loss to the employer. It was held that the dismissal of the employee was justified in the circumstances.

13.7.6 Remedies at common law

Although usually in thinking of termination of a contract of employment we think of the remedies of the employee, it should not be forgotten that the employer also has remedies available to him where it is the employee who wrongfully terminates his employment. For example if the employee has been in breach of some duty which has resulted in loss to the employer, the employer may claim damages. If the employee has made a secret profit, the employer may recover it from him by means of an account. If an employee has compiled a list of his employer's customers, the employer may obtain a court order to force him to deliver up the list. However, the main concern in this regard is the right of the employee who has been wrongfully dismissed. In this regard the main remedy is damages. These are sought by means of a common law action in the courts and are normally based on wages which would have been paid had proper notice of termination been given to the employee. So an employee who is entitled to 4 weeks' notice may, upon wrongful dismissal, claim 4 weeks' wages. Sometimes the amount claimed will be increased. For example, if a waiter is wrongfully dismissed, he may be able to claim for lost tips in addition to the loss of wages. Similarly an actor who is wrongfully dismissed may be able to claim compensation for loss of opportunity to enhance his reputation as well as lost wages.

Conversely on occasion the amount which the employee recovers may be less than the total wages lost. If an employee who is entitled to one year's notice (which is not uncommon in the case of directors' service contracts), the amount he eventually recovers for wrongful dismissal may be reduced because of his common law duty to mitigate his loss (the reduction would be the amount that the court feels he should earn from other employment during the period).

Similarly where wages are claimed for a long period of notice there may be a reduction because the payment is received in a lump sum rather than spread out over the period as wages would be. Although a dismissed employee will no doubt be upset by his dismissal, damages for mental distress may not normally be recovered. In:

Addis v Gramophone Co Ltd (1909)

Addis was a manager employed by the Gramophone Co Ltd. He was given six months' notice of termination of his employment in accordance with the terms of his contract of employment. The company appointed another person to act as manager during the period that Addis was to work out his notice. It was held by the House of Lords that the employers had been in breach of contract in not permitting Addis to continue as manager during his period of notice and he was thus entitled to be paid for the six months' period. He was also entitled to commission that he would have earned had he been allowed to manage the business himself. However, he was not entitled to any compensation for injured feelings or for the loss which he sustained from the fact that his having been dismissed made it more difficult to obtain further employment.

However, following the decision in *Jarvis* v *Swan's Tours Ltd* (see Chapter 10, 10.2.2) in exceptional circumstances an employee who has been wrongfully dismissed may claim for emotional suffering. For example, in:

Cox v Philips Industries Ltd (1975)

Cox was employed by Philips Industries. In breach of his contract of employment, though without any reduction in salary, he was demoted to a position within the firm with less responsibilities. In consequence Cox became ill with depression. It was held that Cox had been wrongfully dismissed (constructive dismissal) and was entitled to five months' salary in lieu of notice.

However, this decision must be seen very much as the exception rather than the rule. Since the Addis decision was one of the House of Lords it is binding. Generally any claim for injured feelings as a result of the manner of dismissal must fail under the rule in the Addis case.

The Cox decision stands very much on its own because it was not in fact concerned with wrongful dismissal at all but rather a claim for damage suffered because of breach of contract during its currency (in other words before the employee brought it to an end by claiming to be constructively dismissed). It was on this basis that it was felt to be analagous to the Jarvis case, since the employer should have had it in contemplation that through his, the employer's, conduct the injury which Cox in fact suffered would be sustained.

Finally it should be noted that if a contract of service contains a restrictive covenant (see Chapter 9, 9.5.6) and is wrongfully terminated by the employer, then the employer may not enforce that restrictive covenant against the employee. In:

General Billposting Co Ltd v Atkinson (1909)

An employee who was subject to a covenent in restraint of trade was wrongfully dismissed. It was held by the House of Lords that the wrongful dismissal justified him in treating himself as being freed from the obligations imposed by the covenant in restraint of trade in his contract of service.

13.8 REDUNDANCY PAYMENTS

The Redundancy Payments Act 1965 recognised for the first time in English law that an employee had what amounted to a proprietory interest in his employment and, in the event of that employment simply disappearing the employee was entitled to be compensated. Although the Redundancy Payments Act 1965 has long been repealed, the principle of entitlement to compensation for redundancy is now contained in the Employment Protection (Consolidation) Act 1978. Before looking at redundancy payments in detail, a few preliminary points should be borne in mind. Firstly, it is comparatively rare that the employee who has been made redundant needs to go to an industrial tribunal for his claim to be determined. Usually payment is made by the employer to the employee in accordance with the detailed provision below. An employee only goes to a tribunal if his entitlement to payment or if the amount of payment is in dispute. Secondly, whereas a claim for wrongful dismissal is brought in the common law courts, a claim for a redundancy payment is heard by an industrial tribunal. This has two important practical consequences. An employee claiming damages for wrongful dismissal must prove his case. It is for him to prove that he has been wrongfully dismissed rather than for the employer to prove that he had good reason for dismissing the employee. (Although at first sight this may look very much like two ways of saying the same thing, it is in fact not the case in practice. If the employee fails to prove wrongful dismissal then he loses his case.) If he loses his case, the employee has to bear his own costs and the costs of the other side. So an employee who has been dismissed and who is likely to be short of funds risks having to pay all the costs in any wrongful dismissal case in which he is unsuccessful. Therefore unless there is a large amount of money at stake, such as where the employee is entitled to a long period of notice, the employee may not feel it is worthwhile to pursue a wrongful dismissal claim. On the other hand, the burden of proof is largely reversed in hearings before the industrial tribunal. All the employee has to do is prove that he has been dismissed, and in fact generally the employer will readily admit this. This having been done, the presumption arises that the employee has been dismissed by reason of redundancy. In other words, if the employer is to avoid making the redundancy payment he must establish that the dismissal was for some reason other than redundancy. Furthermore, it is extremely rare that an industrial tribunal will order that even a losing claimant should pay the costs of the other side. Therefore a dismissed employee who is claiming a redundancy payment can take the necessary proceedings without any serious risk to himself even if he loses the case.

13.8.1 Qualifying employees

Redundancy payments are only available to employees; therefore it is essential to establish that the claimant was, prior to his dismissal, an employee rather than an independent contractor. He must have been continuously employed for a period of 2 years ending with the date of dismissal. He must also have been employed for at least 16 hours in each week of continuous service, though for employees who have been employed for more than 5 years this drops to at least 8 hours per week. The key word in this regard is **continuous**. This, of course, does not mean the same as **uninterrupted**. Obviously almost all employees have their employment interrupted from time to time by their taking time off for such things as holidays or illness. There are also rules, too detailed for consideration here, which provide for continuity of employment where an employer sells his business and his employees continue working in the same jobs for the new employer.

As well as being over the age of 18 the employee, if male, must not have reached the age of 65, and, if female, must not have reached the age of 60. Male employees who have reached the age of 64 and female employees who have reached the age of 59 have one-twelfth deducted from their redundancy claim for every month worked after their attaining that age.

13.8.2 Redundancy

A dismissal is for redundancy if it is attributable wholly or mainly to one of the following two situations:

(a) the fact that the employer has ceased or intends to cease carrying on his business for the purposes for which the employee was employed by him, or has ceased or intends to cease carrying on the business in the place where the employee was so employed.

(b) The fact that the requirement of that business for employees to carry out work of the particular kind or for the employee to carry on work of a particular kind in the place where he was so employed has ceased or diminished or is expected to cease or diminish.

Thus basically redundancy occurs in two cases. Firstly where the employer ceases to exist and secondly where the job ceases to exist. Two of the early cases provide excellent examples of the two situations just described. In:

O'Brien v Associated Fire Alarms (1968)

O'Brien was employed at the Liverpool office of Associated Fire Alarms. This was the regional office for the north and west of England. Work of the type which he was doing diminished in the Liverpool area and Associated Fire Alarms required him to work in Barrow-in-Furness. O'Brien refused to do this because the distance to Barrow-in-Furness from his home was so great that he would be unable to travel to and from home to work on a daily basis. It was held by the Court of Appeal that his dismissal was for reasons of redundancy.

Note that if his contract of service had provided that his employer could require him to work anywhere within the country, as, for example, is generally the case with say a bank manager, then the employee could not claim to be redundant if required to work from somewhere within the area envisaged by the contract. Then an example of the second type of redundancy arose in:

Bromby & Hoare Ltd v Evans (1972)

Evans, a bricklayer, was dismissed when his employers decided that work previously done by employee bricklayers should henceforth be done by independent contractors. It was held that Evans had been made redundant because the business no longer needed to employ bricklayers. The work could be done more economically by self-employed independent contractors.

On the other hand there is not a redundancy if the job continues but the employee simply becomes unsuited to the job. For example in:

Vaux & Associated Breweries Ltd v Ward (1969)

Mrs Ward was employed as a barmaid. It was decided that the public house where she worked should be modernised and younger barmaids employed in the hope of attracting more customers. It was held that Mrs Ward had not been made redundant. The work which the new barmaids were doing in the altered premises was no different from the work which Mrs Ward had been doing previously. Accordingly she had not been made redundant.

Similarly there is no redundancy if established employees are simply unable to settle to new working practices. In:

Johnson v Nottinghamshire Police Authority (1974)

Johnson was one of two clerks employed by the Nottinghamshire Police Authority. The work of these clerks had been reorganised from a 5-day week to a shift system which operated over 6 days a week. Previously they had worked from 9.30 am to 5.30 pm. The new shifts were to run from 8.00 am to 3.00 pm and from 1.00 pm to 8.00 pm.

However, the number of hours worked by the clerks was to remain the same. The clerks refused to change to the new system and consequently were dismissed. It was held by the Court of Appeal that their dismissal was not by reason of redundancy. The work which they had previously done had not diminished, nor was the work to be done by less employees. The only change was in the time when the work was to be done.

Again an employee is not redundant if he simply cannot adapt to new working practices:

North Riding Garages Ltd v Butterwick (1967)

Butterwick had been employed as a mechanic by a garage for many years. He was unable to cope with technological developments in motor vehicles and in consequence was dismissed. It was held that his dismissal was not by reason of redundancy.

13.8.3 Offer of alternative employment

Sometimes, even though an employee finds himself in a redundancy situation within the meaning of the term just described, his employer offers him alternative employment. This might occur, for example, where he is employed by a company within a group. This particular company is closing down but the holding company offers him similar employment within the group. Section 82, Employment Protection (Consolidation) Act of 1978 provides that if an employer makes an employee an offer, before his original contract of employment terminates, to renew his contract or to re-engage him under a new contract on terms that the renewal or re-engagement should take effect either immediately upon the ending of the old contract or within four weeks thereafter, then so long as the principal terms of the contract of employment are the same as the former contract or, if different, constitute an offer of suitable alternative employment, then the employee loses his right to a redundancy payment if he unreasonably refuses the offer.

By the Transfer of Undertakings (Protection of Employment) Regulations 1981 similar provisions apply where there is a change in the ownership of the business and the previous owner terminates the contract of employment of the employee and the new owner offers renewal or re-engagement. Again if the new owner offers to renew the employee's contract or offers suitable alternative employment, the employee will lose his entitlement to a redundancy payment from the outgoing owner if he unreasonably refuses the new employment. When an employee receives an offer of this kind he is allowed a trial period of four weeks during which he may decide on the suitability of the employment offered. If he decides not to continue in employment at the end of the trial period, then upon leaving he may claim to have been dismissed by reason of redundancy as at the date of termination of his earlier contract of employment.

13.8.4 Calculation of redundancy payment

The amount of payment to which an employee is entitled is calculated by means of a formula based upon his age, his weekly earnings (up to a maximum of £172) and his length of service (up to a maximum of 20 years). For each year of service below the age of 22 he receives half a week's pay. For each year of service above the age of 21 and below the age of 41 he receives one week's pay and for each year of service between the age of 41 and retirement he receives 1½ weeks pay. This is illustrated by the following examples:

1   A is made redundant at age 58. He has been in the employment of his firm for 10 years. His weekly wage is £200. His entitlement is 10 × £172 (maximum earnings) × 1½ = £2,580.
2   B is aged 25. He has been in continuous employment for 7 years. He is earning £140 per week when he is made redundant. His entitlement is (5 × £140 = £700) + (2 × £140 × ½ = 140) = £840.
3   C aged 54 is made redundant. He has been in continuous employment for 6 years. His earnings are £100 a week. He is entitled to 6 × 100 × 1½ = £900.

The amount of maximum earnings is amended annually.

13.8.5 Redundancy procedure

Sections 99–107, Employment Protection Act 1975 require that when an employer is to make employees redundant he must consult with recognised trade unions and notify the Secretary of State. Even when he anticipates only a single redundancy he must consult with any recognised trade union as soon as possible. If he proposes to dismiss 10 or more employees on grounds of redundancy at one establishment within a period of 30 days then he must consult with a recognised trade union at least 30 days before the first dismissal takes effect. He must also notify the Secretary of State. If he proposes to dismiss 100 or more employees on the ground of redundancy at one establishment within a period of 90 days or less he must consult with a recognised trade union at least 90 days before the first dismissal occurs. Again he must notify the Secretary of State also. So that there can be proper consultation, the following information must be given to the union:

1   Reasons for the proposed redundancies.
2   Numbers and types of employees concerned.
3   The total number of employees of each type.
4   The method of selection for redundancy.
5   The procedure proposed for carrying out the dismissals.

If an employer fails to consult and notify as required above, a recognised trade union (though not an employee) may apply to an industrial tribunal for what is known as a protective award. If such an award is made the employer must continue to pay the employees for the period of the award. The period of award is such length as the tribunal considers just and equitable, but where 100 or more employees are to be dismissed it cannot exceed 90 days and where 10 or more employees are to be dismissed it cannot exceed 30 days. If less than 10 employees are to be dismissed it cannot exceed 28 days. The purpose of the protective award is to compensate the employee for his lost wages caused by the employer's failure to consult. It is not intended as a punishment of the defaulting employer.

13.9 UNFAIR DISMISSAL

The final possible remedy for the dismissed employee is to claim that he has been unfairly dismissed. As has been said, the concept of unfair dismissal was first introduced into the law in 1971. Until then, so long as an employee was given proper notice of termination of his employment by his employer, he could be dismissed for any reason whatever. He had no entitlement to compensation if he was dismissed because of his trade union connections, religion, political views, marital status, hairstyle or whatever. The only ground of dismissal which gave rise to compensation, and then only from 1965 onwards, was redundancy.

The broad principle of unfair dismissal is that every employee has a right not to be unfairly dismissed. If he is unfairly dismissed he is entitled to compensation from his former employer. As with a claim for a redundancy payment, the remedy is sought in an industrial tribunal. Again, as with a claim for a redundancy payment, all the dismissed employee has to prove is that he has been dismissed. It is then for the employer who wishes to avoid making a payment of compensation to show that he had a good cause to dismiss the employee.

13.9.1 Qualifying employees

As with a claimant for a redundancy payment, so too a claimant for an unfair dismissal payment must establish firstly that he was an employee and secondly that he has been dismissed. He must also have been in continuous employment at the time of the alleged dismissal for two years and employed during that period for at least 16 hours each week. As in the case of redundancy payments, after an employee has been employed for five years the hours worked each week to qualify reduces to 8 hours a week. The employee must also come within certain age limits. He must be above the age of 18 and he must be below the normal retiring age. It should be noted that the upper age limit is slightly different in the case of unfair dismissal from redundancy. The exact wording of s54, Employment Protection (Consolidation) Act 1978 states that the unfair dismissal provisions do not apply if the employee has on or before the effective date of termination attained the age which, in the undertaking in which he was employed, was the normal retiring age for an employee holding the position which he held, or, if a man, attained the age of 65, or, if a woman, attained the age of 60. Thus the State retirement age is only relevant if there is not a different normal retirement age for the post in question. If usually people doing that job retire at 55 then an employee who continues after reaching that age cannot claim to have been unfairly dismissed.

13.9.2 Valid reasons for dismissal

It is obvious that an employer must always reserve the right to dismiss employees for some substantial reason without himself being at risk of being ordered to pay compensation by an industrial tribunal. For example, if an employee is guilty of gross misconduct or if there is no work for him then the employer must be allowed to dispose of his services. The way in which the Act approaches this is by providing that once the employee has shown that he has been dismissed, the employer must establish that the reason for the dismissal was one of the reasons specified in s57(2), Employment Protection (Consolidation) Act 1978.

If the employer can do this, then *prima facie* the dismissal was fair. If he fails to do so then the dismissal was automatically unfair. Even if the tribunal feels that the dismissal was *prima facie* fair, it must then go on to decide whether in all circumstances of the case the employer acted reasonably in treating the reason which he was relying on as a sufficient reason for the dismissal.

Therefore we must consider this in two stages. Firstly, we must consider the permitted reasons in s57(2). Secondly, we must consider the concept of 'reasonableness'.

The following are reasons why a dismissal *may* be fair:

1. The capability or qualifications of the employee for performing work of the kind which he was employed by the employer to do.
   This means the capability of the employee assessed by reference to skill, aptitude, health, or any other physical or mental quality. Extended absence through illness is frequently used as a justification for dismissal on this ground. Similarly an employee who fails to obtain the necessary academic, technical or professional qualification to remain in his job may be dismissed:

Blackman v Post Office (1974)

Blackman was a Post and Telegraph Officer with the Post Office. As such he was required to pass an aptitude test within a specified period of commencing his employment. He took the test the maximum number of times that Post Office rules permitted but failed each time to pass the test. It was held that he had been fairly dismissed since he failed to possess the qualifications for the job which he held. This was notwithstanding the fact that Blackman was able to carry out his duties in practice quite efficiently.

On the other hand, the qualifications of the employee or rather the lack of them, must relate to the job that he was employed to do. For example in:

Woods v Olympic Aluminium Co (1975)

Woods, who had been employed as an accountant was dismissed for reason of lack of management ability. It was held that he had been unfairly dismissed because he had been employed as an accountant not as a manager.

2. The conduct of the employee
   This is an extremely wide ground and covers such conduct as disobedience of disciplinary rules, dishonest conduct, failure to obey reasonable orders, absenteeism, and a hundred and one other forms of misconduct. For dismissal to be justified the misconduct must be serious:

***Smith v St Andrews Scottish Ambulance Service* (1973)**

Smith was an ambulance driver with the St Andrews Scottish Ambulance Service. Although overtime was not compulsory, it was established practice that emergency calls would be given the very highest priority even if this involved drivers in working overtime. Smith failed to answer an emergency call and was dismissed. It was held that this dismissal was fair because of the extreme seriousness of his conduct.

An isolated incident of bad language will not normally be sufficiently serious conduct to justify immediate dismissal. For example in:

***Rosenthall v Butler* (1972)**

An employee swore at a superior on one occasion. It was held that this did not justify immediate dismissal and therefore the dismissal was unfair. For his first offence he should have been given an opportunity to apologise.

On the other hand repeated abuse of superiors may justify dismissal:

***Walters v Top Crust Foods* (1973)**

An employee was asked to do some work which he believed was beyond his normal range of duties. On both occasions that he was asked to do this he swore at his superiors. On the first occasion he had been reprimanded. On the second occasion he was dismissed. It was held that this dismissal was fair.

Sometimes even conduct outside of the course of employment will justify dismissal. For example in:

***Whitlow v Alkamet Construction* (1975)**

Whitlow was required to do some work at the house of a senior fellow employee. While there he had intercourse with the employee's wife. He was subsequently dismissed and claimed that the dismissal was unfair. It was held that the dismissal was justified on the grounds of his conduct. Obviously what had happened would affect relationships at work.

On the other hand the conduct must be such as to be likely to affect the employment relationship. Whitlow's case may be contrasted with:

***Bradshaw v Associated Portland Cement* (1972)**

Bradshaw was a driver with the Associated Portland Cement. He was convicted of incest. The offence had no effect whatever on either the business of the employer or on his fellow employees. He was dismissed. It was held that the dismissal was unfair.

Similarly:

***Grace v Harehills Club* (1974)**

Grace was a 40-year old club steward. He was divorced and living with a 17-year old girl on club premises. He was dismissed. It was held that the dismissal was unfair. The conduct of the steward had no effect on the business of the club at the time of the dismissal. It was not right for the tribunal to pass judgement on the morality of this situation.

3   That the employee was redundant
    It is obvious that an employer who has no work with which to provide his employee to do must be able to dismiss the employee without running the risk of being accused of unfair dismissal. The object of the provision is to prevent duplication of claims by employees who have been made redundant. However, it should be noted that if an employee is unfairly selected for redundancy then he has a claim for unfair dismissal as well as redundancy. An example of unfair selection arose in:

***NC Watling & Co Ltd v Richardson* (1978)**

The company made Richardson, whom they had employed for several months, redundant while keeping on two other men who had only 10 days service on another site. Richardson claimed that he had been unfairly selected for redundancy. The company argued that the customary basis for redundancies in the trade was that selection should be decided on a site basis rather than considering the firm as a whole. It was held by the Employment Appeal Tribunal that even if this were the case it was unreasonable and therefore an unfair selection for redundancy.

(It should be noted that Richardson, who was successful, had only been employed for several months. This is because, at the time, the qualifying period of continuous employment was only 26 weeks. Since it is now 2 years, he would, of course, fail. Nevertheless the case is an excellent example of unfair selection for redundancy.)

4   That the employee could not continue in his job without either the employer or the employee breaking the law
    The most common example of this arises where an employee loses his driving licence. Another example would be where a foreign worker no longer holds the necessary permit to work in England.

5   That the employer can show some other substantial reason of a kind to justify dismissal
    This is a catch-all provision and so a wide range of situations have been considered under it. If two employees are incapable of working together, then the dismissal of one of them may well be seen as necessary and therefore not unfair. Likewise if an employee refuses to submit to a reasonable change in the terms of his contract of employment this would be a substantial reason justifying dismissal. Another example of this ground is the case of:

Creffield v BBC (1975)

Creffield was a cameraman with the BBC. He was found guilty in the Criminal Court of taking indecent photographs of a 13-year old girl. The BBC dismissed him even though the photographs were nothing whatever to do with the BBC. It was held that the dismissal was justified as being for some other substantial reason. The BBC were properly concerned about sending him out on filming assignments as a representative of the BBC.

13.9.3 Was the employer's action reasonable?

By s57(3), Employment Protection (Consolidation) Act 1978 'the determination of the question whether the dismissal was fair or unfair, having regard to the reason shown by the employer, shall depend on whether in the circumstances (including the size and administrative resources of the employer's undertaking) the employer acted reasonably or unreasonably in treating it as a sufficient reason for dismissing the employee; and that question shall be determined in accordance with equity and the substantial merits of the case'.

In deciding whether the employer acted reasonably the tribunal must take into account all the circumstances of the case. Consider, for example, the case of a driver who has lost his driving licence. As has been seen, this is one of the grounds which may justify dismissal. If the driver is employed by a small taxi company, the employer will almost certainly be justified in dismissing him. On the other hand, if the driver is employed by a large industrial concern, the employer should at least consider finding him alternative employment somewhere in the company.

In deciding the reasonableness of an employer's action, the court must have regard only to those facts known to him at the time of his taking the decision to dismiss. This was very clearly stated by the House of Lords in:

Polkey v AE Dayton Services Ltd (1987)

P was employed as a van driver by D. After having been employed for four years, P was dismissed as being redundant. The situation was that D was suffering severe financial losses and decided to reorganise their business overheads by replacing their four van drivers with two van salesmen. In reaching this decision, D decided that three of the van drivers, including P, would not be suitable as salesmen. Accordingly, P dismissed D without prior warning or consultation. He was merely handed a redundancy letter and immediately sent home. He claimed that he had been unfairly dismissed in that the failure of the employer to consult showed that the employer had acted unreasonably in treating the redundancy as a sufficient reason for dismissing the employee and was sufficient to make the redundancy an unfair dismissal.

It was held by the House of Lords that in assessing the reasonableness or otherwise of an employer's action, the tribunal had to have regard to the facts known to the employer at the time of taking the decision to dismiss. It was irrelevant that if the employer had investigated more fully and consulted with the employees he would have reached the same decision to dismiss.

Another matter which would affect the reasonableness or otherwise of a dismissal is whether the employer has conformed with the ACAS Code on Disciplinary Practice Procedure in Employment. This is a code of practice put out by the Advisory, Conciliation and Arbitration Service of the

Department of Employment. Although the code itself is not legally binding, non-compliance does point towards a dismissal being unfair.

There are two main features of the code in connection with disciplinary matters.

Firstly, the employer should always ensure that the employee is notified as to what he has done wrong, and allowed to explain himself. He should also have a right of appeal in the event of his disagreeing with any decision reached.

Secondly, the code favours the practice that an erring employee should be given a first warning, which may be either oral or written, a final written warning, and only then be dismissed. Even here, dismissal should be a very final step taken only after the employer has considered the possibility of other disciplinary measures such as suspension or transfer. The code is not binding and therefore a dismissal is not automatically unfair if its procedures are not followed. If an employee is guilty of gross misconduct, then the employer may dismiss him without going through the various stages of first and second warnings.

13.9.4 Inadmissible reasons for dismissal

If an employee is dismissed either because he was or proposed to become a member of an independent trade union or was not a member of a trade union then such dismissal is automatically unfair. The employer has no defence available to him. This is so notwithstanding that he has not been employed for the usual minimum period of 2 years or that he is over the prescribed age limits.

13.9.5 Dismissal of strikers

The exercise of the right to belong to a trade union must be clearly distinguished from the right to strike. If an employee goes on strike then he is in breach of his contract of employment. As such his employer is entitled to dismiss him. The fact that an employee belongs to a union when he goes on strike and that the strike is official union action does not make the conduct of the strikers any more lawful. They are in breach of their contract of service. The breach is a major breach going to the heart of the contract. They may therefore be dismissed. However, it should be noted that if the employer selects only specified strikers for dismissal then their dismissal is unfair. Thus if he selects only the strike leaders this dismissal is unfair. On the other hand, if the employer dismisses all the strikers, they have no legal cause for complaint.

13.9.6 Written reasons for dismissal

Upon dismissal an employee is entitled to request from his employer a written statement of the reasons for his dismissal. This should be provided to him within 2 weeks of the request. The statement is evidence in any subsequent industrial tribunal hearing and thus must be detailed. A brief comment such as 'misconduct in employment' would not suffice.

13.9.7 Remedies for unfair dismissal

If an employee is found to be unfairly dismissed, the industrial tribunal may recommend re-engagement or re-instatement, or, alternatively, compensation. Re-instatement is a recommendation that the employee should be allowed to return to his former job. Re-engagement is a recommendation that the employee should return to work for the employer though in a different job. These orders are only recommendations and should only be made if there is a possibility that they will work. For example, a recommendation of re-instatement of an employee dismissed from a small family business would probably be futile since the relationship between employer and employee would probably have already broken down.

When an award is made it may consist of up to three elements, a basic award, a compensatory award and a special award. The basic award is assessed in a similar way to the assessment of a redundancy payment. Thus it operates on the basis of a final week's wage (up to a maximum of £172) multiplied by the number of years in employment with a further multiplier to take account of the employee's age. The compensatory award is 'such amount as the tribunal considers just and equitable in all the circumstances having regard to the loss sustained by the complainant in consequence of the dismissal insofar as that loss is attributable to action taken by the employer'. The maximum figure which can be awarded under this head is £8,500. It takes into account matters such as the immediate loss of wages, the manner of the dismissal, future loss of wages and loss of statutory rights eg lost redundancy rights. A special award is a further amount payable in two circumstances:

1. If the dismissal is unfair for reasons connected with trade union membership.
2. If the employee has requested the tribunal to make an order for re-instatement or re-engagement but the employer has refused to comply with the order.

Thus, for example, if John, aged 50, is unfairly dismissed from employment he has enjoyed for 9 years, in circumstances where, at the time of dismissal, he was earning £200 per week, had a company car and was a member of a pension scheme and also had family membership of BUPA paid for by his firm, his compensation would be made up as follows:

basic award 9 × £172	=	£1,548
compensatory award (loss of fringe benefits, difficulty in obtaining further employment, loss of redundancy rights)	= (say)	£4,000
	total	£5,548

If re-engagement or reinstatement had been ordered by the tribune, and the employer had refused to comply, John would then be entitled to a further amount over and above the £5,548 by way of a special award.

13.10 SUMMARY OF REMEDIES FOR DISMISSAL

At the beginning of considering remedies, it is noted that there are three possible remedies for an employee who has been dismissed, damages for wrongful dismissal, redundancy payment, or compensation for unfair dismissal. When considering these remedies in a given situation it is useful to think of a juggler juggling with three balls. One or two of these balls will almost certainly fall to the ground. One, or possibly two, is likely to remain in his hands. Those that remain in his hands are the successful remedies. For example, suppose an employee is dismissed simply because the employer does not like him. The employer pays him wages in lieu of notice. The employee has no claim for damages for wrongful dismissal because he has been paid in lieu of notice. He has no entitlement to redundancy payment because he is not redundant. The ball which remains in the juggler's hands is the unfair dismissal ball.

Quite clearly the employer could not justify the dismissal under any of the heads which make a dismissal fair. A further example to consider is the case of the employee who is laid off because the factory where he works is being closed down. His employer told him that it would close three months after the date of notice of termination was given to the employee. The employee worked the period of notice. Here there is no possibility of a claim for damages for wrongful dismissal since the employee was given proper notice. He is entitled, however, to a redundancy payment given that he has worked for the appropriate 2 years. Since the dismissal is by reason of redundancy, it is not unfair (unless the employees were unfairly selected for redundancy which would almost certainly not be the case where an entire workplace was closing down).

SUMMARY

In this chapter we have been considering the law in relation to individual employment. Essential to understanding this is a knowledge that the contract of employment is much the same as any other contract, but superimposed upon this rather basic contract are a number of statutory provisions which have a considerable effect upon it. A knowledge of the background to employment law is important to this syllabus, though by way of background rather than detailed knowledge.

SELF-TEST QUESTIONS

13.1 Why should an employer be held vicariously liable for the wrongs of his employee?

13.2 What are the factors to be taken into account in deciding whether a person is an employee or an independent contractor?

13.3 List the employer's duties to his employees

13.4 What is the ratio of *Otman* v *Saville Sportswear Ltd* (1960)?

13.5 List the employee's duties

13.6 When may a contract of employment be terminated at common law?

13.7 What is the effect on employees' contracts of employment of the liquidation of the company employing them?

13.8 What is constructive dismissal?

13.9 What are the two main situations in which a person will be dismissed for redundancy?

13.10 Under what circumstances may a dismissal be fair?

Answers on page 327

EXERCISES

Exercise 13.1

What are the main duties owed by an employee?

Exercise 13.2

Two years ago, J obtained a job with B Ltd at its Western site. He was given a written statement from B Ltd which referred him for details of the terms and conditions of his employment to an agreement between B Ltd and the trade union of which J was a member. The agreement stated 'after six months of employment at the Western site, employees of B Ltd may not be moved to the Eastern site without their consent.'

One week ago B Ltd directed J to transfer to the Eastern site (some 30 miles distant). They continued to insist on the transfer despite J's protests. As a consequence, J resigned from his job. Advise J on the action he may take.

Answers on page 328

CHAPTER FOURTEEN

Negotiable instruments—introduction

Negotiable instruments is a subject which almost all students find difficult. This is for two reasons. Firstly the most common negotiable instrument is the cheque. Almost all students have bank accounts of their own and so they are able to relate many of the rules applicable specifically to cheques to their own experience. Cheques, however, are merely a form of a bill of exchange. Bills of exchange are themselves subject to extremely complex rules, many of which have no application to cheques. Unfortunately students often try to relate the rules which they learn about bills of exchange to their own experience in regard to cheques. Often such a relation is impossible. This has the natural result of causing confusion. Secondly many of the more difficult rules which apply to cheques and negotiable instruments arise out of their historical development. If the rules are looked at in the historical context, they make sense. If they are viewed in present day isolation, they are rather more difficult to understand.

14.1 DEVELOPMENT OF THE BILL OF EXCHANGE

Traditionally, the basic business medium for trade was cash. Cash had two major advantages over other mediums of exchange such as barter (ie a straightforward exchange of goods such as would occur where a farmer offered 10 bags of corn to a person who would undertake to plough his field). Firstly cash is legal tender thus it can be used at face value. Secondly it can be transferred with great ease. A person who exchanges goods or services for cash and subsequently receives the cash in good faith obtains good title. In other words, so long as he actually does not know that the person handing over the cash does not have in fact the right to hand it over, the recipient of the cash becomes its full legal owner. A negotiable instrument is rather similar to cash in this latter regard. Although it is not itself legal tender, a person who receives a negotiable instrument in good faith after having given value for it acquires good title. This means that he may sue on the promise contained in the document even though a previous holder's title was in some way defective.

To understand this, look at the following diagram.

TABLE 14.1 **The Classification of Property in English Law**

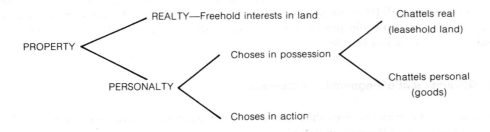

The above diagram shows the basic classification of property in English law. Property is divided into two main types, realty, that is to say land, or more accurately the interests which can be held in freehold land and personalty which is itself divided into two types of property, firstly choses in possession and secondly choses in action. Choses in possession may take the form of chattels real; this is leasehold land which is where a person has a right over land for a limited period of time. There may also be chattels personal which are simply goods such as a pen, a car or a coat. What we are concerned with in this chapter are choses in action. These are what are known as intangible or incorporeal rights. We are concerned specifically with negotiable instruments, but examples of other incorporeal rights are shares in limited companies and what is today known as industrial property, matters such as trademarks, patents and copyright. The word 'incorporeal' means that these rights cannot be physically possessed. They are legal rights and so can only be enforced through the courts. Negotiable instruments create choses in action. As such they are enforceable through the courts, and what we are concerned with in this chapter and the next will be to what extent these rights are enforceable in various circumstances.

To understand the development of negotiable instruments, we need to examine another incorporeal right, a debt. This is money owing by one person to another. In just the same way as if I have £100 in my pocket I can give it to you, so too if I am owed £100 I can assign the right to that money to you.

14.1.1 Assignment of a debt

Look, for example, at the following diagram.

TABLE 14.1.1 **Assignment of a debt**

Anthony owes Brian £100 and Brian owes Colin £100. One way of Brian settling his debt to Colin would be for him to go to Anthony, collect the £100 which he owes and then take it to Colin. Alternatively he could write to Anthony in the terms shown in the box in the diagram requesting Anthony to pay the £100 directly to Colin. This is the most simple assignment of a debt. Brian assigns to Colin the debt which Anthony owes to him (Brian). There is one major difficulty in such an assignment. The assignee (Colin) takes subject to any defect which may exist in the assignors (Brian's) title. For example, suppose the £100 debt owing by Anthony to Brian relates to goods which Brian has supplied to Anthony and which have proved to be defective. In just the same way as Anthony may say to Brian 'I am not paying you because the goods you supplied are defective', so he can say to Colin 'I am not paying you as Brian has requested since the goods which Brian supplied to me are useless'. In legal terms we refer to the assignment of a debt subject to any defects as being 'subject to equities'. Sometimes this terminology is found to be confusing. When we were looking at the development of English law we saw that equity was a separate system of law based on fairness. In this context equities (note the plural) has nothing to do with fairness but is used in the totally different meaning of defect in title.

14.1.2 Development of negotiable instruments

All this looks very far removed from the modern world of negotiable instruments. In reality, however, it is not. Consider the following situation:

TABLE 14.1.2 **Development of negotiable instruments**

Peter owes Quentin £1,000,000
But Peter cannot pay at this moment, though in three months time he will have sufficient funds to do so,
and Quentin needs the money as soon as possible
and Robert has available funds of £1,000,000 which he wants to use to generate more capital.

This is a typical business situation. Peter owes Quentin £1,000,000. Quentin needs the money as quickly as possible but Peter will be unable to pay for three months. He needs to obtain credit therefore for this period of time. Robert, on the other hand, has ample funds to meet the payment of £1,000,000. What Quentin might do in this situation is to go to Robert and explain how he is owed £1,000,000 by Peter. Robert agrees to advance £900,000 to Quentin so long as Quentin agrees that the full £1,000,000 owing from Peter goes straight to Robert when payment is made.

This could be done by way of an assignment, with Quentin assigning to Robert the debt of £1,000,000 owing to him by Peter. However, as has just been seen, the assignment would take place subject to equities. For this reason, in the context of business transactions of this nature, assignments are generally unacceptable. Were there to be an assignment, Robert would not be certain that the title which he had acquired to the £1,000,000 due from Peter was free from any defects without his first investigating the right of Quentin to the money. Obviously in the world of commerce such a procedure would be far too cumbersome to be a practicality. So, in order to get over this difficulty, the negotiable instrument was developed. The word 'negotiable' means transferable free from equities, that is to say free from any defects in title. Thus it provides greatly enhanced security to the recipient of the negotiable instrument who would otherwise merely be receiving an assignment of a debt which was subject to equities.

14.1.3 The negotiable instrument

The negotiable instrument would be made out in the following way:

TABLE 14.1.3

```
                                                        30 June 1990
   To Peter
   Pay Robert, three months after date, the sum of
   one million pounds.

                                                     (Signed) Quentin.
```

This is a typical negotiable instrument. Peter is being required to pay Robert the sum of £1,000,000 in three months time. Peter is not bound by the instrument until he accepts it. Acceptance is a technical term which means that Peter signifies that he is prepared to make the agreed payment at the stipulated time to Robert. He would indicate his acceptance by writing 'accepted' on the front of the document and then signing his name.

Once Peter has accepted the instrument in this way the requirements of all parties are met. Peter will be satisfied because he will have obtained the three months credit which he needed. Quentin will be satisfied because he has obtained immediate payment of the major part of the debt which was not due to be paid for another three months. Robert will be satisfied because he has made satisfactory use of the money in his possession by advancing it on terms which provide him with £1,000,000 profit in three months.

14.2 THE CHARACTERISTICS OF NEGOTIABILITY

There are certain characteristics which distinguish negotiable instruments from other instruments which may be assigned. It is customary when learning about negotiable instruments for these characteristics of negotiability to be dealt with at this stage. It is difficult to see at what other point they can be mentioned, though they will not be fully understood until you have read the remainder of the chapter. For this reason, do not worry if the significance of the characteristics is not apparent on a first reading through of this chapter. Firstly, the rights in the instrument may be transferred simply by delivery or by endorsement and delivery. Sometimes a negotiable instrument is made payable to 'bearer'. In this case all that has to be done to transfer it is simply to hand it over to the intended transferee. Sometimes it is made payable to a named person, as in diagram 14.1.3. In that situation were Robert to want to transfer the instrument to Sam he would have to sign his (Robert's) name on the back of the instrument. This is what is known as endorsement. Having endorsed the instrument he would then hand it to Sam. Secondly the holder of the instrument has a right to sue on the instrument in his own name in order to enforce the promise contained in the instrument. He may do this even though notice of the transfer to him has not been given to the person who actually is liable upon the instrument. In the example we have just been considering therefore Sam, the transferee of the instrument, could sue Peter for the £1,000,000 (so long as Peter has accepted liability on the instrument) notwithstanding that Robert never told Peter of the assignment to Sam. Thirdly a transferee in good faith and for value received good title. This means that he acquires the title to the instrument free from any defects (equities). Fourthly, there is a presumption that consideration has been given for the instrument. Returning to our example, even though Sam may have given Robert no consideration whatever for the assignment to him of the £1,000,000 debt, there is a presumption that consideration was given.

14.3 DEFINITION OF A BILL OF EXCHANGE

A bill of exchange is defined by s3(1), Bills of Exchange Act 1882 in the following way:
'A bill of exchange is an unconditional order in writing, addressed by one person to another, signed by the person giving it, requiring the person to whom it is addressed to pay on demand or at a fixed or determinable future time a sum certain in money to or to the order of a specified person or to bearer.'
In going through this definition it is useful to have in mind diagram 14.1.3, the bill of exchange signed by Quentin requiring Robert to pay Peter £1,000,000. It is an unconditional order requiring Peter to pay Robert three months after date (ie at a fixed or determinable future time) a sum certain in money, namely £1,000,000. This definition is of major importance and it should be learnt by heart. Any instrument which does not satisfy the definition cannot be a bill of exchange.
The bill must be unconditional and it must be an order. For example:

Bavins Junr. & Sims v. London & South Western Bank Ltd (1899)

The case concerned an instrument in the form of a cheque but with the order followed by the phrase 'provided the receipt form at the foot hereof is duly signed, stamped and dated.'
It was held by the Court of Appeal that this was not a negotiable instrument and therefore a bank that acted upon it was not protected by the Bills of Exchange Act 1882.

In the same way words such as 'I should be glad if you would kindly pay' or 'Please pay out of the proceeds of sale of my car' do not constitute a bill of exchange because they are not unconditional. On the other hand, words of courtesy such as 'Please pay' do not prevent an instrument being negotiable. For example:

Ruff v Webb (1794)

The words 'Mr Nelson will very much oblige Mr Webb by paying G Ruff or order, 20 guineas on his account' were held sufficient for a valid bill.

The unconditional order must be in writing. A cheque is defined by s73, Bills of Exchange Act 1882 as 'a bill of exchange drawn on a banker payable on demand'. Thus a cheque has to satisfy all these requirements of the definition of a bill of exchange. A person having a bank account is provided by the bank with what is called a cheque book. A cheque book is not a book of cheques; it is a book of forms on which cheques can be written. Thus if I write a shopping list on one of those cheque forms then all I have is a shopping list rather than a cheque. The shopping list clearly does not comply with the definition of a cheque as contained in the Bills of Exchange Act. Conversely there is nothing in the definition either of a cheque or of a bill of exchange which says that it has to be written on a bank cheque form. So long as it is in writing it may, given that the other criteria are satisfied, be a valid cheque. Thus a cheque may be written on a sheet of paper or on a tablecloth. AP Herbert, the well-known humorous legal writer once wrote a story of a cheque written on the side of a cow. On occasions stories have been carried in the newspapers of people who have written a cheque to cover their tax liability on a shirt. Indeed the only thing on which a cheque may not be written is metal, this being an offence under s5 Coinage Act 1870.

A bill of exchange must be addressed by one person to another and must require the person to whom it is addressed to make some payment to another person or to bearer. This is illustrated in the following diagram:

TABLE 14.3 **Parties to a bill of exchange**

```
                draws              payable
     DRAWER  ─────────→  DRAWEE  ─────────→  PAYEE
              Bill on               to
```

The person who actually draws or signs the bill is the drawer. The person who is ordered to make the payment is the drawee. The person who is going to receive the payment is the payee. Thus, to go back to diagram 14.1.2, Quentin, the drawer, draws a cheque on Peter, the drawee, requiring payment to be made to Peter, the payee.

A bill of exchange must be payable either on demand (ie when the payer requires payment to be made) or at a fixed or determinable future time. An example of a fixed future time is given in diagram 14.1.2, three months after date. An example of a determinable future time would be a bill of exchange payable '30 days after acceptance'; this means 30 days after the drawee has indicated his willingness to make payment in accordance with the bill. In this situation, clearly, the date of payment cannot be known until acceptance takes place.

The bill must be for a sum certain in money. It is obvious that a specific amount must be stated. An order requiring a payment to John of 'somewhere in the region of £250' is clearly too imprecise to be a bill of exchange.

Finally a bill of exchange must be payable either to a named person or to a bearer. Where it is payable to a named person it is called an order bill. Where it is payable to bearer it is known as a bearer bill. The essential difference between an order bill and a bearer bill is that a bearer bill is transferred simply by delivery. An order bill on the other hand is transferred by delivery and indorsement. Thus if I have a cheque which states 'pay bearer the sum of £10', all I have to do to pass the rights in the cheque to you is to hand the cheque over to you. On the other hand, if the cheque provides for payment to me by name, I must sign my own name on the back before handing the cheque over to you.

14.4 HOLDER, HOLDER FOR VALUE AND HOLDER IN DUE COURSE

A person actually in possession of a bill of exchange is referred to as the holder of the bill. There are three types of holder, a bare holder, a holder for value and a holder in due course. The three types of holder progressively acquire increasing rights in the bill which they hold. The holder with the least rights is the bear holder. Look, for example, at the two examples in the following diagram.

TABLE 14.4 **Holder of a cheque**

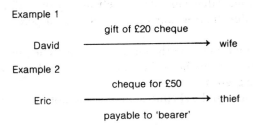

By s2, Bills of Exchange Act 1882, a holder is defined as 'the payee or endorsee of a bill or note who is in possession of it, or the bearer thereof'. A bearer is defined as 'the person in possession of a bill or note which is payable to bearer'. Usually a holder is the person legally entitled to the bill. In the case of a bill payable to bearer, the test of whether a person is a holder is essentially one of possession. Thus a person who finds a bearer bill or a thief who is in possession of it is a holder, though this does not give him rights against the parties to the bill. Indeed a holder cannot himself enforce the bill through the courts, though he can pass good title to the bill to a holder in due course (the significance of which we shall see in a few moments).

In Example 1 above, David gave a cheque for £20 to his wife. The wife as such is a mere holder.

If David requests his bank manager to stop payment on the cheque, his wife cannot sue for the £20 since the cheque was merely a gift.

Similarly, in Example 2, the thief cannot sue on the cheque which he has stolen from Eric. He is a holder by virtue of his being in physical possession of a bearer cheque but he is not the transferee.

14.5 HOLDER FOR VALUE

A holder for value is defined by s27(2), Bills of Exchange Act 1882:
'Where value has at any time been given for a bill, the holder is deemed to be a holder for value as regards the acceptor and all parties to the bill who became parties prior to such time'. Liability therefore arises as soon as value is given for the bill. When such value has been given, the bill is binding on all who were already parties to it and also the party who signed it in return for consideration. The following diagram gives examples of holders for value:

TABLE 14.5 **Holder for value**

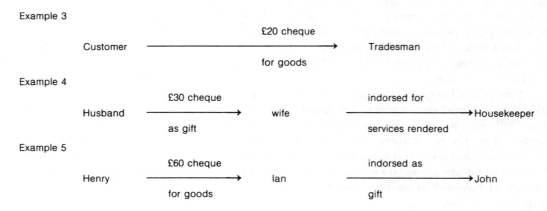

In Example 3, the tradesman to whom the customer gives a £20 cheque is a holder for value since he has provided consideration for the cheque, namely the goods supplied.

In Example 4 the wife who received the £30 cheque as a gift is a mere holder, in just the same way as the wife is in Example 1. However, the housekeeper becomes a holder for value when the wife endorses the cheque and hands it to her, since the housekeeper provides consideration, namely the services supplied, in return for the cheque.

In Example 5 Ian is a holder for value, having supplied goods in return for the cheque for £60 from Henry. John also is a holder for value when the cheque is endorsed and delivered to him by Ian. While John himself has not given consideration, a holder for value is a holder of a bill upon which consideration has **at any time** been given. Ian's giving value for the cheque is sufficient for John to become a holder for value. A holder for value can enforce a cheque against all persons who become parties to it prior to the giving of value. This means that he can sue all perons who signed the bill prior to value being given.

Thus in Example 3 the tradesman may sue the customer on the cheque.

In Example 4 the housekeeper may sue both the wife and the husband on the cheque, since both were parties prior to value being given.

In Example 5, John can sue Henry on the cheque though he cannot sue Ian who became a party only after the giving of value.

A holder for value takes subject to equities. As has been explained, this means that his right to enforce the bill is subject to any defect in title which may attach to it.

Thus in Example 3 if the goods supplied had been defective, the customer could order his bank to stop payment of the cheque, and, if sued by the tradesman on the cheque, he could put up the defence that the goods were not of the standard he was entitled to expect under the contract.

Similarly in Example 4 if the wife had obtained the £30 cheque by threatening the husband with violence, then the husband could refuse to make payment to the housekeeper on the cheque since he had been induced to write it by duress. Finally, in Example 5, if Henry had handed over the £60 cheque to Ian in return for goods which subsequently proved to be defective, Ian would be fully justified in stopping payment to John, the indorsee.

14.6 HOLDER IN DUE COURSE

The holder who obtains the best title of all is the holder in due course. Such a holder is defined in s29(1), Bills of Exchange Act 1882 as 'a holder who has taken the bill, complete and regular on the face of it, under the following conditions: namely:

(a) That he became the holder of it before it was overdue, without knowledge that it had previously been dishonoured, if such was the fact; and
(b) that he took the bill in good faith and for value, and that at the time the bill was negotiated to him he had no notice of any defect in the title of the person who negotiated it.'

The bill must be complete and regular on the face of it, and for this purpose the face of the cheque includes the back. For example, the name of the payee must correspond with the signature of the indorser. There must be no discrepancy between the words and the figures which express the sum of money due. The bill must not be marked with words such as 'not negotiable' or 'not transferable'. An example of a bill not being complete and regular on the face of it is found in:

Arab Bank Ltd v Ross (1952)

Two promissory notes (a form of bill of exchange) were drawn with 'Fathi & Faysal Nabulsy Company' a partnership between Fathi & Faysal Nabulsy. Faysal Nabulsy indorsed the notes 'Fathi & Faysal Nabulsy' and handed them to Arab Bank. It was held by the Court of Appeal that the bank was not a holder in due course although the indorsement was valid to pass title to the notes to the bank, which thus became a holder for value, because of the discrepancy in the name on the front of the notes and the indorser, the bank could not become a holder in due course. The fact that the word 'company' was omitted from the indorsement constituted a sufficient irregularity to cause some doubt as to whether the payee and the indorsee were the same person.

The bill must not be overdue. The reason for this is that when a bill of exchange is issued there is a clear intention that it should be presented for payment on a particular date. Consequently if the date for payment has passed and the bill remains in circulation there must be some cause for suspicion. S36(3), Bills of Exchange Act 1882 provides that a bill payable on demand is overdue 'when it appears on the face of it to have been in circulation for an unreasonable length of time'. What constitutes an unreasonable length of time is a question of fact. Probably it becomes overdue about a week after the date on the bill. Where the bill is one payable other than on demand, it becomes due and payable on the last day of the time of payment fixed by the bill. Thus if a bill is expressed to be payable three months after the date and bears the date 1 June, then the bill becomes overdue on 2 September. If a holder is to be a holder in due course, he must not have notice of the Bill having been previously dishonoured. There are two ways in which a bill may be dishonoured, by non-acceptance and by non-payment. In each instance the effect is the same. The holder has an immediate right of recourse against the drawer of the bill and any person who has indorsed it. A cheque is regarded as dishonoured if it is returned by the bank to the payee with words added such as 'refer to drawer' or 'words and figures differ'.

The holder must have taken the bill in good faith. In effect this means that he must have acted honestly. He must also have given value. He should have given value himself, it not being sufficient that the value was provided by some prior party.

Finally, a holder in due course must take without notice of any defect in the title of the person who negotiated it. In other words, if a person takes a bill knowing that there is some defect in the title of the transferor, he obviously cannot claim himself to be free of those defects.

A holder in due course has very considerable rights in the bill. He can sue on the bill in his own name. He can enforce payment against all parties liable on the bill. He takes good title free from equities and free from any defects in the title of prior parties.

A word of warning needs to be added at this stage in regard to examination questions concerning bills of exchange. It is hardly ever possible to tell from an examination question whether a holder of a bill is a holder in due course. This is because the question will seldom contain all the information required to discover this. For example, it is necessary actually to see a bill to ascertain whether it is complete and regular on the face of it. Again, it is necessary to know the date of the instrument or the date of payment to ascertain whether it is overdue.

It should be noted also that a payee of a bill can never be a holder in due course. This is because a bill has to be negotiated to a holder in due course, in other words the bill is transferred to a holder in due course free from equities. A bill is merely issued to a payee. However, if a payee has negotiated the bill and later has it renegotiated to him, he can then claim the rights of a holder in due course so long as he satisfies the requirements of such a holder under the Bills of Exchange Act.

14.7 LIABILITY ON A BILL OF EXCHANGE

A person does not incur liability on a bill of exchange unless he signs it, whether as acceptor, drawer or indorser. We have already mentioned acceptance. In diagram 14.1.3 (above) Robert would present the bill of exchange to Peter for acceptance. This is because Robert will obviously want to know whether in three months time Peter is in fact willing to pay the £1,000,000 to him. Upon presentment, Peter signifies his acceptance by writing on the bill that he will make the payment as and when necessary and sign his name, though the mere signature of the drawee is sufficient in itself for acceptance. A drawee can never incur any liability on a bill unless and until he does accept it.

The drawer is the one person who is most likely to sign a bill of exchange. Every bill must be signed by a drawer even if it is not accepted or indorsed. If the drawer's signature is forged, the bill of exchange is a nullity. The piece of paper purporting to be a bill of exchange cannot be one since a bill of exchange must by definition be signed by the drawer.

Sometimes bills are signed in a trade name. As a general rule, the signing of a cheque imposes liability upon the person who signs it. This applies equally where the signature is that of an agent. However, an agent may usually avoid personal liability so long as he discloses that he is signing as an agent and adds the name of the principal. Thus a signature 'J Jones, agent' or 'J Jones, director' is insufficient to avoid the agent being personally liable. However, if he signs, 'J Jones, director, for and on behalf of X Limited' then he incurs no personal liability so long as he has correctly stated the company name.

14.8 INDORSEMENT OF A BILL OF EXCHANGE

An indorsement of a bill of exchange consists of the indorser signing the back of the bill, whether with or without the addition of further words. As we saw earlier, bills of exchange are of two kinds, bearer and order. A bearer bill is transferred simply by delivery. Thus a cheque made out 'pay bearer the sum of £25' can be transferred from one person to another simply by being handed over. On the other hand, a cheque 'pay John Smith or order the sum of £25' requires delivery to be accompanied by an indorsement if the transfer is to be effective.

There are various types of indorsement and these will now be considered.

14.8.1 Indorsement in blank

This is where the payee of the bill simply signs the reverse side of it. No indorsee (person to whom the bill is to be transferred) is specified. The effect of an indorsement in blank is to convert the bill into an order bill. Thus after indorsement it can be transferred simply by delivery.

14.8.2 Special indorsement

This is where the indorsee is named in the indorsement. Suppose a cheque has been made payable to J Jones and he wishes to transfer it to J Smith. He indorses the bill 'pay J Smith signed J Jones'. A special indorsement preserves the character of an order bill. Thus the bill remains payable to a designated person, even though that designated person is different from the payee.

If the bill has been indorsed in blank, any holder can convert it to a specially indorsed bill by inserting appropriate words above the signature of the indorser.

14.8.3 Conditional indorsement

This is where the payee indorses the bill and adds a condition, for example, the payee indorses 'pay J Jones provided he passes his examination signed payee'. For such an indorsement there is no need for the drawee to take any notice whatever of the condition. If he so wishes he can check to see whether the indorsee has passed his exams but he is not in breach of duty if he fails to do so.

14.8.4 Restrictive indorsement

Here the payee purports in the words used in the indorsement to ensure that the transfer is only to one specified person, for example, he indorses 'pay J Jones only signed payee'. The effect of this is that the bill becomes non-transferable by the indorsee.

Only J Jones can obtain payment on it.

14.8.5 Indorsement sans recours

As a general rule the only way in which a person can incur liability on a bill of exchange is by signing it. If an indorser wishes to avoid the risk of personal liability, he can put after his signature the words *sans recours* or 'without recourse'. This is very useful in practice. Suppose an accountant is given a cheque which he must pass to a client. The cheque is payable to the accountant. If the accountant makes a simple indorsement in favour of his client and the cheque is subsequently dishonoured, the accountant, by virtue of his having signed the cheque, incurs personal liability upon it. If, however, the accountant adds the words *sans recours* after his signature when indorsing it, this has the effect of simply transferring the cheque to his client without any acceptance of responsibility.

14.8.6 Forged indorsements

If an indorsement is forged, no one taking after the forgery can claim any rights on the bill itself, nor can such a person be a holder in due course since the bill is not complete and regular on the face of it. The only remedy available to a holder of such a bill will be to sue anyone who indorses the bill after the forgery. Thus he will be suing on an implied promise given by every indorser to subsequent indorsees that the bill is valid and that, if it is dishonoured, the amount shown will be paid by the indorser. In other words, the action is on the implied promise of the indorser rather than on the document itself.

14.9 DISHONOUR OF THE BILL OF EXCHANGE

As was said earlier, dishonour occurs if a bill is not accepted when presented by the payee to the drawee for acceptance or if it is not paid on the due date. When there is dishonour, the holder has an immediate right of recourse against all prior parties on the bill. In other words he has a right to claim the sum stated in the bill from all persons who signed the bill in whatever capacity prior to his coming into possession of it. As a general rule, a holder must give notice of the dishonour having occurred to the person against whom he is seeking to enforce the bill as soon as possible. The notice may be in writing or it may be given personally. There is no specified form, though it must identify the bill of exchange and state that it has been dishonoured.

SUMMARY

Negotiable instruments are essential background to the understanding of the law on cheques. Once you understand the nature of them, you are suitably knowledgable to go on to study cheques. The area is slightly artificial in that the only bills of exchange which most people come across are cheques. Nevertheless a sound basic knowledge is needed of this area of law.

SELF-TEST QUESTIONS

14.1 What are the characteristics of a negotiable instrument?

14.2 Complete the definition of a bill of exchange:

'A bill of exchange is an (a) _____ order in (b) _____ addressed by one person to another, (c) _____ by the person giving it, requiring the person to whom it is addressed to pay (d) _____ or at a (e) _____ or (f) _____ a (g) _____ in money to or to the order of a (h) _____ or to (i) _____.'

(j) _____ Act 1882

14.3 Look at the following bill of exchange:

```
1st April 1990                London

Three months after date, pay to
John Smith the sum of five hundred
pounds (£500)

To                            Signed
  Ann Jones
  1 Any Street
  Any Town                    (B. GREEN)
```

(a) Which of the parties is
   (i) the drawer
   (ii) the drawee
   (iii) the payee?
(b) Is the bill payable on demand?
(c) If Ann Jones signs the bill, does she become
   (i) payee
   (ii) indorser
   (iii) acceptor?

14.4 Distinguish between a holder, holder for value and holder in due course

14.5 What are the requirements a person must satisfy in order to show that he is a holder in due course?

14.6 What is meant by 'complete and regular on the fact of it'?

14.7 How does a holder transfer:
(a) a bearer bill
(b) a holder bill?

14.8 Distinguish between:
(a) indorsement in blank
(b) special indorsement
(c) conditional indorsement
(d) restrictive indorsement
(e) indorsement sans recours

Answers on page 330

EXERCISES

Exercise 14.1

Explain what is meant by a bill of exchange and for what purposes it may be used. What is the difference between a holder in due course and a holder for value.

Exercise 14.2

Explain what is meant by 'negotiability', and describe the ways in which bills of exchange may be negotiated.

Answers on page 331

CHAPTER FIFTEEN

Cheques

By s73, Bills of Exchange Act 1882 'a cheque is a bill of exchange drawn on a banker payable on demand'. Thus while not all bills of exchange are cheques, all cheques are bills of exchange. It is because cheques are bills of exchange that we need to know the detailed rules governing bills of exchange which we considered in the previous chapter. In this chapter we are going to look specifically at cheques.

15.1 THE CHEQUE FORM

In the case of a cheque, the drawee is always a banker. If you think of your own cheque book, across the top of the cheque form is the name and address of your bank. Your bank is the drawee of the cheque. The person who is required to make the payment on the cheque can never be anyone other than a banker. A cheque is always payable on demand. It can never, as is the case with other bills of exchange, be payable 'three months after sight', or 'three months after acceptance'. The result of this is that it is very seldom that cheques are negotiated from one holder to another. Because of this, although the rules relating to the transfer of bills of exchange, and holders in due course apply to cheques, they very seldom have any practical importance in this regard.

There are two important ways in which cheques differ from other bills of exchange. Firstly, the rules governing acceptance have no application to cheques. Because of this, a holder of a cheque generally acquires no rights against the banker on whom it is drawn. It will be recalled that liability is only incurred on a bill of exchange by signing it. Since a banker cannot be required to accept a cheque, he will not sign it. Thus he will incur no liability upon it. Secondly the rules relating to crossings are unique to cheques.

These are instructions which are added to the face of a cheque, the purpose of which is to prescribe how the cheque is to be dealt with.

15.2 CROSSINGS

As has just been said, a crossing is an instruction added to the face of a cheque to detail how the cheque should be dealt with. In order to understand this you should have in your mind the following diagram.

TABLE 15.2 **The use of a cheque**

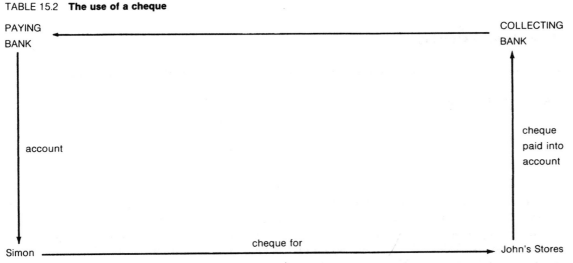

Simon has an account at the bank. He goes to John's Stores and buys some goods for which he pays by cheque. John's Stores will then pay the cheque into his own bank account. The bank then must collect the money from Simon's bank. For this reason the bank into which the cheque was paid is referred to as the collecting bank and Simon's bank is referred to as the paying bank.

The process of collection of money on a cheque is known as clearing. This is the process whereby cheques drawn on one bank but presented for collection at another bank are taken to a place, a clearing house, for payment by the paying bankers. The system of clearing probably originated in the late 18th century when the various banks would send clerks along to a central place with cheques to exchange. At first the clerks used to meet to exchange cheques at an inn in Lombard Street in the City of London. Today the process is effected at the London Clearing House. The crossing of cheques originated in this system of clearing. If you go back to diagram 15.2 (above) you will see that when John's Stores pays Simon's cheque into its account the collecting bank will then collect from the paying bank. In the early days what would happen would be that the collecting bank would hand the cheque to the paying bank. However the paying bank would have no idea where to send the payment. Consequently the practice developed whereby, before handing the cheque to the paying bank, the collecting bank's clerk would write the name of his employer bank across the face of the cheque. As we shall see shortly, this would be today referred to as a specially crossed cheque.

15.2.1 General crossings

The practice of writing instructions on the face of the cheque was gradually adopted by others outside the clearing system. The addition to the face of a cheque of two parallel transverse lines constitutes a general crossing. This is illustrated by diagram 15.2.1.

TABLE 15.2.1 **General crossing**

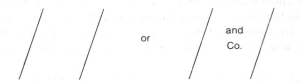

The addition of the words 'and Co.' is not legally necessary. The presence or absence of these words makes no difference to the effect of the general crossing. A cheque which bears a general crossing can only be paid by the paying bank to another bank. Cash cannot be given over the counter by the paying bank to the payee or to any person claiming to be the payee. As such a general crossing offers some protection to the users of a cheque. Clearly it is a hindrance to a person who finds or steals a cheque that payment on the cheque can only be made into a bank account. Since a bank account must be used for the purposes of collection, it is less difficult to trace the finder or thief of a cheque.

15.2.2 Special crossing

The earliest type of crossing was a special crossing, which is illustrated by diagram 15.2.2.

TABLE 15.2.2 **Special crossing**

You see from this that the name of the collecting banker is on the face of the cheque. We have already considered how this practice developed, and the present day effect of such a crossing is that not only must payment be made through a bank account, it must also be made through an account at the named bank. This makes it even more difficult for a person who has wrongfully acquired the cheque to obtain payment. Not only must he use a bank account to get the money, he must use an account at the named bank. A moment's thought will illustrate how much additional security a special crossing gives the payee of a cheque. If you are given a cheque which is crossed specially with the name and branch of your bank and you lose the cheque, a finder, wishing to get the money for himself, must go to your bank and open an account in your name. This obviously would cause suspicion at the branch where you bank. We shall later consider the duties which bankers owe to their customers. It is, however, useful at this stage to note that the effect of a banker making payment on a crossed cheque in cash over the counter is that he may not debit his customer's account with the amount paid. In other words, a banker who pays out over the counter on a crossed cheque is treated as though he has simply given the money to the person to whom he made payment.

15.2.3 Not negotiable crossing

The next type of crossing is that which consists of the words 'not negotiable' being written on the face of the cheque. This is illustrated by diagram 15.2.3.

TABLE 15.2.3 **Crossing 'not negotiable'**

It will be recalled that at the beginning of Chapter 14 it is explained that the word 'negotiable' indicates that the instrument can be transferred to a holder in due course free from equities, that is to say, free from any defects in the title of a prior party. In other words, negotiability consists of two interconnected concepts: firstly, the rights in the instrument can be transferred from one person to another, and secondly such transfer may be free from equities. A crossing 'not negotiable' strikes at the second of these concepts. A cheque crossed 'not negotiable' can still be transferred, but it ceases to be negotiable. Title cannot pass free from equities. Thus there can be no holders in due course on a cheque which is crossed 'not negotiable' and no holder can claim to have a better title than the previous holder. If, of course, previous holders themselves have good title, then this good title will be passed to any transferee of the cheque.

15.2.4 Account payee crossing

Finally in this context, we turn to the crossing 'account payee'. This is illustrated in diagram 15.2.4.

TABLE 15.2.4 **Crossing 'account payee'**

In fact this is not a true crossing. Frequently the words 'account payee' or 'account payee only' appear with a crossing. The words are not a crossing because, strictly speaking, a crossing is a direction to a paying banker, and a paying banker is in no position to ensure that the money goes into a specific account at the collecting bank. The words are merely a direction to the collecting bank as to how the money is to be dealt with after receipt. If the payee's own bank collects for him on the cheque and then fails to follow the direction given by the words, it will be liable to him for any loss so caused. The parallel lines constitute a general crossing and as such are an indication to the paying bank that payment must be made into a bank account.

Difficulty arises when a cheque crossed 'account payee' is negotiated.

In such a situation, the collecting banker is put on enquiry if such cheque is presented for collection by someone other than the payee. Collection for some other account may well be negligence in these circumstances.

15.3 MODERN CLEARING

The more important English banks are members of the London Clearing House. They also act as agents for other bankers who are not members.

Each member has a number of desks at the Clearing House for its employees. The Head Office of each member bank collects together cheques paid in to its different branches. At this stage, the branch will have already specially crossed the cheque in its own name in readiness for collection. These cheques are put into bundles for each other member bank. The bundles are then taken to the appropriate desk of the other banks. Meanwhile, at its own desks, the employees of the member banks will receive similar bundles of cheques which in turn have been drawn on their branches. Balances are arrived at between incoming and outgoing payments and the differences effected by entries made in the books of the Bank of England.

15.4 DUTIES OF THE CUSTOMER

We will turn now to the relationship which exists between the banker and the customer. The relationship is one of debtor and creditor, whether the customer is in credit in which case the banker is the debtor or the customer is in debit in which case he is the debtor. However the relationship is far more than simply one of debtor and creditor. Both banker and customer have important rights and duties and it is these which we shall now examine.

The prime duty of the customer is to take reasonable precautions against possible forgery or alteration of cheques. The leading case on this is:

London Joint Stock Bank Ltd v Macmillan & Arthur (1918)

A clerk employed by the partnership of Macmillan & Arthur was responsible for making out cheques for signature. He presented a cheque to one of the partners in the firm to sign on which he had written the amount of £2 in figures, but left the space for the amount in words blank. Once the cheque had been signed by the partner, the clerk altered the figure of £2 to £120 and wrote one hundred and twenty pounds in words in the appropriate place. Subsequently, the clerk cashed the cheque at the London Joint Stock Bank where his employers had their account. The firm claimed that the bank should debit their account with £2 only; the bank claimed that the firm had been negligent in drawing and signing the cheque in the way in which it had and therefore it was entitled to debit the account to the full £120.

It was held by the House of Lords that the relationship of banker and customer imposed a duty on the customer when drawing cheques to take reasonable precautions against forgery. The alteration in this case was the direct result of a breach of this duty by the firm.

Accordingly the bank was entitled to debit the account with the full £120 paid by them on the cheque.

Furthermore, a customer has a duty to inform his bank of any forgery of a cheque drawn on his account as soon as he becomes aware of it. The customer's duty, however, goes no further than this. For example, he does not owe a duty to his bank to take reasonable precautions to prevent forged cheques being presented for payment.
In:

Tai Hing Cotton Mill Ltd v Liu Chong Hing Bank Ltd (1985)

A clerk had been forging the company's managing director's signature on cheques which he had presented to the bank. The bank had paid out on these cheques and had debited the company's account accordingly. This had gone on for some five years before the fraud was eventually discovered.

When the company sued the bank to recover the amount paid out on the cheques, the bank pleaded that, as the company was in breach of the duty of care owed by customers to examine their statements for unauthorised debit items, it was estopped from claiming the refund. The Privy Council held that no such duty existed. The customer's only duties are to draw cheques in such a way as to prevent forgeries or fraud and to inform the bank immediately of any forgery of which he becomes aware. There is no other duty of care imposed on a bank's customer. In particular he is under no obligation in law to examine regularly his accounts. The company therefore was entitled to recover the money paid out by the bank on the forged cheques.

15.5 DUTIES OF THE BANKER

The banker, not surprisingly, is under more duties. He must not make payments without authority. This means that he should ensure that cheques are properly signed either by the customer or by his authorised agent. For example, in:

Liggett v Barclays Bank (1928)

The bank was mandated by a company only to pay cheques signed by two directors. It paid out on a cheque drawn by a single director. It was held that the bank was not entitled to debit the company's account with the value of the cheque.

An extension of this rule is that the banker is presumed to know his customer's signature. No matter how good a forgery of the customer's signature is, a banker may not debit his customer's account pursuant to paying out on a forged cheque.

There is a limited exception to this rule. A situation may arise where a customer is estopped from denying the validity of a signature which in fact is forged. An example of this is:

Greenwood v Martins Bank (1933)

The plaintiff had an account with Martins Bank. He was the sole authorised signatory on the account, but over a period of time his wife drew on the account by forging his signature. When he learnt of the forgeries, he was persuaded by his wife not to say anything to the bank about what had happened. In return the wife promised not to forge her husband's signature again. Some months later Mr Greenwood determined to tell the bank of the forgeries. He notified his wife and she thereupon committed suicide. The husband sued the bank to recover the sums which had been paid out on cheques bearing forged signatures. It was held by the House of Lords that in delaying, he had become estopped from claiming that the signatures were forgeries. Thus he could not recover.

The bank is also under a duty to honour cheques up to the amount of the customer's credit balance and any agreed overdraft. If a banker dishonours a customer's cheque, he writes or stamps words on the front of the cheque 'not sufficient' or 'refer to drawer' and then refers the cheque to the collecting bank. In the event of funds being available to meet a cheque treated in this way, the use of the words which suggest a lack of funds are defamatory of the drawer. They suggest that the drawer is a man of insufficient funds to meet the cheques which he has written. In such circumstances the drawer may sue the banker for libel. If the customer is a trader, he can claim substantial damages on the banker without having to prove actual loss. On the other hand, non-trader customers may only claim nominal damages unless they can establish that the defamation has in fact caused them actual loss.

The authority of the banker to pay out on cheques bearing the customer's signature may be countermanded by the customer. The leading case on the matter of countermand is:

Curtice v London City & Midland Bank (1908)

Curtice drew a cheque on his bank and the same day he sent a telegram to the bank countermanding payment. The telegram arrived at the bank after business hours and was placed in the bank's letterbox. For some reason, it was two days before the telegram was brought to the notice of the bank manager, by which time the cheque had been paid. Curtice sued his bank for the value of the cheque. It was held that the action must fail. The bank was not liable. To be effective, notice of countermand must actually be received by the manager. The mere presence on the bank's premises of an unopened telegram is not sufficient.

This might appear a rather odd decision and many people feel that it is unfair. It may be that if the case were to arise today it would be decided differently. This was because the case was decided in 1908, which was well before the modern law of negligence was developed in *Donoghue v Stevenson* in 1932 and in *Hedley Byrne v Heller* in 1964 (see Chapter 19). In fact negligence was never pleaded in the Curtice case, but there can be little doubt that were the case to arise today negligence would be pleaded and the decision would go against the bank.

There are a number of other instances where the banker's duty to honour cheques is terminated:

1. Notice of the customer's death.
2. Notice of the customer's insanity.
3. Notice of presentation of bankruptcy petition.
4. Notice of winding up of corporate customer.
5. Notice that customer is an undischarged bankrupt.
6. Notice that customer is drawing cheques for an unlawful purpose.
7. Service of court order restraining the banker from making payment.

A banker is under a duty of secrecy. He must not disclose details of my bank account. This means that not only details of the amount of money I might have or the extent of my overdraft are secret but also where my money is and what I spend it on. Having said this, there are instances where the banker may or even must break the duty of confidentiality. For example, if a bank manager is asked to give a reference for a customer so that the customer can open a credit account with someone, it is obvious that the customer impliedly consents to disclosure of details of his credit-worthiness. Sometimes the court will order a banker to disclose details of a customer's account, for example, in bankruptcy proceedings. If the banker finds that a customer is drawing cheques for an unlawful purpose, for example, to commit fraud, or in breach of trust, then he must disclose this fact to the appropriate authorities. Finally if a customer owes money to a banker by way of an overdrawn account and the banker wishes to recover the money, he must, of course, disclose the amount he is owed if the need arises to sue for it.

The last duty of the banker we must consider is the simple duty to collect cheques paid in by the customer. When a cheque is paid into a bank account, the bank is obliged to contact the paying bank on behalf of the customer and require payment. This is a self-evident duty and needs to be considered no further here.

15.6 PROTECTION OF THE PAYING BANKER

We have already seen that it is the duty of the paying banker to detect forgery of the drawer's signature on a cheque. However, if the customer has failed in his duty of care, the paying banker may nevertheless be protected against the effects of making an unauthorised payment on a forged cheque. It will be recalled that in *Greenwood v Martins Bank Ltd* (1933) (see 15.5) the bank was entitled to debit his customer's account because the customer had neglected to tell the bank that his wife had been forging his signature. This is an instance where the courts themselves develop a common law protection of a banker. There is also extensive protection available to a banker under statute.

The first statutory provision which we must consider is that protecting the paying banker against the risk of his making payment on a valid cheque to the wrong person. For example, in practice almost all cheques which are presented for payment are crossed. The paying banker, as we have seen, must make payment in accordance with any general or special crossing which might be on the cheque. S80, Bills of Exchange Act 1882 provides that the paying banker is protected against the misapplication of the proceeds of crossed cheques so long as he pays a cheque crossed generally to a banker and if crossed specially to the banker to whom it is crossed. So long as he makes the payment in good faith, without negligence and in accordance with the crossing.

An example of how this operates is given in the following scenario.

George draws a crossed cheque payable to Henry and hands it to Henry in payment of a debt. Ivan steals the cheque and forges Henry's indorsement in blank. Ivan then pays the cheque into his own bank which duly presents it to George's bank for payment. George's bank makes payment to Ivan's bank. In this situation, provided that George's bank made the payment in good faith and without negligence, it can debit George's account since the payment was certainly made in accordance with the crossing as it was made to a bank and not over the counter. If George had, however, notified the bank of the loss, then the result would be different since the payment out would not be without negligence. In this instance the bank would not be able to debit George's account.

Further protection is given to a paying bank against a risk of paying out on a cheque which bears a forged or unauthorised indorsement. The reason for such protection is that while it is eminently reasonable that a bank should know the signature of a customer, there is no way in which he could fairly be expected to recognise a forged indorsement, since an indorsement is almost invariably the signature of a person unknown to the bank. The basic rule is that payment on a cheque to a holder in due course discharges all liability on the cheque. By s60, Bills of Exchange Act 1882, a banker may pay on a cheque payable to order which bears an indorsement, knowing that even if the indorsement is forged or unauthorised he may still debit his customer's account provided that the payment was made in good faith and in the ordinary course of business. The phrase 'in the ordinary course of business' means in accordance with normal banking practice. It does not mean the same as without negligence which we have just been considering in relation to the rules on crossings under s80, Bills of Exchange Act 1882. The effects of s60, Bills of Exchange Act 1882, can be illustrated by the following example.

The ABC Bank pays cash over the counter on a crossed cheque to James who claims to be the indorsee of the cheque. The indorsement is in fact forged. In this situation the bank could not debit the drawer's account since the payment was not made in the ordinary course of business. The cheque was crossed and the payment of cash on a crossed cheque is not in accordance with normal banking practice. If the cheque had been uncrossed, the result would have been different so long as payment was made in good faith.

It will be noticed that section 60 applies only to forged or unauthorised indorsements. It doesnot apply where there is no indorsement. Before 1957, banks used to insist that all cheques paid into an account, even by the original payee, should be indorsed. It was estimated, however, that about 97% of all cheques issued were paid directly into a bank account by the payee. In other words, only some 3% were actually negotiated.

Thus the practice of banks in requiring the indorsement of all cheques was of little value and indeed was most time-consuming for both bank staff and their customers. For this reason legislation was recommended which would relieve all concerned of this onerous obligation, and in 1957 the Cheques Act was passed. By s1, Cheques Act 1957, not only is the banker freed from the need to check for an indorsement, he is also given relief where he makes payment on an indorsement which is irregular, say where the name of the payee and the signature of the indorser may not exactly correspond. In both cases, he is only protected so long as he makes a payment in good faith and in the ordinary course of business.

This can be illustrated by the following scenario.

Simon draws a cheque on the ABC Bank in favour of Thomas. The cheque is stolen from Thomas. The thief, instead of negotiating the cheque, opens a bank account at the XYZ Bank in Thomas's name. The XYZ Bank duly collects payment on the unindorsed cheque for their new customer whom they believe to be Thomas. So long as the ABC Bank made their payment out in good faith and in the ordinary course of business, they could debit Simon's account. It would not matter that the cheque was unindorsed because of the protection given by s1, Cheques Act 1957. Had the cheque borne a forged indorsement, then the ABC Bank could still debit Simon's account, but this would be because of the protection given by s60, Bills of Exchange Act 1882, which it will be recalled protects against forged or unauthorised indorsements.

15.7 PROTECTION OF THE COLLECTING BANKER

We turn now to the statutory protection which is available for the collecting banker. At common law, if a banker collected a cheque in circumstances where the customer for whom he had collected had no right to it where, for example, the cheque was stolen, the banker would be liable in the tort of conversion to the true owner. Obviously the collecting banker needs to be protected against such liability so long as he has himself acted properly and this protection is given by s4, Cheques Act 1957. This provides that a banker does not become liable to the true owner of the cheque merely because he collects payment on it provided he does so in good faith, without negligence, and for a customer. The good faith of the banker will rarely be in issue, and the customer is simply a person who has an account with the bank, even if that account was opened with the cheque which is in contention. Problems which have arisen in the cases have mainly been concerned with what constitutes negligence, which is determined by the standard of care used in current banking practice. A good example of this is provided by the case of:

AL Underwood Ltd v Bank of Liverpool and Martins (1924)

AL Underwood was the managing director of and majority shareholder in a small company AL Underwood Ltd. He received some cheques payable to the company which he indorsed and paid into his own private bank account. In an action to recover the money brought on behalf of the company, it was held that the bank had been negligent. The circumstances were such that a bank cashier of ordinary intelligence would have had some doubt as to the proprietory of Underwood's conduct in paying company cheques into a private bank account.

The effect of s4, Cheques Act 1957 can be illustrated by the following example.

Oliver finds a cheque in the street payable to 'H Smith'. He takes it to the ABC Bank where he opens an account in the name of H Smith and pays in the cheque. The ABC Bank subsequently collects the sum due on the cheque. At the time of opening the new account, the bank never asked for reference for Oliver (or H Smith). The true owner of the cheque has now discovered what has happened and brings proceedings against the ABC Bank in conversion. The true owner is very likely to succeed. While the ABC Bank may claim to have acted in good faith and for a customer, it certainly did not act without negligence. Whenever a bank opens an account for a new customer, it should ask for evidence of identity and also take up references of some kind. Since this was not done, the ABC Bank will be liable in conversion.

Finally in regard to protection of the collecting banker, we need to examine the situation where the collecting banker collects in circumstances where he is a holder in due course. Normally when a banker collects, he does so as his customer's agent. Thus if an account is in credit and the customer pays a cheque into his bank, the bank in collecting on that cheque is acting merely as the customer's agent. If the cheque is not duly paid, whether lack of funds or through it being stopped by the drawer, the bank will not suffer. However, in certain circumstances, the bank itself becomes, or is deemed to be, the holder in due course of a cheque on which it is collecting. These circumstances arise where the customer's account is overdrawn, or where the customer is allowed to draw against a cheque before it has been cleared.

For example, suppose a bank account is overdrawn in the sum of £200 and the customer pays in a cheque for £50. The overdraft is thereby diminished by £50 and the bank has effectively given value for the cheque. As such, it is treated as being the holder in due course of the cheque. Likewise if the bank account is standing at exactly zero and a cheque is paid in for £100, and the customer is then allowed to draw £20 in cash, the bank is treated as a holder in due course of that cheque insofar as it has given value for it; that is to say it is treated as a holder in due course for £20. The bank is not prevented from being a holder in due course by the fact that the cheque may not have been indorsed in its favour. By s2, Cheques Act 1957, a bank which gives value or has a lien on a cheque payable to order, has the same rights as it would have had if, upon delivery, the holder had indorsed it in blank. The advantages of the bank being treated as a holder in due course are twofold. Firstly it can itself sue anyone liable on the cheque if the cheque is dishonoured. Secondly, it is protected against any actions brought by previous holders of the cheque.

SUMMARY

A cheque is a bill of exchange drawn on a banker payable on demand. As such it is a very special type of bill of exchange. Unique to cheques are the rules governing crossings and the duties and protection of both banker and customer. It is essential that these are thoroughly understood.

SELF-TEST QUESTIONS

15.1 Define a cheque

15.2 How do cheques differ from other bills of exchange?

15.3 Distinguish between:
(a) a general crossing
(b) a special crossing
(c) not negotiable
(d) account payee or a/c payee

15.4 What duties does the customer of a bank owe to his banker?

15.5 What are the duties of the banker to his customer?

15.6 Why could the bank in *Greenwood v Martins Bank* (1933) debit its customer's account even though the customer's signature on the cheque was forged?

15.7 What protection is given to a paying bank which pays out on a cheque bearing a forged or unauthorised endorsement?

15.8 What protection is afforded to a collecting banker who collects for a customer who had no right to the cheque?

Answers on page 333

EXERCISES

Exercise 15.1

A drew a cheque on the X Bank to pay B. B crossed the cheque generally. It was stolen by C who used it to open an account at the Y Bank in the name of B. Y Bank presented his cheque for payment to the X Bank and received payment.
Advise B.

Exercise 15.2

1   What duties are owed to a customer by his balance in relation to cheques?
2   A was employed by B and Co. A informed B and Co that work had been carried out by C, a non-existent person. B and Co drew a cheque in favour of C. The cheque was obtained by A who indorsed the cheque in C's name. The cheque was presented by A to the X Bank, who gave value to A in good faith. The value of the cheque was paid to the X Bank by the Y Bank, B and Co's bankers.
Advise B and Co.

Answers on page 333

CHAPTER SIXTEEN

The concept of legal personality

Under English law not only may individuals enjoy legal rights and have legal obligations, so too can artificial legal persons. Such artificial legal persons are known as corporations. A corporation may be defined as an association of persons recognised by law as having an existence entirely independent from that of its individual members. There are two types of corporation. Firstly corporations sole where the members of the corporation exist successively, so that at any given time the corporation will consist of only one member. Examples are the Crown, and offices in the established church such as the Archbishop of Canterbury. Secondly there are corporations aggregate which comprise a number of members. The best known of these are limited liability companies.

16.1 CREATION OF CORPORATIONS

The earliest corporations were formed by means of Royal Charter and are known as chartered companies. Some of the earliest examples are the East India Company and the Hudsons Bay Company. The members of these early corporations did not have limited liability, being personally liable to the last pennies of their fortune for the debts of the corporation. The reason for the creation of such corporations was, initially, to give a monopoly to a trading enterprise in a particular area. Thus the Hudsons Bay Company was the only company which was permitted by law to trade in the Hudsons Bay area. Corporations are still formed by Royal Charter today but such as are formed in this way are usually of a charitable or quasi-charitable nature. A typical example is the Chartered Association of Certified Accountants.

In the early days of business enterprise trading was carried on by sole traders or partnerships. A partnership, as we shall see in Chapter 18, is the carrying on in business in common by two or more persons. There was no need for a bigger trading entity since large capital investment was not needed. However, when the Industrial Revolution got under way towards the mid-18th century there was a need for a large scale funding for enterprises such as the railway companies, the canal companies, the gas companies and the like. The need to raise capital from people who were not going to be the proprietors of the business gave the impetus to the creation of the limited liability company. At first such companies were formed by private Acts of Parliament being known as statutory companies. This was the second way in which corporations could be created. Obviously the creation of such a company was an expensive matter and few companies are created in this way today.

The third way in which a limited liability company may be created is by registration under the Companies Act 1985. Creation of a corporation in this way first became possible in the mid-18th century and some two million companies have so far been created in this way, of which over a million are now trading.

16.2 CONSEQUENCES OF INCORPORATION

Once a corporation has been formed it has a number of characteristics. These include:

1. It is a legal entity entirely distinct from its members. As such it can make contracts in its own name and can sue and be sued on those contracts.
2. A corporation also may be responsible vicariously for the acts of its employees (for this see further Chapter 19).
3. A corporation has perpetual succession. Even with a small company where the bulk of the shares are held by one person, the death of that person does not bring the company to an end. The continuance of a corporation is unaffected by changes of membership. This may be

illustrated by the saying 'the king is dead, long live the king'. As was said earlier the Crown is a corporation. Because it can only have one member at a time it is a corporation sole. Even though the king dies the corporation continues. The next in line of succession becomes the king upon the death of the previous king. The death of a king has no effect upon the continuance of the corporation.

4   A corporation may act in its own name. Its powers are limited to those conferred upon it by the documents which created it. A transaction which is beyond those powers is referred to as *'ultra vires'* (literally: 'beyond its powers') and if a registered company acts in this way a transaction entered into which is *ultra vires* may not be enforced by the company, though a third party dealing in good faith with the company may enforce the transaction so long as he was unaware that it was *ultra vires*. Perhaps it should be added that this does not apply to a chartered corporation, although the charter may be forfeited if the corporation acts in an unauthorised manner.

16.3 COMPANIES

A company is the usual name given to a corporation created by registration under the Companies Act 1985. The constitution of the company is set out in two documents, the memorandum of association and the articles of association. The memorandum contains the name of the company, its objects (ie what the company is formed to do and the powers which it enjoys for the attainment of that purpose), a statement that the liability of its members is limited if such is the case, and details of what share capital it may issue. The articles of association contain regulations governing the internal working of the company such as detailed rules regarding the directors and meetings. A copy of the memorandum and articles of association is lodged with the Registrar of Companies and may be inspected by any interested party.

A company is a corporation aggregate and as such may make contracts in its own name. The day-to-day running of the company is by a board of directors, who are elected by the members (the shareholders). Thus a company consists of two separate power groupings, the members acting together in general meeting, and the board of directors. The day-to-day running of the company, as has been said, is with the directors. The members in general meeting, however, have to approve important matters such as a change in the company's constitution or a decision to wind up the company.

Companies may be divided into three types, unlimited companies, companies limited by guarantee and companies limited by shares. An unlimited company is a registered company in which the members do not have limited liability. They are personally fully liable for all debts incurred by the company but not paid. In a company limited by guarantee, the members are guarantors rather than shareholders. They do not, when the company is incorporated, subscribe money to the company. Instead they give a guarantee that in the event of the company going into liquidation (and only in that event) they will pay a specified sum to the liquidator who has responsibility for winding up the company. The usual type of company which is limited by guarantee is a company which does not need a large initial amount of capital from its members, any capital needed being provided by means of subscriptions. Thus a Chamber of Commerce or a private school frequently adopts the form of a company limited by guarantee. By far the most common form of company is one limited by shares, where the members are liable up to the nominal value of their shares. Such a company may be registered either as a public or a private company. A public company is one which satisfies four criteria:

1   Its name indicates that it is a public limited company (plc).
2   It must have a specified minimum amount of share capital (at present the nominal value of its issued share capital must be at least £50,000).
3   Its memorandum must state that it is formed as a public company.
4   The Registrar of Companies must have issued a certificate of incorporation stating that it has been formed as a public company.

All companies which are not public companies are private. Less than 5% of all registered companies are public, though they do include all the biggest companies whose shares are dealt with on the Stock Exchange.

SUMMARY

In this chapter we have briefly looked at the concept of legal personality. The importance of having an understanding of this is that when you come to study company law at Level 2 you will need to understand the meaning of legal personality. At the end of Chapter 18 there is a comparison between partnerships and companies. At this stage it is important that you understand the meaning of a corporation aggregate and the essential characteristics of a corporation.

Legal personality is the right to sue and be sued in the courts. While not every human being enjoys full legal personality (eg infants, drunks, persons under a mental disability) artificial persons (corporations) may enjoy legal personality even though they are obviously not humans. It is important that this is understood before going on to study agency and partnerships.

SELF-TEST QUESTIONS

16.1 What are the characteristics of a corporation?

16.2 What is the meaning and effect of an ultra vires transaction entered into by a corporation?

16.3 List the types of company

16.4 What are the criteria for a public company?

Answers on page 336

EXERCISES

Exercise 16.1

'A corporation may be defined as a legal entity or artificial person' Explain what is meant by this statement and state the main features of artificial personality.

Answers on page 336

242 LAW

Agency

An agent is a person who is authorised to act for another (the principal) in the making of contracts and in the creation of other legal relationships with third parties. Instead of negotiating and forming the contract himself, the principal may give his agent the power to act on his behalf. If the agent acts within the authorisation he has been given, the law will treat the resulting contract as if it had been made by the principal himself.

The agent, in other words, is the channel through whom the principal operates; he is an extension of the principal's powers and when the principal enters a contract through the agent he has the same rights and liabilities as if he had entered the contract himself. The agent is not a party to the transaction. It is directly between the principal and the third party.

Agency is one of the most important modern commercial relationships. For example, one of the basic features of a partnership is that each partner is an agent for the others and for the firm. In company law, although the company is in the eyes of the law a distinct person, being an artificial entity it can act only through human agents. If, for example, a trading company is formed, it will have to make its selling and purchasing contracts through its employees as its agents. The purchasing manager will negotiate a contract between his company and the supplier. The manager as agent will have no rights or duties under this contract.

In this chapter we will look at the ways an agency may be created; at the powers and duties of the agent and the principal; at the effects of agency; and at the ways in which an agency may be ended.

17.1 CREATION OF AGENCY

17.1.1 Introduction

An agency can be created in writing, or orally or simply by the way in which the parties conduct themselves. It does not have to be created by contract, although if it is, the ordinary rules governing simple contracts will apply. If, however, an agent is appointed to execute a deed he must himself be appointed by deed unless he signs the deed with the principal's authority and in the principal's presence.

To be classed as an agent, a person must be able to affect his principal's legal position in relation to third parties. Thus to appoint someone to represent you at, for example, a social function will not be to appoint him your agent. He will have no power to affect your legal position. If, on the other hand, a mother sends her child to the shop to buy a loaf of bread, that child will be an agent. He has the power to alter his mother's position in relation to the shop—he can make a contract on her behalf to buy the goods.

As the contract negotiated by the agent is between his principal and the third party, it follows that it is the principal who must have the contractual capacity to enter the transaction. The agent is merely an extension of the principal's authority. It is as if the principal himself was contracting.

Thus the agent need not have contractual capacity. To be an agent, he merely has to have the ability to consent. So a child can be an agent as long as he has the ability to consent, whereas a mentally disordered person cannot be.

The agent's acts will bind the principal only if the agent acts within the scope of the authority granted him by the principal. For example, if P authorises A to sell P's car, P will not be bound if A makes a contract to sell P's house. A's authority is to sell the car, and P will not be bound if A acts outside this authority.

The scope of the agent's authority (ie the acts by which he can bind his principal) can be discovered by looking at the ways in which the agency was created.

Agency can be created:

1. By agreement, whether contractual or not.
2. By ratification of unauthorised acts by the principal.
3. By estoppel, where the principal makes it appear the agent has authority.
4. By operation of law.

17.1.2 Agency created by agreement

BY CONTRACT

If an agency is created by contract, all the requirements for a valid simple contract must be present. No particular form is required unless the agent is appointed to execute a deed in which case the agency itself must be created by deed.

OTHER THAN BY CONTRACT

If there is no contract, as when, for example, the agent lacks capacity or when he is willing to act without payment, all that has to be shown is that the agent has been expressly appointed by the principal and that the agent has consented to act in this capacity.

AGENCY CREATED BY AGREEMENT GIVES THE AGENT ACTUAL AUTHORITY

The scope of the agent's authority will be discovered by interpreting the words of the contract or agreement. If, on a construction of the agreement, the agent has the power to bind the principal in a particular way, then, even though the third party with whom the agent deals does not know of the authority, both he and the principal will be bound by the agent's act.

IMPLIED AUTHORITY

In looking at the terms of the agent's appointment, it may be discovered that his authority is ambiguous or that he has been given the power to exercise a discretion. For example, if the agent is authorised by the principal to 'obtain a car for principal's use', the agent does not know whether he is supposed to buy a car or merely hire one.

In these circumstances, the court will *imply* an authority into the agreement to enable the agent to carry out his express duties. This does not extend the agent's powers. It merely enables him to fulfil them. For example in the case of:

Comber v Anderson (1808)

A merchant ordered his agent to insure a cargo of corn which was to be transported by sea. No details were given as to the type of policy to be effected nor as to the insurance company which was to be used. The agent insured the cargo under a policy which excluded liability for loss if the ship was stranded. He chose this policy instead of others which did not contain such an exclusion clause. The ship was stranded, the cargo lost, and the merchant found himself unable to claim under the policy. He therefore sued his agent, claiming that, in executing the policy the agent had acted outside the scope of his authority. The court held that the agent had been given a discretion and therefore had implied authority to choose the policy he thought best. He had acted in good faith and was therefore not liable to his principal.

USUAL AUTHORITY

If an agent is appointed in a particular trade or business, he will have the authority to do what is usual in that trade or business. In other words, if the agent belongs to a recognised category (eg auctioneer, estate agent, solicitor, managing director of a company, partner and company secretary) he will have the power to bind his principal by contracts which such agents can normally negotiate, even though the principal has instructed him not to act in this way.

The workings of usual authority are shown in:

***Watteau* v *Fenwick* (1893)**

The manager (A) of a public house was told by the owner, his principal (P), that he was not to buy cigars on credit for the business. A disobeyed these instructions and bought cigars for the business on credit from T, who was unaware of the limits on A's authority. It was held that P was liable on the contract with T. This was the kind of transaction that managers of public houses usually could undertake. P's instructions limiting A's authority could not relieve P of liability.

If, however, the third party knows, or should know, of the restrictions on an agent's authority, he will not be able to enforce a contract entered into by the agent in breach of his instructions. Thus in the case of:

***Daunn* v *Simmins* (1879)**

The manager of a tied public house (ie one which sold alcohol obtained only from certain suppliers) was authorised to buy spirits only from X. The manager, disobeying these instructions, bought spirits from the plaintiff.

The court held that the principal was not liable to the plaintiff. As a person involved in the trade, the plaintiff should have known that managers of tied public houses could buy their alcohol only from specified persons. He also knew that he was not one of these authorised sources.

Only recognised classes of agent have usual authority. These classes were listed above. So, for example, solicitors have such authority, as was shown in:

***Waugh and Others* v *HB Clifford & Sons Ltd* (1982)**

The plaintiffs bought houses built by the defendants. The houses had several faults and the plaintiffs sued for breach of contract and negligence. The defendants initially agreed to compromise (settle) the claim but later changed their minds and wrote to their solicitors withdrawing their authority to compromise. The notice of withdrawal was mislaid by the solicitors' secretarial staff and the solicitor went ahead with the compromise. The plaintiffs asked the court for an order of specific performance against the defendants, requiring them to carry out the terms of the compromise. The defendants argued that they were not bound as they had withdrawn their solicitors' authority to compromise.

The Court of Appeal held that the plaintiffs should succeed. The defendants were bound by the compromise. As between a solicitor and his client, the solicitor has what is in effect usual authority to compromise on action without reference to his client. Also, as between themselves, solicitors have authority to agree to a compromise of an action without the opposing litigant having to obtain proof of the necessary authority.

17.1.3 Agency created by ratification

If an agent makes a contract on his principal's behalf, but in doing so acts without authority or in excess of the authority he has been given, the principal will not be bound. If, however, the principal likes the contract the agent has made, he may adopt the transaction by ratifying it. The effect of such ratification is that it gives the agent authority in arrears. It is as if the agent had been authorised immediately before he made the contract.

EXAMPLE 1

P appoints A to sell P's car. A sees a car he thinks P would like and so, claiming to be acting with P's authority, A buys the vehicle. A has no authority to do so (his actual authority was to sell P's car) so P is not bound by this contract. He does not have to take the car. If, however, P likes the contract A has made, he may ratify the unauthorised act. The effect of ratification is that it is as if A had been authorised all along to buy the vehicle.

Ratification may be made orally or in writing or it may be implied from the parties' conduct. For example, if A, without authority, buys goods from P and P uses these goods, he will be said to have ratified the unauthorised purchase, and will become liable to pay for them.

The principal, however, must have the choice whether to ratify or not. If he has no choice but to accept the unauthorised act he will not be held to have ratified. This is shown in the case of:

Forman & Co. v The Liddesdale (1900)

A shipowner told his captain to have certain damage to his ship repaired. The captain instructed a repairer to carry out the necessary work and also told him to renovate the ship. The repairer carried out all this work even though he knew that the captain's authority was limited. The shipowner recovered his ship and sold it.

The repairer brought this action against the shipowner, claiming the cost of all the work undertaken on the grounds that, by recovering and selling the ship, the shipowner had ratified the contract made by the agent. The Judicial Committee of the Privy Council held that the shipowner's conduct did not amount to ratification. He had no choice but to accept the ship. By taking it 'and making the best he could of it', he could not be said to be ratifying. He could not be expected to leave it with the repairers.

For ratification to be effective, certain conditions must be satisfied:

THE PRINCIPAL MUST EXIST AT THE TIME THE AGENT MADE THE CONTRACT

This rule relates to companies which are in the process of being formed. Until a company is incorporated it is not in existence. So a company cannot ratify a contract made by its promoters on its behalf before it is incorporated. The reason for this is that ratification is retrospective, it relates back to the time of the unauthorised act. In the case of a pre-incorporation contract, the company has not come into existence at the time of making the contract and is therefore unable to act as principal.

This rule is illustrated in:

Kelner v Baxter (1866)

The promoters of a hotel company which was about to be formed bought wine for the company from K. The contract was signed by the promoters on behalf of the company. The wine was delivered, but when the hotel company was incorporated it failed before K had been paid. He sued the promoters claiming that they were personally liable.

The court held that K should succeed. Where a contract is signed by a person professing to sign as agent, but who has no principal existing at the time, that contract would be inoperative unless the one who signed was personally bound. The directors of the proposed company had purported to ratify the contract but this was held to be a nullity as the company did not exist at the time the contract was made.

Thus a company cannot ratify pre-incorporation contracts made on its behalf. By s9(2) European Communities Act 1972 (now s35 Companies Act 1985) an agent who is a party to such a contract will be personally liable, whether he signs the contract in his own name or in the name of the proposed company.

THE PRINCIPAL MUST BE NAMED OR BE ASCERTAINABLE AT THE TIME OF THE ACT

In other words, the principal must either be known, or must be capable of identification, at the time of the unauthorised act. The agent must claim to be acting on behalf of a principal even though he is not. The principal's power to ratify depends, not on what the agent actually intended but rather upon what the third party thought the position was. If the third party believes that the agent is acting for himself, the principal will not be able to ratify. This is shown in:

Keighley Maxstead & Co v Durant (1901)

A was authorised to buy wheat on the joint account of himself and the principal. He was limited as to the maximum price he could pay. A made a contract to buy wheat at a price in excess of the limit. Although he made the contract on behalf of himself and the principal he did not disclose this fact to the third party. The third party, therefore, thought that he was dealing with A alone.

By paying more than he was authorised, A had acted in excess of his authority. The principal later ratified the unauthorised act but failed to honour the contract. The seller of the wheat sued the principal in breach of contract. The court held that the principal was not liable. As the agent had not disclosed that he was acting as agent at the time he purported to make the contract, the principal could not later ratify.

Compare this case with:

Re Tiedemann and Ledermann Frères (1889)

A sold wheat on the principal's behalf. Later, the price of wheat started going up so A, still claiming to be acting for the principal, re-purchased the wheat and sold it to another person at a profit. Although he had acted in the principal's name, A intended the whole transaction to be for his own benefit and to his own account. He had used the principal's name for financial reasons.

When the third party discovered the truth, he tried to avoid the contract claiming that he had entered the contract following A's misrepresentation. The principal then purported to ratify the contract.

The court held that the principal could ratify the contract and therefore the third party was bound by the contract made by A purportedly on the principal's behalf.

THE PRINCIPAL MUST BE AWARE OF ALL THE MATERIAL FACTS

Before he can ratify, the principal must either be aware of all the details of the contract or be taken to accept the contract whatever it involves; in effect, if he ratifies regardless of what the agent has done.

THE PRINCIPAL MUST HAVE CAPACITY AT THE TIME THE AGENT ACTED

In other words, the principal has to be qualified in law to act in the way the agent acted at the time the agent did the unauthorised act. For example, in:

Boston Deep Sea Fishing and Ice Co. v Farnham (1957)

A trawler owned by a French company, P, was in an English port at the time of the German occupation of France in 1940. An English company, A, which had previously acted as P's agent in the course of its business carried on trade using P's trawler, and acting in P's name even though it had not been authorised to do so.

A was assessed as owing tax on its profits of the trade with P's trawler under the Income Tax Act 1918. By this Act, it would only be liable if it were P's 'authorised agent carrying on a regular agency'.

The court held that the only way A could be so authorised would be if P ratified the contract after the war. This ratification, however, would be impossible because, at the time of A's 'agency' P was an alien enemy and therefore could not be a principal since it could not have acted for itself.

THE UNAUTHORISED ACT MUST BE CAPABLE OF BEING RATIFIED

The principal cannot ratify an act which is void or unlawful. Therefore, if the agent, for example, forges the principal's signature, the principal cannot ratify this act.

THE PRINCIPAL MUST RATIFY IN TIME

If the third party is aware that the agent lacks authority he may put a time limit on the principal's ratification. In this case, the principal must ratify within that time. If no time is fixed, the principal must ratify within a reasonable time. What is a reasonable time is a question of fact, depending, for example, on the nature of the goods or services involved.

A principal will also be unable to ratify if, in the meantime, a third party has obtained an interest in the subject matter of the contract. This occurred in:

Bird v Brown (1850)

In this case, the agent, acting without authority for the seller of some goods, purported to stop the goods in transit to a person who had bought them. The buyer was bankrupt and the trustees who were administering his estate then made a formal demand for the goods to be handed over by the captains of the ships in which the goods were being transported. The captains refused and the goods were instead delivered to the seller's agent. The buyer's trustees in bankruptcy made a further demand for the goods from the agent. The demand was again refused. Later the seller ratified his agent's unauthorised stoppage in transit.

The court held that the buyer's trustees had established their right to the goods when they made their formal demand. This had occurred before the attempted ratification and therefore the ratification had been made too late. The goods had to be delivered to the buyer's trustees-in-bankruptcy.

THE PRINCIPAL MUST RATIFY THE WHOLE TRANSACTION

The principal has to ratify all the contract or not ratify at all, he cannot choose to ratify part of the transaction and reject the rest.

THE EFFECTS OF RATIFICATION

As we said earlier, ratification is retrospective in effect. In other words, when the principal ratifies an agent's unauthorised act, it is as if the act had been authorised immediately before it was carried out. So the principal, the agent and the third party have the same rights, duties, and liabilities as if the act had been done with the prior authorisation of the principal.

This is shown in:

Bolton Partners v Lambert (1889)

A was a director of Bolton Partners. On December 8, a third party made an offer to take a lease from Bolton Partners and, on December 13, A accepted this offer on behalf of Bolton, although he had no authority to do so. On January 13, the third party withdrew his offer but later Bolton partners ratified A's unauthorised act.

The court held that Bolton Partners (the principal) could enforce the contract against the third party. When A's act was ratified, it was as if he had been authorised all along to accept this offer. If was as if the contract had been made on December 13 and, therefore, the third party's attempt to withdraw had been too late.

Ratification does not, in effect, put the third party in any worse position than he originally believed. Ratification is possible only where the agent claims to be acting on the principal's behalf and in the principal's name so the third party believes that he is getting a contract with the principal. When the principal ratifies what was, in fact, an unauthorised act, the third party is being put in the position he thought he was in in the first place.

If the principal chooses not to ratify, the third party will have a right of action against the 'agent' in breach of warranty of authority.

17.1.4 Agency created by estoppel

MEANING OF AGENCY BY ESTOPPEL

Agency by estoppel arises when one person, P, has, by his words or conduct, allowed another, A, to appear to a third party or to the world at large, to be his agent. If the third party, relying on this appearance, contracts with A as P's agent, P will be estopped from denying A's authority. In other words, P will be bound by the transaction entered into by A even though P had never intended to give A any authority whatsoever.

Agency by estoppel, therefore, is created by the impression given to the third party by the principal as to the powers of the agent. It is an authority which appears to, but which does not actually, exist.

Such an authority may arise, for example, where a person employed by P as an agent is dismissed. Any people who have dealt with this person as P's agent before the dismissal will be entitled to believe that he is still acting in this capacity until they are informed otherwise. P has given his former employee the appearance of authority and if, relying on this appearance, customers deal with P through the ex-employee, P will be bound by the contract thus made.

For example, in:

Spiro v Lintern (1973)

The defendant, who wanted to sell his house, told his wife that she could find prospective purchasers for the property but did not authorise her to enter a contract of sale. The wife found a prospective purchaser (the plaintiff) and, acting without authority, made a contract to sell the house to him. The defendant, aware of what his wife had done but not informing the plaintiff of her lack of authority, allowed the plaintiff to carry out renovations in the house and to have work done in the garden. The defendant then refused to go through with the sale on the grounds that his wife had not had authority to sell the property in the first place. The plaintiff sued for specific performance of the contract.

The court held that the plaintiff should succeed. The defendant had known that the plaintiff was acting on the mistaken assumption that the defendant's wife had authority to sell and, as he had done nothing to correct this belief, he was estopped from denying the authority. He was bound by the contract.

THERE MUST BE A HOLDING-OUT BY THE PRINCIPAL

For apparent authority to arise, the principal must, by his words or conduct, hold out the agent as having his authority to act in a particular way.

This holding-out must be clear and unequivocal. It must make it appear to the third party or to the world at large that the agent has the power to act in this way.

As it is the principal who is estopped, it is he, and not the agent, who must have made the representation. For example:

Farquharson Bros v King and Co (1902)

The plaintiffs employed a clerk to oversee the distribution of timber which they had sold. The clerk had no authority to sell timber himself. His job was merely to sign delivery orders authorising the release of the wood. The clerk, however, fraudulently sold some timber to the defendants and, when the plaintiffs demanded the return of the goods, the defendants claimed that the plaintiffs were estopped from denying the clerk's authority to sell. The court held that the plaintiffs should succeed. They could recover the timber. They had not held out the clerk as having authority. The holding out, in fact, had been done by the clerk himself. Merely to put someone in a position where he could commit fraud was not sufficient to raise an estoppel. There had to be a positive holding-out that someone had authority to act and no such holding-out had occurred here.

THE REPRESENTATION HAS TO BE MADE TO THE PERSON WHO RELIES ON IT

To be able to plead estoppel, a person has to show that the principal's representation was made either to him specifically or to the world at large (by, for example, the principal giving the agent documents of title to goods or by giving him documents which indicate that the agent has the power to deal in a certain way).

THERE MUST BE RELIANCE ON THE REPRESENTATION

The third party must show that he relied on the representation of authority in entering the contract. So, if the third party knows of the lack of authority, or if he ought to have known, he cannot rely on the estoppel and the principal will not be bound.

SCOPE OF AUTHORITY WHEN AGENCY IS CREATED BY ESTOPPEL

Agency created by estoppel gives rise to the appearance of authority. It is authority which apparently exists because of the principal's words or conduct. The scope of this apparent authority depends on the way in which the agent is held out. He has the power to do things the principal has made it appear he can do. For example:

Dodsley v Varley (1840)

The defendant's (P) agent occasionally employed a sub-agent to buy wool on P's behalf. As we will see, an agent generally has no power to appoint sub-agents so the sub-agent had no authority. Nevertheless, P ratified all the purchases made by the sub-agent from the defendant (T). In June, P told the sub-agent that he was not to make any further purchases on P's behalf. In July, the sub-agent made further purchases from T.

P refused to accept and pay for these purchases. The court held, however, that P was bound. The sub-agent had apparent authority to act in this way. By ratifying all his previous purchases from T, P had held out the sub-agent as having the power to contract in his (P's) name and, even though he had dismissed the sub-agent, P had not told T that the power no longer existed. P was therefore estopped from denying the sub-agent's authority to bind him in contract.

17.1.5 Agency created by operation of law

This most often arises when a sudden, urgent necessity has arisen and the agent had to take on extra powers in order to protect his principal's interests. The emergency which gives rise to the exercise of these powers must be unforeseen and must carry with it a sudden risk to the property or other interests of the person on whose behalf the acts are performed.

Thus captains of ships whose cargo is in danger of perishing may exercise an agency of necessity and sell the cargo before it deteriorates any further. The action, however, must be reasonably necessary in the circumstances, there must be no possibility of communication with the principal and the action must be taken in good faith and for the benefit of all interested parties. With improved communications this agency will be less common nowadays.

An agency of necessity created by operation of law may also arise if a carrier of goods is faced with an emergency relating to the goods. For example:

Great Northern Railway v Swaffield (1874)

The plaintiff railway company was delivering a horse but for various reasons (none of which were the railway's fault) on arrival at its destination the horse was not collected by the consignee. There was nowhere on the railway premises to keep the horse so the plaintiffs had it stabled in T's stables. The defendants, the horse's owners, refused to pay the stabling costs. The court held that the railway had an agency of necessity. Had they not acted as they did the horse would have died. The horse's owners (the principal) were therefore liable to pay the costs of stabling the animal.

In an agency of necessity, however, there must be a pre-existing contract between the principal and the agent. A person who, for example, finds an animal wandering the streets and takes care of the animal to avoid it being harmed or falling ill will be classed as a volunteer and will not be able to recover his expenses. He cannot claim that he was an agent of necessity.

17.2 DUTIES OF AN AGENT

17.2.1 Introduction

If an agency is created by agreement, his duties may be expressed in the agreement itself. If, however, there are no terms, or if the agreement does not cover a situation that has arisen, the obligations will be regulated by the common law, which imposes certain duties on the agent. These duties are as follows:

17.2.2 To perform what he has contracted to perform

The agent must carry out the instructions of his principal so long as they are legal and are not regarded as void by common law or statute. So, for example, if the principal employs his agent to place a bet and the agent fails to do so, he will not be liable as the bet is illegal and void.

17.2.3 To act with care and skill

As well as performing what he has contracted to perform, an agent must carry out his duties with care and skill. This duty arises whether the agent is being paid (contractual agency) or not (gratuitous agency). If the agent claims to be a particular type of agent he must show the appropriate skill that would normally be shown by such an agent. So, for exmple, if he claims to be an estate agent, he must show the degree of skill an estate agent would normally have. This requirement applies whether the agency is contractual or gratuitous.

17.2.4 To perform his duties in person

In other words, an agent must not delegate his duties to another. This is expressed in the Latin phrase '*delegatus non potest delegare*' (a delegate cannot delegate). The reason for this rule is that the principal, by appointing an agent, has put his trust in the personality and skill of that person. This is especially so if the authority granted entails the agent exercising a discretion or if it is coupled with a confidence.

DELEGATION WILL BE ALLOWED IN CERTAIN CIRCUMSTANCES

An agent may delegate, however, if:

1. The principal authorises him to do so either initially or by ratification (see *Dodsley* v *Varley* (17.1.4)).
2. The job delegated is purely administrative (eg typing, filing).

3 The delegation is authorised by custom.
4 The delegation arises by necessary implication as when, for example, a company or a bank is appointed agent. The agent in this case will have to delegate its functions to an individual.
5 There is a sudden emergency such as the appointed agent being taken ill.

In all other cases, delegation is not allowed.

THE EFFECTS OF DELEGATION

If an agent delegates without authority, the principal is not bound by the sub-agent's acts; the agent may be liable in damages for wrongful execution of his duty; and neither the agent nor the sub-agent can claim indemnity or remuneration for the work done by the sub-agent.

If, however, the delegation is allowed, and the agent has a power to appoint a sub-agent either in substitution for or in addition to himself, then there will be privity of contract between the principal and the sub-agent ie the principal can sue the sub-agent for failure to carry out his contractual duty and the sub-agent can sue the principal for his remuneration.

If, however, the sub-agent is appointed merely to assist the agent and not as a substitute for or in addition to him then there will be no privity between the principal and sub-agent. The sub-agent will be liable to the principal only if he performs his duties negligently or in breach of his fiduciary duty.

17.2.5 Not to deny principal's title to money or property

An agent cannot deny his principal's title to any money or property which he is holding for the principal. So, for example, an agent holding goods for his principal must not, without authority, hand over these goods to a third party who claims to have bought them from the principal. If the agent does hand them over without authority and is sued by his principal for breach of the contract of agency he cannot use the third party's claim as a defence to the action.

If the agent is sued by the third party, he can claim indemnification of his costs from the principal.

17.2.6 To act in good faith

An agent is in a fiduciary relationship with his principal and must therefore act in good faith and not allow there to be any conflict between his interests and those of his principal.

Thus, the agent must make full disclosure of any personal interest he has in the subject matter of the agency and, if his interest conflicts or is likely to conflict with his duty, he must inform the principal of all the material facts.

For example, if P appoints A to buy P a house, A cannot sell P a house which A already owns unless he informs P of his ownership, and P consents to the purchase. In the same way, if A is appointed to sell P's house A cannot buy it himself without making full disclosure and obtaining P's consent. In both these cases there is a conflict of duty and interest.

AN AGENT MUST NOT TAKE A BRIBE

As part of his duty to act in good faith, an agent must not take a bribe from the third party. If such a bribe is taken:

1 The agent is liable to be prosecuted under the Prevention of Corruption Acts 1889–1916.
2 The agent is not entitled to pay or indemnity and must return any payment he has received from the principal.
3 The agent may be instantly dismissed, even though the principal suffered no loss because of the bribe.
4 The principal may repudiate any contract made because the agent was bribed.
5 The principal may recover the bribe from the agent.
6 The principal may sue both the agent and the third party if he has suffered any loss. The loss is

usually the amount of the bribe. Once the principal has recovered his loss, however, he cannot then sue the other party and thus make a profit. So, for example, if the principal has recovered the bribe from the agent, and the amount of the bribe is, in effect, the amount the principal has lost, he cannot then sue the third party for extra damages if such damages would result in the principal making a profit. This was decided in the case of *Mahesan v Malaysia Government Officers' Co-operative Housing Society Ltd* (1978) (the facts of which need not concern us).

AN AGENT MUST NOT MAKE A SECRET PROFIT

A bribe is an inducement given to the agent by the third party to, for example, persuade the agent to bind the principal in contract with the third party.

A secret profit, however, is a profit made by the agent without the third party knowing anything about it. If the agent has not been fraudulent in making a secret profit, he must account for this to his principal, but he will nevertheless be entitled to claim his remuneration or commission. This was illustrated in the case of:

Hippisley v Knee Bros (1905)

Auctioneers were appointed to sell the principal's goods. Amongst other things, the principal agreed to pay the auctioneers' advertising and printing expenses as well as commission on the sale. The auctioneers received the normal 10% discount on the costs of printing but, believing that they were entitled to keep this discount as an ordinary perquisite, they charged the principal the full cost. When the principal discovered this, he claimed the discount as a secret profit and refused to pay the defendants their commission.

The Court of Appeal held that the auctioneers had to account for the 10% discount but, as they had acted honestly and had not committed fraud on the plaintiff, they were entitled to their commission.

If, of course, in making a secret profit, the agent is acting fraudulently and knows that he is not entitled to this money, he will not be able to claim his commission from the principal.

17.2.7 To account to the principal for all sums received

Even if the transaction giving rise to the payment is illegal and void, the agent must account for the money to his principal. So, for example, if an agent collects the principal's winnings on a bet, which is illegal and void, he must account to the principal for these winnings. The agent must also keep the principal's property distinct from his own. If he does not do so, anything the agent cannot positively prove to be his own will be presumed to be the principal's.

17.3 RIGHTS OF AN AGENT

17.3.1 A right to indemnity

An agent who has incurred liability or who has paid out his own money in the performance of his duties is entitled to recover this from the principal by way of indemnity. The agent will not be entitled to claim indemnity, however, where he is in breach of his duties or if the loss in question is caused by his own fault.

17.3.2 A right to remuneration

An agent will have a right to be paid if there is an express or implied agreement to that effect with the principal. The amount of payment depends on the terms of the agreement or on any trade usage. In the absence of either of these, the agent will be entitled to claim a reasonable sum.

If the agent is to be paid on commission (ie when he has carried out his duties) he will be entitled to claim the remuneration if the event on which he was to be paid had occurred and if he was the effective cause of this occurrence.

Whether the event on which the agent was to be paid has occurred depends on the wording of the contract. For example, if commission is to be payable on the agent 'finding a purchaser' for the principal's property he will be entitled to claim payment only when a purchaser is found. So, if he is unsuccessful in finding such a person he will not be entitled to commission however much work he has put into the search. If the contract provides that commission is payable 'on completion of sale' the agent will not be entitled to commission if no sale is completed for whatever reason. The event on which he was to be paid has not occurred.

Compare the following cases:

Luxor (Eastbourne) Ltd v *Cooper* (1941)

An estate agent was employed to find purchasers for the principal's cinemas. Commission was payable 'on completion of sale'. The agent introduced a purchaser who was willing to buy but the principal refused to go through with the sale. As there was no 'completion of sale' the agent was not entitled to his commission, but he asked the court to imply a term into the contract that the principal would not, without good cause, act in such a way as to prevent the agent earning his commission. If the court would imply such a clause, the agent claimed damages for its breach.

The House of Lords, however, refused to imply such a term into the contract of agency. When a person is selling property through an estate agent, it is usual for him to put this property on the books of several agents and to make a contract to pay each 'on completion of sale'. It would be against commonsense and ordinary business understanding to say that, when one of these agents found a purchaser for the property, the principal would be liable to pay damages to all the others because he had prevented them from earning their commission.

Conversely in:

Alpha Trading v *Dunnshaw-Patten Ltd* (1981)

An agent was to be paid commission on completion of sale. He introduced a purchaser to the principal who entered into a contract with this purchaser. The principal, however, failed to carry out the contract and had to pay damages to the purchaser. The principal also refused to pay the agent his commission. The agent sued.

The Court of Appeal held that the agent was not entitled to his commission (the sale had not been completed) but that he was entitled to damages for breach of a term which the court implied into the contract that, once the principal had entered into a contract with the third party introduced by the agent, he would not act unreasonably and thus deny the agent his commission.

In other words, once the principal has legally bound himself to the third party, if he breaks that contract and incurs liability to the third party, he will also be liable to the agent.

In Luxor, no contract between principal and third party was made, so the principal could refuse to go through with the sale without incurring any liability to the agent. Once he has made a contract with the third party, however, then business efficacy requires that, if the principal breaks this contract for no good reason, he must be liable to the agent for denying him the right to earn commission.

To be able to claim his commission, the agent must also show that he was the effective cause of the event occurring, even if only indirectly.

For example:

Green v *Bartlett* (1863)

An agent, employed to sell the principal's property at an auction, failed to do so. A person who was present at the auction, however, obtained the principal's name and address from the agent and later made a contract to buy the property directly with the principal. The principal refused to pay the agent his commission but the court held that the agent was entitled to payment. He was the cause of the principal being able to sell the property, albeit indirectly, in that he was the one who gave the purchaser details about the principal. The immediate effect of this was to gain for the principal the transaction required.

In summary, the stage at which the agent can claim his remuneration depends on the terms of the contract. It is only by ensuring that the contract covers the events which may occur that the agent can effectively protect himself against the principal acting in such a way as to deny the agent the right to payment even though the agent has done all that he can to perform his obligations.

17.3.3 A right of lien

A lien is a right to retain the property of another until that person pays the money he owes. In relation to agency, if the principal does not pay what he owes the agent, whether by way of indemnity or remuneration, the agent can retain those goods of the principal which are in the agent's possession until the principal has satisfied his claim.

TYPES OF LIEN

A lien may be either general or particular.

A general lien is a right to hold the principal's property until he has paid all that he owes the agent not just for the transaction connected with the goods but for all other transactions. For example, A sells P's cars by auction and P has not paid A his commission for some previous sales. P then delivers another car to A to be sold. If A holds on to this car until P owes all that is owing he will be exercising a general lien.

You will see that general liens give the agent an advantage over the principal's other creditors so the courts do not like them. They are allowed to only certain categories of agent such as solicitors, bankers and stockbrokers.

A particular lien is a retention of the goods which are the subject matter of the transaction for which the agent is owed money. For example, A sells cars for P, commission payable 'on completion of sale'. A sells a car but P does not pay his commission. A may hold on to this car until P pays. He is holding the actual goods for which P owes him money.

Any agent may exercise a particular lien.

REQUIREMENTS FOR LIEN

To exercise a lien:

1. The agent must have lawful possession of the goods over which he is exercising the right. If the agent obtains the goods by fraud from the principal or from a warehouse where they are being stored, he cannot exercise a lien over them.
2. The agent must have obtained possession in his capacity as agent and not otherwise. For example, a bank cannot exercise a lien over deeds which have been left with it for safe keeping.
3. There must be no express or implied agreement between the principal and the agent which is inconsistent with the exercise of a lien. No lien may be exercised, for example, if the contract expressly states that this right is not available to the agent.

LIEN IS LOST

1. If the principal discharges his obligations to the agent.
2. If the agent freely waives his right of lien by, for example, accepting security from the principal for the amount owing.
3. If the agent freely parts with possession of the goods or property.
4. If the agent changes the character of his possession. For example in:

Barratt v Gough-Thomas (1951)

A solicitor, acting for the principal, was exercising a lien over the title deeds to the principal's land. The principal mortgaged the land to a third party, for whom the solicitor also acted. The solicitor retained the deeds but the Court of Appeal held that, as soon as the mortgage was executed the solicitor held the deeds for the third party. Thus the character of the solicitor's possession had changed and the solicitor lost his lien.

If the principal obtains possession of the property from the agent by fraud, the lien is not ended. The agent can recover the property. Furthermore, as long as the lien attached before the principal deals with the property, and the agent does not assent to the transaction, the lien will continue even though the principal has sold the property to another person.

So, for example, if A is exercising a lien over P's goods for money that P owes A, the fact that P sells the goods to another does not affect A's rights. He can retain the property until he is paid what he is owed.

17.4 EFFECTS OF AGENCY

17.4.1 Where the agent acts for a disclosed principal

As we said earlier, an agent acting for a disclosed principal drops out of the transaction. The contract is between the principal and the third party with whom the agent has made the deal. The principal can sue and be sued by the third party.

This, of course, assumes that the agent has acted within his authority, whether express, implied, usual or apparent, or that, if the agent had no authority, the principal has ratified the unauthorised transaction. If, however, the agent executes a deed on the principal's behalf, the principal will have no rights on the deed unless he is described in the document as a party to the contract and the deed is executed in his name;

or the agent enters into the deed as trustee for the principal;

or the agent is appointed under the Powers of Attorney Act 1971 and executes the deed in pursuance of his powers under that appointment. An agent given a power of attorney under the 1971 Act may bind the principal by any act which a principal may do through an agent.

17.4.2 Where the agent acts for an undisclosed principal

THE MEANING OF UNDISCLOSED PRINCIPAL

An undisclosed principal is one of whose existence the third party is not aware. As far as he knows, the third party is contracting with the agent as the only other contracting party. As a general rule, there is no difference between the rights, duties and liabilities of a disclosed and an undisclosed principal, provided the agent is acting within the scope of this authority.

EXAMPLE 2

Tom sees an advertisement for a car in a newspaper. He goes to the address given in the advertisement and is shown the car by Andrew. Tom believes that Andrew is the one selling the car. He agrees to buy it. He later discovers that the car is, in fact, owned by Pat and Andrew is selling it on Pat's behalf.

Pat is an undisclosed principal. Nevertheless, Tom's contract is with Pat. Both Tom and Pat have the same rights, duties and liabilities in relation to each other as if Andrew had told Tom from the beginning that he (Andrew) was acting as agent for Pat.

So, generally, there is no difference between a disclosed and undisclosed principal's position. There are, however, exceptions to this general rule; cases where the fact that the principal's existence is unknown at the time of the contract affects the rights of the parties. These are as follows:

WHERE THE CONTRACT BETWEEN THE AGENT AND THIRD PARTY EXPRESSLY PROVIDES THAT THE AGENT IS THE ONLY OTHER CONTRACTING PARTY

If the contract expressly states, for example, that only the persons named in the contract are parties to it, an undisclosed principal cannot claim any rights under the contract. The contract contains an express denial of agency.

WHERE THE CONTRACT TERMS ARE INCONSISTENT WITH THE EXISTENCE OF AN AGENCY

This, in effect, is an implied denial of agency. Although the contract does not expressly prevent an undisclosed principal making a claim under it, the terms of the contract mean that no-one other than the parties described may sue. In this event, the undisclosed principal will have no right of action.

This is illustrated in the case of:

Humble v *Hunter* (1848)

A was authorised to charter out P's ship. A contracted to charter the vessel to T, without disclosing that he was doing so as agent. In fact, A described himself in the contract of charter as 'owner' of the 'Good Ship Ann'.

The court held that P could not enforce the contract of charter because to allow evidence to prove that P was the owner of the ship would be to contradict the terms of the contract. A had impliedly contracted that he was the only principal.

WHERE THE IDENTITY OF THE PRINCIPAL OR AGENT IS MATERIAL TO THE THIRD PARTY

If this is the case, an undisclosed principal will have no rights under the contract. It will occur when the third party, for personal reasons, intended to deal only with the agent or when, again for personal reasons, he would not have entered the contract had he known that the agent was acting for this particular principal.

For example:

***Said v Butt* (1920)**

P, a theatre critic, had had a personal disagreement with the managing-director of a theatre and, as a result, P had been banned from going to the theatre. P wanted a ticket for the first night of a play at the theatre so he persuaded a friend of his, A, to buy a ticket for him without disclosing that he was acting on P's behalf. A bought the ticket in his own name and handed it over to P. When P arrived at the theatre he was refused admission.

When P sued, the court held that he should fail. His identity was of great importance to the theatre and, as P was a person with whom the theatre would not have contracted directly, he could not contract with them indirectly by acting through an agent.

THE THIRD PARTY CAN ELECT WHETHER TO SUE THE AGENT OR THE UNDISCLOSED PRINCIPAL

When the third party knows that the agent is acting as agent he knows that the contract is being made between himself and the principal and that his rights will lie against the principal not the agent.

When the principal is undisclosed, however, the third party thinks, at least initially, that he is contracting with the agent as the only other contracting party. It would therefore be unfair to deprive him of the right, which he believed he had, to sue the agent. In the undisclosed principal situation, therefore, the third party may elect to sue either the principal or the agent.

The right to elect will arise only when the existence of the undisclosed principal becomes known to the third party, but once he has made an unequivocal (ie final) election, he cannot then change his mind and sue the other party. What is an unequivocal election is a question of fact. This is shown in the case of:

***Clarkson Booker Ltd v Andjel* (1964)**

T sold goods to A who did not disclose that he was acting for P. T later discovered P's existence and, when the goods were not paid for, T's solicitor wrote to both P and A threatening proceedings in breach of contract. Eventually, T issued a writ against P but P became insolvent. T then issued a writ against A and obtained judgment. A appealed.

The Court of Appeal upheld the judgment against A. The fact that T had started proceedings against P did not amount to a final election, especially in view of the fact that T had never withdrawn his threat to sue A. Thus T had a right to change his mind and sue A instead.

AN UNDISCLOSED PRINCIPAL CANNOT RATIFY

This is because, to be entitled to ratify, the principal must have been named or ascertained at the time of the unauthorised act. If the third party believes he is dealing only with the agent, and the agent is acting without authority, the principal cannot later reveal his existence and claim rights under the contract (see earlier).

17.4.3 Agent's liability to a third party

Generally an agent will have no rights or liability on the contract he negotiates between the principal and the third party unless:

1. He contracts by deed and executes the deed in his own name unless he contracts as trustee for the principal or unless he acts under the authority of the Powers of Attorney Act 1971 (see earlier);
2. He contracts in a dual capacity. This will occur, for example, when the agent negotiates an H-P contract between a customer and the finance company. The agent will be liable for any misrepresentations he makes (see s56 and s75 Consumer Credit Act 1974, discussed in the Chapter 12);
3. He is liable for breach of warranty of authority. This liability will arise when an agent acts without authority. If he knows he lacks authority, he is liable to the third party in the tort of deceit and in breach of warranty of authority.

If the agent acts without authority but is unaware that he is unauthorised he will be liable only in breach of warranty of authority.

This is illustrated by:

Yonge v Toynbee (1910)

A solicitor was conducting a case against the plaintiff. The solicitor's client became insane (thus, as we shall see, automatically ending the solicitor's authority). The solicitor, unaware of this, took further steps in the action and involved the plaintiff in considerable expense. When the solicitor discovered that his client had become insane he immediately stopped the proceedings. The plaintiff sued the solicitor to recover his costs.

The court held that, as soon as his client became insane, the solicitor's authority ended so, although he acted in good faith, he was liable in breach of warranty of authority—he had impliedy promised that he had authority when in fact he did not. The plaintiff could recover his costs as damages.

17.5 TERMINATION OF AGENCY

17.5.1 An agency may be terminated in the following ways:

BY MUTUAL AGREEMENT

The principal and agent may agree that the agency relationship will be ended.

BY CUSTOM

This arises when, by custom, the agent's authority ends at a certain time. For example, there may be a local custom in a particular trade that the agent's authority ends at midnight on the day of appointment. If this is the case, the agency will automatically end at this time.

BY COMPLETE PERFORMANCE

When the agent is appointed to do a particular act, his authority will end when this act is done. For example, if P appoints A to sell P's car, when A has sold the car his authority will automatically end.

BY FRUSTRATION

The agency ends if the subject matter of the agreement is destroyed; in the example above if the car is destroyed before the agent can sell it.

BY THE EXPIRATION OF TIME

If the agent is appointed for a fixed period, the agency automatically ends at the end of this period.

BY REVOCATION BY THE PRINCIPAL

The principal may revoke (or withdraw) the agent's actual authority at any time. Revocation can take any form (even if the appointment is by deed) but the agent must be allowed the period of notice required by the contract, or if there is no such period specified he must be allowed such notice as is customary and reasonable.

The agent's apparent authority will continue until any third party with whom he has dealt in the past as the principal's agent is notified of the revocation.

BY RENUNCIATION BY THE AGENT

The agent can renounce the agency and thus end it, subject to the agent giving the principal the contractual or reasonable notice. The agent's apparent authority again will continue until third parties with whom he has had dealings as the principal's agent are notified.

BY THE DEATH OF EITHER PARTY

BY THE INSOLVENCY OF THE PRINCIPAL

BY THE INSOLVENCY OF THE AGENT

This will end the agency if it results in the agent being unfit to carry out his duties.

BY THE INSANITY OF THE PRINCIPAL OR AGENT

This will end the agency if it prevents them entering into a contract.

WHERE THE AGENCY IS ONE OF NECESSITY, BY THE ENDING OF THE NECESSITY

17.5.2 Limits on the right to terminate

There are certain limits on the right to terminate the agency. Thus

TERMINATION DOES NOT DEPRIVE EITHER PARTY OF ANY VESTED RIGHTS

Vested rights are those rights which either party acquired before the agency terminated. So, for example, if the agent has earned a right to commission or a right to indemnity he will not lose this right merely because the principal has revoked his authority. Also the principal's rights to sue the agent for any breaches of contract are not lost because the agency is ended.

AUTHORITY COUPLED WITH AN INTEREST

If the agent has an interest in the agency other than a right to payment the agency cannot be ended. This interest must amount to a form of security as when, for example, P owes A money and gives A the right to collect the rents from P's properties until the debt is repaid. This is a form of security for the amount of money which P owes and will therefore be an agency coupled with an interest. The principal cannot revoke this agency until A has collected all the money owed to him. If P tries to revoke, A can stop him by obtaining an injunction.

Authority coupled with an interest is unaffected by the principal's bankruptcy, death or insanity.

The Powers of Attorney Act 1971 makes similar provisions enabling a principal to grant an irrevocable power of attorney. Again, this power cannot be ended as long as the interest it was given to protect remains unsatisfied unless the person given the power agrees to the revocation; nor is it affected by the principal's bankruptcy, death or insanity.

17.5.3 Effects of termination

IT IS EFFECTIVE FOR THE FUTURE

Termination, in other words, ends the rights and duties of the principal and the agent for the future although it does not affect vested rights.

THE AGENT MAY STILL HAVE APPARENT AUTHORITY

Even though his actual authority is ended, the agent will still have apparent authority as regards third parties who have dealt with him in the past as the principal's agent and who have not been told that the authority has been terminated. This is shown in the case of:

Drew v Nunn (1879)

A husband allowed his wife to buy goods on his credit. The husband became insane but the wife continued to pledge his credit. When the husband recovered his sanity, he was sued for the price of the goods supplied to his wife during his insanity.

The court held that the husband was liable. He had represented to third parties that his wife was authorised to pledge his credit and had not withdrawn this representation. The fact that he was insane and therefore could not withdraw it was irrelevant.

SUMMARY

As we said in the introduction, agency is one of the most important relationships in commercial law. With the growth in business, both national and international, it is clearly impossible for one person to deal with all the matters which arise on a day-to-day basis. It was therfore inevitable that 'indirect contracting' by means of agents would increase. The law as it has developed is designed in the main to give third parties dealing with agents confidence in the agency relationship. Thus, if a third party deals with an agent who is one of a particular category of agents he can assume that this agent can do everything that agents of this type can do. If the principal has made it appear that an agent has certain powers, the third party can act in confidence on this appearance. If the agent does not disclose he is acting for a principal, the third party need not be bound by the contract if he would not have dealt with the principal in face-to-face negotiations.

For our purposes, the most important aspect of agency is the role it plays in business undertakings. Partnerships, for example, are based on the fact that each partner is an agent for the other partners and for the business. Companies have to rely on agents to enter contracts and to bind the firm in other matters relating to outsiders. In all these cases, the law of agency discussed in this chapter will, in the absence of agreement to the contrary, apply to the relationship between the principal, agent and third party.

SELF-TEST QUESTIONS

1   Why is it not necessary for an agent to have contractual capacity?

2   What is the relationship between an agent's actual (or express), implied and usual authority?

3   Distinguish between *Walteau* v *Fenwick* and *Daun* v *Simmins*

4   What are the requirements for ratification?

5   What kind of authority is an agent given by ratification?

6   What kind of authority did the agent have in the following cases:

(a)   *Re Tiedemann and Ledermann Frieres?*
(b)   *Spiro* v *Lintern?*
(c)   *Farquharson Bros* v *King & Co?*
(d)   *Dodsley* v *Varley?*
(e)   *Yonge* v *Toynbee?*

7   Distinguish between

(a)   a bribe; and
(b)   a secret profit.

8   Complete: as against his principal, an agent has a right to

(a)
(b)
(c)

9   Distinguish *Luxor (Eastbourne) Ltd* v *Cooper* and *Alpha Trading* v *Dunshaw-Patten Ltd*.

10   How may an agency be terminated?

Answers on page 337

EXERCISES

1. (a) In the creation of agency explain what is meant by
    i) agency by ratification.
    ii) agency by estoppel.
    iii) agency by necessity.
   (b) L appointed M as an agent to buy materials from N and other manufacturers. L was dissatisfied with M's work and wrote to him dismissing him. M continued to buy goods on credit from N who believing that M was still L's agent sought payment from L. L later discovered that M had received commission for the orders he placed with several of the manufacturers, and that M had been carrying on a business similar to L's while employed by L. Advise L.
2. Distinguish between the express, implied and usual authority of an agent and explain the doctrine of the undisclosed principal.

Answers on page 338

The law of partnership

In English law business may be carried on in one of three ways, by a sole trader, by a partnership, and by a limited company. An example of a sole trader is where a village shopkeeper or a plumber simply trades by himself; the one-man business. A partnership exists where two or more people carry on the same business together. The concept of the limited company has already been described in Chapter 16 (see particularly 16.3). In this chapter we are going to consider some of the important aspects of the law of partnership.

18.1 INTRODUCTION

There are three general principles which run like golden threads through English partnership law. These need to be learnt by heart because if they are understood then partnership law itself is relatively simple.

They are:

1. Each partner has unlimited liability for the debts and liabilities of his firm.
2. Each partner is an agent both of the firm and of his fellow partners whenever he acts in the partnership business.
3. The affairs of the firm are regulated by the provisions of the Partnership Act 1890 except in circumstances where the partners have specifically agreed to the contrary.

The law of partnership is codified in the Partnership Act 1890. This Act is a fairly comprehensive summary of the rules of law governing the formation of the partnership, the dealings of the partners between themselves and with third parties, and the dissolution of the partnership. As has been said, the Act applies to regulate the affairs of the partnership insofar as the partners have not specifically agreed to the contrary. This is a crucial point in practice. Section 19 Partnership Act 1890 provides 'the mutual rights and duties of partners, whether ascertained by agreement or defined by this Act, may be varied by the consent of all the partners, and such consent may be either expressed or inferred from a course of dealing.' This means that whenever a problem arises in practice concerning a partnership, the person dealing with the problem should first examine any partnership agreement which may exist before turning to the Act itself.

18.2 DEFINITION OF A PARTNERSHIP

Section 1, Partnership Act 1890 defines a partnership as 'the relation which exists between persons carrying on a business in common with a view of profit'. There are a number of points in this definition which need to be noted:

1. **Persons** Because the word 'persons' is in the plural it follows that a partnership cannot be carried on by an individual alone. However, persons are not confined to natural persons. A natural person may be in partnership with a company. There is an upper limit of the number of members which most partnerships may have. By s716 Companies Act 1985 a partnership may not have more than 20 members. This limitation, however, does not apply to solicitors, accountants, members of a recognised stock exchange, and certain other professional partnerships specifically exempted by Department of Trade and Industry Regulations including some consultant engineers, building designers, loss adjusters, actuaries, and estate agents.
2. **A business** By s45 Partnership Act 1890 'business' includes every trade, occupation or profession. For the law to recognise a partnership, there must be a clear intention to carry on the business on a continuing basis. For example, acts carried on by the promoters of a business prior to its incorporation do not render them partners:

Keith Spicer Ltd v Mansell (1970)

Mansell and Bishop decided to go into business together to run a restaurant. To do this they set about forming a limited company. Bishop ordered some goods from Keith Spicer Ltd for use in the restaurant. The goods were never paid for and Keith Spicer Ltd sued Mansell for the price on the basis that a partnership existed between Mansell and Bishop. It was held that the action should fail because there was no evidence that Mansell and Bishop were in partnership together. They were simply preparing to carry on business as a company as soon as they could.

3   **In common**. For a partnership to exist, it is essential that the partners carry on business together (ie by means of a mutual agency where each partner is an agent of both the partnership and his fellow partners for the purposes of the business) and with the intention of sharing the profits.

4   **With a view of profit**. This implies the sharing of net profits (after all expenses have been accounted for, rather than the sharing of gross returns):

Cox v Coulson (1916)

Coulson was the lessee and the manager of a theatre. Mill was the manager of a theatrical company. They entered into an agreement together under which Mill's company was to put on the performance of a play at Coulson's theatre. Coulson was to recieve 60% of the gross receipts and to pay the expenses of the theatre, the lighting, the playbills etc. Mill was to receive the other 40% of the gross receipts and pay for the actors and the scenery. It was held that no partnership existed between them.

Section 2, Partnership Act 1890 states certain rules which must be considered in determining whether a partnership does or does not exist. They are as follows:

1   Joint tenancy, tenancy in common, joint property, common property, or part ownership does not itself create a partnership as to anything so held or owned, whether or not the tenants or owners do not share any profits made by the use thereof.

2   The sharing of gross returns does not of itself create a partnership, whether the persons sharing such returns have or have not a joint or common right or interest in any property from which or from the use of which the returns are derived.

3   The receipt by a person of a share of the profits of a business is prima facie evidence that he is a partner in the business, but the receipt of such a share, or of a payment contingent on or varying with the profits of a business, does not of itself make him a partner in the business; and in particular:
  (a)   The receipt by a person of a debt or other liquidated amount by instalments or otherwise out of accruing profits of a business does not in itself make him a partner in the business or liable as such.
  (b)   A contract for the remuneration of a servant or agent of a person engaged in a business by a share of the profits of a business does not of itself make the servant or agent a partner in the business or liable as such.
  (c)   A person being the widow or child of a deceased partner, and receiving by way of an annuity a portion of the profits made in the business in which the deceased person was a partner, is not by reason only of such receipt a partner in the business or liable as such.
  (d)   The advance of money by way of loan to a person engaged or about to engage in any business on a contract with that person that the lender shall receive a rate of interest varying with the profits, or shall receive a share of the profits arising from carrying on the business, does not of itself make the lender a partner with the person or persons carrying on the business or make him liable as such; provided that the contract is in writing, and signed by or on behalf of all the parties thereto.
  (e)   A person receiving by way of annuity or otherwise a portion of the profits of a business in consideration of the sale by him of the goodwill of the business is not by reason only of such receipt a partner in the business or liable as such.

We shall now examine some of these rules in more detail.

By s2(1), Partnership Act 1890 joint ownership of property does not of itself create a partnership. For example, a husband and wife may jointly own the house in which they live. This does not make them partners in law in the sense envisaged by the Partnership Act. Similarly:

Davis v Davis (1894)

A father left to his two sons (a) his business and (b) three freehold houses in equal shares as tenants in common. They carried on the business together. They let two of the houses to tenants. The rent of one of the houses they shared between them. The rent from the second house they used to improve the second and the third houses. It was held that although they were in partnership in carrying on the business, there was no partnership in respect of the freehold houses.

We have already seen from the case of *Cox v Coulson* (1916) that merely sharing gross returns rather than net profits does not constitute a contract. This case is an illustration of s2(2), Partnership Act 1890.

Section 2(3), Partnership Act 1890 is statutory confirmation of the leading case of:

Cox v Hickman (1864)

A trader who was in financial difficulties assigned (ie transferred the legal title to) his property to trustees on behalf of his creditors. The intention was that the trustees should oversee the conduct of the business so that the creditors could be paid off from the profits of the business. It was held that a partnership had not been created between the trader and his creditors merely because the creditors were sharing in the profits of the business.

Until this case the sharing in profits had been seen as the main indicator of the existence of a partnership. Section 2(3), Partnership Act 1890 only provides that the sharing of profits is a *prima facie* indication of a partnership. In other words the sharing of the profits is evidence but not conclusive evidence of the existence of a partnership. Sub-paragraphs 3(a) to (e) above are instances when sharing the profits does not constitute a partnership.

(a) is in fact based upon the decision in *Cox v Hickman* (1864).
(b) provides that the payment of a bonus based upon profits does not make the employee to whom the bonus is paid a partner.
(c) deals with the situation where a partner has died and his widow or child is paid a share of the partnership profits by the other partners as a pension.
(d) covers the situation where a person lends money to a business on terms that the rate of interest which he shall be paid for the loan will depend on the amount of profits which the business makes.
(e) deals with the sale of the goodwill of a business. The purchaser of goodwill might agree with the vendor that he will pay him a percentage of the profits for a set period of time. All these are instances of persons receiving a proportion of the profits of a business and yet not being partners. The ultimate test for partnership is to examine the intention of the partners themselves. More important than sharing profits is sharing losses. If there appears to be an agreement to share losses then almost certainly there is a partnership in existence.

SALARIED PARTNERS

It is common today, particularly with professional partnerships, to have what are known as salaried partners. These are people working for the firm, whose names appear on the notepaper as partners and so who enjoy a senior position in the firm, but who are remunerated by a salary rather than by a share of the profits. The question is whether such a person whose entitlement to the profits of the firm is zero can be regarded as a partner. The importance of this question lies in deciding whether he is liable for the debts of the firm. The position of salaried partners was considered in the case of:

Stekel v Ellice (1973)

Ellice was the sole surviving member of a firm of chartered accountants. On 1 October 1968 he entered into an agreement with Stekel on the following terms:

(a) They were to be partners until 5 April 1969.
(b) The partnership capital should be provided by and belong to Ellice.
(c) All profits should go to Ellice and he should bear all losses.
(d) Neither Stekel nor Ellice should engage in any other business without the other's consent.
(e) Either Stekel or Ellice could give notice of dissolution of the partnership on specified grounds.
(f) Upon termination of the partnership the capital should go to Ellice.
(g) Stekel should be paid a salary of £2,000 per year.
(h) During this time a full partnership agreement should be entered into.

By 5 April 1969 no full partnership had been entered into and the temporary agreement continued for a further 14 months. Stekel and Ellice fell out and a question arose as to whether the relationship between the two was that of partners or simply that of employer and employee. It was held that on a true construction of the facts the agreement was one of partnership. However, since Stekel had no proprietorial interest in the firm, no order would be made for a winding up of the business. The judge, Megarry, J, said 'it seems to me impossible to say that as a matter of law a salaried partner is or is not a partner in the true sense. He may or may not be a partner depending on the facts. What must be done, I think, is to look at the substance of the relationship between the parties.' In deciding in this case that a partnership existed, the court was influenced by the fact that Ellice had held Stekel out as a partner by such conduct as having his name printed upon the letterheadings.

18.3 CREATION OF A PARTNERSHIP

It will be recalled that a partnership is defined in s1(1) Partnership Act 1890 as 'the relation which subsists between persons carrying on a business in common with a view of profits'. The creation of a partnership requires no formalities. Whether a partnership exists is simply a question of fact. A partnership may exist between persons carrying on business together but who have simply never considered the possibility of their being in partnership.

18.3.1 Illegal partnerships

The law will not recognise an illegal partnership. A partnership is a contract between the partners and the same rules apply regarding illegality as apply to ordinary contracts (see Chapter 9).

An illegal partnership at common law is one which the courts as a matter of public policy will not recognise. So an agreement to share the proceeds of prostitution could not be recognised as a partnership. One of the more interesting cases on this is:

Everett v Williams (1725)

Two highwaymen (Everett and Williams), entered into an agreement to work together in plying their trade, to share all expenses and to share the profits. After successfully trading for some years they fell out and could not agree how the assets of their 'business' should be divided between them. Astonishingly Everett decided to take the matter to court. It was held that the court could not adjudicate on what was essentially an unlawful partnership. The counsel who had dared to represent their clients on such an unlawful matter should bear the costs of the case between them. Everett's solicitor was subsequently deported and the plaintiff and the defendant were both hanged.

Partnerships may also be rendered unlawful by statute. As has been seen, a partnership having more than 20 partners is unlawful unless one of the express exceptions applies (see above 18.2). Section 20, Solicitors Act 1974 states that it is illegal for a solicitor to be in partnership with an unqualified person.

18.3.2 Capacity

The ordinary law of contract applies to the capacity of persons to enter into a partnership. Thus a minor can enter into a partnership agreement, though debts contracted by the firm are unenforceable against him. They may only be enforced by the creditor against adult partners.

18.3.3 The name of the firm

There is almost complete freedom of choice as to what name may be selected for a partnership, though by s34 Companies Act 1985 the last word in the firm's name must not be 'limited'. It should be noted that the use of the word 'and Co' is of no special significance. These words are frequently applied both to incorporated and unincorporated associations.

Having said that there is general freedom in the choice of name by a partnership, there are a few limitations which should be noted:

1. By s2, Business Names Act 1985 the written approval of the Secretary of State is needed for a person to use a name which would be likely to give the impression that the business is connected

with Her Majesty's Government or with the local authority. Consent is also needed from the Secretary of State to use certain technical terms which are specified in delegated legislation.
2 The name chosen must not be such as to deceive members of the public into thinking that they are dealing with a rival firm. In such a case the rival firm may bring an action for passing off to prohibit the use of the name. If the case is proved, the court will grant an injunction prohibiting the use of the offending name.
3 By s4 Business Names Act 1985 where the name of the partnership does not consist of the surnames of all partners without any addition other than their forenames or initials the firm must ensure that all business letters, written orders for goods or services to be supplied, invoices, receipts or written demands for payment of debts state in legible characters the name of each partner and an address at which service of any document relating to the business will be effective. Further, the partnership must display a notice at all places where its business is carried on, detailing the partners' names and the service address. There is an exception in regard to the letterheadings of partnerships having more than 20 partners. In such a case the partners' names may be omitted from the letterheading so long as there is a statement there as to the address of the main office and that a list of the partners' names is there available for inspection. Failure to comply with these provisions may lead to the partners being fined. Moreover, by s5 Business Names Act 1985, the partnership may not enforce a right arising out of a contract made in breach of these provisions if the party with whom they were dealing can show that he has been unable to pursue a claim against the partnership because of the breach or that he has suffered financial loss in connection with the contract as a result of the breach.

18.3.4 The partnership agreement

Because a partnership is something which is brought about so informally, there is no requirement in law that there should even be a partnership agreement. However, it is sensible in practice that there should be some form of written agreement which deals with all major matters which may be of concern to the firm. Section 24, Partnership Act 1890 provides, as we shall see, a number of rules governing the partnership which apply in the absence of contrary agreement. Nevertheless, it is unwise simply to rely upon these general principles.

A properly drawn partnership agreement should provide for the following matters:

1 The name of the partnership.
2 The nature and place of the business.
3 The commencement and duration of the firm.
4 Partnership capital.
5 Entitlement of the partners to profits and drawings and the sharing of outgoings and losses.
6 Banking arrangements and authority to sign cheques.
7 The authority of individual partners to act on behalf of the firm.
8 The management of the business, including any particular powers enjoyed by individual partners and any individual entitlements to salaries.
9 Books of account, annual accounts and accountants.
10 Retirement of a partner.
11 Consequences of death or bankruptcy of a partner.
12 Definition of partnership property.
13 Income tax election under s154, Income and Corporation Taxes Act 1970 which will ensure that the firm is treated as continuing in respect of the payment of income tax.
14 Expulsion—to enable the expulsion of a partner eg for breach of the partnership agreement.
15 Arbitration in case of dispute.

In the absence of an express agreement, then s24 Partnership Act applies. This contains a series of general principles as to the rights and duties of the partners. They are as follows:

1 All partners are entitled to share equally in the capital and profits of the business, and must contribute equally towards the losses whether of capital or otherwise sustained by the firm.
2 The firm must indemnify every partner in respect of payments made and personal liabilities incurred by him.

(a) in the ordinary and proper conduct of the business of the firm, or
(b) in or about anything necessarily done for the preservation of the business or property of the firm.

3. A partner making, for the purpose of the partnership, any actual payment or advance beyond the amount of capital which he has agreed to subscribe, is entitled to interest at the rate of five per cent per annum from the date of the payment or advance.

4. A partner is not entitled, before the ascertainment of profits, to interest on the capital subscribed by him

5. Every partner may take part in the management of the partnership business.

6. No partner shall be entitled to remuneration for acting in the partnership business.

7. No person may be introduced as a partner without the consent of all existing partners.

8. Any difference arising as to ordinary matters connected with the partnership business may be decided by a majority of the partners, but no charge may be made in the nature of the partnership business without the consent of all existing partners.

9. The partnership books are to be kept at the place of business of the partnership (or the principal place, if there is more than one), and every partner may, when he thinks fit, have access to and inspect and copy any of them.

DURATION OF THE AGREEMENT

In the absence of an agreement, for example, that the partnership should be for a fixed duration, it is a partnership at will and, as such, may be brought to an end simply by notice being given by one partner to his fellow partners. By s26, Partnership Act 1890 'where no fixed term has been agreed upon for the duration of the partnership, any partner may determine the partnership at any time on giving notice of his intention so to do to all the other partners'. That one partner may bring the partnership to an end merely by giving notice is probably the most important single reason why there should always be a partnership agreement. This notice does not have to be reasonable. So long as notice is given the dissolution of the firm may be immediate. Accordingly a partnership at will is an extremely unstable trading entity. Because of this, the courts have adopted the view that a partnership at will exists only if there is no indication that the partners intended some other kind of partnership. For example, consider the approach adopted in:

Moss v *Elphick* (1910)

Moss and Elphick were partners in a partnership which was for an undefined duration. A clause in the partnership deed provided that the partnership could only be terminated 'by mutual arrangement'. Moss gave notice to Elphick purporting to dissolve the partnership. It was held by the Court of Appeal that the notice was invalid. Because the agreement stated that the partnership could be terminated 'by mutual arrangement' only, s26, Partnership Act 1890 was inapplicable. There was no partnership at will. Dissolution required mutual consent.

Similarly in:

Abbot v *Abbot* (1936)

On 11 October 1923 a father and his five sons went into partnership. The partnership deed provided that 'the death or retirement of any partner shall not terminate the partnership', and also that 'if any partner shall ... do or suffer any act which would be a ground for the dissolution of the partnership by the court, he shall be considered to have retired'. Years later one of the sons gave notice of dissolution. He commenced proceedings for an order of the court to the effect that the partnership had been dissolved, arguing that he was entitled to give notice since there was no fixed term for the duration of the partnership under s26, Partnership Act 1890. It was held that no such order would be made. The partnership was not one at will. It should therefore continue unless dissolved by the court. So long as there were two partners surviving who had not retired the partnership should continue.

18.3.5 The continuance of the partnership after the expiry date

Section 27, Partnership Act 1890 provides that 'where a partnership entered into for a fixed term is continued after the term has expired, and without any express new agreement, the rights and duties of the partners remain the same as they were at the expiration of the term, so far as is consistent with the incidents of a partnership at will'. This means that if a partnership is entered into for a fixed period of time and the partners continue trading after the expiry date, the partnership will continue as though it were a partnership at will but subject to all other agreements between the partners. A good illustration of this is:

Brooks v Brooks (1901)

A partnership was entered into by the plaintiff and the defendant on 1 January 1889 for 10 years. The agreement provided that the plaintiff could determine the partnership 'by giving the defendant six months' notice, and whether so determined or by effluxion of time' she had the right to purchase the defendant's share of the partnership. The partnership continued after 1 January 1899, its expiry date. The plaintiff claimed she could exercise the right to buy the defendant's share, but the defendant argued that the clause giving her the right to do so was inapplicable because it was inconsistent with a partnership at will. It was held that the plaintiff's action should succeed. The clause was wholly consistent with a partnership at will within the meaning of s27, Partnership Act 1890.

18.4 AGENCY OF THE PARTNERS

In looking at the relationship of the partners to persons who deal with them as a firm, the general principles of the law of agency are of prime importance. By s5, Partnership Act 1890 'every partner is an agent of the firm and his other partners for the purposes of the business of the partnership; and the acts of every partner who does any act or carrying on in the usual way business of the kind carried on by the firm of which he is a member bind the firm and his partners, unless the partner so acting has in fact no authority to act for the firm in the particular matter, and the person with whom he is dealing either knows that he has no authority, or does not know or believe him to be a partner'.

Note from this that each partner has a dual agency. Firstly he is the agent of the firm. Secondly he is the agent of his co-partners. However, the agency is not so wide that he can bind the firm and his co-partners in any matter which he purports to engage in allegedly for the firm. His agency is limited to acts for the purpose of the business of the partnership. It is assumed that every partner enjoys authority to do all necessary acts to carry on the firm's business in the usual way. So if there is a restriction between the partners themselves as to what one partner may do, eg a limitation on a partner in a trading partnership that he may not engage in any buying of goods on behalf of the partnership because he does not have a good eye for a bargain will result in his apparent authority being greater than his actual authority. Thus if, in the example given, the partner who is prohibited from buying on behalf of the firm nevertheless orders goods, the firm will be bound because the buying comes within his apparent authority.

In order to avoid its liability in these circumstances the firm would have to show either that the third party from whom the goods were brought knew of the limitation on the partner's authority or else that he did not know or believe him to be a partner of the firm. An example of the way in which a partner may bind his co-partners, notwithstanding an express agreement to the contrary between them, is to be found in:

Mercantile Credit Co Ltd v Garrod (1962)

Garrod and Parkin were partners in a garage business. The business was primarily concerned with repairing cars and letting lock-up garages. Garrod was a sleeping partner (ie he took no part in the management of the firm). There was a clause in the partnership agreement which prohibited the buying and selling of cars. Parkin, who looked after the day-to-day management of the business, sold a car to the Mercantile Credit Company Ltd who were financing a hire-purchase deal for a customer. Parkin had no right to do this, both because of the prohibition in the partnership agreement and because the car was not his to sell. Mercantile Credit Company Ltd paid Parkin £700 for the car. When it found that Parkin had no right to sell the car, it claimed the £700 from Garrod, his partner. It was held that the claim should succeed. The sale of the car to a finance company was a transaction in the usual way of business of the kind carried on by the firm. Accordingly the transaction fell squarely within s5, Partnership Act 1890, and the firm and Garrod were bound.

It should be noted that the Act in question must not only come within the scope of the business carried on by the firm, but it must also be effected 'in the usual way' of the business. So there will be circumstances where an act, although clearly connected with the firm's business, lies outside the apparent authority of a partner. For example, although partners in a trading firm have an implied authority to borrow money on the firm's credit, partners in a non-trading firm do not. This is illustrated by:

***Higgins v Beauchamp* (1914)**

Beauchamp and Milles were partners in a cinema business. The partnership agreement stated that no partner could contract any debt on account of the partnership without the consent of the other partners. Milles borrowed money from Higgins, who subsequently sued Beauchamp for its return. It was held that the action should fail. The business was not a trading business. Trading implied the buying and selling of goods and a cinema did not buy and sell goods. Therefore Milles had no implied authority to bind the firm in respect of the debt.

18.5 LIABILITY OF THE PARTNERS

18.5.1 Liability in contract

By s9 Partnership Act 1890 'every partner in a firm is liable jointly with the other partners ... for all debts and obligations of the firm incurred while he is a partner; and after his death his estate is also severally liable in due course of administration for such debts and obligations, so far as they remain unsatisfied'. Joint liability means that the plaintiff has only one possible action in respect of a debt owing to him. This could lead to hardship. For example:

***Kendall v Hamilton* (1889)**

A creditor sued the two persons whom he believed to be partners in a firm which owed him money. He claimed judgment against them but was unable to recover from them enough money actually to discharge the debt. He then discovered that there existed a wealthy sleeping partner, Hamilton. Thereupon he commenced an action against him. It was held that since the debt was merely a joint debt and that the creditor had already obtained judgment against some of the members of the firm, the plaintiff could not start fresh proceedings against a sleeping partner.

The hardship of this has been mitigated in two ways. Firstly, the Civil Liability (Contribution) Act 1978 provided that the contractual liability of partners is several as well as joint. This means that a creditor has a right of successive actions against all partners until such time as he has obtained the full satisfaction of his debt. (This does not mean that the creditor can be unduly careless in the way in which he takes proceedings since he may only recover his costs in respect of one proceeding in respect of the same debt). Secondly, by Order 81 of the Rules of the Supreme Court, if the creditor sues the partnership in the firm name this automatically joins in the action all partners who were members of the firm at the time when the cause of action commenced.

18.5.2 Liability in tort

By s10, Partnership Act 1890 'where by any wrongful act or omission of any partner acting in the ordinary course of business of the firm, or with the authority of his co-partners, loss or injury is caused to any person not being a partner in the firm, or any penalty is incurred, the firm is liable therefore to the same extent as the partner so acting or omitting to act'. Thus the firm is liable for the wrongful acts of a partner who is acting in the ordinary course of the business. The operation of this section is illustrated by:

***Hamlyn v Houston & Co* (1902)**

Houston, a partner in the firm of Houston & Co bribed a clerk in a rival firm, Hamlyn, to disclose to him confidential information concerning the contracts and tenders of his employers. As a result, the rival firm suffered a loss and sued Houston & Co for damages. It was held by the Court of Appeal that the action should succeed. Houston & Co were liable for the wrongful act of their partner. On behalf of Houston & Co it was argued that both the obtaining of information concerning competitors and the inducing of the clerk to break his contract were illegal. However, it was found that it was in the ordinary course of business to try to discover information about a trade rival. Since this was in the ordinary course of business, it was immaterial whether the discovery was by lawful or unlawful means.

After the rather general wording of s10, Partnership Act 1890, whereby the liability of the firm for wrongs of the individual partners is dealt with, the rather more specific wrong of misapplying property or money received for or in the custody of the firm is dealt with in s11. By this, 'where one partner acting within the scope of his apparent authority receives the money or property of a third person and misapplies it; and where a firm in the course of its business receives money or property of a third person, and the money or property so received is misapplied by one or more of the partners while it is in the custody of the firm; the firm is liable to make good the loss'. An example of this is to be found in:

Rhodes v *Moules* (1894)

Rhodes, wishing to obtain a loan, mortgaged his property. The matter was dealt with by Rew, a partner in a firm of solicitors Hughes & Masterman. Rew told Rhodes that the mortgagees needed additional security. So Rhodes provided Rew with some share warrants payable to bearer (these are share documents which can be transferred simply by being handed by one person to another; no registration of the transfer is necessary). Rew misappropriated them and Rhodes sued the firm in respect of the loss. It was held by the Court of Appeal that he should succeed since the warrant had been received by the firm in the ordinary course of business.

By s12, Partnership Act 1890 liability for wrongs is joint and several.

18.5.3 The duration of a partner's liabilities

It is important to consider when a partner's liability in respect of the debts and wrongs of his co-partners arises and when it terminates. As a general rule the agency of a partner begins when he becomes a partner and ceases either at the date of his retirement from a firm which is continued by the other partners, or on the date when the winding up of the firm is completed. Accordingly a new partner joining a firm is not liable for debts incurred prior to his joining. By s17, Partnership Act 1890 'a person who is admitted as a partner into an existing firm does not thereby become liable to the creditors of the firm for anything done before he became a partner'. Conversely, and by the same section, 'a partner who retires from the firm does not thereby cease to be liable for partnership debts or obligations incurred before his retirement'. Thus if A, B and C are in partnership and A retires on 31 March 1989 and D joins on 1 April 1989 then A, B and C are jointly and severally liable for the debts and obligations of the firm prior to 1 April 1989 and B, C and D are jointly and severally liable for the debts and obligations of the firm incurred after 31 March 1989. In the normal course of events, when a partner retires, most of the debts of the firm will be discharged. For example, a garage repair bill will usually be paid off during the month following the receipt. However, some contracts are of a more continuing nature. For example, the office premises may be rented. There may be a rental agreement for a photocopying machine. Section 17, Partnership Act 1890 states how these continuous contracts may be dealt with. 'A retiring partner may be discharged from any existing liabilities, by an agreement to that effect between himself and the members of the firm as newly constituted and the creditors, and this agreement may be either express or inferred as a fact from the course of dealing between the creditors and the firm as newly constituted'. This is known as novation. This is essentially a tripartite contractual agreement between the creditor, the partnership as it was, and the partnership as it is after retirement. By means of novation, a new agreement is made with the creditor whereby the partnership as it is to be constituted in future is substituted for the partnership as it was in the past.

The general rule that a retiring partner is not liable for debts incurred after his retirement is subject to the provisions relating to 'holding out'. By s14, Partnership Act 1890 'everyone who by word spoken or written or by conduct himself represents himself, or who knowingly suffers himself to be represented, as partner in a particular firm, is liable as a partner to anyone who has on the faith of any such representation given credit to the firm, whether the representation has or has not been made or communicated to the person so giving credit by or with the knowledge of the apparent partner making the representation or suffering it to be made'. The liability created by this section arises as a result of estoppel. Just as with estoppel in the law of contract (see Chapter 7) estoppel arises where a person holds himself out as a partner or allows others to do so with the result that a third party relies upon the holding out. He is then estopped from denying that he is a partner. A good example of holding out arose in the case of:

Martyn v *Gray* (1863)

Gray allowed the captain of a mine (the manager) in Cornwall to introduce him to Martyn, a merchant, as a capitalist from London and his partner. The merchant gave credit to the captain of the mine on the strength of the representation. It was held that Gray was liable to Martyn, notwithstanding that Martyn did not even know his name. Erle C J, giving judgment, said

'It is not necessary that this person should be identified by his Christian name and surname: it was enough that he should be so pointed at as to be distinctly identified'.

Liability as a result of holding out does not arise merely if a retiring partner is careless in not seeing that all the firm's notepaper bearing his name has been destroyed:

Tower Cabinet Co Ltd v Ingram (1949)

Christmas and Ingram were in business as house furnishers. They traded under the name 'Merry's'. The partnership came to an end in April 1947, but Christmas carried on business using the firm name. In 1948, the Tower Cabinet Co Ltd, which had never previously dealt with Merry's, received an order to supply them some furniture. The furniture was never paid for and Tower Cabinet Co Ltd obtained judgment against Merry's. They sought to enforce judgment against Ingram. The only way in which they knew of Ingram's existence was that his name had appeared on some old headed notepaper which had been used to confirm the order for the purchase of the furniture. Ingram had failed to destroy the notepaper prior to his leaving the firm. It was held that Ingram was not liable under s14, Partnership Act 1890 because he had not 'knowingly' suffered himself to be held out as a partner.

18.6 TERMINATION OF THE PARTNERSHIP

A partnership may be dissolved either by means of a court order or out of court for example pursuant to some provision in the partnership agreement or merely by an agreement between the partners. Before considering the various grounds on which these two types of dissolution may take place, it is important to emphasise that dissolution by the court should always be regarded as very much a last resort. There are two sides to any case in English law, the plaintiff and the defendant. Whichever side loses usually bears the other side's costs. In an application to dissolve a partnership, the plaintiff will be the partner seeking the dissolution. The defendant will be the partnership. If the plaintiff wins, the partnership loses. The partnership will then have to bear the plaintiff's costs. Since the plaintiff is a member of the partnership there will therefore be less assets remaining to share between the partners than would be the case if the dissolution had been without the intervention of the court.

18.6.1 Dissolution without a court order

1   By s32, Partnership Act 1890 'subject to any agreement between the partners a partnership is dissolved
    (a) If entered into for a fixed term, by expiration of that term.
    (b) If entered into for a single adventure or undertaking, by the termination of that adventure or undertaking.
    (c) If entered into for an undefined time, by any partner giving notice to the other or others of his intention to dissolve the partnership.
    The expiration of a fixed term is straightforward. As has been said, if the partnership continues after the expiration of the fixed term, then it continues as a partnership at will. Similarly, if it is entered into for a single adventure, such as the building of a house, then once the house is built and sold the partnership comes automatically to an end. The third instance, where a partnership is entered into for a undefined time, is to be read in conjunction with s26, Partnership Act 1890, partnerships at will. The mere giving of notice is sufficient to dissolve a partnership at will.

2   **Dissolution by bankruptcy or death**
    By s33, Partnership Act 1890 'subject to any agreement between the partners, every partnership is dissolved as regards all the partners by the death or bankruptcy of any partner'. Thus the death or bankruptcy of a partner automatically brings the partnership to an end. To avoid the occurrence of the dissolution of the partnership at what might be an inconvenient time because of the death of a partner, it is very common for partnership agreements to provide that death shall not result in the automatic dissolution of the partnership. Such an exception is not so common in partnership agreements in relation to the bankruptcy of a partner. Often where bankruptcy occurs the remaining partners are only too happy to have the partnership come to an end.

3   **Charging of a partnership share**
    By s33, Partnership Act 1890 'a partnership may, at the option of the other partners, be dissolved if any partner suffers his share of the partnership property to be charged under this

Act for his separate debt'. The making of a charging order on a partner's share does not dissolve the partnership automatically, but the co-partners may dissolve it if they wish. A charging order is an order of the court that the share of the profits and assets due to a partner should be paid over to a third party. If the partners wish to dissolve on this ground they must do so without undue delay and in an unambiguous manner.

4 Illegality

By s34, Partnership Act 1890 'a partnership is in every case dissolved by the happening of any event which makes it unlawful for the business of the firm to be carried on or for the members of the firm to carry on in partnership'. Just as a partnership should not be formed for an illegal purpose, it automatically comes to an end if it becomes illegal. An example of dissolution by illegality is:

R v Kupfer (1915)

Kupfer was a partner in a firm consisting of himself and his two brothers. The two brothers carried on the business of the firm in Frankfurt, while Kupfer himself looked after the London office. The Frankfurt office ordered goods from a Dutch company and payment was to be made for these goods from the London office. On 4 August 1914 war broke out and Kupfer, from the London office, paid the due amount to the Dutch company. He was thereupon charged with the criminal offence of trading with an enemy contrary to Trading with the Enemy Act 1914. One of the matters before the court was whether the partnership had been dissolved by the outbreak of war. It was held by the Court of Criminal Appeal that the partnership had indeed been dissolved for this reason.

5 Notice

If a partnership agreement provides that the partnership may be brought to an end by notice, then if the circumstances in which notice is envisaged arise, notice may be given. For example:

Clifford v Timms (1908)

Clifford and Timms were dentists in partnership. Their agreement provided that if either should be 'guilty of professional misconduct or any act which is calculated to bring discredit upon or injure the other partner or the partnership's business, the other partner shall be at liberty to give notice ... of his intention to determine the partnership ... and thereupon the partnership shall be dissolved'. Clifford advertised a company, The American Dental Institute Limited, in which he (Clifford) was a shareholder by means of pamphlets which Timms felt were unprofessional. Some of the pamphlets suggested that other dental practitioners failed to take the necessary precaution of sterilising their instruments. Timms served notice upon Clifford to dissolve the partnership on the ground of professional misconduct. It was held by the House of Lords that there had indeed been professional misconduct and Timms was entitled to an order dissolving the partnership.

Similarly if a partnership agreement provides that the partnership may be dissolved if a partner commits a flagrant breach of duty, a notice of dissolution may be given if he is convicted of an offence of dishonesty:

Carmichael v Evans (1904)

Carmichael was a partner in a firm of drapers. He was convicted of travelling by train without having obtained a ticket. The partnership agreement provided that if one of the partners were guilty of a flagrant breach of duty then the other partners could by notice dissolve it. Accordingly they served notice upon Carmichael. He, however, applied for an injunction to stop them dissolving the partnership. It was held that the injunction should not be granted. The conviction for dishonesty fell squarely within the expulsion clause. There was full justification for giving notice for dissolution of the partnership.

18.6.2 Dissolution by order of the court

1 Mental incapacity of a partner

By s103, Mental Health Act 1959, a judge may make an order for the dissolution of a partnership of which a patient under the Act is a member. For these purposes a 'patient' is a person who the judge regards as being incapable by reason of mental disorder of managing or administering his property or affairs.

2 Permanent incapacity

By s35 (b) Partnership Act 1890, 'when a partner other than the partner suing, becomes in any way permanently incapable of performing his part of the partnership contract', the other partners may petition for the dissolution of the partnership.

3   **Prejudicial conduct**
    By s35 (c) Partnership Act 1890 'when a partner other than the partner suing, has been guilty of such conduct as, in the opinion of the court, regard being had to the nature of the business, is calculated to prejudicially affect the carrying on of the business' a partner may petition the court for a dissolution. An example of this ground of action would be where a solicitor in partnership steals clients' money or where a medical practitioner in partnership acts unprofessionally.

4   **Persistent or wilful breach of the partnership agreement**
    By s35 (d), Partnership Act 1890 'when a partner, other than the partner suing, wilfully or persistently commits a breach of the partnership agreement, or otherwise so conducts himself in matters relating to the partnership business that it is not reasonably practicable for the other partner or partners to carry on the business in partnership with him', a partner may petition to the court for a dissolution.

5   **Where the partnership may only be carried on at a loss**
    A partner may petition for a dissolution on the ground that 'the business of the partnership can only be carried on at a loss'. Since a partnership is the relation which subsists between persons carrying on a business in common with a view of profit, it is only right that if the profit cannot be made then this failure should be a ground for dissolution.

6   **The just and equitable ground**
    By s35 (f) 'whenever in any case circumstances have arisen which in the opinion of the court render it just and equitable that the partnership should be dissolved' a partner may petition for a dissolution. This is an extremely wide ground of dissolution and leaves the court with great scope to order a dissolution on the ground that justice and equity demand it.

18.6.3 The consequences of dissolution

By s37, Partnership Act 1890, upon dissolution any partner may publicly notify the dissolution and require the other partners to concur for that purpose in all necessary and proper acts to give effect to the dissolution.

The authority of each partner to bind the firm continues, by s38, Partnership Act 1890, so far as is necessary

    (a)   to complete the unfinished transactions of the firm; and

    (b)   to wind up the affairs of the firm.

The effect of this is illustrated by the case of:

Re Bourne (1906)

A partnership was dissolved by the death of one of the partners. The surviving partner carried on the business of the partnership, depositing with a bank the title deeds relating to land owned by the partnership. The purpose of the deposit was to secure an overdraft. The executors of the deceased partner claimed that he should not have done this and that they had a right to the land in preference to the claim of the bank. It was held by the Court of Appeal that the bank had a prior claim since the title deeds had been deposited with the bank so as to wind up the affairs of the partnership.

18.7 DIFFERENCES BETWEEN COMPANIES AND PARTNERSHIPS

It is important to appreciate the differences which exist between companies and partnerships. In Chapter 16 we considered the concept of legal personality. In the present Chapter we have considered the meaning of a partnership. The purpose of the next section of the Chapter is to draw together the various ideas which we have examined and to highlight the two types of trading organisation. There are within the United Kingdom three types of trading organisation, the sole trader, the partnership and the limited liability company. The sole trader is the individual who trades on his own account. For our purposes there is no need to consider him any further. What we shall now concentrate on is the difference between companies and partnerships. For convenience, this is done in the form of a list.

1   A company is a separate legal entity from its members. A partnership is not. It will be recalled that a company is a corporation enjoying separate legal personality. A partnership is simply the relation which subsists between persons carrying on a business in common with a view of profit.

2   The liability of members of a limited company for the debts of the company is restricted to the amount unpaid on their shares. Usually when a company issues shares, those shares are paid for in full by the members at the time they acquire them from the company. This means that in the ordinary course of events, once shares are paid for, a member will not be called upon to make any further payment. On the other hand, a partner in a firm is liable without limit for the debts of the firm. In the event of the firm going into an insolvent dissolution, each partner will find himself liable to the last penny of his fortune for the debts of the firm.

3   By s716, Companies Act 1985 a partnership may not have more than 20 members. There are exceptions to this in the case of certain professions such as solicitors and accountants. There is no limit upon the number of members which a company may have.

4   Each partner may take part in the running of the firm and bind the firm as its agent. Companies are run by their directors. Members, as such, cannot make a contract which is binding on the company. Of course, there is nothing to prevent a member from being a director, in which case, acting as a director he can make a contract binding upon the company.

5   As a general rule a share in the partnership may be transferred only with the consent of all the other partners. The reason for this is that a partner has an implied agency to bind his fellow partners. The corollary of this must therefore be that each partner must have a right to veto any prospective partner of whom he does not approve. Shares within a limited company are freely transferable. There is an exception in the case of companies which by their articles choose to restrict the transferability of shares. In practice, it is very common that there is such a restriction in the articles of a private company. If a company is formed having two shareholders who are also its directors, each will almost certainly wish to ensure that if one sells his shares then the other have a right to veto the new shareholder. This is usually done by means of an article which provides that in the event of a shareholder wishing to sell his shares, the other shareholder shall have a first option to buy them. Alternatively it might be done by an article which provides that in the event of shares being transferred, the new shareholder must be approved by the board of directors of the company.

6   The powers of a company are restricted by the ultra vires rule. A corporation, being a separate legal entity, is restricted in what it can do. It cannot act beyond its powers. If it goes beyond the powers contained in its constitution it is said to be acting ultra vires and as such cannot enforce these contracts, though a third party dealing in good faith with the company can enforce the contract against the company. The powers of a partnership are unlimited. All that is needed to change the powers and objects of a partnership is the unanimous agreement of the partners. If a small partnership trading as greengrocer's decides that it wishes to embark on the business of running an international airline then, so long as there is sufficient capital, the partners may agree to such a change in the nature of the business.

7   Because the liability of the members of a company is limited, the money which has been paid to the company for its shares adopts a particular importance. It forms part of a fund which cannot, without the observation of the strictest formalities, be returned to the shareholders. In the case of a partnership, liability of the partners is, as has been said, unlimited. Because of this there is no problem in returning capital to the partners and the partners can draw out their capital as much as they wish subject only to the consent of their fellow partners.

8   The capital structure of a company is far more flexible than that of a partnership. A partnership may only borrow in the same manner as an ordinary individual. It has open to it sources of credit such as hire-purchase, bank overdrafts and fixed charges. While a company also has these methods of raising capital, it also enjoys a further method, namely the floating charge. This is an equitable charge which was developed in the last century in the Court of Chancery. It is unique to companies and allows the company to utilise its constantly changing assets in order to raise capital. For example, a company manufacturing garden ornaments will at any time have in its possession raw materials, clay, etc from which to fashion the ornaments, ornaments in the course of manufacture, finished ornaments waiting to be sold and book debts owing to the company from the sale of ornaments. At any time these assets might be worth say, £50,000. The company can create over these assets a floating charge which, so long as the company is a going concern, allows the directors to deal with these assets as they will. However, once the charge crystallises (ie becomes fixed upon the assets in the possession of the company at that time, usually upon liquidation or the appointment of an administrative receiver) the directors lose the power to deal with those assets and they become charged for the debt owing by the company to the chargeholder.

9   The conduct of a company is subject to strict statutory provisions. For example, there are specific rules in the Companies Act 1985 requiring an annual audit of accounts, the making of annual returns and the submission of accounts to the Registrar of Companies, the maintenance of registers of members, directors, charges etc. The rules governing the conduct of partnerships are very much less stringent. There is even no statutory provision which requires the keeping of accounts unless the partnership is of sufficient size to warrant VAT registration.

10 Companies and partnerships are taxed differently. Companies are subject to corporation tax. Partnerships are subject to income tax payable by the partners individually.

SELF-TEST QUESTIONS

18.1 The three general principles running through partnership law are?

18.2 Define a partnership.

18.3 When will the sharing of profits not constitute a partnership?

18.4 Why were the partnerships in *Moss* v *Elphick* and *Abbott* v *Abbott* not partnerships at will?

18.5 If a case with facts similar to those in *Kendall* v *Hamilton* came before the courts today, would the decision be different?

18.6 Why were the firms in *Hamlyn* v *Houston & Co* and *Rhodes* v *Moules* liable for the tort of the partner?

18.7 What is the ratio of *Tower Cabinet Co Ltd* v *Ingram*?

18.8 How may a partnership be dissolved without court order?

18.9 Why should a petition to the court to dissolve the firm be used only as a last resort?

18.10 What are the key distinctions between a company and a partnership?

Answers on page 341

EXERCISES

Exercise 18.1

N O and P are partners. What are the rights of the partners:

(i)   to expel a partner
(ii) to dissolve the partnership
(iii) to admit a new partner
(iv) to limit a partner's authority to bind the partnership?

Exercise 18.2

Alan and Jim are partners in a garage. Jim provided the capital and visits the garage only infrequently. Alan works full time for the firm. The agreement between Alan and Jim provides that no partner will incur any debt on behalf of the partnership exceeding £100 unless the other partner consents, that oil shall only be purchased from the Ooze Oil Co and that there shall be no trading in second-hand cars. In contravention of this agreement Alan has bought oil to the value of £200 from another company and has also bought several second-hand cars in the name of the firm.
Advise Jim.

Answers on page 342

Professional negligence and the accountant

As we have already seen, a person who suffers as a result of breach of contract has a remedy against the other contracting party. The law of torts covers the case where a person suffers injury but where that injury emanates, not from a breach of contract, but from a situation where the defendant, the person who did the injury, was perceived by the law as owing some sort of duty in law to the injured person. The usual definition given in textbooks is that a tort is a civil wrong other than a breach of contract or a breach of trust. Since it is a civil wrong, the injured party may seek a remedy in the civil courts. The remedy will usually be damages. Since it is not a breach of contract, the injured party does not have to prove a pre-existing relationship with the defendant. Since it is not a breach of trust, the injured party does not have to prove any pre-existing fiduciary duty owed to him by the defendant.

Probably the most common tort is negligence which we shall shortly be considering, but tort also includes many other different types of conduct such as trespass (ie the direct physical interference with another person's land, possessions or person); nuisance (the indirect interference with a person's enjoyment of his land such as arises when a person causes inconvenience to his neighbour by holding regular noisy parties or having troublesome bonfires in his garden); and defamation of character (which is the publication of a statement which tends to lower a person in the estimation of right thinking members of society generally, or which tends to make that person shunned or avoided by others, or which exposes him to hatred, ridicule or contempt).

What we are concerned with in this chapter is liability in negligence. In particular, we shall be considering the liability of an auditor in respect of the company accounts which he audits. Before we do this, however, it is necessary to remind ourselves of the principle of vicarious liability.

19.1 VICARIOUS LIABILITY

It will be recalled from Paragraph 13.1 that a person may be liable for a tort, not only where he himself has committed it, but also where he has had someone else commit it on his behalf. Obviously the most usual example of vicarious liability is the liability of a master for torts committed by his employee during the course of his employment. In particular it will be recalled that an employer is under a duty to provide a safe system of work. This includes ensuring that fellow employees are competent. Thus in:

Hudson v Ridge Manufacturing Co Ltd (1957)

Hudson was an employee of Ridge Manufacturing. He was injured as a result of being tripped up as a practical joke by a fellow employee who had a reputation for childish behaviour of this type. It was held that Ridge Manufacturing were liable to compensate Hudson for his injuries since there was a duty at common law to ensure that only competent employees were engaged.

Such liability of an employer in tort may arise where an employee has acted in defiance of express instructions. For example:

Limpus v London General Omnibus Co (1862)

This case arose at a time when all bus services in London were provided by private companies. There was considerable competition between the companies and the London General Omnibus Co had given an express instruction to their drivers not to race or obstruct rival vehicles. A driver employed by the company injured Limpus by deliberately driving his bus in such a way as to obstruct the passage of a rival bus and thus be the first at the bus stop to pick up waiting passengers. It was held that the London General Omnibus Co were vicariously liable for this injury notwithstanding that they had ordered their drivers not to race in this way. The reason for so holding was that despite the order prohibiting racing, the racing was done for the purpose of promoting the employer's business, which was part of the driver's duties. The driver was carrying out an authorised act albeit in an unauthorised way.

A similar situation arose in:

Rose* v *Plenty* (1976)

A milkman, as a result of negligent driving, injured a child whom he was carrying on his milkfloat. The child had been acting as his assistant in delivering milk in direct contravention of instructions issued by the employer. It was held by the Court of Appeal that the employers of the milkman were vicariously liable for the child's injuries. Even though the milkman had been in breach of express instructions, he had not ceased to be acting on behalf of his employer.

On the other hand, vicarious liability does not occur where an employee is acting in a manner which in effect removes him from his contract of employment. For example in:

Iqbal* v *London Transport Executive* (1973)

A bus conductor employed by London Transport attempted to drive a bus at a depot. In doing so he injured Iqbal who was a fellow employee. The conductor had been told on several occasions that he must not drive buses. It was held that the employers were not vicariously liable for what the conductor had done, since actually driving the bus was completely different from the usual work of a bus conductor.

An employee may even be held vicariously liable for any act of fraud committed by an employee if that fraud was committed in the course of this employment:

Lloyd* v *Grace, Smith & Co* (1912)

A clerk employed by a firm of solicitors fraudulently induced a client to sign a document transferring certain property which she (the client) had inherited to the clerk. This was done in the course of giving her certain advice for which she had consulted the firm. The clerk then misappropriated the property.
It was held by the House of Lords that the firm of Solicitors was vicariously liable for the fraud.

19.2 INTRODUCTION TO NEGLIGENCE

There can be no doubt that negligence is the most important tort today. It is the cause of action (ie basis of the claim) in the majority of cases brought in tort. The term negligence is also used in the context of breach of contract. An auditor who audits a set of accounts with less than proper care is said to have acted negligently.
To succeed in his action in negligence, the plaintiff must show three things:
(a) That the defendant owed him a duty of care.
(b) That there was a breach of that duty of care by the defendant.
(c) And that such breach of duty resulted in damage to the plaintiff.

The leading case on negligence and the one on which the modern law of negligence is based is:

***Donoghue* v *Stevenson* (1932)**

Donoghue went to a cafe with a friend. There the friend bought Donoghue a bottle of ginger beer. When Donoghue poured the ginger beer from the bottle, she found among the contents a decomposed snail. As a result, Donoghue became ill. She could not sue in contract since the ginger beer had been bought for her by a friend. Moreover the default was not by the seller of the ginger beer but by the manufacturer. It was held by the House of Lords that the manufacturer was liable in negligence to the ultimate consumer. They should have foreseen the probability that a consumer would drink the ginger beer and consequently there was a duty of care owed to the ultimate consumer to ensure there was nothing objectionable such as a decomposed snail in the bottle. Since this duty had been broken the manufacturer was liable to pay damages to Donoghue.

The case is particularly important because in it Lord Atkin explained what is meant by the duty of care:
'the rule that you are to love your neighbour becomes in law, you must not injure your neighbour; and the lawyer's question who is my neighbour? receives a restricted reply. You must take reasonable care to avoid acts or omissions which you can reasonably foresee would be likely to injure your

neighbour. Who, then, in law is my neighbour? The answer seems to be that persons who are so closely and directly affected by my act that I ought reasonably to have them in contemplation as being so affected when I am directing my mind to the acts or omissions which are called in question'.

A few moments thought will reveal that, as a matter of policy, there must be a limit as to who falls within the scope of the duty of care. For example, it is obvious that a car driver owes a duty of care to other road-users, both pedestrians and motorists, to ensure that he does not injure them by his negligent driving. However, he does not owe a duty to an onlooker who might be upset as a result of seeing an accident caused by the driver's negligence. Many people have, from time to time, been upset by seeing a road accident or the result of a road accident, but if all of these people were able to claim compensation from the person who caused the accident this would obviously mean that car insurance premiums would have to rise substantially so as to enable the insurance companies to meet the resulting claims. The limitation of the scope of the duty of care is illustrated by:

Bourhill v *Young* (1943)

A pregnant woman heard the noise of a motorcycle crashing and afterwards, when the debris had been cleared away, she saw blood spilled on the road. As a result she suffered nervous shock and her child was stillborn. She brought an action in negligence against the personal representatives of the motorcyclist who had himself been killed in the crash. It was held that the motorcyclist owed no duty of care to the woman. At the time of the accident she had not been within the area of potential danger. He could not reasonably have been expected to envisage that injury would be caused by the accident to a pregnant woman merely hearing the crash and observing the aftermath.

The number of situations where one person owes a duty of care to another is already a long one, and one which is being added to continually. We have already considered the duty owed by an employer to an employee, a manufacturer to a consumer and a driver to other road-users. It has been held that a local authority owes a duty of care to the occupier of a house in respect of which it has approved plans. For example:

Dutton v *Bognor Regis UDC* (1971)

Mrs Dutton was the second purchaser of a house which had in fact been built on the site of a rubbish tip. The local authority was aware of the fact that the house had been built on a rubbish tip both when it approved the plans and subsequently when it inspected the work on site. The foundations of such a house should have been set much deeper than for a similar house being built on sound land. However, the architect had not designed the house with the necessary deeper foundations and the local authority had not discovered this defect. Subsequently the house was sold to Mrs Dutton who sought damages in negligence from the council when serious structural defects in the house began to emerge. It was held by the Court of Appeal that the local authority was liable for the damages resulting from the negligent approval of the plans.

This decision was approved by the House of Lords in:

Anns v *Merton L B C* (1978)

A block of flats was constructed on foundations which were shallower than those approved by the local authority in the plans which had been submitted to it. Some years later subsidence occurred resulting in substantial damage. Tenants of the flats sought damages from the local authority for their negligent failure to inspect the foundations. It was held by the House of Lords that such liability in negligence existed. The local authority owed a duty of care in carrying out its function in this regard.

Just as a duty of care must have been owed by the defendant to the plaintiff, so too the defendant must have broken his duty by not behaving in the way in which a reasonable person would have behaved in such a position.

The case of:

Latimer v *A E C Ltd* (1953) will be recalled from Chapter 13, 13.4. This was the case where an exceptionally heavy storm caused flooding of A E C's factory. After the flooding had subsided A E C used all sawdust which was available to them to cover the oily surface of the floor. A few areas remained untreated and Latimer slipped on one of these oily patches. It was held that the employers were not liable in negligence because they had done all that could reasonably be expected of them.

It will likewise be recalled from the case of:

***Paris* v *Stepney Borough Council* (1951)** that greater care is demanded when dealing with disabled persons. That case concerned an employee who worked in a garage and who had lost the sight in one eye. He had not been supplied with safety goggles and as a result of an injury at work to his good eye he became completely blind. It was held that the employers had been negligent in failing to supply him with goggles notwithstanding that it was not usual to do so for that type of work. Because of the employee's particular disability there was a duty upon the employers to take effective precautions against the risk of injury.

It goes without saying that the injury must have been caused by the defendant's, rather than the plaintiff's, conduct. It may sometimes be seen upon examination of all the facts of a case that the actual cause of injury was the plaintiff's own act or default rather than that of the defendant. For example in:

Cummings v *Arrol & Co Ltd* (1962)

Cummings was killed as a result of falling from a steel tower. His estate claimed damages from the employers because there had not been safety belts available for Cummings. The court found that as a matter of fact even if the employers had provided safety belts Cummings would not have worn one. He had refused on many occasions to wear a safety belt in the past even when they were readily available. Thus the real cause of death was the behaviour of Cummings himself. Accordingly the court held that no compensation was payable.

As is usual in civil cases, it is the plaintiff who has to prove negligence. Thus he must adduce sufficient evidence to persuade the court that on the balance of probabilities there was negligence on the part of the defendant resulting in injury to the plaintiff. The plaintiff may in appropriate circumstances be aided by the doctrine of '*res ipsa loquitur*'. This phrase means literally 'the thing speaks for itself'. In other words, the circumstances of the incident giving rise to the injury are such that some breach of duty may be inferred. When this doctrine is applied the burden of proof is transferred to the defendant who must then prove on the balance of probabilities that he was not negligent. An early example of the doctrine is the case of:

Byrne v *Boadle* (1863)

While he was passing a warehouse used by Boadle, Byrne was struck by a barrel of flour which had fallen through an open door on an upper floor. It was held that this was itself evidence of negligence. Thus the doctrine of *res ipsa loquitur* applied and the burden of disproving negligence fell to the defendant.

Similarly in:

Ward v *Tesco Stores Ltd* (1976)

The plaintiff slipped on a pool of yogurt while shopping at a Tesco's store. It was held by the Court of Appeal that the accident would not have occurred if spillages had been dealt with promptly.

In circumstances where the plaintiff was himself negligent, the court will then assess the extent of the responsibility of each party for the loss and reduce the damages accordingly under the Law Reform (Contributory Negligence) Act 1945. An example of this is to be found in:

Uddin v *Associated Portland Cement Manufacturers Ltd* (1965)

Uddin was an employee at Associated Portland Cement. He followed a pigeon into a part of the factory which he should not have entered. While trying to catch the bird his clothing became entangled in dangerous machinery and he was severely injured. He claimed damages from Associated Portland Cement. It was held that the employers were liable for failing to provide adequate protection against injury since it was foreseeable that someone would be injured on the machinery in question. However, damages were reduced by 80% to take account of the employee's contributory negligence.

Finally, in regard to the basic principles of the law of negligence, it should be noted that for injury to be recoverable, it must fall within the overall limitations of liability. For this to be the case, the injury must fall within what is referred to as the foreseeability of the defendant. This was laid down in:

The Wagon Mound (1961)

The engineer employed by the defendant company allowed some furnace oil to be spilt from their ship onto the water in Sydney Harbour. Subsequently the oil floated across the harbour to a wharf where oxyacetyline equipment was being used by the plaintiff.

The plaintiff thereupon stopped welding. However, he recommenced on being advised that oil of this kind would not burn on water. Two days later the oil was ignited as a result of molten metal from the welding falling on the oily water. As a result of the fire which followed there was extensive damage caused to the plaintiffs wharf.

The Judicial Committee of the Privy Council found as a fact that it was unforeseeable that the oil would ignite in the circumstances described above. Thus the defendant was not liable.

19.3 ECONOMIC LOSS

At one time it was believed that liability in tort did not extend to economic loss in situations where there was no physical damage incurred. The most widely relied upon suggestion that liability might arise in negligence for economic loss was the dissenting judgment of Lord Denning in:

Candler v Crane, Christmas & Co (1951), the facts of which are not important for our purpose since they concerned accountants preparing accounts knowing that they were to be given to the plaintiffs for a particular purpose. What was significant in the case was Lord Denning's judgment in which he made a number of *obiter dicta* as to what he saw the law to be.

Firstly he considered what persons owed a duty of care. In this regard he felt that a duty of care was owed by persons such as accountants whose profession it is to examine books and accounts and make reports. The key feature of such persons is that they are skilled professional people who engage in a calling which requires special knowledge and skill.

Secondly he considered to whom a duty was owed. It was obviously owed to the client. Beyond this it was also owed to any third person to whom the accounts were shown and to whom the accountants knew the accounts would be shown.

There is little doubt that this was an extremely far-seeing version of the law and way ahead of its time. As such it attracted a certain degree of criticism. However, some twelve years later, the House of Lords recognised that negligent misrepresentation could well be the basis of an action for a breach of duty of care in negligence. This arose in a case we mentioned in Chapters 6 and 9, that of:

Hedley Byrne v Heller & Partners (1964)

Hedley Byrne, a firm of advertising agents, were instructed by a client to place certain advertising contracts. These contracts would involve Hedley Byrne in personal liability to the people with whom they were placing the orders. They made enquiries with Heller & Partners Ltd, who were merchant bankers, and dealt with the client's affairs, regarding their client's creditworthiness. They were told 'in confidence and without responsibility on our part' that the client was good for £100,000. In reliance on this, Hedley Byrne placed orders on behalf of the client but, when the client subsequently went into liquidation, Hedley Byrne suffered losses of £17,000. It was held by the House of Lords that Heller & Partners Ltd was not liable for the losses by reason of their express disclaimer of liability. However, the House of Lords went on to state, obiter, that a negligent though honest misrepresentation could give rise to an action in negligence notwithstanding that no contractual or fiduciary relationship exists between the parties, so long as the person making the statement owed a duty of care to the person to whom it was made. A duty of care would arise in this situation where the person making the statement has some special knowledge or skill and knew or should have known that the person to whom he was making the statement would rely on these qualities being exercised.

This case clearly opened the door to claims for economic loss at least, so long as the economic loss arose out of a special relationship such as existed in this case.

The development came slowly at first. For example in:

Weller v Foot & Mouth Disease Research Institute (1966)

The plaintiffs were a firm of cattle auctioneers. They lost six days' business following an outbreak of foot and mouth disease which they alleged was the fault of the Research Institute which allegedly had allowed the escape of the foot and mouth virus. When the case came to court, the court decided that damages could not be recovered for loss of profits since this was not a recognised head of damages. This would be so even if the Research Institute were to admit carelessness and to admit the foreseeability of the loss and even if causation were found.

However, inroads were made into this shortly afterwards in the case of:

S C M (United Kingdom) Ltd v W J Whittall & Son Ltd (1971)

A workman, who was employed by the defendants, was digging up a road near to the plaintiff's factory when he damaged an electric power cable. The cable supplied power to the plaintiff's factory and the resulting power failure caused loss of one day's profits. It was held by the Court of Appeal that the defendants were liable for the loss of profits.

This has since been extended to situations where there was economic loss without any accompanying damage to property. The loss of profits had been refused, it will be recalled, in *Weller's* case because there had been no damage to property. Clearly in the *Whittall* case there had been damage to property and so an award to cover loss of profits was perhaps easier to make. An extension to the principle arose in:

Midland Bank Trust Co v Hett, Stubbs & Kemp (1979)

A solicitor failed to register an option to purchase a farm for a client who was a prospective purchaser of the farm. The result was that the owner of the farm sold it to someone else. It was held that the plaintiff (or, more accurately, the plaintiff's executors in this case, since the plaintiff had died) could recover for economic loss caused by the negligence of the solicitor.

Similarly in:

Ross v Caunters (1979)

A solicitor executed a will carelessly with the result that a bequest failed. It was held that the disappointed beneficiary could sue the solicitor.

A similar decision was reached in another case mentioned in Chapter 9, that of:

Esso Petroleum Co Ltd v Mardon (1976)

Esso Petroleum granted a tenancy of a filling station to Mardon, claiming that 200,000 gallons would be sold over a period of 3 years. After 3 years, sales had not reached 100,000 gallons. Mardon brought proceedings against Esso Petroleum in negligence and the Court of Appeal held that he was entitled to damages. A special relationship existed. Esso had considerable experience in the trade upon which Mardon was entitled to rely.

It is interesting to note here that the statement made by Esso Petroleum constituted both a misrepresentation in contract, ie it was a pre-contractual statement of fact, and also a statement resulting in liability in negligence. The fact that there is a contractual relationship between the representor and the representee does not preclude the representee from bringing proceedings in negligence.

It should be noted that the standard of care a professional person should show is that of acting honestly and exercising reasonable care. It does not consist of an absolute duty to give correct advice. For example in:

Stafford v Conti Commodity Services Ltd (1981)

Stafford made a number of investments in the commodity markets relying on advice from Conti Commodity Services, a firm of brokers. As a result of the dealings not being successful he lost £19,000. It was held that the brokers had not been negligent, having merely made an error of judgment. Ordinary damages were payable. Error of judgment is not necessarily an indication of negligence.

19.4 EXCLUSION OF LIABILITY

It will be recalled that in the Hedley Byrne case no liability actually arose because the advice given by the defendant merchant bankers had been accompanied by a disclaimer of responsibility, 'in confidence and without responsibility on our part'. Since the Unfair Contract Terms Act 1977 came into force in 1978, such a disclaimer of responsibility for negligent advice is only effective to exclude liability insofar as the exclusion is reasonable. It is suggested that it would be unreasonable for an accountant to seek to exclude liability to a client company if he were negligent in auditing his books.

19.5 THE POSITION OF AUDITORS

The leading judgment as to the standard of skill of auditors is that in the case of:

Re Kingston Cotton Mill Ltd (1896)

The facts of this case are not important for our purposes. What is significant is the statement by Lopes L J as to the skill and care required to be shown by an auditor. 'An auditor is not bound to be a detective, or, as was said, to approach his work with suspicion or with a foregone conclusion that there is something wrong. He is a watchdog, but not a bloodhound. He is justified in believing tried servants of the company in whom confidence is placed by the company. He is entitled to assume that they are honest, and to rely upon their representations, provided he takes reasonable care. If there is anything calculated to excite suspicion he should probe it to the bottom; but in the absence of anything of that kind he is only bound to be reasonably cautious and careful'.

The general duty of auditors was considered in:

Re London and General Bank (No 2) (1895)

Dividends were paid out improperly because assets of the company had been overstated in its balance sheet. It was found that the auditor had been negligent in respect of a particular year's report in that certain loans which had been entered into by the company were valued at face value and in fact they were not realisable. The auditor had failed to draw attention to this fact. Subsequently the members of the company had relied upon the accounts when they resolved to pay a dividend. It was held that the auditor was liable to repay the dividend because he had been in breach of his statutory duty in preparing the accounts. Again the judgment was by Lopes L J who made the following points in regard to auditors' duties:

(a) It is not an auditor's duty to give advice to directors or shareholders.
(b) An auditor has nothing to do with the prudence or imprudence of investments made by the company.
(c) The auditor is under a duty to ascertain and state the true financial position of the company as at the time of the audit.
(d) The auditor must show reasonable care and what constitutes reasonable care in any particular case must depend upon the exact circumstances of that case.
(e) In this particular case the auditors would know that the accounts would be relied upon by the members in voting a dividend.

This was followed in the case of:

Re City Equitable Fire Insurance Co (1925)

The case concerned negligence on the part of the company's auditor in verifying the ownership of certain securities held by the company. At first instance Romer J said that the auditor's duty in this regard is that he must satisfy himself both that securities claimed by the company in fact exist and that they are being held in safe custody. In his opinion, an auditor was never justified in omitting to make a personal inspection of the company's securities where such securities are held by a person with whom it is not proper that they should have been left. The case subsequently went on appeal to the Court of Appeal where Romer J's decision was upheld. The Court of Appeal stressed that the auditor is bound to be reasonably careful rather than suspicious.

Further guidance can be found in the case of:

Fomento (Sterling Area) Ltd v Selsdon Fountain Pen Co Ltd (1958)

Again, in this case, the facts are not important. What is significant is the further guidance given by the court on the standard of care. In the House of Lords, Lord Denning said that it was too narrow a view to adopt that the auditor was simply concerned with figures. Nor is he confined to the mechanics of checking vouchers and making arithmetical computations. He should not be written off as merely a professional 'adder-upper'. His essential task is to ensure that errors are not made whether of computation, omission or commission or downright untruths. While he need not be suspicious of dishonesty, he should nevertheless suspect someone of making a mistake. If he comes across fraud or evidence that a company has gone beyond its power, then he must enquire into it. If he comes across something which requires special knowledge, such as patent matters, he should take separate legal advice.

An example of the situation where an auditor needs to investigate further is the case of:

Re Thomas Gerrard & Son Ltd (1967)

The managing director of a company had falsified the books of the company by altering dates on invoices. The auditors enquired of him in regard to these alterations and accepted the answers given to them. Subsequently, incorrect dividends were paid and tax was overpaid. The auditors were sued in negligence. It was held that they were liable in negligence. Having discovered the altered invoices they should have been put on enquiry and they had failed in their duty to exercise reasonable care and skill.

It is apparent that an auditor's duty lies to the company whose accounts he is auditing. However, does his duty extend to persons unconnected with the company who rely upon the accounts? It was recognised obiter that such a duty did exist in the case of:

J E B Fasteners Ltd v Marks, Bloom & Co (1983)

An auditor prepared accounts in respect of which he failed to notice certain stock deficiencies. Subsequently the accounts were relied upon by a purchaser of the company. The purchaser sued the auditors in negligence. On the facts of the case it was held that there was no liability and the plaintiff's action was dismissed since they would have acted no differently even if they had known of the true financial position of the company. However it was said, obiter, that if the purchasers had in fact relied upon the auditor's account, the auditors would have been liable had they known, or reasonably been able to foresee at the time that the audits were being carried out, that a person might rely upon the accounts for the purpose of deciding whether or not to purchase the company.

Shortly afterwards a Scottish case decided that such liability existed:

Twomax v Dickson McFarlane & Robinson
Gordon v Dickson McFarlane & Robinson (1983)

A firm of accountants was sued by people who had invested in the company in reliance upon negligently audited accounts. It was held that the accountants were liable in damages to these investors when they suffered loss.

The line of argument adopted by the court appears to be that in the case of existing shareholders the removal from office of the auditor gave no adequate redress to a shareholder suffering loss though auditor's negligence. Accordingly, given that a shareholder can establish a breach of duty (which of its nature would ordinarily be hard to establish) he can take proceedings in negligence against the auditor. On the other hand there is no duty of care owed to potential investors in the company. To impose such a duty would be to impose a wider duty upon auditors than exists at common law.

In recent cases, however, the courts are moving away from the approach taken in *J E B Fasteners*. In:

Caparo Industries plc v Dickman and others (1989)

Caparo owned shares in another public company, F. plc, and intended to make a take-over bid for it. As a shareholder in F, Caparo received F's audited accounts and, in reliance on these, later made a successful take-over bid for the company. After the take-over, however, the plaintiffs brought an action against the defendants, F's auditors, alleging that the accounts had been negligently prepared and that the defendants had been negligent in auditing and certifying them. The plaintiffs claimed that the accounts should have shown that F had made a loss of £0.46 million. In fact they showed a reported profit of £1.3 million.

At first instance, the court held that the auditors owed no duty of care to the plaintiffs either as shareholders or potential investors. The plaintiffs appealed to the Court of Appeal which held that there was a sufficient proximity between auditors and existing shareholders to give rise to a duty of care on the auditors' part. The auditors, however, owed no duty of care to potential investors. The duty to members comes about because auditors have a statutory obligation to report to them and members have a statutory right to receive the reports. No such obligation and right exists between auditors and potential investors, nor is there any contractual or other relationship between them.

The Caparo Case has been followed in:

Al Saudi Banque and others v Clarke Pixley (1989)

The plaintiffs were a bank which lent money to GC Ltd, a company providing finance to customers involved in the import-export trade. These customers secured their debts to GC by issuing bills of exchange which were drawn in GC's favour. GC negotiated these bills to the bank as security for the loans. The bills of exchange represented virtually the whole of GC's assets and the plaintiff bank relied on the company's audited accounts, and the auditor's report thereon, to decide whether to grant further loans or to increase or continue existing facilities to GC. The defendants were GC's auditors.

In 1983, GC was compulsorily wound up with debts of £8.6 million owing to unsecured creditors. It had no assets available for distribution and, in fact, its two largest customers were associated with GC's directors and had no underlying business to support the bills of exchange they had issued. The plaintiff alleged that these bills were given merely to enable existing bank indebtedness to be repaid out of fresh advances either from the same or a different bank. The plaintiff claimed that GC's accounts, as audited by the defendant, failed to show that the company was insolvent and so did not give a true and fair view of the company's affairs on the date of audit despite a statement to this effect in the reports on the 1981 and 1982 accounts. The plaintiffs, therefore, sued the defendant auditors in negligence. The court in Chancery Division followed the judgment in Caparo which, said the judge, Millett J, is binding authority for a number of propositions:

- In cases of negligent misstatement, it is necessary to show that it is foreseeable that the plaintiff or someone in a similar position would rely on the statement. Foreseeability of reliance, however, was not itself sufficient to make the defendant liable.
- It is also necessary to show that there is a relationship between the parties sufficient to show that a duty of care existed. This can arise, for example, by a voluntary assumption of responsibility or by a relationship which is "equivalent to contract".
- There is the necessary relationship between a company's members and its auditors. Auditors have a statutory duty to report to members and know that it is intended to send copies of the reports to them.
- There may also be a sufficient relationship where auditors can be taken impliedly to have represented the accuracy of the accounts to the plaintiff and even where they have provided the accounts to the company with the intention,
- or with the knowledge, that it was the company's intention that they were to be supplied to the plaintiff or to persons in a class of which the plaintiff was one.
- It is not necessary that the auditors should have any particular transaction in mind, or that they should intend the recipient of their report to act upon it in any such transaction. As long as the necessary relationship exists, it is enough if it is foreseeable that the recipient of the report may rely on it in some future transaction, whether this is contemplated by the auditors or not.
- The necessary relationship does not exist between a company's auditors and potential investors who are not existing shareholders in the company. The fact that it is foreseeable that the auditor's report may come into the hands of potential investors and be relied upon by them is not enough of itself, to create the relationship.

In the *Al Saudi* case, the auditors did not make their reports to the plaintiff bank or to any other person with the intention or in the knowledge that these reports would be communicated to the plaintiff. At most, it was foreseeable that, if the bank was considering renewing, extending or continuing credit facilities to GC it would call for and rely on copies of the company's latest audited accounts and the report on them.

The fact that a person who relied on the report was an existing creditor of the company did not put that person in the same position as a shareholder. Creditors played no part in appointing auditors, and auditors had no duty to report to them or to supply copies of the report to them; nor did the auditors send their report to the company with the intention or in the knowledge that they would be supplied to them.

With regard to people who were not creditors of the company at the relevant balance sheet date, this is directly comparable to the position of potential investors in *Caparo*. No duty of care is owed to them. The court held therefore that there was no relationship between the banks and the auditors and therefore no duty of care was owed by the auditors. The banks therefore lost their action.

Both the Caparo and Al Saudi cases are going on appeal to the House of Lords for a definitive ruling on the nature and scope of an auditor's liability in the circumstances.

The importance of accounting standards was considered in the recent case of:

Lloyd Cheyham & Co Ltd v Littlejohn & Co (1985)

The facts of this case are not important. What matters is the analysis by Woolf J of the importance of accounting standards. He said:

'While they are not conclusive so that a departure from their terms necessarily involves a breach of duty of care, and they are not as the explanatory foreword makes clear, rigid rules, they are very strong evidence as to what is the proper standard which should be adopted and unless there is some justification a departure will be regarded as constituting a breach of duty. It appears to me important that this should be the position because third parties in reading the accounts are entitled to assume that they have been drawn up in accordance with approved practice unless there is some indication in the accounts which clearly states that this is not the case'.

An auditor is not expected to have the skills of an expert when he values shares:

Whiteoak v Walker (1988)

A company was formed in 1972 to take over the business which had previously been carried on in partnership. Whiteoak was a minority shareholder and former partner in the business. In 1981 he became ill and ceased work. Thereupon he asked the majority shareholder to make him an offer for his shares, claiming them to be worth £135,000. The company was unhappy with that figure and asked the auditor to value the shares, the auditor coming up with the price of £43,000. Whiteoak had to transfer his shares at that price. Subsequently he brought proceedings against the auditor for damages for negligence in valuing the shares. It was admitted by the auditor that he owed Whiteoak a duty of care. The question was as to the standard of this care. Was it the standard of a chartered accountant having specialist skills in valuing unquoted shares (as Whiteoak claimed) or that of a reasonably competent chartered accountant in general practice acting as an auditor who had agreed to a request to undertake the valuation (as the auditor claimed)? It was held that there had been no negligence. The members in this case were seeking a fair result quickly and cheaply and intended the auditor to apply his own skills. They did not intend that he should have the skills of a specialist valuer.

19.6 INSURANCE AGAINST RISK

The development of negligence cases of recent years has been along what is sometimes referred to as the 'deepest pocket principle'. In other words claims are made against the person best able to meet an award. There are two trends which are apparent in the development of professional negligence today. The first is the seemingly ever-widening scope of the duty of care owed by auditors, notwithstanding the *Caparo Industries* case just discussed. The second is the upward movement of settlement figures. A major problem faced by accountants is the level of insurance cover which they should carry to cover them against the risk of liability in a claim made against them. Current advice from the ACCA is that 2.5 times fee income is appropriate as a rough guide. However the level of liability is not related to fee income. What is depended upon is the scale of potential losses. Again, the degree of risk must be borne in mind. The risk involved in carrying out audits is probably quite considerably lower than that incurred in management consultancy or investment advice.

Professional indemnity insurance is expensive and fees for this are simply passed on to clients. At the present time there appears to be a distinct move within the profession towards the possibility of limited liability firms of accountants, notwithstanding that limited liability is quite contrary to the British tradition of professional service. The ongoing expense of adequate insurance cover is a continuing problem for the profession.

SUMMARY

In this chapter we have been looking at liability in negligence with particular reference to liability of accountants. To establish negligence there has to be shown the existence of a duty of care owed to the plaintiff, a breach of that duty and loss resulting to the plaintiff. Liability is now possible for economic loss. Accountants used to be able to avoid liability by the use of a disclaimer, though this is the more difficult to achieve since the Unfair Contract Terms Act 1977. Accountants may seek to protect themselves against the risk of a claim by use of professional indemnity insurance, but this is expensive and it may be that firms of accountants will in the near future become limited liability companies.

PROFESSIONAL NEGLIGENCE AND THE ACCOUNTANT: CHAPTER NINETEEN

SELF-TEST QUESTIONS

19.1 What is the difference between a duty in contract and a duty in tort?

19.2 What is vicarious liability?

19.3 Why were the employers vicariously liable in *Limpus* v *London General Omnibus Co* and not in *Iqbal* v *London Transport Executive*?

19.4 What must be proved for liability in negligence to be shown?

19.5 Why could the plaintiff in *Donoghue* v *Stevenson* not sue in breach of contract?

19.6 Who is 'a neighbour' for the purposes of negligence?

19.7 How does the doctrine '*res ispa loquitur*' help the plaintiff in a negligence action?

19.8 How did *Hedley Byrne* v *Heller & Partners* (1964) extend the scope of negligence?

19.9 What standard of care must be used by an auditor?

19.10 Why were the auditors in Re *Thomas Gerrard & Son Ltd* liable in negligence?

Answers on page 344

EXERCISES

Exercise 19.1

In what circumstances may a person be held vicariously liable for the tort of another?

Exercise 19.2

Explain the decision in *Donoghue* v *Stevenson*.

Answers on page 344

Solutions to Questions

Solutions to Chapter 2 questions

ANSWERS TO SELF-TEST QUESTIONS

2.1 (a) A single system of law from Saxon times

(b) No code of law

(c) Judicial character

(d) Accusatorial

(e) Limited Roman law influence

(f) Uses doctrinal of precedent

2.2 It is a long-established, unified system. To completely codify it now would be very difficult, although in specific areas codification has taken place.

2.3 (a)—(i); (b)—(iii); (c)—(ii); (d)—(i).

2.4 (a) Civil

(b) Private

(c) Substantive

ANSWERS TO EXERCISES

2.1 Codification is the method by which the law contained in a mass of judicial precedent is gathered together into one Act of Parliament. On occasions Parliament takes the opportunity of codification to amend or add to some of the subject matter of the law being codified. Examples of codification are the Partnership Act 1890 and the Sale of Goods Act 1893 (now 1979). Consolidation is the gathering together of all the legislation on a particular area of law, whether such legislation is to be found in a series of statutes or statutory instruments, into a single statute. Consolidation does not involve any change in the law. Examples of consolidation are the Income and Corporation Taxes Act 1970 and the Companies Act 1985.

2.2 This question is answered fully within the chapter. It will be recalled that English law has the following distinctive characteristics:

1 A single continuous system of law from Saxon times.
2 The absence of a code of law.
3 Judicial in character.
4 Accusatorial procedure.
5 Limited influence of Roman law.
6 Doctrine of precedent.

Solutions to Chapter 3 questions

ANSWERS TO SELF-TEST QUESTIONS

3.1 Sentence (b) is true. Equity developed as a result of, and to remedy, defects in the Common Law (see the next answer). Therefore Equity can exist only as a gloss on the Common Law. Although without Equity, the Common Law would have defects, it can nevertheless exist independently of Equity.

3.2 (a) The writ system

(b) No right of appeal

(c) Influence over juniors

(d) Common Law's only remedy was in damages.

3.3 (a) Development of the trust

(b) Development of the mortgage

(c) New remedies other than damages

(d) Modification of extension of some Common Law rules.

3.4 (a) The Common Law is a complete system of law, Equity is not

(b) Equity acts in person, the Common Law is new

(c) The Common Law gives remedies 'as of right', Equitable remedies are discretionary

(d) At Common Law an action must be brought within the time limits of the limitation period; at Equity, the only requirement as to time is that the action must be brought without undue delay. Whether there has been such delay is a question for the court to decide.

3.5 By applying the provision of the Judicature Act that, in cases of conflict between the Common Law and Equity, Equity will prevail.

Solutions to Chapter 4 questions

ANSWERS TO SELF-TEST QUESTIONS

4.1 (a) County Court

(b) Queen's Bench Division of the High Court

(c) Crown Court (it will not be heard in the magistrates' courts as it hears only triable indictment. The magistrates will hold a committal hearing)

(d) Employment Appeals Tribunal.

4.2 (a) Mandamus

(b) Prohibition

(c) Certiorari

4.3 (a) Mandamus: When an individual, body or organisation is not carrying out its duty under law

(b) Prohibition: When a court, tribunal or then judicial or quasijudicial body is exceeding its jurisdiction but has not yet reached a final decision

(c) Certiorari: When a lower court or tribunal has acted in excess of its jurisdiction, or mistakenly in law, or vidation of natural justice.

4.4 When leave to appeal from the Court of Appeal (Civil Division) has been granted. Such leave will be granted only if the point of law in the case is of general public importance.

The House of Lords will hear appeals from the High Court if the 'leap-trap' procedure can be satisfied.

4.5 To interpret provisions of the Treaty of Rome 1957 and of secondary legislation arising from it.

4.6 Some international disputes; guardianship and adoption; affiliation; actions for unpaid rates; licensing; trial court for some crimes; examining courts in committal proceedings; juvenile courts.

4.7 Barristers have a right of audience in all courts; solicitors' right of audience is limited;
Barristers are not employed directly by the client, solicitors are;
Barristers are mainly concerned with work in courts, solicitors with both lower court work and clients' day-to-day legal problems and needs.

4.8 (c) is correct. Barristers and solicitors are separate parts of the profession. A person must qualify either as a solicitor or as a barrister, and practice only in the branch in which he has qualified.

ANSWERS TO EXERCISES

4.1 The county courts have an exclusively civil jurisdiction. They were first established by the County Courts Act 1846 which was passed with the intention of establishing a system of courts to deal with smaller claims. The jurisdiction of the county court is today to be found in the

County Courts Act 1959 which jurisdiction is added to by certain other statutes such as the Rent Act 1977 and the Consumer Credit Act 1974. County courts are to be found in almost all large towns and in many smaller and intermediate towns and their jurisdiction is essentially local in its character. There has to be a link between the action being tried and the county court district in which it is tried. Usually a county court action is brought in the county court of the area where the defendant lives.

There are approximately 400 county court districts in England and Wales which are grouped together into circuits, each circuit having at least one circuit judge. Attached to each court is also a registrar who is a solicitor of at least seven years standing. The function of the registrar is mainly to deal with pre-trial matters though he has a limited jurisdiction to try cases himself.

As has been said the jurisdiction of the county court is limited to small claims. Its present jurisdiction is:

(a) Actions in contract and tort where the sum claimed is less than £5,000.
(b) Actions for the recovery of land of which the net rateable value is below £1,000.
(c) Equitable matters such as the administration of estates, trusts and mortgages where the sum involved is below £30,000.
(d) Contentious probate matters where the net value of the estate at the date of death is below £30,000.
(e) Miscellaneous other matters such as consumer credit and rent act problems, domestic violence, and uncontested divorces.

In addition to this some county courts have a further jurisdiction. For example, about one-third have insolvency jurisdiction, in other words they can deal with bankruptcy matters and the liquidation of companies of which the share capital is below £120,000 and certain county courts near the coast have Admiralty jurisdiction.

The county courts today also have a jurisdiction in arbitration. The Administration of Justice Act 1973 established a power for certain matters to be referred to arbitration. By the rules of the court, the registrar may refer to arbitration any case where the claim is below £500. The parties themselves may ask for a matter to go to arbitration or, if one or both of them object, the procedure may be imposed upon them by the registrar. Even if the claim exceeds £500 the parties may themselves agree for the matter to be resolved by the county court arbitration procedure.

It is usually the registrar of the court who acts as an arbitrator in these matters, but sometimes outsiders may be brought in. The main advantages of arbitration are that it is a quick and informal method of resolving a dispute. The parties are encouraged to present their own cases, thereby reducing considerably the costs which would be incurred were solicitors and barristers to be employed by the parties, and, to cope with the amateur presentation of cases, the rules of evidence may be relaxed. A typical example of the use of the arbitration procedure is in a small consumer claim, for example, where a consumer has bought a pair of shoes which proved to be defective. In this situation the consumer can take action by the use of this informal procedure against the shop from which he or she bought the shoes. As a general rule in arbitration proceedings of this type, no order for costs are made. This again is of advantage to the small claimant. In English law the usual procedure as to costs is that the loser pays. Thus if a consumer brings proceedings in the ordinary courts and fails to prove his case then he will finish up paying not only his own costs but also those of the shop. With the arbitration procedure the consumer is under no such risk. Another advantage of the arbitration procedure is to the county courts themselves. By disposing of the smaller cases in this way the time of the county court judge is saved so that he can concentrate on more serious types of dispute.

Some 90 per cent of all civil cases are commenced in the county court, and of these approximately 90 per cent again involve less than £500. The county court, being local in its character, is far more easily accessible than the High Court and is also much quicker and far less costly.

4.2 In England and Wales the civil courts of first instance are the magistrates' courts, the county courts and the High Court. The magistrates' courts are the most junior of civil courts, deriving their authority from the Magistrates' Courts Act 1980. In England and Wales there are about

1,000 magistrates' courts in which cases are judged either by lay magistrates of whom there are approximately 25,000, or stipendiary (paid) magistrates of whom there are 50. The civil jurisdiction of magistrates is extremely limited, being confined to the issue of licences for the purpose of selling alcoholic drinks and family matters such as maintenance orders and the custody and adoption of children.

The vast bulk of civil litigation takes place in the county courts whose jurisdiction stems from the County Courts Act 1959 as amended and a variety of other statutes. There are a variety of financial limits both of which the county courts have no jurisdiction. For example, they may only decide cases in tort and contract as long as the sum involved does not exceed £5,000. Their jurisdiction in respect of equitable matters such as contested probate actions, mortgages, trusts and partnerships must not exceed £30,000. They may only hear a case for the winding up of a company so long as the capital of the company does not exceed £120,000. An action for the recovery of land cannot be instituted in the county court if the land has a rateable value in excess of £1,000.

Some county courts have jurisdiction to deal with undefended divorce petitions under the Matrimonial Causes Act 1967. All have power to deal with other matters arising out of domestic problems such as the adoption and guardianship of children and violence within the home. County courts also have to deal with problems arising in regard to landlord and tenant and also matters arising under the Fair Trading Act 1973 and problems concerning race relations. About one-third of the county courts have jurisdiction in bankruptcy matters.

It should be noted that the registrar of the county court pays a significant part in the work of the court since the creation of the arbitration scheme by the Administration of Justice Act 1973. Under this legislation, arbitration is automatically the way of determining disputes where the claim is below £500. With the consent of the parties, claims in excess of this figure may also be dealt with by the arbitration procedure. The type of cases where this happens are consumer claims, for example, where the purchaser of goods claims that they are defective and seeks a remedy from the seller and problems concerning hire-purchase agreements. Also claims by landlords for arrears of rent owing by tenants fall within this jurisdiction.

The High Court was divided into three divisions by the Administration of Justice Act 1970. There is no financial limit upon the jurisdiction of the High Court. The Family Division has jurisdiction in a wide range of family matters such as legitimacy, wardship, guardianship and adoption and the validity of the termination of a marriage. The Queen's Bench Division is concerned primarily with contractual and tortious matters, though the Division also includes the specialised Admiralty Court and Commercial Court. Generally matters are dealt with by an individual judge, though there is also a Divisional Court of the Queen's Bench Division which enjoys a supervisory jurisdiction over the activities of all inferior courts, tribunals and bodies making decisions which affect the rights of individuals. This jurisdiction is exercised by what are known as the prerogative orders, of which there are three. Certiorari is an order quashing a decision of an administrative body, prohibition is an order telling an administrative body not to do something. Mandamus is an order instructing an administrative body to do something.

Both the Family and Chancery Divisions have a small appellate jurisdiction confined to appeals on certain matters arising from the county court. The Queen's Bench Division hears appeals from certain administrative tribunals. However, the principal court dealing with civil appeals is the Court of Appeal (Civil Division). In this court there sits the Master of the Rolls, the Lord Chief Justice and 16 Lord Justices of Appeal. Usually three of these judges hear an individual appeal which itself comes either from the county court or the High Court. The usual method of determining appeals is by the use of transcripts of the original trial at first instance and arguments from barristers representing the two sides. Fresh evidence is not usually admitted. The Court of Appeal may either uphold or reverse the decision reached by the lower court or, in very rare circumstances, order a new trial.

The final court of appeal is the House of Lords. Sitting in this court are the Lords of Appeal in Ordinary. Its jurisdiction is to hear appeals from the Court of Appeal. Leave to appeal must be given either by the Court of Appeal which decided the case from which it is sought to lodge a further appeal or from the Appeals Committee of the House of Lords itself. Usually the case is one of public importance. In very limited circumstances an appeal may go direct from the High Court to the House of Lords by means of the 'leap-frog procedure'. For this to happen the trial judge must confirm that the point in issue is one of public importance and that it concerns either statutory interpretation or that the outcome is already subject to a binding precedent of the House of Lords. It is necessary for the House of Lords to give leave for this type of appeal.

In regard to the interpretation of Community Law, the Court of Justice of the European Communities is the ultimate appeal court. The decision is binding authority upon the point of law determined and the national court must then decide the case in the light of such interpretation. Judgments of the Court of Justice of the European Communities are enforced through the national courts of member states.

The Judicial Committee of the Privy Council has a limited appellate jurisdiction in England and Wales. It hears appeals from the Ecclesiastical Courts, from certain tribunals and from the Isle of Man, the Channel Islands and from certain Commonwealth countries.

Solutions to Chapter 5 questions

ANSWERS TO SELF-TEST QUESTIONS

5.1 Customs; Precedent; Statute; the EEC.

5.2 Accurate and consistent law reports; an established hierarchy of courts.

5.3 (a) The House of Lords itself, subject to certain exceptions
The Court of Appeal
The High Court
The County Court
The Magistrates' Courts.

(b) The County Courts
The Magistrates' Courts.

5.4 (a) When there are two conflicting decisions

(b) When a previous decision of the Court of Appeal is inconsistent with a later House of Lords decision

(c) In Criminal Division only, when a 'fall count' decides that the law in a previous decision had been misunderstood or misapplied.

5.5 Law made by, or under the authority of, Parliament.

5.6 (a) Lack of Parliamentary time

(b) Technical detail necessary

(c) Emergencies requiring quick action

(d) Local matters should be dealt with locally.

5.7 By the operation of the doctrine of ultra vires.

5.8 (a) Automatically, by being passed by the Council of Ministers

(b) By the legislature of the member state passing its own law to give effect to the directive.

5.9 (a) Consolidation is the collecting together into one statute the provisions contained in a number of previous statutes. Codification occurs when all the law from all sources on a single area is brought together into a comprehensive code.

(b) Public bills deal with matter of general public importance, private bills with local or individual matters.

5.10 Legislation

ANSWERS TO EXERCISES

5.1 The main sources of English law today are precedent, statute law, custom (to a limited extent) and the European Community. These will be dealt with in this order.

Precedent in English law is based upon the principle that like cases should be treated alike. Decisions of the court made when trying a case are frequently binding upon other courts when they in turn are called upon to try cases of a similar type. Under the system of precedent, sometimes known as the doctrine of stare decisis (let the decision stand) the role of the judge is to apply existing law rather than to make new law. Having said this, if a completely new point arises in a case then it may be necessary for the judge to adapt the existing law to cover this situation. Obviously the proper functioning of a system of precedent depends on the existence of two factors, firstly an established hierarchy of courts and secondly a proper and accurate system for reporting legal decisions.

Legislation is the law made by or under the authority of Parliament. It is a prime characteristic of the English Constitution that Parliament has almost unlimited authority. Although, since we have been a member of the European Communities, in some respects our law has had to comply with the requirements of the Communities, Parliament enjoys a supremacy insofar as an Act of Parliament cannot be challenged in the courts for unreasonableness or on any other basis. Legislation is the main source of new law today. In this role it enjoys certain advantages over precedent. For example, an Act of Parliament can just as easily repeal an existing law as it can create a new one. The alteration of precedent is much more difficult. Legislation by Parliament means that within the Constitution there is a clear division of function between the legislature which makes law and the judiciary which interprets and applies it. Precedent always relates to a set of facts which have happened. Precedent can never anticipate a situation which may happen. Legislation on the other hand, can anticipate situations which may happen in the future. Precedent may only be ascertained by examination of the law reports of which there are vast numbers of volumes. Legislation, on the other hand, can be ascertained by looking at the statute book which, although extensive, is far more restricted than the sum total of the law reports.

Legislation itself falls into three distinct types. The most important type is, of course, the Act of Parliament. This is legislation made by Parliament itself. There are two other types, delegated legislation and autonomic legislation. Delegated legislation is rules, orders, regulations and bylaws made by officers or bodies under a power delegated to them by Parliament. Autonomic legislation is legislation enacted by an autonomous body which enjoys the power to legislate for its own members and, occasionally, for the general public. Examples of bodies having the power to enact autonomic legislation are the Law Society and the Church of England.

Custom used to be an important source of law though today it is of considerably less importance. It is nevertheless capable of producing a legal effect in three different ways:

(a) It may be a source of general law. For example, Mercantile Law was developed as a body of law deriving from the customs and usages of the merchants. Mercantile custom has ceased to be of great importance as a source of law today having been absorbed into statutes such as the Sale of Goods Act 1979 and the Bills of Exchange Act 1882.
(b) Custom may also be a source of local law. For a local custom to exist it must be reasonable, it must conform with statute law, its existence must be as of right (ie without force, openly and without permission) and it must have been in existence since time immemorial.
(c) Custom may also be used as a source of implied terms in contracts. If in a particular trade or in a particular area of commercial operation there are certain terms implied by custom then the existence of such a custom is recognised by the law.

Finally, since the European Communities Act 1972 under which the United Kingdom became a full member of the European Communities, England and Wales are bound by certain obligations imposed by the Community legislation. Of major importance are regulations which emanate from the Communities and are self-executing and take effect upon being passed in just the same way as domestic legislation. Of wider impact in practice are the directives which emanate from the Communities and which, although not themselves law, have to be implemented by the legislatures of the various member states of the Community.

5.2 In English law the prime rule of evidence is that 'he who asserts must prove'. In other words whoever makes an allegation in a case must prove it. In a civil case it is the plaintiff who has to prove his case, in a criminal case it is the prosecution. It is very seldom that a particular fact can be proved with absolute certainty. For instance, a crime often may be proved only by the use of circumstantial evidence. In a civil case the facts sought to be proved must be established on the balance of probabilities. In a criminal case they must be proved beyond reasonable doubt. The expression 'beyond reasonable doubt' means exactly what it says. The prosecution must prove its case in order to establish the guilt of the defendant. The prosecution however need not anticipate and deal with every argument the defence might raise. The jury may find the accused guilty even though it entertains some very slight doubts. If, however, the jury entertains any significant doubts the verdict must be 'not guilty'. This is what is meant by the case being proved beyond reasonable doubt.

The civil standard of proof 'on the balance of probabilities' is a rather lower standard than the criminal standard. In a civil case it is for the plaintiff to prove that it is more likely than not that the allegations he is making are true.

Solutions to Chapter 6 questions

ANSWERS TO SELF-TEST QUESTIONS

6.1 (a) (i) This is the reason for deciding a case. It is the principle of law followed by other lower courts in deciding cases with similar facts.

  (ii) This is 'a thing said by the way'. It is a statement of law, not directly related to the issue at hand. It has persuasive authority.

 (b) (i) This occurs when a higher court in a later case alters a point of law given in the precedent case.

  (ii) This occurs when the actual case which established the ratio is taken on appeal to a higher court and this higher court overturns the lower court's decision.

6.2 When a case is similar to one that has been decided previously, the doctrine of precedent requires that, if the previous decision was made by a court which is superior in the hierarchy to the court deciding the case, the lower court must follow and apply the previous statement of the law. There is therefore certainty in the outcome of the case. This is especially so if the precedent case was decided by the House of Lords.

6.3 Literal Rule; Golden Rule; Mischief Rule; Eiusdem Generis Rule; Expressio unius est exclusio alteruis; Noscitur a sociis.

6.4 By giving the words of the statute their ordinary, plain and natural meaning. If the words are technical, they must be given their normal technical reason.

6.5 Because a literal meaning of the words 'in the vicinity of' in the Official Secrets Act 1920 would have led to the acquittal of a person who was discovered actually on an RAF base. This would have been an absurdity as the act would have covered people near but not actually in prohibited places, so it was interpreted in accordance with the Golden Rule.

6.6 The Licensing Act 1872 was designed to prevent drunken persons going on the highway in charge of some form of transport. The act used the word 'carriage' and the court, using the mischief rule, interpreted this as including bicycles.

6.7 (a) Probably not, as the specific words relate to household pets, so, under the Eiusdem Generis Rule, the general words 'and other animals' will take their meaning from the specific words 'cats and dogs' and refer to animals normally kept as household pets.

 (b) For the reasons given in (a) the act could apply to hamsters although it could be argued that the specific words related to household pets which were normally not kept in cages. If this argument succeeded the act would not apply to hamsters either.

6.8 Because expression of one thing implies exclusion of the others: By referring to cars and lorries and then just to lorries the act impliedly excludes cars from the requirement of a near-side wing mirror.

6.9 Intention is required for criminal liability.

6.10 The act's definition section; the long title.

SOLUTIONS TO QUESTIONS: CHAPTER SIX

ANSWERS TO EXERCISES

6.2 It is the function of judges to interpret statutes. This means that judges must give some meaning to the words used in a statute. In other words, they must construe and interpret it. Any uncertainties or ambiguities in the wording must be resolved by the judges. The main method of construction is the literal rule. This requires judges to interpret an Act according to the ordinary, literal and grammatical meaning of the words which are used in it. If the words are capable of only one literal meaning then this is the meaning which has to be ascribed to the words. This is so even though this meaning goes against the intention of the Act. For example, in *Fisher* v *Bell* (1961) the court had to consider the offence of offering for sale an offensive weapon under the Restriction of Offensive Weapons Act 1959. What happened was that a shopkeeper displayed a flick knife in his shop window. It was held that the shopkeeper, who was accused of the offence of offering for sale an offensive weapon, should be acquitted. The display of the knife in the shop window was an invitation to treat rather than an offer for sale. Both invitation to treat and offer for sale are expressions which have specific meanings in the common law. Accordingly this literal meaning had to be ascribed to the words in the statute.

Although a statute will be construed as far as possible in accordance with the literal rule, if such a method of construction leads to an absurd interpretation the court will apply the golden rule which allows the court to correct and supplement the Act so that it will make sense. Thus if the literal rule can lead to two equally valid interpretations of a word or expression used in the Act the court must adopt whichever interpretation would lead to the least absurd result. An example of this arose in the case of *Adler* v *George* (1964) where the Official Secrets Act 1920 provided that a person would be guilty of an offence if he obstructed HM Forces 'in the vicinity of' a prohibited place. A prosecution was brought under the Act against a person actually found inside an RAF base, a prohibited place. To have applied the words 'in the vicinity of' literally would have meant that the defendant would have been acquitted. This would have been a complete absurdity. The Act was passed to prevent persons getting into such places as RAF bases. Accordingly the Divisional Court decided that an offence had been committed by the defendant who, rather than being in the vicinity of the base, was actually in it.

Sometimes where the wording of the statute read literally leads to an absurdity the judge will look at the common law as it existed before the passing of the Act and ascertain the mischief in the common law which the Act was designed to remedy. This is known as the Mischief Rule of Construction and the Act will be interpreted as though it were passed to correct the particular mischief. This is another way of looking at the decision in *Adler* v *George*. The mischief which the Official Secrets Act 1920 was clearly passed to prevent was the situation where unauthorised persons got into RAF aerodromes.

Sometimes in a statute there is a list of specific words followed by general words. When this occurs the judges apply the ejusdem generis rule which means that where general words follow a series of specific words, the general words have to be read in the context of the specific words. For example in *Powell* v *Kempton Park Racecourse Co* (1899) the court had to interpret a provision in the Betting Act 1853 which prohibited the keeping of any 'house, office, room or other place' for betting. The court had to determine whether Tattersall's Ring at a racecourse was an 'other place' within the meaning of the Act. It was held that it was not. The general words 'or other place' were limited by the specific words 'house, office, room' to include only indoor places. Accordingly a racecourse, being out of doors, was outside the definition.

A further rule for interpreting the meaning of a word in the statute is 'noscitur a sociis'. This means that a statute must be looked upon as a whole and the meaning of words and phrases and clauses obtained from the context in which they appear.

There are also a number of rebuttable presumptions which are used in dealing with the interpretation of a statute. For example it is presumed that an Act does not alter the existing law unless it expressly so states. It is presumed that an Act is not retrospective unless it so states; that it does not deprive a person of existing rights unless it expressly so states that this is its purpose; and that it is not binding upon the Crown unless the Crown is expressly named in the Act as being bound by it.

Finally, there are a number of other aids both within the Act itself and in sources outside the Act which aid judges in the interpretation of statutes. Within the Act there is, for example, a long title which states the general purpose and effects of the Act. This identifies the subject matter of the Act though it does not explain what the purpose of the Act is. Sometimes sections of an Act are grouped under headings which give the general subject matter of those sections. These headings are used by judges when the content of the section is ambiguous or uncertain. Acts also contain marginal notes which are not part of the Acts themselves but which are put in for reference purposes.

Such marginal notes cannot alter the meaning of an Act but judges may look at them to discover the general purpose of the section under review. Of the outside sources, probably the most important is the Interpretation Act 1978 which gives definitions of a number of words commonly found in Acts. It also provides, for example, that words importing the masculine gender shall include the female and that the singular shall include the plural and the plural the singular. These rules of interpretation are, however, only applied when there is no contrary intention, whether express or implied, in the Act itself which is being interpreted.

Solutions to Chapter 7 questions

ANSWERS TO SELF-TEST QUESTIONS

7.1 Offer, acceptance, consideration, capacity, consent, no mistake or misrepresentation, no illegality, possibility of performance.

7.2 Void—contract does not exist and has never existed; voidable—Valid and enforceable unless and until avoided; unenforceable—one that is valid but cannot be enforced by legal action.

7.3 An offer is a definite indication of willingness to be bound by an agreement on the terms proposed. An invitation to treat is an invitation to a person to make an offer.

7.4 By revocation, rejection, lapse of time, non-occurrence of a condition, death.

7.5 (a) acceptance may be by conduct.
   (b) if the offer prescribes a specific method of acceptance, that method must be followed.
   (c) acceptance takes effect from the moment a letter of acceptance is posted.
   (d) acceptance by telex takes effect upon receipt by the offeror.
   (e) silence cannot constitute acceptance.

7.6 By ignoring meaningless terms (*Nicolene* v *Simmonds* (1953)); by looking at trade customs; by looking at previous dealings between the parties (*Hillas & Co* v *Arcos Ltd* (1932)).

7.7 (a) Consideration which has to performed—a promise for a promise.
   (b) Consideration which has been performed under the terms of the contract.
   (c) Consideration which is performed outside the scope of any contract.

7.8 Because the seamen did nothing more than they were contractually obliged to do anyway.

7.9 When the smaller payment is made, at the creditor's request, at a date earlier than that required by the contract or at a different place; when there is payment of a smaller sum plus something different in kind; when the smaller amount is paid by a third party and the creditor agrees to this discharge; when there is equitable promissory estoppel.

7.10 It can never be used as a cause of action—merely as a defence to an action brought to enforce the original contract (*Combe* v *Combe* (1951)).

7.11 Only parties to a contract may sue on it. Strangers to the contract (ie those who did not agree in the first place) have no rights or obligations under it.

7.12 (a) No
    (b) Yes
    (c) No

7.13 (a) contracts for necessaries
    (b) beneficial Contracts of Service

(c) valid and enforceable by and against the minor unless and until he avoids them.

(d) enforceable by the minor to a limited extent but unenforceable against him.

(e) an interest in subject matter of a permanent nature.

(f) those not covered by the other types of contract.

7.14 (a) the assignment must be absolute.

(b) the assignment must be in writing and signed by the assignor.

(c) notice in writing of the assignment must be given to the debtor.

7.15 Because it enables the assignee to sue on the contract in his own name as though he had been a party to the original contract.

ANSWERS TO EXERCISES

7.1 Consideration is the price for the promise. The classic definition is that contained in *Currie* v *Misa* (1875) which provides that consideration may 'consist either in some right, interest, profit or benefit accruing to the one party, or some forebearance, detriment, loss or responsibility given, suffered, or undertaken by the other'. In simple language it is the price given by the one party to the other in return for the promise of that other party. Consideration is an essential element in a valid contract. A bare promise ie one given for no consideration, is not binding upon the parties. Before he can claim for a breach of contract, the plaintiff must show that he either gave or promised to give some advantage to the defendant in return for the defendant's promise to perform his own side of the bargain.

There are a number of basic rules governing consideration. All contracts (other than those contained in a deed) must be supported by consideration. A promise without consideration is unenforceable unless contained in a deed. Consideration need not be adequate though it must have some value. So long as the parties to the contract are themselves satisfied at the value which they have placed on the consideration and have freely entered the agreement the court will not assess the relative value of each party's contribution. Having said this, the consideration must have at least some economic value. An example of the parties being able to place a value themselves on consideration is to be found in the case of *Chappell & Co* v *Nestlé Co* (1960). This concerned a promotional offer by Nestlé of a pop record. They were prepared to sell it to subscribers in return for a 1/6d postal order plus three chocolate bar wrappers. Chappell's were the owners of the copyright of the tune and were entitled to a royalty. The question which the court had to decide was whether the royalty should be based upon the 1/6d or 1/6d plus a value attributed to the three chocolate bar wrappers. It was held that since Nestlé would not have sent out the record without the chocolate bar wrappers then the chocolate bar wrappers must have some value. Accordingly the royalty should be based upon the 1/6d plus the three chocolate bar wrappers.

Consideration must be real. It must be more than something which the promisee is already legally bound to do. The performance of an existing obligation, whether that existing obligation arises by law or under another contract, is insufficient to constitute consideration. For example, in *Stilk* v *Myrick* (1809) two seamen deserted their ship in the course of a voyage. The captain agreed to divide the wages of these deserters between the remaining crew so long as they would finish the voyage short-handed. Upon completion of the voyage the captain failed to honour his promise and members of the crew sued him. It was held that the promise of extra remuneration was not binding. The crew were bound by the terms of their contract to complete the voyage anyway. They had provided no additional consideration for what they had done.

It would have been different if the desertions had resulted in the continuation of the voyage becoming dangerous. For example, in *Hartley* v *Ponsonby* (1857) the facts were very similar to those in *Stilk* v *Myrick* (1809) except that in Hartley the desertions were so numerous that further performance of the voyage would be hazardous. It was held that the promise to the remaining crew members by the captain that he would divide the wages of the deserters between them was binding. It was supported by consideration in that the members of the crew had to work that much harder and in much more dangerous conditions.

Consideration must be legal. It must not be contrary to any rule of law or be tainted with immorality in any way. A contract to commit a crime or to perform an act which is prohibited by statute could not be enforced through the courts.

Consideration must move from the promisee. In *Price* v *Easton* (1833) Easton promised a third party that if that person did certain work for him he would pay some money to Price. The third party duly did the work but Easton failed to pay Price. It was held that Price could not sue. No consideration for the promise had moved from Price to Easton. A party who has not provided the consideration may not, by himself, sue upon the contract. Any action for breach of contract must be brought by the party who gave the consideration.

Consideration must not be past. If an act has been performed prior to the promise being made then that act cannot be used to support the promise and enforce the contract. For example, in Re *McArdle* (1951) McArdle by his will, left a bungalow to his wife for her life and thereafter equally between his children. When McArdle died and while the widow was still living, one of McArdle's sons, together with his wife, went to live at the bungalow with the widow. The wife spent money on improving the house and the other children promised her £188 to reimburse her for the cost of the work. This promise was never kept. When the widow died proceedings were brought by the son and daughter-in-law in an attempt to enforce payment. It was held by the Court of Appeal that there was no obligation on the other children to keep their promise. All the improvements had been complied with before the promise of payment was made. Thus the promise was based upon past consideration and an obligation to pay never arose.

The consideration must not be vague. The promise must be clear and definite since a vague promise is not binding unless such vagueness can be cured by reference to implied terms or to previous dealings between the parties. For example, in *Scammell* v *Ouston* (1941) the contract concerned the acquisition of a motor van on hire-purchase. The order placed for the van was couched in these terms 'This order is given on the understanding that the balance of purchase price can be had on hire-purchase terms over a period of two years'. The question was whether this was sufficient to constitute a contract. It was held that there was no contract. The wording used (ie 'on hire purchase terms') was so vague as to prevent a contract from coming into existence.

Executory consideration is a promise to perform an action at some time in the future. The promise to perform the action forms the basis of the contract. Executed consideration, on the other hand, is an act or forbearance by the promisee which is completed at the moment when the other party's promise is made. The promisee makes the bargain and performs his side of it at one and the same time. Both executory and executed consideration are sufficient to support a valid contract. As has been said, past consideration cannot itself be good consideration. This, however, is a general rule to which there are exceptions. For example, under s27(1) Bills of Exchange Act 1882 consideration whenever given on a bill or cheque is deemed to be good consideration. Again under s23 Limitation Act 1980 while, as a general rule, debts become statute-barred six years after they have been made, (in other words no action can be brought to enforce a contract once a contract is six years old) if one party to a contract acknowledges in writing his liability upon the contract after it is six years old this has the effect of reviving the claim of the other party.

Finally what at first sight might appear to be a past consideration will support a valid contract where the plaintiff acting in the course of business performs a service at the request of the defendant who subsequently promises to pay. For example, Re *Casey's Patents* (1892) Stewart was the owner of certain patent rights. Casey worked for him as a manager and when he had spent two years working promoting the invention which was protected by the patent Stewart wrote to him saying that 'In consideration of your services as practical manager' Casey would be given a one-third share in the patent rights. The promise was never fulfilled and subsequently Casey sued to enforce Stewart's promise. It was held by the Court of Appeal that the promise of a share in the patent rights was enforceable. There was a clear implication that Casey would be rewarded for the work that he was doing in respect of the patent.

7.2 There are four essentials for a valid contract; offer, acceptance, consideration and intention to create legal relations. The offer and the acceptance taken together constitute the agreement.

For the agreement to be enforceable the parties have to intend it to give rise to a legal relationship. Usually in practice this is shown by the payment of consideration. If each of two parties is prepared to give money or money's worth in return for the promise of the other then this is indicative of an intention to make a legally binding agreement. However, there must be a separate element of intention by the parties to be bound by the contract. This intention is separate from and in addition to the presence of consideration. The test for the existence of the intention to create legal relations is an objective test. The intentions of the parties may be expressly stated or they may be presumed by the court. In *Rose and Frank Co* v *Crompton Bros* (1923) Atkin LJ said 'To create a contract there must be a common intention of the parties to enter into legal obligations mutually communicated expressly or impliedly'. In the same case, Scrutton LJ said 'The intention may be implied from the subject matter of the agreement, but it may also be expressed by the parties'. The case concerned a commercial agreement which provided 'This agreement is not entered into . . . as a formal or legal agreement, and shall not be subject to legal jurisdiction in the law courts'. It was held by the House of Lords that the agreement was not a legally enforceable contract. Thus when Crompton refused to honour its obligations under the agreement, Rose and Frank had no remedy.

There is a distinction between commercial agreements, ie those made in business, and what might be termed social or domestic agreements. When a business or commercial agreement is entered into, there is a presumption that it is binding and that legal relations were intended. In other words it is for a party who wishes to establish that a commercial agreement is not legally binding to prove this by evidence which he brings before the court. This was done in *Rose and Frank Co* v *Crompton Bros* (above). There was a provision in the agreement that it was not entered into as a formal or legal agreement.

However, whether a party to a contract has discharged the presumption that it is legally binding is a question of fact to be considered in every case. For example in *Esso Petroleum* v *Commissioners of Customs & Excise* (1976) Esso Petroleum, in a sales promotion, supplied coins commemorating the World Cup Football Series to garages with the intention that one coin should be given away to motorists whenever they bought petrol. The question before the court was whether the handing of the coins to the motorists constituted a sale. It was held by the House of Lords that in fact there was no sale, though a majority of the members thought that there was a contract for the supply of the coins. They reached this decision because Esso Petroleum had failed to prove there was no contractual intent.

If the agreement is a social or domestic agreement, then the presumption goes the other way. Such agreements are presumed not to be legally binding. There is, for example, a general presumption in English law that a husband and wife do not make contracts together. For example in *Balfour* v *Balfour* (1919) the husband was a civil servant based in Ceylon. He came to England on leave with his wife and subsequently returned to Ceylon. On his return his wife had to remain in England because she had health problems. Before leaving the husband promised to pay his wife £30 a month by way of maintenance but he failed to honour his promise. Subsequently the wife sued. It was held that the wife must fail in her action on two grounds, firstly there had been no consideration given for the promise and secondly even if there had been, husbands and wives generally do not tend to make contracts together. On the other hand, if the husband and wife are not living together then there may well be an intention to create legal relations when they make an agreement. For example in *Merritt* v *Merritt* (1970) a husband who was separated from his wife agreed that he would transfer the matrimonial home from their joint names into her name alone so long as she paid off the outstanding mortgage. When the husband failed to transfer the home the wife sued. The husband claimed that there was no legally binding agreement. It was held, however, that the husband's promise was legally binding. This was an arm's length transaction entered into by the parties with the clear intention of being bound.

Similar considerations apply where the contract is made between other close relatives or simply between friends. For example, in *Jones* v *Padavatton* (1969) Mrs Padavatton lived and worked in America. Her mother, Mrs Jones, offered her a monthly allowance if she would give up her job, go to England and read for the Bar. This Mrs Padavatton did though without success in the examinations. Mrs Jones subsequently bought a house in London and allowed the daughter to live there and instead of paying the monthly allowance allowed the daughter to receive the rent from other tenants living in the house. Three years later Mrs Jones sought possession of the house and the daughter counterclaimed for breach of the agreement to pay the monthly allowance. It was held that even though the agreement initially may have been made with both parties intending to enter into a legally binding relationship, it had only been intended to operate for a reasonable time to enable the daughter to pass the Bar examinations. Thus it had lapsed by expiration of time. The subsequent agreement, allowing the daughter to live in the house, had been simply a domestic agreement and there was no intention whatever to create legal relations. Thus the mother's action to recover the house succeeded.

On the other hand in appropriate circumstances friends may be found to have entered into an arm's length transaction. For example, in *Simpkins* v *Pays* (1955) Mrs Pays was a grandmother who, together with her granddaughter and Simpkins, a lodger in Mrs Pays' house, entered into a weekly newspaper competition. All three contributed to the stakes but the entry was in Mrs Pays' name. Eventually one of the entries won a prize of £730. Mrs Pays refused to share this prize with the other two collaborators and Simpkins sued for a one-third share in it. It was held that he was entitled to succeed. This had been a joint enterprise between the three and there was a clear intention that any prize should be shared between them. The agreement had been made with the intention to create a legal relationship.

Finally collective bargaining agreements must be mentioned. These are agreements made between a trade union and an employer. They are concerned with negotiated conditions of service including wages. By s18, Trade Union and Labour Relations Act 1974, there is a presumption that a collective agreement between an employer and a trade union are not legally binding unless there is an express statement to the contrary. If there is a clear statement in the agreement that it is legally binding then and only then is it legally enforceable to the extent stated.

7.3 The question concerns the effect in law of tenders. When tenders are invited for the supply of goods or services as and when demanded, the tender itself is treated as a standing offer. The placing of an order is the acceptance of such an offer. Thus when K submits a tender to J this constitutes a standing offer. There is an acceptance of this standing offer every time J places an order. This means that a separate contract is made on each occasion that an order is placed. Thus a standing offer may be revoked at any time by the person making the offer, except in respect of goods or services for which a definite order has already been placed. There may, however, be a binding agreement between the parties to keep a standing offer open for a set time. For such an agreement to exist there must have been consideration given for it. If a buyer has undertaken to purchase all his goods or services from the person whose tender has been accepted then there is a breach of contract in the event of the goods being bought elsewhere.

(i) Because the relationship between J and K is based on the fact that K has made a standing offer to supply the fuel oil, there will only be a valid acceptance creating a binding agreement when an actual order is placed. There is no obligation on J to place any quantity of orders, or, indeed, any orders at all. There is nothing K can do if J chooses not to place an order. However, if J had undertaken to take all his fuel oil from K, there would have been a breach of contract if orders were placed elsewhere.

(ii) The placing of an order by J was an acceptance of K's standing offer and a separate contract. If K is not able to supply the quantity of fuel oil then he will be liable for breach of contract in relation to that particular order.

(iii) K can revoke his standing offer at any time before acceptance ie at any time before an actual order for fuel oil has been placed. Therefore, provided all orders have been completed by K, he may revoke his standing order provided he communicates the fact to J. It is presumed that no consideration has been provided by K to keep the standing offer open for a specific length of time.

Solutions to Chapter 8 questions

ANSWERS TO SELF-TEST QUESTIONS

8.1 (a) Because no-one else had primary liability

(b) Because the promise was incidental to a larger transaction.

8.2 (c)

8.3 (a) Form; (b) Substance.

8.4 (b)

8.5 That a pre-contractual statement will be a term of the contract if the representee makes it clear that he would not enter the contract unless the statement is true.

8.6 In (a) the court implied a term into the contract because this was necessary to give the contract business efficacy; in (b), although the implication of a term would have helped make better sense of the agreement it was not necessary to give the contract business efficacy and therefore the court refused to imply anything into the agreement.

8.7 (a) These are important terms, breach of which entitle the innocent party to treat the contract as repudiated.

(b) These are minor terms entitling the innocent party to damages but not to treat the contract as repudiated.

(c) These are terms which are not classified as conditions or warranties by the parties, or custom, or the law. In the event of breach of one of those terms, the court will 'wait and see' the effects of breach and award a remedy accordingly.

8.8 (a) Because before the contract was made, an employee had orally misrepresented the effect of the exclusion of this oral description bound the employer.

(b) Because the exclusion had not been incorporated into the contract either expressly or by a previous cause of dealings (this being a consumer sale of *British Crane Corp Ltd* v *Ipswich Plant Hire* (1974)) and because, to exclude liability for negligence, express words to this effect must be used.

(c) Because notice of the exclusion was given after the contract had been made.

(d) Because the exclusion protected the party from liability for breach of implied conditions, but the breach was of one of the express terms.

(e) Because the exclusion as worded would have defeated the main object of the contract.

8.9 (a) Avoidance of liability for death or personal injury caused by negligence.

(b) Avoidance of liability for breach of the implied condition as to title in the Sale of Goods Act 1979 and the Supply of Goods and Services Act 1982.

(c) Avoidance of liability for breach of any other implied terms in the 1979 or 1982 Acts if the contract is a consumer dealing.

(d) Avoidance of liability by a manufacturer by means of a guarantee.

8.10 One in which
(a) the buyer does not buy or hold himself out as buying in the course of business, and
(b) the seller does sell in the course of a business and
(c) the goods are of a type ordinarily supplied for private use or consumption.

ANSWERS TO EXERCISES

8.1 The terms of a contract are those parts of the contract which actually contain the obligations under the contract. In the case of documents in writing, whether they are in the form of a deed or are merely simple contracts reduced into writing, the discovery of the express terms of the contract is easy. They are written into the document. In both these instances, the court will generally not allow oral evidence to 'add to, vary or contradict' the written agreement unless such evidence is necessary to prove a custom or trade usage, or to show that the contract had not been intended to come into existence until the occurrence of an event which had not yet occurred or, as is usual, if the court decides that the parties have not reduced all of their agreement into writing and so must bring oral evidence to prove the unwritten part of the agreement.

The traditional distinction made in regard to terms is that they are either conditions or warranties. The importance of the distinction lies in the remedies available for breach. If the term broken is a condition, the innocent party may repudiate the contract at once and incur no further liability upon it. A condition is a term which goes to the heart of the contract. If any benefit has been paid over by one party to the other then it must be returned in the event of a breach of condition. The injured party may also bring an action for damages if he has suffered any extra loss which is recoverable. If the injured party does not wish to treat the breach of condition in such a way as to enable him to repudiate the contract, he may rather treat the contract as continuing and merely sue for breach of warranty. This will enable him to claim damages.

A warranty is merely subsidiary or collateral to the main purpose of a contract. Where the term broken is a warranty, the innocent party cannot repudiate the contract. His only remedy is to sue for damages, the contract remaining in existence.

The distinction between conditions and warranties lies, as has been said, in the fact that the condition is a term of prime importance whereas the warranty is subsidiary to the main purpose of the contract. Whether a term is a condition or a warranty depends upon the intention of the parties as shown in the contract. Words used by the parties are not necessarily conclusive though, of course, if the parties refer to a term as a condition then that is persuasive that a condition is intended. The distinction between conditions and warranties is illustrated by the cases of *Poussard* v *Spiers & Pond* (1876) and *Bettini* v *Gye* (1876). In the Poussard case an actress was taken ill and so was unable to honour a contract which she had made to take the lead in an operetta. By the time she had recovered sufficiently to resume her part, the operetta was in the second week of its run. Meanwhile a substitute had been called in and had taken her place. It was held that she had herself gone in breach of condition and so the producers were able to treat the contract as discharged. On the other hand in the Bettini case, a singer who had been engaged for the whole season turned up for rehearsal three days before the opening night. The contract provided that the singer should rehearse for six days. It was held that, since the rehearsal clause was subsidiary to the main purpose of the contract, the singer's employers could not treat the contract as repudiated. They could merely treat the breach as one of warranty and not of condition. Sometimes terms are easily and obviously divisible into conditions and warranties. On other occasions the division may be more difficult. When terms are not categorised into conditions and warranties by the parties or by statute or custom they are referred to as innominate or intermediate terms. The remedy for a breach of an innominate or intermediate term depends upon the harm caused by the breach. In *Cehave MV v Bremer Handelsgeselleschaft* mbH. (1976) the court had to consider a term in a contract that citrus pulp pellets should be shipped 'in good condition'. Upon arrival the pellets proved to be damaged though the buyer was able to use them for the purpose for which they had been bought, namely the preparation of cattle food. The buyer claimed there had been a breach of condition but the court held that the requirement that the pellets should be in good condition was an innominate term. The remedy should depend on how harmful the breach had been to the innocent party. Put another way the court would adopt a 'wait and see' approach. Since in this case the pellets were usable there had not been a breach of condition. The contract should be allowed to stand. The buyer was entitled merely to damages for breach of warranty as to the quality of the pellets.

It should be noted that terms may be implied into a contract by statute, for example, the Sale of Goods Act 1979, the Supply of Goods and Services Act 1982 and the Consumer Credit Act 1974. These statutes expressly divide terms into conditions and warranties. When the term under consideration is one implied in this way by an Act of Parliament, the court must apply this division.

8.2 (a) A deed is sometimes referred to as a specialty contract. Such a contract depends for its validity upon its form rather than its content. The agreement is put into writing and the written document is then signed, witnessed by an outsider and delivered by the party making it.

Certain agreements are not binding in law unless they are made by deed. The most important of these are legal mortgages of interests in land and leases of land for more than three years. Conveyances of land also have to be by deed. Another type of agreement which has to be in this form to be valid is a contract unsupported by consideration. Since a deed takes its validity from the form in which it is entered into rather than from its content, there is no need for consideration for the contract to be binding.

If an existing simple contract dealing with the same subject matter as a deed becomes embodied in the deed, the simple contract is said to be merged in the deed and ceases to have any effect.

A statement made in a deed may not be denied unless the party who made it can show that he executed the deed under duress or as a result of some fraud or illegality. A deed operates from the date of delivery and right of action under it becomes statute-barred by the Limitation Act 1980 after 12 years as opposed to action on a simple contract which becomes statute-barred after only six years.

(b) While the general rule is that simple contracts may take any form, some simple contracts have to be in writing in order to be enforceable. This requirement always derives from an Act of Parliament. Thus the Bills of Exchange Act 1882 provides that all bills of exchange and promissory notes must be in writing. The Copyright Act 1956 requires that any assignment of a copyright must be in writing. The Companies Act 1985 provides that the transfer of shares in a registered company must be in writing. The Consumer Credit Act 1974 states that if a consumer credit agreement is not in writing then it is unenforceable unless the court, in the light of all the circumstances of the case, decides otherwise. Contracts for the sale of land have to be in writing.

(c) Certain other simple contracts have to be evidenced in writing in order to be enforceable. The requirement that the contract to which this rule applies should be evidenced in writing dates from the Statute of Fraud 1677. The Act was passed because, at the time, parties to certain actions could not themselves give evidence in court. Thus a special form of proof was introduced for contracts which were considered to be most open to fraud. The requirement for evidence in writing applies even today to contracts of guarantee.

If a contract which should be evidenced in writing is in fact not so evidenced then it is valid but unenforceable at common law. The importance of the unenforceability arises if one of the parties breaks the contract. On the other hand, if the contract is performed then the transaction stands.

Solutions to Chapter 9 questions

ANSWERS TO SELF-TEST QUESTIONS

9.1 When the opinion contains an element of fact and the representor has no reasonable grounds for his claim to hold the opinion (*Smith* v *Land and House Property Corporation* (1884); when the giver of the opinion has expert knowledge of the circumstances surrounding the opinion (*Esso Petroleum Co Ltd* v *Mardon* (1976)).

9.2 (a) change of circumstances

(b) half-truth

(c) fiduciary relationship

(d) contracts of the utmost good faith.

9.3 (a) Fraudulent misrepresentation arises when the representor knows that his statement is false, or makes it without believing it to be true, or recklessly, careless whether it be true or false

(b) If a representation is not fraudulent it is presumed negligent unless the representor can show that he did believe and had reasonable grounds to believe in the truth of what he was saying. If he can so show, the representation will be

(c) wholly innocent.

The remedies for misrepresentation are:

(a) if it is fraudulent—rescission and damages for deceit

(b) if negligent—rescission and damages under s 2(1) Misrepresentation Act 1967

(c) if wholly innocent—rescission. The court may award damages in lieu.

9.4 The representee will be able to avoid (ie set aside) the contract by telling the representor, or by doing some other act which shows the intention to avoid. Instead of, or as well as, doing this, the representee may apply to the court for an order of rescission. This is a formal cancellation of the contract by the court. It will be applied for especially where property is involved and the representee wants the court to order the representor to return the benefits he has received under the contract.

9.5 (a) Representee had left it too late to rescind

(b) Restitutio in integrum was not possible.

9.6 (a) Both parties make the same mistake.

(b) Both parties make a mistake, but each makes a different mistake.

9.7 (a) The identity of the rogue was not vital to the creation of the contract, therefore there was

9.8 (a) The signature must have been induced by a trick or fraud

(b) There must be a substantial difference in nature or character between the document the signer thought he was signing and the document he actually was signing.

(c) The signer must not have acted negligently.

9.9 (a) By granting rescission on terms

(b) By refusing specific performance

(c) By rectification

9.10 (a) The contract is illegal from the outset. Generally, neither party can sue or be sued on the contract

(b) The party who performed the contract illegally has no rights or remedies. If the other is innocent of the illegality, his rights remain unaffected.

9.11 (a) As the illegal scheme had already been substantially effected, repentance was too late

(b) The illegal scheme had not been executed, so it was possible to repent the illegal purpose.

9.12 (a) There is an interest worthy of protection

(b) The restriction is reasonable in the interests of the parties

(c) The restriction is reasonable in the interests of the public.

ANSWERS TO EXERCISES

9.1 The word 'mistake' in relation to contract has a very specific meaning. Generally a mistake by one or both of the parties to a contract will not be sufficient to render the contract invalid. However, some mistakes are considered to be so fundamental that they have the effect of nullifying the consent of the parties and so prevent a contract being formed at all. There are a number of forms that such a fundamental mistake may take.

Firstly a contract is void for mistake if at the time of making the contract both parties are mistaken as to the existence of the subject matter of the contract. So, if, at the time of the contract, the goods have been destroyed and the parties are contracting under a common mistake then such mistake is sufficient to avoid the contract. For example, in *Couturier* v *Hastie* (1843–60), a contract was entered into for the sale of a cargo of corn. Unknown to both parties the corn had ceased to exist as a commercial entity since it had already been sold to another person. It was held that the contract had been entered into under a mistake and was therefore void. Further if the parties have made a common mistake about a matter which is essential to the agreement then there can be no binding contract. For example, in *Galloway* v *Galloway* (1914) a separation deed made between a man and a woman was declared to be a nullity since it had been made under the assumption that they were married to each other. In fact they were not married and so the whole basis of the separation agreement was mistaken.

Secondly, if the parties have entered into a contract under a mutual mistake and are acting at cross-purposes to the extent that the offer of the one party and the acceptance by the other do not in fact coincide, then there can be no agreement because again the mistake is an operative one. For example, in *Raffles* v *Wichelhaus* (1864) the plaintiff purported to sell to the defendant some cotton 'to arrive ex Peerless from Bombay'. In fact there were two ships called Peerless sailing from Bombay that year, one which was sailing in October and one in December. The one party had in mind the one ship and the other the other. It was held that there was an operative mistake sufficient to avoid the contract.

The third kind of mistake is mistake as to the expression of intention. If the offeror makes a mistake in expressing his intention and the offeree knows or is deemed to know of the mistake, then the error is sufficient to constitute an operative mistake in law and any resulting contract will be void. For example, in *Smith* v *Hughes* (1871) a contract was made for the sale of oats which were believed by one party to be warranted to be 'good old oats' and not intended by the other party to be so warranted. It was held that because the parties were at cross-purposes, there was a sufficient mistake to avoid the contract.

The fourth kind of mistake which operates to avoid a contact is unilateral mistake by one party as to the identity of the other contracting party. This type of mistake does not generally cause a contract to be void but rather voidable as a result of fraud. Where a seller intends to sell to another person who is present at the time of the contract there arises a presumption that the identity of the buyer is not relevant to the transaction. Thus the contract is valid until such time as it may later be avoided because of the fraud. In *Lewis* v *Averay* (1972) a contract was entered into with a rogue for the sale to the rogue of a motor car. The rogue stated to the seller that he was a well-known actor. Subsequently the rogue sold the car to a third party. The seller sought to recover the car from this innocent sub-purchaser. If the contract between the seller and the rogue were void for mistake then the rogue would have been unable to pass any title to the car to the innocent third party. If, on the other hand, the contract was merely voidable because of the rogue's fraud then the innocent third party would have obtained good title since, at the time of the resale to him, the original contract had not been avoided. It was held that the first contract between the seller of the motor car and the rogue was voidable for fraud rather than void for mistake. On the other hand, however, where the parties enter into a contract by correspondence and are not in each other's presence when the contract is concluded then the mistake as to identity may render the contract void. For example, in *Cundy* v *Lindsay* (1878) the plaintiffs, who were sellers of handkerchiefs, received an order from a rogue called Blenkarn for handkerchiefs. Blenkern gave his address as 37, Wood Street, Cheapside. He had signed his name on the order to make it look like Blenkiron & Co. a respectable firm known by the plaintiffs and carrying on business at 123, Wood Street. The plaintiffs despatched the handkerchiefs to 'Blenkiron & Co., 37, Wood Street' where Blenkarn took possession of them. He never paid for the goods but resold them to the defendant. It was held that there was no contract between the plaintiffs and Blenkarn. The plaintiffs intended dealing with Blenkiron not with Blenkarn. The mistake was known to Blenkarn. Thus no property in the handkerchiefs passed to Blankarn, so he could pass no property to the defendant. Accordingly the handkerchiefs could be recovered from the defendant by an action in conversion.

The final type of mistake which may be operative to avoid a contract is where there is a unilateral mistake as to the nature of a document signed. As a general rule a party is bound by the terms of any document which he signs even if he has not read or understood the contents of the document. However, there is an exception where the document is signed under a complete mistake as to the nature of the document and without negligence on the part of the person signing it. It was established in Thoroughgood's case (1584) that if a person who cannot read executes a deed after it has been incorrectly read to him, he will not be bound by the deed. He can plead 'non est factum' (ie it is not my deed). However, this doctrine is very severely restricted. It only applies where the signer is mistaken as to the nature, as opposed to the contents, of the document and where the signer has not been negligent. For example, in *Saunders* v *Anglia Building Society* (1971) a widow wanted to help her nephew to raise some money on the security of her house. To do this she agreed to execute a deed of gift in favour of the nephew. When ultimately the deed of gift was presented to her for signing, she signed it without reading it. The document was indeed a deed of gift though not in favour of the nephew but for a third party. It was held that the widow was bound by the document. She had not been mistaken as to what she was signing. She understood full well that it was a deed of gift. Moreover she had been negligent in signing it without reading it through.

Common law only provides a remedy to a party to a contract made under a mistake where the mistake is so fundamental as to prevent the contract from being a true agreement. When this occurs the remedy at common law is for the contract to be declared void. If the mistake is not an operative mistake, however, there may still be the possibility of some equitable relief. The first equitable remedy which may be granted is rescission. This will be granted if it can be shown that, although the contract is valid at common law, it would be against the principles of equity to allow the other party to take full advantage of his contractual rights. So in *Solle* v *Butcher* (1950) a flat was let at a rental of £250 per annum. The parties mistakenly thought that the flat was free from rent control, whereas in fact it was subject to rent control legislation and the maximum rent chargeable was £140 per annum. If the landlord had been aware of this at the time of entering into the lease, he could have increased the rent to £250 per annum because of work which had been done by him to the flat. However, he had no entitlement to make such an increase during the currency of a lease which was already existing. The tenant brought proceedings to establish that the rent he should be required to pay was £140 per annum and an order that the excess rent paid should be repaid to him. The landlord counterclaimed for rescission of the lease. It was held that the lease should be rescinded on terms which did justice to both parties.

Specific performance will be refused on any contract which, even though valid at common law, was entered into under a mistake by one of the parties in circumstances where it would be unduly harsh to force him to comply with the contract. So in *Day* v *Wells* (1861) Wells instructed an auctioneer to sell cottages thinking that he had instructed the auctioneer to place a reserve price on them. In fact the auctioneer sold them without reserve at a much lower price. It was held that Day, the purchaser, could not obtain an order of specific performance to compel performance of the contract. If a written agreement is entered into which does not accurately express the agreement reached by the parties, then an order for rectification of the agreement may be made by the court so that the writing does in fact conform with the actual agreement. Before rectification will be ordered, however, there must have been a mistake in expressing the terms of some agreement which had been properly entered into by the parties.

9.2 This problem concerns the effect of misrepresentation upon a contract. What has happened is that James has made honest misrepresentations to Peter about the dining chairs which Peter subsequently bought. For a representation to be a misrepresentation so as to affect the enforceability of the contract, it must be a statement of fact made by one party to the other with the intention that the party to whom it was made should rely upon in entering into the contract.

Thus the first point to consider is whether James's representations are representations of fact. This is because representations of law, or opinion or intention are not actionable. James stated that the chairs were 'beyond doubt 18th century'. He added that they 'might well have come from Chippendale's own workshop'. The latter statement that they 'might well have come from Chippendale's own workshop' is no more than a statement of opinion and thus is not actionable. However, the statement that they are 'beyond doubt 18th century' is a statement of fact. Often there is a fine line between a statement of fact and a statement of opinion but if the party making the statement has or appears to have some special skill or knowledge in regard to the matter on which he is making the statement, it is likely to be treated by the court as a statement of fact. James is an antique dealer who is alleged to have a special knowledge of 18th century English furniture. Thus the statement that the chairs are '18th century' is a statement of fact. It would appear from the facts of the question that Peter did indeed rely upon the statement by James and entered into the contract as a result of such reliance. Thus the essential elements of an actionable misrepresentation appear to exist. Peter's remedies are firstly to seek rescission of the contract and secondly to claim damages under s2, Misrepresentation Act 1967. Rescission is only possible if restitutio in integrum is possible, in other words the parties must be restored to their identical position prior to the contract. It would appear here that restutio is possible. There has been no acquisition of rights by a third party in the subject matter of the contract. Peter appears to have acted quickly. By s1, Misrepresentation Act 1967, the fact that the contract has been performed does not prevent rescission.

Additionally Peter may claim damages under s2(1), Misrepresentation Act 1967. James may, however, seek to avoid liability under this by proving that he had reasonable grounds to believe and honestly did believe that the representation was true both at the time when he made it and up to the time of making the contract. On the facts of the case, James would have difficulty in discharging this burden of proof. There is a label on the underside of the seat stating 'Made by CAR Penter, Watford, 1937'. Thus it would seem to suggest that James simply was negligent in not examining the chairs.

It may be that James's statement amounts to a warranty which is actually a term of the contract rather than a mere representation. In *Dick Bentley (Productions) Limited* v *Harold Smith (Motors) Limited* (1965) it was said that 'if a representation is made in the course of dealings for a contract for the very purpose of inducing the other party to act on it, and it actually induces him to act on it by entering into the contract, that is prima facie ground for inferring that the representation was intended as a warranty'. This principle appears to apply to the facts of this problem. The distinction between warranties and mere representations is important in that a misrepresentation which is neither negligent nor fraudulent does not generally attract damages under the Misrepresentation Act 1967, whereas if a breach of warranty can be established the representee is entitled to damages without having to establish the negligence of the representor.

Solutions to Chapter 10 questions

ANSWERS TO SELF-TEST QUESTIONS

10.1 (a) by performance

(b) by agreement

(c) by frustration

(d) by breach

10.2 (a) The builder had performed only part of the work, and the other party had no choice but to accept the part performance. The builder therefore was not entitled to claim payment for his part performance

(b) The contract had been *substantially* performed. The defects were trivial. The contractor, therefore, was entitled to be paid the contractual price less the cost of remedying the defects.

10.3 A contract will be frustrated when, without the fault of either party, further performance becomes impossible because of some inevitable outside cause.

10.4 (a) Because the contract was for personal services and, because of ill health, it could not be fully performed

(b) Because the contract depended upon the occurrence of an event which did not occur

(c) Because there was a change in the law making such contracts unlawful to perform.

10.5 The Law Reform (Frustrated Contracts) Act 1943 will apply unless the relevant contract is not covered by the Act or the parties have agreed to exclude its provisions.

10.6 It is a breach of contract which occurs before the time for performance has arrived or before the contract has been fully performed. The innocent party may treat the contract as ended at once, claiming damages, or wait until the time for performance has arrived and then sue.

10.7 In *Hadley* v *Baxendale* (1854) it was held that damages will be awarded for
(a) losses arising naturally from the breach or otherwise within the reasonable contemplation of the parties

(b) losses outside the natural course of events only if the special circumstances causing the loss were brought to the defendant's notice at the time the contract was made.

10.8 (a) The special circumstances were, or should have been, known to the defendant at the time of the contract and therefore he was liable to compensate the plaintiff for all his loss

(b) Loss of normal profits arose naturally from the breach and so could be claimed as a head of damages. Loss incurred from circumstances which were outside the contemplation of the defendant and which had not been brought to the defendant's notice at the time of the contract were too remote and so could not be recovered.

10.9 To compensate the innocent party.

10.10 That damages may be recovered for mental distress and inconvenience in suitable cases. In the

Jarvis case, for the upset caused by a faulty holiday, in *Cox* for breach of the contract of employment, in *Heywood* for wrongful performance of his duties by a solicitor.

10.11 Liquidated damages are a genuine pre-estimate of loss that will be suffered in the event of breach. Penalties are sums stated in the contract designed to deter breach of contract. The test for the distinction depends on the parties' intentions, but guidelines for determining the difference were given by Viscount Dunedin in *Dunlop Pneumatic Tyre Co Ltd* v *New Garage and Motor Co Ltd* (1915).

10.12 (a) Contracts for personal performance of continuous successive acts. These cannot be supervised by the Courts

(b) Contracts to build or repair property, again because of the need for the court to supervise and control (but note the exception to this rule)

(c) Contracts for the loan of money, because the loan can be raised elsewhere

(d) Contracts for the sale of goods which are not unique, rare or in short supply.

In both (c) and (d) damages would be an adequate remedy.

10.13 (a) Where the contract does not provide how much the plaintiff is to be paid

(b) Where there is not full provision for payment

(c) A minor's contract for necessaries

(d) Where the plaintiff is prevented from completing his work by the other party's breach

(e) Where the contract is partially performed.

10.14 (a) 6 years

(b) 12 years

ANSWERS TO EXERCISES

10.1 Parties to a contract are discharged from their obligations under the contract if, after its making, the contract becomes incapable of performance. Frustration occurs because some event for which neither party is responsible causes the object of the contract to become unattainable. Frustration occurs in the following circumstances. Firstly, where there is a destruction of some specific thing essential to the performance of the contract. For example in *Taylor* v *Caldwell* (1863) Caldwell agreed to rent a music hall to Taylor for four concerts to be held there. Before the date that the first concert was due to be held, the hall was destroyed by fire. Taylor claimed damages for Caldwell's failure to make the premises available. It was held that the claim for breach of contract must fail since it had become impossible to perform the contract. Secondly, the personal incapacity of a party to a contract for personal services will render the contract frustrated. For example in *Condor* v *Barron Knights Ltd* (1966) a drummer engaged to play in a pop group was bound by his contract to work on seven nights a week as and when work was available. He suffered an illness and was advised to play no more than four nights a week. It was held that the drummer's contract of employment had been frustrated. His intervening illness had effectively brought the contract to an end. Thirdly, the non-occurrence of an event which forms the basis of the contract will cause frustration. For example in *Krell* v *Henry* (1903) Henry hired a room from Krell for two days so that he and his family could watch the Coronation procession of King Edward VII. The King was taken ill which caused the Coronation procession to be postponed. It was held that Henry was excused from paying the rental for the room. The Coronation procession was regarded by both parties as an essential prerequisite for the performance of the contract. Fourthly, Governmental interference striking at the root of the contract will terminate a contract. For example in *Metropolitan Water Board* v *Dick Kerr & Co* (1918) a company agreed to build a reservoir for the Metropolitan Water Board. The construction was to take place over a period of six years. Two years into the contract, the company was required to cease work because of a statute passed during the first world war prohibiting contract work of this nature during war. It was held that this was sufficient to frustrate a contract. The interruption was of such a nature as to make the contract, if ever it was resumed, a totally different contract. Finally, the change in the law may render the main object of the agreement illegal. For example in Re *Shipton* (1915) a contract was made for the sale of some wheat lying in a warehouse. Subsequently the Government requisitioned the wheat under a wartime emergency regulation. It was held that the seller was excused from further performance of the contract since it was now impossible to deliver the goods.

There are certain instances when, although a contract might appear to be frustrated, it is not discharged. There is no frustration of the performance of a contract if it is merely made more difficult or more expensive. For example in *Tsakiroglou & Co Ltd* v *Noblee Thorl GmbH* (1962) there was a contract for the carriage of Sudanese groundnuts to be shipped from Sudan to Hamburg during the period of November/December 1956. The Suez Canal was closed from 2 November 1956 until April 1957. Consequently the delivery did not take place since it was argued that shipment around the Cape was commercially and fundamentally different. It was held that the contract was frustrated. The change in the circumstances was not fundamental. The mere fact that the contract became more expensive was insufficient to frustrate it. Frustration must not be self-induced. In *Maritime National Fish Limited* v *Ocean Trawlers Limited* (1935) Maritime chartered a vessel from Ocean which could only operate with an otter trawl. It was an offence to use such a trawl without a Government licence. Maritime was granted three such licences but chose to use them in respect of three other vessels. In consequence Ocean's vessel could not be used. It was held that the charter party had not been frustrated and thus Maritime was liable to pay the charter fee. Maritime had elected freely of its own volition not to licence Ocean's vessel. Thus their inability to use the vessel was a direct result of their own deliberate act.

As a general rule there cannot be frustration if the parties expressly provide in the contract for the frustrating event. However, if the event is more extreme than anything envisaged by the contract, the court has to decide whether, on construction of the contract the event had been provided for. Finally, it is generally believed that the doctrine of frustration does not apply to leases.

The general result of frustration is to discharge the contract. There is some relief provided to the parties by the Law Reform (Frustrated Contracts) Act 1943. Under this all sums paid to the frustrating event may be recovered by the party claiming them. This is so whether the failure of consideration was total or partial. Any money payable prior to the frustrating event under the contract ceases to be payable. The court may then order compensation to be paid for any expenses incurred or benefits obtained. The amount of such compensation is entirely at the discretion of the court.

10.2 (a) The purpose of damages is to compensate a party injured as a result of a breach of contract for the loss which he has suffered as a result of the breach. In order to arrive at an appropriate level of compensation the court has to consider the rules governing remoteness of damage and those governing the measure of damages. By considering these rules the court must satisfy itself that the loss suffered by the plaintiff was not too remote a consequence of the breach of contract by the defendant and also assess exactly how much may be recovered by the plaintiff. The general rule covering remoteness of damages was stated in *Hadley* v *Baxendale* (1854). In this case the driveshaft of a mill was taken for repair. There was a delay on the part of the carrier in getting the shaft back to the plaintiff. As a result of this the mill was idle for a period of time and the plaintiff lost profits. It was held that the plaintiff could only recover damages for losses which arose naturally from the breach of the contract. In other words the damages must have arisen in the usual course of events and be within the reasonable contemplation of the parties at the time when they made the contract. It was held that in this case that since the plaintiff would normally be expected to keep a spare driveshaft, the loss of profits occasioned by the delay in getting the repaired shaft back was not in the contemplation of the defendant carrier when the contract was made. Exactly what does fall within the contemplation of the parties is a question of fact to be considered in each separate case. In the case of *Heron II* (1967) Lord Morris explained 'it is a question of what the parties contemplated. Even without notice of special circumstances or special considerations there may be situations where it is plain that there was a common contemplation'.

An example of this arose in the case of *Victoria Laundry (Windsor) Limited* v *Newman Industries Limited* (1948). In this case a laundry ordered a new boiler. As a result of late delivery, the laundry lost not only considerable profits for anticipated expansion of trade but also a particularly lucrative dyeing contract placed with them by a Government department. It was held that the defendant should be liable for the loss of the business profits. It was not, however, liable for the loss of the dyeing contract of which it was not aware.

When the court comes to assess the amount of damages to be awarded, it attempts to award such sum of money that reflects the loss suffered by the plaintiff. For example in *W L Thompson Limited* v *Robinson (Gunmakers) Limited* (1955) the defendants failed to take delivery of a Standard Vanguard car which they had contracted to buy from the plaintiffs. The plaintiffs were unable to sell the car elsewhere and so had to return it to the supplier. It was held that the measure of damages payable was the loss of profit on the sale.

In arriving at the sum which reflects the plaintiff's loss, the court will consider whether in the contract the parties have themselves made some provision for an amount to be paid in the event of a breach. For example, very frequently in building contracts there is a proviso that in the event of the building not being completed by a specified date the total sum payable to the builder will be reduced by a specified amount for each week of delay. This is known as a liquidated damages clause so long as it is a genuine pre-estimate of the loss. However, if the sum is greater than that occasioned by the breach of contract then it is known as a penalty clause which the court will not enforce. In *Dunlop Pneumatic Tyre Co* v *New Garage & Motor Co* (1915) the Dunlop company supplied tyres to the New Garage under a price maintenance agreement whereby the garage agreed not to tamper with certain marks on the goods, not to sell below listed prices, not to supply certain people with the tyres, not to exhibit or export any tyres without consent and to pay £5 by way of liquidated damages for each tyre sold in breach of the agreement. It was held that the sum of £5 was liquidated damages. Although £5 might appear a rather large amount having regard to the date of the case in the event of a single tyre being sold below list price, account had to be taken of resulting damage to Dunlop's general sales organisation since news of the undercutting would soon spread in the trade. Thus the £5 was a reasonable attempt to quantify the damage and not an extravagant figure.

The plaintiff must take reasonable steps to mitigate any loss which he suffers. In the event of his failing to mitigate his loss then he is penalised in the amount of damages which he may receive. For example in *Brace* v *Calder* (1895) a partnership agreed to employ Brace as its manager for two years. After five months the partnership was dissolved. This constituted a breach of Brace's service contract. A new partnership was formed which agreed to employ Brace on exactly the same basis as before. Brace refused to work for it and sought by way of damages the amount of salary he would have earned if he had served the full two years. It was held that only nominal damages were recoverable since Grace had failed in his duty to mitigate the loss suffered.

Damages may also be claimed for any mental distress and inconvenience caused by the breach of contract. The plaintiff must, however, not make a profit out of his action for damages. The leading case on damages for mental suffering is *Jarvis* v *Swan's Tours Limited* (1973). Jarvis booked a holiday with Swan's Tours. Many of the promises made in the sales brochure were not carried out and the holiday was a total disaster. It was held that Jarvis could recover not only the price of the holiday but also an additional sum for the mental distress suffered as a result of the holiday being such a disaster.

(b) This problem concerns a breach of contract as between H and I. Although goods of the correct quality and quantity were delivered by H he was two weeks late in making the delivery. Whether or not the time of delivery is essential in a contract depends upon the terms of the contract. The mere fact that delivery is to be by a specified date does not necessarily make time of the essence. On the other hand in this case if I has informed H that time is of the essence to the agreement and that delivery must be by the date specified, then the time of delivery may well be interpreted by the court as a condition of the contract. If it were treated as a breach of condition, then I could treat the contract as repudiated and sue for any loss which he has incurred as a result of the breach. However, in this particular case I has accepted delivery which means that by so doing he has lost his right to treat the contract as being at an end. Notwithstanding this he may still sue for damages for any loss which he has suffered as a result of the late delivery of the goods.

Included in the contract is a term to cover the amount of damages paid in the event of a breach occurring. The £500 is referred to as 'liquidated damages'. However, it must be decided whether the 'liquidated damages' is a genuine attempt to pre-estimate the loss or whether it constitutes a penalty. If it constitutes a penalty then it will not be upheld by the court. The House of Lords in the case of *Dunlop Pneumatic Tyre Co* v *New Garage Co* (1915), referred to above, laid down guidelines to be followed by the court in such a situation. These are firstly, the use of the term 'liquidated damages' by the parties is not conclusive. Secondly, the intention of the parties at the time of the contract is paramount. Thirdly, the sum should not be excessive when compared with the greatest loss which can arise from the breach. Fourthly, the breach contemplated may not be just the non-payment of money. Fifthly, if one sum is to be paid for a whole variety of possible breaches, it is likely to be considered to be a penalty. Sixthly, difficulty in estimating the consequences of a breach will not prevent the sum from being considered a genuine pre-estimate and thus acceptable as liquidated damages.

In this case it is necessary for I to prove that the sum of £500 is a genuine pre-estimate of the anticipated loss which will arise from the breach of contract. The success or otherwise of this will depend upon the interpretation put on the amount by the court and the seriousness of the breach envisaged in comparison to the contract as a whole. It will be necessary for I to convince the court that, at the time the contract was made, both he and H were seeking genuinely to anticipate the loss which would occur. On the facts of the case this may be difficult since the contract would appear to envisage one sum being payable regardless of how serious is the breach.

Solutions to Chapter 11 questions

ANSWERS TO SELF-TEST QUESTIONS

11.1 A contract for the sale of goods is one whereby the seller transfers or agrees to transfer property (ie ownership) in the goods to the buyer for a money consideration called the price (s 2(1) SGA 1979).

11.2 (a) These are terms actually agreed in the contract by the parties

(b) These are terms, not agreed by the parties, but brought into the contract by operation of law eg the SGA 1979.

11.3 By ss 34 and 35:

(a) when the buyer says he accepts

(b) when, after a reasonable opportunity for examination, he acts in a manner inconsistent with the seller's rights

(c) when he keeps the goods for a reasonable time without notice of rejection (see *Bernstein* v *Pamsons Motors (Golders Green) Ltd* (1987)).

11.4 By s 11 (4) the buyer has to treat a breach of condition as a breach of warranty. In other words, he has lost his right to reject the goods for breach of conditions. All he can do is sue the seller in damages ie he must treat the breach of condition as a breach of warranty.

11.5 Implied condition and warranties as to title (s 12)
Implied condition as to description (s 13)
Implied condition as to merchantable quality (s 14 (2))
Implied condition as to fitness for purpose (s 14(3))
Implied condition in a sale by sample (s 15)

11.6 To transfer ownership in the goods from the buyer to the seller.

11.7 When the goods are unascertained;
When specific goods are bought as 'a thing corresponding with a description'.

11.8 Those words necessary to identify the nature of the goods.

11.9 (a) fit for the purpose or purposes

(b) reasonable

(c) the description

(d) the price

(e) 14 (6)

11.10 By showing that, to be merchantable, goods need only be fit for one of their normal purposes, even though this is not the purpose for which the buyer bought them.

11.11 In *Grant*'s case the goods were intended for immediate use and so had to be merchantable at the time of sale and delivery. In *Heil*'s case, the reasonable person would know that the goods had to have some process applied to them before they were used (ie they had to be cooked) so they needed to be merchantable only when this had been done.

11.12 (a) The correct answers would be (ii) and (iii)—the car is not of merchantable quality (not fit for its ordinary purpose) nor is it fit for the buyer's specific purpose, made known to the garage at the time of sale

Point (i) relates to sale by description, which is irrelevant here and point (iv) gives the definition of merchantable quality.

The condition as to merchantable quality is contained in s 14 (2) (point (ii)).

(b) (i) condition

(c) (i) Yes—there is no implied condition as to merchantable quality if the buyer has examined the goods before sale and the actual examination undertaken would have revealed the defect.

11.13 (a) When the parties intend it to pass (s 17) but, failing such an intention, according to the 5 rules in s18

(b) The risk of accidental loss passes with the property; seller can claim the purchase price and is not restricted to a claim in damages.

11.14 If a contract is entire, breach or acceptance of part of the contract will affect the whole contract. If it is divisible, however, and the goods are delivered by instalments, breach of one or more instalments will mean that the court will look at the ratio the part in breach bears to the rest of the contract and the likelihood of the breach being repeated (*Maple Flock Co Ltd* v *Universal Furniture Products (Wembley) Ltd* (1934) and *Munro & Co Ltd* v *Meyer* (1930)).

11.15 (a) Lien

(b) Stoppage in transit

(c) Resale

11.16 (a) (ii)—the contract is for work and materials—the main point of the contract is to 'improve' John's goods

(b) (i)—Fred has not executed the work with reasonable care and skill. Fred was acting in the course of business.

ANSWERS TO EXERCISES

11.1 (a) By s17, Sale of Goods Act 1979, property in goods passes at the time the parties intend it to pass. In the case of unascertained goods, property does not pass unless and until those goods have been ascertained (s16, SGA.) Of course, when a person is entering into a contract for the sale of goods it is very seldom that he thinks about when the property is to pass. Because of this there are rules contained in s18 which apply in the absence of contrary intention. Firstly, where there is an unconditional contract for the sale of specific goods in a deliverable state, property in those goods passes when the contract is made (Rule 1). This is irrespective of the fact that the time of payment or the time of delivery may be postponed. For example, in *Tarling* v *Baxter* (1827) a contract was made for the purchase of a haystack. Before the buyer was able to take it away it was destroyed by fire. It was held that the property had passed and thus the loss fell on the buyer. By s62 SGA goods are in a deliverable state when they are in such a state that the buyer would be bound to take delivery of them under contract. Secondly, where there is a contract for the sale of specific goods which have still to be put in a deliverable state, property in those goods does not pass unless this has been done and the buyer has been given notice of the fact (Rule 2). Thirdly, in the case of a contract for the sale of specific goods in a deliverable state, where the price is still to be ascertained by the seller by his weighing or measuring them, property does not pass until this is done and the buyer has notice of this (Rule 3). Fourthly, where goods are goods are delivered on approval or on sale or return or on some similar terms, the property passes to the buyer either when he signifies his approval or acceptance to the seller, or when he does any other act adopting the transaction, or when he retains the goods without giving notice of the rejection within a reasonable time (Rule 4). Finally, in the case of a sale of unascertained or future goods which are sold by description, property passes when goods of that description and in a deliverable state are unconditionally appropriated to the contract by one party with the consent of the other (Rule 5). For example, this might happen by the seller delivering the goods to the buyer or to a carrier on his behalf without reserving the right of disposal. In this situation the buyer's assent to the appropriation may be given before or after the appropriation or it may be implied. For example in *Pignataro* v *Gilroy* (1919) a seller of some bags of rice which were to be collected by the buyer from the seller's place of business informed the buyer that the bags were ready. The buyer, however, did nothing further for over three weeks during which time the bags were stolen. It was held that the buyer by his action had assented to the appropriation so that the property in the goods had passed to him.

By s20, SGA unless otherwise agreed, the goods remain at the seller's risk until the property therein is transferred to the buyer, but when the property therein is transferred to the buyer, the goods are at the buyer's risk whether delivery has been made or not. Thus the risk of accidental loss or damage to the goods falls on the owner of the goods, regardless of whether he is in possession of those goods. For example in *Tarling* v *Baxter* (above) the risk lay with the buyer since the ownership of the goods had passed to the buyer. Similarly in *Pignataro* v *Gilroy* (above) the risk lay with the buyer, again notwithstanding the fact that the possession of them was with the seller. This is because by the time the bags of rice were stolen the ownership had passed to the buyer.

(b) This question concerns the passing of property and risk. It appears from the facts that L has agreed to buy from M the quantity of paper which M has put on one side. By s20, SGA the passing of risk and ownership is concurrent. Accordingly we have to look to whether the property has passed. The supply of paper would appear to be a contract for the sale of unascertained goods. By s18, r5 property passes in such goods when goods of that description and in a deliverable state are unconditionally appropriated to the contract by one party with the consent of the other. It is quite obvious from the question that M has appropriated the paper. It would appear also that L has assented to this if only by implication since M has telephoned L to inform him of the appropriation.

Thus, assuming that there has indeed been an unconditional appropriation of the paper to the contract, both property and risk will have passed to L. Accordingly M is advised that he may sue L for the price of the paper.

11.2 (a) The *nemo dat* rule is a general rule whereby a party to a contract cannot give a better title to the goods the subject matter of the contract then he himself possesses. Thus, as a general rule, a thief cannot pass good title to stolen property to a third party. Over the years there have developed a number of exceptions to this rule, mainly for the purpose of protecting a bona fide purchaser for value who does not have notice of any defect in the title of the seller. These exceptions to the general rule will now be considered. Firstly under s21(1), SGA 1979 the property in goods may pass where 'the owner of the goods is by his conduct precluded from denying the seller's authority to sell'. Thus, for example, in *Henderson & Co* v *Williams* (1895) the owner of certain goods laying at a warehouse was induced by the fraud of a rogue to instruct the warehouseman to transfer the goods to the order of the rogue. Thus the goods were placed at the rogue's disposal. He then sold the goods to an innocent purchaser who was informed by the warehouseman that they were held to his, the innocent purchaser's, order. When the fraud was discovered, the warehouseman refused to deliver the goods. The purchaser brought proceedings against the warehouseman for the goods. It was held that since the warehouseman had acknowledged the rights of the third party, he was thereby estopped from denying the purchaser's title to the goods and his refusal to deliver amounted to conversion.

Secondly, by s2, Factors Act 1889 if a mercantile agent is in possession of goods with the consent of the owner, or in possession of documents of title to goods with the consent of the owner, then any sale or disposition of the goods while acting in the ordinary course of business will give the purchaser good title.

Thirdly, by s22 SGA where goods are sold in market overt according to the usage of the market, the buyer acquires good title to the goods so long as he buys in good faith and without notice of any defect or want of title on the part of the seller. The expression market overt means any public and legally constituted market and every shop in the City of London.

Fourthly, by s23 SGA where the seller of goods has a voidable title thereto but his title has not been avoided at the time of the sale, the buyer acquires a good title to the goods, provided he buys in good faith and without notice of the seller's defect of title.

Fifthly, by s24 SGA a person who, having sold goods, continues in possession of them or the documents of title to the goods and sells or disposes of them to another who buys in good faith and without notice of any defect in title, the purchaser obtains a good title. Conversely by s25 SGA where a buyer with the consent of the seller obtains possession of goods or documents of title to goods and then transfers possession of the goods or documents of title to a third party who receives in good faith and without notice of the defect in title, then the third party obtains good title.

Finally there are a number of special exceptions to the general *nemo dat* rule created by other statutes or delegated legislation. For example, under the Rules of the Supreme Court, the High Court may order the sale of goods which are of a perishable nature or likely to deteriorate if kept or if for any other good reason it is desirable to sell them forthwith. When such an order is made a third party acquiring the goods receives good title. Similarly there are statutes such as Torts (Interference with Goods) Act 1977 and the Innkeepers Act 1878 which give persons such as bailees and innkeepers a statutory power to sell goods of which they are in possession in appropriate circumstances.

(b) This question concerns the implied conditions as to quality and fitness under the Sale of Goods Act 1979. The contract in question is a contract of sale of goods since it is a contract whereby the seller transfers or agrees to transfer the property in the goods to the buyer for a money consideration called the price. By s14(2) SGA where a seller sells goods in the course of a business there is an implied condition that the goods supplied under the contract are of merchantable quality. In this context merchantable quality means that the goods must be as fit for the purpose or purposes for which goods of their kind are commonly bought as it is reasonable to expect having regard to any description applied to them, the price and all the other circumstances. This implied condition of merchantable quality does not apply, however, if the circumstances are such that the seller specifically drew the defects in question to the attention of the buyer prior to the making of the contract or if the buyer examines the goods before the contract is made, as regards defects which that examination should have revealed. In this particular case it was pointed out to L that the typewriter had a minor fault that needed repair. Whether a fault costing £50 to repair on a typewriter costing only £100 is a minor fault is something which the court would have to consider. If it were found not to be a minor fault and if L had not examined the typewriter before purchase then he would have a claim under s14(2). Even if he had inspected the typewriter, he may also have a claim for misrepresentation, again assuming that the fault was not a minor fault.

L will more certainly have a claim under s14(3) SGA. Under this provision there is an implied condition that goods supplied in the course of business must be fit for the purpose for which they are supplied. The typewriter was sold in the course of business by M. L impliedly made known the purpose for which the typewriter was required, since a typewriter has only one purpose. Moreover L specified that he required a machine suitable for beginners, and thus made the purpose clearly known to M.

Thus in conclusion L will almost certainly have a claim under s14(3) SGA, and possibly under s14(2) SGA and for misrepresentation.

Solutions to Chapter 12 questions

ANSWERS TO SELF-TEST QUESTIONS

12.1 (a) Credit given in such a way that it can only be sued by the debtor to finance an agreed purchase (eg HP)

(b) Credit given to the debtor with no control over the way he spends it (eg a bank overdraft).

12.2 (a) creditor

(b) £15,000

(c) individual

(d) partnership

(e) fixed sum

(f) running account

12.3 (a) debtor cannot bind himself to enter the agreement

(b) the creditor is liable for pre-contractual statements

(c) debtor may withdraw

12.4 If the agreement is executed when the debtor signs, he must be given a copy when he signs. If it is not executed on his signature he must be given a copy when he signs and a further copy within 7 days of its execution by the creditor. Note the variations if the agreement is cancellable.

12.5 (d)

12.6 (a) three

(b) misrepresentation

(c) breach of contract

(d) creditor

(e) jointly

(f) severally

12.7 When the payments are grossly exhorbitant or the agreement otherwise grossly contravenes the ordinary principles of fair dealing.

12.8 When oral representations are made in antecedent negotiations in the debtor's presence *and* the debtor signs other than at the place of business of the creditor, a negotiator or a party to a linked transaction.

12.9 The cancellation period runs until the end of the fifth day following the day upon which the debtor receives his second notice of cancellation.

12.10 (a) He must pay all the instalments outstanding

(b) He may have to bring the total amount paid to ½ total HP price (or less if stated by the agreement or the court).

(c) He must allow the creditor to re-possess the goods

(d) He must pay damages if he has failed to take reasonable care of the goods.

12.11 These are goods, in the possession of the debtor under an HP or conditional sale agreement, and for which the debtor
(a) Has paid ⅓ total HP price, and

(b) Is in breach of his contract, and

(c) Has not terminated the agreement

(d) The goods must still be in the ownership of the seller.

ANSWERS TO EXERCISES

12.1 Under a hire-purchase contract, the owner of goods agrees to hire them to a person wishing to acquire them (the hirer) on the understanding that, having completed payment of all the instalments of the contract of hire, the hirer has an option actually to become the owner of the goods. This is usually done by the payment of some nominal amount as an option to purchase the goods. The owner is usually a finance house though not necessarily so. The ownership of the goods remains with the owner until such time as the final instalment has been paid. Hereupon ownership passes to the hirer. Consumer credit agreements are governed by the Consumer Credit Act 1974 which requires that certain formalities must be complied with. Firstly, the agreement must be in writing. Secondly, it must be signed by the hirer and also by or on behalf of all the other parties to the agreement. Thirdly, it must contain a full statement of the total cash price, the total hire-purchase price, the amount to be paid at each instalment and the date on which the instalments fall due. Fourthly, the agreement must describe the articles being acquired under the contract. Fifthly, if the agreement is signed other than at trade premises, two copies of the agreement must be delivered to the hirer. The first copy must be given to him at the time of making the agreement or sent to him. The second copy must be sent to the hirer by post within seven days of the making of the agreement. If the agreement is actually signed by both parties at the trade premises then only one copy of the agreement need be given to the hirer. Copies of the agreement must comply with regulations of the Department of Trade and Industry regarding legibility and layout. Sixthly, if the agreement is signed other than at trade premises and following oral representations during the antecedent negotiations in the presence of the hirer and by or on behalf of the creditor, there must be contained in the agreement a statement of the hirer's right of cancellation. In this case again a further copy must be sent to him or alternatively, if a copy of the agreement is given to him at the time of its making, a copy of his right of cancellation. Finally the agreement must contain a statement that there is a limitation on the owner's right to recover possession of the goods once a third of the total hire-purchase price has been paid.

It is essential that these formalities are complied with. If they are not, the agreement is only enforceable against the hirer by means of a court order. The owner may only recover the goods forming the subject matter of the agreement following an order of the court, and the owner may only enforce any security such as a guarantee under the agreement by means of an order of the court. In any of these instances before the court will make an order it must be satisfied that in all the circumstances of the case it is just that an order should be made.

12.2 (a) One of the greatest problems in the early days of hire-purchase was the manner in which the owner of goods subject to a hire-purchase agreement would seize them back after the hirer had paid most of the instalments. As legislation began to control hire-purchase, provisions were introduced to stamp out this abuse. If a hirer fails to make a payment which is due under the agreement or goes in breach of the agreement in any other way, the owner is obliged to serve upon him a default notice requiring reparation of the default within a period of not less than seven days. No matter how little has been paid under the hire-purchase agreement, the owner may not terminate agreement without going through this procedure and the hirer having remained in default throughout the entire period up to the moment of repossession. Any provision in a hire-purchase agreement is void if it seeks to authorise the owner to go onto the premises of the debtor to repossess goods which are the subject matter of a regulated hire-purchase agreement.

The strongest protective provision to be found in the Consumer Credit Act is that once one-third of the total hire-purchase price has been paid, the goods become known as 'protected goods'. This means that the owner may not take any action to recover possession from the debtor other than through the court. Any repossession of the goods by the owner contrary to this constitutes a termination by the owner of the agreement and entitles the hirer to recover all monies which he has paid under the agreement.

(b) This problem concerns the provisions of the Consumer Credit Act 1974 which deal with protected goods and the way in which further goods added to an agreement under which the goods are already protected themselves become protected.

As was stated above, once one-third of the total hire-purchase price of goods has been paid, the goods become 'protected goods'. In this situation the creditor cannot enforce any right to recover possession of the goods from the hirer other than by means of court action. The Act further provides that if goods are being acquired under a hire purchase agreement and, after one-third of the total hire-purchase price has been paid, the owner and the hirer enter into a further agreement in relation to the whole or part of the goods, then the goods forming the subject matter of the second agreement themselves become protected goods.

Thus in the problem being considered both the television and the cooker are protected goods. The television is protected since one-third of the total hire-purchase price has been paid. The cooker is protected since it has become the subject matter of a further agreement with the owner relating to goods which are already protected.

Thus the creditor has no right to take back either the coloured television or the cooker without first obtaining a court order. Were he to take back the goods without the necessary court order, this would constitute a termination by him of the agreement and John would be entitled to be repaid all sums which he has so far paid under the agreement and moreover would be under no further liability. Having said this, were the creditor to bring the case to court, John's conduct would obviously be a matter to which the court would take into account in determining what sort of order to make. Thus John should be advised to write back to the creditor explaining about any financial difficulties which he may be experiencing and perhaps offering to pay reduced instalments over a prolonged period.

Solutions to Chapter 13 questions

ANSWERS TO SELF-TEST QUESTIONS

13.1 (a) Employer has ultimate control

(b) Employer in better position to insure against third party liability

(c) Employer is the ultimate profit maker

(d) Employee is an extension of the employer.

13.2 Look at the whole arrangement between the worker and the employer. Consider the factors such as

(a) method of payment of wages

(b) are income tax or social security contributions deducted by the employer before payment to worker?

(c) who provides the tools and equipment for the job?

(d) may the worker profit from his own management of the task?

(e) is the worker regarded as an integral part of the employer's business?

13.3 (a) To pay wages

(b) To provide work

(c) To provide a safe system of work

(d) To indemnify the employee

(e) To give references.

13.4 If the written contract of employment is silent on the question of the payment of wages during periods of illness, such wages will be payable unless the employer can prove otherwise.

13.5 (a) To act reasonably and to co-operate

(b) Not to delegate

(c) To obey lawful orders given by the employer

(d) To act in good faith

(e) To exercise reasonable care.

13.6 (a) by passage of time

(b) impossiblity of performance

(c) insolvency of the employer

(d) notice

(e) dismissal without notice.

13.7 When liquidation of an insolvent company commences following a court order, or shareholders' resolution, the employees are automatically discharged. They may claim damages for wrongful dismissal because they have not been given notice.

13.8 This occurs when the employer is in breach of duty to the employee and, in effect, forces the employee to leave. This will occur, for example, when the employee's pay is reduced, or he is demoted, or he fails to maintain adequate working temperatures, or there is a change in the employee's place of work.

13.9 (a) When the employer has ceased or intends to cease carrying on his business for the purposes for which the employee was employed or has ceased or intends to cease carrying on the business in the place where the employee was employed

(b) When the need for employees of this type has ceased.

13.10 (a) The employee's lack of capability or qualifications for performing work of the kind he was employed to do

(b) The conduct of the employee

(c) Redundancy

(d) Continuation impossible without breaking the law

(e) Some other substantial reason.

ANSWERS TO EXERCISES

13.1 The answer to this question is to be found in the text between pages 200 and 202. The main duties of the employee are to act reasonably and co-operate, to perform personally his duties under the contract, to obey lawful orders, to act in good faith and to act with reasonable care. For further details on this the student is referred to the text.

13.2 This problem concerns the termination of a contract of employment. Where an employee is dismissed he has possible remedies for unfair dismissal, wrongful dismissal and/or redundancy. The first point to establish, however, is that the employee in question was dismissed.

Thus J must establish that he has been dismissed from his employment. As well as an outright dismissal of an employee by an employer, dismissal also takes place where an employee resigns as a result of a repudiatory breach of contract by the employer. This is known as constructive dismissal. Whether there has been a repudiatory breach in this problem depends upon the term in the contract of employment as to where J is to work. Unless a contract of service gives an employer the right to require an employee to move to a distant site, such an order will often constitute a repudiatory breach of contract. It would appear in this problem that the collective agreement with the trade union that after six months of employment at the Western site, employees could not be moved to the Eastern site without their consent has become incorporated in J's own contract of service. Thus since by the term B Ltd cannot move J from the Western site to the Eastern site without his consent, B has committed a repudiatory breach and so J has been constructively dismissed.

Therefore the three possible remedies detailed above must be considered. A claim for wrongful dismissal is brought in the ordinary court, in this case it would be the county court. The amount of damages claimable in this situation is the amount that J would have earned during the period of notice to which he was entitled. Since he has been employed for two years, his minimum notice entitlement under the Employment Protection (Consolidation) Act 1978 is two weeks. J should be advised that in bringing an action at common law, the burden of proving his case falls upon him and, should he lose, he will have to pay the other side's costs. Since the amount being claimed is going to be relatively small, this may be a course of action considered not really to be worth taking.

A redundancy payment under the Employment Protection (Consolidation) Act 1978 may be claimed at an Industrial Tribunal if the reason for J's dismissal is indeed redundancy. We are not told in the question why B Ltd requires J to move to the Eastern site. It may be that there is no more work at the Western site of the kind which J was employed to undertake. It may be that the Western site is closing down altogether. In either of these cases J would be entitled to a redundancy payment. An advantage of claiming through the Industrial Tribunals is that once the employee has proved that he has been dismissed (and in most circumstances the employer will admit this) it is for the employer to prove why the dismissal took place. In this situation where a redundancy payment is claimed, if B Ltd could prove that the repudiatory breach of contract was other than because of redundancy, then no redundancy payment could be awarded.

The final remedy to be considered is unfair dismissal which is also claimed before an Industrial Tribunal. Again J must prove that he has been dismissed. Once he has done this it is for B Ltd to establish its reason for the dismissal. This could be done, for example, if J could be shown to be guilty of misconduct in refusing to move from the Western site to the Eastern site when requested so to do. Since there appears to be a provision in his contract of service that he may not be so required to move after being employed for six months, it would appear that his refusal to move is not misconduct. Having said this, it should be noted that one good reason for dismissal being fair is redundancy. Thus the remedies of redundancy payments and unfair dismissal are generally mutually exclusive, though a dismissal for redundancy may be found to be unfair if the employee concerned was unfairly selected for dismissal.

If J's dismissal is found to be unfair, then as well as claiming compensation, he may in the alternative claim reinstatement or re-engagement.

Since as a general rule costs are never awarded by Industrial Tribunals, J should be advised to consider bringing a claim for either redundancy or unfair dismissal. Because of the risk of incurring costs and because of the relatively small amount which could be claimed at common law, he should be advised against a wrongful dismissal claim in the present circumstances.

Solutions to Chapter 14 questions

ANSWERS TO SELF-TEST QUESTIONS

14.1 (a) Rights may be transferred by delivery or by indorsement and delivery

(b) The holder for the time being may sue in his own name to enforce the promise

(c) A transferree in good faith and for value receives good title

(d) There is a presumption that consideration has been given for the instrument.

14.2 (a) unconditional

(b) writing

(c) signed

(d) on demand

(e) fixed

(f) determinable future time

(g) sum certain

(h) specified person

(i) bearer

(j) Bills of Exchange

14.3 (a) (i) Drawer is B Green
(ii) Drawee is Ann Jones
(iii) Payee is John Smith

(b) No. It is payable at a fixed or determinable future time ie three months after 1 April 1990

(c) (iii)

14.4 A holder is a person legally in possession of a bill, or who is in possession of a bearer bill without authority

A holder for value is one who is in possession of a bill for which consideration has at some stage been given. Such a holder takes subject to equities

If the bill he is holding is subject to some defect in the title of one of the prior parties, a holder for value's claim will be defeated by this defect unless he can show that he is a holder in due course

A holder in due course is one who comes within the definitions in s 29(1) of the 1882 Act.

14.5 (a) he took the bill complete and regular on the fact of it

(b) before it was overdue

(c) without knowledge of dishonour if such was the case

(d) in good faith

(e) for value

(f) without notice of any defect in title of the person who negotiated it.

14.6 The bill is regular both on its front and its back eg the name of the payee must correspond with the indorser's signature—see *Arab Bank Ltd* v *Ross* (1952).

14.7 (a) by mere delivery

(b) by indorsement and delivery

14.8 (a) holder's signature with nothing more—this converts an order bill into a bearer bill

(b) an indorsement which names the indorsee

(c) an indorsement which adds a condition

(d) an indorsement which uses words which ensure that the transfer is to one specified person only

(e) an indorsement with the words 'sans recours' or 'without recourse' put after the signature. The indorsee will incur no liability on the bill.

ANSWERS TO EXERCISES

14.1 By s3, Bills of Exchange Act 1882 a bill of exchange is defined as 'an unconditional order in writing addressed by one person to another signed by the person giving it, requiring the person to whom it is addressed to pay on demand or at a fixed or determinable future time a sum certain in money to or to the order of a specified person or to bearer'. A bill of exchange has three vital characteristics. Firstly, title passes by delivery if the instrument is simply payable to bearer and by delivery and indorsement in other cases. Secondly, a transferee of a negotiable instrument may obtain a good title even though the transferor had no title himself or had a defective title so long as the instrument was negotiable and so long as the transferee received in good faith for value and without notice of the defect in title. Thirdly, the holder of a bill of exchange can sue upon it in his own name.

For the statutory definition of a bill of exchange to be satisfied, the bill must contain an order to pay and not a mere request. In other words the wording must be in the imperative. The order must be unconditional as between drawer and drawee. Thus an order to pay £x's 'out of the proceeds of sale of my car' does not constitute a valid bill of exchange. It goes without saying that the order must be in writing. A 'person' may be a body of persons such as a partnership or corporation. The payee cannot, however, be a fictitious person. If the payee is fictitious, the bill will be treated as payable to bearer. There is nothing to prevent the drawer and the drawee being the same person. A bill of exchange is of no effect until it is signed by the drawer, though this need not be done at the time that the other parts of the bill of exchange are made out. The order must be for the payment of a sum certain in money. This may include foreign money and it can also relate to a single sum or to a series of instalments. Payment of the bill must be either on demand or at a fixed or determinable future time.

A bill of exchange may operate as a form of credit since the possibility that it will be payable at a fixed or determinable time eliminates the need to pay cash immediately. It is a means of assigning a debt while at the same time giving all parties the advantages of a negotiable instrument. It is a way whereby credit may be allowed to the buyer of goods while ensuring the prompt payment of the seller.

By s29, Bills of Exchange Act 1882 a holder in due course is defined as a holder who has taken a bill complete and regular on the face of it provided that he became the holder before it was overdue and took it without notice that it had been previously dishonoured. He must also have taken the bill in good faith, for value and without notice of any defect in the title of the person who negotiated it to him. By s27, Bills of Exchange Act, a holder for value is a person in possession of a bill for which value has at some time been given. The value may have been given by the holder himself or by some previous party to the bill. Once consideration has been given, all subsequent holders are holders for value. The important distinction between a holder for value and a holder in due course is that, in the case of the former, the bill is taken subject to 'equities' (ie defects in title) and thus may be met by the defences of fraud, duress or illegality by parties liable on the bill at or at any time before the occurrence of the fraud, duress or illegality. A holder for value may also have his entitlement challenged on the basis of a right of set-off or counter-claim enjoyed by the drawee.

There is a presumption that the holder of a bill of exchange is a holder in due course.

14.2 Bills of Exchange are negotiable instruments. Negotiation is the transfer of a bill from one person to another in such a way as to make the transferee the holder of the bill. Such a holder may be a holder for value or a holder in due course. The latter may enforce the bill notwithstanding any defect in his title. To be a holder in due course there are certain conditions which have to be satisfied. Firstly, value must have been given for the bill by the holder. Secondly, he must have acted in good faith and without any knowledge of a defect in title. Thirdly, the bill must be complete and regular on the face of it. Fourthly, the bill must be capable of negotiation. Finally, the bill must not be overdue.

The method of negotiation depends upon whether the bill is payable to bearer or to a named person. If it is payable to bearer or is otherwise a bearer instrument having been indorsed in blank, then transfer takes place simply by delivery. By s55, Bills of Exchange Act, an indorser warrants firstly that the drawer's signature and any subsequent indorsements are in order and secondly that at the time of indorsement the bill was valid and that he, the indorser, had good title to it. The indorser must compensate any subsequent holder if this proves not to be the case. For a valid indorsement it must be of the entire bill, be written on the bill itself and made by all payees or indorsees.

There are various kinds of indorsement. An indorsement in blank is where the bill is signed by the indorser without stating to whom it is payable. This has the effect of converting the bill into a bearer bill. A special indorsement is one which specifies the name of the indorsee. A conditional indorsement is one where the indorser makes the payment of the bill conditional upon the occurrence of some event. A restrictive indorsement is one which prevents further negotiation of the bill. An indorsement 'sans recours' is one on which the indorser disclaims any liability for the bill.

Solutions to Chapter 15 questions

ANSWERS TO SELF-TEST QUESTIONS

15.1 A cheque is a bill of exchange drawn on a banker payable on demand (s73 Bills of Exchange Act 1882).

15.2 (a) The rules of acceptance do not apply to cheques.

(b) The rules relating to crossing are unique to cheques.

15.3 (a) This is a crossing with or without the words 'and Co'. It means that the paying bank must only pay the cheque to another bank and not cash it across the counter.

(b) A crossing which contains the name of the collecting banker. The paying bank must pay only into an account in the named bank.

(c) The document cannot be passed free from equities—ie a holder can obtain no better title than his predecessors had.

(d) A direction to the collecting banker as to the account into which the money is to be paid. If person other than the payee presents the cheque for collection the collecting bank is put on inquiry to check the rights of this person.

15.4 (a) To take reasonable precautions against forgery or alteration of the cheque.

(b) To inform the bank of any forgery of a cheque drawn on his account as soon as he becomes aware of it.

15.5 (a) To pay only on his customer's signature and to his customer's directions.

(b) To honour customer's cheques up to the amount of the customer's credit balance and any agreed overdraft.

(c) To keep his customer's business secret.

(d) To collect on cheques paid in by the customer.

15.6 Because, by not telling the bank when he discovered the forgeries, the customer was estopped from denying the validity of the signature.

15.7 Section 60 Bills of Exchange Act 1882 provides that a bank which pays on a cheque payable to order, but on which an indorsement is forged or unauthorised, is not liable for so doing provided it makes the payment in good faith and in the ordinary course of business.

15.8 (a) S4 Cheques Act 1957

(b) Bank proves it is a holder in due course.

ANSWERS TO EXERCISES

15.1 This question concerns the rights of parties to a cheque which is stolen and subsequently presented. A cheque is a bill of exchange drawn on a banker payable upon demand. In this problem A is the drawer, B is the payee and the X Bank is the drawee. The rules governing negotiation apply to cheques in just the same way as they apply to other negotiable instruments.

A cheque may be crossed by the drawer or any subsequent holder. The crossing may be general or special. B appears here to have made a general crossing which constitutes a notice to the paying banker to make payment only into an account at another bank. Any bank paying on a cheque drawn upon it other than in accordance with the crossing is liable to the true owner for any loss caused by such unauthorised payment.

By s80, Bills of Exchange Act 1882 if a bank pays out on a crossed cheque in accordance with the crossing and in good faith and without negligence, it is placed in the same position as if it had paid the true owner. Thus if a cheque with a general indorsement is stolen so long as the paying banker pays into another bank account in good faith and without negligence then it has the same rights in regard to debiting the customer's account as if the transaction had been correctly carried out in every way.

B cannot sue the X Bank because the bank paid on the cheque to the Y Bank even though C had no title to the cheque at the time that he presented it to the Y Bank for collection. This is because the X Bank was protected by s80 Bills of Exchange Act 1882. B has no right to sue A since s80, Bills of Exchange Act also provides that a drawer (in this case A) enjoys the same rights and is in the same position as if the cheque had been paid to the true owner. A may not be sued by B. Likewise B has no right to sue the Y Bank since it is protected by s4, Cheques Act 1957 so long as it acted in good faith and without negligence in collecting the cheque from X Bank.

15.2 (a) The following are the duties owed by bankers to their customers in relation to cheques:
1. A duty to obey the instructions of the customer.
   A bank has a duty to honour cheques drawn by a customer so long as the cheques are properly drawn and so long as the customer has sufficient funds in his account or is within his agreed overdraft limits. Damages may be sought for defamation if a bank wrongly refuses to pay on a cheque. The bank must not make any payments from the customer's account other than in accordance with the customer's mandate.
   If a bank receives instructions not to pay a cheque, then the bank is liable if it pays on the cheque in contravention of this instruction.

2. A duty to render an account.
   There is a general duty of care owed by a bank to its customers as part of the contractual relationship. It must take care in the conduct of the customer's affairs and should provide him with an accurate statement of his account upon which he can rely. When drawing cheques upon his account, a customer may assume that his credit balance is correct.

3. A duty of secrecy.
   A bank owes a duty of secrecy when dealing with a customer's affairs. It should not disclose to third parties matters concerning the customer except in limited circumstances such as where the customer consents (as in the case where a customer gives the banker's name for a reference), where the bank is suing for its own protection (eg when suing to recover an overdraft) or where the bank makes disclosure under a court order.

4. There are various other duties which a bank owes of a more general nature. It must not pay post-dated cheques before the date due for payment. If it wishes to close an account which is in credit then it must give reasonable notice of this intention to the customer. It must not pay cash over the counter on a crossed cheque.

(b) This question concerns the duty of a bank in relation to cheques. B & Co have drawn a cheque in favour of C. In this case C is a non-existent person being merely a name invented by A for the purpose of extracting money from B & Co. Cheques drawn in these circumstances are treated as bearer cheques. B & Co will no doubt consider bringing an action to recover the money from the X Bank who have given value for the cheque to A. Under the Bills of Exchange Act no title to a cheque can pass on a forged or unauthorised indorsement. A bearer cheque may be negotiated by delivery without indorsement. By s7, Bills of Exchange Act, where a cheque has a fictitious or non-existent payee then it is treated as a bearer cheque payable upon delivery. Thus since the cheque drawn by B & Co is treated as a bearer cheque, the forged indorsement by A will have no effect upon the title of X Bank. The bank gave value for the cheque and obtained good title as a holder in due course. Thus the bank has right to receive payment from the Y Bank.

Moreover, s4, Cheques Act 1957 also protects the X Bank as the collecting bank. A bank which in good faith and without negligence receives payment of a cheque for a customer or, having credited a customer's account, receives payment for itself is protected by this provision. So long as the bank collected for the customer in good faith and without negligence then the bank is under no liability to the true owner. It may in this situation be difficult for the X Bank to show that it was not negligent in making the payment to A. For example it may be that the bank should have been put on enquiry when presented with a cheque drawn by A's employers in favour of a third party in circumstances where the cheque is negotiated to A himself.

If the X Bank has been negligent but has acted in good faith then it may still be protected in an action in conversion by B & Co. Section 29, Bills of Exchange Act provides that so long as a bank has acted in good faith then it is protected from an action in conversion by being a holder in due course of the cheque who has given value without notice of dishonour. The X Bank will be deemed to have given value in this case since it has given value to A.

The Y Bank will also be protected in this case by s60, Bills of Exchange Act so long as it paid the cheque in good faith and in the ordinary course of business.

Thus unless B & Co can prove negligence on the part of the X Bank, they must seek the return of the value of the cheque from A.

Solutions to Chapter 16 questions

ANSWERS TO SELF-TEST QUESTIONS

16.1 (a) it is a legal entity distinct from its members.

(b) it may be vicariously liable.

(c) it has perpetual succession.

(d) it may act in its own name.

16.2 An ultra vires act is one which is beyond the powers granted to a corporation by its document. An ultra vires transaction may not be enforceable by the company, although a third party dealing with the company is not affected by the ultra vires nature of the transaction provided he acts in good faith and without knowledge of the fact that the company was acting outside its power.

16.3 Unlimited companies
Companies limited by guarantee
Companies limited by shares.

16.4 (a) the name must indicate that it is a public limited company (plc)

(b) it must have a specified minimum share capital (£50,000)

(c) its memorandum must state that it is a public company

(d) it must have a certificate of incorporation from the registrar of companies stating that it has been formed as a public company.

ANSWERS TO EXERCISES

16.1 A legal person is regarded in law as having legal rights and duties. There are two main types of legal persons, natural persons and artificial persons. Artificial persons are corporations which are a person or body of persons recognised in law as having an existence distinct from their members. Corporations may be sole or aggregate. Examples of corporations sole are offices such as that of the Prime Minister, the Monarch, the Archbishop of Canterbury or the Treasury Solicitor. Corporations aggregate may be corporations formed under Royal Charter such as the Hudson's Bay Company or the Law Society or the Chartered Association of Certified Accountants. Corporations aggregate may also be statutory, such as the British Railways Board. The most common corporations aggregate are those registered under the Companies Act 1985.

    A corporation, being a separate legal entity, may make contracts in its own name and may carry on all normal business functions without recourse to individual members or shareholders. It may be made liable upon contracts which are broken or not performed and the usual remedies for damages and specific performance may be enforced against it. A corporation may also sue and be sued in the law of tort and may be held liable both individually and vicariously in the same circumstances as a private individual. A corporation may own property in its own name and may buy and sell such property. A corporation has perpetual succession which means that it does not cease to exist upon the death of an individual member. In the case of a company even if all the members were to die the company would still continue as a separate legal person.

Solutions to Chapter 17 questions

ANSWERS TO SELF-TEST QUESTIONS

17.1 Because he is acting as an extension of his principal's powers. The contract will be between the principal and the third party. The agent has no part in it. If, however, the agent does lack capacity, it will mean that, if he breaks his agreement with the principal the principal will have no right of action against him.

17.2 Implied authority enables the agent to fulfil his express function, usual authority extends the agent's express powers.

17.3 In Watteau, the third party had no notice of the limitation on the agent's powers: in Daun he had. The notice came from the type of public house involved.

17.4 (a) Principal must exist when the Act was done.
  (b) Principal must be named or ascertainable.
  (c) Principal must be aware of the material facts.
  (d) Principal must have capacity.
  (e) Act must be capable of being ratified
  (f) Principal must ratify in time.
  (g) Principal must rafity the whole transaction.

17.5 Actual authority given in arrears for this one transaction.

17.6 (a) Actual authority given in arrears by ratification.
  (b) Apparent authority.
  (c) None.
  (d) Apparent authority.
  (e) Actual then none.

17.7 (a) A bribe occurs when the agent is given an inducement to, or a reward for, entering the contract by the third party.
  (b) A secret profit occurs when the agent obtains some benefit from the transaction but the third party is unaware of this.

17.8 (a) Indemnity.
  (b) Remuneration.
  (c) Lien.

17.9 In Alpha Trading, the transaction has reached the stage where the principal was contractually bound to the third party. To act in such a way as to prevent the agent earning his commission, the principal would have to break his contract with the third party and so the court held, that, in these circumstances, the principal would be in breach of an implied term in the contract of agency that he would not behave unreasonably in denying the agent his commission. In Luxor, the principal had not reached the stage of contracting with the third party.

17.10 (a) Agreement.
  (b) Custom.
  (c) Performance.
  (d) Frustration.

(e) Time.
(f) Renunciation.
(g) Death.
(h) Bankruptcy.
(i) Insolvency.
(j) Insanity.
(k) Ending of the necessity.

ANSWERS TO EXERCISES

17.1 i) In the normal course of agency the authority of the agent is derived from his contractual arrangement with the principal. If the authority given to the agent is exceeded the principal incurs no liability. However, a principal may ratify the agent's action notwithstanding that it is in excess of his authority either expressly or by implication by the way in which he behaves. For ratification to be effective the following conditions must be satisfied.

(1) the agent must have claimed throughout that he was acting as an agent and must have stated who his principal was.
(2) the principal must have had contractual capacity throughout to make the contract.
(3) the principal, at the time of the purported ratification, must have been fully aware of all the relevant facts concerning the contract.
(4) ratification must take place within a reasonable time.
(5) the contract must be one which is valid in law.

If the principal ratifies he gives the agent authority 'in arrears'. It is as if the agent had been authorised all along to carry out the act.

ii) Estoppel is a rule of evidence which prevents a person from denying the existence or the truth of something which he has previously stated. Thus if one person leads another to believe that he has given authority to someone to act as his agent, then that person is usually estopped from denying the existence of the agency relationship, even though one may never have come into being. Agency by estoppel would occur where a person is appointed as an agent and then dismissed but the third parties with whom the agent has dealt in the past are not informed by the principal of the agent's dismissal. The principal is estopped from denying the existence of the agency.

iii) An agency of necessity arises where an agent, because of some emergency situation, finds it necessary to exceed his authority. For an agency of necessity to arise the following conditions must be satisfied:

(1) it must have been impossible for the agent to communicate with the principal.
(2) there must have been an emergency or necessity situation.
(3) the agent must have acted in good faith and in what he believed to be the best interest of the principal.
(4) there must already have existed a contractual relationship between the principal and the agent.

If these points are satisfied the principal will be bound by the agent's act.

(b) There is here a principal/agent relationship between L and M. L the principal is bound by contracts which M makes with a third party so long as M is acting within his authority. There is no dispute as to the terms of the agency in that M was appointed as agent to buy materials from N and other third parties. In any agency situation there is an implied authority for the agent to do anything necessary to the carrying out of his functions.

L is dissatisfied with the way in which M is working and brings the agency contract to an end. However, after termination, M continues to buy goods on credit from N who now seeks payment from L. As a general rule, upon the cessation of an agency, the agent ceases to have any authority and thus cannot bind his principal. However, circumstances may arise where a principal is estopped from denying the existence of an agency. Thus L is still liable for contracts made by M even after the termination of the agency relationship since the third parties, in dealing with M, relied on M's previous authority. Thus L is liable to pay N for the materials supplied pursuant to the orders from M. This would not apply if L were able to establish that he had informed N of the termination of the agency, though this does not appear to be the situation from the facts given in the question. Similarly there would be no liability if L could establish that N knew in some other way that M was no longer his agent.

Turning now to the commission which M received for placing orders, the relationship between agent and principal is a fiduciary relationship. As such, an agent is obliged to account to his principal for any secret profit received. A commission paid secretly, as in this case, constitutes a bribe and so L is entitled to claim these sums from M. It is not necessary in this case for L to prove that he has suffered any loss as a result of the bribe.

Moreover L may refuse to pay any remuneration to M. M has gone in breach of his contractual obligations. He has disallowed himself any rights under the contract. Moreover L may refuse to perform his part of any contract entered into by M with a third party paying a secret commission.

Another matter raised by the question is the obligation of an agent not to allow his personal interest to conflict with his business interest. It appears that M has been carrying on a business similar to L's. It could be argued that by so doing there arose a conflict. If this is the case it matters not that there was no intention to defraud. This obligation not to permit a conflict to arise between business and personal interests continues even after the termination of the agency relationship in that the agent may not use knowledge acquired during the course of his agency. Again in this situation the remedy is to withhold any commission owing to M or to bring proceedings for damages if L can prove loss caused as a result of M's private business.

17.2 The central feature of agency is the manner in which an agent can bring his principal into a contractual relationship with third parties. This capacity to enter into a binding relationship on behalf of the principal arises from the authority of the agent. An agent's authority takes three forms.

Express or actual authority is the authority given to the agent by the agreement itself. To discover the agent's actual authority, therefore, the court will look at the terms of the agreement, applying the ordinary rules of construction. So, if the agreement is in the form of a deed, known as a power of attorney, the court will restrict itself to looking at the wording of the deed and will, generally, not permit oral evidence to add to, vary or contradict that wording. If, however, the agency agreement is in writing other than by deed, or is completely oral, the courts adopt a more flexible attitude and will for example, imply powers to the agent if his express instructions are ambiguous.

If an agent acts within his express authority, he will have the power to bind the principal and the third party in contract whether the third party knows of the agency agreement or not.

Implied authority arises when the agent's express instructions are ambiguous or when they give the agent a discretion, as occurred in the case of *Comber* v *Anderson*. In these cases, if the agent acted in good faith and in what he believed were the best interests of the principal, the principal will be bound even if the result achieved by the agent is not what he wanted. This is again illustrated in the case of *Comber* v *Anderson*. Implied authority does not extend the agent's powers. It is an authority necessarily granted to enable him to carry out his express instruction and it is derived from an interpretation of these express instructions.

Usual authority is also derived from the agent's actual authority. An agent appointed to a particular job, or acting in a particular capacity, such as a solicitor, stockbroker, or a manager of a public house, will have the authority to perform all acts which agents of that type usually can perform. This authority arises even though the principal has expressly forbidden the agent from acting in this way. Usual authority, in other words, extends the agent's powers to cover all contracts into which agents of that type normally can enter. It is intended to protect a third party who deals with such an agent in the belief that this agent can do what agents of this type usually can do.

Usual authority is relevant when the principal has attempted to limit the agent's powers. Unless the principal can show that a third party dealing with the agent knew that the authority was restricted, he will be bound by any contracts entered into by the agent within the scope of his usual authority (*Watteau* v *Fenwick*). The only way in which the principal may avoid liability is by showing that the third party knew or should have known of the restriction, as he was able to do in the case of *Daun* v *Simmins*.

In this case, the fact that the agent was a manager of a *tied* public house should have given the third party notice that the agent's powers to buy alcohol for the business were restricted.

An agent who acts within his powers, be they express, implied or usual, will bind the principal and third party in any contract he makes whether he discloses that he is acting for a principal or not. In other words, as a general rule, there is no difference in the rights, duties or liabilities of a principal who is disclosed and one who is undisclosed. An undisclosed principal is one of whose existence the third party is unaware. He believes that he is acting with the agent as the only other contracting party. There are, however, exceptions to this general rule. That is, situations where the fact that the agent is acting for a principal who has not been disclosed will make a difference to the rights of the parties.

These are:
(a) Where the contract the agent makes with the third party expressly states that there is no principal involved in the transaction. In these cases, the undisclosed principal cannot claim rights under the contract.
(b) Where the contract terms are inconsistent with the existence of an agency, again the principal cannot claim any rights. This occurred in the case of *Humble* v *Hunter*.
(c) Where the identity of the principal or agent is important to the third party who would not have entered the contract had he known that the agent was acting for a principal or that the agent was acting for this particular principal. In this case, again the principal has no rights under the contract, as was shown in the case of *Said* v *Butt*.
(d) The third party has a right to elect, or choose, whether he wishes to sue the agent or the principal (*Clarkson Booker Ltd* v *Andjel*).
(e) An undisclosed principal cannot ratify an unauthorised act of the agent.

These are, however, exceptions to the general rule. That is, they are the few cases where there is any difference between the rights duties and liabilities of disclosed and undisclosed principals.

Solutions to Chapter 18 questions

ANSWERS TO SELF-TEST QUESTIONS

18.1 (a) Unlimited liability of partners.

(b) Agency of each partner both for the firm and his fellow partners when acting in the partnership business.

(c) The Partnership Act 1890 governs the affairs of the firm in the absence of any agreement to the contrary.

18.2 The relation which exists between persons carrying on a business in common with a view of profit. PA 1890, s2.

18.3 When, without the evidence, the sharing of the profits is for one of the reasons listed in PA 1890, s2(3).

18.4 In *Moss* v *Elphick*, the agreement provided for dissolution 'by mutual agreement' and in *Abbot* v *Abbot* the agreement provides that the partnership should, in effect, be indissoluble except by order of the court.

18.5 Yes. Following the Civil Liability (Contribution) Act 1978, the creditor could bring an action against the sleeping partner and succeed, although he could not recover costs. Liability of partners joint and several following the 1978 Act. Alternatively, the creditor could sue the firm in the firm's name and thus, by RSC Ord 81, automatically join to the action the partners who were members at the time the debt arose.

18.6 Because the partner in each case was acting in the ordinary course of business when he committed the tort.

18.7 That, for s14 PA 1890 to operate, a partner who has left a firm must knowingly hold himself out as still being a partner for estoppel to apply and render him liable for the firm's debts incurred after he has retired.

18.8 (a) By s32 PA 1890.

(b) By death or bankruptcy

(c) By changing of a share in the partnership.

(d) By illegality.

(e) By notice.

18.9 Because whoever loses will probably have to pay costs. So, the party bringing the action for dissolution will lose whatever happens—either he has to pay the costs and thus loses the money directly or the firm has to pay which means that each partner's share will be reduced, in which case the party petitioning for dissolution will lose indirectly.

18.10 Company

(a) A company has separate legal personality.

(b) Limited liability of shareholders.

Partnerships

(a) A partnership does not have separate personality.

(b) Unlimited liability of partners.

(c)	Unlimited membership.	
(d)	Members are not agents for the company.	
(e)	Public companies' shares are freely transferable.	
(f)	Company has restricted powers as to the transactions into which it may enter.	
(g)	Money paid by shareholders generally cannot be returned to them.	
(h)	Easier to raise money.	
(i)	Governed by strict rules as to accounts.	
(j)	Has to pay corporation tax.	

(c)	Limits on numbers of partners.	
(d)	Partners are agents for the firm.	
(e)	Partnership share transferable only with all other partners' consent.	
(f)	Partnerships have unlimited powers.	
(g)	Partnership money can be drawn on by partners subject only to the other partners agreeing.	
(h)	Can raise money only in the same way as an individual can.	
(i)	No rules apply as to strict account presentation.	
(j)	No separate taxations provisions—partners pay income tax.	

ANSWERS TO EXERCISES

18.1 Section 1, Partnership Act 1890 defines a partnership as the relation which subsists between persons carrying on a business in common with a view of profit. The relationship is essentially contractual. It may be express, as where there is a partnership deed. It may be implied from the business existing between the partners. Given that there is a partnership agreement, the matters with which this question is concerned may well be dealt with by the agreement itself. This answer, however, proceeds on the basis that the agreement is silent in respect of these matters. Given that this is the situation, we have to apply the rules laid down in the Partnership Act 1890. In this case the answers to the problems posed are as follows:

i) if the partners wish to expel a partner, all must agree. By s25 Partnership Act 1890, no majority of the partners may expel any other partner unless there is an express power to this effect in the partnership agreement. Even where this is the case the power must be executed in good faith, which implies that there must be good cause for the expulsion.

ii) where a partnership is for a fixed term or where the partnership agreement provides for dissolution in certain circumstances then dissolution occurs on the expiration of the term or on the occurrence of the dissolving event envisaged in the agreement. On the other hand if the agreement contains no provision for dissolution the partnership is a partnership at will. In this circumstance it may be brought to an end by any partner merely giving notice of dissolution. By s26, Partnership Act 1890, such notice has the effect of dissolving the partnership.

iii) if a new partner is to join the partnership agreement then by s24, Partnership Act 1890, all the partners must agree. This is a matter of major significance within the partnership and a majority vote is insufficient to admit a new partner in normal circumstances. The reason for this is that by ss 5 and 8 Partnership Act 1890, there is an implied agency on the part of each partner both for the partnership and for his fellow partners. It is obvious that the principal in an agency agreement such as this must have a right to veto the coming into effect of the agency.

iv) By s24, Partnership Act 1890, each partner is entitled to take part in the management of the firm. If there is to be a restriction on the rights of any of the partners to take part in management, all the partners including that partner whose rights are to be restricted, must agree.

18.2 As a general rule partners may bind both the firm and their fellow partners on any matter which falls within the normal business of the firm. This is so even though there is an agreement between the partners that they should not do so, so long as the third party with whom they are dealing has no notice of the restriction on the partner's authority. Sections 5 and 8, Partnership

Act 1890 provide that a partner has an implied agency both for his fellow partners and the partnership. Limits such as occur in this problem governing restrictions as to suppliers and the upper limits of contractual capacity are essentially internal rules and cannot be used by Jim to restrict his liability to third parties.

It would be expected that a garage would normally deal in fuel and also in second-hand cars. Thus the purchase of the oil for £200 is binding on the firm notwithstanding that it was in excess of the agreed limit and from a company other than the Ooze Oil Company. The purchase of the second-hand cars is again the sort of business which it would be expected that a garage would do, though perhaps if the garage were merely a filling station and the person with whom Alan dealt knew of the restriction the contracts would not be binding on the partnership or on Jim. Having said this, this seems unlikely on the facts, and almost certainly the contract is binding. By s21, Partnership Act 1890 any property which is bought by money which belongs to the firm is deemed to have been bought on account of the firm and thus belongs to the firm.

A similar situation to this arose in the case of *Mercantile Credit Co v Garrod* (1962). Here the active partner in a two-man garage business bought cars in contravention of the partnership agreement. It was held that the transactions into which he entered were binding on the firm since they fell within the normal course of business of a firm of that kind.

Finally Alan has clearly committed a wilful breach of the partnership agreement and Jim could commence proceedings under s35(*d*), Partnership Act 1890 for the dissolution of the firm.

Solutions to Chapter 19 questions

ANSWERS TO SELF-TEST QUESTIONS

19.1 A duty in contract arises by virtue of the agreement between the parties. A duty in tort arises from the law, independently of any agreement.

19.2 Liability incurred for a tort committed by another person.

19.3 Because in Iqbal's case the employee was acting outside the scope of his employment.

19.4 (a) Duty of care.

(b) Breach of that duty.

(c) Damage resulting from breach.

19.5 Because of the doctrine of privity.

19.6 Anyone the defendant can reasonably foresee as being likely to be harmed by his acts.

19.7 By removing from him the need to prove negligence in cases where the event that occurred would not have done so had there been no negligence.

19.8 It provided that a negligent misrepresentation leading to economic loss could be actionable.

19.9 '... to be reasonably careful and cautious' per (Lopes L J in *Re Kingston Cotton Mill Ltd*; to ascertain and state the financial position of the company as at the time of audit (per Lopes L J in *Re London and General Bank (No2)*).

19.10 Because they had been put on enquiry and, by failing to follow up the enquiry, had not exercised reasonable care and skill.

ANSWERS TO EXERCISES

19.1 Vicarious liability is the liability of one person for torts committed by another. For vicarious liability to be established two elements must be proved. Firstly, the relationship between the person committing the tort and the actual defendant in the case must be shown usually to have been that of employee and employer. Secondly, the tort must have been committed during the course of the employee's employment. As a general rule vicarious liability does not apply when an employee uses an independent contractor to perform a task. In this regard it is important to sort out the difference between an employee and an independent contractor. There is no single decisive test to settle this issue, there being three tests which the court from time to time has applied. The oldest test is referred to as the 'control' test. In short, this involves asking the question whether the employer could not only tell the employee what to do but how to do it. The second test is the 'organisation' test which involves asking whether the employee was an integral part of the organisation. Perhaps the most common test today is the 'multiple' test which requires the court to look at all the circumstances of the case and to reach a decision as to whether the person concerned was or was not an employee.

The second condition is that the wrongful act must normally have been committed during the course of an employee's employment. An act may come within the scope of employment notwithstanding that it is a wrongful way of performing the employment. For example, in *Century Insurance Co* v *Northern Ireland Road Transport Board* (1942) a driver of a petrol tanker was at a garage undertaking the transfer of petrol from his lorry to a storage tank. While doing this he lit a cigarette and threw away the match. An explosion resulted which caused a considerable amount of damage. The employers sought to avoid liability by claiming that the lighting of a cigarette was wholly outside of the contract of employment. It was held, however, that the driver had been acting in his employment in unloading the petrol and that by smoking he had simply been doing what he had been employed to do in a careless way. On the other hand, of course, if the employee completely absents himself from his employment then no question of vicarious liability can arise. For example, in *Iqbal* v *London Transport Board* a bus conductor drove a bus in spite of this being totally contrary to his instructions. In so doing he injured a fellow employee. It was held that his employers were not liable. The conductor had absented himself from his employment by his conduct. Similarly in *Warren* v *Henlys* (1948) an employee at a garage assaulted a customer in an over-exuberant attempt to persuade the customer to pay for some petrol of which he had just taken possession. It was held that the employers were not vicariously liable for the assault since the act of the employee was totally outside the scope of his duties.

Just because an act is prohibited does not necessarily mean that it will fall outside the scope of employment. For example, in *Limpus* v *London General Omnibus Co* (1862) there was a prohibition against bus drivers racing each other. One bus driver cut across the path of another vehicle which resulted in injury to a third party. It was held that the employers were liable for this negligence. Again in *Rose* v *Plenty* (1976) an employer specifically instructed milk roundsmen employed by him not to carry children on their milkfloats and not to allow children to deliver milk. In contravention of this a milkman allowed a 13-year old boy to ride on the milkfloat and to deliver milk. Due to the negligence of the milkman the boy was injured. It was held that the employers were liable.

19.2 The facts of *Donoghue* v *Stevenson* (1932) were that the appellant drank some ginger beer bought for her by a friend and manufactured by the respondent. The manufacturer had sold the ginger beer to a retailer and the retailer had subsequently re-sold it to the appellant's friend. Thus there was no contract between the manufacturer and the appellant. The appellant poured herself a glass of ginger beer and drank it. When she came to pour herself a second glass from the bottle the remains of a partly decomposed snail emerged from the bottle. Because of this the appellant became ill and brought proceedings against the manufacturers in negligence.

It was held by the House of Lords that there was liability on the part of the manufacturers to the ultimate consumer. When he sells products in the form in which he intends them to reach the ultimate consumer and knowing that there is no probability of intermediate examination, he owes a duty to the consumer to take reasonable care. In giving the leading judgment in the case, Lord Atkin said 'You must take reasonable care to avoid acts or omissions which you can reasonably foresee would be likely to injure your neighbour . . . (these are) persons so closely and directly affected by my act that I ought reasonably to have them in contemplation as being so affected when I am directing my mind to the acts or omissions which are called in question'.

This dictum is the cornerstone of the modern law of negligence. It has been adapted in a number of cases to establish liability in negligence in a wide variety of situations. For some time it was thought that it was inapplicable when the resulting injury was purely economic. However, in *Hedley Byrne* v *Heller & Partners* (1964) it was held by the House of Lords that in the absence of an adequate disclaimer a person giving advice on which he knows the recipient will rely will incur liability in the event of that advice proving to have been negligent.

Additional questions

Students are encouraged to attempt these questions. However, the answers are provided only in the manual issued to lecturers. Lecturers may obtain a free copy of the manual by writing to: Sales & Marketing Department, Longman Group UK Ltd, 21–27 Lamb's Conduit Street, London WC1N 3NJ.

Chapter 4

1. How far is it true to say that the courts have a monopoly on the right to resolve disputes?

2. Describe the jurisdiction and composition of magistrates' courts (June 1984)

3. Describe the jurisdiction of the civil courts of first instance and explain the system of appeals in civil courts

4. Explain the function of the following:
    (a) the Lord Chancellor
    (b) the Lord Chief Justice
    (c) the Master of the Rolls

5. What are the main advantages and disadvantages of administrative tribunals?

6. Distinguish between the role and function of solicitors and barristers

7. There are many industrial and commercial disputes settled today by administrative tribunals:
    (a) What are administrative tribunals?
    (b) Why were they established?
    (c) How are they controlled?

8. Arthur has recently bought a brand new car for £17,000 from Shifty Garages Ltd. He claims that the car has several defects but Shifty Garages Ltd will not give a refund or repair the vehicle. Arthur says he will take 'Shifty Garages Ltd to the highest court in the land'. Explain how such a case might be pursued through the court system (including appeals). What alternatives might there be to going to court and the factors that Arthur should consider before taking legal action?

Chapter 5

1. Explain what you understand by statute law. What would you regard as the main advantages and disadvantages of statute law?

2. What is delegated legislation? What are its main advantages and disadvantages?

3. To what extent is (a) the House of Lords, and (b) the Court of Appeal bound by its own previous decisions?

4. What are the main purposes for which an Act of Parliament might be passed?

Chapter 6

1. In what different ways may a judicial decision be treated when it comes to be considered by the court?

2. How far can it be said that judges make law?

3. (a) Explain what is meant by *ratio decidendi* and *obiter dicta* (**6 marks**)

   (b) What are the advantages and disadvantages of the doctrine of binding precedent? (**8 marks**)

   (c) When, if at all, can or should a court refrain from following a binding precedent? (**6 marks**)

4. What do you understand by delegated legislation? What are its main advantages and disadvantages?

5. 'In interpreting a statute a judge can come to almost any decision he likes; the rules of statutory interpretation impose very few limits on his discretion.' Discuss

6. Section 1 of the Unfair Musical Instruments Act 1986 provides that: 'It is an offence to blow, squeeze or bang any musical instrument in any house, shed or other place after 10.00 pm for the purpose of entertainment'. Explain how this provision would be interpreted by the court in the following circumstances:

   (a) Jake, an amateur musician, has a penny whistle which he blows when he finds it difficult to sleep. At 12.30 pm one evening, he starts playing the penny whistle since he cannot get to sleep

   (b) Slick, a punk rocker, wishes to take the music world by storm by creating new musical sounds. He therefore connects some rubber tubing to an old dustbin, attaches a mouthpiece to the tubing, and one evening at 10.30 pm commences blowing into it. This produces a thundering noise. Sometime later that night some friends go round to Slick's house and he re-commences blowing into the contraption for his friends' entertainment

   (c) Maud plays her harp in an underground soundproof apartment at 11.00 pm to some friends who find the music soothing

Chapter 7

1. (a) Distinguish between executed, executory and past consideration and explain the importance of the distinction

   (b) Tom has lent Fred £500 which is due for repayment on 1 December. Tom asks Fred in early November for immediate repayment because he is short of money. Fred replies that he can give Tom only £400. Tom agrees to accept £400 in settlement of the debt. Would Tom be able to sue for the outstanding £100? Would your answer be different if Fred had asked to settle the debt by giving Tom a cheque for £400 on 1 December?

   (June 1975)

2. (a) Outline the rules governing the contractual liability of a minor (**12 marks**)

   (b) Advise Rupert, aged 17, as to his contractual liability in the following situations:
   (i) He borrowed £500 from his uncle which he never repaid
   (ii) He took a two year lease on a flat at a monthly rental of £80. He paid three months rent in advance and moved into the flat. After one month he now wishes to leave the flat.
   (iii) He bought a sports car, for which he is now unable to pay. He told the dealer who sold it to him that he was 19 years of age. (**8 marks**)

   (June 1983)

3 (a) 'It is always necessary to communicate acceptance of an offer to the other party to the contract'
Explain whether or not you agree with this statement **(12 marks)**

(b) A wrote to B offering to sell him a consignment of goods. In the letter he asked B to telephone his decision to C, A's agent. Is there a valid contract between A and B in each of the following situations:
  (i) B does not telephone C but writes to A accepting his offer. The letter is delayed and A sells the goods elsewhere.
  (ii) B sends a telex to A accepting the offer. **(8 marks)**
(December 1984)

4 (a) State the rules which govern the acceptance of an offer in the law of contract **(10 marks)**

(b) Explain whether a contract exists in the following situations:
  (i) A sees a suitcase in a shop window with a price label of £20. He goes into the shop to buy the suitcase and is told that the wrong label has been attached and the price is £30.
  (ii) B offers to sell his guitar to C for £100. C says he can only afford to pay £75 and B says it is not enough. Later in the evening C goes to B's house to say he will buy the guitar for £100. **(10 marks)**
(June 1984)

5 (a) When, if ever, does payment of a smaller sum discharge a debt owed to a creditor? **(10 marks)**

(b) D owned a fleet of lorries.
  (i) He agreed with E to deliver E's grain to his warehouse. E then asked D to deliver the grain to a different destination 50 miles away, and offered him extra remuneration. E did not pay the extra remuneration.
  (ii) He agreed with E to deliver F's steel to G. G agreed to assist D with unloading the steel. When the steel was delivered G refused this assistance.
  Advise D. **(10 marks)**
(June 1987)

6 A's car broke down and the garage informed him that it would take fourteen days to repair it. His neighbour, B, offered to take A to work during this time. At the end of the fourteen days, A said he would pay B £50. He failed to make the payment. Can B sue A for money? **(8 marks)**
(December 1983)

7 Explain whether Paul must fulfil his promises in the following situations:
(a) He promises to sell his very expensive car to Arthur for £10

(b) He returns home to find that the windows of his house have been cleaned by Bernard; he promises Bernard £1 for his trouble

(c) He promises to pay Charles £100 for painting his house, the contract to be completed within one week. Subsequently, when it appears that the work is getting behind, he promises Charles a further £20 if he finishes on time

(d) He promises to deliver goods to David in return for a payment to him of £50 by Eric

(e) He promises to release Frank from a debt of £500 if Frank pays him £400

8 In *Dunlop Pneumatic Tyre Co Ltd* v *Selfridge Co Ltd* (1915) it was said to be a 'fundamental principle' that 'only a person who is a party to a contract can sue on it'.
Explain this statement and consider the extent to which third parties can acquire rights under a contract.

9 Why is it necessary that the parties to a contract should have an intention to create legal relations if the contract is to be binding upon them? How is the intention ascertained?

10 On Monday 6 November, Smith offered to sell to Jones a bicycle for £60 and said that the offer would remain open for three days. What is the position in each of the following situations:

(a) On Tuesday 7 November, Jones tells Smith that he will buy the bicycle for £50. Smith refuses this, whereupon Jones says he will pay £60.

(b) On Wednesday 8 November, Jones tells Smith that he accepts the offer; in fact Smith had, on 7 November, sold the bicycle to Brown.

(c) On Friday 10 November, Jones tells Smith that he accepts the offer.

Chapter 8

1 Mr and Mrs Jorrocks, who were on a touring holiday in Cornwall, arrived at the Pencrockett Motel and booked in for one night. They explained that they wanted to be away early next morning and paid for the room in advance. Having signed the register, they were shown to their room where there was a notice that the Motel would not accept responsibility for any articles lost or stolen unless handed to the management for safe keeping. The couple later went to the Motel restaurant for a meal and Mrs Jorricks left her fur coat in their bedroom. Mrs Jorricks suggested that in view of the notice, it might be wiser to take it with her, but she said that it was a warm night and anyway they would not be away for long. Accordingly, the coat was left in the room. Mr and Mrs Jorricks locked the door and deposited the key at reception. While they were in the restaurant, a thief took the key and stole the fur coat.

Advise Mrs Jorricks whether she has any claim against the Motel. Would your answer be any different if the notice seeking to avoid the Motel's liability had been on display at reception?

2 'By virtue of recent developments in the law relating to exclusion clauses, it is becoming increasingly difficult for a person to exclude or limit his liability in the event of a breach of contract.'

Discuss.

3 Give examples of:

(a) Contracts which must be in the form of a deed.

(b) Contracts which must be in writing; and

(c) Contracts which must be evidence in writing

What is the effect of these requirements not being complied with?

4 (a) Define a guarantee and explain how it differs from a contract of indemnity.

(b) P orally agreed with A that A should act as his agent in the sale of some valuable paintings. As part of the contract, A guaranteed P against failure of any of A's clients to pay for the paintings they bought. State whether this guarantee is enforceable.

Chapter 9

1 What is meant by misrepresentation in the law of contract? What remedies are available if misrepresentation has taken place?

(December 1988)

2 (a) What principles does the court apply to decide whether a covenant, which is in restraint of trade in a contract, is void?

(b) Fred sold his private petrol filling station to a large petrol company which had petrol stations all over England and Wales. A clause in the contract of sale provided that he would not operate a competing business within a 10 mile radius of the station being sold or within a 10 mile radius of any other filling station operated by the purchasers for the next 10 years following completion of the sale. For six years after the sale Fred found no work which he could settle to, and so he eventually opened, on the seventh anniversary of the sale, a small petrol filling station some 225 miles away from the station previously owned by him but within six miles of one of the purchasers's other stations. The purchaser company is now seeking an injunction to prevent Fred from trading from the new site.
  Advise Fred.

3 Explain, giving case-law examples:
(a) the distinction between void, voidable and unenforceable contracts,

(b) the effect of the distinction when the goods the subject matter of such contracts are transferred to third parties

4 Martin, a wealthy bachelor, agreed with the Society for the Promotion of Marriage, a charitable organisation, that, if the Society would arrange for him to receive an award in the next Honours List and would also find him a wife suitable for a man of his standing, he would pay the Society £10,000. He made an immediate down payment of £1,000 as a 'deposit', but a few weeks later he wrote to the Society saying that he now wished to withdraw from the arrangement. The Society refuses to return the £1,000 'deposit', and is seeking a further £200 for work allegedly done and expenses allegedly incurred in furtherance of the contract.
  Advise Martin.

5 (a) Explain the equitable remedies for a mistake, which is not recognised as an operative mistake at common law

(b) James, an accountancy student, advertised his Skoda car for sale for £2,000. A rogue, posing as 'Sir Stephen', a wealthy barrister, called on James and offered to buy the car. James accepted 'Sir Stephen's' offer and received a cheque signed 'Sir Stephen'. He was worried that the cheque might prove worthless since 'Sir Stephen' was not dressed as well as James expected a barrister to dress and also looked rather shifty. 'Sir Stephen', however, produced a membership card showing him to be a member of the Outside Temple Law Library. Thus satisfied with 'Sir Stephen's' identity, James handed over the registration papers and allowed 'Sir Stephen' to drive away the Skoda. The rogue, now posing as James, has sold the car to Martin, who bought in good faith believing the rogue to be James.
  James has just learnt from his bank that the cheque from 'Sir Stephen' has been dishonoured.
  Advise James whether he can reclaim the Skoda car from Martin.

6 Gregg owns an old-established coal merchant's business in the High Street of Doomsville. Following a practice established many years before by his great-grandfather, he required every assistant in the business to give a written undertaking that he (the assistant) will not be employed in any business selling, supplying, purveying or otherwise providing solid fuel to the general public if the main place of business shall be within five miles of the Dogs' Watering fountain in the middle of Doomsville. Bold, an assistant for many years in Gregg's business, has recently joined another firm in the middle of Doomsville whose business is selling coal. Gregg is upset and angry about this.
  Has he any legal redress against Bold?

7 Skullion offered for sale the Wheae Ronald mine. The offer for sale was accompanied by exaggerated and unreliable statements as to the mine's earning capacity. A potential buyer, Zikster, agreed to accept the offer if Skullion's statements could be verified. Zikster thereupon appointed experienced agents to investigate the whole of the matter. These agents duly visited the mine, where they were offered every facility for forming a judgment. Subsequently, they reported to Zikster that in their opinion Skullion's statements were true. Accordingly Zikster completed the purchase. He now wishes to rescind the transaction on the basis of misrepresentation by Skullion.

Advise Zikster.

8   (a)   What are the legal consequences so far as the parties are concerned where a contract has been made which was illegal from the outset

       (b)   A supplied B with oxyacetylene equipment which A knew B intended to use for safe-breaking. A was promised a share in the proceeds of the break-in but has just learnt that B has decided to abandon the enterprise.

Can A recover the equipment from B? Would your answer be different if B had sold the equipment to a garage proprietor and A wished to recover the price of the equipment from him?

9   In English law, the parties to a contract are, as a general rule, free to make whatever bargain they can; and such a contract is enforceable notwithstanding that it is a bad bargain for them. However, there are limits, and the law will interfere to relieve a party from a contract arising from certain pressures put upon him. What sort of 'pressures' does the law regard as illegitimate?

10   James is a sole trader in business running a garage. His secretary places in front of him a pile of documents and says, 'these are order forms for spares from Supersales Ltd. Will you, please, sign them?' James duly signs the forms, though without really reading them through. Supersales Ltd is a well-known firm of car accessory suppliers. One of the forms which James signs reads 'in consideration of your supplying Egbert with the parts which are listed in this order, I will indemnify you against the cost'. Egbert is in fact a close friend of James' secretary. Subsequently Supersales Ltd delivers the parts to Egbert, and when Egbert fails to pay on the invoice, Supersales Ltd sends James a bill for them.

Advise James as to his possible liability.

11   (a)   In what circumstances, if any, will proof of mistakes render a contract invalid?

       (b)   A had notepaper printed showing the addresses of some large, but non-existent, factory premises and a whole string of offices abroad. Using this notepaper, he ordered and obtained from B a quantity of goods, which he promptly resold to C, who acted in good faith. A has now disappeared with the proceeds of the sale.
Advise B.

Chapter 10

1   (a)   In what circumstances will a contract be discharged through frustration? (**12 marks**)

       (b)   D engages E to sing in a series of concerts. In each of the following situations what is the legal position if before the first concert can take place:
           (i)   the theatre in which the concerts are to be held is seriously damaged by fire and the concerts are cancelled?
           (ii)   E is found guilty of drug smuggling and is sent to prison for two years?

(**8 marks**)
(December 1984)

2   What remedies are available to a plaintiff in an action for breach of contract?

(June 1984)

3   (a)   Describe the rules governing remoteness of damage and the measure of damages in the law of contract. (**10 marks**)

       (b)   H promised to deliver goods to I on a specified date. There was a term in the contract which provided for the payment of liquidated damages of £500 in the event of a breach of contract.

H delivered goods of the right quality and quantity but two weeks late. I accepted the goods. Later I decided to sue H for breach of contract and to claim £500 damages. Advise I. (June 1987)

4   (a) What principles will the court supply in assessing unliquidated damages for breach of contract?

(b) A boards an express coach to London for a business meeting at which he is to finalise an important contract which will bring him a profit of £50,000. On the journey the coach breaks down. As a result A is very late arriving in London and in consequence he loses the contract.
What is the liability of the coach company?

5   (a) Explain the circumstances under which the equitable remedies of (i) specific performance and (ii) injunctions are granted by the court in actions upon contracts

(b) Harry, a student, signs, in March 1988, a contract with the XYZ Language School, whereby during the summer vacation he will work exclusively with the company as a teacher of English. In April 1988, Harry is offered a better paid job with another company, and writes to the XYZ Language School cancelling his contract with them. Advise XYZ as to their legal rights.

6   How may a contract be discharged? (June 1983)

7   (a) In what circumstances is impossibility a defence to an action for breach of contract?

(b) Tourifrisk Ltd owned a plot of land on the South Devon coast and obtained planning permission to erect a luxury hotel. Specblock Ltd are contracted to carry out the construction work for £50,000. Unknown to either party the site was unsuitable for building, but this fact was undiscovered until Tourifrisk Ltd had already paid £200,000 to Speckblock Ltd and then later had expended £100,000 under the contract. It could be shown that the sale of rubble from the initial construction work would realise £10,000. How would the court determine the rights of the parties.

8   (a) 'In a proper case damages for mental distress can be recovered in contract', per Lord Denning M.R. in *Jarvis* v *Swan's Tours Ltd* (1973). Discuss.

(b) Jenkin booked, through a travel agent, a touring holiday on which he was to stay at a number of hotels in Wales. The price of the holiday was £600. Jenkin paid this to the travel agent, and included in the price was the entire cost of the holiday. The agent's brochure described the holiday as 'a delightful excursion, calling at superb hostelries and replete with good companionship'. Jenkin has just returned from the holiday and is complaining that he had a 'dreadful time'. He seeks your advice, telling you that he has received demands for £400 for his accommodation because they had not been paid by the travel agent and that he found his fellow travellers most uncongenial.
Advise Jenkin as to (a) whether he is liable to make this payment of the further £400 and (b) any entitlement he may have to compensation from the travel agent for having to put up with uncongenial company.

9   (a) In what circumstances is loss arising from a breach of contract too remote to recover by an action for damages?

(b) The parties to a contract agreed that in the event of a breach of contract, the party in default shall pay to the other a fixed sum by way of damages. Explain whether this agreed sum will be recoverable or not recoverable in the courts.

10 Superstar Films Ltd was making a film of 'Othello' and contracted with Sid Gentle, a famous actor, to play the leading role. Considerable expenses were also incurred in engaging a script editor and a director. Sid Gentle's other filming commitments were such that he was unable to

perform the contract and so he announced his withdrawal from the film. Superstar Films Ltd has reluctantly accepted the repudiation but was unsuccessful in finding a suitable replacement.

Advise Superstar Films Ltd whether it can:
(a) sue Sid Gentle for specific performance
(b) recover the expenses incurred before the contract in form of salaries.

Chapter 11

1 (a) Explain the conditions and warranties implied into contracts for the sale of goods by the UK Sale of Goods Act 1979. **(12 marks)**

   (b) F purchased an electric toaster from a shop owned by W. A week later, while she was using the toaster, she suffered a relatively severe electric shock and the toaster ceased to function. F took the toaster back to the shop and demanded a refund of her money from W. W informed her she should complain to the manufacturers as the shop was not responsible for a manufacturing fault.

   After F had left the shop, W looked at the conditions of sale which he had agreed with the manufacturers of the toaster. He discovered the agreement included a clause which excluded the manufacturers from liability for any expenses or implied conditions or warranties concerning the quality and fitness of the toasters they had supplied to him.

   Advise F and W. **(8 marks)**
   (June 1983)

2 (a) State the rules which govern the passing of property in a contract for the sale of goods, and explain why it is important to ascertain the time at which the property in goods passes from the seller to the buyer. **(12 marks)**

   (b) It delivers by lorry a consignment of goods which he has contracted to sell to J. The goods are unloaded in J's yard by the lorry driver. Later that day J examines the goods and discovers they do not comply with the contract description.

   Advise J. **(8 marks)**
   (December 1984)

3 (a) What remedies are available to an unpaid seller of goods against (i) the goods, and (ii) the buyer? **(10 marks)**

   (b) J agreed to buy goods from K. He examined them only after they had been delivered. J found the goods did not comply with the contract description. J informed K of this fact, that he did not accept the goods and that K should collect the goods from J's premises. K did not collect the goods from J's premises, and they deteriorated. K later sued J for the price of the goods.

   Advise J. **(10 marks)**
   (June 1987)

4 M purchased a used car from D for £750. D informed M the car was generally in excellent condition, although the clutch might need some minor adjustments in the future. M then purchased sheepskin covers and a stereo cassette player for the car from C. After fitting these items to the car, M discovered that the seat covers were not real sheepskin as indicated by the ticket in the shop. Also, the cassette player was faulty and could not be heard above the sound of the engine. M returned to C's with the seat covers and the cassette player.

   C refused to exchange them, or refund M's money, pointing to a sign on the wall which read, 'No goods may be returned or exchanged'. A week later, the car engine completely seized up and could not be repaired.

   Advise M. (December 1983)

5 (a) Explain briefly in what circumstances the terms implied in a contract for the sale of goods by the Sale of Goods Act 1979 can be excluded from a contract by agreement between the parties.

(b) A bought a car from B's Garages Ltd. The car was described as 'new'. In the sale documents was a clause purporting to exclude 'all conditions and warranties, express or implied'. After he had taken delivery of the car and driven it for three days, A discovered that it had been driven for about 600 miles before he had taken delivery of it. Advise A as to what remedies, if any, he might have.

6 In what circumstances has a buyer the right to reject goods which he has bought and repudiate his obligations under the contract of sale? When does a buyer lose this right to reject the goods?

7 Jim wishes to buy his son a car as a birthday present. He approaches Henry, a retailer of car accessories, who he knows engages in buying and selling motor vehicles occasionally. Henry offers to sell Jim a second-hand car; he explains that the brakes are defective and require attention, and reduces the price of the car to take account of this. He adds that he will accept no responsibility for this or any other defect with the car. Jim accepts Henry's offer without examining the car. Had he done so, he would have noticed that the tyres were badly worn.

Jim drives the car away from Harry's premises, but, because of its defects, fails to negotiate a bend in the road. The car strikes a wall and is damaged beyond repair.

Advise Jim as to what rights he may have against Henry.

8 (a) When there is a contract for sale of goods, what are the rules which govern the passing of risk?

(b) M sells to N 100 gallons of white spirit out of a large quantity in a tank on a wharf. No appropriation to the contract is made, but a delivery warrant is issued to N. The warrant is not acted upon for some time, and in the meantime the spirit deteriorates. Upon whom does the loss fall?

9 (a) What are the provisions of the Sale of Goods Act 1979 as to when a buyer is deemed to have accepted the goods delivered to him?

(b) How, if at all, are these provisions limited if a buyer has not had a reasonable opportunity to examine the goods after they have been delivered to him?

10 (a) What terms are implied in a contract for the sale of goods by sample?

(b) A contract for sale by sample provided that payment was to be made on arrival, against shipping documents. The buyer accordingly paid for the goods before he had an opportunity to examine them. On examination he found that the bulk did not correspond with the sample.

Can he reject the goods and, if so, on what grounds?

11 Smith, a manufacturer of furniture and bedding, made a contract in writing to buy from Jones 100 tons of rag flock. Deliveries of the rag flock were to be made in weekly loads of one and a half tons, each load to be separately paid for. Smith can prove that the fifteenth load was not up to the agreed standard. He suggests that he is not obliged to accept any further deliveries.

Is he correct? Give reasons for your answer.

12 What is meant by an unpaid seller's lieu and in what circumstances does it arise?

13 What are the main terms which are implied in a contract for the supply of services?

Chapter 12

1 In relation to a consumer credit agreement explain what is meant by a 'cancellable agreement'. What are the rights of the debtor under such an agreement and what are the effects of cancellation? (December 1984)

2 (a) What is a hire-purchase contract? How does it differ from a credit sale contract and a conditional sale contract?

(b) Charles buys a second-hand sports car from Peter after reading Peter's advertisement in the local newspaper. Charles pays Peter in cash the £500 agreed price and takes delivery of the car. Two days later Charles is visited by a representative of the Bunter Finance Company who informs him that the car is subject to hire-purchase agreement with Peter who has not paid all the instalments. Charles refuses to surrender the car. Discuss the legal position.

3 (a) What are the main obligations of the hirer under a contract of hire-purchase?

(b) Andrew, Bernard and Cedric take identical goods on hire-purchase from Fleecure plc, a finance company. The total purchase price is £300 payable by 15 monthly instalments of £20. Andrew terminates his agreement after paying two instalments and before the third instalment is due. Bernard terminates his agreement after paying nine instalments and before the tenth instalment is due. Cedric terminates his agreement after paying seven instalments, but after the eighth has become due. Each returns the goods in good order and condition to Fleecure plc on terminating the agreement.

To what extent is (a) Andrew, (b) Bernard and (c) Cedric liable under their respective agreements?

Chapter 13

1 How does the law seek to ensure that employees are made aware of major terms and conditions of their contracts of employment? Why has such awareness become more significant in recent years?

2 (a) What are the most important duties owed by an employee to an employer?

(b) Jim and John were respectively the lorry driver and mate of the Bigwagon Haulage Co Ltd. Jim negligently injures John in the course of their work by reversing the lorry over John's foot.
Advise John.

3 Henry, an operator of a coach-firm, secures a contract to take a large party of businessmen to a major sporting event. Because a number of his coaches are undergoing repairs, he engages Race, an independent contractor, to help with carrying some passengers. Robert, a driver employed by Henry, and Speed have a bet as to who can complete the journey in the fastest time. Because of their careless driving, there is a collision between the two coaches. Several passengers in both coaches are injured.
What are the legal liabilities of Henry, Robert and Speed?

4 (a) How does the illness of an employee affect his employment?

(b) David is employed by Eric, a grocer, as an assistant. Part of his duties is delivering groceries by bicycle. One evening he breaks his leg while playing football. When Eric learns of this, he dismisses David.
Advise David.

5 Minicabs Ltd is the operator of a fleet of taxis. It engages James as a driver. The taxi driven by James is provided and maintained by Minicabs Ltd who also pay for all fuel used. James has undertaken only to do taxi work for Minicabs Ltd. James is not paid a wage, earning instead a commission on his taxi fares. What journeys he makes are entirely at his discretion.

(a) Is James an employee or an independent contractor?

(b) Why might a contract of service be of importance in this case?

6 (a) Explain the duty of loyal and faithful service owed by an employee to his employer.

(b) Andy and Berny are employed as repairers of television sets. Their employer has recently discovered that Andy is repairing television sets for friends at weekends and Berny is working several nights a week as a barman at a local hotel.
On what grounds, if any, may an employer object to these part-time activities?

7 Consider the redundancy entitlement of the following employees:
   (a) A is employed for a two year fixed term contract which is due to expire

   (b) B has been warned that his firm will shortly be closing down. He has acquired another job elsewhere, and has left his former employment

   (c) C has resigned from his employment because his employer has been asking him to take risks for which he was not employed and which he is not prepared to take

   (d) D's job is coming to an end, but he agrees to try another job with the same employer for six weeks to see whether he likes it. After three weeks he leaves

   (e) E has been away from work for over a year through illness. He has now been told that his job has ended.

8 'Terms and conditions of employment may be derived from various sources.'
What are these sources?

9 (a) In what circumstances is an employer justified in summarily dismissing an employee?

   (b) Albert, a waiter, has been summarily dismissed after slipping on a wet floor and dropping a tray of plates. After he goes, his employer discovers that he has regularly been taking money from the till.
   Advise Albert.

Chapter 14

1 Discuss the meaning of negotiability and explain the main characteristics of bills of exchange and promissory notes. (December 1984)

2 Explain what is meant by a bill of exchange and for what purposes it may be used. What is the difference between a holder in due course and a holder for value? (December 1983)

3 (a) Where a negotiable instrument is dishonoured, who can sue to enforce it and whom can he sue?

   (b) Explain the liability on a bill of exchange of (i) the drawer, (ii) the drawee, and (iii) an indorser

4 State, giving reasons, whether the following are valid bills of exchange:
   (a) Pay on demand to Frank Greystock the sum of £100 provided he passes the foundation Examination in April 1989

   (b) Pay to Sir Florian Eustace the sum of £1,000 from the proceeds of sale of the Eustace diamonds

   (c) After a celebration dinner, the host finds he has left his cheque book at home. In a slightly inebriated state he writes, in pencil, on the back of the menu card, 'To the Barchester Bank, Silverbridge. Pay to the Green Dragon, the sum of £40 or order'.
   You may assume that in each the bills are correctly signed and dated.

5 What is meant by the discharge of a bill and what are its legal consequences?
State with reasons whether the bill is discharged in the following cases:
   (a) The holder of a bill endorses it to the sole acceptor after maturity

   (b) The holder of a bill writes to the acceptor after its maturity that he renounces all claims against him, but does not return the bill to him

   (c) The holder of the bill before maturity strikes out the acceptor's signature, intending to cancel it, but keeps the bill and afterwards negotiates it before it matures

Chapter 15

1. What is the extent of the protection afforded by the law to:
   (a) a paying banker who pays a cheque to a person who is not its rightful owner; and
   (b) a collecting banker who collects a cheque for a person who is not its rightful owner?
   (December 1984)

2. (a) Discuss the nature of the duties owed by a banker to his customer in relation to cheques
   (b) Nationwide Bank Ltd, which had been mandated by Faith Company Limited to pay cheques drawn by two directors, paid a cheque drawn by one director only. Advise Faith Company Limited whether Nationwide Bank Ltd can debit their account

3. R draws a cheque in favour of S for £50. The cheque was stolen by T who forged S's signature as an indorsement and obtained £50 in cash from a garage. The garage paid the cheque into their account with the Blue Bank. The Blue Bank then obtained the value of the cheque from the White Bank where R had his account.
   Discuss the legal position. (December 1987)

4. (a) State four duties which a banker owes to his customers
   (b) Eric has an account at the local branch of the Barchester Bank. He draws a cheque in favour of Flash Ltd, a hardware store, for an electric razor. On reaching home he finds that the razor does not work. In consequence, he sends a telegram to his bank stopping the cheque. The manager, Grimm, is on holiday, and Horace, the under manager, decides not to open the telegram until the manager returns. By the time the manager opens the telegram, the cheque has been paid.
   Advise Eric.

5. (a) What is the effect of the words 'not negotiable' on a cheque?
   (b) What is the effect of the words 'a/c payee'?
   (c) Charles draws an uncrossed cheque in favour of David. David has an account at the Barchester Bank Ltd in Barchester and he is going to have to pay the cheque in by post. What advice would you give him regarding crossing the cheque?
   Give reasons for your answer.

6. (a) Explain the effect of a 'not negotiable' crossing on:
   (i) a cheque;
   (ii) a bill of exchange other than a cheque. **(10 marks)**
   (b) Bundys Bank plc operates a computerised system of dealing with its customers' accounts. Because of a problem with the computer, several cheques drawn by the bank's customers have been dishonoured and returned to the payees with the words 'Refer to drawer' across the front. Some customers whose cheques have been so dealt with are traders.
   Advise Bundys Bank plc as to its legal liability. **(10 marks)**

7. (a) What is meant by an indorsement on a bill of exchange, and in what circumstances is indorsement necessary? What is the legal position of an indorser?
   (b) H's wife, W, over a period of some months obtained money from H's bank by using H's cheque book and forging his signature on cheques which she drew in favour of herself. When H discovered the fraud he informed the bank and claimed to be entitled to reimbursement by the bank for the amounts wrongly debited against him. Advise the bank.
   Would it make any difference to your answer if it could be shown that H had discovered W's fraud some weeks before he reported it to the bank?

8. A steals two cheques from his employer, B. One, which is payable to bearer, he cashes immediately at the Midchester Bank on which it is drawn. The other cheque is made payable to

C but A forges C's indorsement on the cheque and negotiates it to D as payment for a record player. D has been paid by the bank in respect of this cheque. B is intending to sue the Midchester Bank in respect of the payment of the two cheques. What defences, if any, might the bank be able to raise?

Chapter 16

1 What is a corporation? In what ways may a corporation be created?

2 (a) What do you understand by the expression 'legal personality' and why is legal personality of importance?

   (b) Explain what you understand by the expression 'ultra vires' and give three examples to illustrate its significance.

Chapter 17

1 Explain how agency may be created and discuss the duties owed by an agent to his principal.
   (December 1984)

2 (a) Outline five duties owed by an agent to his principal.

   (b) What, in agency, is meant by the doctrine of ostensible authority?

3 (a) How may an agency arise by implication?

   (b) A was P's agent and on P's behalf made several contracts with T over a period of some years. P later terminated A's agency but failed to notify T. A continued to deal with T, in his own name and on his own behalf, but became insolvent. T as a result suffered losses and now wishes to claim damages by way of compensation from P. Advise P.

4 (a) In what ways can a contract of agency be brought into existence?

   (b) Ivan is the manager of a shop selling shoes. The shop is owned by Jerry Shoes Ltd. The board of directors has expressly told Ivan that under no circumstances is he to buy any polish from anywhere other than Kashmarts Ltd to sell in the shop. One day, Len, a representative from Multishine Ltd, calls on Ivan and persuades him to buy six gross tins of polish for resale. Jerry Shoes Ltd are refusing to pay for the polish. Advise Multishine Ltd.

5 (a) What conditions must be satisfied before a principal may adopt a contract entered into by his agent acting without authority?

   (b) Pierre, a restaurant owner, sometimes commissions Jules to buy wine for the business. On one occasion, Jules buys a quantity of wine from Henri which he believes Pierre will like. Henri refuses to deliver the wine because he can get a better price elsewhere. Later, when Pierre learns of Jules' purchase, he agrees to take the wine.
   Advise Pierre.

6 (a) How may an agent's authority come to an end?

   (b) Colin is an agent who sells paint on behalf of David and wallpaper on behalf of Eric. He agrees to sell a quantity of both paint and wallpaper to Frank. At the time of the sale, unknown to both Chris and Frank, David has withdrawn Colin's agency and Eric has died. In consequence of this, Colin is unable to deliver the goods.
   Advise Frank as to his rights under these contracts.

7 (a) When does an agent incur personal liability in respect of a contract which he has entered into on behalf of his principal?

(b) Harry has sold goods to Peter on behalf of John. Peter paid Harry for the goods, but Harry has now disappeared with the money. When may John claim the price of the goods from Peter?

Chapter 18

1 F and G are partners in a firm which specialises in the production of wrought iron gates. F, contrary to the partnership agreement, ordered new welding equipment from E, but F and G later refused to pay for the equipment.
   Advise E.   (December 1983)

2 In what circumstances will dissolution of a partnership be ordered by the court?

3 In the absence of contrary agreement, what are the rights of a partner as between himself and his fellow partners in regard to the application of partnership property on dissolution? How are these rights enforceable?

4 Explain and contrast a liability for debts of a firm of
   (a) a limited;
   (b) a dormant; and
   (c) a retired partner

5 What is the meaning of the expression 'partnership property', and what is its importance in partnership law?

6 (a) What is meant by joint and several liability in partnership law?
   (b) A and B are in partnership as butchers. While driving the firm's van delivering meat, A negligently ran down and injured T. T has brought proceedings against A, who is found to be heavily insolvent.
      Advise B as to his personal liability and that of the firm.

7 Compare and contrast the main features of a limited liability company with those of a partnership.

Chapter 19

1 When may a person be held to be vicariously liable for the tort of another?

2 Explain the decision in the case of *Donoghue* v *Stevenson*

3 'In the varied web of affairs, the law must abstract some consequences as relevant, not perhaps on grounds of pure logic but simply for practical reasons.'
   Explain what consequences the law regards as relevant.

4 James, an accountant, fails to notice serious stock deficiencies while auditing the accounts of Bright Sparks Ltd. Some months later, Grogg Ltd takes over Bright Sparks Ltd, basing the price it pays for the shares on the underlying asset value as shown by the accounts audited by James. Bright Sparks Ltd has now discovered that the shares are not worth what they paid for them.
   Advise James.

5 (a) What facts have to be proved to establish negligence?

(b) Kojak is a private investigator. He is asked by Len, a local garage proprietor, to investigate and report on the creditworthiness of Max, who desires to open a credit account. Kojak makes a very cursory investigation and reports, 'I believe Max to be absolutely safe so far as allowing credit is concerned'. After two months of operating the account, Max absconds and cannot be found. The account is £180 in debit.

Advise Len.

6 In the tort of negligence who is my neighbour and why does it matter?

The Chartered Association of Certified Accountants

December 1989

**Level 1 — Preliminary Examination
Paper 1.4(E)**

LAW

Time allowed — 3 hours
Number of questions on paper — 8
FIVE questions ONLY to be answered

1 Describe and explain the relative importance of the sources of English Law.

(20 marks)

2 E is a successful manufacturer of specialist spectacle lenses. He has a number of important clients who value the specialised and efficient service provided by E and his staff. Following rapid expansion of his business E is considering the employment of a production manager for his factory, but he is concerned that any such employee would have complete access to his secret manufacturing process and also access to the names and addresses of all his clients. E is worried that if such an employee left E's employment he would be able to make use of the information gained during the course of his employment with E. Accordingly, E wishes to include a clause in the contract of employment of the new production manager restricting the scope of any future employment he might hold so as to protect his own commercial interests.

Advise E as to the extent by which he might achieve such an object by the insertion of such a clause into the contract. (20 marks)

3 **Describe the structure and jurisdiction of the courts of civil jurisdiction and the system of appeals in civil cases.** (20 marks)

4 In mid-1989 the World Billiards Championships were due to be held in London. Late in 1988, C, a billiards enthusiast, in anticipation of the championships, agreed by written contract with D to lease a flat from her for the six weeks duration of the championships. The flat was situated very close to the venue for the championships and was convenient for the billiards halls which would be used for the competition. Because of its close proximity to the venue and because of the very high demand for accommodation at the time of the championships the rent for the flat was fixed at £500 per week. C paid £500 rent to D in advance. D subsequently spent £300 in installing a new shower in the flat. Because of political differences between some of the major billiards-playing nations a boycott of the championships was organised in the days leading up to the beginning of the competition and at a late stage the championships were cancelled.

C no longer wishes to stay in the flat and he wishes to recover the £500 he has already paid to D. D refuses to refund the £500 and insists that C pays a further £2,500, being the balance of the rent for the six week period.

Advise C (20 marks)

5 (a) **Explain what is meant by 'an intention to enter into legal relations' as a requirement of a valid contract.** (10 marks)

(b) **Explain the proposition that in the law of contract 'consideration must be sufficient but it need not be adequate'.** (10 marks)
(20 marks)

6 (a) **In relation to the Consumer Credit Act 1974 explain what is meant by the following:**

(i) a regulated consumer credit agreement;
(ii) a regulated consumer hire agreement;
(iii) an exempt agreement. (10 marks)

(b) Three days ago at Q's request Q was visited by R, a roof insulation salesman, in his home. Following a discussion between Q and R, Q entered into a written credit sale agreement for the purchase of £2,000 worth of roof insulation. The insulation was delivered to Q's house the following day. Q now regrets entering into the agreement and wishes to rescind the contract.

Advise Q. (10 marks)
(20 marks)

7 Describe fully, with examples, the duties owed

(a) **by an agent to a principal;**
(b) **by a principal to an agent.** (20 marks)

8 (a) **In what circumstances, if any, may the purchaser of goods acquire a valid title from the vendor where the vendor is not the owner of the goods?** (10 marks)

(b) S owns a personal computer which he uses for word processing. Following a malfunction S took the machine to T Ltd, a firm in business selling and repairing personal computers. T Ltd told S that the repair would be a straightforward matter, but it took them over five months to repair the machine and return it to S. When the machine was returned its plastic cover was badly scratched and damaged in several places. An invoice was sent with the machine saying 'Parts — £3·00; two hours labour — £80·00'. S is extremely annoyed at what he considers to be the gross delay in repairing the machine, the damage to its cover and at what he thinks is an exorbitant charge for the repair.

Advise S as to his rights, if any, under the Supply of Goods and Services Act 1982 (10 marks)
(20 marks)

End of Question Paper

Reproduced by kind permission of the Chartered Association of Certified Accountants.

Authors' model answers to this examination paper are on page 365.

Authors' model answers to December 1989 ACCA Law paper

1   This question is in two parts. The various sources of English law must be described and the relative importance of each explained. There are three major sources (precedent, statute and EEC) and four subsidiary sources (custom, law merchant, canon law and text books).

English law is a common law system. The common law is based on judicial precedent, otherwise known as case law. Precedent is the law made by judges in the course of trying a case; it is the application of the law in one case to the facts of another, similar case coming before the lower courts at a later date. In other words, the doctrine of precedent is recognition that decided cases are evidence of the existence of a legal rule.

There are two types of precedent: binding and persuasive. A binding precedent is one which as a general rule, a lower court must follow. A persuasive precedent, although authoritative, need not be followed in later cases.

For the doctrine of precedent to be effective, there must be an accurate system of law reporting and an established hierarchy of courts. Until 1865 the reporting of cases was left to individuals and so was unreliable. In 1865, however, the General Council of Law Reporting was established to regularise the system, and since this date the official law reports have provided an accurate, reliable source of case law. The General Council was replaced by the Incorporated Council of Law Reporting for England and Wales and there are now five official Law Reports published. There are also a number of private reports which are used by lawyers.

The importance of a decision depends on the status of the court in which the case was decided. The highest court in the country is the House of Lords. Decisions of the Lords bind all lower courts but, since 1966, the House may depart from its own previous decisions where it appears right to do so in the interests of justice or where to follow the precedent would unduly restrict the proper development of the law.

Below the House of Lords is the Court of Appeal, which is bound by the Lords but itself binds all lower courts. The Court of Appeal is also bound by its own previous decisions unless there are two conflicting precedents for the same point. In this case, the Court of Appeal may choose one and reject the other, thus impliedly overruling it. It also does not have to follow a previous decison where this is inconsistent with a later House of Lords case or where the previous decision was given *per incuriam*. Where the Court of Appeal (Criminal Division) is sitting as a full court it may refuse to follow a precedent of the court where it decides that the previous decision was based on law misunderstood or misapplied.

The next court in the hierarchy is the High Court. This court is bound by the House of Lords and the Court of Appeal and itself binds all lower courts. Although not bound by its own decisions, in practice the High Court generally follows them.

The decisions of courts lower in the hierarchy, such as the County Courts and magistrates courts, have no binding effect at all.

The binding element of a decision is the *ratio decidendi*. This is the application, directly or by analogy, of rules of law to the material facts of a case. In the course of giving a judgment, however, a judge may make a statement of law to illustrate a point or as a commentary, or may develop a principle of law wider than the actual decision requires. These precedents, known as *obiter dicta*, have only persuasive force. Other examples of persuasive precedents are dissenting judgments, decisions of inferior courts, decisions of Scottish, Irish and Commonwealth courts, and precedents set by the Judicial Committee of the Privy Council. Persuasive precedents do not have to be followed by the lower courts although they may be adopted as the ratio in later cases. An example of this is the doctrine of equitable promissory estoppel which was formulated in an obiter by Denning J in *Central London Property Trust Ltd* v *High Trees House Ltd* (1947) but adopted as the ratio in the later case of *Tool Metal Manufacturing Co Ltd* v *Tungsten Electric Co Ltd* (1955).

The second major source of law is statute or legislation. There are two main types of legislation – Acts of Parliament and delegated legislation. Acts are the most important source of law nowadays.

As acts are passed by Parliament, which is the supreme law making body in the country, legislation can be made for any purpose whatsoever. It can be used to amend and update existing law; to create new law; to codify or consolidate or revise existing laws; and to raise revenue. All statutes, however, presuppose the existence of common law rules and are passed to alter or add to the common law. In other words, common law remains the basis of the English legal system but, because statutes are passed by Parliament, if there is any conflict between them and the common law, the statutes will prevail. Statutes are the pre-eminent source of modern law.

Statutes have several advantages over the common law. For example, a statute is equally effective in abolishing as in creating law, whereas the common law can change the law only if a case is brought to court and either the judge is not bound by the precedent (because it was set by a lower court) or can distinguish the case on the facts. Also, unlike common law, statute can anticipate situations which may arise rather than having to make law in arrears. Statutes are also easily accessible and provide for an efficient division of functions between the legislators and the judiciary. Parliament makes the law, the judges interpret it. The interpretation given will set a precedent for later, lower courts to follow when they are called upon to deal with the Act.

As Parliament is the supreme law making body, it can delegate the power to make laws to other persons or bodies. Delegated legislation takes several forms. It may be made by Order in Council, or by Statutory Instrument or by bye-laws. Delegated legislation is now the most prolific source of law in the country.

There are a number of reasons why this is so. It is better suited than an Act of Parliament to deal with technical and detailed matters and with local business. It also saves Parliamentary time and can be passed quickly thus making it suitable to deal with emergencies.

The power to make delegated law is limited by the terms of the statute which created the power. If legislation is made outside the scope of these powers it will be *ultra vires* and can be challenged in the courts. If the *ultra vires* allegation can be proved the legislation will be held void. Delegated legislation, therefore, is controlled by both the statute which created the power and by the Common Law courts.

The final major source of Law is European Economic Community. There are various types of EEC legislation which have an effect on member states' legal systems. The European Council has the power to make regulations which, if stated to be of general application, will be directly applicable to all member-states and their citizens. They will apply without member-states having to take any further action to implement them. The council may also issue directives. These do not have immediate effect. They have to be implemented by national legislation within the member-states. In other words, directives instruct each member-state to change its law to bring it into line with the directives' requirements. In England, directives are implemented by means of Acts of Parliament. For example, the Companies Act 1989 implements the 7th and 8th Directives. If there is any conflict between EEC and UK law, EEC law prevails.

Of the subsidiary sources of law, the most important is custom. This is the oldest source of law in England, having its origin in the usage or practice of people in doing a certain thing in a certain way. In the early stages of the development of the common law custom was the major source of law in England but it has now largely been absorbed into the common law itself. The only customs which are now of legal effect are local customs which will be recognised and enforced by the courts provided they have existed since time immemorial, are limited to a particular locality, are reasonable, certain and clearly defined, and are consistent with the existing law. The law merchant is a form of customary law being based on the usages of merchants and traders. It has now been absorbed into statutes such as the Sale of Goods Act 1893 (now 1979) and the Bills of Exchange Act 1882. Canon law was the law administered by the Ecclesiastical Courts which, as well as dealing with matters involving the Church, also had jurisdiction over such matters as marriage, legitimacy of children, and wills of property other than land. These matters are now within the jurisdiction of the High Court and are almost entirely regulated by statutes.

The final source of law is text books. Text books used not to be treated as authority in court however respected the views of the authors were. Nowadays, however, text books may be cited in court and, although they are not authority in themselves, they may be used to guide the court in its thinking.

2 This question relates to the doctrine of restraint of trade and requires advice to be given to E as to how, in the event of their leaving his employment, he can prevent his employees from using information they

gain whilst working for him for the benefit of either themselves or E's competitors.

All restraints of trade are *prima facie* void but can be enforced if the party relying on them can show that he has an interest worthy of protection and that they are reasonable in the interests of the parties (that is, they do not give a wider protection than can be justified) and in the interests of the public (that is, they do not harm the public good). The burden of proving that there is an interest and that the restriction is reasonable lies with the employer; in the problem the duty will lie with E.

E could not try to stop a former employee from merely using his skill, even if this skill was obtained in E's service. The two interests which the law recognises as being worthy of protection are trade secrets and influence over clients. For example, in the case of *Forster & Sons Ltd v Suggett* (1918), an employee who had been instructed in his employers' secret manufacturing processes could be validly prevented from carrying on, or being interested in, the manufacture of glass bottles or in any other business relating to glass making for a period of five years after leaving the plaintiff's employment. The employer had an interest which was worthy of protection.

In *Home Counties Dairies v Skilton* (1970), the defendant, a milkman, had a covenant in his contract of employment which provided that, for six months after leaving the dairies, he would not serve or sell milk or dairy produce to anyone who had been a customer of the plaintiffs.

The court held that the plaintiff had an interest worthy of protection. The defendant had influence over his previous customers and could be prevented from using this influence for the benefit of one of the plaintiff's competitors.

The fact that E's employees would have complete access to his secret manufacturing process and to the names and addresses of all his clients means that E has an interest worthy of protection. He can therefore restrict the scope of any future employment which his new production manager might undertake.

Any restriction, however, must be no wider than is reasonably necessary to protect E's interests. In deciding the validity of a restraint, the court will consider both the area covered and the length of time for which the restraint is to apply. For example, in *Empire Meat Co Ltd v Patrick* (1939), the contract of employment of a retail butcher provided that, after leaving his employment, he would not be employed in, or carry on the business of, retail butchering within five miles of the employer's place of business. The court held that, as the employer's business was drawn from a much smaller area, the five mile restriction was unreasonably wide. It was therefore unenforceable against the employee.

In *Fitch v Dewes* (1921), on the other hand, a solicitor's managing clerk was restricted from practising as a solicitor within seven miles of his former employer's office. The court held that this restriction was valid. The clerk had influence over his employer's clients. The area covered was a rural one with low-density population and therefore the seven mile restriction was reasonable. Furthermore, the fact that the restraint was to last for the rest of the managing clerk's life was also reasonable, as solicitors' clients tend to be 'for life'.

As well as showing that he has an interest worthy of protection and that the restriction he has imposed is no wider than is necessary to afford him reasonable protection, E will also have to be able to prove that the restraint is reasonable in the interests of the public. In employment cases, the public interest issue rarely defeats a restraint of trade clause. One case where it was held that a restriction should fail because it operated against the public interest was that of *Hensman v Trail* (1980). Here, a doctor who was a partner in a general practice had a clause in his contract preventing him from working as a doctor within seven miles of the practice for five years after leaving the firm. The court held that this restriction was too wide and that it operated against the public interest. It would have meant that this particular community would have been deprived of the services of this doctor.

E, therefore, should be advised that he can prevent his new production manager from harming E's commercial interests by putting a restrictive covenant in the manager's contract of employment. E certainly has interests worthy of protection. In drafting the restraint, however, he must ensure that it is reasonable in the interest of the parties and of the public. If he fails to do so, the restriction will be held to be void and will be unenforceable. In other words, unless E is reasonable in the limits he imposes on the manager he will be unable to prevent subsequent competition if and when the manager leaves E's employment. In these circumstances, E's only hope would be to rely on the manager's common law duty not to disclose confidential information gleaned in the course of his work under a contract of employment (*Faccenda Chicken Ltd v Fowler* (1986)).

3   The lowest civil courts of first instance are the magistrates' courts. These have a limited civil jurisdiction dealing mainly with matrimonial matters such as matrimonial disputes, other than

divorce petitions, cases concerning guardianship, adoption and affiliation. The magistrates also have the power to hear actions relating to claims for unpaid rates and to grant applications for licences. Appeal from the magistrates' courts on matrimonial proceedings lies to the Family Division of the High Court and on licensing to the Crown Court.

Magistrates' Courts are presided over by either stipendiary or lay magistrates. Stipendiary magistrates are appointed from barristers or solicitors of at least seven years' standing. They will usually sit alone in hearing a case and are paid a salary. Lay magistrates, known as justices of the peace (JPs) have no legal qualifications. They usually sit in panels comprising three to seven justices and are advised on points of law and procedure by the Clerk of the Court. The Clerk will be a barrister or solicitor of at least five years' standing. JPs are unpaid.

The next civil court in the hierarchy is the County Court. There are over 400 county courts in England and Wales and they were established to deal with small civil claims within their area. The jurisdiction of the court, in fact, is restricted to the locality within which it is situated. Actions in a particular county court may be brought only if the defendant lives or carries on business within that court's district or if it was in that district that the cause of action arose. County courts are presided over by judges who are either circuit judges or Recorders. Exceptionally, a judge of the High Court or the Court of Appeal may hear county court cases, but as a general rule a circuit judge sitting alone will hear the actions. If, however, the case involves an allegation of fraud, or if it is a defamation action remitted from the High Court, the judge may sit with a jury of eight people. The judge will be assisted by a Registrar who is appointed from amongst solicitors of at least seven years' standing. The Registrar acts as clerk of the court but will also deal with smaller cases under the small claims procedure.

The county court's jurisdiction includes:

actions in contract and tort where the amount claimed is less than £5,000. Contractual claims involving higher amounts may also be heard if the parties agree to waive the £5,000 limit and the limit does not apply to actions in defamation;

equitable matters such as trusts, dissolution of partnerships and actions relating to mortgages where the sum involved does not exceed £30,000;

unlimited jurisdiction to deal with insolvencies is granted to some county courts outside London. These courts also have jurisdiction to wind-up companies with a paid-up share capital not exceeding £120,000;

actions relating to the title to, and recovery of possession of, land, the net annual rateable value of which does not exceed £1,000;

undefended divorces;

matters required by statute to be dealt with by the county court eg the Consumer Credit Act 1974.

The county court may also conduct arbitration under the small claims procedure. The procedure is set out in guidelines laid down by the Lord Chancellor. Small claims cases are usually heard by the Registrar and will apply to actions involving sums of £500 or less. The procedure is kept simple. It starts with an attempt to reach agreement between the parties and it is only if this fails that the action will proceed to a hearing. The only costs allowed in these cases are those relating to the cost of the summons, the costs of enforcing any award made, and any legal expenses which have been incurred because the party ordered to pay the costs has behaved unreasonably. In practice, any action in the county court which involves claims for less than £500 will automatically be referred to small claims arbitration unless the action involves complicated issues of law or fact, or if fraud is alleged in the case, or if both parties agree to the case going to trial or if, in the light of the subject matter of the claim or of the interests of the parties or the circumstances of the case, arbitration would be unreasonable. In these cases, any referral to the small claims procedure will be rescinded by the Registrar following application by one of the parties.

Appeals from county court decisions are made to the Court of Appeal (Civil Division). The appeal may be on questions of law and/or fact.

The next court in the civil court hierarchy is the High Court. This court has jurisdiciton to try any cases other than those allocated by statute to another court. The High Court is divided into three divisions, each of which deals with different types of case. The divisions are:

Queen's Bench Division (QBD)
This division deals with common law cases not dealt with in the other divisions. It has jurisdiction over Admiralty and Commercial matters and, in particular, it deals with claims in contract and tort for sums exceeding £5,000. The QBD also has the power of judicial review. This enables the Division to protect individuals against injustice by preventing abuse of power by inferior courts and tribunals or by national or local government departments or by individuals. The QBD is headed by the Lord Chief Justice and has around forty puisne judges. The court hears appeals from Rent Tribunals.

Chancery Division (Ch D)
This division deals with trust, mortgages, bankruptcy, company and partnership matters. It also has jurisdiction over specific performance of contracts and disputes relating to wills, such as their validity or meaning. It also deals with questions relating to intestacy. Ch. D is headed by the Vice-Chancellor and has ten puisne judges. It has appeal from bankruptcy courts outside London and from the Special Commissioners of Income Tax.

Family Division (Fam)
This division deals with family matters such as contested divorces, annulment of marriages, judicial separations and wardship cases. The Division is headed by the President and has 16 puisne judges. It hears appeals from decisions on matrimonial matters made by the magistrates' courts.

Appeals from High Court decisions are to the Court of Appeal (Civil Division). Since the Administration of Justice Act 1969 it is also possible to appeal directly to the House of Lords by means of the 'leap-frog' procedure. Such an appeal will be allowed when a High Court judge certifies that a sufficient case for a direct appeal has been established. This will occur where the point of law involved relates wholly or mainly to the interpretation of a statute or statutory instrument and is based on a decision of the Court of Appeal or the House of Lords and involves a point of law of general public importance. The procedure may only be used if both the House of Lords and the parties to the case agree to it.

The final civil court of first instance is the Restrictive Practices court. This court is on a level with the High Court and deals with cases under the Restrictive Trade Practices Act 1976. It decides whether an agreement comes within the Act and, if it does, whether it can be justified on one of the grounds given in the Act. The court is staffed by High Court judges and a number of laymen selected because of their experience in industry, commerce or public affairs. The quorum in the court is one judge and two other members. The judge decides questions of law, and questions of fact are decided by a majority of the court. Appeals on points of law go to the Court of Appeal (Civil Division).

As well as the appeal function of the Divisional Courts of the High Court, the other civil courts of appeal are the Employment Appeals Tribunal, the Court of Appeal (Civil Division) and the House of Lords. The Employment Appeals Tribunal (EAT) hears appeals almost exclusively on points of law from Industrial Tribunals on applications under various pieces of employment legislation. It will hear cases relating, for example, to redundancy payments, equal pay, labour relations and sex discrimination. The EAT is staffed by judges (nominated by the Lord Chancellor) and by lay members selected from both sides of industry. A quorum is a judge and two lay members. The EAT is on a level with the High Court.

The Court of Appeal (Civil Division) hears appeals from the High Court, other superior courts and county courts. The court considers the whole case that was argued before the lower court, using the notes made by the shorthand writer and the judge. In its decision, the Court of Appeal may uphold, reverse or amend the lower court's decision, or order a retrial. The Court of Appeal (Civil Division) comprises the Master of the Rolls and 16 Lord Justices of Appeal and, in practice, three judges will hear a case.

The House of Lords comprises the Lord Chancellor, nine Lords of Appeal in Ordinary and any other members of the House who have held high judicial office. The House of Lords is the highest civil court of appeal in the United Kingdom. It hears appeals from the Court of Appeal but only if the appellant can obtain leave to appeal from either the Court of Appeal or from the House of Lords itself.

Leave to appeal will be granted only if the relevant point of law is one of general public importance. The Lords will also hear appeals from the High Court under the 'leap-frog' procedure.

Finally, mention should be made of the Court of Justice of the European Communities. Although this court is not part of the hierarchy of English courts, it has an important role in the interpretation of the Treaty of Rome 1957. By Article 177 of the Treaty, if a point of EEC law arises in a case heard by the highest court in a member state (in England, the House of Lords), that court must refer the issue to the European Court for a ruling on the interpretation of the relevant point of law. Courts other than the highest court may, but do not have to, refer questions of interpretation to the European Court. If such questions are referred, the interpretation given must be applied by the national court and will thus bind all lower courts under the doctrine of precedent. Judges of the European Court are drawn from member states, who are assisted in their work by Advocates-General who provide the court with information and guidance.

4 C's rights and remedies depend on whether or not his contract with D has been frustrated. A contract will be frustrated when further performance of it is prevented by some outside cause for which neither of the contracting parties is to blame. In other words, the rules relating to frustration apply to cases where a contract fails because of subsequent impossibility.

There are several grounds on which a court will hold that a contract has been frustrated. One of these is where the contract was made for some commercial purpose which has failed to materialise. This failure must mean that the whole purpose of the contract has gone, not merely that it has become commercially different (*Tsakiroglou & Co Ltd v Noblee Thorl GmbH* (1962)). For example, in the case of *Krell v Henry* (1903) the plaintiff had agreed to hire a room to the defendant for a day to watch the coronation procession of King Edward VII. The procession, however, was cancelled because the King was ill and the defendant refused to pay the balance of the rent for the room, claiming that the commercial purpose of the contract had gone. The owner of the room brought this action for the money but failed, the court holding that the contract was frustrated. The coronation procession was the basis of the contract and both parties were aware of this, so when the procession was cancelled the contract was discharged by frustration and the parties were released from their obligations to each other.

In the case of *Herne Bay Steam Boat Co v Hutton* (1903), however, a boat was hired for the day to take paying passengers around the fleet, which was assembled to celebrate Edward VII's coronation, and to 'view the naval review'. Because of the King's illness the review was cancelled but, as the fleet had assembled, the court held that the contract for the hire of the boat had not been frustrated. Although one of the purposes of the hire (to view the review) had gone, the other purpose (to sail around the fleet) could still be achieved and therefore the contract was still valid.

The question to be posed in C's case, therefore, is whether the cancellation of the World Billiards Championships is sufficient to frustrate his contract for the lease of D's flat. D was aware of the purpose of the lease and, from the facts of the problem, would seem to have charged C a high rent because the property was close to the venue of the Championship and because of the high demand for property during this period. It would therefore appear that the holding of the Championship was fundamental to the existence of the contract. As the Championships were cancelled, the contract for the lease of the flat will be frustrated (*Krell v Henry*).

D might argue that, although there were no Championships being held, C could still have the use of the property for the six-week period. This argument, however, would probably fail. Although the contract for the lease was still capable of being performed, it had been granted for a short period and for a specific purpose. As this purpose could no longer be achieved the contract is frustrated.

The rights and liabilities of the parties in these circumstances are governed by the Law Reform (Frustrated Contracts) Act 1943. This act provides that, as a general rule, any money paid before the frustrating event may be recovered and any money which was payable ceases to be payable. The court has the power to allow any party who has incurred expenses in performing the contract before frustration to recover payment for this from the other party. Furthermore, if either party has received a valuable benefit under the contract, he must pay for it. The court decides how much should be awarded.

As C's contract with D has been frustrated both parties are discharged from any further obligations. C, therefore, does not have to pay the balance of the rent. Under the 1943 Act, C can recover the £500 advance payment which he made to D. D, however, may be able to retain part of this sum to cover her costs in installing the new shower. In other words, she may attempt to set off this sum against C's claim. If such a set-off is made the court may decide that it would take into account the fact that this work has increased the value of the flat for D and that it is an amenity which D will enjoy in the future. C could also argue that it was not a requirement of the lease that a shower should be installed. The money, if any, which D will be allowed to retain will be based on a finding of fact by the court. It may allow her to retain the full £300 or some of this sum or none of it. The court has a complete discretion in the matter.

5 **(a)** Even if there is offer, acceptance and consideration and there has been no misrepresentation, mistake or duress, an agreement will not be a valid contract unless there is an intention by the parties to enter into legal relations. In other words, for an agreement to be a valid binding contract, the parties must intend it to be enforceable by legal action. It is this intention to create a legal relationship that distinguishes contracts from, for example, mere social arrangements.

The law in this area is based on a number of presumptions. The basic presumption is that, in the case of commercial agreements, there is an intention that the agreements should be legally binding. As with all presumptions, this may be rebutted if a contrary intention can be shown. For example, in the case *Rose and Frank and Co v Crompton Bros Ltd* (1925) an agreement stated that it was 'not entered into . . . as a formal or legal agreement, and shall not be subject to legal jurisdiction in the law courts.' The House of Lords held that this agreement was not a legally enforceable contact.

Whether a party to an agreement has discharged the presumption that it is legally binding is essentially a question of fact in each case.

In relation to domestic and social arrangements, on the other hand, the general presumption is that, if the parties are closely related, there is no intention to create a legal relationship. Thus, for example, in the case of *Balfour v Balfour* (1919) it was held that a promise by a husband to pay his wife a monthly sum of money as maintenance was unenforceable. As the parties were married, there was a presumption that they did not intend to create a legal relationship. This presumption was capable of being rebutted but had not been in this case.

If, however, a husband and wife make a contract after they have separated, this may be sufficient to rebut the presumption. This was held in the case of *Merritt v Merritt* (1970). Because of the separation, the husband and wife were dealing at arms' length and therefore the agreement made between them was a legally enforceable contract.

The presumption that there is no intention to create a legal relationship will also apply in the case of agreements between a parent and child. This was held in *Jones v Padvatton* (1969). Again, this presumption may be rebutted by the parties.

The more remote the relationship between the parties, however, the less likely the courts are to presume that there was no intention to create a legal relationship. In the case of *Simpkins v Pays* (1955) for example, it was held that an arrangement between the defendant, her granddaughter and her lodger whereby they entered a weekly newspaper competition was intended to give rise to a legal relationship. When one of the entries was successful it was held that the plaintiff, the lodger, was entitled to a share in the prize money.

The other presumption relating to intention to create a legal relationship arises in the case of collective bargaining agreements. These are agreements made between a trade union and an employer relating to conditions of services including wages. By section 18 of the Trade Union and Labour Relations Act 1974, there is a presumption that a collective agreement between an employer and a trade union is not legally binding unless there is an express statement to the contrary in the agreement. If there is such a statement, the agreement is legally enforceable to the extent stated.

(b) As long as a contract is supported by consideration, the courts will not enquire into the fairness of otherwise of the bargain made. Provided the consideration has some economic value, the courts will not question its adequacy. In the case of *Chappell & Co Ltd v Nestle Co Ltd* (1960), for example, the House of Lords held that chocolate bar wrappings, although destroyed upon receipt, were capable of forming part of the consideration as the recipient had required them to be tendered as payment for gramophone records and therefore regarded them as part of the bargain.

Although consideration need not be adequate, however it must nevertheless have some value in the eyes of the law. In other words, it must be sufficient. The courts will decide whether or not the consideration is sufficient. For example, in the case of *White v Bluett* (1853), it was held that a son's promise to his father to stop complaining about the fact that he had been disinherited was not good consideration for the father's promise to release him from a promisory note. The promise was not capable of expression in terms of value and, in any case, the son had no right to complain and so was not giving up anything in return for the father's agreement.

A promise to perform an existing legal or contractual duty will also not be regarded as sufficient consideration by the courts. Thus, in *Collins* v *Godefroy* (1831), the plaintiff was subpoenaed to give evidence for the defendant in an action to which the defendant was a party. The defendant promised the plaintiff a sum of money if he appeared but, despite the fact that the plaintiff did give evidence, the defendant refused to pay. The plaintiff sued but failed in his action. He had not given consideration for the promise. He had been subpoenaed to appear and was therefore obliged by law to do so. By appearing, he was doing nothing more than performing his legal duty.

If, however, a person promises to act in excess of an existing legal duty this will provide good consideration. In the case of *Glasbrook Bros Ltd* v *Glamorgan County Council* (1925), for example, the police were asked to provide a permanent guard on a colliery during a miners' strike. The police believed that this was greater protection than was necessary but agreed to provide the permanent protection in return for the colliery owner's promise to pay a sum of money to the police. When the colliery owners refused to pay, arguing that the police were merely doing their public duty in protecting property and had therefore not provided any consideration, the police authority sued. The court held that, by giving greater protection than they believed to be necessary, the police were acting in excess of their public duty and therefore had provided good consideration. There was therefore a valid contract and Glasbrook had to pay. The same approach was adopted in *Ward* v *Byham* (1956) where a woman's promise to keep her illegitimate child well and happy was held to be good consideration for the father's promise to pay her £1 a week. By statute, the mother of an illegitimate child had to care for it but, by agreeing to keep it well and happy, the mother had acted in excess of her legal duty.

The same principle applies in relation to exisitng contractual obligations. A promise to perform such an obligation will not be good consideration for an undertaking to provide additional consideration. In *Stilk* v *Myrick* (1809), following desertion by two sailors, the captain of a ship promised to pay the remaining crew extra money if they sailed the vessel shorthanded. They agreed to do so, but, when the voyage was over, the captain failed to honour his promise. When the crew sued, the court held that they were not entitled to the payment. Sailing a ship with this type of shortage was one of the normal incidents of the crew's contract. They were therefore doing nothing more than they had contracted to do and therefore had not provided any consideration for the captain's promise.

In *Hartley* v *Ponsonby* (1857), however, so many crew deserted the ship that it was dangerous to sail. The court held that, by sailing a ship in these circumstances the rest of the crew had acted in excess of their contractual duties and had therefore provided good consideration for the captain's promise to pay them a bonus.

Another case illustrating this point is *Williams* v *Roffey Bros & Nicholls (Contractors) Ltd* (1989) in which the defendant building contractors sub-contracted some carpentry work to the plaintiff for £20,000. The plaintiff discovered that he could not complete the job at the price agreed and the defendants offered him a further £10,300 for him to complete the work on time. Had the completion been delayed, the defendants would have had to make penalty payments to their own employers. The plaintiff completed the work on time but the defendants refused to pay the £10,300 arguing that he had done nothing more than he had contracted to do and therefore not provided any consideration for the promise. The defendants cited *Stilk* v *Myrick* as authority. The court of Appeal, however, held that the plaintiff's claim should succeed.

This decision would seem to move away from the ratio in *Stilk* v *Myrick*, although the Court of Appeal said it merely 'refined and limited' the *Stilk* principle. The position will be uncertain until the House of Lords decides the issue.

An important aspect of the rule that performance of an existing contractual duty cannot provide good consideration relates to part payment of a debt. This is the rule in *Pinnel's* case. This rule, too, will be affected by the decision in *Williams* v *Roffey Bros*.

Finally, consideration will be sufficient where the plaintiff agrees to perform a contractual duty which he owes to a third party. This was held in the case of *New Zealand Shipping Co Ltd* v *Satterthwaite & Co Ltd* (1975).

6 (a) (i) A regulated consumer credit agreement is defined by section 8 of the Credit Act 1974 as being an agreement whereby a person (the creditor) provides credit not exceeding £15,000 to an individual or partnership (the debtor). The creditor may be an individual, a partnership, or an incorporated or unincorporated association. In other words, any entity known to the law may be a creditor. The debtor, however, must be an individual or a partnership. If the debtor is a body corporate the agreement will not be regulated by the 1974 Act.

The word 'credit' applies to any form of financial assistance on terms of repayment either in cash or in any other form. It includes, for example, cash loans from banks or other bodies, hire-purchase contracts, overdraft and credit card agreements. The £15,000 limit applies to the financial accommodation given to the debtor. In calculating this sum, the interest and credit charges paid on the loan etc will be disregarded as will any deposit paid by the debtor.

Credit may be either fixed sum or running account. Fixed sum credit occurs where the amount is fixed at the beginning of the agreement. Fixed sum bank loans and hire-purchase contracts will come within this category. Running account credit occurs where a debtor is entitled to draw money up to an agreed credit limit. Bank overdrafts and credit card agreements are examples of this type of credit transaction.

(ii) A regulated consumer hire agreement is defined by s 15 CCA as being an agreement between the owner of goods and an individual (the hirer) for the bailment of the owner's goods to the hirer. The agreement must not be for the hire-purchase of the goods (this will be a regulated consumer credit agreement); it must be capable of continuing for more than three months; and it must not require the hirer to make payments exceeding £15,000.

(iii) The 1974 Act exempts certain agreements in whole or in part from its requirements. The agreements which are totally exempt include:

mortgages for house or land purchase where the lender is a building society or a local authority or is one of the bodies listed in regulations made under s 16 CCA eg insurance companies or charities.

Debtor–creditor–supplier (D–C–S) agreements (other than H–P or conditional sale) for fixed sum credit where the credit is repayable in four or fewer instalments.

(D–C–S) agreements for running account credit where the debt is repayable in a single instalment e.g. American Express.

Debtor–Creditor agreements where the annual percentage charge for credit does not exceed 13% or 1% above the highest base rate of the London and Scottish Clearing Banks.

The only way in which the CCA applies to these contracts is if they are extortionate credit bargains and in relation to the controls imposed on the lender seeking business from the creditor.

Agreements which are partly exempt include small agreements and non-commercial agreements. Small agreements are those which are either unsecured or secured only by a guarantee or indemnity and which provide credit of £50 or less. H–P and conditional sale agreements are specifically excluded from this category. Small D–C–S agreements for restricted-use-credit are generally exempted from the CCA's provisions relating to formalities and cancellation but are still subject to the Act as regards default, termination and control by the courts.

Non-commercial agreements are those not made by the creditor in the course of a business carried on by him. These will not be affected by the formalities and cancellation provisions of the Act nor will the lender be jointly and severally liable with the supplier of the goods and services under s 75 CCA. The rest of the Act, however, will apply to these transactions.

(b) Q regrets having entered the agreement with R and wishes to end it. His best course of action would be to cancel the contract but to do so he must be able to show that his case falls within the cancellation provisons of the CCA.

To be cancellable an agreement must have been concluded following oral representations made in antecedent negotiations in the debtor's presence and the debtor must have signed the agreement at a place other than the place of business of the creditor, a negotiator or a party to a linked transaction. The oral representation must have been made by an individual acting as, or on behalf of, the negotiator.

In Q's case, presumably R had made some oral representations to Q before the agreement was concluded, and the agreement was signed at Q's home. The agreement, therefore is cancellable. Q's right to cancel has to be stated both on the copy of the agreement he is given after he has signed and on the second copy of the agreement he is sent within seven days of the execution of the contract. If the agreement was executed when Q signed it, he must be sent a notice of cancellation within seven days. The notice of the right of cancellation must indicate a person to whom notice of cancellation can be sent.

As the agreement is cancellable, Q is given the right to end the contract. He can do this by serving notice of cancellation on the person specified in the documents which informs him of his rights. Notice must be served during the cancellation period. This period lasts until the end of the fifth day following the day on which Q received his second notice of cancellation. If notice of cancellation is served by post, it takes effect from the moment of posting irrespective of whether, or when, it actually arrives.

Once notice of cancellation has been served, the finance agreement and any linked transaction are automatically ended. The parties are put in the position they would have been in had the contract never been made.

If he cancels, therefore, Q is released from any liability to make payments under the credit sale agreement. If he has already paid a deposit to R he can recover this money. He must, however, allow R to recover the insulation which has been delivered and, until re-delivery, Q must take reasonable care of it. His duty of care, however, comes to an end after 21 days. If R does not return all the money which Q has paid, Q has lien over the goods until R settles with him in full.

Q therefore should be advised that, as the agreement is cancellable, he should cancel it as soon as possible and in any event before the expiry of 5 days following his receipt of the second notice of cancellation. By doing this he will effectively rescind the contract and incur no liability whatsoever to R.

7 (a) Where an agency is created by agreement, the rights and duties of the parties may be set out in that agreement. Where there is no formal agreement, or where the parties have not covered an eventuality which has occured, the law implies certain rights and duties into the relationship. These rights and duties will apply unless the parties agree otherwise.

The main duty of the agent is to perform what he has agreed to perform. He must carry out the instructions of his principal unless these instructions are illegal or void by common law or statute. Failure to do this will make the agent liable in damages. This duty arises whether the agency is contractual or gratuitous: that is, whether or not the agent is being paid for his services.

Another duty which is imposed on all agents is the duty to act with due care and skill. The standard of skill to be used depends on how the agent has held himself out to the principal. If he has claimed to have a particular expertise, he must show the standard of skill and care which a reasonable person with such expertise would be expected to show.

An agent, it is presumed, is appointed because of his personal skill and experience. It follows, therefore, that an agent cannot delegate his duties. This is expressed in the Latin maxim *'delegatus non potest delegare'*: an agent must perform his duties in person. There are, however, a number of cases where delegation is permitted. It is allowed, for example, where it is expressly authorised by the principal or where unauthorised delegation is ratified as in the case of *Dodsley* v *Varley* (1840). Delegation will also be permitted where the work is purely administrative, such as typing and filing; or where it is authorised by trade custom; or when it arises by necessary implication as when, for example, a company or bank is appointed agent; or when there is a sudden emergency, such as the appointed agent being taken ill.

If an agent delegates without authority, the principal will not be bound by the sub-agent's acts. The agent will also be liable in damages for wrongful execution of his duty and neither the agent nor the sub-agent can claim remuneration or indemnity from the principal (*John McCann & Co v Pow*) (1975).

If, however, the delegation is allowed and the agent has a power to appoint a sub-agent either in substitution for or in addition to himself, then there will be privity of contract between the principal and the sub-agent. If, however, a sub-agent is appointed merely to assist the agent, there will be no privity of contract between the principal and sub-agent. The sub-agent will be liable only if he is negligent or acts in breach of his fiduciary duty.

Another duty of the agent is that he must not deny his principal's title to money or property. He must not, without authority, hand over the goods he is holding on behalf of the principal to a third party. If he does so hand them over he will be liable to the principal.

Agency is a fiduciary relationship and therefore the agent has a duty to act in good faith and not to allow there to be any conflict between his interests and those of his principal. The agent must make full disclosure of any personal interest he has in the subject matter of the agency.

One aspect of this duty is that the agent cannot make a secret profit out of the agency. A secret profit is a profit made by the agent without the third party knowing anything about it. If, however, the agent has not been fraudulent in making a secret profit, he must account for this to his principal but will nevertheless be entitled to claim his remuneration or commission. This was held in the case of *Hippisley v Knee Bros* (1905).

Another part of the agent's duty to act in good faith is that he must not take a bribe from the third party. If such a bribe is taken, the principal has a number of remedies:

the agent is liable to be prosecuted under the Prevention of Corruption Acts 1889–1916;

the agent is not entitled to pay or indemnity and must return any payment he has received from the principal;

the agent may be instantly dismissed, even though the principal suffered no loss because of the bribe;

the principal may repudiate any contract made because the agent was bribed;

the principal may recover the bribe from the agent;

the principal may sue both the agent and the third party if he has suffered any loss. If he recovers from one of these, however, he cannot sue the other and thus make a profit. This was held in *Mahesan v Malaysia Government Officers' Co-operative Housing Society Ltd* (1978).

(b) The principal owes two main duties to the agent: to pay the agent and to indemnify him against any loss or expenses incurred in carrying out his duties.

An agent's right to payment will arise only if there is an express or implied agreement that the work will be remunerated. The amount of payment depends on the terms of the agreement or on any trade usage. If neither of these apply, the agent will be entitled to a reasonable remuneration which can be fixed by the court. An agent who is paid on commission will be entitled to claim payment if the event on which payment is to be made has occurred and if the agent was the effective cause of this occurrence. Whether this event has occurred depends on the wording of the contract (*Luxor (Eastbourne) Ltd v Cooper* (1941) and *Alpha Trading v Dunnshaw-Patten Ltd* (1981)).

If the agent is an estate agent, section 18 Estate Agents Act 1979 provides that he has a duty to tell the principal what is the event on which commission will be charged and how that commission will be calculated.

If an agent has incurred liability or has paid out his own money in the performance of his duties, he will be entitled to recover this from the principal by way of indemnity. Indemnity, however, cannot be claimed where the agent is in breach of his duties or where he was responsible for his own loss.

Until the principal pays the agent what he owes, the agent has a lien over those goods of the principal which are lawfully in his possession.

8 (a) The general rule of law is that a person who does not own goods cannot give a valid title to those goods to another, however innocent that other may be. This is expressed in the maxim *nemo dat quod non habet* (no-one can give what he does not have). This rule, however, proved inconvenient in commercial transactions. In certain circumstances, therefore, the law recognised cases where, although the seller did not own the goods he could nevertheless give a valid title to an innocent third party purchaser.

The exceptions to the *nemo dat* rule are:

Sales under a court order (s 21(2)(b)SGA)
The *nemo dat* rule does not apply to sales by courts of a competent jurisdiction. For example, sales by bailiffs of the goods of a judgment debtor where these goods have been seized under a warrant of execution will operate to pass good title in the goods to the purchaser.

Sales by a mercantile agent (s 21(2)(a)SGA)
By section 26 SGA, a mercantile agent is defined as a person who, in the ordinary course of his business as such agent, has the authority to sell goods, or to consign goods for the purpose of sale, or to buy goods or to raise money on the security of goods.

By section 2 of the Factors Act (1889), if a mercantile agent is, with the consent of the owner, in possession of goods or documents of title to them, then any sale or other disposition made by him when acting in the ordinary course of business as a mercantile agent, will be as valid as if it had been expressly authorised by the owner, provided the person taking the goods does so in good faith and without notice that the mercantile agent lacks authority.

Section 21(2)(a) SGA preserves these provisions of the Factors Act and thus creates another exception to the *nemo dat* rule.

Estoppel (s 21(1)SGA)
Where the owner of goods acts in such a way as to make it appear to the buyer that the person selling the goods has the right to do so, and the buyer acts in reliance on this appearance, the true owner is stopped from denying the seller's right to sell (*Henderson & Co* v *Williams* (1895)). For the doctrine of estoppel to apply to a sale, the owner must have made a positive holding-out of the non-owner as having the right to sell (*Eastern Distributors* v *Goldring* (1957)).

Sale in a market overt (s 22(1)(SGA)
If goods are sold in a market overt in accordance with the normal usage of the market, the buyer acquires a good title even though the seller had none. A market overt is an open, public and legally constituted market established by Act of Parliament, Royal Charter or by long usage. A sale in a market overt will operate to pass good title in goods if the purchaser takes in good faith and without notice of the seller's lack of title (*Reid* v *Commissioner of Police of Metropolis* (1973).

The purchaser in a market overt must take in good faith and without notice of the seller each of title.

Sale under a voidable title (s 23 SGA)
A voidable title is a title which is valid and enforceable unless and until it is avoided. Such a title will arise following a misrepresentation or if a contract is made under duress.

If an innocent purchaser, acting in good faith and without notice, buys goods from a seller who has a voidable title to them before that title has been avoided, the purchaser obtains a valid title to the goods (*Lewis* v *Averay* (1972)).

Sale by a seller in possession (s 24 SGA)
If a person who sells goods remains in possession of them with the consent of the buyer and later sells the same goods to another purchaser who takes in good faith and without notice of the original sale, the second buyer will acquire good title provided he obtains physical possession of the goods.

As long as the seller remains in possesion of the goods until the second sale, it does not matter that this possession is not as seller but is in some other capacity such as hirer (*Worcester Works Finance Ltd* v *Cooden Enginerring Co Ltd* (1971)).

Sale by a buyer in possession (s 25 SGA)
Where a person who has bought or agreed to buy goods obtains possession of them with the consent of the seller, then any sale by this buyer to another person who takes without notice of the original contract operates to transfer title to the second purchaser, provided he obtains physical possession of the goods and the first buyer sells as if he were a mercantile agent (even though he is not).

Sale of a motor vehicle being hired under a hire purchase contract
This exception to the *nemo dat* rule is contained in Part III Hire Purchase Act 1964, as substituted by Sched 4 Consumer Credit Act 1974. Where a person who is hiring a motor vehicle on hire purchase sells the vehicle to a private person (that is, a person who is not engaged in the business of buying or selling motor vehicles or of providing finance for such purchases) then that person obtains good title to the goods provided he takes in good faith and without notice of the original H-P transaction.

(b) S's complaints relate to the faulty repair work carried out on his computer, the time taken to complete the work, and the charges being claimed by T Ltd. His actions will be based on T's breach of the Supply of Goods and Services Act 1982, sections 13-15.

Section 13 of the 1982 Act provides that where a person, acting in the course of business, supplies a service, there is an implied term that this service will be carried out with reasonable care and skill. The standard of care and skill to be shown is a question of fact and depends amongst other things on what could be expected in the relevant trade or profession.

As the computer was returned badly scratched and damaged in several places, and as T Ltd's business was selling and repairing personal computers, it would seem that T is in breach of section 13 of the 1982 Act and therefore S is entitled to claim damages from the firm.

Section 13 is a statutory declaration of the pre-1982 rules of common law. Its operation can therefore be illustrated by common law cases such as *Levison* v *Patent Steam Carpet Cleaning Co* (1977).

By section 14 of the 1982 Act, when a supplier is acting in the course of business and no time for performance is agreed in the contract, nor is it left to be agreed in a manner specified in the contract, nor can it be determined by a course of dealings between the parties, then there is an implied term that the supplier will carry out the service within a reasonable time. What constitutes a reasonable time is a question of fact (*Charnock* v *Liverpool Corporation* (1968)).

The five-month repair period in the problem would seem to be unreasonable and therefore S has an action against T Ltd in breach of section 14 of the 1982 Act.

Section 15 of the 1982 Act provides that, if no price is fixed in the contract, nor is left to be agreed in a manner specified in the contract, nor can it be determined by a course of dealings between the parties, there is an implied term that the person acquiring the service will pay a reasonable price. What constitutes a reasonable price is a question of fact. S therefore can insist that he pays T Ltd a reasonable sum for the repair rather than the amount claimed by the firm. What is reasonable would depend on what the average computer repairer would charge for this type of work.

Glossary

Agent A person having authority to act for another (the principal)

Appellant The party bringing an appeal before a higher court.

Assets The property available for the payment of debts.

Assignment The disposition or transfer of rights, property or interests to another person.

Attorney-general The government's chief legal adviser.

Bailment The delivery of goods into the possession of a person who is not the owner of such goods.

Bankrupt A person unable to pay his debts and who has been adjudicated bankrupt by the court.

Bar The barristers' profession.

Barrister-at-law A member of the Inns of Court. A person who is a barrister-at-law may practise as counsel in the Courts.

Beneficiary One entitled under a will or trust.

Bona fide In good faith.

Breach Non-fulfilment of a contractual obligation.

By-laws (sometimes spelt bye-laws) Delegated legislation made under statutory authority.

Caveat emptor Let the buyer beware.

Certiorari Short for certiorarai volumus—'we wish to be informed'.

Chancery A division of the High Court.

Charge A security for a debt attached to property.

Chattel Movable personal property.

Chose in action Intangible personal property not capable of physical possession and enforceable only by action.

Collateral contract A subsidiary contract but for which the main contract would not have been made.

Common law Either English law as opposed to continental systems; or case law as opposed to statute, or the law of the common law courts as opposed to equity.

Condition A major term of a contract, breach of which entitles the innocent party to treat the contract as ended.

Condition precedent A condition which must be fulfilled before a contract can take effect.

Consensus ad idem Agreement as to the same thing.

Consideration The price paid for the promise received. The element of bargain to a contract.

Contingent Operative only on the occurrence of an uncertain event.

Contract A binding agreement which is intended to be and is legally enforceable.

Counsel Barrister-at-law.

Counterclaim A cross action brought by a defendant against the plaintiff.

County courts Civil courts dealing with inferior civil matters.

Court of appeal The court hearing appeals from the county courts and High Court, and also some appeals from the Crown Court.

Covenant A promise contained in a deed.

Crown Court The branch of the Supreme Court dealing with criminal matters.

Damages The money award made to the winning party in a civil action.

Deed A written document signed, sealed and delivered.

Delegatus non potest delegare A person entrusted with a duty cannot appoint another person to perform that duty.

De minimis non curat lex The law is not concerned with trifles.

Eiusdem generis General words following specific words must be construed as relating to things of a similar kind to those specifically listed.

Equity A supplement to the common law deriving from the former Court of Chancery.

Estate An interest in land.

Estoppel A rule of evidence which prevents a party from denying facts which he has led another to assume to be true and on which that other has relied.

Executed Performed or completed.

Execution The enforcement of a judgement.

Executory Not yet completed.

Ex officio By virtue of an office.

Frustration The termination of a contract by some external intervening event for which neither party is liable, making performance impossible.

General damages Unascertained damages to be assessed by the judge.

Habeas corpus A writ addressed to one person who is detaining another person in custody requiring him to produce that person to the court.

High Court The main civil court, includes Queen's Bench, Family and Chancery Divisions.

House of Lords The highest court with appellate jurisdiction in both civil and criminal matters.

Incorporeal Intangible (rights or interests).

Indorsement Something written on the back of a document.

Injunction An order of the court forbidding the breaking of an obligation.

In lieu of In place of.

Innominate (or intermediate) term A term of the contract not categorised into a condition or warranty.

Inns of Court The societies to which barristers-at-law belong; there are four inns: Inner Temple, Middle Temple, Lincoln's Inn and Gray's Inn.

In personam (Right) against an individual.

In re (or Re) In the matter of.

In rem (Right) against goods or land.

Inter alia Amongst other things.

Interim Provisional.

Inter se Between themselves.

In toto Completely.

In transitu In passage from one place to another.

Intra vires Within the powers of the body, organisation, company or person in question.

Ipso facto By the very fact itself.

Joint Where two or more persons share a right or obligation in circumstances where their interest is in the entire subject-matter.

Judgment The decision of a court.

Jurisdiction The authority of a court to hear and decide a case.

Laches Delay in pursuing a legal remedy. This defeats a claim in equity.

Law report A report of a decided case; the report is made by a barrister-at-law and printed.

Law Society The governing body of English solicitors.

Lease A letting of land or the document creating such letting.

Licence A permission eg to enter land or other real property.

Lien The right of retention of some property belonging to another pending satisfaction of some claim by the holder of the lien, usually the payment of a debt due from the owner of the property.

Limitation period The statutory period within which a claim must be commenced.

Liquidated damages Damages assessed either by the parties or by the court.

Liquidation The winding up of a company.

Lord Chancellor The person who presides over the House of Lords in both its legislative and judicial capacities.

Lord Chief Justice The head of the Queen's Bench Division.

Lord Justice of Appeal A judge of the Court of Appeal.

Lord of Appeal in Ordinary A judge of the House of Lords.

Magistrates' courts The most inferior criminal court where all criminal cases are commenced and where summary offences are dealt with.

Mandamus A prerogative order from a superior court commanding an inferior tribunal, public official or corporation to take some specific action.

Master of the Rolls The head of the Court of Appeal.

Mortgage A transfer of property as security for a loan.

Nisi Unless, (usually in relation to a decree or order of the court which will be made absolute "unless" some sufficient cause is shown to the contrary).

Non sequitur It does not follow.

Noscitur a sociis A rule of interpretation meaning that words must be interpreted in the context of the document in which they appear.

Obiter dictum Things said by the way; a statement made by a judge not forming part of the decision.

Onus of proof Burden of proof; who has to prove the case?

Pari passu Equally, on an equal footing.

Parol By word of mouth.

Partnership The relationship which exists between persons carrying on a business in common with a view to profit.

Penalty A sum provided to be payable in a contract if a breach occurs, such a sum amounting to a punishment of the party in breach rather than a genuine attempt at calculating the loss.

Per curiam In the opinion of the court.

Per incuriam A decision which has not taken account of a previous binding precedent or a statute.

Per se By itself.

Plaintiff The person who commences a civil action.

Post After.

Post mortem After death.

Precedent The doctrine whereby a court follows its own previous decisions or the decisions of a higher court.

Prima facie At first sight.

Privy council The final court of appeal from certain Commonwealth countries.

Pro rata In proportion.

Pro tanto So far, to that extent.

Pro tempore For the time being.

Public policy The courts' concept of what is in the interests of the public as a whole.

Puisne judge Ordinary judge of the High Court.

Quaere But question whether this is correct (sometimes written—SED QUAERE).

Quantum How much.

Quantum meruit The amount which a specific piece of work is worth.

Queen's Bench A division of the High Court.

Queen's Counsel A senior barrister.

Qui facit per alium facit per se Whoever employs another person to do something, does it himself.

Ratification Authorisation of an unauthorised act.

Ratio decidendi The reason for the decision, the main part of a judgment.

Re (or in re) In the matter of, concerning.

Rectification Correction by the court of a document to ensure that it expresses the true intention of the parties.

Repudiation Refusal by a party to a contract to perform his obligations under it.

Res Thing, matter, affair.

Seal Formerly piece of wax attached to a document and impressed usually with a signet ring (hence the expression document or contract under seal).

Set-off The diminution or extinction of the plaintiff's claim by a counterclaim by the defendant.

Sheriff The Queen's officer in a county, he is responsible for the enforcement, through the bailiff or sheriff's officer, of judgments of the superior courts.

Simple contract A contract not under seal.

Solicitor A qualified member of the Law Society, whose function is to ensure that clients are correctly advised as to their legal position.

Special damages Compensation for loss which, although not the direct consequence of the breach, is in the contemplation of the parties at the time the contract is made.

Specialty contract A contract under seal.

Specific performance An equitable remedy enforcing the plaintiff's contractual rights by making the defendant do as he was obliged to do under the contract.

Status quo (ante) The position in which things were previously.

Stipendiary magistrate A paid, legally qualified magistrate who can sit alone.

Subpoena A writ compelling the person to whom it is addressed to appear in court.

Subrogation The right of being able to bring an action in the name of another.

Sue To proceed at law in civil proceedings.

Sui generis Of its own kind, unique.

Sui juris Of full legal capacity.

Third party A person not privy to a contract.

Tort A civil wrong not dependent on contract.

Trust The holding of the legal title to property by trustees for the benefit of others (beneficiaries).

Uberrimae fidei Of utmost good faith.

Ultra vires Beyond those powers recognised by the law as belonging to the person or body in question.

Unliquidated damages Damages which are to be assessed.

Unsolicited goods Goods which are sent without any prior request being made for them.

V. (Versus) Against.

Vicarious liability Liability of one person for the torts of another.

Vis major Irresistible force

Volens Willing.

Volenti non fit injuria No wrong is done to the person who consents to it.

Warranty A term of a contract not a condition but collateral to the main purpose of the contract.

Writ The document used to commence a civil action.

Table of Cases

Abbott v Abbott [1936] 3 All ER 823; 81 Sol Jo 58	266
Adams v Lindsell (1818) 1 B & Ald 681; 106 ER 250	59
Addis v Gramophone Co Ltd [1909] AC 488; [1908-10] All ER Rep 1; 78 LJKB 1122, HL	207
Adler v George [1964] 2 QB 7; [1964] 2 WLR 542; [1964] 1 All ER 628, DC	48
Aldridge v Johnson (1857) 7 E & B 885; 26 LJQB 2906; 5 WR 703	160
Alpha Trading v Dunnshaw-Patten Ltd [1981] QB 290; [1981] 2 WLR 169; [1981] 1 All ER 482, CA	253
Al Saudi Banque and others v Clarke Pixley [1989] Ch D	282
Aluminium Industrie Vaasen BV v Romalpa Aluminium [1976] 1 WLR 676; [1976] 2 All ER 552; 120 SJ 95, CA	157
Anderson Ltd v Daniel [1924] 1 KB 138; [1923] All ER Rep Ext 783; 40 TLR 61, CA	117
Andrews v Hopkinson [1957] 1 QB 229; [1956] 3 All ER 422; 100 SJ 768	66
Andrews Bros (Bournemouth) Ltd v Singer & Co [1934] 1 KB 17; [1933] All ER Rep; 103 LJKB 90, CA	89
Anns v Merton LBC [1978] AC 728; [1977] 2 WLR 10224; 121 SJ 377, HL	277
Appleby v Myers [1861-73] All ER Rep 452; 16 LT 669; 36 LJCP 331	130
Arab Bank v Ross [1952] 2 QB 216; [1952] 1 All ER 709; 96 SJ 229, CA	225
Archbolds (Freightage) Ltd v Spanglett [1961] 1 QB 374; [1961] 2 WLR 170; 105 SJ 149, CA	115
Ashington Piggeries Ltd v Hill (Christopher) Ltd [1972] AC 441; [1971] 2 WLR 1051; 115 SJ 223	151, 154
Atkinson v Denby [1861-73] All ER Rep Ext 2294; 10 WR 389	118
A-G v Fulham Corporation [1921] 1 Ch 440; 90 LJCh 281; 125 LT 14	39
Associated Japanese Bank (International) Ltd v Credit du Nord SA [1988] 3 All ER 902	107
Attwood v Small [1838] 6 Cl and Fin 232	99
Avery v Bowden (1856) 26 LJQB 3; 5 WR 45; 28 LTOS 145	132
Baker v Jones [1954] 1 WLR 1005; [1954] 2 All ER 553; 98 SJ 473	120
Balfour v Balfour [1919] 2 KB 571; [1918-19] All ER Rep 860; 88 LJKB 1054, CA	67
Bannerman v White (1861) 10 CBNS 844; 31 LJCP 28; 4 LT 740	79
Barclay v Pearson [1893] 2 Ch 154; 62 LJCh 636; 42 WR 74	119
Barratt v Gough-Thomas [1951] Ch 242; [1950] 2 All ER 1048; 94 SJ 760, CA	254
Bartlett v Marcus (Sydney) Ltd [1965] 1 WLR 1013; [1965] 2 All ER 753; 109 SJ 451; CA	153
Baster v London & County Printing Works [1899] 1 QB 901; 68 LJQB 622; 80 LT 757, DC	207
Bastin v Davies [1950] 2 KB 579; [1950] 1 All ER 1095; 66 TLR (Pt 2) 719, DC	41
Bavins Junior & Sims v London & Western Bank Ltd [1899] 1 QB 270; 69 LJQB 164; 81 LT 655, CA	222
Beach v Reed Corrugated Cases Ltd [1956] 1 WLR 807; [1956] 2 All ER 652; 100 SJ 472	136
Beale v Taylor [1967] 1 WLR 1193; [1967] 3 All ER 253; 111 SJ 668, CA	150
Behrend v Produce Brokers [1920] 3 KB 530; [1920] All ER Rep 125; 90 LJKB 143	163
Bell v Lever Bros Ltd [1932] AC 161; [1931] All ER Rep 1; 101 LJKB 129, CA	106
Bentley (Dick) (Productions) Ltd v Smith (Harold) (Motors) Ltd [1965] 1 WLR 623; [1965] 2 All ER 65; 109 SJ 329, CA	78
Bernstein v Pamsons Motors (Golders Green) Ltd [1987] 2 All ER 220; [1987] RTR 384	147
Bettini v Gye [1874-80] All ER Rep 242; 1 QBD 183; 45 LJQB 209	83
Bigg v Boyd Gibbins Ltd [1971] 1 WLR 913; [1971] 2 All ER 183; 115 SJ 406, CA	55
Bigos v Bousted [1951] 1 All ER 92; 95 SJ 180; 211 LT 346	118
Bird v Brown (1850) 4 Exch 786; 19 LJEx 154; 154 ER 1433	247
Bisset v Wilkinson [1927] AC 177; 96 LJPC 12; 136 LT 97, PC	96
Blackman v Post Office [1974] ICR 151; [1974] ITR 122; [1974] IRLR 46, NIRC	212
Bolton v Mahadeva [1972] 1 WLR 1009; [1972] 2 All ER 1322; 116 SJ 564, CA	127
Bolton Partners v Lambert (1889) 41 ChD 302, CA	248
Boston Deep Sea Fishing and Ice Co v Ansell [1886-90] All ER Rep 65; 39 ChD 339; 59 LT 345, CA	201, 208
—— v Farnham [1957] 1 WLR 1051; [1957] 3 All ER 204; 101 SJ 834	247
Bourhill v Young [1943] AC 92; 111 LJPC 97; 167 LT 261, HL	277
Bourne, Re [1906] 2 Ch 427; 75 LJCh 779; 95 LT 131, CA	272
Bowmakers Ltd v Barnet Instruments Ltd [1945] KB 65; [1944] 2 All ER 579; 114 LJKB 41, CA	117
Brace v Calder [1895] 2 QB 253; [1895-9] All ER Rep 1196; 64 LJQB 582, CA	136
Bradshaw v Associated Portland Cement [1972] IRLR 46	213
Brinkibon Ltd v Stahag Stahl und Stahlwarenhandelsgesellschaft mbH [1983] AC 34; [1982] 2 WLR 264; [1982] 1 All ER 293, HL	60
British Crane Hire Corp Ltd v Ipswich Plant Hire [1974] QB 303; [1974] 2 WLR 856; [1974] 1 All ER 1059, CA	86
British Reinforced Concrete Engineering Co Ltd v Schelff [1921] 2 Ch 563	122
British Syphon Co v Homewood [1956] RPC 27	201
Brogden v Metropolitan Railway Co (1877) 2 App Cas 666, HL	58
Bromby & Hoare v Evans (1971) 12 KIR 160; sub nom Brobley & Hoare v Evans [1972] ITR 76, NIRC	209
Brooks v Brooks (1901) 85 LT 456	267
Bushwall Properties Ltd v Vortex Properties Ltd [1976] 1 WLR 591; [1976] 2 All ER 283; 120 SJ 183, CA	60
Byrne v Boadle (1863) 2 H & C 722; 33 LJEx 13; 9 LT 450	278
—— v Van Tienhoven (1880) 5 CPD 344; 49 LJQB 316; 42 LT 371	57
Cammel Laird & Co v Management Bronze and Brass [1934] AC 402; [1934] All ER Rep 1; 103 LJKB 289, HL	155
Candler v Crane Christmas & Co [1951] 2 KB 164; [1951] 1 All ER 426; 95 SJ 171; CA	279

Caparo Industries v Dickman & Others [1989] 1 All ER 798 .... 282, 284
Car and Universal Finance Co v Caldwell [1965] 1 QB 525; [1964] 2 WLR 600; [1964] 1 All ER 290, CA 102
Carlill v Carbolic Smoke Ball Co [1893] 1 QB 256; [1891–94] All ER Rep 127; 62 LJQB 257, CA 56, 59
Carlos Federspiel & Co SA v Twigg (Charles) & Co Ltd [1957] 1 Lloyd's Rep 240; [1957] JBL 296 160
Carmichael v Evans [1904] 1 Ch 486; 73 LJCh 329; 90 LT 573 271
Casey's Patents, Re [1892] 1 Ch 104; 61 LJCh 61; 36 Sol Jo 77, CA 62
Cehave NV v Baremer Handelgesellschaft mbH [1976] QB 44; [1975] 3 WLR 447; [1975] 3 All ER 739, CA 84
Cellulose Acetate Silk Co Ltd v Widnes Foundry Ltd [1933] AC 20; [1932] All ER Rep 567; 101 LJKB 694, HL . 137
Central London Property Trust Ltd v High Trees House Ltd [1947] KB 130; [1946] 1 All ER 256; 93 SJ 414..... 46, 65
Chapelton v Barry UDC [1940] 1 KB 532; [1940] 1 All ER 213; 1109 LJKB 213, CA 85
Chaplin v Hicks [1911] 2 KB 786; [1911–13] All ER Rep 224; 80 LJKB 1292, CA 136
Chappel & Co v Nestlé Co Ltd [1960] AC 87; [1959] 3 WLR 168; [1959] 2 All ER 701, CA 63
Charnock v Liverpool Corporation [1968] 1 WLR 598; [1971] 2 All ER 588; 115 SJ 265, CA.................... 171
Charter v Sullivan [1957] 2 QB 117; [1957] 2 WLR 528; [1957] 1 All ER 809, CA 166
City Equitable Fire Insurance Co, Re [1925] 1 Ch 407; [1924] All ER Rep 485; 94 LJCh 445, CA 281
Clarkson Booker Ltd v Andjel [1964] 2 QB 775; [1964] 3 WLR 466; 108 SJ 580, CA 256
Clifford v Timms [1908] AC 12 affg [1907] 2 Ch 236; 76 LJCh 627, HL.. 271
Clough Mill v Martin [1985] 1 WLR 111; [1984] 3 All ER 982; 128 SJ 850, CA................................. 158
Combe v Combe [1951] 2 KB 215; [1951] All ER 767; 95 SJ 317, CA.. 65
Comber v Anderson [1808] 1 Camp 523 244
Condor v The Barron Knights Ltd [1966] 1 WLR 87; 110 SJ 71 .... 129, 204
Conway v Rimmer [1968] AC 910; [1968] 2 WLR 998; [1968] 1 All ER 874, CA 36
Cooper v Micklefield Coal and Lime Co Ltd (1912) 56 Sol Jo 706, 107 LT 457................................ 72
—— v Phibbs (1867) LR 2 HL 149; 16 LT 678; 15 WR 1049, HL 108, 111
Corkery v Carpenter [1951] 1 KB 102 48
Corpe v Overton (1833) 10 Bing 252; 3 Moos & S 738; 3 LJCP 24 69
Cort v Ambergate Railway Co (1851) 17 QB 127; 20 LJQB 460; 17 LTOS 179................................... 132
Couturier v Hastie [1843–60] All ER Rep 280; 5 HL Cas 673; 25 LJEx 253, HL 107
Cox v Coulson [1916] 2 KB 177; 85 LJKB 1081; 114 LT 599, CA 262
Cox v Hickman (1860) 8 HL Cas 268; 11 ER 431, HL... 263
Cox v Philips Industries Ltd [1975] ICR 138; [1976] 1 WLR 638 208
Craddock Bros Ltd v Hunt [1976] 1 WLR 638; [1976] 3 All ER 161; 119 SJ 760 112
Craven-Ellis v Canons Ltd [1936] 2 All ER 1066; [1936] 2 KB 403; 105 LJKB 767, CA 141
Creffield v BBC [1975] IRLR 23, Industrial Tribunal.. 214
Cricklewood Property & Investment Trust Ltd v Leighton's Investment Trust Ltd [1945] AC 221; [1945] 1 All ER 252; 114 LJKB 110, HL... 131
Crowther v Shannon Motor Co [1975] 1 WLR 30; [1975] 1 All ER 139; [1975] RTR 201, CA 154
Cummings v Arrol & Co [1962] 1 WLR 295 278
Cundy v Lindsay [1874–80] All ER Rep 573; 3 App Cas 459; 47 LJQB 481, HL 108
Currie v Misa (1895) LR 10 Exch 153; 44 LJEx 94; 23 WR 450... 61
Curtice v London City & Midland Bank [1908] 1 KB 293; 77 LJKB 341; 98 LT 190, CA......................... 233
Curtis v Chemical Cleaning and Dyeing Co [1951] 1 KB 805; [1951] 1 All ER 631; 95 SJ 253, CA............ 85, 171
Czarnikow Ltd v Koufos, see Koufos v Czarnikow
D & C Builders Ltd v Rees [1966] 2 QB 617; [1966] 2 WLR 288; [1965] 3 All ER 837, CA 64, 65, 128
Daunn v Simmins [1879] 41 LT 783 245
Davie v New Merton Board Mills [1959] AC 604; [1959] 2 WLR 331; [1959] 1 All ER 346, HL 199
Davis v Davis [1894] 1 Ch 393; 63 LJCh 219; 70 LT 265.. 262, 263
De Francesco v Barnum [1886–90] All ER Rep 414; 45 ChD 430; 60 LJCh 63 69
Demby Hamilton & Co Ltd v Barden [1949] 1 All ER 435; [1949] WN 73 156
Derry v peek [1886–90] All ER Rep 1; 14 App Cas 337; 61 LT 265, HL 100
Dickinson v Dodds (1876) 2 ChD 463; 45 LJCh 777; 34 LT 607, CA.. 57
Dimes v Grand Junction Canal Properties (1852) 3 HL Cas 759; 19 LTOS 317; 10 ER 301, HL 17
Dodsley v Varley (1840) 12 Ad & El 632; 5 Jur 316 249
Donoghue v Stevenson [1932] AC 562; 101 LJPC 119; 48 TLR 494, HL 4, 233, 276
Doyle v Olby (Ironmongers) Ltd [1969] 2 QB 158; [1969] 2 WLR 673; [1969] 2 All ER 119, CA 104
Drew v Nunn [1874–80] All ER Rep 114; 4 QBD 661; 48 LJQB 591, CA 258
Duncan v Cammel Laird & Co [1942] AC 624; 22 MLR 187; 79 LQR 153....................................... 36
Dunlop Pneumatic Tyre Co Ltd v New Garage and Motor Co Ltd [1915] AC 79; [1914–15] All ER Rep 739; 83 LJKB 1574, HL... 137
—— v Selfridge & Co Ltd [1915] AC 847; [1914–15] All ER Rep 333; 84 LJKB 1680, HL 65
Durham Bros v Robertson [1898] 1 QB 765; 67 LJQB 484; 78 LT 438, CA 71
Dutton v Bognor Regis UDC [1972] 1 QB 373; [1972] 2 WLR 299; [1971] 116 SJ 16, CA..................... 277
Edgington v Fitzmaurice [1884] 29 ChD 459; 53 LT 369, 32 WR 848, CA.................................... 97, 100, 139
Empire Meat Co Ltd v Patrick [1939] 2 All ER 85 121
Entores v Miles Far East Corporation [1955] 2 QB 327; [1955] 3 WLR 48; [1955] 2 All ER 493, CA 59
Errington v Errington & Woods [1952] 1 KB 290; [1952] 1 All ER 149; 96 SJ 119, CA 57
Esso Petroleum v Commissioners of Customs & Excise [1976] 1 WLR 1; [1976] 1 All ER 117, HL 68
—— Co Ltd v Commissioners of Customs & Excise [1975] 1 WLR 406; 119 SJ 205, CA......................... 169
—— Co Ltd v Harpers Garage (Stourport) Ltd 1967 123
—— Co Ltd v Mardon [1976] 2 WLR 583; 120 SJ 131, CA... 97, 104, 280
Evans (J) & Son (Portsmouth) v Andrea Merzaria [1976] 1 WLR 1078; [1976] 2 All ER 930; 120 SJ 734, CA 88
Everett v Williams (1725) 9 LQR 197 264
Farquharson Bros v King & Co [1902] AC 325; 71 LJKB 667; 46 Sol Jo 584; HL............................. 249
Felthouse v Bindley (1863) 1 New Rep 401; 7 LT 835; 11 WR 429 60
Financings Ltd v Stimson [1962] 1 WLR 1184; [1962] 3 All ER 386, CA 58
Fisher & Co v Apollinaris Co (1875) 10 Ch App 277; 44 LJCh 500; 32 LT 628............................... 116
Fitzgerald v Dressler (1859) 7 CBNS 374; 29 LJCP 113; 33 LTOS 43 77

Fletcher v Krell (1873) 42 LJQB 55; 28 LT 105; 37 JP 198	97
Foakes v Beer [1881–5] All ER Rep 106; 9 App Cas 605; 54 LJQB 130, HL	64
Fomento (Sterling Area) Ltd v Selsdon Fountain Pen Co [1958] 1 WLR 45; [1958] 1 All ER 11; 102 SJ 283, CA	281
Ford Motor Co (England) Ltd v Armstrong (1915) 31 TLR 267; 59 Sol Jo 362, CA	138
Forman & Co v Liddesdale, The [1900] AC 190; 669 LJPC 44; 82 LT 331, PC	246
Foster v Driscoll [1929] 1 KB 470; [1928] All ER Rep 130; 98 LJKB 282, CA	116
Friedeberg-Seeley v Klass [1957] 101 SJ 275; *The Times*, 19 February	113
Frost v Aylesbury Dairies [1905] 1 KB 608; [1904–7] All ER Rep 132; 74 LJKB 386, CA	155
Galloway v Galloway (1914) 30 TLR 531, DC	107
General Billposting Co Ltd v Atkinson [1909] AC 118; [1908–10] All ER Rep 619; 78 LJCh 77, HL	208
Gerrard (Thomas) & Son; *Re* [1968] Ch 455; [1967] 3 WLR 84; [1967] 2 All ER 525	282
Gibson v Manchester City Council [1979] 1 WLR 294; [1979] 1 All ER 972; 123 SJ 201, HL	55
Glassbrook Bros v Glamorgan County Council [1925] AC 270	64
Glynn v Margetson & Co [1893] AC 351; 62 LJQB 466; 9 TLR 437, HL	88
Godden, *Re see* R v Kent Police Authority, *ex parte* Godden	
Godley v Perry, Burton & Sons [1960] 1 WLR 9; [1960] 1 All ER 36; 104 SJ 16	156
Goodwin v Robarts (1875) LR 10 Exch 337; 44 LJEx 157; 33 LT 272, HL	40
Gordon v Dickson, McFarlane & Robinson 1983	282
—— v Gordon (1821) 3 Swan 400; 36 ER 910	98
—— v Selico Co Ltd (1986) 278 EG 53	99
Gosling v Anderson (1872) *The Times*, 8 February, CA	103, 105
Goss v Nugent [1824–34] All ER Rep 305; 5 B & AD 58; 2 LJKB 127	127
Grace v Harehills Club (1974) (unreported)	213
Grant v Australian Knitting Mills [1936] AC 85; [1936] All ER Rep 209; 105 LJPC 6, PC	150, 152
Great Northern Railway v Swaffield (1874) L R Exch 132; 43 LJEx 89; 30 LT 562	250
Green v Bartlett (1863) 14 CBNS 681; 32 LJCP 261; 8 LT 503	253
Greenwood v Martins Bank [1933] AC 51; [1932] All ER Rep 318; 101 LJKB 623, HL	234
Gregory v Ford [1951] 1 All ER 121	200
Griffiths v Conway (Peter) Ltd [1939] 1 All ER 685, CA	154
Hadley v Baxendale [1843–60] All ER Rep 461; 9 Exch 341; 23 LTOS 69	134, 141, 165
Hamlyn v Houston & Co [1903] 1 KB 81; 72 LJKB 72; 87 LT 500, CA	268
Harris v Nickerson (1873) 42 LJQB 17; 28 LT 410; 37 JP 536	56
Harris v Sheffield United Football Club Ltd [1987] 2 All ER 838	64
Hartley v Ponsonby (1857) 7 E & B 872; 26 LJQB 322; 29 LTOS 195	63
Hartog v Colin & Shields [1939] 3 All ER 566	110
Harvey v Facey [1893] AC 552; 62 LJPC 127; 69 LT 504, PC	55
Head v Tattersall (1871) LR 7 Exch 7; 41 LJEx 4; 25 LT 631	128
Hedley Byrne & Co v Heller & Partners Ltd [1964] AC 465; [1963] WLR 101; [1963] 2 All ER 575, CA	46, 104, 233, 279
Heil v Hedges [1951] 1 TLR 512; 95 SJ 140	152
Hensman v Traill (1980) 124 SJ 776; *The Times*, 22 October	121
Herne Bay Steam Boat Co v Hutton [1903] 2 KB 683; [1900–3] All ER Rep 627; 72 LJKB 879, CA	129
Heydon's Case (1584) 3 Co Rep 7a; Moore KB 128; 76 ER 637	48
Heywood v Wellers [1976] QB 446; [1976] 2 WLR 101; [1976] 1 All ER 300, CA	137
Higgins v Beauchamp [1914] 3 KB 1192; [1914–15] All ER Rep 937; 84 LJKB 631, DC	268
—— (W) Ltd v Northampton Corporation [1927] 1 Ch 128; 96 LJCh 38; 136 LT 235	108
Hillas & Co Ltd v Arcos Ltd [1932] All ER Rep 494; 147 LT 503; 38 Com Cas 23, HL	61
Hippisley v Knee Bros [1905] 1 KB 1; 74 LJKB 68; 92 LT 20	252
Hitchcock v Post Office [1980] ICR 100, EAT	196
Hochster v De la Tour [1843–60] All ER Rep 12; 22 LJQB 455; 22 LTOS 171	132
Hoenig v Isaacs [1952] 2 All ER 176; [1952] 1 TLR 1360, CA	126
Hollier v Rambler Motors [1972] 2 QB 71; [1972] 2 WLR 401; [1972] 1 All ER 399; CA	86
Holwell Securities Ltd v Hughes [1974] 1 WLR 155; [1974] 1 All ER 161; 117 SJ 912, CA	59
Horsfall v Thomas (1862) 1 H & C 90; 2 F & F 785; 6 LT 462	99
Houghton v Trafalgar Insurance [1954] 1 QB 247; [1953] 3 WLR 985; [1953] 2 All ER 1409, CA	87
Hudson v Ridge Manufacturing Co Ltd [1957] 2 QB 348; [1957] 2 WLR 948; [1957] 2 All ER 229	275
Humble v Hunter (1838) 12 QBD 310; 17 LJQB 350; 11 LTOS 265	255
Humming Bird Motors v Hobbs [1986] RTR 276	101
Hutton v Warren (1836) 1 M & W 466; 5 LJEx 234; 150 ER 517	81
Hyde v Wrench (1840) 3 Beav 334; 4 Jur 1106; 49 ER 132	57
Ingram v Little [1961] 1 QB 31; [1960] 3 WLR 504; [1960] 3 All ER 332, CA	110
Interfoto Picture Library Ltd v Stilletto Visual Programmes Ltd [1988] 1 All ER 348	87
IRC v Hinchy [1960] AC 748; [1960] 2 WLR 448; [1960] 1 All ER 505, CA	47
Iqbal v London Transport Executive (1973) *The Times*, 7 June, CA	276
Jackson v Union Marine Insurance Co Ltd [1874–80] All ER 317; 44 LJCP 27; 312 LT 789	131
—— v Horizon Holidays [1975] 3 All ER 92	137
Jarvis v Swan's Tours Ltd [1973] 1 QB 233; [1972] 3 WLR 954; [1973] 1 All ER 71, CA	136, 207
JEB Fasteners Ltd v Marks, Bloom & Co [1983] 1 All ER 583; [1981] 3 All ER 289; [1982] Com LR 226, CA	282
John v Mendoza [1939] 1 KB 141	116
Johnson v Nottinghamshire Police Authority [1974] 1 WLR 358; [1974] 1 All ER 1082; 118 SJ 166, CA	210
Jones v Padavatton [1969] 1 WLR 328; [1969] 2 All ER 616; 112 SJ 965, CA	67
Kearley v Thomson (1890) 24 QBD 742	118
Keighley Maxstead & Co v Durant 1901	246
Keith Spicer Ltd v Mansell 1970, *see* Spicer (Keith) Ltd v Mansell	
Kelner v Baxter (1866) 36 LJCP 94; 15 LT 213; 15 WR 278	246
Kendall v Hamilton [1874–80] All ER Rep 932; 4 App Cas 504; 48 LJQB 705, HL	268
Kimber v William Willett Ltd [1947] KB 570; [1947] 1 All ER 361; 91 SJ 206, CA	170

Kingston Cotton Mill Ltd, *Re* [1896] 2 Ch 279	281
Kleinwort Benson Ltd *v* Malaysian Mining Corp Bhd [1989] 1 All ER 785	68
Krell *v* Henry [1903] 2 KB 740; [1900-3] All ER Rep 20; 72 LJKB 794, CA	129
Koufos *v* Czarnikow Ltd (The Heron II) [1969] 1 AC 350; [1967] 3 WLR 1491; 111 SJ 848, CA	134
Langston *v* AUEW [1974] 1 WLR 185; [1974] 1 All ER 980; 118 SJ 97, CA	198
Latimer *v* AEC Ltd [1953] AC 643; [1953] 3 WLR 259; [1953] 2 All ER 449, CA	199, 277
Laws *v* London Chronicle [1959] 1 WLR 698; [1959] 2 All ER 285; 103 SJ 470, CA	207
Leaf *v* International Galleries [1950] 2 KB 86; [1950] 1 All ER 693; [1950] 66 TLR (Pt 1) 1031, CA	102, 106
Legal and General Assurance Society *v* General Metal Agencies (1969) 113 SJ 876; 20 P & CR 953	108
Leslie *v* Sheill [1914] 3 KB 607	70
L'estrange *v* Graucob [1934] 2 KB 394; [1934] All ER Rep 16; 103 LJKB 730; 152 LT 164, DC	85, 88
Levison *v* Patent Steam Carpet Cleaning Co [1978] QB 69; [1977] 3 WLR 90; [1977] 3 All ER 498, CA	171
Lewis *v* Averay [1971] 3 WLR 603 [1971] 3 All ER 907; 115 SJ 755, CA	110
Liggett (B) (Liverpool) Ltd *v* Barclays Bank [1928] 1 KB 48; [1927] All ER Rep 451; 97 LJKB 1	233
Limpus *v* London General Omnibus Co (1862) 1 HeC 526; 32 LJEx 34; 7 LT 641	275
Lister *v* Romford Ice & Cold Storage Co Ltd [1957] AC 555; [1957] 2 WLR 158; [1957] 1 All ER 125, CA	202
Littlewoods Organisation Ltd *v* Harris [1978] 1 All ER 1026; [1977] 1 WLR 1472; 121 SJ 727, CA	121
Lloyd *v* Grace, Smith & Co [1912] AC 716	276
Lloyd Cheyham & Co Ltd *v* Littlejohn & Co (1985) (unreported)	283
Lloyd's Bank Ltd *v* Bundy [1975] QB 326; [1974] 3 WLR 501; [1974] 3 All ER 757, CA	113
London and General Bank (No 2), *Re* [1895] 2 Ch 673; [1895-9] All ER Rep 953; 64 LJCh 866	281
London Joint Stock Bank Ltd *v* MacMillan & Arthur [1918] AC 777; [1918-19] All ER Rep 30; 119 LT 387, HL	232
London Street Tramways Ltd *v* London County Council [1898] AC 375; 67 LJQB 559; 78 LT 361, HL	36
Long *v* Lloyd [1958] 1 WLR 753; [1958] 2 All ER 402; 102 SJ 488, CA	147
Lumley *v* Wagner (1852) 5 De Ge Sm 485; 19 LTOS 127; 64 ER 1209	139
Luxor (Eastbourne) Ltd *v* Cooper [1941] AC 108; [1941] 1 All ER 33; 110 LJKB 131, HL	253
McArdle, *Re* [1951] Ch 669; [1951] 1 All ER 905; 95 SJ 284, CA	62
McClelland *v* Northern Ireland General Health Services Board [1957] 1 WLR 594; [1957] 2 All ER 129; 101 SJ 355, HL	205
Mahesan *v* Malaysia Government Officers' Co-operative Housing Society Ltd [1979] AC 374; [1978] 2 WLR 444; [1978] 2 All ER 405, PC	252
Mahmoud & Ispahani, *Re* [1921] 2 KB 716; [1921] All ER Rep 217; 90 LJKB 821, CA	117
Maidstone BC *v* Mortimer [1980] 3 All ER 552; [1981] JPL 112; 256 EG 1013, DC	48
Maple Flock Co Ltd *v* Universal Furniture Products (Wembley) Ltd [1934] 1 KB 148; [1933] All ER Rep 15; 103 LJKB 513, CA	164
Maritime National Fish Ltd *v* Ocean Trawlers Ltd [1935] AC 524; [1935] All ER Rep 86; 104 LJPC 88, PC	130
Marles *v* (Phillip) Trant and Sons Ltd (No 2) [1954] 1 QB 29; [1953] 2 WLR 564; [1953] 1 All ER 651, CA	117
Marrison *v* Bell [1939] 2 KB 187; [1939] 1 All ER 745; 108 LJKB 481, CA	204
Martyn *v* Gray (1863) 14 CBNS 824; 143 ER 667	269
May & Butcher *v* R [1934] 2 KB 17; 103 LJKB 556; 151 LT 246, HL	145
Mears *v* Safecar Security Ltd [1983] QB 54; [1982] 3 WLR 366; [1982] 2 All ER 865, CA	198
Mendelssohn *v* Normand Ltd [1970] 1 QB 177; [1969] 3 WLR 139; [1969] 2 All ER 1215, CA	88
Mercantile Credit Co Ltd *v* Garrad [1962] 3 All ER 1103	267
Mercer *v* Denne [1905] 2 Ch 538; [1904-7] All ER Rep 80; 74 LJCh 723, CA	34, 35
Merritt *v* Merritt [1970] 1 WLR 1211; [1970] 2 All ER 760; 114 SJ 455, CA	67
Metropolitan Water Board *v* Pick Kerr & Co [1918] AC 119; [1916-17] All ER Rep 122; 87 LJKB 370, HL	130
Microbeads *v* Vinhurst Road Markings Ltd [1975] 1 WLR 218; [1975] 1 All ER 529; 119 SJ 81, CA	148
Miller *v* Karlinsky (1945) 62 TLR 85, CA	115
Midland Bank *v* Shepherd [1988] 3 All ER 17	114
Midland Bank Trust Co *v* Hett, Stubbs & Kemp [1979] Ch 496; [1979] 2 WLR 594; [1979] 2 All ER 193, CA	280
Mihalis Angelos, The (1969) 114 SJ 30	133
Miliangos *v* Frank (George) (Textiles) Ltd [1976] AC 443; [1975] 3 WLR 758; [1975] 3 All ER 801, CA	36
Mitchell (George) (Chesterhall) Ltd *v* Finney Lock Seeds Ltd [1983] 2 AC 803; [1983] 3 WLR 163; [1983] 2 All ER 737, HL	91
Moorcock, The [1886-90] All ER Rep 530; (1889) 14 PD 64; 58 LJP 73, CA	81, 170
Moore & Co *v* Landauer & Co, *Re* [1921] 2 KB 519; [1921] All ER Rep 466; 90 LJKB 731, CA	150
Maordaunt Brothers *v* British Oil and Cake Mills Ltd [1910] 2 KB 502; 79 LJKB 967; 103 LT 217	167
Morgan *v* Manser [1948] 1 KB 184; [1947] 2 All ER 666	203
Morris *v* Beardmore [1981] AC 446; [1980] 3 WLR 283; [1980] 2 All ER 753, DC	50
Moss *v* Elphick [1910] 1 KB 846; [1908-10] All ER Rep Ext 1202; 79 LJKB 631, CA	266
Mount (DF) Ltd *v* Jay and Jay (Provisions) Co Ltd [1960] 1 QB 159; [1959] 3 WLR 537; [1959] 3 All ER 307	168
Mountford *v* Scott [1975] 2 WLR 114; [1975] 1 All ER 198; 118 SJ 755, CA	63
Mountstephen *v* Lakeman (1871) LR 7 QB 196; 41 LJKB 67; 25 LT 755, HL	77
M/S Aswan Engineering Establishment Co *v* Lupdine [1987] 1 WLR 1; [1987] 1 All ER 135	152
Munro (Robert A) & Co Ltd *v* Meyer [1930] 2 KB 312; [1930] All ER Rep 241; 99 LJKB 703	164
Nanka Bruce *v* Commonwealth Trust Ltd [1926] AC 77; 94 LJPC 169, 134 LT 35, PC	159
Nash *v* Inman [1908] 2 KB 1; [1908-10] All ER Rep 317; 77 LJKB 626, CA	69
National Westminster Bank *v* Morgan [1985] 1 All ER 821	114
Niblett Ltd *v* Confectioner's Materials Co Ltd [1921] 3 KB 387; [1921] All ER Rep 459; 90 LJKB 984, CA	148
Nicolene *v* Simmonds [1953] 1 QB 543; [1953] 2 WLR 717; [1953] 1 All ER 822, CA	60
Nordenfelt *v* Maxim Nordenfelt Guns and Ammunition Co [1894] AC 535; [1891-4] All ER Rep 1; 63 LJCh 908, HL	122
North Riding Garages Ltd *v* Butterwick [1967] 2 QB 56; [1967] 2 WLR 571; [1967] 1 All ER 644, DC	210
Nottingham Patent Brick & Tile Co *v* Butler (1886) 16 QBD 778; 55 LJQB 280; 54 LT 444, CA	98
O'Brien *v* Associated Fire Alarms [1968] 1 WLR 1916; [1969] 1 All ER 93; 112 SJ 232, CA	209
Olley *v* Marlborough Court Ltd [1949] 1 KB 532; [1949] 1 All ER 127; 93 SJ 40, CA	87
Orman *v* Saville Sportswear Ltd [1960] 1 WLR 1055; [1960] 3 All ER 105; 104 SJ 212	198

Case	Page
Oscar Chess Ltd v Williams [1957] 1 WLR 370; [1957] 1 All ER 325; 101 SJ 186, CA	78
Ottoman Bank v Chakarian [1930] AC 277; 99 LJPC 97; 142 LT 465, PC	201
Overseas Tankship (UK) v Morts Dock and Engineering Co (The Wagon Mound) [1961] AC 388; [1961] 2 WLR 126; [1961] 1 All ER 404, PC	4, 278
Paris v Stepney Borough Council [1951] AC 367; [1951] 1 All ER 42; 94 SJ 837, HL	199, 278
Parkinson v College of Ambulance Ltd and Harrison [1925] 2 KB 1; [1924] All ER Rep 325; 93 LJKB 1066	116, 117
Parkinson & Co Ltd v Commissioners of Works and Public Buildings [1949] 2 KB 632; [1950] 1 All ER 208; 210 LT 25, CA	140
Partridge v Crittendon [1968] 1 WLR 1204; [1968] 2 All ER 421; 112 SJ 582, DC	55
Pearce v Brooks (1866) 4 H & C 358; 35 LJEx 134; 14 LT 288	116
Pearce v Foster (1886) 17 QBD 536	206
Pengelly v Bell Punch Company Ltd [1964] 1 WLR 1068; [1968] 2 All ER 945; 108 SJ 461, CA	49
Petrofina (GB) v Martin [1966] Ch 146; [1966] 2 WLR 318; [1966] 1 All ER 126, CA	122
Pfizer Corp v Minister of Health [1965] AC 512; [1965] 2 WLR 387; [1965] 1 All ER 450, CA	171
Pharmaceutical Society of GB v Boots Cash Chemists (Southern) Ltd [1953] 1 QB 401; [1953] 2 WLR 427; [1953] 1 QB 401; [1953] 2 WLR 427; [1953] 1 All ER 482, CA	54
Phillips v Alhambra Palace Co [1901] 1 KB 59; 70 LJQB 26; 83 LT 431, DC	205
Photo Production Ltd v Securicor Transport Ltd [1980] AC 827; [1980] 2 WLR 283; [1980] 1 All ER 556, HL	89, 91
Pignataro v Gilroy and Son [1919] 1 KB 459; 88 LJKB 726; 120 LT 480, DC	160
Planche v Colburn (1831) 8 Bing 14; 1 Moo & S 51; 1 LJCP 7	126, 140
Polkey v AE Dayton Services Ltd [1987] 1 WLR 1147; [1987] 1 All ER 984; [1987] ICR 301, CA	214
Poussard v Spiers and Pond (1876) 1 QBD 410; 45 LJQB 621; 34 LT 572	83, 204
Powell v Kempton Park Racecourse Company [1889] AC 143; [1895-9] All ER Rep Ext 1488; 68 LJQB 392, HL	49
Priest v Last [1903] 2 KB 148	154
R v Kent Police Authority [1971] 2 QB 662; [1971] 3 WLR 416; 115 SJ 640, CA	17
—— v Kupfer [1915] 2 KB 321; 84 LJKB 1021; 112 LT 1138, CCA	271
—— v Miah [1974] 1 WLR 683; 118 SJ 365; sub nom Waddington v Miah [1974] 2 All ER 377, HL	51
Raffles v Wichelhaus (1864) 2 H & C 906; 33 LJEx 160; 159 ER 375	108
Ramsgate Victoria Hotel Co v Montefiore [1861-73] All ER Rep Ext 2232; (1866) LR 1 Exch 109; 4 H & C 164	58
Ready Mixed Concrete (South East) Ltd v Minister of Pensions and National Insurance [1968] 2 QB 497; [1968] 2 WLR 775; [1968] 1 All ER 433	196
Redgrave v Hurd (1881) 20 ChD 1; [1881-5] All ER Rep 77; 51 LJCh 113, CA	99
Rhodes v Moules 1894	269
Rickards (Charles) Ltd v Oppenheim [1950] 1 KB 616; [1950] 1 All ER 420; 94 SJ 161, CA	163, 171
Roberts v Gray [1913] 1 KB 520	69
Rogers v Parish (Scarborough) Ltd [1987] QB 933; [1987] 2 WLR 353; [1987] 2 All ER 232, CA	152
Rose v Plenty [1976] 1 WLR 141; [1976] 1 All ER 97; 119 SJ 592, CA	276
Rose (Frederick) (London) Ltd v Pim (William) & Co Ltd [1953] 2 QB 450; [1953] 3 WLR 497; [1953] 2 All ER 739, CA	112
Rose and Frank Co v Crompton (JR) & Bros Ltd [1925] AC 445; [1924] All ER Rep 245; 94 LJKB 120, HL	67
Rosenthal v Butler [1972] IRLR 39	213
Ross v Caunters [1980] Ch 279; [1979] 3 WLR 605; [1979] 3 All ER 580	280
Routledge v McKay [1954] 1 WLR 615; [1954] 1 All ER 855; 98 SJ 247, CA	79
Rowland v Divall [1923] 2 KB 500; [1923] All ER Rep 270; 92 LJKB 1041, CA	148
Royal College of Nursing of United Kingdom v DHSS [1982] AC 800; [1981] 2 WLR 279; [1981] 1 All ER 545, CA	51
Ruff v Webb (1794) 1 Esp 130, NP	222
SCM (United Kingdom) Ltd v Whittal (WJ) & Son Ltd [1971] 1 QB 137; [1970] 3 WLR 694; [1970] 3 All ER 245, CA	280
Said v Butt [1920] 3 KB 497; [1920] All ER Rep 232; 90 LJKB 239	256
Sanders v Parry [1967] 1 WLR 753; [1967] 2 All ER 803; 111 SJ 296	201
Saunders (Executrix of the Estate of Rose Maud Gallie) v Anglia Building Society [1971] AC 1004; [1970] 3 WLR 1078; sub nom Saunders v Anglia Building Society 114 SJ 885, HL	110
Schawel v Reade (1913) 46 ILT 281, HL	79
Schuler (L) A/G v Wickman Machine Tool Sales [1974] AC 235; [1973] 2 WLR 683; [1973] 2 All ER 39, CA	82
Secretary of State for Employment v ASLEF (No 2) [1972] 2 QB 455; [1972] 2 WLR 1370; [1972] 2 All ER 949, CA	200
Shanklin Pier Ltd v Dettel Products Ltd [1951] 2 All ER 471; 95 SJ 563	66
Sharp Bros and Knight v Chant [1917] 1 KB 771; 86 LJKB 608; 116 LT 185, CA	106
Shipton Anderson & Co v Harrison Bros Arbitration [1915] 3 KB 676; 113 LT 1009, DC	130
Simpkins v Pays [1955] 1 WLR 975; [1955] 3 All ER 10; 99 SJ 563	67
Simpson v London & North Western Railway Co (1876) 1 QBD 274; 45 LJQB 182; 33 LT 805	135
—— v Welles (1872) LR 7 QB 214; 41 LJMC 105; 26 LT 163	34
Sky Petroleum Ltd v VIP Petroleum Ltd [1974] 1 WLR 576; [1974] 1 All ER 954; 118 SJ 311	138
Smith v Land and House Property Corporation (1884) 28 ChD 7; 51 LT 718; 49 JP 182, CA	97
—— v Mawhood (1845) 14 M & W 453; 15 LJEx 149; 153 ER 552	115
—— v St Andrews Scottish Ambulance Service 1973	213
—— v Wilson (1832) 3 B & Ad 728; 1 LJKB 194; 110 ER 266	34
Solle v Butcher [1950] 1 KB 671; [1949] 2 All ER 1107; 94 SJ 465, 482, 514, CA	111
Spicer (Keith) Ltd v Mansell [1970] 1 WLR 333; [1970] 1 All ER 462; 114 SJ 30, CA	262
Spiro v Lintern [1973] 1 WLR 1002; [1973] 3 All ER 319; 117 SJ 584, CA	248
Stafford v Conti Commodity Services Ltd [1981] 1 All ER 691; [1981] 1 Lloyd's Rep 466; [1981] Com LR 10	280
Steinberg v Scala (Leeds) Ltd [1923] 2 Ch 452; 92 LJKB 944; 129 LT 624, CA	70
Stekel v Ellice [1973] 1 WLR 191; [1973] 1 All ER 465; 117 SJ 843	263
Stevenson v McLean (1880) 5 QBD 346; 49 LJQB 701; 42 LT 897	57
Stilk v Myrick (1809) 2 Camp 317; 6 Esp 129; 170 ER 1168, NP	63
Strickland v Turner (1852) 7 Exch 208; 22 LJEx 115; 155 ER 919	107

Case	Page
Suisse Atlantique Société D'Armement Maritime SA v NV Rotterdamsche Kolen Centrale [1967] 1 AC 361; [1966] 2 WLR 944; [1966] 2 All ER 61, CA	89
Sumpter v Hedges [1898] 1 QB 673; 67 LJQB 545; 78 LT 378, CA	125, 126, 140
Sweet v Parsley [1970] AC 132; [1969] 2 WLR 470; [1969] 1 All ER 347, DC	50
Tai Hing Cotton Mill v Liu Chong Hing Bank [1985] 3 WLR 317; [1985] 2 All ER 947; 129 SJ 503, PC	232
Tamplin (FA) Steamship Co Ltd v Anglo-Mexican Petroleum Products Co Ltd [1916] 2 AC 397; [1916-17] All ER Rep 104; 85 LJKB 1389, HL	130
Taylor v Bowers (1876) 1 QBD 291; 46 LJQB 39; 34 LT 938, CA	118
Teheran-Europe Co Ltd v Belton (ST) (Tractors) Ltd [1968] 2 QB 545; [1968] 3 WLR 205; [1968] 2 All ER 886, CA	155
Tempest v Kiher (1846) 3 CB 249	49
Thomas Gerrard & Son Ltd, Re, see Gerrard (Thomas) & Son	
Thompson v London, Midland & Scottish Railway Co [1930] 1 KB 41; 98 LJKB 615; 141 LT 382, CA	85
Thompson (WL) Ltd v Robinson (Gunmakers) Ltd [1955] Ch 177; [1955] 2 WLR 185; [1955] 1 All ER 154	165
Tiedemann and Ledermann Frères, Re [1889] 2 QB 66; 68 LJQB 852; 81 LT 191	246
Tinn v Hoffman & Co (1873) 29 LT 271	56
Tower Cabinet Co Ltd v Ingram [1949] 2 KB 397; [1949] 1 All ER 1033; 93 SJ 404, DC	270
Trollope and Colls Ltd v NW Metropolitan Regional Hospital Board [1973] 1 WLR 601; [1973] 2 All ER 260; 117 SJ 355, HL	81
Tsakiroglov & Co Ltd v Noblee & Thorl GmbH [1962] AC 93; [1961] 2 WLR 633; [1961] 2 All ER 179, HL	129, 130
Twomax v Dickson McFarlane and Robinson [1983] SLT 454	282
Uddin v Associated Portland Cement Manufacturers Ltd [1965] 2 QB 582; [1965] 2 WLR 1183; [1965] 2 All ER 213, CA	278
Underwood Ltd v Burgh Castle Brick and Cement Syndicate [1922] 1 KB 343; [1921] All ER Rep 515; 91 LJKB, CA	159
—— (AL) Ltd v Bank of Liverpool and Martins [1924] 1 KB 775; [1924] All ER Rep 230; 93 LJKB 690, CA	235
United Railways of Havana and Regla Warehouses Ltd, Re [1961] AC 1007; [1960] 2 WLR 969; [1960] 2 All ER 332, HL	36
Unwin v Hanson [1891] 2 QB 115; 60 LJQB 531; 65 LT 511, CA	48
Vancouver Malt and Sake Brewing Co Ltd v Vancouver Breweries Ltd [1934] AC 181	122
Vaux and Associated Breweries Ltd v Ward (1968) 112 SJ 761; [1968] ITR 385, DC	209
Victoria Laundry (Windsor) Ltd v Newman Industries Ltd [1949] 2 KB 528; [1949] 1 All ER 997; 93 SJ 371, CA	135
Vigers v Pike (1842) 8 Cl & Fin 562; 8 ER 220	102
Wagon Mound, The (1961) see Overseas Tankship (UK) v Morts Dock and Engineering Co (The Wagon Mound)	4, 278
Wait, Re [1927] 1 Ch 606; [1926] All ER Rep 433; 71 Sol Jo 56, CA	145
Walsh v Lonsdale (1882) 21 ChD; 52 LJCh 2; 46 LT 858	11
Walters v Top Crust Foods [1972] IRLR 108	213
Ward v Tesco Stores Ltd [1976] 1 WLR 810; [1976] 1 All ER 219; 120 SJ 555, CA	278
—— (RV) Ltd v Bignall [1967] 1 QB 534; [1967] 2 WLR 1050; [1967] 2 All ER 449; CA	168
Warman v Southern Counties Car Finance Corp Ltd [1949] 2 KB 576; [1949] 1 All ER 711; 93 SJ 319	184
Warner Brothers Pictures Inc v Nelson [1937] 1 KB 209; [1936] 3 All ER 160; 106 LJKB 97	139
Watling (NC) & Co Ltd v Richardson [1978] 13 ICR 1049; [1979] ITR 333; [1978] IRLR 255, EAT	213
Watteau v Fenwick [1893] 1 QB 346; [1891-4] All ER Rep 897; 67 LT 831	245
Waugh and Others v MB Clifford & Sons Ltd [1982] Ch 374; [1982] 2 WLR 679; [1982] 1 All ER 1095, CA	245
Welby & Drake (1825) 1 Ce P 557, NP	64
Weller v Foot & Mouth Disease Research Institute [1966] 1 QB 569; [1965] 3 WLR 1082; [1965] 3 All ER 560	279
Western Excavating (EEC) Ltd v Sharp 1978	206
Western Electric Ltd v Welsh Development Agency [1983] 2 WLR 897; HL	59
White and Carter (Councils) Ltd v MacGregor [1962] AC 413; [1962] 2 WLR 17; [1961] 3 All ER 1178; HL	132
Whiteoak v Walker (1988) 4 BCC 122	284
Whitlow v Alkamet Construction [1975] IRLR	213
Whittington v Seale Hayne (1900) 82 LT 49; 16 TLR 181; 44 Sol Jo 229	103
Williams v Bayley (1866) 35 LJCh 717; 14 LT 802; 12 Jur NS 875, HL	113
Wilson v Rickett, Cockerell & Co [1954] 1 QB 598; [1954] 2 WLR 629; [1954] 1 All ER 868, CA	151
With v O'Flanagan [1936] 1 All ER 727; [1936] Ch 575; 105 LJCh 247, CA	98
Wolstanton Ltd v A-G of Duchy of Lancaster v Newcastle-under-Lyme BC [1940] AC 860; 109 LJCh 319; 163 LT 187, HL	34
Wolverhampton Corporation v Emmons [1901] 1 KB 515; [1900-3] All ER Rep Ext 1570; 70 LJKB 429, CA	139
Wood v Scarth (1855) 2 K & J 33; 26 LTOS 87; 4 WR 31	108, 112
Woodman v Photo Trade Processing (1981) (unreported)	90
Woods v Olympic Aluminium Co [1975] IRLR 356	212
Wroth v Tyler [1974] Ch 30; [1973] 2 WLR 405; [1973] 1 All ER 897	135
Yonge v Toynbee [1910] 1 KB 215; [1908-10] All ER Rep 204; 79 LJKB 208, CA	257
Young and Marten Ltd v McManus Childs Ltd [1969] 1 AC 454; [1968] 3 WLR 630; [1968] 2 All ER 1169, HL	168, 169

Index

Accusatorial procedure, 4
Acts of Parliament, 38
Administrative tribunals, *see* Tribunals
Admiralty Division, *see* Probate, Divorce and Admiralty Division
Adversarial procedure, 4
Agency, 161, 243-60
   agent's liability to third party, 256-7
   authority—
      actual, 244
      apparent, 258-9
      coupled with interest, 258
      implied, 244
      usual, 244-5
   commission, 252-3
   creation, 243-52
      by agreement, 244-5
      by estoppel, 248-9
      by operation of law, 249-50
      by ratification, *see* Ratification
   delegation, 250-1
   disclosed principal, 254-5
   duties of agent—
      care and skill, 250
      good faith, 251-2
      no secret profit, 252
      not to deny principal's title, 251
      not to take bribe, 251-2
      performance, 250
      personal performance, 250-1
      to account for sums received, 252
   mercantile agents, 161
   of necessity, 249-50
   of partners, 267-8
   rights of agent—
      indemnity, 252
      lien, 253-4
      remuneration, 252-3
   termination, 257-9
      effects of, 258-9
      limits on right to, 258
      vested rights and, 258
   undisclosed principal, 255-6
Appeal, 9
   civil courts of—
      Court of Appeal, 18
      European Court of Justice, 19-20
      High Court, 18
      House of Lords, 18-9
      JCPC, 20
      leap-frog procedure, 19
   criminal courts of—
      Court of Appeal, 24-5
      Crown Court, 23-4
      House of Lords, 25
      Queen's Bench Division, 24
Appeal Court, *see* Court of Appeal
Arbitration—
   Advantages, 28
   conduct of, 27
   disadvantages, 28
   supervision, 27-8
Arm's length transaction, 67
Assignment, 70-3
   by act of parties, 71-2

   equitable, 71-2
   legal, 71
   rights unassignable, 72
   subject to equities, 72
   upon bankruptcy, 72-3
   upon death, 72
Auctions, 55-6
Auditors, liability for negligence, 280-2
   further investigation needed, 281-2
   reliance on accounts, 282-3
   share valuation, 282

Barristers, 15, 28-9
Bentham, Jeremy, 9
Bills of exchange, *see* Cheques; Negotiable instruments
Bribes, 251-2

Canon law, 41
Capacity—
   drunken persons, 70
   mentally disordered, 70
   minors, 68-70
   to create partnership, 264
Cases, citation, 35
Caveat emptor, 106
Certiorari orders, 17, 26
Chancery Division, 9, 16, 18
Cheques, 229-37
   clearing, 230-2
   crossing, 229-31
      account payee, 231
      general, 230
      non-negotiable, 231
      special, 231-2
   duties of bankers, 232-4
      collecting cheques paid, 234
      honouring cheques, 233
      secrecy, 233-4
   duties of customers, 233
   form, 229
   protection of collecting banker, 235-6
   protection of paying banker, 234-5
   see also Negotiable instruments
Citation of cases, 35
Civil courts—
   first instance—
      county courts, 14-5
      High Court, *see* High Court
      magistrates' courts, 14
      restrictive practices court, 18
   of appeal, *see* Appeal, civil courts of
   structure, 13-4
Civil law, 5
Codification, 4, 37
Collateral contract, 66
Collective bargaining arrangements, 68
Common law—
   and equity, 10-1
   contract terms implied by, 81
   contracts illegal by, 114
   contracts void at, 119-22
   damage remedy, 8
   historical development, 7
   presumption against alteration, 50
Common Pleas Division, 9

Companies, 240, 272-4
Condition subsequent, 128
Consideration, *see* Contract, consideration
Consolidation, 4, 37
Consumer credit, 175-93
    cancellation—
        cancellable agreements, 187
        effects of, 188-9
        methods, 187
        period, 188
    credit brokers, 176
    credit reference agencies, 176
    debt collecting agencies, 176
    debt counsellors and adjusters, 176
    ending contract—
        cancellation, *see* cancellation
        creditor's termination for breach, 190-1
        creditor's termination on default, 191
        debtor repudiation for breach of condition, 189-90
        H-P or conditional sale agreement, 190
        paying off early, 190
        rescission for misrepresentation, 189
    excluded agreements, 181
    exempt agreements, 181
    individual or partnership debtor, 180
    linked transactions, 180-1
    non-commercial agreements, 181
    protection of debtor and contract—
        copies, 183-5
        extortionate credit bargains, 186
        formalities, 183
        implied terms, 184
        liability of creditor, 184-6
        loss of credit token, 186
        right to information, 186
    protection of debtor before agreement—
        cannot be bound, 182
        pre-contractual statements, 182
        withdrawal from contract, 183
    protection of debtor by court, 191-3
    recovery of goods, 192
    regulated consumer agreements, 179-80
    small agreements, 182
    terminology, 176-8
        debtor-creditor agreements, 177-9
        debtor-creditor-supplier agreements, 177-9
        restricted and unrestricted use credit, 177
    types of, 175
Contra proferentem rule, 87
Contract—
    acceptance—
        communication of, 59-60
        conduct not acceptance, 59
        nature of, 58-60
        silence, 60
        see also Sale of goods
    arm's length transaction, 67
    assignment, *see* Assignment
    breach, *see* Discharge
    capacity, *see* Capacity
    collateral, 66
    consideration, 171
        adequate, 63
        meaning of, 61
        moves from promisee, 62
        past, 61-2
        sufficient, 63-5
    contents, 77-91
    credit, *see* Consumer credit
    deeds, 75
    discharge, *see* Discharge
    divisible, 126, 164
    duress, 112
    employment, *see* Employment contracts
    equitable estoppel, 65
    evidenced in writing, 76-9
    exclusion clauses—
        construction of, 87-9
        constructive notice, 86
        contra proferentem rule, 87
        fundamental breach and, 88-90
        incorporation in contracts, 85-7
        main purpose rule, 87-9, 91
        notice after contract made, 87
        oral representations and, 89-90
        reasonable notice, 85
    for work and materials, 146
    form of, 53-74, 75-9, 92
    frustration, *see* Discharge
    fundamental breach, 88-9
    guarantees, 76-7, 91
    hire-purchase, 145-7
    illegal, 114-23
        as formed, 116-7
        as performed, 117
        at common law, 115-6
        by statute, 115
        recovery after, 117-9
    implied promises, 62
    in writing, 76
    invalidation, 95-124
    land or interest in land, 77-9
    legal relations, 66-8
        collective bargaining arrangements, 68
        commercial arrangements, 67-8
        domestic and social, 66-7
    misrepresentation, *see* Misrepresentation
    mistake, *see* Mistake
    necessary elements, 53
    of indemnity, 77
    offer—
        auctions, 55-6
        communication of, 56
        conditional, 58
        counter-offer, 57
        death of offerer or offeree, 58
        declaration of intention, 55-6
        display of goods, 54-5
        invitation for tenders, 55
        invitation to treat, 55-6
        nature of, 54-6
        rejection of, 57-8
        revocation, 56-7
        statement of selling price, 55
        termination, 56-8
        time lapse, 58
    ousting court jurisdiction, 120
    parties' intentions, 84
    performance, *see* Discharge; Sale of goods
    privity of, 62, 65-6
    remedies, *see* Remedies for breach
    representations, 80-2
    restraint of trade, 120-3
    restrictive trade practices, 119-120
    sale of goods, *see* Sale of goods
    supply of goods, 169-170
    supply of services, 170
    terms, 78-80
        certainty of, 60-1
        classification, 82-4
        conditions, 83
        express, 80
        implied, 80-1, 170-1, 184; *see also* Sale of goods
        innominate, 83-5
        standard terms of business, 91
        warranties, 83
    under seal, 75, 77, 79
    undue influence, 112-3
    unenforceable, 54
Unfair Contract Terms Act, 89-9
    guarantees, 91
    misrepresentation liability, 91, 105
    negligence liability, 89
    sale or supply of goods liability, 89-91

INDEX

scope, 91
standard terms of business, 91
valid, 95
void, 54, 95
   at common law, 120-3
   by statute, 119-20
voidable, 54, 95
wagering, 119
Conversion, 235-7
Conveyancing, 15
Corporations, see Legal personality
Corruption, 115
County courts, 10
   function of, 15
   jurisdiction, 15
   personnel, 14-5
   precedent and, 37
   small claims procedure, 15
Court of Appeal, 9, 18, 24-5
   composition in criminal appeal, 25
   precedent and, 36
Courts—
   alternatives to, 25-8
   civil and criminal, see Civil and Criminal courts
   county, see County courts
   Crown Courts, see Crown Courts
   divorce, 9
   High Court, see High Court
   historical development, 7-8
   juvenile, 22
   magistrates', see Magistrates' courts
   of appeal, see Appeal; Court of Appeal
   of first instance and of appeal, 13
   of record and not of record, 13
   precedent and, 35-7
   Probate, 9
   restrictive practices, 18
   superior and inferior, 13
   Supreme Court, 9
Credit, see Consumer credit
Criminal courts—
   first instance—
      Crown Courts, 23
      magistrates' courts, 21-3
   of appeal, see Appeal
   structure, 20-1
Criminal law, 5
Crown Courts, 23
   appeals from magistrates' courts' decisions, 23-4
      composition of court, 24
      powers, 24
   composition, 23
   offences classification for, 23
Custom, 33-4
   contract terms implied by, 83

Damages, 8, 9, 10
   for misrepresentation, 105-6
   see also Remedies, for breach; Sale of goods, personal remedies
Death—
   assignment upon, 71
   contract frustration by, 128
   of offeror or offeree, 58
Debt—
   assignment of, 220
   see also Consumer credit
Deeds, 75
Defamation action, 14
Delegated legislation, 39-40
Delegation, agency and, 250-1
Director of Public Prosecutions, 22
Discharge, 125-33
   bilateral, 127-8
   breach—
      anticipatory, 132-3
      failure of performance, 133

implied repudiation, 135
   remedies, see Remedies for breach
condition subsequent, 128
frustration, 128-2, 203-4
   agency termination by, 258
   changes in law, 130
   definition, 129
   effects of, 131
   frustrating events, 130-1
   limitations, 131-2
   non-frustrating events, 130-1
novation, 128
performance, 125-7
   divisible contracts, 126
   failure of, 133
   partial, 77-8, 126, 140
   prevention of complete, 126
   specific, 9, 111, 138-9
   substantial, 126-7
   time of, 127
   unilateral, 129
Dismissal, see Employment contracts, termination
Divisional courts, 36-7
Divorce court, 9
Domestic tribunals, 27
Duress, 112

Ecclesiastical law, 41
Economic loss, 279-80
Eiusdem generis rule, 49
Employment Appeal Tribunals, 18, 26
Employment contracts, 195-217
   contract of and for service, 195-6
   employees and independent contractors, 196-7
   employee's duties—
      act reasonably and co-operate, 200
      good faith, 201-3
      obedience, 200-1
      personal service, 200
      reasonable care, 202
   employer's duties—
      indemnifying employees, 200
      payment of wages, 197-8
      provision of work, 198
      reasonable care, 198-9
      references, 200
   formation of, 197
   redundancy, 208-11
      alternative employment offers, 210
      payments, 208, 210-1
      procedure, 211
      qualifying employees, 209
      remedies for dismissal, 216
      unfair dismissal, 215-6
      wrongful dismissal, 207-8
   statement of employment, 197
   termination, 202-16
      constructive dismissal, 205-7
      dismissal without notice, 205-7
      impossibility of performance, 203-4
      insolvency of employer, 204-5
      notice, 205
      passage of time, 203
      remedies, see remedies for dismissal
      wrongful dismissal, 207-8
      see also redundancy; unfair dismissal
   unfair dismissal, 211-6
      qualifying employees, 211-2
      reasonableness, 212-4
      remedies, 215-6
      strikes and, 215
      trade unions and, 215
      unreasonable dismissals, 214-5
      valid dismissals, 212-4
      written reasons, 215
Equity—
   and common law, 10-11

concept of, 8-9
historical development, 8-9
laches, 10, 141
Estoppel—
   agency creation by, 248-9
   equitable, 65
   transfer of title, 161
European Communities, 41-3
   decisions, 42
   directives, 42
   evidence, 42-3
   regulations, 42
European Court of Justice—
   composition, 20
   interpretative role, 19-20
   procedure, 20
Evidence—
   European Communities law, 42-3
   in writing of contracts, 76-9
Exchequer Division, 9
Exclusion Clauses, see Contract, exclusion clauses
Expressio unius est exclusio alterius, 49

Family Division, 9, 16, 18
Forbearance, 53
Fraud, 14
   limitation and, 141
Frustration, see Discharge

Golden rule, 48
Goods, 144
   future, 145
   protected, 192
   sale of, see Sale of goods
   specific, 144
   supply, see Supply of goods
   unascertained, 145, 160
Guarantees, 76-7, 91

Habeas corpus, 17
High Court, 9, 16-7
   civil appeals in, 18
   precedent and, 37
   see also individual divisions
Hire-purchase, 145-6
   see also Consumer credit
Historical development—
   common law, 7, 10-1
   early courts, 7-8
   equity, 8-9, 10-1
   from Saxon times, 3-4
   Judicature Acts (1873-1875), 9-10
Holder, holder for value, holder in due course, see Negotiable instruments
House of Lords—
   civil appeals, 18-9
      from Court of Appeal, 19
      from High Court, 19
   criminal appeals, 25
   precedent and, 36

Immoral contracts, 114-5
Incorporation, see Legal personality
Indemnity, contract of, 77
Indorsement of bill—
   conditional, 226-7
   forged, 227
   in blank, 226
   restrictive, 227
   sans recours, 227
   special, 226
Industrial tribunals, 18, 26
Injunctions, 9, 10, 139
Inns of Court, 28-9
Inquisatorial procedure, 4
Institute of Legal Executives, 29
Insurance against risk, 283

Intention, 50
Interpretation, 47-51, 52
   eiusdem generis rule, 49
   expressio unius est exclusio alterius, 49
   golden rule, 48
   intrinsic aids to, 51
   literal rule, 47-8
   mischief rule, 48
   noscitur a sociis, 49

JCPC, see Judicial Committee of the Privy Council
Judges—
   circuit, 14
   county court, 14
   decisions 46
   making law, 46
   see also Interpretation
Judicial Committtee of the Privy Council, 20
Judicial precedent, see Precedent
Judicial review, 16
Jurisdiction—
   contracts to oust, 119
   county courts, 15
   offences triable either way, 22
   offences triable only on indictment, 21-2
   offences triable only summarily, 21
Juvenile courts, 22

Laches, 10, 141
Law—
   accusatorial procedure, 4
   characteristics of, 3
   codification, 4, 37
   consolidation, 4, 37
   criminal and civil, 5
   definition, 3
   history of, see Historical development
   inquisatorial procedure, 4
   judicial character, 4
   precedent doctrine, 5
   public and private, 5
   Roman, 5, 41
   sources, see Sources of law
   substantive and procedural, 5
   see also under individual aspects
Law Commission, 41
Law merchant, 40-1
Law reports, 34-5
Law Society, 29
Leap-frog procedure, 19
Legal assignment, see Assignment
Legal executives, 29-30
Legal personality, 239-41
   companies, 240, 272-4
   creation of corporations, 239
   incorporation consequences, 239-40
Laegal relations, intent to create, 66-8
Legislation—
   delegated, 39-40
   process, 38-9
   retrospective, 51
Liability—
   economic loss, 279-80
   exclusion of, 280
   for misrepresentation, 91, 105
   for negligence, see Negligence
   of agent to third party, 256-7
   of auditors, 281-3
   of creditor, 184-6
   of minors, 70
   of partners, 268-70
   on bills of exchange, 226
   sale or supply of goods, 89-91
   vicarious, 275-6
Lien, 164
   right of agent, 253-4
   loss of, 254

requirements, 254
types of lien, 254
Limitation—
  contract frustration, 131-2
  in remedies for breach, 141
  period, 10
Literal rule, 47-8
London Clearing House, 230, 232

Magistrates' courts, 14
  criminal jurisdiction, 21-2
  examining magistrates, 22
  juvenile courts, 22
  precedent and, 37
Main purpose rule, 87-9, 91
Mandamus orders, 16-7, 26
Matrimonial jurisdiction, 9
Mentally handicapped persons, 70
Merchant law, 40-1
Minors—
  capacity—
    liability in tort, 70
    valid contracts, 68-9
    voidable contracts, 69-70
  contracts for necessaries, 140
Mischief rule, 48
Misrepresentation, 10, 91, 96-105
  exclusion of liability for, 91, 105
  expert knowledge, 97
  fraudulent, 100, 104
  future intention, 97
  negligent, 100, 104-5
  opinions, 96-7
  reliance upon, 99
  remedies—
    avoid contract, 101
    damages, 104-5
    recission, 101-4
  sales talk, 96
  silence as, 97-99
  statement of fact not law, 96
  untrue statement, 97
  wholly innocent, 101-2
Mistake—
  common—
    as to ownership, 107-8
    as to state of affairs, 107
    as to subject matter, 107
  errors of judgment, 106
  mutual, 108
  nature of document signed, 110
  not affecting contract, 105-6
  relief granted by equity, 110-2
    rectification, 111-2
    rescission on terms, 111
    specific performance refusal, 111
  unilateral—
    as to identify, 108-9
    as to intention, 110
Mortgage, 9

National security, 115
Negligence, 276-9
  economic loss, 279-80
  insurance against risk, 283
  liability for 89-91
  plaintiff must prove, 278
  res ipsa loquitur, 278
  see also Liability
Negotiable instruments, 219-28
  assignment of debt, 220
  bearer, 221
  bills of exchange, 219-21
    definition, 222-3
    dishonour of, 227
    holder, 223-4
    liability on, 226

    overdue, 225
    trade name signing, 226
    see also Indorsement of bill
  consideration presumption, 222
  delivery, 221
  development of, 220-1
  holder for value, 224
  holder in due course, 225-6, 236
  negotiability, 221-2
  sample of, 221
  transfer of, 221-2
  see also Cheques
Noscitur a sociis, 49
Notetaking, 2
Novation, 128, 269

Obiter dicta, 45-6
Offers, *see* Contract, offer

Part performance, 76-7, 126, 140
Partnerships, 261-78
  agency of partners, 267-9
  agreement—
    after expiry date, 266-7
    duration, 266
  business in common, 262
  companies and, 272-4
  creation—
    capacity, 264
    illegal partnerships, 264
    name of firm, 264-5
  definition, 261-4
  dissolution, 270-2
    by order of court, 271-2
    consequences, 272
    without court order, 270-1
  liability of partners—
    duration of, 269-70
    holding out, 269-71
    in contract, 268
    in tort, 268-9
    retiring partner, 269-70
  novation, 269
  rules determining existence, 262-3
  salaried partners, 263-4
  with view of profit, 262
Performance, *see* Discharge; Sale of goods
Personality, legal, *see* Legal personality
Precedent, 5, 45-7, 52
  advantages and disadvantages of, 47
  authority of courts, 35-7
  case citation, 35
  judicial decisions, 46
  Law reports, 34-5
  persuasive and binding, 47
  ratio decidendi and *obiter dicta*, 45-6
  statute law and, 51
Prerogative orders—
  certiorari, 17, 26
  habeas corpus, 17
  mandamus, 16-7, 26
  prohibition, 17
Private law, 5
Privity of contract, 62, 65-6
Probate, Divorce and Admiralty Division, 9
Problem solving, 2
Procedural law, 5
Prohibition orders, 17
Property, 143-4
Public law, 5
Public policy, 114, 118

Quantum meruit, 133, 140-1
Queen's Bench Division, 9, 16
  criminal appeals in, 24
Queen's Counsel, 29

Ratification, 245-8
   effects of, 248
   in time, 247
   not by undisclosed principal, 256
   whole transaction, 247
   see also Agency
Ratio decidendi, 45-6
Rectification, 111-3, 140
Redundancy, *see* Employment contracts
Registrar, 14
Remedies, *see* Remedies for breach; Sale of goods
Remedies for breach, 133-41
   damages, 133-8
      assessment difficulties, 136-7
      liquidated, 137-8
      mental distress and inconvenience, 136-7
      mitigation of loss, 136
      penalties, 137-8
      purpose, 135-6
      reasonableness, 134-5
      remoteness, 134
      special damages, 135
      see also Damages
   equitable claims, 141
   injunctions, 9, 10, 139
   limitations of actions, 141
   quantum meruit, 133, 140-1
   rectification, 111-2, 140
   rescission, *see* Rescission
   specific performance, 9, 111, 138-9
Repentance plea, 117
Res ipsa loquitur, 278
Rescission, 102-5
   damages instead of, 104-5
   for misrepresentation, 101-4, 189
   impossible, 102
   loss of right, 102-3
   on terms, 111
   remedy for breach, 140
   Restitutio in integrum, 102
Restitutio in integrum, 102
Restraint of trade, 119-22
   imposed on sale of business, 120-1
   imposed upon employees, 119-21
   solus agreements, 121-2
Restrictive agreements, 118-9
Restrictive practices court, 18
Revocation, 56-7, 257
Risk, insurance against, 283
Roman law, 5, 41
Romalpa clause, 157-8

Sale of goods, 143-68
   acceptance, 147
   bulk of goods sold by sample, 156
   contracts covered by SGA, 143-5
   de minimis rule, 151, 163
   fit for buyer's purposes, 153-6
   hire-purchase contracts, 145-6
   implied terms, 146-56
      as to title, 147-9
      conditions, 147, 149-56
      sale by description, 149-51
      types of, 147
      warranty, 147, 148-9
   merchantable quantity, 151-3, 155-6
   performance—
      buyer's duty, 165
      delivery of wrong quantities, 163
      duty to deliver, 165
      instalment delivery, 163-4
      seller's duty to deliver, 162-3
      time of delivery, 163
   personal remedies, 165-6
      available market, 165-6
      for lost sub-sale, 166
      measure of damages, 165

      price, 145
   real remedies—
      lien, 166-7
      retention of goods, 167-8
      right of resale, 168
      stoppage in transit, 167
      unpaid seller, 166
   transfer of property and possession, 156-60
      deliverable state, 158-9
      risk, 156-7
      Romalpa clause, 157-8
      sale or return, 159-61
      section 18 rules, 158-60
      when intend to pass, 157-8
   transfer of title, 161-2
      agency, 161
      buyer in possession, 162
      estoppel, 161
      market overt, 161
      seller in possession, 162
      voidable title, 162
   work and materials contracts, 146
   see also Goods; Supply of goods
Sealing, *see* Contract, under seal
Secret profit, 252
Services, supply, *see* Supply of services
Silence, misrepresentation and, 97-9
Small claims procedure, 15
Social Security Appeal Tribunals, 26
Solicitors, 15, 29
Solus agreements, 121-2
Sources of law, 33-43
   custom, 33-4
   European Communities, 41-3
   precedent, *see* Precedent
   statute law, *see* Statute law
   subsidiary—
      canon or ecclesiastical law, 41
      Law Commission, 41
      merchant law, 40-1
      Roman law, 41
      text books, 41
Specific performance, 9, 138-9
   refusal, 111
Statute law—
   Acts of Parliament, 38
   contract terms implied by, 81
   contracts illegal by, 114
   contracts void by, 118-9
   interpretation, *see* Interpretation
   judicial precedent and, 51
   legislation—
      delegated, 39-40
      process of, 38-9
   presumptions, 49-51
Substantive law, 5
Supply of goods—
   implied terms, 170
   SGSA, 168-70
Supply of services, 170-1
   consideration, 171
   implied terms, 170-1
   reasonable care and skill, 170-1
   reasonable time, 171
Supreme Court, 9

Terms of contract, *see* Contract, terms
Tort, *see* Liability; Negligence
Tribunals—
   administrative, 25-7
      advantages, 26-7
      composition, 26
      control of, 26
      disadvantages, 27
      precedent and, 37
   domestic, 27
   Employment Appeal Tribunals, 18, 26

industrial, 18, 26
Social Security Appeal Tribunals, 26

Undue influence, 112-3
Unfair Contract Terms Act, *see* Contract

Unfair dismissal, *see* Employment contracts, unfair dismissal

Vicarious liability, 275-6

Wagering contracts, 118
Warranties, 83, 147-8